WRITING NATURE

An Ecological Reader for Writers

WRITING NATURE

An Ecological Reader for Writers

Carolyn Ross
Stanford University

St. Martin's Press
New York

Senior editor: Karen J. Allanson
Associate editor: Sam Potts
Managing editor: Patricia Mansfield Phelan
Associate project editor: Nicholas Webb
Production manager: Patricia Ollague
Art director: Sheree Goodman
Photo research: Barbara Salz
Cover design: Rod Hernandez
Cover art: Andy Goldsworthy, *Iris blades pinned together with thorns filled in
    five sections with rowan berries fish attacking from below difficult to keep
    all the berries in nibbled at by ducks.* Yorkshire Sculpture Park, West
    Bretton. Courtesy of the artist and Galerie Lelong, New York.

For information, write:
St. Martin's Press, Inc.
175 Fifth Avenue
New York, NY 10010

ISBN: 0–312–10391–3

50% TOTAL RECYCLED FIBER
10% POST-CONSUMER

PRINTED WITH
SOY INK™

Acknowledgments
Acknowledgments and copyrights can be found at the back of the book on pages
641–43, which constitute an extension of the copyright page.
    It is a violation of the law to reproduce these selections by any means whatsoever
without the written permission of the copyright holder.

To my family;
my teachers;
and my students,
past, present, and future

Preface

Writing Nature is the first ecologically themed reader to feature an extensive exploration of rhetorical issues. Thematically, the text presents diverse readings about human experiences of nature and relationships between people and the natural world. Rhetorically, *Writing Nature* explores the writing process and relationships between writers and readers with particular attention, supported throughout the apparatus, to questions of audience and purpose. The book offers perspectives on its theme through a selection of rich interdisciplinary and cross-cultural readings while encouraging students to understand their own and others' writing as a complex personal, social, and rhetorical process.

The overall progression of the readings and rhetorical apparatus, from relatively personal to more public forms of writing, will be familiar to composition teachers. By engaging students in the writing process and in an exploration of nature, the organization of the text asks students to build broad understandings on personal ones. It has been my experience in years of teaching that students explore more deeply and write more effectively about broad social issues or literary themes when they *own* their subjects with some intimacy, and that they write more convincingly of personal experience or revelation when they are aware of the larger implications of their subjects. Thus, the goal of *Writing Nature* is to encourage students to understand their individual relationships to nature within a wider social context just as it encourages them to understand each writing task within the context of the writing process and as part of a wider discourse. It is my further hope that these thematic and rhetorical goals will be achieved not side by side, but hand in hand.

Environmentalism is a subject of real concern in students' lives. They are ready to read, to think critically, to speak, and to write about it. Many students have not fully related their own and their culture's attitudes about nature and human beings' roles in the natural order to the ethics and politics of environmental awareness, but I hope that this text will help them do so. Reading and writing about nature and the environment, and about inherently related subjects in science and technology, invites not only a healthy interdisciplinary perspective; it invites students to relate their personal lives to their academic lives, and their academic lives to their lives as members of both social and ecological communities.

In much of the most recent writing about nature, the environment, and the ethics of science and technology, there is an appropriate urgency. We must reassess our individual and collective attitudes about our relationships to nature and come to understand the world in ecological terms in order both to know who we are and to resolve the many crucial environmental problems we now face. These problems will multiply and intensify as we enter the next millennium, and students currently in their teens and twenties will feel the full brunt of environmental concerns soon enough. We need citizens who understand both themselves and the environment, who grasp the personal and public dimensions of environmental issues, their context and complexity, and who can think critically and communicate clearly if we are to expect success in meeting the challenges ahead.

FEATURES

Unique among environmental readers, Writing Nature *is a single-theme reader for writers with extensive rhetorical instruction.* The readings in *Writing Nature* explore and elucidate the theme of human relationships to nature. The progression of the chapters from personal to public modes of expression guides students through the writing process while developing their analytical skills and their awareness of ecological issues.

Writing Nature is divided into four parts that reflect a unity of theme and rhetoric. These four parts comprise eight chapters, each with an extensive introduction focusing on writing strategies *and* a separate thematic discussion of the chapter's readings. Each rhetorical introduction is a detailed discussion that provides students with practical information about crucial aspects of researching and writing about their subjects. The rhetorical focus of each chapter is reinforced by the chapter's headnotes, reading selections, questions for critical thinking and for writing following each reading, and end-of-chapter questions that encourage students to make connections among readings. The brief thematic introduction to each chapter connects the issues and concerns raised by the readings to students' experiences in the world. The text concludes with a detailed appendix on researching, organizing, and documenting the research paper. Also included in the appendix is a substantially documented student essay in the MLA format.

Since essays are what students most frequently write, essays constitute the majority of the readings in this text. However, Chapter 1 features journals and letters, because journal work is important to the writing process and letters introduce important questions about audience and purpose in writing. Fictional works make up the readings of Chapter 5, in which the rhetorical emphasis is on writing about literature. Within each chapter, the readings are presented chronologically, with the exception of Chapter 8, which features three reading cycles on three essential environmental debates. This organization, I believe, best displays an historical perspective and a sense of the evolution of individual and cultural thought about human relationships to the natural world.

The readings included in Writing Nature *reflect diverse perspectives and genres.* American nature writing has deep roots in our literary tradition, but literary essayists have not been the only ones to take up human-and-nature themes. Poets, novelists, journalists, historians, sociologists, political scientists, economists, biologists, anthropologists, and other writers in many fields and disciplines have explored themes of humans' relations to nature, providing a rich array of flexible writing models representing many perspectives and motives for writing. Assembling readings for this text, I have made a determined effort to achieve several types of diversity. In addition to selecting writing of quality that reflects a real spectrum of historical, cultural, gendered, and aesthetic American experiences of nature, I have tried to achieve a similar diversity of professional and disciplinary perspectives.

For students, one of the appeals of *Writing Nature* should be that the readings demonstrate that good writing belongs to everyone, to people with wide-ranging interests from various fields, inside and outside the academic world. The diversity of the readings should help students— whose own personal and academic interests vary similarly—relate writing to their own interests, and their own interests to writing.

Throughout Writing Nature *there is a consistent emphasis on audience and purpose in writing.* In the rhetorical introductions to each chapter, in questions and ideas for writing that follow each reading, and in end-of-chapter discussion, research, and writing questions, *Writing Nature* asks students to consider the unique "contract" between the writer and the reader in any given piece of writing. The book calls on students to look consistently at writing, whether from a reader's or a writer's perspective, in terms of audience, purpose, and genre:

- *Purpose:* What does the writer want to say and why? What effect on the reader does the writer hope to achieve?
- *Audience:* Who is the reader? Why is he or she reading this particular piece? What does the reader need to know, and what does he or she already know?
- *Genre:* Within the form or discipline in which the writer is writing, what are the special requirements of genre?

Whenever possible, this text offers ideas for writing that will extend students' audiences outside the classroom. For example, students who have written argumentative essays for class might also articulate their arguments in letters to the editor and drop them in the nearest mailbox, or students might research and write fact sheets for local environmental organizations or reports for local historical societies.

Student writing features prominently in each chapter. Although students learn a great deal about writing from studying the work of professional writers, they may feel at times that these works set an unattainable standard. *Writing Nature* contains eleven strong pieces of student writing with which other student writers may more readily identify. To illustrate the writing process, student works include journal selections and early drafts, in addition to finished works. Student writers introduce themselves and their work with headnotes in which they explain their goals and strategies in writing, providing personal and practical contexts in which other student writers may consider these readings.

The student pieces provide examples of writing adapted to a variety of purposes (a fact sheet, a newsletter article, personal and analytical essays) and executed in a range of styles and modes (description, process analysis, narration, writing about literature, cause-and-effect analysis, reporting, investigation, argumentation, and single as well as multiple source essays).

The appendix, "Weaving the Threads: An Overview of the Research Process," contains both instruction on writing the documented essay and one student research paper. The book concludes with detailed information on researching, structuring, and drafting single-source and multiple-source essays. I have included an overview of the most widely accepted documentation styles in the disciplines (MLA, APA, and CBE), which should be valuable to instructors and students. I have provided in-depth explanations and examples of documentation in the MLA style, which the student research paper in the appendix illustrates, since this is the more frequently used format in the humanities.

Distinctively comprehensive headnotes provide historical, biographical, and critical contexts for the readings. When researching and writing the headnotes, I attempted in all cases to exceed bare-bones bibliography and biography. Each headnote provides important historical and critical contexts for reading as well as information about the author's audience and purpose in writing. Most headnotes include commentary by the authors themselves on writing and the writing process, especially as they relate to the rhetorical focus of the chapter that contains them. Many headnotes relate readings within and among chapters.

Writing Nature *contains an alternate thematic table of contents.* Instructors and students who prefer a more thematic focus will appreciate the provision of an alternate table of contents in which readings are indexed by theme.

ACKNOWLEDGMENTS

I am deeply grateful for the encouragement and the contributions of many people who have helped me shape *Writing Nature,* but I owe the greatest debt of thanks to my students. These bright, spirited, articulate, and hard-working people have taught me most of what I know about writing, and they have taught me how to teach, reminding me, constantly, of what needs to be learned. They have set a standard of excellence for my own work, provided the test of its relevance, and been a constant source of renewal of energy and optimism for me. That these people are our future leaves me extraordinarily hopeful. To those students who have contributed their fine work to this text, I am especially grateful. They have been my coauthors in a very real sense, generously contributing not only their writing but parts of themselves to this book and helping to form its character.

My thanks in several categories go to my editors at St. Martin's Press. Of the several editors with whom I discussed this project early on, Karen Allanson, senior editor at St. Martin's, was the only one who really and immediately *got it.* Sam Potts, my associate editor at St. Martin's, sustained a perspective on the entire project which, when I was absorbed in pieces of the whole, was invaluable to me. How he accomplished this while combing the minutiae of the text and coordinating details of permissions and production is quite beyond me. Karen's and

Sam's understanding of composition rhetoric and their sensitivity to the issues of teaching and learning, combined with their editorial finesse, have contributed greatly to the shape and character of this text. I am finally grateful to both Karen and Sam for providing essential encouragements at exactly the right moments.

Also deserving of thanks for their diligent work are Alda Trabucchi and Nick Webb, the project editors who guided the manuscript through the many stages of production; Rod Hernandez, who designed the cover and the interior of the book; and Laura Ann Robb, who secured a large number of permissions well within the budget. Each has contributed tremendously with patience, thoughtfulness, and excellent ability.

I would also like to thank my talented and committed colleagues in the Program in Writing and Critical Thinking at Stanford University and elsewhere who have contributed so much to my understanding of pedagogy over the years. In particular, Rich Holeton, Dennis Matthies, and Ann Watters of Stanford, and Jon Ford of the College of Alameda have been generous with their advice and encouragement throughout the long process of my developing this text. I am especially grateful to Marjorie Ford of Stanford, an extraordinary teacher and an extraordinary friend, for her unfailing support, including her well-timed kicks in my posterior. I extend a very special and grateful acknowledgment to Scott Baker for his diligent, intelligent, and articulate work on the instructor's manual.

Finally, I thank all the people involved in the Community Service Writing Project and the Writing across the Curriculum Program at Stanford. They have provided support and inspiration as we work to dissolve the exclusionary boundaries between community and academy and among disciplines of study, enhancing purpose in writing and living, in teaching and learning. In these categories, my special thanks go to Nora Bacon, Joyce Moser, Claude Reichard, Leslie Townsend, and Ann Watters of the Program in Writing and Critical Thinking, and to Ken Fields, director of Writing and Critical Thinking; to Ann Beaufort of the School of Education; and to Janet Luce and Tim Stanton of the Haas Center for Public Service.

I was fortunate to receive positive evaluation and helpful criticisms from the professors and writing instructors who reviewed *Writing Nature* at various stages of its development. For their perceptive comments and encouragement, I thank Carl G. Herndl, New Mexico State University; Zita Ingham, Arkansas State University; Barbara Lounsberry, University of Northern Iowa; John P. O'Grady, University of California—Davis; Linda Palmer, California State University—Sacramento;

Timothy M. Russell, Sullivan County Community College; Ellen Sparks-Olson, Western State College; Sandar W. Stephan, Youngstown State University; H. Lewis Ulman, The Ohio State University; and Richard Zbracki, Iowa State University.

In the process of undertaking research for *Writing Nature*, my appreciation for good librarians has been refined. I extend my thanks to Kathy Kerns of Green Library at Stanford for her help with research and Nancy Hemingway, Lynn Murray, and Kerry Livingston of the Marin County (California) Libraries for going out of their ways to fill my tall and sometimes esoteric book orders.

Finally, my gratitude goes to the members of my family, especially Carol, Caitlin, and Ruffin, for their patience in accommodating their lives and needs to a partner and parent who was at times unreasonably preoccupied with her work. Their love has been central. To my mother (a writer and editor) and my father (an author and English professor), I owe thanks for much more than the usual parental support.

Carolyn Ross

Contents

Chapter 3: Descriptions of Process   132

PART III   NARRATIONS: HUMAN ENCOUNTERS WITH THE NATURAL WORLD   187

Chapter 4: Personal Narratives   191

Chapter 5: Fictional Accounts   254

Appendix: Weaving the Threads: An Overview of the Research Process 598

Alternate
Thematic Contents

Women

Writing about Writing

I

EXPLORATIONS

The Landscape and Language
of Discovery

In setting out to explore, we begin where we are, placing one foot in front of the other, moving from the familiar, into the less familiar, into the foreign, and finally into the altogether unknown. Exploration is an act of faith; discovery is by nature unpredictable. And writing is as much an act of exploration and discovery as the mapping of a continent.

Though perhaps we have some vague goal and a rough map before setting out—an assignment perhaps—often we don't know exactly what it is we are searching for until we find it. We may not know how long the search will take or what will be required of us along the way. What we discover may not be at all what we expected. There are certainly risks in exploration, but there is an inherent value in the process itself. We can hardly avoid learning from it.

Journeys of exploration come in many shapes: the broad, meandering loop; the straightforward there-and-back-again round trip; the one-way journey, a migration to a new and yet undiscovered homeland. But no matter what our final destination is—and whether or not we anticipated it—we arrive there changed by the journey itself (and by the act of describing, questioning, and analyzing it) in ways we could not have imagined on the day of starting out.

Whether our primary goal is to explore exterior or interior landscapes, whether the search is for an overland trading route or a writing subject, language allows us to keep an account of what we encounter along the way. But beyond this, in many cases creating a record—the

1

act of articulation and communication with a reader—actually shapes and directs the nature of our exploration. Writing is an act of attention to a subject that escalates our understanding of that subject.

Explorations in writing, especially early in the writing process, help us plot the route toward discovery of what it is we want to write about, what we know about the subject and have yet to learn, and what we want to say about it to ourselves and others as we shape our experience into words.

CHAPTER 1

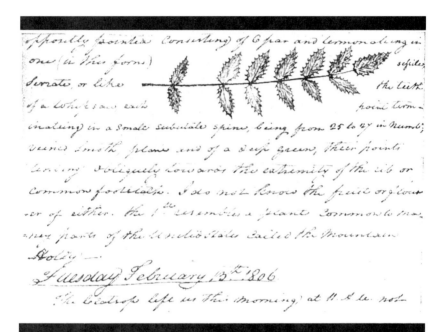

From the Lewis and Clark Journals *manuscript* (Culver Pictures)

JOURNALS AND LETTERS

RHETORIC: ENGAGING
IN READING AND WRITING

LITERATURE: WHAT YOU ARE READING
AND WHAT YOU ARE WRITING

In the readings in this book, you will encounter literature in some, but not all, of its many forms. Literature, in its broadest meaning, includes anything that is written down. However, literature can be classified into four major kinds or *genres: prose fiction, poetry, drama,* and *nonfiction prose.*

Imaginative literature generally refers to prose fiction (including short stories, novels, myths, and parables), poetry, and drama. *Nonfiction prose* includes specific genres as varied as journalistic writing; historical, biographical, and autobiographical works of varying lengths (including the journals and letters in this chapter); textbooks; literary criticism; and other forms. It is important for you to realize that not only the writing you *study,* but much of the writing you *do*—whether in the form of college themes or your own poetry or fiction—is literature.

Thinking in terms of genres can help us understand the nature of both the parts and the whole of literature, but the labels can be somewhat misleading. For example, although imaginative literature is invented, it is also "true" in the sense that it is true to life, reflecting the realities of emotion, of human nature, and of natural and human events.

Nonfiction prose relates facts and actual events, but it requires of its writers a flexible intelligence, which is a kind of imagination.

The nonfiction writing you do—for example, the essays you write in college—necessitates not only critical thinking and basic communication skills, but considerable imagination as you explore your subjects, discover connections between complex ideas (perhaps making intuitive leaps toward perception and understanding), and search for the most effective ways to communicate your understanding to your reader.

JOURNALS AND LETTERS

The purpose of journals and letters, including those which comprise the readings of Chapter 1, are to record, clarify, and communicate the process of exploration and discovery. In journals and letters, writers engage in and celebrate writing as a process more clearly than in any other literary form.

Most of us associate journal writing with an exclusively private purpose and an audience of one—namely the writer himself or herself. If you have ever kept a personal journal or diary, its primary function has probably been to keep track of events that affect you or to map personal change. You may also have enjoyed having at least one place where you could write freely, experimenting with thoughts and playing with language, without feeling the pressure of having to do it "right." You, like many others, may dread writing in more formal contexts (such as for school or work), for readers with exacting expectations, but love sitting down to discover and sketch out your thoughts in your journal or to share what's been going on in your life in a letter to a family member or friend.

For many of us, the urge to articulate and explain, if only to ourselves, is strong. We find that sitting down with pen and paper or at a computer keyboard and reviewing the events of our lives or working through our thoughts or feelings can help shape and clarify them. We may feel, afterwards, less chaotic, more certain, and better equipped to act. Writing for personal reasons may help us learn more about ourselves and reach a certain self-understanding. It may help us come to terms with our past, allowing us to make valuable connections and comparisons that may not otherwise have come to light; or it may help us face the future by clarifying our needs and desires and defining our goals and interests.

For most of us, perhaps, the absence of a reader for our journal writing or the assurance that the reader of our intimate letters is friendly and uncritical is what makes these forms of writing both productive and pleasurable. When a less than intimate reader enters the picture, especially if that reader occupies some position of authority (a teacher or employer, for example), we often lose track of ourselves in the process and our comfort in writing may evaporate.

It may be difficult for some of us to imagine a journal that is simultaneously motivated by the urge to explore and the need to communicate this open-ended process to a less than familiar reader. The fact that most of the journal selections of Chapter 1 were written with specific audiences and particular purposes in mind, and that all have been published, may seem strange and contrary to what many of us have come to see as the private purpose of journal writing. But there are many kinds of journals, just as there are many audiences and purposes for letter writing, and the urge to articulate frequently evolves into the urge, or the requirement, to communicate with a reader. And when a reader enters the writing process, his or her presence affects the content, structure, and style of what we write. If we as writers can successfully balance our own purposes with our readers' expectations, our writing process may be enriched.

The Class Journal

One kind of journal with a very specific purpose is the class journal. You might find it useful to keep one, especially for a class that involves both reading and writing. The primary purpose of a class journal is to help you to keep track of the ongoing process of your own thinking and writing, to give you an opportunity to record, explore, experiment, and think on the page. A class journal will certainly have personal dimensions, but its purpose is more than personal, and it may even speak to an audience beyond yourself—your instructor, perhaps, and possibly at times your classmates.

A class journal is not only a writing journal, but a reading journal and field or research notebook as well. Use it to record and explore any information or ideas relevant to your writing and reading, your course theme, and course work. A class journal provides a safe, informal place in which to explore, shape, or abandon ideas for writing—a place to prewrite, draft, and revise. As an active reader, you can use it as a place to reflect upon the readings in this text, and as a member of a community of writers and readers, as a place to continue and extend class discussions. Your class journal will offer you the opportunity to engage in reading and writing as processes in which understanding evolves and its expression gradually takes shape on the page.

WRITING AS PROCESS: AN OVERVIEW

Although we may admire good writing, we may also feel intimidated by it. We may assume that the work of professional writers has somehow sprung, whole and shining, from a talent far beyond our own. But the fact is, good writing takes time and hard work to produce—as virtually any professional writer will tell you. It evolves from a process not only of persistent revising and editing, but also of gradual understanding.

Although the writing process is never exactly the same for any two writers and may also vary for any one writer from one writing task to another, it is helpful to think of writing as a process that can be undertaken in relatively distinct stages.

Many see the writing process as consisting of three fundamental stages: prewriting, drafting, and revising. But within each stage there tend to be a multitude of substages, and, because the writing process also tends to be *recursive,* most writers move back and forth between stages. Thus, rather than moving forward in a straight line, writing generally tends to move in more of a zigzag.

Prewriting

Prewriting is perhaps the most complex, and for many writers the most time-consuming, stage of the writing process because it encompasses so many purposes. In it, we discover (or invent) our subjects for writing; we explore and learn about them; we organize our thoughts and reach at least tentative conclusions; and we begin to determine the best strategies for communicating with our readers. These goals of prewriting, and hence your prewriting activities, may involve the following, in roughly chronological order:

- *Assessing the writing task* by making sure you understand the assignment, if there is one, and the audience and purpose of the writing.
- *Searching for a subject,* if one has not been assigned; or, if one has been assigned, searching for an approach to, or angle on, the subject.

- *Learning about the subject* and, based on what you learn, *deciding what you have to say.*
- *Planning organizational and rhetorical strategies* that best suit you, your reader, and the function your writing will serve.

You may have already determined that the term "prewriting" is misleading, since much of the work you are likely to do at this stage of the writing process actually involves quite a lot of writing, including journal writing, note taking, outlining, or in any number of other forms.

At each stage of the prewriting process, you have a range of tools and techniques to draw upon, as the following possibilities suggest.

TO ASSESS YOUR WRITING TASK:

- If you are working with an assigned subject, check your peers' understanding of the assignment, its audience and purpose, with your own.

- Another way of clarifying an assigned topic is to ask for further information from the person who gave you the assignment. You might ask for details about or even an example of the kind of writing that is expected, and whether he or she can offer any useful suggestions. Write down any new information.

- In your journal or in another informal written form, describe the writing task, characterize your reader, and clarify your writing's purpose.

TO LOCATE YOUR SUBJECT OR DETERMINE YOUR APPROACH TO A SUBJECT:

- Share and explore your writing ideas in conversation with friends, classmates, or your instructor.

- Take a solitary walk to mull over possibilities.

- Perhaps in your journal, try *freewriting* (or *invisible writing*), *clustering*, or *brainstorming*.

During a *freewriting* session of five to fifteen minutes, simply write whatever comes into your mind without stopping to edit either your thoughts or your writing. If you begin to get stuck, force yourself to keep writing—anything, even if it seems to make no sense, even if it is the same word over and over—until the next thought or image comes to you. At the end of the session, read back over what you have written, and determine what the main idea or dominant impression is. If there doesn't seem to be one, pick out the most intriguing detail. Use this idea or detail as the starting point for your next freewriting session. Keep up the freewriting sessions until you have a coherent idea, one of genuine interest to you.

Invisible writing takes freewriting one step further. If you use a computer to write, try dimming the screen or throwing a T-shirt over it so you can't see what you are writing. The critical voice in us is sometimes almost impossible to quiet, and frequently it will attempt to edit a writing idea before that idea has had a chance to develop, "fine-tuning" it right out of existence. Invisible writing may make you nervous at first, but it will hush the premature editor in you.

Clustering (or *mapping*) is often used in combination with freewriting to clarify vague or abstract ideas and to uncover significant details associated with them. To begin a cluster, write in the middle of a blank sheet of paper a word or phrase that suggests the subject you want to explore. Draw a circle around it. As you begin to think of words, phrases, ideas, and images that you associate in any way with your central thought, write each down and circle it as well, drawing a line to connect it with the word, phrase, idea, or image that engendered it, along with additional lines to illustrate its relationship to other images and ideas. Do not stop to edit yourself; there is no wrong response. If you get stuck, draw more circles to fill. The cluster will begin to resemble a spider web in pattern and complexity. When your cluster feels complete, freewrite for five or ten minutes, weaving the images, ideas, and associations of your cluster into a sequence that makes sense to you, leaving out what feels irrelevant and ending with a reference to the idea, word, or image with which you began your freewrite. Clustering and the freewriting that grows out of it should help you focus your topic and see how it might be developed and illustrated.

Brainstorming works best when writers have at least a general topic in mind. Brainstorming takes the form of listing anything about, or associated with, the topic that comes to mind. The list may include images, memories, seemingly inexplicable associations, questions, words, and phrases. It is important, as in freewriting and clustering, that you not censor or edit yourself in a brainstorming session. After fifteen minutes or so, look back over your list and see if you can pick out central ideas or relationships between ideas. This may help you understand not only where your topic is headed but how you might develop it.

Brainstorming may also work well for groups in generating ideas for collaborative writing. In a group brainstorming session involving more than a few people, try designating one person as the secretary. That person's job will be to record all ideas, no matter how odd or irrelevant they might seem. In a group brainstorming session, no one's ideas should be criticized or dismissed. Set a time limit on the session before it begins, and when the time is up, consider and discuss all ideas fairly, as a group.

TO LEARN ENOUGH ABOUT YOUR SUBJECT TO DRAW A CONCLUSION:

- If your subject is a physical object, observe it carefully on several different occasions. Record your observations in your journal, along with any insights that accompany your observations. Examine the object from various perspectives, up close and from a distance, and from someone else's point of view. Record not only visual impressions, but sounds, smells, textures, and tastes as well. Notice how your subject changes from one observation to another, and how it fits and functions in its setting.

- If you are observing someone or something from memory, try freewriting, clustering, or brainstorming to recall the details and clarify the overall impression. Talk with someone who was there to help you remember more clearly, or to see your subject from another point of view.

- Learning about your subject often involves critical reading and research of primary or secondary sources. Primary sources may be the subject of your writing (the object of scrutiny itself), experts on your subject whom you would like to interview, or groups of people you would like to survey. Secondary sources are written (or otherwise recorded) observations about your subject that others have produced. Whether you are probing primary or secondary sources for information and insight, you will want to record what you learn in notes.

TO DETERMINE WRITING STRATEGY AND TO ORGANIZE YOUR THOUGHTS:

- Consider how audience and purpose will—and should—affect your writing strategies. Who is the reader, and what are his or her expectations, if any? Is your reader expecting a report, an argument, a personal essay? What are the requirements of the kind of writing that's called for?

- Take the journalistic approach, asking yourself *who, what, when, where, how,* and *why?* Answer these questions in journal freewrites. A structure should begin to emerge.

- In your journal, make a rough or formal outline, depending on the relative complexity of the writing project, in order to chart the progression your thoughts will take, establishing the relationships between the main idea, your central points, and supporting details before you begin your first draft.

Not all kinds of writing require all these steps in the prewriting stage. If a specific subject has been assigned to you, obviously you will not have to brainstorm to find one; if your subject is fresh and entirely personal, the only source you will have to consult is yourself; and if you are writing a personal narrative, the structure of your writing may be self-evident and an outline may be a waste of time. You may find that you move back and forth between prewriting stages, letting one inform and further the other, just as you may use certain prewriting strategies—such as freewriting—repeatedly in the prewriting process and beyond.

Drafting

After you have decided what it is you are going to write about, explored and learned enough about the subject to be in a position to draw some valid conclusions about it, and established some general idea as to how you will organize your writing and what rhetorical approach might work best, you are ready to begin drafting (that is, if you haven't already begun).

There is no one correct way to go about a first draft. You may have written a sentence or two, or a paragraph here and there, in the prewriting process, but these may or may not find their way into your first draft, and, if they do, they may or may not make it to the final draft. In drafting, you might begin at the beginning and end at the end. Or you might decide to start within the body of the essay, learning still more about what you think as you go and leaving the opening paragraph until you are certain you know what your conclusions will be, how you will frame your main idea, and how best to capture your reader's attention from the outset.

You may write your first draft in one sitting, or you may write the opening paragraph five different times and decide (probably rightly so) that you are stuck and need to take a long walk and come back to drafting, with a fresh approach, later.

It is important in drafting, as it is in prewriting, that you not be overly critical—that you not get bogged down in details at the expense of allowing yourself to build momentum. Many writers who begin drafting too early find that they are working on sentence structure before they have anything much to say, either in the sentence or in the whole essay. If you have confidence in your subject and an idea of what can be gained in writing about it, then the draft is the place to experiment with structure and style in writing. What is your main idea? How will you explain it and flesh it out? What distinguishes the central point of one paragraph from that of the next? How do ideas relate? How will you frame and phrase information and ideas precisely and interestingly? How will you drive your point home? If you have allowed prewriting to serve its purpose, the answers to these questions will come more easily in the drafting stage. It is important to remind yourself that at the drafting stage, what you write is not set in stone.

Revising

There is, or should be, a distinction between revising and editing, and many of us make the mistake of thinking that editing is all that revision entails. Some prefer the term *re-visioning* to revising, because it more accurately describes what this part of the writing process really entails: the reworking of ideas and the rearrangement of fairly large chunks of writing or thinking. As you draft and revise, you should be involved in a continuing process of re-evaluating your subject, rethinking your conclusions, and reconsidering the most effective ways to communicate with your reader. You may find that the piece of writing you end up with is not what you originally had in mind. When writing is approached as a relatively fluid process, rather than a one-shot deal, it can offer room for the writer to evolve his or her perceptions, sometimes even to change his or her mind radically, about the subject. This, after all, is learning.

Editing occurs at a more minute level than revising. It is the final step before you declare a piece of writing "done." It is your opportunity to polish phrasing and refine word choice, to catch grammatical and spelling errors, and to make sure that the finished writing looks good on the page. Editing is extremely important to the overall effectiveness of a piece of writing, but editing in itself does not constitute revision.

If you approach your writing as simply a matter of leaping into and knocking out a first (and final) draft based on preconceived notions (instead of information-gathering and reflection), relying on a once-over reading to edit for grammatical errors before delivering it to your reader, you will probably have done yourself, your subject, and your reader a disservice. Nothing in particular is learned; nothing in particular is gained.

It could be argued that even so-called final drafts are not set in stone, that writing is never truly finished; one simply finishes with any given piece and moves on to something else. If you have worked hard you should be content in knowing that you have done the best you could, given what you knew and the time you had, to say precisely what you meant.

THE READING PROCESS: READING WITH A WRITER'S EYE

The term *critical reading* is used to describe an active rather than a passive reading process. A critical reader is not, as the term perhaps suggests, one that is impossible to please; he or she is simply curious. Critical readers approach reading with an open and inquiring mind, probing as they read. Beyond a literal understanding of a written text, critical readers are interested in understanding the text's implications and how it relates to other texts, ideas, and experience. And critical reading within the context of a writing course implies a further dimension: reading with a writer's eye. Writers are interested in understanding how other authors have constructed their work, how and why they have succeeded or failed in developing their ideas in writing and in having an impact on their readers. Developing your critical reading skills will help you become a more effective writer.

When we read for pleasure, we may or may not read a text more than once. When we are reading explicitly to learn, multiple readings are important if we are to understand the depth and complexity of ideas, relate those ideas to other ideas, and appreciate how a writer has constructed his or her writing. A careful reading process, like a careful writing process, may be best approached in stages; but these stages, like those of the writing process, may be recursive, or one stage may be more important than another, depending upon the complexity of the text, the individual's reading style, and the purpose associated with the reading. In college, you may not always have the time to read every text assigned to you two or three times, but when the text is especially complex or your understanding of it is especially important, multiple readings are a very good idea indeed.

Previewing: Getting Oriented

In previewing, you browse, familiarizing yourself with what you are about to read in more depth and orienting yourself. Scan titles and subheadings to gather what the piece is about; then read the first paragraph or two. Take note of how the writing looks on the page, its length and density, getting a sense of its style and purpose. Is it factual or fictional? Argumentative, analytical, or anecdotal? Scholarly or popular? Traditional or nontraditional? Is it dense or light reading? Does its subject or style remind you of anything else you have read? Does it bring to mind any experience you have had?

Read any background on the text that is provided. Are there headnotes that supply historical or biographical information? Is the author a man or a woman? Where is he or she from? What qualifies him or her as an expert on the subject? When was the piece originally published, and in what form? For what audience was the writer originally writing and for what purpose? If the reading appears in a textbook such as this one, and if there are discussion questions following it, scan them in advance.

Knowing something about the nature and context of the reading before you start will help you better understand and engage in it. Highlight, underline, or circle information that seems of particular interest and jot it down, along with your initial impressions, in prereading notes in your journal or notebook.

Initial Reading: Gathering a First Response

In your first reading, read quickly for an overall impression of meaning and the writing's effect. If you encounter passages that you do not fully understand, note them with a question mark. Underline passages that articulate key points. Put exclamation marks next to portions that seem especially well-written, interesting, or with which you emphatically agree. Put *X*'s next to passages that seem especially poorly written or with which you emphatically disagree. As you would in freewriting, try not to get bogged down in the details. Instead, read for an overall impression, and don't worry if your response seems "merely" subjective at this stage.

In your journal or notebook, sum up your initial impressions. What is the author's central idea? Jot down in question form points you may not yet be clear on. What is your emotional and/or intellectual response to the reading? Do you find the writing engaging? In what ways does it challenge you? What is your general impression of the writer's style? Does this piece of writing bring to mind, in its ideas or style, anything else you have read or anything you have written? Reread your notes before you read the piece again more closely.

Close Reading: Interpreting and Evaluating

Reading closely, in depth, you will read more slowly and more carefully. You will probably read some passages more than once. In the margins of your text, flesh out the shorthand notes you made in your first reading. Have the passages you marked with question marks come clearer with subsequent reading? If not, is the writer being unclear, or do you need to try again? Try to articulate in notes what it is you like or dislike about the passages you marked with exclamation points or X's. Have you changed your mind about any of them?

By now, you should have a pretty clear idea of what the author's central idea is; now pay particular attention to how he or she develops and supports it. Take note of how the writer has organized the writing. Try writing a one-sentence summary of each paragraph's central idea or dominant impression. If there are major shifts in focus, point of view, or style, mark them. In argumentative or analytical writing, are the reasons convincing and well-supported by evidence? List the author's supporting points in your journal or notebook. In descriptive or narrative writing, how do descriptive and narrative details, action, character, dialogue, and point of view, as well as the author's writing style, contribute to the writing's theme or convey the author's attitudes?

If ideas or images seem related in any way to you, circle and connect them, explaining the connections to yourself in marginal notations. If the writer uses a particular rhetorical strategy more than once, underline and note it. For every general observation you make about the writing's meaning or the writer's style, make note of a sentence or two that exemplifies or illustrates your own critical observation. In notes in your journal or notebook, compare this piece to others you have read. How is this piece similar to or different from other writing you have encountered on the same subject? How do this author's ideas, methods of development, or writing style compare to those of other authors you have read? Collect examples from both texts that support these comparisons.

As a writer yourself, you should approach a close reading of any text with the intention of grasping not only what the author is saying but how he or she has constructed the writing to express it. Reading with a writer's eye will promote more than your literal understanding of what you read; it will also improve your understanding of what works and what doesn't work in writing. These are lessons you can then take back with you to your own writing process.

READINGS: MAPPING EXPLORATION

WRITING IN TIME

Journals and letters are intimate expressions, open-ended and often rough, and literature seems to stand as solid as a public statue before the city library, finished and unalterable. We may see literature as a destination, and journals and letters as stops on the road. And it's true that most writers' journals are not ends in themselves but provide momentum, raw material, or drafting space for other writing projects. Similarly, most personal letters are never published, since publication runs contrary to their purpose. For some writers, though, journals and letters *are* literature. Part of such writings' liveliness, their unique literary character, has precisely to do with their unique function and the fact that they exist within time: Journals and letters are designed to illuminate and illustrate key *processes*—the process of exploration and discovery, and the process of articulation.

Journal entries and letters are also historical documents, since they are defined within the context of the moments, hours, and days in which they were written. Although they serve an immediate purpose, offering a location and occasion for the writer to observe, explain, and record within the moment, their significance often grows or comes into focus when they are understood by writer or reader as pieces of a larger picture, as steps in an ongoing process of discovery and articulation. They are like snapshots that might be heaped haphazardly in a shoebox in the basement, or, on the other hand, may be sorted and organized into albums to share.

The journal selections and letters included in Chapter 1 chart the progress of the authors' explorations and record their moments of discovery. All of these writers are searching for something, and the promise of its discovery lies within the natural world. But where some writers represented in this chapter are primarily concerned with observing flora and fauna or mapping terrain, others are tracking themselves. And some are doing both at once: In scanning a mountainous horizon or studying the geometry of a flower, a writer may find his or her or all of our faces reflected there.

Some of the written "snapshots" you will find in this chapter have a clear historical resonance born of the purpose that inspired them and highlighted as we look back at them through time. Most of us can appreciate, for example, how important Lewis and Clark's discovery of an overland route to the Pacific was for westward expansion in the United States because we are living with the effects, and Lewis and Clark's journals, the written record of their expedition, exist as a historically significant document. Others of these "snapshots," however, are much more personal in scope. Yet they too are pieces of history and have important things to say about nature and culture, as well as about the inner lives of the individuals who wrote them.

Some of the journal selections included here were originally written as private diaries, including those of John Muir and George G. Swan (included within Ivan Doig's journal), and were published posthumously. Most, however, were intended to be read.

The journals of the early American explorers Lewis and Clark grew from an assignment and were part of the requirements of a specific job. The primary audience were Lewis and Clark's employers, Thomas Jefferson and the U.S. Congress. Though they were official documents, the *Original Journals of the Lewis and Clark Expedition* found their way into broader publication and were eagerly consumed by an interested public. The journal selections by Todd Dickson also arose from an assignment—in this case a class assignment—to keep a class journal, one purpose of which was to explore possible writing subjects.

Contemporary journal writers Peter Matthiessen and Ivan Doig are well-established writers who set out to write their journals with the awareness that publication, though perhaps not assured, was certainly a strong possibility. Although this by no means implies that they had no personal impetus in writing, the prospect of publication no doubt affected how these writers perceived and undertook their writing, and the care each took in communicating something important to the reader.

The letters included in Chapter 1—John Muir's letter to his friend Jeanne Carr and Isabella Bird's letter to her sister—are intimate letters, and were not originally intended for publication. Since they are letters, they have to communicate clearly, even if to a single and familiar reader.

How, when we are aware of it, does the existence of a reader at the far end of writing affect not only the style, but the subject, the content, and the structure of our writing? How do we approach subjects differently, depending upon the purpose our writing serves?

WRITERS AND WILDERNESS

Confronted with such vast wilderness, few white explorers or settlers of the American West from the mid-1700s through the mid- to late 1800s felt much inclined toward nature worship. Wilderness was fearsome and deadly, and it served no purpose until conquered, cultivated, and developed; then it promised great material riches. Meriwether Lewis, though appreciative of nature's abundance and respectful of its power, describes it with the eye of a surveyor.

Henry David Thoreau, writing from the tame New England wilderness of Walden Pond in the mid-1800s, was probably the first white American to propose that wilderness had in and of itself an intrinsic value, a concept later put into action by John Muir, one of our earliest conservationists, who founded the Sierra Club in 1892 and was instrumental in establishing our National Parks system. Since Muir's time, the American wilderness has dwindled and popular appreciation of it has generally increased; we hardly know how to accommodate all our wilderness tourists.

For the growing number of American writers who, perhaps ironically, seem inclined to write of wilderness that is so steadily disappearing, the realm of wilderness may have shifted. Wilderness journals have become more and more introspective, charting an interior landscape, as if the last true wilderness were the human heart and mind.

■ **MERIWETHER LEWIS**
Up Jefferson's River

Meriwether Lewis was born near Charlottesville, Virginia, in 1774. His life as an explorer and naturalist developed with his military and political careers and his ongoing association with Thomas Jefferson. As President Jefferson's private secretary from 1801 to

1803, Lewis was groomed to head a transcontinental expedition to explore an overland route to the Pacific, a dream that Jefferson and Lewis held in common. Lewis selected, with Jefferson's approval, fellow Virginian, frontier soldier, and Indian agent William Clark to help lead the expedition. The Lewis and Clark Expedition, for which Congress appropriated $2,500 in 1803 but which cost $5,000 before it was over, was key to the opening of a vast American wilderness to westward expansion. Following the successful completion of the expedition, Jefferson appointed Lewis governor of the Louisiana Territory, a position he occupied for only three years before his death in 1809. Plagued by both personal financial problems and questions regarding his use of public monies, Lewis set out for Washington, D.C. to put his affairs in order but died en route near Nashville, Tennessee, a victim, apparently, of either murder or suicide.

Lewis was a well-educated man, but his spelling and punctuation in the journals are quirky. As you read the following selection from the Original Journals of the Lewis and Clark Expedition, 1804–1806, *a passage describing an area that lies along what is now the Idaho-Montana border, keep in mind that these journals were commissioned; that is, they were part of Lewis's job, and therefore had a very particular purpose and audience. Not only were Lewis and Clark's* Journals *submitted to the president and Congress, but they were published (and in most editions "corrected") and eagerly consumed by an interested public.*

Sunday, July 28th, 1805

Both Captain C. and myself corrisponded in opinion with rispect to the impropriety of calling either of these streams the Missouri and accordingly agreed to name them after the President of the United States and the Secretaries of the Treasury and state having previously named one river in honour of the Secretaries of War and Navy. In pursuance of this resolution we called the S.W. fork, that which we meant to ascend, Jefferson's River in honor of that ullustrious personage Thomas Jefferson (the author of our enterprise.) The Middle fork we called Madison's River in honor of James Madison, and the S.E. Fork we called Gallitin's River in honor of Albert Gallitin. the two first are 90 yards wide and the last is 70 yards. all of them run with great velocity and throw out large bodies of water. Gallitin's River is reather more rapid than either of the others, is not quite as deep but from all appearances may be navigated to a considerable distance. Capt. C. who came down Madison's river yesterday and has also seen Jefferson's some distance thinks Madison's reather the most rapid, but it is not as much so by any means as Gallitin's. the beds of all these streams are formed of smooth pebble and gravel, and their waters perfectly transparent; in short they are three noble streams. there is timber enough here to support an establishment, provided it be erected with brick or stone either of which would be much cheaper than wood as all the materials for such a work are immediately at the spot. there are several small sand-bars along the shores at no great distance of pure sand and the earth appears as if it would make good brick. I had all our baggage spread out to dry this morning; and the day proving warm, I had a small bower or booth erected for the comfort of Capt. C. our leather lodge when exposed to the sun is excessively hot . . . in the evening about 4 O'Ck the wind blew hard from the South West and after some little time brought on a Cloud attended with thunder and Lightning from which we had a fine refreshing shower which cooled the air considerably; the showers continued with short intervals untill after dark. in the evening the hunters all returned they had killed 8 deer and 2 Elk, some of the deer were in excellent order. . . .

Tuesday, July 30th, 1805

Capt. Clark being much better this morning and having completed my observations we reloaded our canoes and set out, ascending Jeffersons river. Sharbono, his woman two invalleds and myself walked through the bottom on the Lard. side of the river about 4½ miles when we struck it again at the place the woman informed us she was taken prisoner. here we halted untill Capt. Clark arrived which was not until after one P.M. the water being strong and the river extremely crooked. we dined and again proceeded on; as the river now passed through the woods the invalleds got on board together with Sharbono and the Indian woman. I passed the river and continued my walk on the Stard. side. saw a vast number of beaver in many large dams which they had maid. I directed my course to the high plain to the right which I gained after some time with much difficulty and wading many beaver dams to my waist in mud and water. I would willingly have joined the canoes but the brush was so thick, the river crooked and bottoms intercepted in such manner by the beaver dams, that I found it uceless to attempt to find them, and therefore proceeded on up the river in order to intersept it where it came near the plain and would be more collected into one channel.

at length about sunset I arrived at the river only about six miles from my calculation on a direct line from the place I had left the canoes but I thought they were still below me. I found the river was divided where I reached it by an Island and was therefor fearful that they might pass without my seeing them, and went down to the lower point of the large island; here I discovered a small island, close under the shore on which I was; I passed the narrow channel to the small island and examined the gravely bar along the edge of the river for the tracks of the men, knowing that from the appearance of the river at this place if they had passed they would have used the cord on the side where I was. I saw no tracks and was then fully convinced that they were below me. I fired my gun and hallooed but could hear nothing of them. by this time it was getting nearly dark and a duck lit on the shore in about 40 steps of me and I killed it; having now secured my supper I looked out for a suitable place to amuse myself in combating the musquetos for the ballance of the evening. I found a parsel of drift wood at the head of the little island on which I was and immediately set it on fire and collected some willow brush to lye on. I cooked my duck which I found very good and after eating it layed down and should have had a comfortable nights lodge but for the musquetoes which infested me all night. late at night I was awakened by the nois of some animal running over the stoney bar on which I lay but did not see it; from the weight with which it ran I supposed it to be either an Elk or a brown bear.

Wednesday, July 31st, 1805

This morning I waited at my camp very impatiently for the arrival of Capt. Clark and party; I observed by my watch that it was 7 A.M. and they had not come in sight. I now became very uneasy and determined to wait until 8 and if they did not arrive by that time to proceed on up the river taking it as a fact that they had passed my camp some miles last evening. just as I set out to pursue my plan I discovered Sharbono walking up shore some distance below me and waited untill he arrived. I now learnt that the canoes were behind, they arrived shortly after. their detention had been caused by the rapidity of the water and the circuitous rout of the river. they halted and breakfasted after which we all set out again and I continued my walk on the Stard. shore. the river now becomes more collected the islands tho' numerous ar generally small. the river continues rapid and is from 90 to 120 yds. wide has a considerable quantity of timber in its bottoms. toward evening the bottoms became much narrower and the timber much more scant. . . .

August 1st, 1805

At half after 8 A.M. we halted for breakfast and as had been previously agreed on between Capt. Clark and myself I set out with 2 men in quest of the Snake Indians. the men I took were the two interpreters Drewyer and Sharbono and Sergt. Gass. the rout we took lay over a rough high range of mountains on the North side of the river. the river enetered these mountains a few miles above where we left it. . . .

The mountains are extremely bare of timber and our rout lay through the steep valleys exposed to the heat of the sun without shade and scarcely a breath of air; and to add to my fatigue in this walk of about 11 miles I had taken a doze of glauber salts in the morning in consequence of a slight desentary with which I had been afflicted for several days; being weakened by the disorder and the opperation of the medecine I found myself almost exhausted before we reached the river. I felt my sperits much revived on our near approach to the river at the sight of a herd of Elk of which Drewyer and myself killed two. we then hurried to the river and allayed our thirst. I ordered two of the men to skin the Elk and bring the meat to the river while myself and the other prepared a fire and cooked some of the meat for our dinner. we made a comfortable meal of the Elk and left the ballance of the meat on the bank of the river for the party with Capt. Clark. this supply was no doubt acceptable to them as they had had no fresh meat for two days except one beaver Game being very scarce and shy. we had seen a few deer and some goats but had not been fortunate enough to kill any of them. after dinner we resumed our march and encamped about 6 M. above on the Stard. side of the river.

Shortly after I left Capt. Clark this morning he proceeded on and passed through the mountains; they formed tremendious clifts of ragged and nearly perpendicular rocks; the lower part of this rock is of the black grannite before mentioned and the upper part a light coloured freestone. these clifts continue for 9 miles and approach the river very closely on either side. he found the current very strong. Capt. C killed a big horn on these clifts which himself and party dined on. after passing this range of mountains he entered this beautiful valley in which we also were. just at the upper side of the mountain there is a bad rappid. here the toe line of our canoe broke in the shoot of the rapids and swung on the rocks and had very nearly overset.

Friday, August 2cd, 1805

We resumed our march this morning at sunrise. finding that the river still boar south I determined to pass it if possible in order to shorten our rout; this we effected by wading the river about 5 miles above our encampment of the last evening. we found the current very rapid waist deep and about 90 yds. wide. bottom smooth pebble with a small mixture of coarse gravel. this is the first time I ever dared to wade the river, tho' there are many places between this and the forks where I presume it might be attempted with equal success. The valley along which we passed today, and through which the river winds it's meandering course is from 6 to 8 miles wide and consists of a beatifull level plain with but little timber and that confined to the verge of the river; the land is tolerably fertile, and is either black or dark yellow loam, covered with grass from 9 inches to 2 feet high. the plain ascends gradually on either side of the river to the bases of two ranges of high mountains. the tops of these mountains are yet covered partially with snow, while we in the valley are nearly suffocated with the intense heat of the mid-day sun; the nights are so cold that two blankets are not more than sufficient covering . . .

Saturday, August 3rd, 1805

Set out early this morning, or before sunrise; still continued our march through the level valley on the lard. side of the river. the valley much as yesterday only reather wider; I think it is 12 Miles wide, tho' the plains near the mountains rise higher and are more broken with some scattering pine near the mountain. in the leveler parts of the plain and river bottoms which are very extensive there is no timber except a scant proportion of cottonwood near the river. The Mountains continue high on either side of the valley and are but scantily supplyed with timber; small pine appears to be the prevalent growth; it is of the pitch kind, with a short leaf. at 11 A.M. Drewyer killed a doe and we halted 2 hours and breakfasted, and then continued our rout till night without halting . . . .

Capt. Clark set out this morning as usual. he walked on shore a small distance this morning and killed a deer. in the course of his walk he saw a track which he supposed to be that of an Indian from the circumstance of the large toes turning inward. he pursued the track and found that the person had ascended a point of a hill from which his camp of the last evening was visible; this circumstance also confirmed the belief of its being an Indian who had thus discovered them and ran off. They found the river as usual much crowded with islands, the currant more rapid & much more shallow than usual. in many places they were obliged to double man the canoes and drag them over the stone and gravel. this morning they passed a small creek on Stard. at the entrance of which Reubin Fields killed a large Panther. we called the creek after that animal Panther Creek. they also passed a handsome little stream on Lard. which is form of several springs which rise in the bottoms and along the base of the mountains with some little rivulets from the melting snows. in the evening they passed a very bad rappid where the bed of the river is formed entrely of solid rock and encamped on an island just above. the men wer compelled to be a great proportion of their time in the water today; they have had a severe days labour and are much fortiegued.

Tuesday, August 6th, 1805

about five miles above the forks I heard the hooping of the party to my left and changed my rout towards them; on my arrival found that they had taken the rapid fork and learnt from Capt. Clark that he had not found the note which I left for him at that place and the reasons which had induced him to ascend this stream. it was easiest & more in our direction, and apd. to contain as much water. he had however previously to my comeing up with him, met Drewyer who informed him of the state of the two rivers and was on his return. One of their canoes had just overset and all the baggage wet, the medicine box among other articles and several articles lost a shot pouch and horn among with all the implements for one rifle lost and never recovered.

I walked down to the point where I waited their return. on their arrival found that two other canoes had filled with water and wet their cargoes completely. Whitehouse had been thrown out of one of these canoes as she swing in a rapid current and the canoe had rubbed him and pressed him to the bottom as she passed over him and had the water been inches shallower must inevitably have crushed him to death. our parched meal, corn, Indian presents and a great part of our most valuable stores were wet and much damaged on this ocasion. to examine, dry and arrange our stores was the first object; we therefore passed over to the lard. side opposite the entrance of the rapid fork where there was a large gravly bar that answered our purposes; wood was also convenient and plenty. here we fixed our camp, and unloaded all our canoes and opened and exposed to dry such articles as had been wet. a part of the load of each canoe consisted of the leaden canestirs of powder which were not in least injured, tho' some of them had remained upwards of an hour under water. about 20 lbs. of powder which we had in a tight Keg or at least one we thought sufficiently so got wet and entirely spoiled. this would have been the case with the other had it not been for the expedient which I had fallen on of securing the powder by means of the lead having the latter formed into canesters which were filled with the necessary proportion of powder to discharge the lead when used, and those canesters well secured with corks and wax. in this country the air is so pure and dry that any vessel however well seasoned the timber may be will give way or shrink unless it is kept full of some liquid. we found that three deer skins which we had left at a considerable height on a tree were taken off which we supposed had been done by a panther. we sent out some men to hunt this evening they killed 3 deer and four Elk which gave us plentifull supply of meat once more.

Shannon had been dispatched up the rapid fork this morning to hunt, by Capt. Clark before he met with Drewyer or learnt his mistake in the rivers. when he returned he sent Drewyer in surch of him, but he rejoined us this evening and reported that he had been several miles up the river and could find nothing of him. we had the trumpet sounded and fired several guns but he did not join us this evening. I am fearful he is lost again. this is the same man who was separated from us 15 days as we came up the Missouri and subsisted 9 days of that time on grapes only. . . .

■ CONSIDERATIONS OF MEANING AND METHOD

1. How are Meriwether Lewis's purposes in journal keeping reflected in his writing—in content (that is, in what he notices) and in style (that is, in how he records in language what he notices)?

2. What can you discern about Lewis's attitudes toward wilderness and exploration from this journal entry?

3. Put yourself in President Jefferson's and Congress's place as Lewis and Clark's employers, sponsors, and primary readers.

Did Lewis do his job in keeping this journal? Do the errors in spelling and punctuation seem sloppy to you, given the journals' audience? How much do they matter?

■ POSSIBILITIES FOR WRITING

1. You are President Jefferson. Compose a letter to Meriwether Lewis evaluating his performance as expedition journal keeper.

2. In a letter to Meriwether Lewis and William Clark, describe the consequences of their discovery of an overland route to the West. You may have to do a little library research to fill any gaps in your knowledge.

3. In your journal write an account, as an outside observer, of alien territory. Visit a place you've never been—an unfamiliar place, or a place where an unfamiliar activity takes place—and describe what you encounter. For example, you might visit a forest at night or a soup kitchen, or attend a social event or a religious or cultural ceremony that is new to you. Notice, record, reflect, and speculate to a reader who, like you, is unfamiliar with what you are describing and has asked you to explore and report.

■ JOHN MUIR
Journal Entry, April 3, 1871
Letter to Jeanne C. Carr, Christmas Day, 1872
An Unexpected Adventure

Naturalist John Muir was one of America's first conservationists. He believed that wilderness was worth preserving for its own intrinsic value and that it should not be seen simply in terms of profit—not the prevailing opinion of the day. He was instrumental in establishing early forest conservation policies, and it is largely due to his efforts that his beloved Yosemite and other wilderness areas have been preserved as national parks. In 1892 John Muir founded The Sierra Club.

Born in 1838 in Dunbar, Scotland, Muir emigrated with his family to a Wisconsin homestead in 1849. He was educated at the University of Wisconsin but never graduated, electing to pursue his own interests in philosophy and science rather than an officially sanctioned course of study. Muir was an inveterate wanderer whose adventures and observations, both scientific and philosophical, are recorded in his extensive journals, most of which ultimately saw publication. His travels included a walk in 1867 from Indiana to Florida; many forays into the wilderness regions of the California Sierra range; subsequent exlorations of Nevada, Utah, Washington, Oregon, and Alaska; and expeditions late in his life to locations as far-flung as South America, Africa, and Australia. He died in 1914.

John Muir's voluminous writings provide one of the foundation blocks of American writing and thought about nature and wilderness. Muir's appreciation of landscape and natural history is both technically precise and grandly spiritual. Thomas J. Lyon, author of This Incomperable Lande: A Book of American Nature Writing, *describes Muir as possessing a "scientific-poetic faith that all that is required, in order to transcend the usual limitations of thought, is to [as Muir himself said] 'study and mingle with nature more.'" He wrote a great deal for publication, although "raw" journal writing was his preferred medium, and he was a dedicated correspondent. Among the most notable of his letters were those to Jeanne C. Carr, the wife of Ezra Carr, a professor of his at the University of Wisconsin. His affection for Mrs. Carr is clear, and they shared a spiritual affinity and an ecstatic enthusiasm for the natural world.*

The following selections by Muir include a journal entry describing an adventure he had at Yosemite Falls in 1871, a letter written in 1872 to Mrs. Carr in which he expresses his feelings about writing for public consumption, and a description of his Yosemite Falls adventure revised for publication in 1912. As you read them, consider how the nature of Muir's writing accommodates itself to a changing audience and purpose.

Journal Entry, April 3, 1871

At night the lunar bows in the spray make a most impressive picture. There was the huge dark cavern of the gorge filled with tempestuous foam and the scud and roar of many storms. The fall above hung white, ghostlike, and indistinct. Slowly the moon coming round the domes sent her white beams into the wild uproar, and lo, among the tremendous blasts and surges at the foot of the pit, five hundred feet below the ledge on which I stood, there appeared a rainbow set on end, colored like the solar bow only fainter, strangely peaceful and still, in the midst of roaring, surging tempestuous power. Also a still fainter secondary bow.

I had intended to stay all night, but an hour ago I crept out on a narrow ledge that extends back of the fall, and as the wind swayed the mighty column at times a little forward from the face of the precipice, I thought it would be a fine thing to get back of the down-rushing waters and see them in all their glory with the moonlight sifting through them. I got out safely, though the ledge is only about six inches wide in one place, and was gazing up and out through the half-translucent edge of the fall, when some heavy plashes striking the wall above me caught my attention; then suddenly all was dark, and down came a dash of outside gauze tissue made of spent comets, thin and harmless to look at a mile off, but desperately solid and stony when they strike one's shoulders. It seemed as if I was being pelted with a mixture of choking spray and gravel. I grasped the angle of the ledge and held hard with my knees, and submitted to my frightful baptism with but little faith. When I dared look up after the pelting had nearly ceased, and the column swaying back admitted the light, I hastily pounced back of a block of ice that was frozen to the ledge, squeezing myself in between the ice and the wall, and no longer feared being washed off.

When the moonbeams again slanted past the ever-changing edge of the torrent, I took courage and made a dash for freedom and escaped, made a fire and partially warmed my benumbed limbs, then ran down to my cabin, reached it sometime towards morning, changed my clothing, got an hour or two of sleep, and awoke sane and comfortable, some of the earthiness washed out of me and Yosemite virtue washed in, better, not worse, for my wild bath in lunar bows, spent comet-tails, ice, drizzle, and moonshine. . . . Wonderful that Nature can do such wild passionate work without seeming extravagant, or that she will allow poor mortals so near her while doing it.

Letter to Jeanne C. Carr, Christmas Day, 1872

Book-making frightens me, because it demands so much artificialness and retrograding. Somehow, up here in these fountain skies [of Yosemite] I feel like a flake of glass through which light passes, but which, conscious of the inexhaustibleness of its sun fountain, cares not whether its passing light coins itself into other forms or goes unchanged—neither charcoaled nor diamonded! Moreover, I find that though I have a few thoughts entangled in the fibres of my mind, I possess no words into which I can shape them. You tell me that I must be patient and reach out and grope in lexicon granaries for the words I want. But if some loquacious angel were to touch my lips with literary fire, bestowing every word of Webster, I would scarce thank him for the gift, because most of the words of the English language are made of mud, for muddy purposes, while those invented to contain spiritual matter are doubtful and unfixed in capacity and form, as wind-ridden mist-rags.

These mountain fires that glow in one's blood are free to all, but I cannot find the chemistry that may press them unimpaired into booksellers' bricks. True, with that august instrument, the English language, in the manufacture of which so many brains have been broken, I can proclaim to you that moonshine is glorious, and sunshine more glorious, that winds rage and waters roar, and that in "terrible times" glaciers guttered the mountains with their hard cold snouts. This is about the limit of what I feel capable of doing for the public— the moiling, squirming, fog-breathing public. But for my few friends I can do more because they already know the mountain harmonies and can catch the tones I gather for them, though written in a few harsh and gravelly sentences.

An Unexpected Adventure

A wild scene, but not a safe one, is made by the moon as it appears through the edge of the Yosemite Fall when one is behind it. Once, after enjoying the night-song of the waters and watching the fomation of the colored bows as the moon came round the domes and sent her beams into the wild uproar, I ventured out on the narrow bench that extends back of the fall from Fern Ledge and began to admire the dim-veiled grandeur of the view. I could see the fine threads of the fall's filmy border by having the light in front; and wishing to look at the moon through the meshes of some of the denser portions of the fall, I ventured to creep further behind it while it was gently wind-swayed, without taking sufficient thought about the consequences of its swaying back to its natural position after the wind-pressure should be removed. The effect was enchanting: fine, savage music sounding above, beneath, around me; while the moon, apparently in the very midst of the rushing waters, seemed to be struggling to keep her place, an account of the ever-varying form and density of the water masses through which she was seen, now darkly veiled or eclipsed by a rush of thick-headed comets, now flashing out through openings between their tails. I was in fairyland between the dark wall and the wild throng of illuminated waters, but suffered sudden disenchantment; for, like the witch-scene in Alloway Kirk, "in an instant all was dark." Down came a dash of spent comets, thin and harmless-looking in the distance, but they felt desperately solid and stony when they struck my shoulders, like a mixture of choking spray and gravel and big hailstones. Instinctively dropping on my knees, I gripped an angle of rock, curled up like a young fern frond with my face pressed against my breast, and in this attitude submitted as best I could to my thundering bath. The heavier masses seemed to strike like cobblestones, and there was a confusing noise of many waters about my ears—hissing, gurgling, clashing sounds that were not heard as music. The situation was quickly realized. How fast one's thoughts burn in such time of stress! I was weighing chances of escape. Would the column be swayed a few inches away from the wall, or would it come yet closer? The fall was in flood and not so lightly would its ponderous mass be swayed. My fate seemed to depend on a breath of the "idle wind." It was moved gently forward, the pounding ceased, and I was once more visited by glimpses of the moon. But fearing that I might be caught at a disadvantage in making too hasty a retreat, I moved only a few feet along the bench to where a block of ice lay. I wedged myself between the ice and the wall, and lay face downwards, until the steadiness of the light gave me encouragement to rise and get away. Somewhat nerve-shaken, drenched, and benumbed, I made out to build a fire, warmed myself, ran home, reached my cabin before daylight, got an hour or two of sleep, and awoke sound and comfortable, better, not worse, for my hard midnight bath.

■ CONSIDERATIONS OF MEANING AND METHOD

1. Compare Muir's journal entry, written hours after his adventure, and his later account, revised for publication more than forty years later. In what ways are the accounts similar, and how do they differ? Which do you prefer and why?

2. Do you agree with Muir's assessment, in his letter to Mrs. Carr in 1872, of the fundamental inadequacy of language to capture and convey thought and emotion, or even to describe the physical world accurately? Do you, as did Muir, find it easier to write to an intimate reader than to a less familiar or wider readership? Why or why not?

3. How does Muir's letter to Mrs. Carr accommodate itself to its reader? From the content and tone of the letter, can you describe the nature of their relationship?

■ Possibilities for Writing

1. Write a journal account of a memorable encounter you have had with nature. Revise the account for a general reader. Write a third version in the form of a letter to a friend who has both an interest in you and your life and in your subject. When you are finished, write a paragraph or two describing how the specific focus and your writing style differ from version to version, depending upon audience and purpose.

2. Write an essay in which you compare your experiences in writing for personal reasons and writing for a distant reader. With which form are you more comfortable and why? If you have used journal writing or freewriting as a prewriting technique to help you produce more formal writing, what purpose does informal writing serve? How do your writing strategies and styles change when a less than intimate reader enters the picture?

3. John Muir's commitment to wilderness conservation grew from his intimate experiences with nature. He was much more at home as a naturalist in the field than as an activist in political circles, and yet he engaged in the second endeavor to preserve the quality of the first. Have you ever had to reveal, explain, or defend in a public forum (writing, speaking, political involvement, or even informal conversation) what seemed an intimate part of your life? If you have, consider writing, in an essay, about the experience and any conflicts that may have arisen from it.

■ **ISABELLA BIRD**
Estes Park, Colorado, October 1873

For someone compelled to travel in search of improved health, nineteenth-century Englishwoman Isabella Bird was a hearty explorer indeed, often traveling in remote areas alone on horseback. Her 1873 ascent of Long's Peak, in Estes Park, Colorado, an adventure which Bird recounts here, took place only five years after its first documented ascent by explorer John Wesley Powell. Anne La Bastille, in her book Women and Wilderness, *calls Bird "every inch a lady," but she was certainly a lady who defied the conventions of her time. Although she may not have considered herself an explorer, others did; in 1892 she was the first woman elected to the Royal Geographical Society of England.*

Born on October 15, 1831, in Yorkshire, England, Bird was well-known in the 1800s for her travels, and her many books chronicling them were widely read. Her Pacific and Asian explorations included an eight thousand–mile solo trek through China. La Bastille notes that "her account of the period she spent in Colorado in the fall and winter of 1873 . . . is as vivid, perceptive, and eloquent a portrayal of the western wilderness as any early female writer has bequeathed us." Isabella Bird died on October 7, 1904, in Edinburgh, Scotland.

Although the following selection from A Lady's Life in the Rocky Mountains *(1879) has the appearance of a journal account, it is actually a series of long letters Bird wrote to her sister in England describing her travels. Bird did not originally intend to publish them, but was urged to do so after they were written. As you read Bird's account of her ascent of Long's Peak, bear in mind how unusual it was at the time for a woman to travel alone, and especially to undertake wilderness adventure.*

As this account of the ascent of Long's Peak could not be written at the time, I am much disinclined to write it, especially as no sort of description within my powers could enable another to realize the glorious sublimity, the majestic solitude, and the unspeakable awfulness and fascination of the scenes in which I spent Monday, Tuesday, and Wednesday.

Long's Peak, 14,700 feet high, blocks up one end of Estes Park, and dwarfs all the surrounding mountains. From it on this side rise, snow-born, the bright St. Vrain, and the Big and Little Thompson. By sunlight or moonlight its splintered grey crest is the one object which, in spite of wapiti and bighorn, skunk and grizzly, unfailingly arrests the eyes. From it come all storms of snow and wind, and the forked lightnings play round its head like a glory. It is one of the noblest of mountains, but in one's imagination it grows to be much more than a mountain. It becomes invested with a personality. In its caverns and abysses one comes to fancy that it generates and chains the strong winds, to let them loose in its fury. The thunder becomes its voice, and the lightnings do it homage. Other summits blush under the morning kiss of the sun, and turn pale the next moment; but it detains the first sunlight and holds it round its head for an hour at least, till it pleases to change from rosy red to deep blue; and the sunset, as if spell-bound, lingers latest on its crest. The soft winds which hardly rustle the pine needles down here are raging rudely up there round its motionless summit. The mark of fire is upon it; and though it has passed into a grim repose, it tells of fire and upheaval as truly, though not as eloquently, as the living volcanoes of Hawaii. Here under its shadow one learns how naturally nature worship, and the propitiation of the forces of nature, arose in minds which had no better light.

Long's Peak, "the American Matterhorn," as some call it, was ascended five years ago for the first time. I thought I should like to attempt it, but up to Monday, when Evans left for Denver, cold water was thrown upon the project. It was too late in the season, the winds were likely to be strong, etc.; but just before leaving, Evans said that the weather was looking more settled, and if I did not get farther than the timber line it would be worth going. Soon after he left, "Mountain Jim" came in, and he would go up as guide, and the two youths who rode here with me from Longmount and I caught at the proposal. Mrs. Edwards at once baked bread for three days, steaks were cut from the steer which hangs up conveniently, and tea, sugar, and butter were benevolently added. Our picnic was not to be a luxurious or "well-found" one, for, in order to avoid the expense of a pack mule, we limited our luggage to what our saddle horses could carry. Behind my saddle I carried three pair of camping blankets and a quilt, which reached to my shoulders. My own boots were so much worn that it was painful to walk, even about the park, in them, so Evans had lent me a pair of his hunting boots, which hung to the horn of my saddle. The horses of the two young men were equally loaded, for we had to prepare for many degrees of frost. "Jim" was a shocking figure; he had on an old pair of high boots, with a baggy pair of old trousers made of deer hide, held on by an old scarf tucked into them; a leather shirt, with three or four ragged unbuttoned waistcoats over it; an old smashed wideawake, from under which his tawny, neglected ringlets hung; and with his one eye, his one long spur, his knife in his belt, his revolver in his waistcoat pocket, his saddle covered with an old beaver skin, from which the paws hung down; his camping blankets behind him, his rifle laid across the saddle in front of him, and his axe, canteen, and other gear hanging to the horn, he was as awful-looking a ruffian as one could see. By way of contrast he rode a small Arab mare, of exquisite beauty, skittish, high spirited, gentle, but altogether too light for him, and he fretted her incessantly to make her display herself.

Heavily loaded as all our horses were, "Jim" started over the half-mile of level grass at a hard gallop, and then throwing his mare on her haunches, pulled up alongside of me, and with a grace of manner which soon made me forget his appearance, entered into a conversation which lasted for more than three hours, in spite of the manifold checks of fording streams, single file, abrupt ascents and descents, and other incidents of mountain travel. The ride was one series of glories and surprises, of "park" and glade, of lake and stream, of mountains on mountains, culminating in the rent pinnacles of Long's Peak, which looked yet grander and ghastlier as we crossed an attendant mountain 11,000 feet high. The slanting sun added fresh beauty every hour. There were dark pines against a lemon sky, grey peaks reddening and etherealizing, gorges of deep and infinite blue, floods of golden glory pouring through canyons of enormous depth, an atmosphere of absolute purity, an occasional foreground of cottonwood and aspen flaunting in red and gold to intensify the blue gloom of the pines, the trickle and murmur of streams fringed with icicles, the strange *sough* of gusts moving among the pinetops—sights and sounds not of the lower earth, but of the solitary, beast-haunted, frozen upper altitudes. From the dry, buff grass of Estes Park we turned off up a trail on the side of a pine-hung gorge, up a steep pine-clothed hill, down to a small valley, rich in fine, sun-cured hay about eighteen inches high, and enclosed by high mountains whose deepest hollow contains a lily-covered lake, fitly named "The Lake of the Lilies." Ah, how magical its beauty was, as it slept in silence, where *there* the dark pines were mirrored motionless in its pale gold, and *here* the great white lily cups and dark green leaves rested on amethyst-colored water!

From this we ascended into the purple gloom of great pine forests which clothe the skirts of the mountains up to a height of about 11,000 feet, and from their chill and solitary depths we had glimpses of golden atmosphere and rose-lit summits, not of "the land very far off," but of the land nearer now in all its grandeur, gaining in sublimity by nearness—glimpses, too, through a broken vista of purple gorges, of the illimitable Plains lying idealized in the late sunlight, their baked, brown expanse transfigured into the likeness of a sunset sea rolling infinitely in waves of misty gold.

We rode upwards through the gloom on a steep trail blazed through the forest, all my intellect concentrated on avoiding being dragged off my horse by impending branches, or having the blankets badly torn, as those of my companions were, by sharp dead limbs, between which there was hardly room to pass—the horses breathless, and requiring to stop every few yards, though their riders, except myself, were afoot. The gloom of the dense, ancient, silent forest is to me awe inspiring. On such an evening it is soundless, except for the

branches creaking in the soft wind, the frequent snap of decayed timber, and a murmur in the pine tops as of a not distant waterfall, all
tending to produce *eeriness* and a sadness "hardly akin to pain."
There no lumberer's axe has ever rung. The trees die when they have
attained their prime, and stand there, dead and bare, till the fierce
mountain winds lay them prostrate. The pines grew smaller and more
sparse as we ascended, and the last stragglers wore a tortured, war-
ring look. The timber line was passed, but yet a little higher a slope of
mountain meadow dipped to the south-west towards a bright stream
trickling under ice and icicles, and there a grove of the beautiful silver
spruce marked our camping ground. The trees were in miniature, but
so exquisitely arranged that one might well ask what artist's hand had
planted them, scattering them here, clumping them there, and training their slim spires towards heaven. Hereafter, when I call up memories of the glorious, the view from this camping ground will come
up. Looking east, gorges opened to the distant Plains, then fading
into purple grey. Mountains with pine-clothed skirts rose in ranges,
or, solitary, uplifted their grey summits, while close behind, but
nearly 3,000 feet above us, towered the bald white crest of Long's
Peak, its huge precipices red with the light of a sun long lost to our
eyes. Close to us, in the caverned side of the Peak, was snow that,
owing to its position, is eternal. Soon the afterglow came on, and before it faded a big half-moon hung out of the heavens, shining
through the silver blue foliage of the pines on the frigid background
of snow, and turning the whole into fairyland. The "photo" which
accompanies this letter is by a courageous Denver artist who attempted the ascent just before I arrived, but, after camping out at the
timber line for a week, was foiled by the perpetual storms, and was
driven down again, leaving some very valuable apparatus about 3,000
feet from the summit.

Unsaddling and picketing the horses securely, making the beds of
pine shoots, and dragging up logs for fuel, warmed us all. "Jim" built
up a great fire, and before long we were all sitting around it at supper.
It didn't matter much that we had to drink our tea out of the battered
meat tins in which it was boiled, and eat strips of beef reeking with
pine smoke without plates or forks.

"Treat Jim as a gentleman and you'll find him one," I had been
told; and though his manner was certainly bolder and freer than that
of gentlemen generally, no imaginary fault could be found. He was
very agreeable as a man of culture as well as a child of nature; the desperado was altogether out of sight. He was very courteous and even

kind to me, which was fortunate, as the young men had little idea of showing even ordinary civilities. That night I made the acquaintance of his dog "Ring," said to be the best hunting dog in Colorado, with the body and legs of a collie, but a head approaching that of a mastiff, a noble face with a wistful human expression, and the most truthful eyes I ever saw in an animal. His master loves him if he loves anything, but in his savage moods ill-treats him. "Ring's" devotion never swerves, and his truthful eyes are rarely taken off his master's face. He is almost human in his intelligence, and, unless he is told to do so, he never takes notice of any one but "Jim." In a tone as if speaking to a human being, his master, pointing to me, said, "Ring, go to that lady, and don't leave her again to-night." "Ring" at once came to me, looked into my face, laid his head on my shoulder, and then lay down beside me with his head on my lap, but never taking his eyes from "Jim's" face.

The long shadows of the pines lay upon the frosted grass, an aurora leaped fitfully, and the moonlight, though intensely bright, was pale beside the red, leaping flames of our pine logs and their red glow on our gear, ourselves, and Ring's truthful face. One of the young men sang a Latin student's song and two Negro melodies; the other "Sweet Spirit, hear my Prayer." "Jim" sang one of Moore's melodies in a singular falsetto, and all together sang, "The Star-spangled Banner" and "The Red, White, and Blue." Then "Jim" recited a very clever poem of his own composition, and told some fearful Indian stories. A group of small silver spruces away from the fire was my sleeping place. The artist who had been up there had so woven and interlaced their lower branches as to form a bower, affording at once shelter from the wind and a most agreeable privacy. It was thickly strewn with young pine shoots, and these, when covered with a blanket, with an inverted saddle for a pillow, made a luxurious bed. The mercury at 9 P.M. was 12° below the freezing point. "Jim," after a last look at the horses, made a huge fire, and stretched himself out beside it, but "Ring" lay at my back to keep me warm. I could not sleep, but the night passed rapidly. I was anxious about the ascent, for gusts of ominous sound swept through the pines at intervals. Then wild animals howled, and "Ring" was perturbed in spirit about them. Then it was strange to see the notorious desperado, a red-handed man, sleeping as quietly as innocence sleeps. But, above all, it was exciting to lie there, with no better shelter than a bower of pines, on a mountain 11,000 feet high, in the very heart of the Rocky Range, under twelve degrees of frost, hearing sounds of wolves, with shivering stars looking through the fragrant canopy, with arrowy pines for bed-posts, and for a night lamp the red flames of a camp-fire.

Day dawned long before the sun rose, pure and lemon colored. The rest were looking after the horses, when one of the students came running to tell me that I must come farther down the slope, for "Jim" said he had never seen such a sunrise. From the chill, grey Peak above, from the everlasting snows, from the silvered pines, down through mountain ranges with their depths of Tyrian purple, we looked to where the Plains lay cold, in blue-grey, like a morning sea against a far horizon. Suddenly, as a dazzling streak at first, but enlarging rapidly into a dazzling sphere, the sun wheeled above the grey line, a light and glory as when it was first created. "Jim" involuntarily and reverently uncovered his head, and exclaimed, "I believe there is a God!" I felt as if, Parsee-like, I must worship. The grey of the Plains change to purple, the sky was all one rose-red flush, on which vermilion cloud-streaks rested; the ghastly peaks gleamed like rubies, the earth and heavens were newly created. Surely "the Most High dwelleth not in temples made with hands!" For a full hour those Plains simulated the ocean, down to whose limitless expanse of purple, cliff, rocks, and promontories swept down.

By seven we had finished breakfast, and passed into the ghastlier solitudes above, I riding as far as what, rightly or wrongly, are called the "Lava Beds," an expanse of large and small boulders, with snow in their crevices. It was very cold; some water which we crossed was frozen hard enough to bear the horse. "Jim" had advised me against taking any wraps, and my thin Hawaiian riding dress, only fit for the tropics, was penetrated by the keen air. The rarefied atmosphere soon began to oppress our breathing, and I found that Evans's boots were so large that I had no foothold. Fortunately, before the real difficulty of the ascent began, we found, under a rock, a pair of small overshoes, probably left by the Hayden exploring expedition, which just lasted for the day. As we were leaping from rock to rock, "Jim" said, "I was thinking in the night about your traveling alone, and wondering where you carried your Derringer, for I could see no signs of it." On my telling him that I traveled unarmed, he could hardly believe it, and adjured me to get a revolver at once.

On arriving at the "Notch" (a literal gate of rock), we found ourselves absolutely on the knifelike ridge or backbone of Long's Peak, only a few feet wide, covered with colossal boulders and fragments, and on the other side shelving in one precipitous, snow-patched sweep of 3,000 feet to a picturesque hollow, containing a lake of pure green water. Other lakes, hidden among dense pine woods, were farther off, while close above us rose the Peak, which, for about 500 feet, is a smooth, gaunt, inaccessible-looking pile of granite. Passing through the "Notch," we looked along the nearly inaccessible side of the Peak, composed of boulders and *debris* of all shapes and sizes, through which appeared broad, smooth ribs of reddish-colored granite, looking as if they upheld the towering rock mass above. I usually dislike bird's-eye and panoramic views, but, though from a mountain, this was not one. Serrated ridges, not much lower than that on which we stood, rose, one beyond another, far as that pure atmosphere could carry the vision, broken into awful chasms deep with ice and snow, rising into pinnacles piercing the heavenly blue with their cold, barren grey, on, on for ever, till the most distant range upbore unsullied snow alone. There were fair lakes mirroring the dark pine woods, canyons dark and blue-black with unbroken expanses of pines, snow-slashed pinnacles, wintry heights frowning upon lovely parks, watered and wooded, lying in the lap of summer; North Park floating off into the blue distance, Middle Park closed till another season, the sunny slopes of Estes Park, and winding down among the mountains the snowy ridge of the Divide, whose bright waters seek both the Atlantic and Pacific Oceans. There, far below, links of diamonds showed where the Grand River takes its rise to seek the mysterious Colorado, with its still unsolved enigma, and lose itself in the waters of the Pacific; and nearer the snow-born Thompson bursts forth from the ice to begin its journey to the Gulf of Mexico. Nature, rioting in her grandest mood, exclaimed with voices of grandeur, solitude, sublimity, beauty, and infinity, "Lord, what is man, that Thou art mindful of him? or the son of man, that Thou visitest him?" Never-to-be-forgotten glories they were, burnt in upon my memory by six succeeding hours of terror.

You know I have no head and no ankles, and never ought to dream of mountaineering; and had I known that the ascent was a real mountaineering feat I should not have felt the slightest ambition to perform it. As it is, I am only humiliated by my success, for "Jim" dragged me up, like a bale of goods, by sheer force of muscle. At the "Notch" the real business of the ascent began. Two thousand feet of solid rock towered above us, four thousand feet of broken rock shelved precipitously below; smooth granite ribs, with barely foothold, stood out here and there; melted snow refrozen several times presented a more serious obstacle; many of the rocks were loose, and tumbled down when touched. To me it was a time of extreme terror. I was roped to "Jim," but it was of no use; my feet were paralyzed and slipped on the bare rock, and he said it was useless to try to go that way, and we retraced our steps. I wanted to return to the "Notch," knowing that my incompetence would detain the party, and one of the young men said almost plainly that a woman was a dangerous encumbrance, but the trapper replied shortly that if it were not to take a lady up he would not go up at all. He went on the explore, and reported that further progress on the correct line of ascent was blocked by ice; and then for two hours we descended, lowering ourselves by our hands from rock to rock along a boulder-strewn sweep of 4,000 feet, patched with ice and snow, and perilous from rolling stones. My fatigue, giddiness, and pain from bruised ankles, and arms half pulled out of their sockets, were so great that I should never have gone half-way had not "Jim," *nolens volens*, dragged me along with a patience and skill, and withal a determination that I should ascend the Peak, which never failed. After descending about 2,000 feet to avoid the ice, we got into a deep ravine with inaccessible sides, partly filled with ice and snow and partly with large and small fragments of rock, which were constantly giving away, rendering the footing very insecure. That part to me was two hours of painful and unwilling submission to the inevitable; of trembling, slipping, straining, of smooth ice appearing when it was least expected, and of weak entreaties to be left behind while the others went on. "Jim" always said that there was no danger, that there was only a short bad bit ahead, and that I should go up even if he carried me!

Slipping, faltering, gasping from the exhausting toil in the rarefied air, with throbbing hearts and panting lungs, we reached the top of the gorge and squeezed ourselves between two gigantic fragments of rock by a passage called the "Dog's Lift," when I climbed on the shoulders of one man and then was hauled up. This introduced us by an abrupt turn round the south-west angle of the Peak to a narrow shelf of considerable length, rugged, uneven, and so overhung by the cliff in some places that it is necessary to crouch to pass at all. Above, the Peak looks nearly vertical for 400 feet; and below, the most tremendous precipice I have ever seen descends in one unbroken fall. This is usually considered the most dangerous part of the ascent, but it does not seem so to me, for such foothold as there is is secure, and one fancies that it is possible to hold on with the hands. But there, and on the final, and, to my thinking, the worst part of the climb, one slip, and a breathing, thinking, human being would lie 3,000 feet below, a shapeless, bloody heap! "Ring" refused to traverse the Ledge, and remained at the "Lift" howling piteously.

From thence the view is more magnificent even than that from the "Notch." At the foot of the precipice below us lay a lovely lake, wood embosomed, from or near which the bright St. Vrain and other streams take their rise. I thought how their clear cold waters, growing turbid in the affluent flats, would heat under the tropic sun, and eventually form part of that great ocean river which renders our far-off islands habitable by impinging on their shores. Snowy ranges, one behind the other, extended to the distant horizon, folding in their wintry embrace the beauties of Middle Park. Pike's Peak, more than one hundred miles off, lifted that vast but shapeless summit which is the landmark of southern Colorado. There were snow patches, snow slashes, snow abysses, snow forlorn and soiled looking, snow pure and dazzling, snow glistening above the purple robe of pine worn by all the mountains; while away to the east, in limitless breadth, stretched the green-grey of the endless Plains. Giants everywhere reared their splintered crests. From thence, with a single sweep, the eye takes in a distance of 300 miles—that distance to the west, north, and south being made up of mountains ten, eleven, twelve, and thirteen thousand feet in height, dominated by Long's Peak, Gray's Peak, and Pike's Peak, all nearly the height of Mont Blanc! On the Plains we traced the rivers by their fringe of cottonwoods to the distant Platte, and between us and them lay glories of mountain, canyon, and lake, sleeping in depths of blue and purple most ravishing to the eye.

As we crept from the ledge round a horn of rock I beheld what made me perfectly sick and dizzy to look at—the terminal Peak itself—a smooth, cracked face or wall of pink granite, as nearly perpendicular as anything could well be up which it was possible to climb, well deserving the name of the "American Matterhorn."[1]

Scaling, not climbing, is the correct term for this last ascent. It took one hour to accomplish 500 feet, pausing for breath every minute or two. The only foothold was in narrow cracks or on minute projections on the granite. To get a toe in these cracks, or here and there on a scarcely obvious projection, while crawling on hands and knees, all the while tortured with thirst and gasping and struggling

---

[1]Let no practical mountaineer be allured by my description into the ascent of Long's Peak. Truly terrible as it was to me, to a member of the Alpine Club it would not be a feat worth performing.

for breath, this was the climb; but at last the Peak was won. A grand, well-defined mountain top it is, a nearly level acre of boulders, with precipitous sides all round, the one we came up being the only accessible one.

It was not possible to remain long. One of the young men was seriously alarmed by bleeding from the lungs, and the intense dryness of the day and the rarefication of the air, at a height of nearly 15,000 feet, made respiration very painful. There is always water on the Peak, but it was frozen as hard as a rock, and the sucking of ice and snow increases thirst. We all suffered severely from the want of water, and the gasping for breath made our mouths and tongues so dry that articulation was difficult, and the speech of all unnatural.

From the summit were seen in unrivalled combination all the views which had rejoiced our eyes during the ascent. It was something at last to stand upon the storm-rent crown of this lonely sentinel of the Rocky Range, on one of the mightiest of the vertebrae of the backbone of the North American continent, and to see the waters start for both oceans. Uplifted above love and hate and storms of passion, calm amidst the eternal silences, fanned by zephyrs and bathed in living blue, peace rested for that one bright day on the Peak, as if it were some region

Where falls not rain, or hail, or any snow,
Or ever wind blows loudly.

We placed our names, with the date of ascent, in a tin within a crevice, and descended to the Ledge, sitting on the smooth granite, getting our feet into cracks and against projections, and letting ourselves down by our hands, "Jim" going before me, so that I might steady my feet against his powerful shoulders. I was no longer giddy, and faced the precipice of 3,500 feet without a shiver. Repassing the Ledge and Lift, we accomplished the descent through 1,500 feet of ice and snow, with many falls and bruises, but no worse mishap, and there separated, the young men taking the steepest but most direct way to the "Notch," with the intention of getting ready for the march home, and "Jim" and I taking what he thought the safer route for me—a descent over boulders for 2,000 feet, and then a tremendous ascent to the "Notch." I had various falls, and once hung by my frock, which caught on a rock, and "Jim" severed it with his hunting knife, upon which I fell into a crevice full of soft snow. We were driven lower down the mountains than he had intended by impassable tracts of ice, and the ascent was tremendous. For the last 200 feet the boulders were of enormous size, and the steepness fearful. Sometimes I drew myself up on hands and knees, sometimes crawled; sometimes "Jim" pulled me up by my arms or a lariat, and sometimes I stood on his shoulders, or he made steps for me of his feet and hands, but at six we stood on the "Notch" in the splendor of the sinking sun, all color deepening, all peaks glorifying, all shadows purpling, all peril past.

"Jim" had parted with his *brusquerie* when we parted from the students, and was gentle and considerate beyond anything, though I knew that he must be grievously disappointed, both in my courage and strength. Water was an object of earnest desire. My tongue rattled in my mouth, and I could hardly articulate. It is good for one's sympathies to have for once a severe experience of thirst. Truly, there was

> Water, water, everywhere,
> But not a drop to drink.

Three times its apparent gleam deceived even the mountaineer's practiced eye, but we found only a foot of "glare ice." At last, in a deep hole, he succeeded in breaking the ice, and by putting one's arm far down one could scoop up a little water in one's hand, but it was tormentingly insufficient. With great difficulty and much assistance I recrossed the "Lava Beds," was carried to the horse and lifted upon him, and when we reached the camping ground I was lifted off him, and laid on the ground wrapped up in blankets, a humiliating termination of a great exploit. The horses were saddled, and the young men were all ready to start, but "Jim" quietly said, "Now, gentlemen, I want a good night's rest, and we shan't stir from here to-night." I believe they were really glad to have it so, as one of them was quite "finished." I retired to my arbor, wrapped myself in a roll of blankets, and was soon asleep.

When I woke, the moon was high shining through the silvery branches, whitening the bald Peak above, and glittering on the great abyss of snow behind, and pine logs were blazing like a bonfire in the cold still air. My feet were so icy cold that I could not sleep again, and getting some blankets to sit in, and making a roll of them for my back, I sat for two hours by the camp-fire. It was weird and gloriously beautiful. The students were asleep not far off in their blankets with their feet towards the fire. "Ring" lay on one side of me with his fine head on my arm, and his master sat smoking, with the fire lighting up the handsome side of his face, and except for the tones of our voices, and an occasional crackle and splutter as a pine knot blazed up, there was no sound on the mountain side. The beloved stars of my far-off home were overhead, the Plough and Pole Star, with their steady light; the glittering Pleiades, looking larger than I ever saw them, and "Orion's studded belt" shining gloriously. Once only some wild animals prowled near the camp, when "Ring," with one bound, disappeared from my side; and the horses, which were pick-eted by the stream, broke their lariats, stampeded, and came rushing wildly toward the fire, and it was fully half an hour before they were caught and quiet was restored. "Jim," or Mr. Nugent, as I always scrupulously called him, told stories of his early youth, and of a great sorrow which had led him to embark on a lawless and desperate life. His voice trembled, and tears rolled down his cheek. Was it semi-conscious acting, I wondered, or was his dark soul really stirred to its depths by the silence, the beauty, and the memories of youth?

We reached Estes Park at noon of the following day. A more suc-cessful ascent of the Peak was never made, and I would not now ex-change my memories of its perfect beauty and extraordinary sublim-ity for any other experience of mountaineering in any part of the world. Yesterday snow fell on the summit, and it will be inaccessible for eight months to come.

■ CONSIDERATIONS OF MEANING AND METHOD

1. Why do you think Isabella Bird chose to write in the form she did, in letters to her sister and in journal format? What effect do you think her audience-of-one might have had on the content and style of her writing?

2. Both Bird and Mountain Jim are vivid "characters." How do they deviate from or conform to the image you have of the Eng-lish lady and the desperado of the Old West? Why do they seem to get along so well?

3. Consider the difficulties you or women you know may have en-countered in solitary travel. To what extent do you think times have or have not changed?

■ POSSIBILITIES FOR WRITING

1. Imagine a discussion between Mountain Jim and the two young men who accompanied them when Isabella Bird was out of hear-ing range. What might they have had to say about her in their private conversation? Write a dialogue among the three.

2. In a narrative essay, describe an experience you've had in going somewhere you supposedly didn't belong. Were you accepted or rejected by those who did "belong"?

3. Have you ever been skiing or rock climbing, or engaged in any other sport or activity which required your strength, endurance, and/or skill in surmounting a natural obstacle? Describe in an essay, perhaps for a reader unfamiliar with the activity, what is especially difficult or unusual about it.

■ PETER MATTHIESSEN
from *The Snow Leopard*

Peter Matthiessen is widely considered one of the most important wilderness writers of this century. In both fiction and nonfiction works, he explores endangered natural environments and endangered human cultures. Literary critic Terrence Des Pres writes that Matthiessen is "quietly obsessed with one of the uglier truths of our age: that nothing lasts, that no place, culture, bird or beast can survive in the path of Western—and now Eastern— greed."

Matthiessen was born in New York City in 1927, though he grew up in rural New York State and Connecticut. His writing career was launched in 1950 when he won the prestigious Atlantic Prize for short fiction, the same year he received his B.A. degree from Yale University. He stayed at Yale for a short time to teach creative writing, but, having spent his junior year at the Sorbonne, he returned to Paris, where he continued to write and cofounded The Paris Review, *one of the best-known literary journals in English and for which he still serves as an editor. Returning to the United States in 1954, Matthiessen lived in Montauk, Long Island, and worked for several years as a commercial fisher and as captain of a charter fishing boat. He served as a trustee for the New York Zoological Society from 1965 to 1978. Matthiessen still lives at the tip of Long Island, when he is not traveling.*

Over the past four decades, Matthiessen has traveled in and written widely of exotic locales, among them the polar North, the Amazon, East Africa, Nepal, and New Guinea. Many of his approximately two dozen books, as divergent as his encyclopedic Wildlife in America *(1959) and the novel* At Play in the Fields of the Lord *(1965), have been extremely popular.* Wildlife in America *enjoys a place on the shelf in the permanent library collection at the White House. Matthiessen's writing has been widely recognized for its literary and scientific merit. Critical essayist Vernon Young has noted that Matthiessen "combines the exhaustive knowledge of a naturalist . . . with a poet's response to far-out landscapes." The Snow Leopard (1978) won the National Book Award and the American Book Award, and Sand Rivers (1981) won a gold medal for distinction in natural history from the Academy of Natural Sciences.*

Peter Matthiessen is a practitioner of Zen Buddhism. In his prologue to The Snow Leopard, *he describes his journey into the mountains of "northwest Nepal, near the frontier of Tibet" as not only the occasion "to study the bharal, or Himalayan blue sheep" but as "a true pilgrimage." The snow leopard, "that rarest and most beautiful of the great cats . . . this near-mythic beast," becomes a symbol of Matthiessen's "journey of the heart."*

November 3

There is so much that enchants me in this spare, silent place that I move softly so as not to break a spell. Because the taking of life has been forbidden by the Lama of Shey, bharal and wolves alike draw near the monastery. On the hills and in the stone beds of the river are fossils from blue ancient days when all this soaring rock lay beneath the sea. And all about are the prayer stones, prayer flags, prayer wheels, and prayer mills in the torrent, calling on all the elements in nature to join in celebration of the One. What I hear from my tent is a delicate wind-bell and the river from the east, in this easterly wind that may bring a change in the weather. At daybreak, two great ravens come, their long toes scratching on the prayer walls.

The sun refracts from the white glaze of the mountains, chills the air. Old Sonam, who lives alone in the hamlet up the hill, was on the mountain before day, gathering the summer's dung to dry and store as cooking fuel; what I took for lumpish matter straightens on the sky as the sun rises, setting her gaunt silhouette afire.

Eleven sheep are visible on the Somdo slope above the monastery, six rams together and a group of ewes and young; though the bands begin to draw near to one another and sniff urine traces, there is no real sign of rut. From our lookout above Sonam's house, three more groups—six, fourteen, and twenty-six—can be seen on the westward slopes, across Black River.

Unable to hold the scope on the restless animals, GS calls out to me to shift the binoculars from the band of fourteen to the group of six sheep, directly across the river from our lookout. "Why are those sheep running?" he demands, and a moment later hollers, "Wolves!" All six sheep are springing for the cliffs, but a pair of wolves coming straight downhill are cutting off the rearmost animal as it bounds across a stretch of snow toward the ledges. In the hard light, the blue-gray creature seems far too swift to catch, yet the streaming wolves gain ground on the hard snow. Then they are whisking through the matted juniper and down over steepening rocks, and it appears that the bharal will be cut off and bowled over, down the mountain, but at the last moment it scoots free and gains a narrow ledge where no wolf can follow.

In the frozen air, the whole mountain is taut; the silence rings. The sheep's flanks quake, and the wolves are panting; otherwise, all is still, as if the arrangement of pale shapes held the world together. Then I breathe, and the mountain breathes, setting the world in motion once again.

Briefly, the wolves gaze about, then make their way up the mountainside in the unhurried gait that may carry them fifty miles in a single day. Two pack mates join them, and in high yak pasture the four pause to romp and roll in dung. Two of these were not among the five seen yesterday, and we recall that the old woman had seen seven. Then they trot onward, disappearing behind a ridge of snow. The band of fourteen sheep high on this ridge gives a brief run of alarm, then forms a line on a high point to stare down at the wolves and watch them go. Before long, all are browsing once again, including the six that were chased onto the precipice.

Turning to speak, we just shake our heads and grin. "It was worth walking five weeks just to see that," GS sighs at last. "That was the most exciting wolf hunt I ever saw." And a little later, exhilarated still, he wonders aloud if I remember "that rainy afternoon in the Serengeti when we watched wild dogs make a zebra kill in that strange storm light on the plain, and all those thousands of animals running?" I nod. I am still excited by the wolves seen so close yesterday, and to see them again, to watch them hunt blue sheep in such fashion, flying down across the cliffs within sight of our tents at Shey Gompa—what happiness!

After years of studying the carnivores, GS has become fascinated by the Caprini—the sheep and the goats—which have the attraction of inhabiting the remote high mountains that he loves. And among the Caprini, this "blue sheep" is a most peculiar species, which is one reason we have come so far to see it. It is presumed that the sheeps and goats branched off from a common ancestor among the Rupicaprini, the so-called goat-antelopes, which are thought to have evolved somewhere south of the Himalaya; this generalized ancestor may have resembled the small goat-antelope called the goral, which we saw last month in the dry canyon of the Bheri. Besides the six species of true goat *(Capra)* and the six of true sheep *(Ovis),* the Caprini include three species of tahr *(Hemitragus),* the aoudad or Barbary sheep *(Ammotragus),* and the bharal or Himalayan blue sheep *(Pseudois),* all of which exhibit characters of both sheep and goat. The tahrs, which in their morphology and behavior appear to be intermediate between goat-antelopes and true goats, are classified as goats, and the sheeplike aoudad is mostly goat as well. *Pseudois,* too, looks very like a sheep; it recalls the Rocky Mountain sheep, not only in its general aspect but in type of habitat—rolling upland in the vicinity of cliffs. Certain specimens, GS says, possess the interdigital glands on all four feet which were thought to be a diagnostic character of *Ovis,* and the species lacks the strong smell, beard, and knee callouses that are found in *Capra.* Nevertheless, GS considers it more goat than sheep, and hopes to establish this beyond all doubt by observation of its behavior in the rut.

Hunters' reports account for most of what is known of the wild goats and sheep of Asia, which may be why the classification of *Pseudo* is still disputed. Since the blue sheep is now rare in world collection the one way to resolve the question is to observe the animal in its own inhospitable habitat—above timberline, as high as 18,000 feet, in the vicinity of cliffs—in one of the most remote ranges of any animal on earth: from Ladakh and Kashmir east across Tibet into northwest China, south to the Himalayan crest, and north to the Kuenlun and Altyn mountains. In Nepal, a few bharal are found on the western and southern flanks of Dhaulagiri (this is the population that we saw near the Jang Pass), as well as in the upper Arun Valley, in the east, but most are found here in the northwest, near the Tibetan border.

This morning, through the telescope, I study blue sheep carefully for the first time. Like the Rocky Mountain sheep, they are short-legged, strong, broad-backed animals, quick and neat-footed, with gold demonic eyes. The thick-horned male is a handsome slaty blue, the white of his rump and belly set off by bold black face marks, chest, and flank stripe, and black anteriors on all four legs; the black flank stripes, like the horns, become heavier with age. The female is much smaller, with dull pelage and less contrast in the black, and her horns are spindly, as in female sheep. Those of the males, on the other hand, are heavy, curving upward, out, and back. Also, the basio-occipital bone at the base of the skull is goatlike, and so are the large dew claws and the prominent markings on the fore sides of the legs. In this confused situation, the rutting behavior will be a deciding factor, yet from the limited reports available, even the rutting is ambiguous. For example, the courting sheep rarely raises its tail above the horizontal, whereas the goat may arch it back onto its rump: perhaps for lack of the odorous tail-gland secretions of true goats that the arched tail may help disseminate, both tahr and bharal compromise by erecting the tail straight up into the air.

Although the male herds are still intact—this sociability of rams is a trait of Caprini—the males are mounting one another, as much to establish dominance as in sexuality; among many sheep and goats, the juvenile males and the females are quite similar in appearance, and tend to imitate the behavior of the other, so that rams may fail to differentiate between them, treating all of these subordinates alike. A few are displaying the bizarre behavior (heretofore unreported) that GS calls "rump-rubbing," in which one male may rub his face against the hind end of another. In the vicinity of females, the male "kicks"— a loose twitch of the leg in her direction that appears to be a mounting preliminary and may also serve to display his handsome markings. Also, he thrusts his muzzle into her urine stream, as if to learn whether or not she is in estrus, and licks in agitation at his penis. But the blue sheep stops short of certain practices developed by the markhor of Pakistan and the wild goat (the ancestor of the domestic goat, ranging from Pakistan to Greece), both of which take their penises into their mouths, urinate copiously, then spit on their own coats; the beard of the male goat is an adaptive character, a sort of urine sponge that perpetuates the fine funky smell for which the goats are known.

The itch of the rutting season has begun, and even the young animals play at butting and sparring, as if anxious not to miss the only lively time in the blue sheep's year. GS wonders at the scarcity of the young, concluding that a 50 percent mortality must occur in the first year, due as much to weakness or disease caused by poor range condition as to predation by wolves and leopard. Perhaps one juvenile in three attains maturity, and this may suffice to sustain the herds, which must adjust numbers to the limited amount of habitat that remains snow-free all the year. This region of the Tibetan Plateau is a near desert of rock and barren slopes dominated by two thorn shrubs *Caragana* and a bush honeysuckle, *Lonicera;* the blue sheep will eat small amounts of almost any growth, including the dry everlasting and the oily juniper, and the adaptations of the Caprini for hard abrasive forage permit limited browsing of this thorny scrub as well. But excepting a few tufts among the thorns, almost all the native grasses that are its preferred food have been eradicated by the herds of yak and sheep and goats that are brought here from distant villages in summer, and the overgrazing has led already to erosion.

November 9

From the path that leads beyond Tsakang, along the precipices of the Black River Canyon, there is a stirring prospect of the great cliffs and escarpments, marching northward toward the point where this Yeju-Kangju flows into the great Karnali River. The path is no more than a ledge in many places and, on the northward face of each ravine, is covered by glare ice and crusted snow. Even on the southward face, the path is narrow, and concentrating hard on every step, I come upon what looks like a big pug mark. Because it is faint, and because GS is too far ahead to summon back, and because until now we have found no trace of leopard, I keep quiet; the mark will be there still when we return. And just at this moment, looking up, I see that GS has paused on the path ahead. When I come up, he points at a distinct cat scrape and print. The print is faded, but at least we know that the snow leopard is here.

Mostly we spend the day apart, meeting over the clay oven for breakfast and supper, but whenever we act like social animals, the impulse has brought luck. A little farther on there is another scrape, and then another, and GS, looking ahead to where the path turns the cliff corner into the next ravine, says, "There ought to be a leopard scat out on that next point—it's just the sort of place they choose." And there it is, all but glowing in the path, right beneath the prayer stones of the stupa—the Jewel in the Heart of the Lotus, I think, unaccountably, and nod at my friend, impressed. "Isn't that something?" GS says, "To be so delighted with a pile of crap?" He gathers the dropping into one of the plastic bags that he keeps with him for this purpose and tucks it away into his rucksack with our lunch. Though the sign is probably a week old, we are already scanning the sunny ledges and open caves on both sides of the river that we have studied for so many days in vain.

On the ledge path we find two more scats and a half dozen scrapes, as well as melted cat prints in the snow on the north face of the ravines. Perhaps this creature is not resident but comes through on a hunting circuit, as the wolves do: the wolves have been missing now for near a week. On the other hand, this labyrinth of caves and ledges is fine haunt for leopard, out of the way of its enemy, the wolf, and handy to a herd of bharal that is resident on the ridge above and often wanders down close to these cliffs. Perhaps, in the days left to us, we shall never see the snow leopard but it seems certain that the leopard will see us.

Across the next ravine is the second hermitage, of earth red decorated in blue-gray and white. It lacks stacked brush or other sign of life, and its white prayer flags are worn to wisps by wind. In the cliffs nearby are smoke-roofed caves and the ruins of cells that must have sheltered anchorites of former times; perhaps their food was brought them from Tsakang. This small gompa, half-covering a walled-up cave, is tucked into an outer corner of a cliff that falls into Black Canyon, and like Tsakang it faces south, up the Black River. Because the points of the Shey stupas are just visible, its situation is less hallucinatory than the pure blue-and-white prospect at Tsakang, but the sheer drop of a thousand feet into the gorge, the torrent's roar, the wind, and the high walls darkening the sky all around make its situation more disturbing. The hermitage lies on the last part of a pilgrim's path that climbs from Black River and circles round the Crystal Mountain, striking Black Canyon once again on the north side of this point and returning to Shey by way of Tsakang; but most of the path is lost beneath the snows.

Taking shelter on the sunny step, leaning back into the warmth of the wooden door, I eat a green disc of Phu-Tsering's buckwheat bread that looks and tastes like a lichened stone mandala from the prayer walls. Blue sheep have littered this small dooryard with their dung, a human hand has painted a sun and moon above the lintel, yet in this forlorn place, here at the edge of things, the stony bread, the dung and painted moon, the lonely tattering of flags worn to transparence by the wind seem as illusory as sanity itself. The deep muttering of boulders in Black River—why am I uneasy? To swallow the torrent, sun, and wind, to fill one's breath with the plenitude of being . . . and yet . . . I draw back from that sound, which seems to echo the dread rumble of the universe.

Today GS is stumbling on the ledges. He speculates about atmospheric ions that affect depression, as in the mistral winds of southern France (there are recent speculations that negative ions, which seem to be positive in their effect on animals and plants, may be somehow related to *prana,* the "life energy"), and we agree that one is clumsy when depressed, but he feels that his own stumbling is a sign of incipient sickness, a cold coming on or the like. Perhaps he is right, perhaps I imagine things, but earlier on this same ledge, as if impelled, my boots sought out the loose stones and snow-hidden ice, and I felt dull and heavy and afraid; there was a power in the air, a random menace. On the return, an oppression has lifted, I am light and quick. Things go better when my left foot is on the outside edge, as it is now, but this cannot account for the sudden limberness, the pleasure in skirting the same abyss that two hours ago filled me with dread. Not that I cease to pay attention; on the contrary, it is the precise bite and feel and sound of every step that fills me with life. Sun rays glance from snow pinnacles above and the black choughs dance in their escadrilles over the void, and dark and light interpenetrate the path, in the all-pervading presence of the Present.

November 14

Crossing Black River, I climb the west slope trail, out of the night canyon, into the sun. In the matted juniper is a small busy bird, the Tibetan tit-warbler, blue-gray with a rufous cap, and an insistent cat note, *t-sip:* what can it be insisting on, so near the winter?

On this bright morning, under the old moon, leopard prints are fresh as petals on the trail. But perhaps two hundred yards short of the trip line to GS's camera, the tracks appear to end, as if the cat has jumped aside into the juniper; the two prints closer to the trip line have been made the day before. Beyond the next cairn, where the path rounds the ridge high above the river and enters the steep snow-covered ravine below Tsakang, more fresh tracks are visible in the snow, as if the snow leopard had cut across the ridge to avoid the trip line, and resumed the path higher up, in this next ravine. Close by one print is an imprint of lost ages, a fernlike fossil brachiopod in a broken stone.

From Tsakang comes the weird thump of a *damaru,* or prayer drum, sometimes constructed of two human skulls; this instrument and the *kangling* trumpet, carved from the human thigh bone, are used in Tantrism to deepen meditation, not through the encouragement of morbid thoughts but as reminders that our time on earth is fleeting. Or perhaps this is the hollow echo of the cavern water, dripping down into the copper canister; I cannot be sure. But the extraordinary sound brings the wild landscape to attention: somewhere on this mountainside the leopard listens.

High on the ridge above Tsakang, I see a blue spot where GS is tracking; I come up with him in the next hour. "It fooled me," he calls by way of greeting. "Turned up the valley just below the trip line, then over the ridge, not one hundred yards from where I was lying, and down onto the path again—typical." He shifts his binoculars to the Tsakang herd, which has now been joined by the smaller bands of the west slope. "I've lost the trail now, but that leopard is right here right this minute, watching us." His words are borne out by the sheep, which break into short skittish runs as the wind makes its midmorning shift, then flee the rock and thorn of this bare ridge, plunging across deep crusted snow with hollow booming blows, in flight to a point high up on the Crystal Mountain. Blue sheep do not run from man like that even when driven.

The snow leopard is a strong presence; its vertical pupils and small stilled breaths are no more than a snow cock's glide away. GS murmurs, "Unless it moves, we are not going to see it, not even on the snow—these creatures are really something." With our binoculars, we study the barren ridge face, foot by foot. Then he says, "You know something? We've seen so much, maybe it's better if there are some things that we *don't* see." He seems startled by his own remark, and I wonder if he means this as I take it—that we have been spared the desolation of success, the doubt: is this *really* what we came so far to see?

When I say, "That was the haiku-writer speaking," he knows just what I mean, and we both laugh. GS strikes me as much less dogmatic, more open to the unexplained than he was two months ago. In Kathmandu, he might have been suspicious of this haiku, written on our journey by himself:

> Cloud-men beneath loads.
> A dark line of tracks in snow.
> Suddenly nothing.

Because his sheep, spooked by the leopard, have fled to the high snows, GS accompanies me on my last visit to Tsakang. There we are met by Jang-bu, who has come as an interpreter, and by Tukten, who alone among the sherpas has curiosity enough to cross the river and climb up to Tsakang of his own accord. Even that "gay and lovable fellow," as GS once said of Phu-Tsering, "hasn't the slightest curiosity about what I am doing; he'll stand behind me for two hours while I'm looking and taking notes and not ask a single question."

Once again, the Lama of Shey lets us wait on the stone terrace, but this time—for we are here by invitation—the aspirant monk Takla has prepared sun-dried green yak cheese in a coarse powder, with *tsampa* and buttered tea, called *so-cha*, served in blue china cups in the mountain sun. The sharp green cheese and bitter tea, flavored with salt and rancid yak butter, give character to the *tsampa,* and in the cool air, this hermit's meal is very very good.

Takla lays out red-striped carpeting for us to sit upon, and eventually the Lama comes, wrapped in his wolf skin. Jang-bu seems wary in the Lama's presence, whereas Tukten is calm and easy and at the same time deferential; for the first time since I have known him, indoors or out, he doffs his raffish cap, revealing a monk's tonsure of close-cropped hair. Tukten does most of the translation as we show the Lama pictures from our books and talk animatedly for several hours. Lama Tupjuk asks about Tibetan lamas in America, and I tell him about Chögyam Trungpa, Rinpoche (*rinpoche,* or "precious one," signifies a high lama), of his own Karma-pa sect, who left Tibet at the age of thirteen and now teaches in Vermont and Colorado. For GS, he repeats what he had told me about the snow leopard and the argali, pointing across Black River at the slopes of Somdo.

Horns high, flanks taut, the blue sheep have begun a slow descent off the Crystal Mountain, in a beautiful curved line etched on the snow. The leopard is gone—perhaps they saw it go. Through binoculars, now and again, a ram can be seen to rear up wildly as if dancing on the snow, then run forward on hind legs and descend again, to crash its horns against those of a rival.

In the high sun, snows shift and flow, bathing the mind in diamond light. Tupjuk Rinpoche speaks now of the snow leopard, which he has seen often from his ledge, and has watched carefully, to judge from the accuracy of all his observations: he knows that it cries most frequently in mating time, in spring, and which caves and ledges it inhabits, and how it makes its scrape and defecation.

Before we leave, I show him the plum pit inscribed with the sutra to Chen-resigs that was given me by Soen Roshi, and promise to send him my wicker camp stool from the tea stall on the Yamdi River. The Lama gives me a white prayer flag—*lung-p'ar,* he calls it, "wind pictures"—printed with both script and images from the old wood blocks at Shey; among the Buddhist symbols is an image of Nurpu

Khonday Pung-jun, the great god of mountains and rivers, who was here, says the Lama, long before the B'on-pos and the Buddhists: presumably this was the god who was vanquished by Drutob Senge Yeshe and his hundred and eight snow leopards. Nurpu is now a Protector of the Dharma, and his image on flags such as this one is often placed on bridges and the cairns in the high passes, as an aid to travelers. The Lama folds it with greatest concentration, and presents it with the blessing of his smile.

The Lama of the Crystal Monastery appears to be a very happy man, and yet I wonder how he feels about his isolation in the silences of Tsakang, which he has not left in eight years now and, because of his legs, may never leave again. Since Jang-bu seems uncomfortable with the Lama or with himself or perhaps with us, I tell him not to inquire on this point if it seems to him impertinent, but after a moment Jang-bu does so. And this holy man of great directness and simplicity, big white teeth shining, laughs out loud in an infectious way at Jang-bu's question. Indicating his twisted legs without a trace of self-pity or bitterness, as if they belonged to all of us, he casts his arms wide to the sky and the snow mountains, the high sun and dancing sheep, and cries, "Of course I am happy here! It's wonderful! *Especially* when I have no choice!"

In its wholehearted acceptance of *what is,* this is just what Soen Roshi might have said: I feel as if he had struck me in the chest. I thank him, bow, go softly down the mountain: under my parka, the folded prayer flag glows. Butter tea and wind pictures, the Crystal Mountain, and blue sheep dancing on the snow—it's quite enough!

Have you seen the snow leopard?

No! Isn't that wonderful?

■ CONSIDERATIONS OF MEANING AND METHOD

1. What does Matthiessen mean when he writes,

   Have you seen the snow leopard?
   No! Isn't that wonderful?

2. Matthiessen's journal seems to have dual subjects, dual purposes, and dual writing styles. Explain and illustrate with examples.

3. Is Matthiessen targeting readers who are specialized in any way? In what respects is he himself an expert?

4. Why do you think Matthiessen chose the journal as his literary form in *The Snow Leopard* over other possibilities? A more typi-

cal approach, perhaps, for a nonfiction book would have been to break the general subject down and address its specific aspects in distinct chapters.

■ POSSIBILITIES FOR WRITING

1. In the sciences and social sciences, repeated observations of subjects of study are an important way of gathering information about behavior. Find a location in which people gather on a regular basis, and for a particular reason—a coffee house or café, or a classroom, for example. Observe the scene several times over a period of days, possibly at the same time every day. Use your journal to record details of the scene and the people in it, individual behavior and interactions, events, and your own reflections about them. When you are finished with your observations, read over your notes and pull the information together into an essay in which you describe the scene and the kind of social interaction that takes place there.

2. Visit a zoo, if you can. Choose an animal with which you are not very familiar and observe its appearance and behavior closely over a reasonably long period of time, recording your observations in detail in your journal or notebook. In your library, locate information about the same animal in the wild. In an essay, compare your own observations with those you have read.

■ IVAN DOIG
from *Winter Brothers*

The son of a ranch worker, Ivan Doig was born in White Sulphur Springs, Montana, in 1939. He has been an editor and journalist as well as a freelance writer. His best-known book, This House of Sky: Landscapes of a Western Mind *(1978), is a memoir of his childhood, depicting "a sense of the land and how it shapes us." His enduring interest in "the American people and the westering expanse of this continent they happened to come to" has led him to write about the West in many forms.* Winter Brothers: A Season at the Edge of America *(1980), from which the following excerpt is taken, is a concurrent diary in which Doig intersperses his own reflections about the landscape, history, and people of the Olympic Peninsula Region of Washington state, as well as about writing, with the diaries of James Gilchrist Swan, an early white settler of the area.*

In 1849, James Swan abandoned the security of a prosperous ship-fitting business, polite Boston society, and his wife and two children for the wilds of the Pacific Northwest Coast, where, according to historian Norman H. Clark, in 1852 "he was one of perhaps two dozen white Americans then on the Pacific Coast north of the Columbia River." Near Port Townsend, Swan settled among the Indians, whom he came to know intimately and to respect well during a time when they were, as Clark puts it, "passing between the twilight of their tranquility and the night of their most desperate affliction. The hour was late: smallpox, measles, and syphilis had already swept grimly over a bewildered people. Since their first contact with Europeans in the eighteenth century, the mortality among some groups was as high as 90 percent." Systematic violence, unequal justice, and cultural genocide at the hands of business and government interests intent on reaping the riches of Northwest lumber and aquaculture during the 1850s all but finished them off.

An untutored but meticulous anthropologist, Swan wrote several books documenting the culture of Indians of the Pacific Northwest Coast, and was a prolific diarist of his days and decades among them. His books include The Northwest Coast, The Indians of Cape Flattery, *and* The Haidah Indians of Queen Charlotte's Island, British Columbia. *"In his moments of solemn clarity . . . ," Clark says, "[Swan] could see himself as both observer of and participant in a barbaric invasion." Swan died in 1900 at the age of 82.*

In the following selection from Doig's Winter Brothers, *James Swan chronicles a week at Neah Bay, and Ivan Doig speculates on the motivation of such a dedicated diarist as Swan who over a period of "forty years . . . [penned] two and a half million words by hand."*

Day Seventeen

Neah Bay, mid-January 1864: a week of Swan's winter.

Sunday. *Russian Jim came in this evening and requested me to intercede with his squaw who has recently left him and try and induce her to return. Jim told me that when any one came to my door at night I should always ask "Who is there" for the Skookums sometimes came to peoples doors and did mischief. I told him I was not afraid of the powers of the air at all. He said I had a skookum tumtum*—a strong heart.

Monday. *This is my birth day 46 years old. Cleaned up the school house today, piled the lumber, and placed things in order. I shall be glad when the building is completed for the constant interruption I have and the various duties I am called on to perform prevent my giving that attention to the children I wish to. I have no time that I can call my own or in which I am not liable to interruptions except evenings and then I am generally alone but I can find but little time to write for my sight is getting too poor to attempt writing much except by daylight.*

The Indians think I have a skookum tumtum to live alone in this great house. I do not suppose one of them would dare sleep here alone for anything they are so afraid of spirits. I think the spirits of the earth are more to be feared, both spirituous liquors and evil prowling Indians but I don't apprehend any dangers or alarms from any source and thus far never have been more peacefully situated.

Tuesday. *Today took an inventory of Government property for Mr. Webster. Billy Balch came in this evening and gave me a very lucid explanation why the spirits of the dead did not molest me. He says that it is because we have a cellar to the house and a floor over it, but in Indian houses there is nothing but the bare ground or sand. That when any of the Indians are alone in a great house and make a fire and cook, that the memelose or dead come up through the earth and eat food and kill the Indian, but he thinks they can't come up through our floor altho as he says he would be afraid to try to sleep alone here for there might be some knot hole or crack in the floor through which they could come.*

Billy also related an interesting tradition. He says that . . . at not a very remote period the water flowed from Neeah Bay through the Waatch prairie, and Cape Flattery was an island. That the water receded and left Neeah Bay dry for four days and became very warm. It then rose again without any swell or waves and submerged the whole of the cape and in fact the whole country except the mountains. . . . As the water rose those who had canoes put their effects into them and floated off with the current which set strong to the north. Some drifted one way and some another and when the waters again resumed their accustomed level a portion of the tribe found themselves beyond Nootka where their descendants now reside and are known by the same name as the Makahs. . . .

There is no doubt in my mind of the truth of this tradition. The Waatch prairie shows conclusively that the waters of the ocean once flowed through it, and as this whole country shows marked evidences of volcanic influences there is every reason to believe that there was a crust which made the waters to rise and recede as the Indian stated.

Wednesday. *Very heavy surf during the night and this morning, showing there must have been strong winds outside the cape recently. . . . At 8 PM Jackson & Bob came to the door and informed me that a vessel had run on the rocks on the north end of Waadda Island. I went out on the beach and saw a light in that direction, but after watching it some time I concluded it was as likely to be a vessel at anchor in the harbor as one on the rocks. The Indians refused to go off to ascertain, as the wind was blowing too strong, so I came back to the house and after going up to my room in the upper part of the turret, where I had a better chance to judge I concluded from the appearance of the light that it was the US Rev Cutter* Joe Lane *. . . expected here with Mr Smith the keeper of Tatooche Light.*

Thursday. *My surmise last evening proved correct, it was the cutter* Joe Lane *which arrived. Mr Webster came down and breakfasted with me and then went on board the cutter in a canoe with five Indians who afterward conveyed him to Baadah.*

Yowarthl brought one cord oven wood today. Paid him 12 buckets of potatoes.

Went to Baadah this PM Mr Webster gave me a letter to send to the Cutter, which I sent by Hopestubbe & Yachah, who carried it and delivered it safe. Wrote this evening. . . .

Friday. *7:30 AM The Cutter got under way and stood out of the bay bound to Barclay Sound in search of Bark* Narramissic, *said to be lost or missing. . . .*

Saturday. *Went to Baadah to pay off Indians. Peter says that a short time since a Quillehuyte Indian named Towallanhoo came across by way of the Hoko river and from thence down on foot to Baadah where he arrived at night and reconnoitered Mr Webster's premises and then passed on to Waatch. This may account for the Indians asking me if I was not afraid to be alone in this great house and also the reason why Russian Jim cautioned me not to open my door to any one without enquiring who was there, for the Indians say that the*

Quillehuytes have threatened to come here and attack the whites. This may or may not be true and may be only some scheme of these people to do mischief and charge it on the Quillehuytes.

Day Eighteen

Swan's day-upon-day sluice of diary words: why?

Was the diarying habit something which surfaced out of instinct, the unslakable one that murmurs in some of us that our way to put a mark on the world is not with sword or tool, but pen? Or did contents mean more to him than the doing of it—the diary a way to touch out into life as it flowed past him and skim the most interesting as an elixir? Either way Swan clearly was not using his pen nib merely to pass the time. So much interested him, inside the covers of books and wherever else his glance fell along this coastline, that boredom seldom seems to have found him. I do accept that the brown-inked words helped to keep straight in memory what he was seeing or being told; Swan possessed a granny's passion for gossip, and a broker's fixity on exact sums and issues. But passions and fixities do not commonly last for forty years and two and a half million words by hand. Any of us serve summer terms as diarists, generally at some moonstruck time of our lives. Somewhere in the tumble of family items in a closet of this room is interred, deservedly, the five-year diary I began in my final year of high school. I lasted at the routine a few months and am now told nothing by it but a recitation of football and basketball scores and journeys between my boarding place in town and the family's sheep ranch. That dry stick of a youngster tracing such items into my life, I can scarcely recognize. Almost twenty years passed before I undertook a diary again—oddly, the occasion was the same as that earliest eddy of Swan's torrent of paper, a time spent in Britain—and even yet I dodge behind the constant excuse that a page should be a hireling, not the field boss, to evade for days, weeks, at a time. This journal of winter, ninety days of exception, I face down into regularly because it must be kept, as a ship's log must. To navigate by; know the headway. But Swan's diary plainly masters him. Pulls his hand down onto each day's page like a coaxing lover. How far beyond the surface of the paper he ever can be coaxed is yet to be seen. Swan's days and the land and people of them get scrupulous report; less so his own interior. Unlike that other tireless clerk, Pepys of plague-time London, Swan does not confess himself every second sentence, gaily jot down whom he last tumbled to bed with and is eyeing next nor repent every hangover nor retaste every jealousy. Much more assessor than confessor, is Swan. Yet, yet, his words do configure, make enough significant silhouette that I stare hard for the rest. No, the Swan style of diary-keeping—this dialogue of a man with his days—is not merely maintenance but more like architecture, the careful ungiddy construction of something grand as it is odd. Swan works at these pages of his as steadily, incessantly, as a man building a castle out of pebbles.

Castling his own life, I suppose, while I have the luck to look on in curiosity.

■ CONSIDERATIONS OF MEANING AND METHOD

1. What is the difference, if any, between a diary and a journal?

2. Have you ever caught anyone reading your private diary or journal? What was your response, and why? If you have ever willingly shared a private diary or journal entry with a friend, were you nervous about doing so? If so, what was it that made you nervous?

3. Does the historical aspect of Swan's journal entries, as we look back at them with Doig across the distance of so many years, make them inherently more or less interesting?

■ POSSIBILITIES FOR WRITING

1. Write an essay for your local historical society in which you recount "legends" regarding your hometown's (or state's) terrain, tracing the evolution and assessing the accuracy of such reports. To gather information, you might interview long-time residents and/or peruse published local histories.

■ TODD DICKSON
Journal Selection

Todd Dickson offers the following statement about himself and his journal excerpts.

As someone who had lived in ten different towns during the first twenty years of my life, I found a crucial constant in the world outdoors. The wilds, though stunningly diverse, are all endowed with

*the constance of creation, the Spirit that speaks a language all
humans can understand. There I have a permanent address.
The future will likely find me still mobile, perhaps involved with
developing countries. My studies in Eurasian history and
mechanical engineering may find their meeting place in an
overseas mission.*

*My journal entry was an exploration of my perceptions and
feelings about a day skiing. I wrote it to discover in words how I
saw my surroundings and my place in them. I discovered an
analogy to an intimate relationship. I discovered images that
approach the beauty of the sight, sound, smell on location. I wrote
it for myself. As I read it over now, I see that the relationship I was
exploring while I wrote in my journal was not an earthly romance
at all. If I hadn't hidden myself behind the woman and the
mountain, I would have seen God, and my search would have
been rewarded, not repulsed.*

1–11–92

Today we drove out to Hope Valley where Sorensen's Ski Ranch
is located. While most of Zapata's troops commenced operations at
Heavenly Valley just to the south of our lakeshore encampment, our
small select group of three tactical members pointed the camouflaged
personnel carrier towards Luther Pass, aloft in the white heights. As
the crew advanced steadily, stealthily, our thoughts focused on the
task ahead. Not even the darkening of the near bright sun nor the
blowing snow distracted our attention. The "golden oldies" punctuated by static bursts gave meter and tempo to our conversation and
readiness-making. Topping the grade, we caught a first distant
glimpse of our playing field. The Sorensen Ski Ranch lay below,
where the corral gates were open and about 25 vehicles stood already
parked.

We replenished our incomplete supplies of eqpt. at the rental
lodge, glanced at the map like usual first-time tourists, loaded up and
parked at the trailhead just out of sight of the lodge. Shuffling about
and selecting our personal gear, we packed our needed items in a
minute, hid the rest, and locked the vehicle. Continuing under the
ruse of first-time tourists and beginning skiers, we set off up the trail
towards our target.

We had planned our journey carefully and knew our mission down to the last detail. We would climb by the Brucinch trail to

I'm not sure where this is going. It's tough to keep up the b.s., when I know I have got to break it sooner or later, the "mission" I had built the whole story around didn't have anything to do with the story. On the other hand, that could show a real contrast to this para-military stuff and the sublimity of nature. I'll have to mull on that. I'm going to bed.

1–13

Some day I'll develop this—one *kamikaze* (down-wind) can change such lofty plans . . . remember the mogul fleet? But for now the assignment calls for something more introspective, more intimate (as I see it). So.

1–13 Cont'd

Recently I mounted the double-chair for the summit opposite Carson Pass. My reunion with the earth was less than graceful, awed as I was by the pure fantasy of the scene.

The jewel-white dazzle of the morning snow enveloped the tree trunks, as a wool blanket in a cool cabin. The soft pillowy face and limbs of the mountain contrasted with the severe and grand cliffs of the summit. Gliding up this silver screen of surreality, only the brmm-brmm of the chairlift past the supports and the nearby stunted pine boughs groping skyward as if to brush my cheek convinced my senses that the scene was real and I was a living part of it. Scaling the final steep of the mountain's shoulder, a stiff west wind tumbled over from the distant unfamiliar side, setting fire to my face.

Standing now on the collarbone of the great mountain's strong mute body, the wind's muscles fought to launch me off my narrow perch. All my desire to hold the western view in my eyes vanished with the sting of the thousand wasps on my crimson cheeks. The mountain—still silent. She shared not a word, nor a whisper. Ski tips poised over the empty altitude, I released the 10,321 foot collarbone. I dropped smoothly down and across her icy, hard chest, plying the surface with my freshly prepared skis. A quick stop and a breather to collect myself, explore my arms, my legs, my fingers, knees and skis. A subconscious review of the pushing, pulling, tearing, straining, holding punctuating and singing we call skiing, and I sought anew the slopes for my future. Eyes ahead, skis informing, quads responding, I began a monologue with the mountain. Looking for my future, I found a furrow of snow where another had lost a struggle with the hillside. I found a mogul, creased on both sides by the pasts of the person before me. I found a rock, refusing the aid of the winter's white comforter. I found the tuft of a seven-foot jack pine, spending its first January Sunday in the January sun. I found a modest jump that would force a response from the mountain. Or so I thought. She was not eager to share her secrets, this staggering living snowdrift. Another run, starting again at the icy collarbone and descending to the treetops, gullies, divots and moguls. My cacophonous efforts reached a campfire cowboy's crooning. Again I searched. I found the mountain's silhouette; I found other seekers of snow, their past and present; I found the vestiges of a vibrant life about me. But beyond every snowdrift, behind every tree trunk, on the far peaks on the horizon, everywhere I looked to find my future. Another ascent into the stiff wind of the west. This time a whisper inside me. A prayer socked deep in my soul. Drop onto the paths of my searching. This time not my future in focus, but the prayer is my path. My muscles tense, then loose. Rippling, feeling, soothing, giving, taking, asking, listening, responding. No, not my future. Here on the silvery blinding spectacular slopes I've found something else. The whisper within grows, broadens, lightens its step, and spreads into a careful song. The sounds of the brmm-brmm, skiers shouting, snowmobiles, airplanes and helicopters vanish from the sacred mountain air. Only the vibrations of my ski edges against the singing snow punctuate the stillness. The swoosh-shwik-shh play the rhythm section in the ever-louder song in my soul. A joy rushes through me.

The joy alone can't carry the tune, and my search falters. A misplaced edge elicits a savage rebuke from the mountain beneath the soles of my feet. My left ski is ripped across my right, and I pack my left ear like a pile driver into numbing cold. A moment to pause and consider my muscles, my ear, my hat & glasses. The song? Yes, a bit fainter, but ever so symphonic. I rise and push ahead. Put the faux pas in your pack and move on. Feeling, asking, answering, giving, taking. There I'd given quite a bit. Took my fair share too. I should have asked. Or listened. But each turn tells me she forgives the ones who listen to the song. The symphony grows, adding parts, grandeur and beauty. The spiritual drive of the melody lifts me away. The joy rushes back. Attentive this time. The moguls meander peacefully beneath my toes, my movements all in harmony with the song of the Manna I've found. I know this song. It swoops me to the top of the mountain, where the west wind spares my cheek and unfolds to my eyes the glowing splendor of the western Below. Ripples of mountain limbs, sharp ridges raking the sky, families of trees celebrating in togetherness. The steep and the gentle. Each plays a song. Each song blends in the auditorium of my ear, and my soul hears the joy of the ages. The beauty of the concert is the beauty of its origin. I lean against the granite of the mountain I know, the mountain I speak with. The song of the Manna I found on the snow's surface calls to me from the hardened jack pine. The moguls, the cliff, the icy collarbone, the smooth slips in the trees, the divots, the tufts, the snow's harbor—all sing out to me—glory. The glory shines from every crevice in the cliff. The glory tickles my feet by the seven-foot pine. The glory smiles at me, stroking my westward cheek. The outrageous delight—I feel my lungs bursting to join the song. I sing fully to the one whose song this is, sparing not a note. My voice folds into the vastness of the wilds as wonderful as my mountain who speaks to me. My song joins the mountain air, the sleeping mammals, the birds on wing, the very soil. My song, though silent, reaches on to grasp forever.

> I noticed
> analogy to relationship with a woman (mountain)
> lesson on mistakes—how to keep on
> analogy to music—mountain
> home
> love—when you're singing the same song
> All the "ing" words get you there

■ CONSIDERATIONS OF MEANING AND METHOD

1. In his class journal entries, Todd Dickson is looking for a specific writing subject, but he is also experimenting with a way in which to approach the subject and a language with which to articulate it. Why do you think Dickson abandoned his first journal exploration?

2. In his longer entry of January 13, why are Dickson's second two paragraphs so much longer than his first two?

3. At the end of his second entry of January 13, Dickson lists some of the things he noticed about his writing in this journal exploration. What can you add to his list?

■ **POSSIBILITIES FOR WRITING**

1. Try your hand at the assignment Todd Dickson was responding to in his writing. In a series of journal explorations—through brainstorming, clustering, and/or freewriting—explore a possible writing subject of interest to you. You might write about an experience you've had, or an incident you've observed, that has illustrated something interesting to you about your own or others' relationship to nature, or you could ruminate on some question or policy of environmental concern.

2. Try taking the above assignment a step further. When you are finished exploring the subject in journal entries, select a specific reader (an individual or a group) who would have a sincere interest and practical stake in a particular aspect of your subject. Examples of possible readers might be a company, organization, or institution, an individual in a position of authority, an editor (as in letters to the editor), a mentor, a current or former teacher, your classmates. Compose a letter to your reader with a specific goal in mind: How do you want your writing to influence or motivate your reader? When you are finished with your letter, mail or otherwise deliver it to your reader.

MAKING CRITICAL CONNECTIONS:
QUESTIONS FOR DISCUSSION, RESEARCH, AND WRITING

1. Look at the Chapter 1 readings from an historical perspective. Taken in sequence, what do these readings tell you about exploration and settlement of the land over the past nearly two hundred years? Where are the new wilderness frontiers? In discussion or in writing, compare the major concerns of the early journal writers represented here with those of the more recent journal writers.

2. Several of the journal writers in this chapter's readings refer to the problem of articulation. Can language express our experience of the world? In discussion or in writing, assess from a reader's point of view the effectiveness of these journal selections in describing landscape, thought, and emotion. Use specific references to at least three of this chapter's readings to support and illustrate your points.

3. Choose one of the journal writers of Chapter 1 whose work particularly interests you, whether in style, subject matter, or the nature of his or her exploration. As Ivan Doig has done in *Winter Brothers,* write a series of interactive journal entries, to share with your instructor and classmates, in which you intersperse reflections, questions, speculations, and experiences of your own which the reading brings to mind. What is it in this writer's accounts that is especially compelling to you?

4. Many "wilderness" areas, including Muir's Yosemite Valley and Bird's Estes Park, have become popular vacation destinations. In this country and in other parts of the world, wilderness tourism is a booming industry. In a letter to John Muir or Isabella Bird, explain what our national parks and wilderness areas are like today (this may require some research), and what you think drives so many Americans to seek the "wilderness experience." Describe in your letter to Muir or Bird the consequences of this popularity, and speculate about whether or not, or in what form, you think wilderness will survive into the next century.

II

OBSERVATIONS AND REFLECTIONS

Looking at Nature, Seeing Ourselves

In recording my impressions of the natural scene I have striven above all for accuracy, since I believe there is a kind of poetry, even a kind of truth, in simple fact. But the desert is a vast world, an oceanic world, as deep in its way and complex and various as the sea. Language makes a mighty loose net with which to go fishing for simple facts, when facts are infinite. If a man knew enough he could write a whole book about the juniper tree. Not juniper trees in general but that one particular juniper tree which grows from a ledge of naked sandstone near the old entrance to Arches National Monument. What I have tried to do then is something a bit different. Since you cannot get the desert into a book any more than a fisherman can haul up the seas with his nets, I have tried to create a world of words in which the desert figures more as medium than material. Not imitation but evocation has been the goal.

Edward Abbey, "Author's Introduction," *Desert Solitaire*

Exploration is a defining process, leading us through a wilderness of facts and experience to the object of our search, the specific subject of our interest. Through our explorations we may discover subjects that take us completely by surprise—Edward Abbey's particular juniper tree, for example. We may rediscover old subjects, approaching them from new angles; powerful memories about people, places, or events from our past may puzzle us until current events bring them into clearer focus. Or we may discover what specifically interests us about a general subject or how our general interests apply in practice. For example, a general interest in biology could combine with another general interest in anthropology to ignite a passionate interest in a specific subject, perhaps how indigenous cultures in Brazil have developed in harmony with rain forest ecology, and how both are threatened by deforestation.

As writers, our interests in particular subjects may be personal, even intuitive; they may be practical or academic. Our interests may arise from a combination of these motivating factors. Subjects that provoke a real interest in us intrigue us in ways we don't yet fully understand, and won't until we investigate them more thoroughly. As exploration is a defining process, examination of subject is a focused learning process.

We learn by observing, and observation comes in many forms. It may be a process by which we examine the subject (whether an inanimate or living subject or a subject in the form of written text) literally, at close range—studying it with our full attention and focused awareness, noting, recording, and reflecting upon details and implications as they emerge. It may also involve recollection, or searching our memories to reconstruct details of subjects obscured by time. In its broader sense, observation may involve research—searching out experts on the subject, either in person or in various forms of records (written, filmed, or spoken) in order for these experts' experiences, observations, and conclusions to improve our own understanding.

With close observation, understanding emerges, and with understanding writers move from subject to theme. If you examine a subject long enough, and carefully enough, it will speak to you. It will tell you a truth—probably not the *only* truth, but a truth nonetheless. It is then that you take the next step, asking yourself, *What's the most effective way to explain this to my reader?*

CHAPTER 2

Whooping Crane, pl. 261 © National Aubudon Society
(Photo Researchers)

DESCRIPTIONS OF PLACES AND LIVING THINGS

RHETORIC:
TRAVELING FROM SUBJECT
TO CENTRAL IDEA

A SUBJECT OF INTEREST

In locating a subject of interest, the writer enters into a learning process as well as an extended negotiation with audience and purpose. Ultimately, if the writer has something important to say and communicates it effectively to the reader, this learning process will evolve into a teaching process. Developing a piece of writing around any particular subject requires that the writer (1) study the subject carefully, (2) come to understand the context in which examination of the subject is worthwhile, (3) be in a position to draw interesting conclusions about the subject, and (4) determine the most effective way to present the subject and conclusions to the reader.

As the writer trains his or her focus on a specific subject, questions abound. Careful writers understand that before they can communicate something worth reading to their audience, they will need to develop a full and accurate understanding of the subject at hand, building upon and clarifying what they already know. And writers must also understand who the reader will be and what function the writing will serve (since this will predict the direction and form of the writing). Will a subject of real interest and consequence to the writer be as compelling to the reader? How familiar is the reader likely to be with the subject? How much does the writer know about the subject? How much more will he or she need to learn? How will the writer go about gathering additional information?

As the writer prepares to write, more questions will arise, having to do with the form the writing will take, as well as its tone and style:

- What effect does the writer want his or her writing to have on the reader?
- How will the writer structure and style the writing to achieve this effect?
- What, if any, are the reader's expectations regarding the writing's purpose and form?
- How will the writer balance his or her own purpose with the reader's expectations?

CHOOSING A SUBJECT

Many writers claim that choosing a writing subject is the most difficult part of the writing process. Part of this challenge for the writer involves finding a subject that will sustain his or her interest during a focused thinking and writing process—a subject, that is, with which the writer is actively engaged and about which he or she will have something compelling to say. Our instinct for self-preservation advises us, if we listen, to avoid subjects that we find tedious. But when we write with readers in mind, our choice of subject gets more complicated, raising questions such as:

- What are the readers' expectations, and what is the purpose of the writing?
- How do readers' expectations and the function the writing serves mold our writing, including our choices of subject?

Writing on Assigned Topics

In writing on assigned topics—for many types of academic writing, for example, as well as much of the writing we do, or will do, on the job—we are called upon by people who are in positions of authority (and who may know more about our subjects than we do), to address specific subjects, often from a particular point of view and in a specified form. Naturally we want to please these readers, and we want to prove our mettle. In academic writing on assigned topics, the purpose may seem clear, and also daunting: to prove our knowledge of the material. This kind of writing often may feel uncomfortably like a test, and often it *is* a test.

There is a difference, though, between understanding and responding to the reader's expectations, and second-guessing that reader to the point where there is nothing left of you, the writer, in what and how you are writing. Most college teachers do not want to read uninspired rehashes of lectures and reading assignments, or distorted reflections of what the student may have interpreted as the analysis or conclusions the instructor wants to hear. Most instructors want to see students analyze, relate, and apply what they have learned in an original way that demonstrates an ability to think critically and creatively, and shows that students can communicate their observations and ideas clearly and effectively.

Your first challenge in writing on an assigned topic is to choose a specific area within the general one that truly interests and excites you, that provokes your curiosity, and that challenges you, in ways that feel personally relevant, to learn more. When your learning and writing processes are motivated by a sincere interest, the depth and breadth of your thinking as well as the quality of your writing will likely reflect that interest, which will, in turn, excite your reader.

Although it may be a challenge to come up with your own angle on an assigned subject while at the same time meeting a reader's expectations in content and form, there are advantages in writing on assigned topics. For one thing, your reader is likely to be inherently interested in what you write. When you can assume the reader's interest as well as a certain level of familiarity with the subject, you will not have to work quite so hard to establish *exigence*—the reader's need to know or the writing's reason for being—or to explain or demonstrate to the reader how the writing is relevant to his or her life, as you do in many other kinds of writing.

Writing on Open Topics

When there is more freedom in determining subject and purpose in writing, writers often experience both relief and the simultaneous realization that such freedom makes for a more complex writing challenge. Not only are we confronted with the need to observe carefully, understand fully, and articulate clearly, but first we have to determine for ourselves (a) what constitutes a good writing subject and (b) how to interest a reader who has no explicit need to know about the subject we have determined is important. We have to work much harder to capture the reader's interest; the challenge is to convince a neutral reader that what he or she is reading is worth reading, and that it bears some relevance to the reader's life.

In many instances, the selection of subject in academic writing may be left up to you, although the mode of development may be specified. In assigning open topics in a composition class, your instructor probably has certain rhetorical goals; for instance, he or she may want you to practice descriptive or narrative techniques. Learning to write effective description and narration is not only useful in and of itself, but these rhetorical strategies, used in combination with others—in analytical or argumentative writing, for instance—can enhance the overall effectiveness of various kinds of writing designed for many different purposes.

When you are asked to write a descriptive essay or a personal narrative and the choice of topic is left up to you, how do you decide what makes for a good writing subject? The advice offered above, for choosing a specific area of an assigned subject, applies here as well. Don't choose a subject based solely on an assumption about what you think the reader wants to read; choose a subject that inspires in you a real interest, one that will motivate you in a careful examination of your subject and in your desire to communicate clearly and effectively what you come to learn about it. Avoid subjects about which you think you already know everything, which may make your thinking and writing automatic and predictable; instead, choose a subject about which you would like to think and learn more. Writing offers us an opportunity for learning: the process of exploring, analyzing, and articulating a subject in language forges our understanding of it in ways that passive or random thought does not. It is an opportunity for self-clarification, with the additional pleasure of recreating our perceptions and experiences vividly in writing for a reader.

We all understand, in selecting from among the infinite in open topics, that we should select subjects that are not only interesting and significant to us, but will be similarly compelling for our readers. But here is where many of us, as writers, will encounter crises of confidence, prompting thoughts like the following: *What I think of as interesting and significant is actually uninteresting and insignificant, because it comes straight from me and my life. Nothing of interest or significance ever happens to me, and my perceptions are far from profound. I'm going to bore my reader to death!*

Have confidence; have faith. If you are like most readers, you recognize sincerity and honesty—at least when they come from *other* writers—as important qualities in good writing. You know that compelling observations and conclusions can and often do come from ordinary subjects and everyday events. In fact, readers tend to identify best with subjects they recognize from their own experience, as opposed to subjects that seem far removed, abstract, or theoretical; readers appreciate writing and writers that provide them with the opportunity to examine the familiar in a new light.

WHO'S THE EXPERT?

There are some subjects about which you are already an expert, and these tend to be of a personal or introspective nature. Even these subjects, however, require further "research" in the form of observation, recollection, reflection, and analysis when you have decided to focus attention upon them in writing. In some cases, you may even need to collect information from outside sources to establish an effective context, even for personal or introspective writing. With writing subjects that fall further outside the range of your experience to date, you will have to earn your expertise from the ground up, through careful and thorough study. This will mean expanding your knowledge through investigation of outside sources, as well as through reflection and analysis. Your readers will not find your writing credible and persuasive if they are not convinced of your expertise.

Expertise comes in many forms, however. Some of the authors of the readings in Chapter 2 are acknowledged specialists in their fields. Other authors in the chapter study their subjects with such precision, communicating details and conclusions to their readers with such care, that their expertise is earned. Although we may or may not be certified specialists in the fields in which we write, we are obliged, through our learning, thinking, and writing processes, to become experts on the specific subjects we have chosen. It is important to know that there are many ways in which to go about that learning.

LEARNING ABOUT YOUR SUBJECT: OBSERVATION AND OTHER FORMS OF STUDY

Whether you have chosen a personal subject for writing or one further removed from your personal experience, you will have to study that subject carefully in order to have anything particularly worthwhile to communicate about it to your reader. Depending upon your purpose (is it to entertain, to report, to explain, to persuade?), you will have to supply enough information, whether in the form of descriptive detail or factual evidence (or both) to give the reader a basis upon which to understand and accept the conclusions you draw.

If you think about it, perhaps you will agree that all writing is inherently persuasive. Even in descriptive writing, when your purpose is "merely" to describe your subject in vivid detail, you are really writing an argument on behalf of your own perceptions. In such writing, style is certainly important, but without having observed your subject thoroughly, you will have nothing to describe, no mood or experience to recreate for your reader. Most forms of writing require the writer to adopt multiple approaches to studying a subject. But, depending upon the subject and purpose of the writing, one of the following approaches may predominate.

Observation

Observation does not only apply to the process of learning about a static subject in the physical world through a physical examination of it; it also applies, in its broadest sense, to the study of documents and occurrences, both ordinary and extraordinary, in the form of data, written texts, works of art, staged or unstaged events.

Observation as a form of research and a method of learning is familiar to anyone who has written in the sciences. When you take notes in your lab notebook, observing the details of a lab experiment as it unfolds, and when you write these notes up in the form of a lab report, you are relying upon observation as a crucial research and learning tool.

Similarly, in descriptive writing—whether your subject is a person or any other animate subject, an inanimate object, or a place—the vividness and impact of what you write, as well as the conclusions you draw, will depend not only on your use of language, but also on your careful observation of details and your own understanding of how these details contribute to the conclusions you draw. In narrative writing, as well as in other forms, description of observed details will probably serve an important function, providing you and your reader with a way of "seeing," of being concretely engaged, and a means for conveying an overall impression, mood, or point. Through description of observed details writers can recreate their subjects, and the process by which they have come to understand them, for their readers.

As you would when observing a lab experiment, record the details of your observation in process. Don't rely upon memory if you can help it. If you are observing a physical subject, observe it not once, but several times. Take note of its properties and characteristics using all your senses, not just your eyes. How does it smell, feel, sound, taste? Observe it at various times of day or under various circumstances. How does it look up close? At a distance? Note not only the specific, isolated subject, but also how it fits in its setting and how it interacts or corresponds with its environment. If your subject is an event rather than a static subject, try to observe the event, or variations upon it (which may, in fact, enrich it), on multiple occasions.

If you are observing a staged event—a film, a play, or a recording, for example—try to see or listen to it more than once, since your appreciation and understanding of it will deepen with repeated exposure. If you cannot take notes during the event, allow yourself the time and space to do so immediately after. If you are observing data or texts—whether you are analyzing population statistics or a short story—read them carefully and repeatedly, taking notes, recording information, and posing questions, in the margins of the texts and/or in your journal or notebook.

You do not have to interact with your subject physically in order to engage it: use your senses and your intellect to probe it in observation. In all forms of observation, it is important to record not only the details of your subject's properties and attributes, but to reflect upon and analyze their possible significance and implications in your notes as well.

Recollection

There is a special poignancy in remembered subjects. We are often attracted to writing about them because these places, objects, people, and events have lingered in our memories for good reasons. They are significant, and over time we are likely to have come to understand their importance better than we do places, objects, people, and events that are newer and less familiar to us, ones that have not yet found a clear context in our experience. In writing from memory, we tend to know better before we start what it is we are writing about.

But in some respects, writers who write from memory are at a disadvantage when compared to those who can observe their subjects firsthand. Memory can be selective, and it can be sketchy. We may have a distinct impression of objects, events, people, and places drawn from memory, but over time we may have lost many of the details that originally contributed to our impressions. The main challenge for the writer who has chosen to write from memory is the *recollection*, rather than collection, of details.

Many of the free-association techniques in prewriting described in Chapter 1 will help you in the process of recollection. Freewriting and clustering in your journal, for example, may help you uncover the details of a remembered subject.

Describing the subject in conversation with friends, classmates, or your instructor will also help you recall the details about it that made it so memorable. These listeners are likely to ask questions, since they will want a complete picture and will see where the gaps in information are. Filling these gaps in conversation will help you reach deeper into your memories for important details and context. Exploring your remembered subject in conversation is really a first step in recreating your subject for your reader: consider it a first draft in oral form.

Another important strategy in uncovering details of, and establishing background for, remembered subjects is to talk with people who were there when "it happened." If you are writing about your old neighborhood, talk to your family and your old playmates to see what they remember. Let your conversations with them provoke, accelerate, and enrich your own memories. What was the experience of the neighborhood like for them? If you are writing about the death of a grandparent, talk to members of your family. It may be difficult or it may feel gratifying (or both) to share these memories. Ask not only what they remember about the experience from their points of view, but also what they remember about you and your reactions during that time.

Use your journal or notebook to jot down details and reflections during or immediately after a clarifying conversation about your subject. If you make a specific arrangement to talk to someone about your subject—especially if this person is an "eyewitness" or a participant—consider tape-recording the conversation, since much of what this person says is likely to be of clear and specific interest, and you might even want to quote him or her. (Make sure in advance that tape-recording is all right with the person you're talking to.)

Whatever strategy or combination of strategies the writer uses, uncovering the sometimes obscured details of a remembered subject is important because only in reconstructing the remembered subject fully will the writer be able to recreate it vividly in language.

Outside Sources

Sometimes, even when our writing subjects are personal or immediate and it would seem that observation or recollection should be enough to teach us what we need to know to write effectively about them, we encounter gaps in our understanding. And in filling these gaps, we may find it necessary to go to outside sources to find the answers to our questions.

When you go "straight to the horse's mouth," you are consulting primary sources. *Primary source* material can come in two fundamentally different forms. A primary source can be the subject itself: the original document or text about which you may be writing. Primary source material can also come in the form of original research, such as interviews you conduct or questionnaires or surveys of your own design. When you interview someone with a specialized knowledge or understanding of your subject—an expert, a participant, or eyewitness—you are consulting a primary source, whether you are interviewing your grandmother about your family history or a meteorologist about weather patterns.

Filling gaps in understanding may be as simple as looking up in a botany text the correct terminology to use in describing the anatomy of a flower, if that is your writing subject, or as complex as researching the physics of conductivity if you are describing an electrical storm. These two examples involve examination of *secondary source* material. Secondary source material is anything that has been written (or recorded in any other form) by others *about* your subject. To provide yourself with information about or analysis of your subject, you might seek out secondary source material in a variety of forms: newspaper or magazine articles, books, documentary films, official documents or reports, or interviews conducted by someone else.

In consulting primary or secondary source material, take careful notes, not only of factual information, summaries, paraphrased ideas, and quotations, but of bibliographic information as well. Remember too that learning about your subject through studying source material involves more than an accumulation of facts, information, and examples; it also requires careful analysis of these facts, information, and examples, a questioning process that should be recorded in your notes as well.

No matter how carefully you go about it, observation and recollection may not always provide you with full knowledge of your writing subject, and you may have to expand your search for information to outside sources. It does seem to be true at times that the more we learn, the more we discover we don't know. But writers who allow unanswered questions to guide the learning process, and who understand that there are a variety of ways to go about learning, are more likely to write with both authority and purpose.

MOVING FROM SUBJECT TO CENTRAL IDEA: APPROACHES TO STRUCTURING AN ESSAY

In the process of studying your subject—whether through observation, recollection, use of outside source material, or a combination of these approaches—you have been reflecting upon and analyzing it. In addition to recording details of fact in notes and journal writing, you have recorded your reflections, including questions, speculations, interpretations, and associations. These are what begin to carry you, as your understanding of your subject takes a more definite shape, from the subject of your writing to your essay's central idea.

Both in the process of studying your subject and at the point at which you consider what fundamental point you want to make about that subject in your writing, questioning is a useful tool. Try a journalistic approach, even in descriptive and narrative writing. Ask yourself the questions *who, what, when,* and *where* to help clarify context and organize the details of your subject. Next ask the more probing questions *how* and *why* in order to focus your analysis, helping you to define and articulate your central idea.

The Central Idea

The most fundamental point the writer makes is an essay's central idea. It can be articulated overtly in a thesis statement, or conveyed more subtly through a dominant impression or mood, depending upon the kind of writing the writer is engaged in and its intended purpose.

Most of us have been taught that every essay should have a thesis statement, presented succinctly in one or two sentences, probably at the end of the opening paragraph, and that the rest of the essay should be dedicated to proving and defending this thesis statement. In many kinds of writing—in analytic, interpretive, or argumentative writing especially—this may indeed be the most effective approach. But this approach does not work equally well in all writing situations.

For example, the most persuasive form of argument in some cases could be for the author to recreate a situation in which the reader will have a vicarious experience that is likely to lead him or her to the conclusion the writer intends. This argument appeals more to sentiment than to logic, and it is probably more effectively supported by anecdote than by any aggressive proof. Some essays are meant to be exploratory rather than absolute, to provoke rather than to defend, and their central ideas may be expressed more speculatively, rather than in the form of direct statements. David Quammen, in his essay "The Face of a Spider" (see Chapter 4), articulates his thesis in the form of a question: "How should a human behave toward the members of other living species?" Although his essay explores this question thoroughly, Quammen does not arrive at any absolute answers.

In descriptive writing, a thesis or central idea—whether of a single paragraph or an entire essay—may not be stated outright; rather, it may be implied through a dominant impression or mood, as is the case in many of the readings in this chapter.

Deductive and Inductive Patterns

When a writer makes a general statement and then develops, supports, and illustrates it with particulars, the writer is following a *deductive* pattern. The more traditional approach to structuring the essay—the one in which the thesis statement comes at the end of the opening paragraph—is deductive. Similarly, a deductive paragraph is one in which the topic sentence opens the paragraph and the details which follow are intended to illustrate, support, and defend that paragraph thesis. A deductive approach, whether to paragraphs or entire essays, works well when the writer wants to prove a point unambiguously, even aggressively.

When the writer designs a paragraph, or an entire essay, that moves from particulars—descriptive or narrative details, facts, examples, or illustrations—to a general statement, the writer is using an *inductive* pattern. The strength of deductive patterns in writing lies in their demonstration of logic. Inductive patterns, on the other hand, actively engage the reader in the recreation of the process by which the writer arrived at his or her conclusion. Thus, the effect of inductive patterns in writing is cumulative.

Induction, therefore, lends itself to both descriptive and narrative writing by virtue of the fact that it involves readers more effectively in the mood of the writing and engages them in the immediacy of events. It allows readers to participate in the writing at a more visceral level and to gather and form their own impressions and conclusions as they go—guided, of course, by the careful writer's selection of detail and his or her writing style.

CREATING A DOMINANT IMPRESSION: TECHNIQUES FOR DEVELOPING THE DESCRIPTIVE ESSAY

In a descriptive essay (or within descriptive paragraphs), your main objective will be to recreate a vivid picture or experience for your reader rather than to prove a point. The effectiveness of the description you write will lie in your ability to show, rather than simply tell, your readers what you want them to know. Just as in argumentative writing, where it is important to select factual evidence or reasoning to develop and support your thesis, it is crucial in descriptive writing to select details and present them in such a way that they develop and support a dominant impression or central idea, thereby fulfilling your purpose in writing.

In descriptive writing, it is important to decide in advance what dominant impression you want to convey to your reader. Is there a mood you would like to get across to the reader in your description of the subject? If so, what is the emotional impression you want to convey? Furthermore, you should also decide in advance how this dominant impression translates into the tone you will take in writing: Are you sympathetic? Angry? Amused? Detached?

In some descriptive writing—for example, in many kinds of scientific description—you will want to avoid explicit mood and tone as much as possible. If this is the case, you will have to be careful *not* to inject emotion, to keep description as well as your tone neutral and factual, leaving your reader with a vivid but impartial view of the subject.

As with any other form of evidence, not all descriptive details are equally relevant. In any descriptive writing, accuracy is crucial. Whether you interpret accuracy as being true to fact or true to emotion, or both, you will want to focus only on details which contribute clearly to a coherent and unified picture. Focusing on relevant details while letting irrelevant ones go is a way of supporting your central idea. In description, be as concrete as possible, avoiding abstract or general statements in favor of concrete detail. If the dominant impression you are attempting to convey has an emotional or interpretive quality to it, build to a climax. Once you have selected them, let details and facts speak for themselves; your reader's understanding should grow from them, and you shouldn't have to attach explanations.

Descriptive Language

In any kind of writing, writers must take care to choose words which convey precisely, rather than approximately, what they mean and the tone they wish to convey. At times, even when we think we are using concrete descriptive language—say, adjectives like "wonderful" or "awesome"—we are really using generic terms, and a little further thought will help us discover more precise words or images that express the subtlety and uniqueness of what we mean. Before writers use figurative language—metaphors, similes, and analogies—they should make sure that they are describing their subjects accurately and concretely through careful word choice. This is the foundation for effective descriptive writing.

If you take a look at the excerpt from Richard Wright's *Black Boy* in this chapter, for example, you will notice that the quality of Wright's description relies more on the vividness and accuracy of descriptive language than on figurative language. When Wright writes, "There was the delight I caught in seeing long straight rows of red and green vegetables stretching away in the sun to the bright horizon" or "There was the disdain that filled me as I tortured a delicate, blue-pink crawfish that huddled fearfully in the mudsill of a rusty tin can," he is painting a vivid picture in the reader's mind through accurate observation of detail and careful choice of words and phrasing.

Richard Wright is also aware of other qualities of language, beyond precise word choice, that contribute to the effectiveness of descriptive writing. He is aware that both rhythms in phrasing and the texture of language in descriptive writing can be emphasized to achieve a mood. In the repetition of "There was" and "There were" at the beginning of each descriptive passage, Wright creates a kind of revery of childhood for the reader, a dreamlike quality that enhances the spell of looking back through time. And when he describes "a chicken [leaping] about blindly after its neck had been snapped by a quick twist of my father's wrist," he knows that the abruptness of the word "snapped" and the sharp internal rhyme of "twist" and "wrist" will impart not only meaning but a stunned emotional quality to the scene. Words, isolated or in combinations of phrasing, often have a certain quality of sound and/or rhythm that a good descriptive writer understands can either enhance or contradict the mood of a piece of writing.

Figurative Language: Simile, Metaphor, and Analogy

In using figurative language, in the form of similes, metaphors, and analogies, in descriptive writing, we go beyond the boundaries of the literal, drawing on associations and comparisons to enhance meaning. Whether a comparison is a simile, a metaphor, or an analogy is partly a matter of phrasing and partly a matter of scope.

A *simile* is a comparison of specific qualities of two essentially dissimilar things, using "like" or "as." A *metaphor* employs the same kind of comparison, but in stating the comparison more directly, the writer does not use "like" or "as." For example, in "The Dry Salvages," T. S.

Eliot writes " . . . the river / Is a strong brown god." This is a metaphor. Had Eliot phrased the comparison as a simile, it would have read, " . . . the river / Is *like* a strong brown god."

Analogies are extended similes. Beyond comparing isolated characteristics of two essentially dissimilar things, analogies compare whole systems. Annie Dillard, in her essay "Sojourner" (see Chapter 3), draws an analogy between a mangrove island floating at sea, drifting "anywhere in an alien ocean, feeding on death and growing, netting a makeshift soil as it goes, shrimp in its toes and terns in its hair," and our planet, which has "accumulated a great and solacing muck of soil, of human culture . . . bearing it with us across nowhere."

Effective writers use similes, metaphors, and analogies to clarify and emphasize important themes in their writing. In another of her essays, titled "Heaven and Earth in Jest," Annie Dillard describes cattle that come down to Tinker Creek to drink as "a human product like rayon. They're like a field of shoes. They have . . . tongues like foam insoles." She is using simile to enhance our understanding of her point that these creatures are essentially manufactured through breeding, more a product of human commerce than of nature. She goes on to write, " . . . they have beef fat behind their eyes, beef stew." Here she is using metaphor, stating the figurative comparison emphatically without using "like" or "as." We are not likely to take her literally, though we certainly get her point. In its directness, metaphor is often more effective than simile.

Because they are complex, and because there are generally multiple points of comparison that the writer needs to sustain, analogies are much more difficult to develop than are simple similes or metaphors. In "Heaven and Earth in Jest," Dillard describes the waning of a windy day: "Clouds slide east as if pulled from the horizon, like a table-cloth whipped off a table." This is simile, comparing clouds to table-cloths, with the suggestion of magic in the comparison, contributing to the meaning and mood of the writing. But Dillard extends the comparison, building upon the original simile to develop an analogy:

> I walk home. By five-thirty the show has pulled out. Nothing is left but an unreal blue and a few banked clouds low in the north. Some sort of carnival magician has been here, some fast-talking worker of wonders who has his act backwards. "Something in this hand," he says, "something in this hand, something up my sleeve, something behind my back . . . " and abracadabra, he snaps his fingers, and it's all gone. Only the bland, blank-faced magician remains, in his unruffled coat, bare-handed, acknowledging a smattering of muffled applause. When you look up

again the whole show has pulled up stakes and moved on down the road. It never stops. New shows roll in from over the mountains and the magician reappears unannounced from a fold in the curtain you never dreamed was an opening. Scarves of clouds, rabbits in plain view, disappear into the black hat forever. Presto chango. The audience, if there is an audience at all, is dizzy from head-turning, dazed.

Dillard has extended her original simile, her metaphoric understanding of nature as a magic act, in an analogy long enough and complex enough to create a twist in meaning: nature may be like a magic act, but a magic act in reverse, and therefore doubly mystifying.

Trite Language

Effective use of figurative language depends to a large extent on its originality, its surprising qualities. Many of the metaphors and similes we are tempted to use in descriptive writing turn out to be so timeworn that they are a liability rather than an asset to our writing. Expressions like "Her lips are like cherries" or "It was raining cats and dogs" were at one time marvelously original, but they have long since lost their effectiveness. The writer, as well as the reader, relates to them as a kind of perceptual shorthand; we write and read them with a glassy eye. An essay riddled with trite expressions suggests, probably correctly, that the writer has only a superficial or automatic understanding of the thing he or she is trying to describe, that he or she has not looked carefully enough, probed deeply enough, or articulated precisely enough. Trite language leaves the reader uninformed and uninspired—but worse, it suggests that the writer is in the same state.

READINGS: THE SUBJECT
IN NATURE

Kinds of writers, kinds of readers, subjects, and purposes in writing are many and various; one might think of them as infinite, in fact—as varied as individual human beings and the ways in which they might communicate. But in our vast, ongoing discourse, we are really all members of the same special interest group: the human species. In our attempts to understand the world around us, to discover how it works and decode its meaning, to communicate to one another in speaking and writing what we have come to learn, and to add our own voices to the cultural dialogue, we discover that perhaps we have more in common than we think.

In studying and interpreting subjects in the natural world—locations in nature, inanimate entities, and plant and animal species—the writers in this chapter are really engaged in an attempt to understand the human place in the natural order. John James Audubon, in describing the White-headed Eagle, our national symbol, is also writing political commentary. In describing a battle between two "races" of ants, Henry David Thoreau, in "Brute Neighbors," draws an analogy to the struggle between human groups. In "A Very Warm Mountain," Ursula K. Le Guin chooses to see Mount St. Helens in feminist terms as "a woman . . . not a mother but a sister," describing "her" eruption as the act of a "well-behaved, pretty, serene, domestic creature peaceably yielding herself to the uses of man all of a sudden [saying] NO." These are acts of interpretation.

Is anthropomorphism—the attribution of human characteristics to non-human animals or things—pure ego? Is it pure sentimentality? Is an objective, impersonal description of nature possible? And if so, is it desirable? Student writer Kiran Pandeya found in writing natural histories for the San Francisco Zoo's volunteer program that her project supervisor at the Zoo, Nicolette Heaphy, insisted in no uncertain terms that these histories be devoid of sentiment and that projecting human qualities onto the animals described was contrary to the zoo's conservation goals. If, in looking at these animals, volunteers and visitors to the zoo see only teddy bears and talking mynahs, Ms. Heaphy believes, they are not really appreciating the animals themselves and will not support their preservation on the animals' own terms and for their own intrinsic value.

However, it is difficult for us to see a subject outside ourselves without relating it back to ourselves. In criticizing the coolly detached method of scientific description of animals in which the "*anima,* [the animal's] vital spirit" is missing, Henry David Thoreau wrote that "In describing brutes, as in describing men, we shall naturally dwell most on the particulars in which they are most like ourselves,—in which we have most sympathy with them." Thus, the magnifying lens we use to examine the natural world often seems to function more as a mirror.

■ JOHN JAMES AUDUBON

White-headed Eagle
(Bald Eagle, *Haliaeetus Leucocephalus*)

The illegitimate son of Frenchman Jean Audubon and a Creole woman, Mademoiselle Rabin, famed ornithologist and artist John James Audubon was born in Les Cayes, Santo Domingo (now Haiti), in 1785. He spent his early years with his father and adoptive mother in France, and as a young man came to the United States, where he and his father settled near Philadelphia. Audubon began his study of American birds in 1804 with his first bird-banding expedition. A talented painter, Audubon financed many of his subsequent expeditions into the American wilderness by painting portraits of wealthy patrons and supported himself over the years as a tutor, drawing teacher, and sign painter. Audubon's attempts to find an American publisher for his drawings of birds were unsuccessful, so in 1826 he took his drawings to Europe, where they enjoyed a more favorable reception. He was elected to the Royal Society of Edinburgh in 1827 and was engaged to prepare drawings and text for his first book. Audubon was elected to the American Academy in 1830, and by the time he returned to the United States a year later, his reputation as a foremost American naturalist was established. He settled in New York City, on his estate, "Minnie's Land," which is now Audubon Park, and died in New York in 1851.

Although Audubon's extraordinary talent in rendering birds in rich and exquisitely detailed drawings and paintings is indisputable, most of the scientific information in the text of his many books seems to have been supplied by others. His classic ornithological works include Birds of America *(four volumes, 1827–1838) and* Ornithological Biography *(five volumes, 1831–1838), from which the following selection is taken. In* Ornithological Biography, *Audubon describes not only birds but also his wilderness adventures, and although he wrote the work in collaboration with Scottish naturalist William McGillivray, it has, at times, a distinctly American patriotic thrust.*

The figure of this noble bird is well known throughout the civilized world, emblazoned as it is on our national standard, which waves in the breeze of every clime, bearing to distant lands the remembrance of a great people living in a state of peaceful freedom. May that peaceful freedom last forever!

The great strength, daring, and cool courage of the White-headed Eagle, joined to his unequalled power of flight, render him highly conspicuous among his brethren. To these qualities did he add a generous disposition towards others, he might be looked up to as a model of nobility. The ferocious, overbearing, and tyrannical temper which is ever and anon displaying itself in his actions, is, nevertheless, best adapted to his state, and was wisely given him by the Creator to enable him to perform the office assigned to him.

To give you, kind reader, some idea of the nature of this bird, permit me to place you on the Mississippi, on which you may float gently along, while approaching winter brings millions of waterfowl on whistling wings, from the countries of the north, to seek a milder climate in which to sojourn for a season. The Eagle is seen perched, in an erect attitude, on the highest summit of the tallest tree by the margin of the broad stream. His glistening but stern eye looks over the vast expanse. He listens attentively to every sound that comes to his quick ear from afar, glancing now and then on the earth beneath, lest even the light tread of the fawn may pass unheard. His mate is perched on the opposite side, and should all be tranquil and silent, warns him by a cry to continue patient. At this well known call, the male partly opens his broad wings, inclines his body a little downwards, and answers to her voice in tones not unlike the laugh of a maniac. The next moment, he resumes his erect attitude, and again all around is silent. Ducks of many species, the Teal, the Wigeon, the Mallard and others, are seen passing with great rapidity, and following the course of the current; but the Eagle heeds them not: they are at that time beneath his attention. The next moment, however, the wild trumpet-like sound of a yet distant but approaching Swan is heard. A shriek from the female Eagle comes across the stream—for, kind reader, she is fully as alert as her mate. The latter suddenly shakes the whole of his body, and with a few touches of his bill, aided by the action of his cuticular muscles, arranges his plumage in an instant. The snow-white bird is now in sight: her long neck is stretched forward, her eye is on the watch, vigilant as that of her enemy; her large wings seem with difficulty to support the weight of her body, although they flap incessantly. So irksome do her exertions seem, that her very legs are spread beneath her tail, to aid her in her flight. She approaches, however. The Eagle has marked her for his prey. As the Swan is passing the dreaded pair, starts from his perch, in full preparation for the chase, the male bird, with an awful scream, that to the Swan's ear brings more terror than the report of the large duck-gun.

Now is the moment to witness the display of the Eagle's powers. He glides through the air like a falling star; and, like a flash of lightning, comes upon the timorous quarry, which now, in agony and despair, seeks, by various manoeuvers, to elude the grasp of his cruel talons. It mounts, doubles, and willingly would plunge into the stream, were it not prevented by the Eagle, which, long possessed of the knowledge that by such a stratagem the Swan might escape him, forces it to remain in the air by attempting to strike it with his talons from beneath. The hope of escape is soon given up by the Swan. It has already become much weakened, and its strength fails at the sight of the courage and swiftness of its antagonist. Its last gasp is about to escape, when the ferocious Eagle strikes with his talons the under side of its wing, and with unresisted power forces the bird to fall in a slanting direction upon the nearest shore.

It is then, reader, that you may see the cruel spirit of this dreaded enemy of the feathered race, whilst, exulting over his prey, he for the first time breathes at ease. He presses down his powerful feet, and drives his sharp claws deeper than ever into the heart of the dying Swan. He shrieks with delight, as he feels the last convulsions of his prey, which has now sunk under his unceasing efforts to render death as painfully felt as it can possibly be. The female has watched every movement of her mate; and if she did not assist him in capturing the Swan, it was not from want of will, but merely that she felt full assurance that the power and courage of her lord were quite sufficient for the deed. She now sails to the spot where he eagerly awaits her, and when she has arrived, they together turn the breast of the luckless Swan upwards, and gorge themselves with gore.

■ CONSIDERATIONS OF MEANING AND METHOD

1. How does Audubon characterize these birds? This piece can be interpreted as political commentary as well as natural history. Explain and illustrate with examples from the text.

2. What writing techniques does Audubon use to draw the reader in?

3. Is a visual portrait—a painting, a drawing, or even a photograph—any more or less objective, or more or less subjective, than a verbal portrait? Examine some of Audubon's drawings or paintings of birds, such as ones used as illustrations in his *Ornithological Biography*. Can you compare them to this text? To what extent does Audubon record information, and how much does he interpret what he sees in writing and in painting?

■ POSSIBILITIES FOR WRITING

1. Based on observation or recollection, write a brief description of an animal subject, one with which you are quite familiar although your reader may not be (a pet, for example, or the squirrel that lives in the tree outside your window). In your description, record nothing beyond the facts, in as careful detail as you can. Then write a different kind of description of the same subject, in which you allow your interpretation of it—how you feel about it, or what it means to you—to come forward in your selection of detail and your descriptive language. Which was more challenging to write, and why?

2. Choose as a writing subject a natural object which also functions as a powerful symbol, as the white-headed eagle (or bald eagle) is a symbol of American independence and power, or the Rock of Gibraltar is a symbol of enduring strength. In a short essay, describe the subject objectively, in detail; then explain how its physical qualities contribute to and enhance its symbolic significance.

■ HENRY DAVID THOREAU
Brute Neighbors from *Walden*

*Writer, naturalist, moral philosopher, and activist Henry David
Thoreau is preeminent among American nature writers. He helped
establish the tradition of nature writing later developed by John
Burroughs and John Muir, and his writing and thinking serve as
an important point of reference for contemporary writers in that
genre. A protégé of American Transcendentalist Ralph Waldo
Emerson, Thoreau believed that humans were perfectible; that if
human beings wished to know themselves, they had to look to
nature; and that truth lay in a correlation between the human
spirit and the spirit inherent in nature. He also believed that in a
materialistic society where there was a great and increasing
pressure to conform, especially at a time of urban and industrial expansion, each individual had a right, even an obligation, to shape
his or her life according to inner principles. Thoreau's famous essay
"Civil Disobedience" (which he originally titled "Resistence to
Civil Government") influenced Ghandi and Martin Luther King,
Jr., among many others. In it, Thoreau defended his belief that private conscience, not majority rule, should provide the standard for
moral action.*

    *Thoreau spent virtually his whole life in Concord,
Massachusetts, where his family owned a pencil factory. Unable to
support himself by writing, he worked in his family's business and
as a surveyor, even while living his contemplative life on a few
acres of land provided him by Emerson at Walden Pond. At
Walden, he meticulously observed the workings of the natural
world and reflected upon both nature and human nature.
Constantly writing, Thoreau accumulated a great body of work
over his lifetime, much of it published posthumously. He himself
published his first book,* A Week on the Concord and Merrimack
Rivers *(1849), after it had been consistently rejected by publishers.
The following selection, "Brute Neighbors," is from what is generally acknowledged as Thoreau's greatest work,* Walden: or, Life in
the Woods *(1854). Scholars Robert Finch and John Elder have
noted that Thoreau's "descriptions of wild animals [in* Walden] *(including the famous battle of the ants) remain among the finest of
their kind, ground-breaking in their conscious metaphoric
overtones and Thoreau's deliberate exploration of the role of the
self-aware narrator as both observer and participant." Thoreau's*

journal writings, which eventually ran to thirty-nine manuscript volumes, were published in Journals *(1906) well after his death in Concord in 1862.*

I was witness to events of a less peaceful character. One day when I went out to my wood-pile, or rather my pile of stumps, I observed two large ants, the one red, the other much larger, nearly half an inch long, and black, fiercely contending with one another. Having once got hold they never let go, but struggled and wrestled and rolled on the chips incessantly. Looking farther, I was surprised to find that the chips were covered with such combatants, that it was not a *duellum*, but a *bellum*, a war between two races of ants, the red always pitted against the black, and frequently two red ones to one black. The legions of these Myrmidons covered all the hills and vales in my wood-yard, and the ground was already strewn with the dead and dying, both red and black. It was the only battle which I have ever witnessed, the only battle-field I ever trod while the battle was raging; internecine war; the red republicans on the one hand, and the black imperialists on the other. On every side they were engaged in deadly combat, yet without any noise that I could hear, and human soldiers never fought so resolutely. I watched a couple that were fast locked in each other's embraces, in a little sunny valley amid the chips, now at noonday prepared to fight till the sun went down, or life went out. The smaller red champion had fastened himself like a vice to his adversary's front, and through all the tumblings on that field never for an instant ceased to gnaw at one of his feelers near the root, having already caused the other to go by the board; while the stronger black one dashed him from side to side, and, as I saw on looking nearer, had already divested him of several of his members. They fought with more pertinacity than bulldogs. Neither manifested the least disposition to retreat. It was evident that their battle-cry was "Conquer or die." In the meanwhile there came along a single red ant on the hillside of this valley, evidently full of excitement, who either had despatched his foe, or had not yet taken part in the battle; probably the latter, for he had lost none of his limbs; whose mother had charged him to return with his shield or upon it. Or perchance he was some Achilles, who had nourished his wrath apart, and had now come to avenge or rescue his Patroclus. He saw this unequal combat from afar,—for the blacks were nearly twice the size of the red,—he drew near with rapid pace till he stood on his guard within half an inch of the combatants; then, watching his opportunity, he sprang upon the black warrior, and commenced his operations near the root of his right fore leg, leaving the foe to select among his own members; and so there were three united for life, as if a new kind of attraction had been invented which put all other locks and cements to shame. I should not have wondered by this time to find that they had their respective musical bands stationed on some eminent chip, and playing their national airs the while, to excite the slow and cheer the dying combatants. I was myself excited somewhat even as if they had been men. The more you think of it, the less the difference. And certainly there is not the fight recorded in Concord history, at least, if in the history of America, that will bear a moment's comparison with this, whether for the numbers engaged in it, or for the patriotism and heroism displayed. For numbers and for carnage it was Austerlitz or Dresden. Concord Fight! Two killed on the patriots' side, and Luther Blanchard wounded! Why here every ant was a Buttrick,— "Fire! for God's sake fire!"—and thousands shared the fate of Davis and Hosmer. There was not one hireling there. I have no doubt that it was a principle they fought for, as much as our ancestors, and not to avoid a three-penny tax on their tea; and the results of this battle will be as important and memorable to those whom it concerns as those of the battle of Bunker Hill, at least.

I took up the chip on which the three I have particularly described were struggling, carried into my house, and placed it under a tumbler on my window-sill, in order to see the issue. Holding a microscope to the first-mentioned red ant, I saw that, though he was assiduously gnawing at the near fore leg of his enemy, having severed his remaining feeler, his own breast was all torn away, exposing what vitals he had there to the jaws of the black warrior, whose breastplate was apparently too thick for him to pierce; and the dark carbuncles of the sufferer's eyes shone with ferocity such as war only could excite. They struggled half an hour longer under the tumbler, and when I looked again the black soldier had severed the heads of his foes from their bodies, and the still living heads were hanging on either side of him like ghastly trophies at his saddlebow, still apparently as firmly fastened as ever, and he was endeavoring with feeble struggles, being without feelers and with only the remnant of a leg, and I know not how many other wounds, to divest himself of them; which at length, after half an hour more, he accomplished. I raised the glass, and he went off over the window-sill in that crippled state. Whether he finally survived that combat, and spent the remainder of his days in some Hôtel des Invalides, I do not know; but I thought that his industry would not be worth much thereafter. I never learned which party was victorious, nor the cause of the war; but I felt for the rest of that day as if I had had my feelings excited and harrowed by witnessing the struggle, the ferocity and carnage, of a human battle before my door.

Kirby and Spence tell us that the battles of ants have long been celebrated and the date of them recorded, though they say that Huber is the only modern author who appears to have witnessed them. "Aeneas Sylvius," say they, "after giving a very circumstantial account of one contested with great obstinacy by a great and small species on the trunk of a pear tree," adds that "'this action was fought in the pontificate of Eugenius the Fourth, in the presence of Nicholas Pistoriensis, an eminent lawyer, who related the whole history of the battle with the greatest fidelity.' A similar engagement between great and small ants is recorded by Olaus Magnus, in which the small ones, being victorious, are said to have buried the bodies of their own soldiers, but left those of their giant enemies a prey to the birds. This event happened previous to the expulsion of the tyrant Christiern the Second from Sweden." The battle which I witnessed took place in the Presidency of Polk, five years before the passage of Webster's Fugitive-Slave Bill.

■ CONSIDERATIONS OF MEANING AND METHOD

1. In what respects is Thoreau both an observer and a participant in the events he describes in "Brute Neighbors"? How does this role affect his point of view in writing?

2. In "Brute Neighbors," Thoreau's analogy of the battle of the ants to human warfare provides a strong reflective element. How does he develop this analogy in this piece? Does the analogy seem appropriate to you? How much do you need to know about the history of Thoreau's time to appreciate the analogy fully?

3. Writing conventions—not only in terms of style, but also grammar and usage—change over time. In what respects might Thoreau's style of writing feel antiquated to readers today? What in his writing might even be considered mistakes by today's stylistic and grammatical standards?

■ POSSIBILITIES FOR WRITING

1. In an essay for general readers, describe an animal subject and try

to capture "its *anima*, its vital spirit" (Thoreau, *Journals*) as well as its physical characteristics, habits, and habitats.

■ RICHARD WRIGHT
From *Black Boy*

Novelist, short story writer, poet, and essayist Richard Wright, born near Natchez, Mississippi, in 1908, was largely self-educated. His formal education, frequently interrupted by his family's moves, ended when he was fifteen, although he read widely after that, following his own wide-ranging interests. He was a clerk at the U.S. Post Office in Chicago during the 1920s, and during the Great Depression he worked with the Works Progress Administration (WPA) Federal Writers' Project in Chicago and New York. In 1946, Wright was invited by the government of France to visit that country; after a six-month stay, he decided to live there permanently. He died in 1960, at the age of 52, in Paris.

Wright was one of the most influential American writers of the century, and his earliest work of fiction, Uncle Tom's Children *(1938), a collection of four novellas, attracted attention and acclaim. Wright, in retrospect, was dissatisfied: "... I had written a book [about racial oppression] which even bankers' daughters could read and weep over and feel good. I swore to myself that if I ever wrote another book, no one would weep over it; that it would be so hard and deep that they would have to face it without the consolation of tears."* Native Son *(1940) was that book.*

However, many critics consider Black Boy *(1937) to be his most important work. In this autobiography (some consider it to be an autobiographical novel), Wright describes his childhood in the South. Novelist Ralph Ellison writes that "in* Black Boy *Wright has used his own life to probe what qualities of will, imagination, and intellect are required of a Southern Negro in order to possess the meaning of his life in the United States.... And like blues sung by such an artist as Bessie Smith, its lyrical prose evokes the paradoxical, almost surreal image of a black boy singing lustily as he probes his own grievous wound...."*

Richard Wright is certainly not a nature writer, although in his work, as in the work of many writers in many forms, both fictional and autobiographical, the natural world emerges as a powerful influence. In this brief passage from Black Boy, *Wright poignantly evokes, in the "lyrical prose" Ellison describes, his experience of nature as a child—a time when most of us experience the least separation from the natural world.*

Each event spoke with a cryptic tongue. And the moments of living slowly revealed their coded meanings. There was the wonder I felt when I first saw a brace of mountainlike, spotted, black-and-white horses clopping down a dusty road through clouds of powdered clay.

There was the delight I caught in seeing long straight rows of red and green vegetables stretching away in the sun to the bright horizon.

There was the faint, cool kiss of sensuality when dew came on to my cheeks and shins as I ran down the wet green garden paths in the early morning.

There was the vague sense of the infinite as I looked down upon the yellow, dreaming waters of the Mississippi River from the verdant bluffs of Natchez.

There were the echoes of nostalgia I heard in the crying strings of wild geese winging south against a bleak, autumn sky.

There was the tantalizing melancholy in the tingling scent of burning hickory wood.

There was the teasing and impossible desire to imitate the petty pride of sparrows wallowing and flouncing in the red dust of country roads.

There was the yearning for identification loosed in me by the sight of a solitary ant carrying a burden upon a mysterious journey.

There was the disdain that filled me as I tortured a delicate, blue-pink crawfish that huddled fearfully in the mudsill of a rusty tin can.

There was the aching glory in masses of clouds burning gold and purple from an invisible sun.

There was the liquid alarm I saw in the blood-red glare of the sun's afterglow mirrored in the squared panes of whitewashed frame houses.

There was the languor I felt when I heard green leaves rustling with a rainlike sound.

There was the incomprehensible secret embodied in a whitish toadstool hiding in the dark shade of a rotting log.

There was the experience of feeling death without dying that came from watching a chicken leap about blindly after its neck had been snapped by a quick twist of my father's wrist.

There was the great joke that I felt God had played on cats and dogs by making them lap their milk and water with their tongues.

There was the thirst I had when I watched clear, sweet juice trickle from sugar cane being crushed.

There was the hot panic that welled up in my throat and swept through my blood when I first saw the lazy, limp coils of a blue-skinned snake sleeping in the sun.

There was the speechless astonishment of seeing a hog stabbed through the heart, dipped into boiling water, scraped, split open, gutted, and strung up gaping and bloody.

There was the love I had for the mute regality of tall, moss-clad oaks.

There was the hint of cosmic cruelty that I felt when I saw the curved timbers of a wooden shack that had been warped in the summer sun.

There was the saliva that formed in my mouth whenever I smelt clay dust potted with fresh rain.

There was the cloudy notion of hunger when I breathed the odor of new-cut, bleeding grass.

And there was the quiet terror that suffused my senses when vast hazes of gold washed earthward from star-heavy skies on silent nights . . .

■ CONSIDERATIONS OF MEANING AND METHOD

1. Take a close look at the structure of Wright's sentences in this passage, noticing how he sets up the powerful rhythms of his prose, creating the sense of an incantation that carries the reader into a kind of revery. Aside from the repetitions of "There was" and "There were" at the beginning of virtually every sentence, what other patterns are repeated? How does he vary the patterns?

2. Go through the passage word by word and image by image, distinguishing between descriptive language (describing a thing as it is) and figurative language (comparing it to something else). Underline every simile and metaphor you encounter. To what extent does Wright rely upon figurative language as opposed to simpler descriptive language in creating vivid images?

■ POSSIBILITIES FOR WRITING

1. Immediately after reading this passage, while you are still caught up in its rhythms and images, sit down with your journal and compose a series of imagistic memories from your childhood, in vivid descriptive and/or figurative language and in a rhythmic

form similar to Wright's. Try beginning each sentence with "I remember . . . ." If memories of your impressions of nature don't
provide enough material, expand into other childhood memories,
other themes.

2. In a descriptive essay, recreate for members of your writing com-
    munity, your classmates, a specific place from your childhood
    that elicited in you a strong emotional response—perhaps a place
    in which you felt especially secure, comfortable, or happy, or one
    which made you extremely anxious, uncomfortable, or sad.
    Begin in your journal with brainstorming, clustering, and/or
    freewriting. In the essay, try *not* putting yourself in the scene;
    rather, focus your description upon the place itself, letting the
    concrete details of the scene and the rhythm and texture of your
    language produce the dominant emotional impression you want
    to convey to your reader. That is, try to show rather than tell.

■ N. SCOTT MOMADAY
Introduction from *The Way to Rainy Mountain*

*N(avarre) Scott Momaday, born in 1934, is a Kiowa Indian who
grew up among the Jemez Indians in New Mexico. His father is of
the Kiowa tribe; his mother, although she is primarily of Anglo
descent, strongly identifies with her great-grandmother's Cherokee
heritage as well as that of the Kiowas, her adoptive tribe.
Momaday's parents instilled in him a strong sense of Indian history
and cultural heritage. He earned his A.B. degree from the
University of New Mexico and his M.A. and Ph.D. from Stanford
University. He is currently professor of English at the University of
Arizona, Tucson. Momaday is an artist as well as a writer of major
importance. His first novel,* House Made of Dawn *(1968), won a
Pulitzer Prize. The following selection is from the introduction to
his book* The Way to Rainy Mountain *(1969), which blends history
and personal reflection with a retelling of Kiowa Indian legends
and folktales.*

*"When I was growing up on the reservations of the Southwest, I
saw people who were deeply involved in their traditional life, in
the memories of their blood. They had, as far as I could see, a
certain strength and beauty that I find missing in the modern
world at large," Momaday stated in a 1984 interview. "I believe,"
he continued, "that the Indian has an understanding of the
physical world and of the earth as a spiritual entity that is his, very*

*much his own. The non-Indian can benefit a good deal by having
that perception revealed to him." In* The Way to Rainy Mountain,
*Momaday—who is, like many of us, a product of mixed cultures—
sets out to discover as well as to teach others about the most crucial
aspects of his Kiowa cultural heritage.*

A single knoll rises out of the plain in Oklahoma, north and west of
the Wichita Range. For my people, the Kiowas, it is an old landmark,
and they gave it the name Rainy Mountain. The hardest weather in
the world is there. Winter brings blizzards, hot tornadic winds arise
in the spring, and in summer the prairie is an anvil's edge. The grass
turns brittle and brown, and it cracks beneath your feet. There are
green belts along the rivers and creeks, linear groves of hickory and
pecan, willow and witch hazel. At a distance in July or August the
steaming foliage seems almost to writhe in fire. Great green and yellow grasshoppers are everywhere in the tall grass, popping up like
corn to sting the flesh, and tortoises crawl about on the red earth,
going nowhere in the plenty of time. Loneliness is an aspect of the
land. All things in the plain are isolate; there is no confusion of objects in the eye, but *one* hill or *one* tree or *one* man. To look upon
that landscape in the early morning, with the sun at your back, is to
lose the sense of proportion. Your imagination comes to life, and
this, you think, is where Creation was begun.

I returned to Rainy Mountain in July. My grandmother had died
in the spring, and I wanted to be at her grave. She had lived to be very
old and at last infirm. Her only living daughter was with her when
she died, and I was told that in death her face was that of a child.

I like to think of her as a child. When she was born, the Kiowas
were living the last great moment of their history. For more than a
hundred years they had controlled the open range from the Smoky
Hill River to the Red, from the headwaters of the Canadian to the
fork of the Arkansas and Cimarron. In alliance with the Comanches,
they had ruled the whole of the southern Plains. War was their sacred
business, and they were among the finest horsemen the world has
ever known. But warfare for the Kiowas was preeminently a matter
of disposition rather than of survival, and they never understood the
grim, unrelenting advance of the U.S. Cavalry. When at last, divided
and ill-provisioned, they were driven onto the Staked Plains in the
cold rains of autumn, they fell into panic. In Palo Duro Canyon they
abandoned their crucial stores to pillage and had nothing then but
their lives. In order to save themselves, they surrendered to the sol-

diers at Fort Sill and were imprisoned in the old stone corral that now stands as a military museum. My grandmother was spared the humiliation of those high gray walls by eight or ten years, but she must have known from birth the affliction of defeat, the dark brooding of old warriors.

Her name was Aho, and she belonged to the last culture to evolve in North America. Her forebears came down from the high country in western Montana nearly three centuries ago. They were a mountain people, a mysterious tribe of hunters whose language has never been positively classified in any major group. In the late seventeenth century they began a long migration to the south and east. It was a journey toward the dawn, and it led to a golden age. Along the way the Kiowas were befriended by the Crows, who gave them the culture and religion of the Plains. They acquired horses, and their ancient nomadic spirit was suddenly free of the ground. They acquired Tai-me, the sacred Sun Dance doll, from that moment the object and symbol of their worship, and so shared in the divinity of the sun. Not least, they acquired the sense of destiny, therefore courage and pride. When they entered upon the southern Plains they had been transformed. No longer were they slaves to the simple necessity of survival; they were a lordly and dangerous society of fighters and thieves, hunters and priests of the sun. According to their origin myth, they entered the world through a hollow log. From one point of view, their migration was the fruit of an old prophecy, for indeed they emerged from the sunless world.

Although my grandmother lived out her long life in the shadow of Rainy Mountain, the immense landscape of the continental interior lay like memory in her blood. She could tell of the Crows, whom she had never seen, and of the Black Hills, where she had never been. I wanted to see in reality what she had seen more perfectly in the mind's eye, and traveled fifteen hundred miles to begin my pilgrimage.

Yellowstone, it seemed to me, was the top of the world, a region of deep lakes and dark timber, canyons and waterfalls. But, beautiful as it is, one might have the sense of confinement there. The skyline in all directions is close at hand, the high wall of the woods and deep cleavages of shade. There is a perfect freedom in the mountains, but it belongs to the eagle and the elk, the badger and the bear. The Kiowas reckoned their stature by the distance they could see, and they were bent and blind in the wilderness.

Descending eastward, the highland meadows are a stairway to the plain. In July the inland slope of the Rockies is luxuriant with flax and buckwheat, stonecrop and larkspur. The earth unfolds and the limit of the land recedes. Clusters of trees, and animals grazing far in the distance, cause the vision to reach away and wonder to build upon the mind. The sun follows a longer course in the day, and the sky is immense beyond all comparison. The great billowing clouds that sail upon it are shadows that move upon the grain like water, dividing light. Farther down, in the land of the Crows and Blackfeet, the plain is yellow. Sweet clover takes hold of the hills and bends upon itself to cover and seal the soil. There the Kiowas paused on their way; they had come to the place where they must change their lives. The sun is at home on the plains. Precisely there does it have the certain character of a god. When the Kiowas came to the land of the Crows, they could see the dark lees of the hills at dawn across the Bighorn River, the profusion of light on the grain shelves, the oldest deity ranging after the solstices. Not yet would they veer southward to the caldron of the land that lay below; they must wean their blood from the northern winter and hold the mountains a while longer in their view. They bore Tai-me in procession to the east.

A dark mist lay over the Black Hills, and the land was like iron. At the top of a ridge I caught sight of Devil's Tower upthrust against the gray sky as if in the birth of time the core of the earth had broken through its crust and the motion of the world was begun. There are things in nature that engender an awful quiet in the heart of man; Devil's Tower is one of them. Two centuries ago, because they could not do otherwise, the Kiowas made a legend at the base of the rock. My grandmother said:

Eight children were there at play, seven sisters and their brother. Suddenly the boy was struck dumb; he trembled and began to run upon his hands and feet. His fingers became claws, and his body was covered with fur. Directly there was a bear where the boy had been. The sisters were terrified; they ran, and the bear after them. They came to the stump of a great tree, and the tree spoke to them. It bade them climb upon it, and as they did so it began to rise into the air. The bear came to kill them, but they were just beyond its reach. It reared against the tree and scored the bark all around with its claws. The seven sisters were borne into the sky, and they became the stars of the Big Dipper.

From that moment, and so long as the legend lives, the Kiowas have kinsmen in the night sky. Whatever they were in the mountains, they could be no more. However tenuous their well-being, however much they had suffered and would suffer again, they had found a way out of the wilderness.

My grandmother had a reverence for the sun, a holy regard that now is all but gone out of mankind. There was a wariness in her, and an ancient awe. She was a Christian in her later years, but she had come a long way about, and she never forgot her birthright. As a child she had been to the Sun Dances; she had taken part in those annual rites, and by then she had learned the restoration of her people in the presence of Tai-me. She was about seven when the last Kiowa Sun Dance was held in 1887 on the Washita River above Rainy Mountain Creek. The buffalo were gone. In order to consummate the ancient sacrifice—to impale the head of a buffalo bull upon the medicine tree—a delegation of old men journeyed into Texas, there to beg and barter for an animal from the Goodnight herd. She was ten when the Kiowas came together for the last time as a living Sun Dance culture. They could find no buffalo; they had to hang an old hide from the sacred tree. Before the dance could begin, a company of soldiers rode out from Fort Sill under orders to disperse the tribe. Forbidden without cause the essential act of their faith, having seen the wild herds slaughtered and left to rot upon the ground, the Kiowas backed away forever from the medicine tree. That was July 20, 1890, at the great bend of the Washita. My grandmother was there. Without bitterness, and for as long as she lived, she bore a vision of deicide.

Now that I can have her only in memory, I see my grandmother in the several postures that were peculiar to her: standing at the wood stove on a winter morning and turning meat in a great iron skillet; sitting at the south window, bent above her beadwork, and afterwards, when her vision failed, looking down for a long time into the fold of her hands; going out upon a cane, very slowly as she did when the weight of age came upon her; praying. I remember her most often at prayer. She made long, rambling prayers out of suffering and hope, having seen many things. I was never sure that I had the right to hear, so exclusive were they of all mere custom and company. The last time I saw her she prayed standing by the side of her bed at night, naked to the waist, the light of a kerosene lamp moving upon her dark skin. Her long, black hair, always drawn and braided in the day, lay upon her shoulders and against her breasts like a shawl. I do not speak Kiowa, and I never understood her prayers, but there was something inherently sad in the sound, some merest hesitation upon the syllables of sorrow. She began in a high and descending pitch, exhausting her breath to silence; then again and again—and always the same intensity of effort, of something that is, and is not, like urgency in the human voice. Transported so in the dancing light among the shadows of her room, she seemed beyond the reach of time. But that was illusion; I think I knew then that I should not see her again.

Houses are like sentinels in the plain, old keepers of the weather watch. There, in a very little while, wood takes on the appearance of great age. All colors wear soon away in the wind and rain, and then the wood is burned gray and the grain appears and the nails turn red with rust. The windowpanes are black and opaque; you imagine there is nothing within, and indeed there are many ghosts, bones given up to the land. They stand here and there against the sky, and you approach them for a longer time than you expect. They belong in the distance; it is their domain.

Once there was a lot of sound in my grandmother's house, a lot of coming and going, feasting and talk. The summers there were full of excitement and reunion. The Kiowas are a summer people; they abide the cold and keep to themselves, but when the season turns and the land becomes warm and vital they cannot hold still; an old love of going returns upon them. The aged visitors who came to my grandmother's house when I was a child were made of lean and leather, and they bore themselves upright. They wore great black hats and bright ample shirts that shook in the wind. They rubbed fat upon their hair and wound their braids with strips of colored cloth. Some of them painted their faces and carried the scars of old and cherished enmities. They were an old council of warlords, come to remind and be reminded of who they were. Their wives and daughters served them well. The women might indulge themselves; gossip was at once the mark and compensation of their servitude. They made loud and elaborate talk among themselves, full of jest and gesture, fright and false alarm. They went abroad in fringed and flowered shawls, bright beadwork and German silver. They were at home in the kitchen, and they prepared meals that were banquets.

There were frequent prayer meetings, and great nocturnal feasts. When I was a child I played with my cousins outside, where the lamplight fell upon the ground and the singing of the old people rose up around us and carried away into the darkness. There were a lot of good things to eat, a lot of laughter and surprise. And afterwards, when the quiet returned, I lay down with my grandmother and could hear the frogs away by the river and feel the motion of the air.

Now there is a funeral silence in the rooms, the endless wake of some final word. The walls have closed in upon my grandmother's house. When I returned to it in mourning, I saw for the first time in my life how small it was. It was late at night, and there was a white moon, nearly full. I sat for a long time on the stone steps by the kitchen door. From there I could see out across the land; I could see the long row of trees by the creek, the low light upon the rolling plains, and the stars of the Big Dipper. Once I looked at the moon and caught sight of a strange thing. A cricket had perched upon the handrail, only a few inches away from me. My line of vision was such that the creature filled the moon like a fossil. It had gone there, I thought, to live and die, for there, of all places, was its small definition made whole and eternal. A warm wind rose up and purled like the longing within me.

The next morning I awoke at dawn and went out on the dirt road to Rainy Mountain. It was already hot, and the grasshoppers began to fill the air. Still, it was early in the morning, and the birds sang out of the shadows. The long yellow grass on the mountain shone in the bright light, and a scissortail hied above the land. There, where it ought to be, at the end of a long and legendary way, was my grandmother's grave. Here and there on the dark stones were ancestral names. Looking back once, I saw the mountain and came away.

■ CONSIDERATION OF MEANING AND METHOD

1. This selection serves as the introduction to Momaday's book *The Way to Rainy Mountain,* a retelling of Kiowa stories and legends. To what extent is this selection a portrait of Momaday's grandmother, a portrait of his people, a portrait of the landscape, or a self-portrait? Why, given the function this selection serves, did he focus on historical and "scenic," as well as personal, elements?

2. How, and upon what, does Momaday's opening paragraph focus the reader's attention? Why didn't he begin with the second paragraph? How do the opening and closing paragraphs relate? Does Momaday draw conclusions? Is his central idea stated or implied?

3. Explain the significance of the image of the cricket, whose silhouette from Momaday's perspective "filled the moon like a fossil"? Why did the image evoke such "longing" in Momaday?

■ POSSIBILITIES FOR WRITING

1. In an essay for a reader outside your family circle, describe an elder of your family in an outdoor setting. Is he or she comfortable or uncomfortable, at home or out of place there? Let details

of the description of both setting and person reflect and enhance each other.

2. Describe in detail a family event or holiday celebration that will vividly illustrate to your reader, whose cultural background may be different from yours, important elements of your own cultural heritage.

■ LEWIS THOMAS
Ponds

Lewis Thomas, born in 1913 in Flushing, New York, died in 1993 of Waldenstrom's Disease, a rare form of cancer. He enjoyed a distinguished career as a physician, researcher, and teacher, and, more recently, as a writer. His reputation as an essayist was established in 1974 with the publication of The Lives of a Cell: Notes of a Biology Watcher, *winner of the National Book Award. This book of essays and his subsequent book* The Medusa and the Snail: More Notes of a Biology Watcher *(1979), which won the American Book Award for science in 1981 and from which "Ponds" is taken, grew out of his popular column, "Notes of a Biology Watcher," a regular feature in the* New England Journal of Medicine *since 1971. His other books include* The Youngest Science: Notes of a Medicine-Watcher *(1983) and* Late Night Thoughts on Listening to Mahler's Ninth Symphony *(1984).*

Thomas was somewhat embarrassed at the success of The Lives of a Cell. *He told one interviewer, "I mean it's not really fair to have a book with a cover and everything when you never wrote a book, except in such little tiny bits." But Thomas was humble, and he was certainly no stranger to success. His list of achievements in medicine is long. He had been a professor of pediatrics and pathology at Johns Hopkins, Tulane, and New York Universities; dean of the School of Medicine at Yale University; and president and chief executive officer as well as chancellor of the Memorial Sloan-Kettering Cancer Center in New York City.*

Although Thomas published widely in specialized medical journals and texts, in his popular works he demonstrates an ability to write clearly and evocatively of scientific concepts for general readers. Symbiosis—the mutually advantageous association of different organisms living attached to one another—is a recurrent theme in his writing. Thomas explained that "There is a tendency

for living things to join up, establish linkages, live inside one
another, return to earlier arrangements, get along wherever
possible. . . . The whole dear notion of one's own . . . isolated island
of a Self . . . is a myth." Thomas's message is finally optimistic,
though it may also be disturbing. In The Lives of a Cell *he writes:*

We are told that the trouble with Modern Man is that he has been trying
to detach himself from nature. . . . Man comes on as a stupendous lethal
force, and the earth is pictured as something delicate, like rising bubbles
at the surface of a country pond. . . . But it is an illusion to think that
there is anything fragile about the life of the earth; surely this is the
toughest membrane imaginable in the universe, opaque to probability,
impermeable to death. We are the delicate parts, transient and vulnerable
as cilia.

"Ponds" is a fanciful celebration of the adaptability of living
things, as well as a commentary on the human tendency to perceive
natural processes as somehow rude, if not downright threatening.

Large areas of Manhattan are afloat. I remember when the new Bellevue Hospital was being built, fifteen years ago; the first stage was the
most spectacular and satisfying, an enormous square lake. It was
there for the two years, named Lake Bellevue, while the disconsolate
Budget Bureau went looking for cash to build the next stage. It was
fenced about and visible only from the upper windows of the old
hospital, but pretty to look at, cool and blue in midsummer, frozen
gleaming as Vermont in January. The fence, like all city fences, was
always broken, and we could have gone down to the lake and used it,
but it was known to be an upwelling of the East River. At Bellevue
there were printed rules about the East River: if anyone fell in, it was
an emergency for the Infectious-Disease Service, and the first measures, after resuscitation, were massive doses of whatever antibiotics
the hospital pharmacy could provide.

But if you cleaned the East River you could have ponds all over
town, up and down the East Side of Manhattan anyway. If you lifted
out the Empire State Building and the high structures nearby, you
would have, instantly, an inland sea. A few holes bored in the right
places would let water into the subways, and you'd have lovely underground canals all across to the Hudson, uptown to the Harlem
River, downtown to the Battery, a Venice underground, without pi-
geons.

It wouldn't work, though, unless you could find a way to keep out the fish. New Yorkers cannot put up with live fish out in the open. I cannot explain this, but it is so.

There is a new pond, much smaller than Lake Bellevue, on First Avenue between Seventieth and Seventy-first, on the east side of the street. It emerged sometime last year, soon after a row of old flats had been torn down and the hole dug for a new apartment building. By now it is about average size for Manhattan, a city block long and about forty feet across, maybe eight feet deep at the center, more or less kidney-shaped, rather like an outsized suburban swimming pool except for the things floating, and now the goldfish.

With the goldfish, it is almost detestable. There are, clearly visible from the sidewalk, hundreds of them. The neighborhood people do not walk by and stare into it through the broken fence, as would be normal for any other Manhattan pond. They tend to cross the street, looking away.

Now there are complaints against the pond, really against the goldfish. How could people do such a thing? Bad enough for pet dogs and cats to be abandoned, but who could be so unfeeling as to abandon goldfish? They must have come down late at night, carrying their bowls, and simply dumped them in. How could they?

The ASPCA was called, and came one afternoon with a rowboat. Nets were used, and fish taken away in new custodial bowls, some to Central Park, others to ASPCA headquarters, to the fish pound. But the goldfish have multiplied, or maybe those people with their bowls keep coming down late at night for their furtive, unfeeling dumping. Anyway, there are too many fish for the ASPCA, for which this seems to be a new kind of problem. An official stated for the press that the owners of the property would be asked to drain the pond by pumping, and then the ASPCA would come back with nets to catch them all.

You'd think they were rats or roaches, the way people began to talk. Get those goldfish out of that pond, I don't care how you do it. Dynamite, if necessary. But get rid of them. Winter is coming, someone said, and it is deep enough so that they'll be swimming around underneath the ice. Get them out.

It is this knowledge of the East River, deep in the minds of all Manhattan residents, more than the goldfish themselves, I think. Goldfish in a glass bowl are harmless to the human mind, maybe even helpful to minds casting about for something, anything, to think about. But goldfish let loose, propagating themselves, worst of all *surviving* in what has to be a sessile eddy of the East River, somehow threaten us all. We do not like to think that life is possible under some conditions, especially the conditions of a Manhattan pond. There are four abandoned tires, any number of broken beer bottles, fourteen shoes and a single sneaker, and a visible layer, all over the surface, of that grayish-green film that settles on all New York surfaces. The mud at the banks of the pond is not proper country mud but reconstituted Manhattan landfill, ancient garbage, fossilized coffee grounds and grapefruit rind, the defecation of a city. For goldfish to be swimming in such water, streaking back and forth mysteriously in small schools, feeding, obviously feeding, looking as healthy and well-off as goldfish in the costliest kind of window-box aquarium, means something is wrong with our standards. It is, in some deep sense beyond words, insulting.

I thought I noticed a peculiar sort of fin on the undersurface of two of the fish. Perhaps, it occurs to me now in a rush of exultation, in such a pond as this, with all its chemical possibilities, there are contained some mutagens, and soon there will be schools of mutant goldfish. Give them just a little more time, I thought. And then, with the most typically Manhattan thought I've ever thought, I thought: The ASPCA will come again, next month, with their rowboat and their nets. The proprietor will begin pumping out the pond. The nets will flail, the rowboat will settle, and then the ASPCA officials will give a sudden shout of great dismay. And with a certain amount of splashing and grayish-greenish spray, at all the edges of the pond, up all the banks of ancient New York landfill mud, crawling on their new little feet, out onto the sidewalks, up and down and across the street, into doorways and up the fire escapes, some of them with little suckers on their little feet, up the sides of buildings and into open windows, looking for something, will come the goldfish.

It won't last, of course. Nothing like this ever does. The mayor will come and condemn it in person. The Health Department will come and recommend the purchase of cats from out of town because of the constitutional boredom of city cats. The NIH will send up teams of professionals from Washington with a new kind of antifish spray, which will be recalled four days later because of toxicity to cats.

After a few weeks it will be finished anyway, like a lot of New York events. The goldfish will dive deep and vanish, the pond will fill up with sneakers, workmen will come and pour concrete over everything, and by next year the new building will be up and occupied by people all unaware of their special environmental impact. But what a time it was.

■ CONSIDERATIONS OF MEANING AND METHOD

1. What is the dividing line between fact and fantasy in Lewis Thomas's "Ponds"?

2. Thomas says that neighborhood people's "complaints against the pond . . . [are] really against the goldfish"; their stated disdain masks a deeper, unstated one. What is it about the proliferation of goldfish in this "sessile eddy of the East River" that is so deeply disturbing?

3. How would you characterize Thomas's humor in "Ponds"? Underline words, phrases, sentences, and passages from the essay that you found particularly funny. How, specifically, does he convey humor in his writing?

4. In what ways is Thomas especially well qualified to write this fanciful observation of nature and human nature? Who is his audience?

■ POSSIBILITIES FOR WRITING

1. The province of nature does not, of course, begin at the outer edge of the city limits. In an essay describe the occurrence of a natural phenomenon within a city or suburban landscape and the effect it has on people there. Your readers might be the people about whom you are writing but who, to some extent, may lack awareness or perspective.

2. Invent an evolutionary fable in which you explain how a creature developed, with a specific attribute or adaptation, to its current state. You could invent the evolution but not the creature ("How the Leopard Got Its Spots," for example), or invent both the creature and its evolution. Your reader might be a child—or someone who hasn't yet forgotten what it was like to be a child.

■ JOHN McPHEE
from *Basin and Range*

John McPhee was born in 1931 in Princeton, New Jersey, was educated at Princeton University, and is currently Professor of Journalism there. He has nearly two dozen nonfiction books to his credit, on subjects ranging from bark canoes to basketball. McPhee sees himself as "fundamentally . . . a working journalist"; in fact, many of his books are collections of essays which have appeared in The New Yorker, *for which he has been a staff writer since 1964. He has also been associate editor of* Time *magazine. Some of his many books are* The Pine Barrens *(1968),* Encounters with the Archdruid *(1972),* The Survival of the Bark Canoe *(1975),* Coming into the Country *(1977), and* Basin and Range *(1981).*

McPhee's occupation as a journalist has led him to take on a wide range of subject material, earning through research, interviews, and field study his expertise in area after area. In addition to describing American places and events, his books provide portraits of people, as well as American occupations and preoccupations. McPhee claims that "most of [my subjects] orginate when they strike an echo from my earlier experience, like The Survival of the Bark Canoe. *When I was quite young, my father took me to a summer camp [where] our canoe trips were a big thing, and I dearly loved them. What you hope is that some subject will interest you, and then you will have to deal with it on its own terms."*

Several books by McPhee, who is a member of the Geological Society of America and in 1982 won the American Association of Petroleum Geologists Journalism Award, have been on geological subjects. One of the theories McPhee describes in Basin and Range *suggests that movement of huge geologic plates on land and under the Pacific will eventually cause the west coast of the United States to separate from the continent, "thus making California an island." (Novelist and critic Evan Connell comments in a review of McPhee's work that "Metaphorically, of course, many people believe this has already happened.") In the following excerpt from* Basin and Range, *McPhee both parodies and delights in the special-ized language geologists use in their profession.*

I used to sit in class and listen to the terms come floating down the room like paper airplanes. Geology was called a descriptive science, and with its pitted outwash plains and drowned rivers, its hanging tributaries and starved coastlines, it was nothing if not descriptive. It was a fountain of metaphor—of isostatic adjustments and degraded channels, of angular unconformities and shifting divides, of rootless mountains and bitter lakes. Streams eroded headward, digging from two sides into mountain or hill, avidly struggling toward each other until the divide between them broke down, and the two rivers that did the breaking now became confluent (one yielding to the other, giving up its direction of flow and going the opposite way) to become a single stream. Stream capture. In the Sierra Nevada, the Yuba had captured the Bear. The Macho member of a formation in New Mexico was derived in large part from the solution and collapse of another formation. There was fatigued rock and incompetent rock and inequigranular fabric in rock. If you bent or folded rock, the inside of the curve was in a state of compression, the outside of the curve was under great tension, and somewhere in the middle was the surface of no strain. Thrust fault, reverse fault, normal fault—the two sides were active in every fault. The inclination of a slope on which boulders would stay put was the angle of repose. There seemed, indeed, to be more than a little of the humanities in this subject. Geologists communicated in English; and they could name things in a manner that sent shivers through the bones. They had roof pendants in their discordant batholiths, mosaic conglomerates in desert pavement. There was ultrabasic, deep-ocean, mottled green-and-black rock—or serpentine. There was the slip face of the barchan dune. In 1841, a paleontologist had decided that the big creatures of the Mesozoic were "fearfully great lizards," and had therefore named them dinosaurs. There were festooned crossbeds and limestone sinks, pillow lavas and petrified trees, incised meanders and defeated streams. There were dike swarms and slickensides, explosion pits, volcanic bombs. Pulsating glaciers, Hogbacks. Radiolarian ooze. There was almost enough resonance in some terms to stir the adolescent groin. The swelling up of mountains was described as an orogeny. Ontogeny, phylogeny, orogeny—accent syllable two. The Antler Orogeny, the Avalonian Orogeny, the Taconic, Acadian, Alleghenian Orogenies. The Laramide Orogeny. The center of the United States had had a dull geologic history—nothing much being accumulated, nothing much being eroded away. It was just sitting there conservatively. The East had once been radical—had been unstable, reformist, revolutionary, in the Paleozoic pulses of three or four orogenies. Now, for the last hundred and fifty million years, the East had been stable and conservative. The far-out stuff was in the Far West of the country—wild, weirdsma, a leather-jacket geology in mirrored shades, with its welded tuffs and Franciscan mélange (internally deformed, complex beyond analysis), its strike-slip faults and falling buildings, its boiling springs and fresh volcanics, its extensional disassembling of the earth.

There was, to be sure, another side of the page—full of geological language of the sort that would have attracted Gilbert and Sullivan. Rock that stayed put was called autochthonous, and if it had moved it was allochthonous. "Normal" meant "at right angles." "Normal" also meant a fault with a depressed hanging wall. There was a Green River Basin in Wyoming that was not to be confused with the Green River Basin in Wyoming. One was topographical and was *on* Wyoming. The other was structural and was *under* Wyoming. The Great Basin, which is centered in Utah and Nevada, was not to be confused with the Basin and Range, which is centered in Utah and Nevada. The Great Basin was topographical, and extraordinary in the world as a vastness of land that had no drainage to the sea. The Basin and Range was a realm of related mountains that all but coincided with the Great Basin, spilling over slightly to the north and south. To anyone with a smoothly functioning bifocal mind, there was no lack of clarity about Iowa in the Pennsylvanian, Missouri in the Mississippian, Nevada in Nebraskan, Indiana in Illinoian, Vermont in Kansan, Texas in Wisconsinan time. Meteoric water, with study, turned out to be rain. It ran downhill in consequent, subsequent, obsequent, resequent, and not a few insequent streams.

As years went by, such verbal deposits would thicken. Someone developed enough effrontery to call a piece of our earth an epiengeosyncline. There were those who said interfluve when they meant between two streams, and a perfectly good word like mesopotamian would do. A cactolith, according to the American Geological Institute's *Glossary of Geology and Related Sciences,* was "a quasi-horizontal chonolith composed of anastomosing ductoliths, whose distal ends curl like a harpolith, thin like a sphenolith, or bulge discordantly like an akmolith or ethmolith." The same class of people who called one rock serpentine called another jacupirangite. Clinoptilolite, eclogite, migmatite, tincalconite, szaibelyite, pumpellyite. Meyerhofferite. The same class of people who called one rock paracelsian called another despujolsite. Metakirchheimerite, phlogopite, katzenbuckelite, mboziite, noselite, neighborite, samsonite, pigeonite, muskoxite, pabstite, aenigmatite. Joesmithite. With the X-ray diffractometer and the X-ray fluorescence spectrometer, which came into general use in geology laboratories in the late nineteen-fifties, and then with the electron probe (around 1970), geologists obtained ever closer examinations of the components of rock. What they had long seen through magnifying lenses as specimens held in the hand—or in thin slices under microscopes—did not always register identically in the eyes of these machines. Andesite, for example, had been given its name for being the predominant rock of the high mountains of South America. According to the machines, there is surprisingly little andesite in the Andes. The Sierra Nevada is renowned throughout the world for its relatively young and absolutely beautiful granite. There is precious little granite in the Sierra. Yosemite Falls, Half Dome, El Capitan—for the most part the "granite" of the Sierra is granodiorite. It has always been difficult enough to hold in the mind that a magma which hardens in the earth as granite will—if it should flow out upon the earth—harden as rhyolite, that what hardens within the earth as diorite will harden upon the earth as andesite, that what hardens within the earth as gabbro will harden upon the earth as basalt, the difference from pair to pair being a matter of chemical composition and the differences within each pair being a matter of texture and of crystalline form, with the darker rock at the gabbro end and the lighter rock the granite. All of that— not to mention such wee appendixes as the fact that diabase is a special texture of gabbro—was difficult enough for the layman to remember before the diffractometers and the spectrometers and the electron probes came along to present their multiplex cavils. What had previously been described as the granite of the world turned out to be a large family of rock that included granodiorite, monzonite, syenite, adamellite, trondhjemite, alaskite, and a modest amount of true granite. A great deal of rhyolite, under scrutiny, became dacite, rhyodacite, quartz latite. Andesite was found to contain enough silica, potassium, sodium, and aluminum to be the fraternal twin of granodiorite. These points are pretty fine. The home terms still apply. The enthusiasm geologists show for adding new words to their conversation is, if anything, exceeded by their affection for the old. They are not about to drop granite. They say granodiorite when they are in church and granite the rest of the week.

When I was seventeen and staring up the skirts of Eastern valleys, I was taught the rudiments of what is now referred to as the Old Geology. The New Geology is the package phrase for the effects of the revolution that occurred in earth science in the nineteen-sixties, when geologists clambered onto sea-floor spreading, when people began to discuss continents in terms of their velocities, and when the interactions of some twenty parts of the globe became known as plate tectonics. There were few hints of all that when I was seventeen, and now, a shake later, middle-aged and fading, I wanted to learn some geology again, to feel the difference between the Old and the New, to sense if possible how the science had settled down a decade after its great upheaval, but less in megapictures than in day-to-day contact with country rock, seeing what had not changed as well as what had changed. The thought occurred to me that if you were to walk a series of roadcuts with a geologist something illuminating would in all likelihood occur. This was long before I met Karen Kleinspehn, or, for that matter, David Love, of the United States Geological Survey, or Anita Harris, also of the Survey, or Eldridge Moores, of the University of California of Davis, all of whom would eventually take me with them through various stretches of the continent. What I did first off was what anyone would do. I called my local geologist. I live in Princeton, New Jersey, and the man I got in touch with was Kenneth Deffeyes, a senior professor who teaches introductory geology at Princeton University. It is an assignment that is angled wide. Students who have little aptitude for the sciences are required to take a course or two in the sciences en route to some cerebral Valhalla dangled high by the designers of curriculum. Deffeyes' course is one that such students are drawn to select. He calls it Earth and Its Resources. They call it Rocks for Jocks. . . .

■ CONSIDERATIONS OF MEANING AND METHOD

1. All areas of specialty (professions, disciplines, sports, social groups) have a specialized vocabulary, or jargon. From a textbook, a manual, lyrics to a song, reconstructed conversation, or in whatever other form you can find it, locate an example of specialized language and bring it to share with the class. What functions does jargon serve? As an insider, how does it feel to encounter it in writing or conversation? How does it feel as an outsider?

2. McPhee says that "Geology was called a descriptive science, and with its pitted outwash plains and drowned rivers, its hanging tributaries and starved coastlines, it was nothing if not descriptive." He goes on to cite terms that "sent shivers through the bones" and "terms to stir the adolescent groin." Underline in your text examples of a few of the richer descriptive terms and try to explain the source of their richness.

3. Not all geologic terms are as richly descriptive. What other kinds of terminology and usage does McPhee identify? Underline examples of this jargon in the text and explain their effect on you. What does the evolution of the language of geology have to do with the "Old Geology" and the "New Geology"?

■ POSSIBILITIES FOR WRITING

1. Use the example of jargon you located in response to question 1 above, or write your own. Now translate the example in terms accessible to any reader. What is lost in the translation, and what is gained?

2. Locate a map of the area surrounding the place you grew up or the place you attend school. Make a list of some of the more interesting or colorful place names, then try writing a poem or story—nonsensical, if you like—in which you incorporate as many of them as possible.

3. In an essay intended to inform local readers without any specialized knowledge, describe and explain the geology of your area (your hometown or county, or the area surrounding your campus). In order to accomplish this, you will probably have to learn more about your subject through observation and through outside sources, primary and/or secondary. You might follow McPhee's lead in consulting a primary source and ask a geology professor or major to accompany you on a walking or driving tour of the area. You could write this essay simply to impart information, but if that doesn't satisfy you, try writing an essay in which you attempt to convey, besides basic information, a certain *feeling* or *atmosphere* through your conscious use of descriptive and figurative language.

■ URSULA K. LE GUIN
A Very Warm Mountain

A prolific and versatile writer, Ursula K. Le Guin, born in 1929, the daughter of anthropologist Alfred L. Kroeber and writer Theodora Kroeber, is widely known for her science fiction and fantasy works, although she has also written poetry, essays, and children's books. Among her best known books are The Left Hand of Darkness *(1969),* The Lathe of Heaven *(1971),* The Dispossessed *(1974), and* The Earthsea Trilogy *(1977). Her writing has earned many prestigious awards, including several Nebula and Hugo Awards for science fiction, a Newberry Honor Medal for children's literature, and a National Book Award.*

Le Guin dislikes the labels "science fiction" and "fantasy" because she feels they have come to connote a "second-class" literature. She has said that her science fiction is based on "social science, psychology, anthropology, [and] history." The result, as scholar Keith Hull points out, "is an emphasis on culture." Another critic, Robert Scholes, observes that "Le Guin works . . . with an ecology, a cosmology, a reverence for the universe as a self-regulating structure." In her writing, both fiction and nonfiction, Le Guin frequently explores the use of myths as a way of understanding both nature and culture.

In 1980, as she recovered from surgery in her home in Portland, Oregon, her window framed the eruption of Mount St. Helens, forty-five miles away. She describes this event in "A Very Warm Mountain," interpreting various responses to it, including her own, as a personal and cultural phenomenon. Nature is frequently personified in feminine terms, although in her essay, Le Guin adds a twist to this ancient perception, personifying Mount St. Helens in feminist terms.

> An enormous region extending from north-central Washington to northeastern California and including most of Oregon east of the Cascades is covered by basalt lava flows. . . . The unending cliffs of basalt along the Columbia River . . . 74 volcanoes in the Portland area . . . A blanket of pumice that averages about 50 feet thick. . . .
>
> —*Roadside Geology of Oregon*
> Alt and Hyndman, 1978

Everybody takes it personally. Some get mad. Damn stupid mountain went and dumped all that dirty gritty glassy gray ash that flies like flour and lies like cement all over their roofs, roads, and rhododendrons. Now they have to clean it up. And the scientists are a real big help, all they'll say is we don't know; we can't tell, she might dump another load of ash on you just when you've got it all cleaned up. It's an outrage.

Some take it ethically. She lay and watched her forests being cut and her elk being hunted and her lakes being fished and fouled and her ecology being tampered with and the smoky, snarling suburbs creeping closer to her skirts, until she saw it was time to teach the White Man's Children a lesson. And she did. In the process of the lesson, she blew her forests to matchsticks, fried her elk, boiled her fish, wrecked her ecosystem, and did very little damage to the cities: so that the lesson taught to the White Man's Children would seem, at best, equivocal.

But everybody takes it personally. We try to reduce it to human scale. To make a molehill out of the mountain.

Some got very anxious, especially during the dreary white weather that hung around the area after May 18 (the first great eruption, when she blew 1300 feet of her summit all over Washington, Idaho, and points east) and May 25 (the first considerable ashfall in the thickly populated Portland area west of the mountain). Farmers in Washington State who had the real fallout, six inches of ash smothering their crops, answered the reporters' questions with polite stoicism; but in town a lot of people were cross and dull and jumpy. Some erratic behavior, some really weird driving. "Everybody on my bus coming to work these days talks to everybody else, they never used to." "Everybody on my bus coming to work sits there like a stone instead of talking to each other like they used to." Some welcomed the mild sense of urgency and emergency as bringing people together in mutual support. Some—the old, the ill—were terrified beyond reassurance. Psychologists reported that psychotics had promptly incorporated the volcano into their private systems; some thought they were controlling her, and some thought she was controlling them. Businessmen, whom we know from the Dow Jones Reports to be an almost ethereally timid and emotional breed, read the scare stories in Eastern newspapers and cancelled all their conventions here; Portland hotels are having a long cool summer. A Chinese Cultural Attaché, evidently preferring earthquakes, wouldn't come farther north than San Francisco. But many natives were irrationally exhilarated, secretly, heartlessly welcoming every steam-blast and earth-tremor: Go it, mountain!

Everybody read in the newspapers everywhere that the May 18 eruption was "five hundred times greater than the bomb dropped on Hiroshima." Some reflected that we have bombs much more than five hundred times more powerful than the 1945 bombs. But these are never mentioned in the comparisons. Perhaps it would upset people in Moscow, Idaho or Missoula, Montana, who got a lot of volcanic ash dumped on them, and don't want to have to think, what if that stuff had been radioactive? It really isn't nice to talk about it, is it. I mean, what if something went off in New Jersey, say, and *was* radioactive—Oh, stop it. That volcano's way out west there somewhere anyhow.

Everybody takes it personally.

I had to go into hospital for some surgery in April, while the mountain was in her early phase—she jumped and rumbled, like the Uncles in *A Child's Christmas in Wales,* but she hadn't done anything spectacular. I was hoping she wouldn't perform while I couldn't watch. She obliged and held off for a month. On May 18 I was home, lying around with the cats, with a ringside view: bedroom and study look straight north about forty-five miles to the mountain.

I kept the radio tuned to a good country western station and listened to the reports as they came in, and wrote down some of the things they said. For the first couple of hours there was a lot of confusion and contradiction, but no panic, then or later. Late in the morning a man who had been about twenty miles from the blast described it: "Pumice-balls and mud-balls began falling for about a quarter of an hour, then the stuff got smaller, and by nine it was completely and totally black dark. You couldn't see ten feet in front of you!" He spoke with energy and admiration. Falling mud-balls, what next? The main West Coast artery, I-5, was soon closed because of the mud and wreckage rushing down the Toutle River towards the highway bridges. Walla Walla, 160 miles east, reported in to say their street lights had come on automatically at about ten in the morning. The Spokane-Seattle highway, far to the north, was closed, said an official expressionless voice, "on account of darkness."

At one-thirty that afternoon, I wrote:

It has been warm with a white high haze all morning, since six A.M., when I saw the top of the mountain floating dark against yellow-rose sunrise sky above the haze.

That was, of course, the last time I saw or will ever see that peak.

Now we can see the mountain from the base to near the summit. The mountain itself is whitish in the haze. All morning there has been this long, cobalt-bluish drift to the east from where the summit would be. And about ten o'clock there began to be visible clots, like cottage cheese curds, above the summit. Now the eruption cloud is visible from the summit of the mountain till obscured by a cloud layer at about twice the height of the mountain, i.e., 25–30,000 feet. The eruption cloud is very solid-looking, like sculptured marble, a beautiful blue in the deep relief of baroque curls, sworls, curled-cloud-shapes—darkening towards the top—a wonderful color. One is aware of motion, but (being shaky, and looking through shaky binoculars) I don't actually see the carven-blue-sworl-shapes move. Like the shadow on a sundial. It is *enormous*. Forty-five miles away. It is so much bigger than the mountain itself. It is silent, from this distance. Enormous, silent. It looks not like anything earthy, from the earth, but it does not look like anything atmospheric, a natural cloud, either. The blue of it is stormcloud blue but the shapes are far more delicate, complex, and immense than stormcloud shapes, and it has this solid look; a weightiness, like the capital of some unimaginable column—which in a way indeed it is, the pillar of fire being underground.

At four in the afternoon a reporter said cautiously, "Earthquakes are being felt in the metropolitan area," to which I added, with feeling, "I'll say they are!" I had decided not to panic unless the cats did. Animals are supposed to know about earthquakes, aren't they? I don't know what our cats know; they lay asleep in various restful and decorative poses on the swaying floor and the jiggling bed, and paid no attention to anything except dinner time. I was not allowed to panic.

At four-thirty a meteorologist, explaining the height of that massive, storm-blue pillar of cloud, said charmingly, "You must understand that the mountain is very warm. Warm enough to lift the air over it to 75,000 feet."

And a reporter: "Heavy mud flow on Shoestring Glacier, with continuous lightning." I tried to imagine that scene. I went to the television, and there it was. The radio and television coverage, right through, was splendid. One forgets the joyful courage of reporters and cameramen when there is something worth reporting, a real Watergate, a real volcano.

On the 19th, I wrote down from the radio, "A helicopter picked the logger up while he was sitting on a log surrounded by a mud flow." This rescue was filmed and shown on television: the tiny figure crouching hopeless in the huge abomination of ash and mud. I don't know if this man was one of the loggers who later died in the Emanuel Hospital burn center, or if he survived. They were already beginning to talk about the "killer eruption," as if the mountain had murdered with intent. Taking it personally . . . Of course she killed. Or did they kill themselves? Old Harry who wouldn't leave his lodge and his whiskey and his eighteen cats at Spirit Lake, and quite right too, at eighty-three; and the young cameraman and the young geologist, both up there on the north side on the job of their lives; and the loggers who went back to work because logging was their living; and the tourists who thought a volcano is like Channel Six, if you don't like the show you turn it off, and took their RVs and their kids up past the roadblocks and the reasonable warnings and the weary country sheriffs sick of arguing: they were all there to keep the appointment. Who made the appointment?

A firefighter pilot that day said to the radio interviewer, "We do what the mountain says. It's not ready for us to go in."

On the 21st I wrote:

Last night a long, strange, glowing twilight; but no ash has yet fallen west of the mountain. Today, fine, gray, mild, dense Oregon rain. Yesterday afternoon we could see her vaguely through the glasses. Looking appallingly lessened—short, flat—That is painful. She was so beautiful. She hurled her beauty in dust clear to the Atlantic shore, she made sunsets and sunrises of it, she gave it to the western wind. I hope she erupts magma and begins to build herself again. But I guess she is still unbuilding. The Pres. of the U.S. came today to see her. I wonder if he thinks he is on her level. Of course he could destroy much more than she has destroyed if he took a mind to.

On June 4 I wrote:

Could see her through the glasses for the first time in two weeks or so. It's been dreary white weather with a couple of hours sun in the afternoons.—Not the new summit, yet; that's always in the roil of cloud/plume. But both her long lovely flanks. A good deal of new snow has fallen on her (while we had rain), and her SW face is white, black, and gray, much seamed, in unfamiliar patterns.

"As changeless as the hills—"

Part of the glory of it is being included in an event on the geologic scale. Being enlarged. "I shall lift up mine eyes unto the hills," yes: "whence cometh my help."

In all the Indian legends dug out by newspaper writers for the occasion, the mountain is female. Told in the Dick-and-Jane style considered appropriate for popular reportage of Indian myth, with all the syllables hyphenated, the stories seem even more naive and trivial than myths out of context generally do. But the theme of the mountain as woman—first ugly, then beautiful, but always a woman—is consistent. The mapmaking whites of course named the peak after a man, an Englishman who took his title, Baron St. Helens, from a town in the North Country: but the name is obstinately feminine. The Baron is forgotten, Helen remains. The whites who lived on and near the mountain called it The Lady. Called her The Lady. It seems impossible not to take her personally. In twenty years of living through a window from her I guess I have never really thought of her as "it."

She made weather, like all single peaks. She put on hats of cloud, and took them off again, and tried a different shape, and sent them all skimming off across the sky. She wore veils: around the neck, across the breast: white, silver, silver-gray, gray-blue. Her taste was impeccable. She knew the weathers that became her, and how to wear the snow.

Dr. William Hamilton of Portland State University wrote a lovely piece for the college paper about "volcano anxiety," suggesting that the silver cone of St. Helens had been in human eyes a breast, and saying:

> St. Helens' real damage to us is not . . . that we have witnessed a denial of the trustworthiness of God (such denials are our familiar friends). It is the perfection of the mother that has been spoiled, for part of her breast has been removed. Our metaphor has had a mastectomy.
>
> At some deep level, the eruption of Mt. St. Helens has become a new metaphor for the very opposite of stability—for that greatest of twentieth-century fears—cancer. Our uneasiness may well rest on more elusive levels than dirty windshields.

This comes far closer to home than anything else I've read about the "meaning" of the eruption, and yet for me it doesn't work. Maybe it would work better for men. The trouble is, I never saw St. Helens as a breast. Some mountains, yes: Twin Peaks in San Francisco, of course, and other round, sweet California hills—breasts, bellies, eggs, anything maternal, bounteous, yielding. But St. Helens in my eyes was never part of a woman; she is a woman. And not a mother but a sister.

These emotional perceptions and responses sound quite foolish when written out in rational prose, but the fact is that, to me, the eruption was all mixed up with the women's movement. It may be silly but there it is; along the same lines, do you know any woman who wasn't rooting for Genuine Risk to take the Triple Crown? Part of my satisfaction and exultation at each eruption was unmistakably feminist solidarity. You men think you're the only ones can make a really nasty mess? You think you got all the firepower, and God's on your side? You think you run things? Watch this, gents. Watch the Lady act like a woman.

For that's what she did. The well-behaved, quiet, pretty, serene, domestic creature peaceably yielding herself to the uses of man all of sudden said NO. And she spat dirt and smoke and steam. She blackened half her face, in those first March days, like an angry brat. She fouled herself like a mad old harridan. She swore and belched and farted, threatened and shook and swelled, and then she spoke. They heard her voice two hundred miles away. Here I go, she said. I'm doing my thing now. Old Nobodaddy you better JUMP!

Her thing turns out to be more like childbirth than anything else, to my way of thinking. But not on our scale, not in our terms. Why should she speak in our terms or stoop to our scale? Why should she bear any birth that we can recognize? To us it is cataclysm and destruction and deformity. To her—well, for the language for it one must go to the scientists or to the poets. To the geologists. St. Helens is doing exactly what she "ought" to do—playing her part in the great pattern of events perceived by that noble discipline. Geology provides the only time-scale large enough to include the behavior of a volcano without deforming it. Geology, or poetry, which can see a mountain and a cloud as, after all, very similar phenomena. Shelley's cloud can speak for St. Helens:

I silently laugh
At my own cenotaph . . .
And arise, and unbuild it again.

So many mornings waking I have seen her from the window before any other thing: dark against red daybreak, silvery in summer light, faint above river-valley fog. So many times I have watched her at evening, the faintest outline in mist, immense, remote, serene: the center, the central stone. A self across the air, a sister self, a stone. "The stone is at the center," I wrote in a poem about her years ago. But the poem is impertinent. All I can say is impertinent.

When I was writing the first draft of this essay in California, on July 23, she erupted again, sending her plume to 60,000 feet. Yesterday, August 7, as I was typing the words "the 'meaning' of the eruption," I checked out the study window and there it was, the towering blue cloud against the quiet northern sky—the fifth major eruption. How long may her labor be? A year, ten years, ten thousand? We cannot predict what she may or might or will do, now, or next, or for the rest of our lives, or ever. A threat: a terror: a fulfillment. This is what serenity is built on. This unmakes the metapors. This is beyond us, and we must take it personally. This is the ground we walk on.

■ CONSIDERATIONS OF MEANING AND METHOD

1. Le Guin remarks repeatedly that, despite the variety in individual reactions to Mount St. Helens' eruption, "everybody takes it personally," and, in her conclusion, that "we must take it personally." What does she mean? In what ways does Le Guin herself take the eruption of Mount St. Helens personally?

2. Do you agree that nature has been generally characterized as female, as Le Guin claims? Think of examples (like "Mother Nature") that support her assertion. To what extent do you think a feminine characterization of nature makes sense? What does it say, if anything, about culture as well as about nature?

3. How might Le Guin's circumstances and her literal vantage point in viewing the eruption of Mount St. Helens have influenced her point of view in writing? How are these factors reflected in the structure and style of her essay, the way in which she develops it?

4. Can you compare the point Lewis Thomas makes in "Ponds" and any point Le Guin makes in "A Very Warm Mountain"?

■ POSSIBILITIES FOR WRITING

1. If you have ever been caught in a cataclysmic natural event (a flood, a wildfire, an earthquake, a tornado, or a hurricane, for example), recall and describe the event from the point of view of a participant in an essay for readers who weren't there. The purpose of your description, beyond reporting what happened, might be to describe to them how it felt.

2. Do you recall hearing of a significant natural disaster in the past few years, reports of which made a real impression upon you? In your library, look up several different popular magazine or newspaper reports of the event. Most of these reports are intended to inform people who were not directly affected by the event. Analyze the articles, and write an essay in which you identify and illustrate what seems to be most compelling about the event from the outside observer's point of view. What do people seem to want to know about it? What apparently interests them most?

■ KIRAN PANDEYA
Rough-legged Hawk

In the following statement, student Kiran Pandeya introduces herself and describes the assignment that produced her fact sheet about the Rough-legged Hawk.

I was raised in West Des Moines, Iowa, where as a high school student I planned on being a doctor and nurtured a secret ambition of being a writer. As a sophomore in college, I have altered my course considerably, and I am now aiming for a degree in International Relations. Although I have no idea what specific career I want to pursue after college, I still maintain my desire to be a novelist some day. The most difficult problem I encounter in writing is trying to determine exactly what I want to say and the style that would be most effective for saying it.

Those questions were not a problem for me with this particular project, however, due to the assignment's clear purpose and its strict parameters. This fact sheet was written for the Volunteer Program at the San Francisco Zoo as part of a Community Service Writing Project in my Freshman English class. In Community Service Writing, each student chooses a nonprofit organization with which to work and takes on a writing task that the organization assigns. The projects vary tremendously; the students in my class wrote everything from press releases to pamphlets.

Nicolette Heaphy, the liaison at the San Francisco Zoo, was extremely helpful in clarifying the assignment and supplying information to get me started. I chose the Rough-legged Hawk from a list of animals she needed fact sheets on. She also provided a list of reputable sources to begin with (although I spent a lot of time gathering additional sources from the university library) and an example of the format she wanted. I expected to have difficulty excluding emotion from the text, but instead I discovered that I enjoy writing in this factual format. The fact sheets on the animals would be used to teach teenagers who volunteer at the zoo about the animals so that they can teach zoo visitors. I always consider purpose and audience as I write, but I focused especially on these aspects with this project. Knowing that these students would be reading my writing as fact truly impressed upon me my responsibility as a writer to present the truth.

Teachers often tell students to write as if the audience were someone other than just themselves, and as if the purpose were for something other than a grade. With this project, I learned that my writing was satisfactory in the professional world, and this gave me a completely different type of satisfaction than a good grade on a paper. Knowing that I wrote something that will be used to help other people (not to mention the animals) makes me feel as if I have done something beneficial for others as well as for myself.

Aves Ciconlisormes Accipitridae
Buteo Lagopus

<u>Geographic Range</u>: This species inhabits North America and is most commonly found near the Great Basin and in the northern Great Plains, avoiding the western coastline and the southeastern corner of the United States. Most concentrated populations are found within national wildlife refuges.

<u>Habitat</u>: Nests are often built in treetops of coniferous trees or sometimes on edges of steep banks or cliffs. Nests are composed of sticks, grass, weed stalks, and excrement; they are lined with grass, down, and feathers.

<u>Diet</u>: Primary food sources are lemmings and meadow mice, although this species also eats other small mammals and occasionally small birds. All prey are captured on the ground.

<u>Description</u>: Species displays melanistic plumage. During melanistic morph, feathers are uniformly sooty-black except for the base of the wing feathers and the base of the tail, which are whitish. Normally the feathers are marginated whitish with grayish-brown. The wings and tail show gray and white bars; the underside is spotted or has a dark band across the abdomen. The tips of the wings are usually black. The young have similar coloring, except for the tail and body, which are darker. The young develop adult plumage after two years.

This hawk received its name because of its legs, which are feathered completely to the talons. This unique trait can be helpful in identifying the bird.

<u>Weight</u>: 940–1,040 grams.

<u>Total Length</u>: Males are twenty inches; females are twenty-two inches.

<u>Habits and Adaptations</u>: These hawks hunt at dusk and are considered semi-nocturnal. They are known to hover over one area or perch on posts while hunting.

These hawks migrate in loose flocks to the same location each winter. The migration is induced by weather; precipitation and temperature are important, but the amount of snow affects migration more than intensity of cold.

Although they roost communally, these birds mate for life. Their nests are reused each year. The spacing of these nests is random and patchy; this may reflect the distribution of their food supply.

Reproductive Information: The number of birds pairing, mating, and producing young is directly affected by the abundance of the food supply. The male does most or all of the foraging during the fledging of the young. The eggs are usually laid in early June; the fledging occurs in August. Each clutch contains between two and seven greenish-white eggs that weigh sixty grams. The incubation period is thirty-one days. The young hatch asynchronously.

Miscellaneous: Other common names are American Rough-legged Hawk or Rough-legged Buzzard.

Humans are this species' worst enemy. These birds are often shot or hit by cars while consuming road kills.

Bibliography

Audubon, John. *Birds of America.* Garden City, NY: Garden City Publishing Company, 1936.

Ehrlich, Paul R., et al. *The Birder's Handbook: A Field Guide to the Natural History of North American Birds.* New York: Simon and Schuster, 1988.

Johnson, Donald R. *The Study of Raptor Populations.* Rev. ed. Moscow, Idaho: University Press of Idaho, 1981.

Newton, Ian. *Population Ecology of Raptors.* Vermillion, SD: Buteo Books, 1979.

Poole, K. G., et al. "Interrelationships within a Raptor Guild in the Central Canadian Arctic." *Canadian Journal of Zoology* 66.10 (1988): 2275–2282.

Root, Terry Louise. *Atlas of Wintering North American Birds.* Chicago: University of Chicago Press, 1988.

Terres, John K. *The Audubon Society Encyclopedia of North American Birds.* 1st ed. New York: Knopf, 1980.

■ CONSIDERATIONS OF MEANING AND METHOD

1. Imagine that you are Kiran Pandeya's intended reader: a teenage volunteer at a zoo whose job it is to relate information to visitors about the animals displayed there. In what ways, specifically, do you find the content, style, and format of Pandeya's fact sheet on the Rough-legged Hawk effective or ineffective?

2. How do writing style and usage in this description of the Rough-legged Hawk compare to those you would expect to find in a description of an animal in essay form? How does this description specifically compare to descriptions of animals elsewhere in this chapter?

3. Nicolette Heaphy, the coordinator of the San Francisco Zoo's volunteer program, insisted that the authors of these fact sheets should make sure to stick to the facts and not project any human characteristics onto the animals or inject any commentary into their writing. Has Pandeya succeeded in this? Why is this important to Heaphy and consistent with a zoo's mission?

■ Possibilities for Writing

1. Choose an animal that intrigues you, one that is relatively easy to observe firsthand, whether in a zoo, at home, or in the wild. Write two different descriptions of the animal—one scientific and objective, the other nonscientific and subjective. In both cases, your purpose will be to inform a reader who cares about animals; the question is, to inform the reader of what, exactly? What differences in emphasis, content, and style did you notice? In which writing were you more comfortable, and why?

2. Contact a zoo or a wildlife conservation or rehabilitation organization in your area. See if the organization needs a volunteer to help them produce public relations, informational, or educational materials. In writing for such an organization, pay particular attention to audience and purpose, and the differences you perceive between academic writing and writing in the world of work and political activity.

MAKING CRITICAL CONNECTIONS:
QUESTIONS FOR DISCUSSION, RESEARCH, AND WRITING

1. In discussion or in writing, compare Audubon's "White-headed Eagle" with student writer Kiran Pandeya's fact sheet on the Rough-legged Hawk. In what ways, specifically, do the writers' purposes seem to differ? How do point of view, form, and use of language in each differ, contributing to differences in purpose?

2. Find out more about the historical contexts in which Audubon's "White-headed Eagle" and Thoreau's "Brute Neighbors" were written. Report to your class, either orally or in written form, about what you learn. Compare the two works, explaining how and to what extent events of the time may have influenced both authors.

3. In the work of a great many writers who, like Richard Wright, are not generally considered to be nature writers, the natural world is nonetheless an important feature in terms of setting or theme. Think back over your experience as a reader to writing you have enjoyed in the past—essays, novels, short stories, poems, or plays. Have the authors of any of these works used nature in an interesting way that you may or may not have recognized when you first read the work? Review one of these works closely with this question in mind, and in an oral or written analysis, explain (1) the role nature plays in this work and (2) the writer's treatment of, or attitude about, nature as it is conveyed through his or her writing, citing examples from the work to illustrate and support your views.

4. Interview specialists in three distinctly different fields at your school—for example, a literary scholar, a research scientist, and an economics or business professor. Ask each person what determines the standards for writing in his or her discipline. What are the characteristics of good writing in the field, and what are the characteristics of poor writing? What purpose does writing serve in each field, and in what ways do the standards of quality adapt themselves to purpose? Compare what you learn from your interviews—about the standards for writing in different fields and their relationship to purpose—and write up the results in essay form, or report them orally to your class.

5. Many of the readings in this chapter raise questions, directly or indirectly, about *anthropomorphism* (the projection of human characteristics and qualities onto nonhuman entities). Which readings do this, and how? What is the difference between seeing

and interpreting nature as it is and anthropomorphizing it? What purpose does anthropomorphism serve? What do we stand to gain or lose through this way of seeing the natural world? In discussion or in writing, compare two or more of the readings in this chapter in light of these questions.

CHAPTER 3

Storm Front, © Joel Gordon 1981

DESCRIPTIONS OF PROCESS

RHETORIC:
DEVELOPING IDEAS
AND PURPOSE IN WRITING

KINDS OF WRITING

An essay (from the French word *essayer,* to attempt) is a relatively short nonfiction prose work of limited scope, intended to prove a particular point or to illustrate or interpret a specific subject. This broadly defined literary form includes many different kinds of writing and accommodates many different purposes. There is often a good deal of overlap in the purpose of essays and in the ways in which writing strategies may be used to accomplish purpose effectively. It may be helpful to understand kinds of essays, and their most fundamental purposes, within certain categories. The writer's primary purpose in some writing is to report, in other writing to explain, and in still other writing to persuade the reader. These purposes affect all of the elements that contribute to the development of writing in essay form: the writer's point of view, the tone and style of the writing, rhetorical strategies the writer undertakes in developing his or her ideas, and the writing's form and format. And inherent in purpose is the writer's understanding of who the reader will be, and what effect the writer hopes to have on that reader.

Reporting

In a piece of writing whose primary purpose is to report, the writer's objectivity is crucial. In an essay in which reporting is the primary purpose, the goal is to convey information in the most unbiased form pos-

133

sible. The writer's task is to relate an event or describe an object, scene, or situation completely and accurately without analyzing or interjecting commentary. Such writing satisfies the reader's need to know the facts, providing a foundation upon which the reader can begin to develop his or her own judgments and conclusions, combining these with other kinds of information and experience.

Journalism, of course, is one area in which we find—or expect to find—objective reporting in written form. However, anyone who reads newspaper or magazine reports of events, or anyone who has attempted to write a thoroughly objective report of an event (or even an object) will realize that objectivity is difficult to achieve at best. The very act of observation, the absorption of information in any form, is to some degree subjective and interpretive. The information we receive is filtered through our individual perceptions, which, in turn, are informed by our personal experience. The process of transcribing information, perception, and experience into language is subjective: we choose one detail over another based on what we deem is more or less important, and the words we select are inherently full of nuances of interpretation. Pure objectivity may in fact be impossible to achieve in writing.

In reporting, the modes of development most frequently used by writers are description and narration. As you know, description and narration can also be, and often are, used by writers to provoke a specific intellectual or emotional response in readers, when evoking such an effect is in keeping with the writer's purpose. But in addition to writing to achieve certain effects, when the writer's purpose is to relate information to the reader as objectively as possible, description and narration are the reporter's most useful rhetorical tools. Often, in writing, the author's overall purpose may be one thing (such as to explain or to persuade). Still, however, in some part of the essay the writer may need to step back and report, providing the reader with background information or a factual point of reference before going on to analyze, interpret, prove, or persuade.

Explaining

When the writer's primary purpose in an essay is to explain, without arguing for one view or interpretation over another, clarity is essential. The purpose in such writing goes beyond providing information to the reader; in an essay which explains an event, a situation, an object, a process, or an idea, the writer's primary purpose is to lead the reader to an understanding of the context and complexities of the subject.

The act of analysis in essays that explain something is more subjective than the acts of observing and reporting, since analysis demonstrates the writer's individual style of thought as well as more overtly reflecting his or her experience. The writer's task in an explanatory essay is not to exclude himself or herself altogether, but rather to maintain an openness and flexibility in exploring and articulating a range of possible explanations related to the subject rather than promoting one particular view over another.

Because of their analytic qualities, essays in which the writer's primary goal is to explain are likely to employ a broader range of rhetorical strategies than essays that simply report. The writer may use description or narration to provide background information, describing an object, setting a scene, or relating an event. But he or she will go on to use other strategies—such as definition, classification, cause and effect analysis, illustration and example, and comparison and contrast, for example—either alone or in combination, to explain the significance of these things.

Persuading

A writer whose primary purpose in an essay is to persuade the reader to accept one view over others will likely employ many of the strategies of both reporting and explaining: description, narration, definition, classification, cause and effect analysis, illustration and example, and comparison and contrast. In addition, though, the writer will need to demonstrate skill in logic and reasoning, offer a variety of convincing evidence to support his or her assertions, and possess an understanding of other interpretations or opposing views in order to write persuasively.

The term "argument" is perhaps misleading, if not damaging. Argument implies conflict, and some forms of persuasive writing do degenerate into mere wars of words. But the wider intent of persuasive writing is to advance a dialogue on an issue of controversy in which solutions are widely debatable and open to interpretation. The writer's purpose is (1) to articulate to the reader how and why he or she has arrived at a particular interpretation or come to take a particular stand on an issue, and (2) to motivate a similar response in the reader.

The audience for persuasive writing is directly related to its purpose. The more aggressive and absolute the argument is, the narrower the audience is likely to be. Because they are defensive, one-sided arguments are likely to appeal only to those who are already convinced that the writer's interpretation is correct. A persuasive essay that takes a fair look at all sides, and then draws a sensible conclusion based on a broad critical view, is likely to appeal to more readers, including both those who are predisposed to accept the writer's conclusion and those who are more neutral. It may even be more likely than the *harangue*, or one-sided argument, to cause those with opposing viewpoints to reconsider them. When we write persuasive essays, our real goal may be not so much to change the minds of those disinclined toward our interpretation or view, as to move neutral readers closer toward our position or even to motivate those who already share our views to act on them.

MODES OF DEVELOPMENT

Modes of development, including description of process (highlighted in this chapter's readings), are specific rhetorical strategies writers use to achieve their purposes in writing. Most writers in most forms use a combination of these strategies to develop, demonstrate, and articulate their ideas in writing and to promote the overall purpose of any given piece of writing. In the introduction to Chapter 2, we examined description as a strategy of development. In the introduction to Chapter 4, narration will be discussed in detail; in the Chapter 6 introduction, we will look at cause and effect analysis more closely; and in Chapter 8, we will consider strategies of argumentation in more depth. Meanwhile, five other important modes of development will be discussed here: description of process, definition, classification, illustration and example, and comparison and contrast.

Description of Process

Much of our writing—particularly, by its very nature, process writing—evolves through one kind of assignment or another. Often the subject is clearly defined, the reader is identified by the nature and function of the writing, and we are left to work within these boundaries. When process writing subjects are assigned to us, we are being asked to demonstrate our understanding of the process and, generally, its function or significance, through a clear articulation of it to a reader with a functional need to know.

We encounter process writing frequently in our daily lives. Pick up a cookbook, the instruction manual for assembling your new bicycle, or the methods section of a biology lab report, and you will have encountered process writing. The process writer's job is to recreate the process in language, to explain it accurately enough for the reader to achieve a clear understanding of it, or to articulate a clear set of instructions with which the reader can reproduce a specific result—a decent meal, a bicycle that works, or a lab experiment, for example.

Process writing often comes in the form of explicit instructions, written in the imperative (*Do this,* or *Do that*) and in the present tense when the reader is expected to duplicate both process and results. But even in more subtle forms of process writing, where the writer's purpose is more complex than simply to create a recipe or a set of directions, readers often discover an instructive quality to the writing; the reader may be invited to participate intellectually or emotionally, as the process unfolds moment by moment, by the writer's use of the present tense and/or direct address of the reader as "you."

In process writing, we are describing repeatable events, which can and do occur over and over and can be repeatedly observed or recreated. Like journal writing and narration, process writing is temporal by nature, and like other types of descriptive and expository prose, its effectiveness depends upon close observation and careful recording of detail. From the writer's point of view, and as far as organization is concerned, the relatively easy part of describing processes is that the writing tends to organize itself, logically, according to steps in a chronological sequence. If you have studied your subject carefully enough and have a firm understanding of it, you should be able to explain the process clearly to your reader. The challenge for the writer is to make sure that (a) no crucial steps are missing, (b) the explanation of each step and the relationship between one step and the next is accurate, thorough, and well-balanced, and (c) the context for explanation of the process is clearly established. The writer's purpose in some kinds of process writing is to report the facts as objectively as possible; in other cases, the writer's purpose will be to analyze or interpret the process he or she describes.

Although description of process can function as the primary mode of development, the foundation upon which an essay is built, it is frequently used in combination with other rhetorical approaches. For example, in Annie Dillard's "Sojourner," in which the author's description of the formation of mangrove islands is used as an analogy to human culture, description of process works in partnership with reflection and analysis. And in student Lizabeth Clabaugh's essay "On Belay? Belay On," the process described—in this case, rappelling—is embedded within a narrative. How a writer integrates description of process, or any other mode of development in writing, depends upon his or her purpose, and the function the writing serves.

Definition

Definition is seldom used as the sole mode of development in a piece of writing. More commonly, a writer will realize the necessity of establishing with the reader a common understanding of the definition of key words and concepts in order to further explanation or analysis in an essay. Because definition provides a foundation for understanding, writers frequently use it early in an essay, or when they introduce new concepts or ideas in the course of writing.

The first step in using definition as a mode of development is for the writer to recognize which terms require definition. A writer may need to clarify a term with which he or she is unfamiliar. The writer who tries to base his or her report, explanation, or argument on a lack of understanding, or misunderstanding, of a key term or concept is not going to succeed in writing effectively. If the writer understands a technical term that the average reader is not likely to understand, the writer will have to define the term to establish a foundation of understanding. Sometimes the writer and the reader may have two different interpretations of the meaning or application of a term, and the writer will have to articulate through definition exactly what he or she means by the term rather than assuming a common understanding.

Using a dictionary definition in writing will not always be enough. Dictionaries frequently list several definitions of one word, assigning them equal weight, and they do not generally offer examples to illustrate how definitions apply. In addition to its literal meanings, a word may have connotations that will need to be explored more subtly than a dictionary definition allows. A good definition in writing will clarify the writer's exact use of the term, distinguishing that use from other possible uses and interpretations and relating it to the broader subject. The writer of definition should also illustrate the concept in order to clarify it. Such a writer may find it especially effective to provide examples and illustrations that will not only relate the term clearly to the subject being explored, but will also relate the subject and definition of the term to the reader's experience.

Classification

In classifying, writers break down a subject or an idea into its component parts, examining each part carefully in turn, and then relating the way each part functions back to the workings of the whole, with a more complete understanding. Successful classification in writing depends upon the writer's ability to recognize which elements of the subject are most important and how they interrelate. Sometimes these elements are mechanical, as in process writing, when the writer presents component parts in a chronological sequence. But often these elements are more abstract, and in categorizing them in writing, the writer will have to determine not only the relative importance of the various elements, but also in which order it is most logical and effective to present the discussion of them. To accomplish this, the writer will have to understand what relationship these elements have to one another.

A careful examination of how separate elements function will amount to next to nothing unless the writer is able to explain clearly, in a conclusion, how these elements and their interrelationships affect the whole. The purpose of classification in writing is to lead the reader through the understanding the writer has reached in exploring his or her subject. The purpose of classifying, from the writer's point of view, is to facilitate his or her own understanding of the subject. The writer of classification should therefore avoid drawing premature conclusions; the process of analysis itself should reveal conclusions to the writer.

Illustration and Example

Illustrations and examples are fundamental to clear and effective writing of all sorts. Illustration is a way of offering convincing evidence, and it provides an opportunity for the writer to apply general concepts in concrete ways, often relating them effectively to the reader's personal experience. Offering illustrations and examples is a way of showing rather than simply telling, and it makes writing more concrete, more meaningful, and more convincing. Without illustration and example, writers run the risk of stringing together series of abstractions and generalizations that discourage depth of understanding on the writer's part and that will have little or no—or even a negative—effect on the reader.

As a strategy of development, illustration and example works effectively in combination with nearly all other modes of development. In description, narration, process writing, definition, classification, cause and effect analysis, comparison and contrast, and argumentation, writers need to provide illustrations and examples to demonstrate how general statements apply in specific ways. Such illustrations and examples come in many different forms. In description, they could include the details of a scene that the writer has interpreted in a general way. If a writer were to describe a room as chaotic, the reader would have no way of visualizing this, and the statement would have little meaning unless the writer went on to describe the details of the scene. In interpretive writing—say, if the writer is analyzing a poem, for example—the reader would not be much convinced if the writer were to claim that the poet was being self-indulgent without offering *examples* from the text to *illustrate* this self-indulgence. And in argumentation, if the writer claims that an opposing view is not logical, the writer must offer proof to support this statement in the form of specific examples and a reasoned analysis of them.

As a rule of thumb, whenever a writer makes a general statement or characterizes something with an abstraction, he or she should offer illustrations or examples to clarify or demonstrate the point. It is generally a good idea to offer more than one illustration or example in each case, since the reader will be likely to see, through multiple illustrations, that the generality or abstraction applies not only in a single case but more widely. The writer should make sure that the illustration or example offered is directly, not approximately, applicable to the general statement and that it will be familiar to the reader.

Comparison and Contrast

One of the most natural ways of clarifying an idea is to compare how it applies in two related instances. Comparison and contrast employs techniques of illustration and example and is frequently used as the primary strategy of development in essays. It may also be used on a smaller scale, within particular parts of an essay, to furnish background information or to illustrate the nuances or applications of a point.

When we use comparison and contrast as a mode of development in writing, we examine similarities and differences between two (or occasionally more, though multiple comparisons can be extremely complicated) similar things—the study habits of two students or the geology of two mountain ranges, for example. We are seeking not only to understand the intricacies of the two subjects of comparison, but to understand something about the ideas that relate them. In examining the study habits of two students, we may want to draw conclusions about which study habits produce the best results in terms of grades or in controlling anxiety. In examining the geology of two mountain ranges, we may be seeking to understand what factors contribute to the formation of mountains under different geological conditions or within different time periods.

Comparison and contrast is sometimes confused with analogy (see Chapter 2), but they differ in fundamental ways. Analogy points out a similarity between things that are fundamentally different, usually comparing something familiar with something less familiar. In using analogy it is not the author's intent to establish a literal relationship between the two, but to promote a novel way of looking at the dominant partner in the analogy. Comparison, on the other hand, establishes the likenesses and differences between things that are fundamentally similar and seeks to clarify both subjects equally and demonstrate a real relationship between them.

In developing comparison and contrast, the writer must select significant points of comparison. These are the most important respects in which the two subjects, despite their illuminating differences, are similar. In this respect, comparison and contrast is structured like classification: the writer breaks the subject down into component parts. In order to write effective comparison and contrast, the writer must observe accurately and analyze carefully, and he or she must have a thorough knowledge of both—not just one—of the things being compared.

Comparison and contrast offers the writer special challenges since the material must be organized in two ways at once—by subject (the things being compared) and by points of comparison (the ways in which they are being compared). There are several options, each addressing the need, in comparison and contrast, for the writer to provide an equal treatment of each subject:

1. The writer can present all the points about the first subject of comparison, and then, in the same sequence, all the points about the second subject of comparison. Depending upon how long and fully developed the comparison is, this could be accomplished in two paragraphs, each focusing on one subject, or in a series of many paragraphs developed point-by-point and proceeding from the first subject to the second.

2. The writer can discuss each point of comparison as it applies to each subject, applying each point to one subject and then to the next subject before moving on to the next point. Depending upon how long and fully developed the analysis of each point is, the writer could discuss in one paragraph how each point relates to both subjects, or, in two separate paragraphs, how the point relates to one subject and then the next before proceeding to discussion of the next point of comparison.

3. In simple comparisons, the writer can alternate sentences, commenting on how a particular point of comparison applies to the first subject, then the second—thus moving point-to-point and subject-to-subject within one paragraph.

DEVELOPING THE PARAGRAPH

It is useful for writers to have an understanding of how the paragraph works in developing ideas and purpose in writing, regardless of which strategy of development is being used.

Opening and Closing Paragraphs: Framing the Essay

Opening and closing paragraphs frame an essay, providing context, clarifying the central idea, and articulating conclusions. Opening and closing paragraphs should work in partnership; they should relate, without repeating one another. Introductions and conclusions do not always take place conveniently in one paragraph each. Sometimes a writer will need more than one paragraph to accomplish his or her goals in either introducing a subject or drawing conclusions about it.

In an opening paragraph or paragraphs, the writer has several tasks. First he or she needs to capture the reader's interest. The writer also needs to establish the purpose and tone of the writing, as well as his or her point of view. Is the writer an observer? Is this a narrative in which the author is a participant? Is the writer reflective or absolute in defense of a position? Is the tone serious or satirical? Often, the writer will state his or her thesis in the opening paragraph or paragraphs; often he or she will not. Whether or not the thesis is explicitly stated in the opening paragraph or paragraphs, the reader should have a definite indication of what the writing will be about, the context in which the subject will be examined and, if not what the writer's conclusion is in advance, then at least an understanding of the questions or dilemmas the writing will explore.

In drafting essays most student writers begin at the beginning and end at the end, composing their opening paragraphs first, then moving through the body of the essay to the conclusion. Many make the mistake, however, of not going back and reexamining the opening paragraph or paragraphs carefully for consistency. In the course of thoroughly exploring a subject in the body of the essay, and in drawing conclusions based on this process of learning and articulation, the writer will frequently have made great progress in both thought and writing style. Often early paragraphs will require more revision than later paragraphs, since the writer's ideas may not have been fully formed at that early point. In terms of writing style, the writer may have just been getting warmed up, and the early writing may feel stilted or awkward in comparison to later paragraphs.

In the closing paragraph or paragraphs, the writer will have an opportunity to communicate with the reader for the last time. A writer should ask himself or herself what he or she wants the reader's last thought to be, what kernel of the subject is most crucial, most powerful. A closing paragraph may be the most effective place to state the thesis, since conclusions arise naturally out of close examination of the subject. The conclusion of an essay should resonate; it should suggest the larger implications of the subject, and the reader should be able to relate to it in a meaningful way.

A closing paragraph should not reiterate statements made in an opening paragraph. It should fit with the opening paragraph the way a question and answer fit, or it should suggest the broader relevance of the interpretation or argument the writer has presented. A closing paragraph is not the place to introduce altogether new ideas since there is no time for the writer to develop new points adequately. In a closing paragraph, writers are often tempted to claim broader conclusions than the evidence warrants. Be honest in writing conclusions; if your essay has explored its subject in depth, your conclusions, whatever their scope, will be valuable.

Interior Paragraphs

Regardless of the mode of development a writer employs in any given paragraph, the paragraph is a unit in which a single central idea or dominant impression is thoroughly developed. The central idea of a paragraph may be stated in a topic sentence (which will appear at the beginning of a deductive paragraph and at the end of an inductive paragraph), or it may be implied through the creation of a dominant impression. The sentences of each paragraph should contribute clearly to the development of its central idea, and the central idea of each paragraph should relate clearly to the central idea of the whole essay. Thus, a paragraph can be seen as a kind of mini-essay.

Short paragraphs can be symptomatic of ideas which are not thoroughly enough developed. Long paragraphs, on the other hand, may indicate that a writer is trying to cover too much in one paragraph and that the ideas might be broken down into parts, then developed separately and perhaps more thoroughly. Sometimes there are stylistic reasons to use extremely short—perhaps even one-sentence—paragraphs. These are effective when the writer wants to establish extra emphasis, or when, in dialogue, conventions and clarity require that there be paragraph breaks to distinguish between one speaker and the next. Decisions about where to create paragraph breaks—that is, breaking down the examination of a large central idea into smaller component parts—are to some extent a matter of style and interpretation. But a writer should be aware that his or her reader is likely to have trouble digesting a huge block of prose in long paragraph form, even if the writer can demonstrate that there is a single, if broad, unifying idea.

"Unity" and "coherence" are words that student writers are likely to recognize from teachers' comments in the margins of papers. But you may or may not know what these terms mean. Paragraph unity refers to the extent to which all the elements of the paragraph relate clearly to the development of its central idea. A disunified paragraph may attempt to develop more than one central idea at once, or it may offer a list of details that seem random and unrelated to a central idea. Coherence in paragraph development refers to the order in which the writer presents details or evidence. If a paragraph is coherent, then the sequence of sentences will be logical. If a paragraph is incoherent, the sentences will seem to jump around, moving at random or illogically rather than fluidly and straight ahead; or there may be important gaps in information that the writer has failed to recognize.

Transitions between Paragraphs

If a writer is certain of what his or her writing is about, how the ideas developed in each paragraph relate to one another and why they are presented in the sequence in which they are, transitions between paragraphs should come naturally. Articulating the relationship between ideas, these transitions will move the writer steadily toward drawing valid and honest conclusions. Of course, it will be difficult for a writer to create a fluid transition between paragraphs if he or she has to strain to see the relationship between ideas, or if little or no relationship exists.

In many forms of writing, an outline will provide you with the opportunity to test the relationships between ideas before you begin drafting. When organizing a piece of writing, you are not simply listing points, you are determining how these points relate and the best sequence in which to present them. This will prompt an understanding of their relationships and provide you with a basis upon which to draw conclusions.

One good way to check overall unity and coherence in an essay is to read the opening and closing paragraphs together to make sure that the conclusion, rather than repeating the opening paragraph, really does draw a conclusion. Similarly, after drafting an essay, you can check paragraph unity and the coherence of transitions between paragraphs by writing on a separate piece of paper the opening and closing sentences of each paragraph. Do the first and last sentences indicate unity in each paragraph's central idea? Do the closing sentence of one paragraph and the opening sentence of the next establish the relationship between these two central ideas?

A well-conceived and well-executed essay is a work of verbal architecture: Its form facilitates its function, and its symmetry satisfies us intellectually and aesthetically.

READINGS: PROCESSES NATURAL AND UNNATURAL

We are surrounded by processes of all kinds, and our understanding of the workings of the world—nature and human endeavor, cycles of life and death—depends upon our ability to examine and analyze these processes. In our attempts to understand how these processes overlap and interrelate, we begin to understand the ecology of natural and human events, how they relate in a functioning (and sometimes malfunctioning) system.

The readings in this chapter illustrate many approaches to recording and explaining natural and human processes in writing, and a variety of purposes in doing so. Often the authors of these selections are active participants in the processes they describe, as is Noel Perrin in "Falling for Apples," Gretel Ehrlich in "Rules of the Game: Rodeo," or Maxine Kumin in "Building Fence." In Rachel Carson's "The Changing Year," the writer's role is more explicitly that of an outside observer. In Annie Dillard's "Sojourner," the author not only observes from outside the processes she describes, but her role is that of detached analyst or commentator.

The process writer's role in observing, recording, and communicating, and in reflecting upon process within a certain context of understanding, requires an act of attention which to some extent sets the writer apart from the process, even when he or she is an active participant. The point of view inherent in process writing highlights some interesting thematic questions in writing about nature. Many of the selections in this chapter ask, in one form or another, to what extent we, as human beings, are part of or separate from nature. The answers to this question are neither absolute nor completely consistent with one another, but the role of the process writer as a critical observer—both involved in, and standing outside, the process—perhaps implies an answer.

■ RACHEL CARSON
The Changing Year

Scientist and writer Rachel Louise Carson was born in 1907 in Springfield, Pennsylvania, and died of cancer in 1964. As an undergraduate she attended Pennsylvania College for Women, and she did her graduate work at Johns Hopkins University and the Marine Biological Laboratory at Woods Hole, Massachusetts. Early in her career, she taught zoology at the University of Maryland. She joined the staff of the U.S. Bureau of Fisheries (now the Fish and Wildlife Service) in Washington, D.C., as an aquatic biologist in 1936, and from 1949 to 1952 she served as editor in chief for the Bureau's publications. From 1952 until the time of her death, she dedicated herself full-time to her own research and writing. Carson was a careful scientist and a committed and influential conservationist with a gift for explaining complex biological processes in clear and moving prose.

Her best known books include Under the Sea-Wind: A Naturalist's Picture of Ocean Life *(1941);* The Sea Around Us *(1951), which won the National Book Award and from which the following selection, "The Changing Year," is taken;* The Edge of the Sea *(1955); and her most influential work,* Silent Spring *(1962). The year before her death, she was recognized as Conservationist of the Year by the National Wildlife Federation.*

Her immensely popular The Sea Around Us *had sold 338,000 copies and entered its ninth printing by October of its year of publication and was made into an Academy Award-winning documentary the following year. A* Time *magazine critic praised Carson for "catching the breadth of science on the still glass of poetry."* Silent Spring, *Carson's famous exposé of the extraordinary dangers that unbridled use of pesticides and poisonous fertilizers posed to animals, birds, and humans, was, if more sobering and less beautiful than her earlier books, even more popular. The book created a public outcry and prompted President John F. Kennedy to initiate a federal investigation into the problem. The 1963 report of the President's Science Advisory Committee agreed with Carson's indictment of agricultural practices that relied excessively on pesticide use; the Committee recommended stricter regulations and further research.*

Thus with the year seasons return.

Milton

For the sea as a whole, the alternation of day and night, the passage of the seasons, the procession of the years, are lost in its vastness, obliterated in its own changeless eternity. But the surface waters are different. The face of the sea is always changing. Crossed by colors, lights, and moving shadows, sparkling in the sun, mysterious in the twilight, its aspects and its moods vary hour by hour. The surface waters move with the tides, stir to the breath of the winds, and rise and fall to the endless, hurrying forms of the waves. Most of all, they change with the advance of the seasons. Spring moves over the temperate lands of our Northern Hemisphere in a tide of new life, of pushing green shoots and unfolding buds, all its mysteries and meanings symbolized in the northward migration of the birds, the awakening of sluggish amphibian life as the chorus of frogs rises again from the wet lands, the different sound of the wind which stirs the young leaves where a month ago it rattled the bare branches. These things we associate with the land, and it is easy to suppose that at sea there could be no such feeling of advancing spring. But the signs are there, and seen with understanding eye, they bring the same magical sense of awakening.

In the sea, as on land, spring is a time for the renewal of life. During the long months of winter in the temperate zones the surface waters have been absorbing the cold. Now the heavy water begins to sink, slipping down and displacing the warmer layers below. Rich stores of minerals have been accumulating on the floor of the continental shelf—some freighted down the rivers from the lands; some derived from sea creatures that have died and whose remains have drifted down to the bottom; some from the shells that once encased a diatom, the streaming protoplasm of a radiolarian, or the transparent tissues of a pteropod. Nothing is wasted in the sea; every particle of material is used over and over again, first by one creature, then by another. And when in spring the waters are deeply stirred, the warm bottom water brings to the surface a rich supply of minerals, ready for use by new forms of life.

Just as land plants depend on minerals in the soil for their growth, every marine plant, even the smallest, is dependent upon the nutrient salts or minerals in the sea water. Diatoms must have silica, the element of which their fragile shells are fashioned. For these and all other microplants, phosphorus is an indispensable mineral. Some of these elements are in short supply and in winter may be reduced below the minimum necessary for growth. The diatom population must tide itself over this season as best it can. It faces a stark problem of survival, with no opportunity to increase, a problem of keeping alive the spark of life by forming tough protective spores against the stringency of winter, a matter of existing in a dormant state in which no demands shall be made on an environment that already withholds all but the most meager necessities of life. So the diatoms hold their place in the winter sea, like seeds of wheat in a field under snow and ice, the seeds from which the spring growth will come.

These, then, are the elements of the vernal blooming of the sea: the "seeds" of the dormant plants, the fertilizing chemicals, the warmth of the spring sun.

In a sudden awakening, incredible in its swiftness, the simplest plants of the sea begin to multiply. Their increase is of astronomical proportions. The spring sea belongs at first to the diatoms and to all the other microscopic plant life of the plankton. In the fierce intensity of their growth they cover vast areas of ocean with a living blanket of their cells. Mile after mile of water may appear red or brown or green, the whole surface taking on the color of the infinitesimal grains of pigment contained in each of the plant cells.

The plants have undisputed sway in the sea for only a short time. Almost at once their own burst of multiplication is matched by a similar increase in the small animals of the plankton. It is the spawning time of the copepod and the glassworm, the pelagic shrimp and the winged snail. Hungry swarms of these little beasts of the plankton roam through the waters, feeding on the abundant plants and themselves falling prey to larger creatures. Now in the spring the surface waters become a vast nursery. From the hills and valleys of the continent's edge lying far below, and from the scattered shoals and banks, the eggs or young of many of the bottom animals rise to the surface of the sea. Even those which, in their maturity, will sink down to a sedentary life on the bottom, spend the first weeks of life as freely swimming hunters of the plankton. So as spring progresses new batches of larvae rise into the surface each day, the young of fishes and crabs and mussels and tube worms, mingling for a time with the regular members of the plankton.

Under the steady and voracious grazing, the grasslands of the surface are soon depleted. The diatoms become more and more scarce, and with them the other simple plants. Still there are brief explosions of one or another form, when in a sudden orgy of cell division it comes to claim whole areas of the sea for its own. So, for a time each spring, the waters may become blotched with brown, jellylike masses, and the fishermen's nets come up dripping a brown slime and containing no fish, for the herring have turned away from these waters as though in loathing of the viscid, foul-smelling algae. But in less time than passes between the full moon and the new, the spring flowering of Phaeocystis is past and the waters have cleared again.

In the spring the sea is filled with migrating fishes, some of them bound for the mouths of great rivers, which they will ascend to deposit their spawn. Such are the spring-run chinooks coming in from the deep Pacific feeding grounds to breast the rolling flood of the Columbia, the shad moving in to the Chesapeake and the Hudson and the Connecticut, the alewives seeking a hundred coastal streams of New England, the salmon feeling their way to the Penobscot and the Kennebec. For months or years these fish have known only the vast spaces of the ocean. Now the spring sea and the maturing of their own bodies lead them back to the rivers of their birth.

Other mysterious comings and goings are linked with the advance of the year. Capelin gather in the deep, cold water of the Barents Sea, their shoals followed and preyed upon by flocks of auks, fulmars, and kittiwakes. Cod approach the banks of Lofoten, and gather off the shores of Iceland. Birds whose winter feeding territory may have encompassed the whole Atlantic or the whole Pacific converge upon some small island, the entire breeding population arriving within the space of a few days. Whales suddenly appear off the slopes of the coastal banks where the swarms of shrimplike krill are spawning, the whales having come from no one knows where, by no one knows what route.

With the subsiding of the diatoms and the completed spawning of many of the plankton animals and most of the fish, life in the surface waters slackens to the slower pace of midsummer. Along the meeting places of the currents the pale moon jelly Aurelia gathers in thousands, forming sinuous lines or windows across miles of sea, and the birds see their pale forms shimmering deep down in the green water.

By midsummer the large red jellyfish Cyanea may have grown from the size of a thimble to that of an umbrella. The great jellyfish moves through the sea with rhythmic pulsations, trailing long tentacles and as likely as not shepherding a little group of young cod or haddock, which find shelter under its bell and travel with it.

A hard, brilliant, coruscating phosphorescence often illuminates the summer sea. In waters where the protozoa Noctiluca is abundant it is the chief source of this summer luminescence, causing fishes, squids, or dolphins to fill the water with racing flames and to clothe themselves in a ghostly radiance. Or again the summer sea may glitter with a thousand thousand moving pinpricks of light, like an immense swarm of fireflies moving through a dark wood. Such an effect is produced by a shoal of the brilliantly phosphorescent shrimp Meganyctiphanes, a creature of cold and darkness and of the places where icy water rolls upward from the depths and bubbles with white ripplings at the surface.

Out over the plankton meadows of the North Atlantic the dry twitter of the phalaropes, small brown birds, wheeling and turning, dipping and rising, is heard for the first time since early spring. The phalaropes have nested on the arctic tundras, reared their young, and now the first of them are returning to the sea. Most of them will continue south over the open water far from land, crossing the equator into the South Atlantic. Here they will follow where the great whales lead, for where the whales are, there also are the swarms of plankton on which these strange little birds grow fat.

As the fall advances, there are other movements, some in the surface, some hidden in the green depths, that betoken the end of summer. In the fog-covered waters of Bering Sea, down through the treacherous passes between the islands of the Aleutian chain and southward into the open Pacific, the herds of fur seals are moving. Left behind are two small islands, treeless bits of volcanic soil thrust up into the waters of Bering Sea. The islands are silent now, but for the several months of summer they resounded with the roar of millions of seals come ashore to bear and rear their young—all the fur seals of the eastern Pacific crowded into a few square miles of bare rock and crumbling soil. Now once more the seals turn south, to roam down along the sheer underwater cliffs of the continent's edge, where the rocky foundations fall away steeply into the deep sea. Here, in a blackness more absolute than that of arctic winter, the seals will find rich feeding as they swim down to prey on the fishes of this region of darkness.

Autumn comes to the sea with a fresh blaze of phosphorescence, when every wave crest is aflame. Here and there the whole surface may glow with sheets of cold fire, while below schools of fish pour through the water like molten metal. Often the autumnal phosphorescence is caused by a fall flowering of the dinoflagellates, multiplying furiously in a short-lived repetition of their vernal blooming.

Sometimes the meaning of the glowing water is ominous. Off the Pacific coast of North America, it may mean that the sea is filled with the dinoflagellate Gonyaulax, a minute plant that contains a poison of strange and terrible virulence. About four days after Gonyaulax comes to dominate the coastal plankton, some of the fishes and shellfish in the vicinity become toxic. This is because, in their normal feeding, they have strained the poisonous plankton out of the water. Mussels accumulate the Gonyaulax toxins in their livers, and the toxins react on the human nervous system with an effect similar to that of strychnine. Because of these facts, it is generally understood along the Pacific coast that it is unwise to eat shellfish taken from coasts exposed to the open sea where Gonyaulax may be abundant, in summer or early fall. For generations before the white men came, the Indians knew this. As soon as the red streaks appeared in the sea and the waves began to flicker at night with the mysterious blue-green fires, the tribal leaders forbade the taking of mussels until these warning signals should have passed. They even set guards at intervals along the beaches to warn inlanders who might come down for shellfish and be unable to read the language of the sea.

But usually the blaze and glitter of the sea, whatever its meaning for those who produce it, implies no menace to man. Seen from the deck of a vessel in open ocean, a tiny, man-made observation point in the vast world of sea and sky, it has an eerie and unearthly quality. Man, in his vanity, subconsciously attributes a human origin to any light not of moon or stars or sun. Lights on the shore, lights moving over the water, mean lights kindled and controlled by other men, serving purposes understandable to the human mind. Yet here are lights that flash and fade away, lights that come and go for reasons meaningless to man, lights that have been doing this very thing over the eons of time in which there were no men to stir in vague disquiet.

On such a night of phosphorescent display Charles Darwin stood on the deck of the *Beagle* as she plowed southward through the Atlantic off the coast of Brazil.

> the sea from its extreme luminousness presented a wonderful and most beautiful appearance [he wrote in his diary]. Every part of the water which by day is seen as foam, glowed with a pale light. The

vessel drove before her bows two billows of liquid phosphorus, and in her wake was a milky train. As far as the eye reached the crest of every wave was bright; and from the reflected light, the sky just above the horizon was not so utterly dark as the rest of the Heavens. It was impossible to behold this plain of matter, as it were melted and consuming by heat, without being reminded of Milton's description of the regions of Chaos and Anarchy.*

Like the blazing colors of the autumn leaves before they wither and fall, the autumnal phosphorescence betokens the approach of winter. After their brief renewal of life the flagellates and the other minute algae dwindle away to a scattered few; so do the shrimps and the copepods, the glassworms and the comb jellies. The larvae of the bottom fauna have long since completed their development and drifted away to take up whatever existence is their lot. Even the roving fish schools have deserted the surface waters and have migrated into warmer latitudes or have found equivalent warmth in the deep, quiet waters along the edge of the continental shelf. There the torpor of semi-hibernation descends upon them and will possess them during the months of winter.

The surface waters now become the plaything of the winter gales. As the winds build up the giant storm waves and roar along their crests, lashing the water into foam and flying spray, it seems that life must forever have deserted this place.

For the mood of the winter sea, read Joseph Conrad's description:

The greyness of the whole immense surface, the wind furrows upon the faces of the waves, the great masses of foam, tossed about and waving, like matted white locks, give to the sea in a gale an appearance of hoary age, lustreless, dull, without gleams, as though it had been created before light itself.**

But the symbols of hope are not lacking even in the grayness and bleakness of the winter sea. On land we know that the apparent lifelessness of winter is an illusion. Look closely at the bare branches of a tree, on which not the palest gleam of green can be discerned. Yet, spaced along each branch are the leaf buds, all the spring's magic of swelling green concealed and safely preserved under the insulating,

---

*From *Charles Darwin's Diary of the Voyage of H.M.S. Beagle,* edited by Nora Barlow, 1934 edition, Cambridge University Press, p. 107.
**From *The Mirror of the Sea,* Kent edition, 1925, Doubleday-Page, p. 71.

overlapping layers. Pick off a piece of the rough bark of the trunk; there you will find hibernating insects. Dig down through the snow into the earth. There are the eggs of next summer's grasshoppers; there are the dormant seeds from which will come the grass, the herb, the oak tree.

So, too, the lifelessness, the hopelessness, the despair of the winter sea are an illusion. Everywhere are the assurances that the cycle has come to the full, containing the means of its own renewal. There is the promise of a new spring in the very iciness of the winter sea, in the chilling of the water, which must, before many weeks, become so heavy that it will plunge downward, precipitating the overturn that is the first act in the drama of spring. There is the promise of new life in the small plantlike things that cling to the rocks of the underlying bottom, the almost formless polyps from which, in spring, a new generation of jellyfish will bud off and rise into the surface waters. There is unconscious purpose in the sluggish forms of the copepods hibernating on the bottom, safe from the surface storms, life sustained in their tiny bodies by the extra store of fat with which they went into this winter sleep.

Already, from the gray shapes of cod that have moved, unseen by man, through the cold sea to their spawning places, the glassy globules of eggs are rising into the surface waters. Even in the harsh world of the winter sea, these eggs will begin the swift divisions by which a granule of protoplasm becomes a living fishlet.

Most of all, perhaps, there is assurance in the fine dust of life that remains in the surface waters, the invisible spores of the diatoms, needing only the touch of warming sun and fertilizing chemicals to repeat the magic of spring.

■ CONSIDERATIONS OF MEANING AND METHOD

1. How does Carson indicate her purpose in the opening paragraphs? Who is her audience?

2. Make a list of the opening sentences of all the paragraphs of the essay. What does this list tell you about how Carson has structured "The Changing Year"?

3. What specific techniques does Carson use to make the seasonal cycles of the sea more familiar to a reader who may be unfamiliar with life in the sea?

4. In addition to description of process, what other modes of development does Carson use in writing this essay?

■ **POSSIBILITIES FOR WRITING**

1. In a process essay, describe the natural patterns and rhythms of your favorite season. Pay attention not only to a full and accurate description of the process, but also to your opening and closing paragraphs. How will you capture your reader's attention and imagination in the opening paragraph? How will you relate your experience to your reader's? What is the central idea or the dominant impression you wish to convey to your reader?

2. In an essay that employs both the strategies of description of process and comparison and contrast, compare two processes— for example, the begging strategies of dogs and cats, or how to grow and tend tulips and roses.

3. In a process essay, describe the effect that one environmental pollutant has on the ecosystem. You may have to consult outside sources if you lack a complete picture of this process. Consider your primary purpose in writing: is it to report, to explain, or to persuade?

■ NOEL PERRIN
Falling for Apples

An avid proponent of rural living and a dedicated New Englander, Noel Perrin teaches English and environmental studies at Dartmouth College in Hanover, New Hampshire. He was born in 1927 in New York City, attended Williams College for his B.A., Duke University for his M.A., and Trinity Hall College at Cambridge University in England for his M. Litt. Perrin is the author of both scholarly and historical works, but his best-known writings are his popular essays about life in rural New England and his experiences as a "sometime farmer" (many of which were first published in magazines such as Vermont Life *and* Country Journal).

The following essay, "Falling for Apples," is from Perrin's Second Person Rural: More Essays of a Sometime Farmer *(1980); there are two other books in this series,* First Person Rural: Essays of a Sometime Farmer *(1978) and* Third Person Rural: Further Essays of a Sometime Farmer *(1983). Many of the essays in these books are instructional, offering the reader practical advice on subjects that range from keeping pipes from bursting during cold snaps to cidering. However, critic Stephen Goodwin has noted that the essays of* Second Person Rural *"are more reflective, less concerned with* How-to *than with the meatier question,* Why?*"*

The number of children who eagerly help around a farm is rather small. Willing helpers do exist, but many more of them are five years old than fifteen. In fact, there seems to be a general law that says as long as a kid is too little to help effectively, he or she is dying to. Then, just as they reach the age when they really could drive a fence post or empty a sap bucket without spilling half of it, they lose interest. Now it's cars they want to drive, or else they want to stay in the house and listen for four straight hours to The Who. That sort of thing.

There is one exception to this rule. Almost no kid that I have ever met outgrows an interest in cidering. In consequence, cider making remains a family time on our farm, even though it's been years since any daughter trudged along a fencerow with me, dragging a new post too heavy for her to carry, or begged for lessons in chain-sawing.

It's not too hard to figure out why. In the first place, cidering gives the child instant gratification. There's no immediate reward for weeding a garden (unless the parents break down and offer cash), still less for loading a couple of hundred hay bales in the barn. But the minute you've ground and pressed the first bushel of apples, you can break out the glasses and start drinking. Good stuff, too. Cider has a wonderful fresh sweetness as it runs from the press.

In the second place, making cider on a small scale is simple enough so that even fairly young children—say, a pair of nine-year-olds—can do the whole operation by themselves. Yet it's also picturesque enough to tempt people of any age. When my old college roommate was up last fall—and we've been out of college a long time—he and his wife did four pressings in the course of the weekend. They only quit then because I ran out of apples.

Finally, cider making appeals to a deep human instinct. It's the same one that makes a housewife feel so good when she takes a bunch of leftovers and produces a memorable casserole. At no cost, and using what would otherwise be wasted, she has created something. In fact, she has just about reversed entropy.

Cidering is like that. You take apples that have been lying on the ground for a week, apples with blotches and cankers and bad spots, apples that would make a supermarket manager turn pale if you merely brought them in the store, and out of this unpromising material you produce not one but two delicious drinks. Sweet cider now. Hard cider later.

The first step is to have a press. At the turn of the century, almost every farm family did. They ordered them from the Sears or Montgomery Ward catalogue as routinely as one might now order a toaster. Then about 1930 little presses ceased to be made. Pasteurized apple juice had joined the list of American food-processing triumphs. It had no particular flavor (still hasn't), but it would keep almost indefinitely. Even more appealing, it was totally sterile. That was the era when the proudest boast that, let's say, a bakery could make was that its bread was untouched by human hands. Was touched only by stainless-steel beaters and stainless-steel wrapping machines.

Eras end, though, and the human hand came back into favor. One result: in the 1970s home cider presses returned to the market. They have not yet returned to the Sears catalogue, but they are readily available. I know of two companies in Vermont that make them, another in East Aurora, New York, and one out in Washington state. If there isn't someone making them in Michigan or Wisconsin, there soon will be. Prices range from about 175 to 250 dollars.

Then you get a couple of bushels of apples. There *may* be people in the country who buy cider apples, but I don't know any of them. Old apple trees are too common. I get mine by the simple process of picking up windfalls in a derelict orchard that came with our place. I am not choosy. Anything that doesn't actually squish goes in the basket.

With two kids to help, collecting takes maybe twenty minutes. Kids tend to be less interested in gathering the apples than in running the press, but a quiet threat of no-pickee, no-pressee works wonders. Kids also worry about worms sometimes, as they scoop apples from the ground—apples that may be wet with dew, spiked with stubble, surrounded by hungry wasps. Occasionally I have countered with a short lecture on how much safer our unsprayed apples are than the shiny, wormless, but heavily sprayed apples one finds in stores. But usually I just say that I have yet to see a worm in our cider press. That's true, too. Whether it's because there has never been one, or whether it's because in the excitement and bustle of grinding you just wouldn't notice one little worm, I don't dare to say.

As soon as you get back with the apples, it's time to make cider.

Presses come in two sizes: one-bushel and a-third-of-a-bushel. We have tried both. If I lived in a suburb and had to buy apples, I would use the very efficient third-of-a-bushel press and make just under a gallon at a time. Living where I do, I use the bigger press and make two gallons per pressing, occasionally a little more.

The process has two parts. First you set your pressing tub under the grinder, line it with a pressing cloth, and start grinding. Or, better, your children do. One feeds apples into the hopper, the other turns the crank. If there are three children present, the third can hold the wooden hopper plate, and thus keep the apples from bouncing around. If there are four, the fourth can spell off on cranking. Five or more is too many, and any surplus over four is best made into a separate crew for the second pressing. I once had two three-child crews present, plus a seventh child whom my wife appointed the official timer. We did two pressings and had 4¼ gallons of cider in 43 minutes and 12 seconds. (Who won? The second crew, by more than a minute. Each crew had one of our practiced daughters on it, but the second also had the advantage of watching the first.)

As soon as the apples are ground, you put the big pressing plate on and start to turn the press down. If it's a child crew, and adult meddling is nevertheless tolerated, it's desirable to have the kids turn the press in order of their age, starting with the youngest: at the end it takes a fair amount of strength (though it's not beyond two nine-year-olds working together), and a little kid coming after a big one may fail to produce a single drop.

The pressing is where all the thrills come. As the plate begins to move down and compact the ground apples, you hear a kind of sighing, bubbling noise. Then a trickle of cider begins to run out. Within five or ten seconds the trickle turns into a stream, and the stream into a ciderfall. Even kids who've done it a dozen times look down in awe at what their labor has wrought.

A couple of minutes later the press is down as far as it will go, and the container you remembered to put below the spout is full of rich, brown cider. Someone has broken out the glasses, and everybody is having a drink.

This pleasure goes on and on. In an average year we start making cider the second week of September, and we continue until early November. We make all we can drink ourselves, and quite a lot to give away. We have supplied whole church suppers. One year the girls sold about ten gallons to the village store, which made them some pocket money they were prouder of than any they ever earned by baby-sitting. Best of all, there are two months each year when all of us are running the farm together, just like a pioneer family.

■ CONSIDERATIONS OF MEANING AND METHOD

1. As an introduction to an essay about cidering (considering that cidering is not mentioned there), how effective is Perrin's opening paragraph? What purpose does the paragraph serve? How does Perrin relate this paragraph to the rest of the essay?

2. How do Perrin's word choice and sentence structure throughout the essay establish and sustain his tone? Give specific examples from the text. How does Perrin's tone relate to his audience?

3. For Perrin, what are the most gratifying aspects of cidering? What is his central idea? Is it stated or implied? What, beyond cidering, does the process of cidering produce?

4. Make a list of all the paragraphs' opening sentences. What does this list tell you about how Perrin has organized the essay? What do these sentences tell you about his writing style?

5. In the seventh and eighth paragraphs, Perrin gives us a history of the availability of the cider press in twentieth-century America. Is this a digression? What purpose does it serve?

■ POSSIBILITIES FOR WRITING

1. Write an essay in which you incorporate a recipe or a set of instructions into a narrative (keep it concrete, avoiding abstractions). With this recipe or set of instructions, your reader should be able to duplicate the process, although the narrative that surrounds it will be unique to your experience.

2. In an essay, describe an activity with which you are familiar but that is likely to be unfamiliar to your reader. Make clear not only the process, but also its significance or your feelings about it.

■ ANNIE DILLARD
Sojourner

Annie Dillard, born in 1945, grew up in Pittsburgh, Pennsylvania, and attended Hollins College, where she received her B.A. and M.A. degrees. In 1974, Dillard published her first two books, Tickets for a Prayer Wheel, *(poetry), and* Pilgrim at Tinker Creek, *which won the Pulitzer Prize for general nonfiction that year. Few young writers achieve such early and resounding success. The following essay, "Sojourner," is taken from* Teaching a Stone to Talk *(1982). Some of her more recent books include* An American Childhood *(1987),* The Writing Life *(1989), and* The Living *(1992). Dillard teaches poetry and creative writing at Wesleyan University.*

Dillard's character and voice as a writer come from the intensity of her awareness as well as from her rich associative imagery and her carefully sculpted poetic prose. A critic for Commentary *magazine observed, "Like a true transcendentalist... Dillard understands her task to be that of full alertness, of making herself the conscious receptacle of all impressions. She is a connoisseur of the spirit, who knows that seeing, if intense enough, becomes vision." Dillard, who has described herself as "a poet... with a background in theology and a penchant for quirky facts," has brought together in "Sojourner" both theology and quirky facts. She has built this essay on an analogy, a comparison of two processes, two systems—one small, a microcosm within the other, larger one: "the mangrove island [that] wanders on, afloat and adrift" and "the planet itself... a sojourner in airless space, a wet ball flung across nowhere." She asks the fundamental question,* What are we doing here?

If survival is an art, then mangroves are artists of the beautiful: not only that they exist at all—smooth-barked, glossy-leaved, thickets of lapped mystery—but that they can and do exist as floating islands, as trees upright and loose, alive and homeless on the water.

I have seen mangroves, always on tropical ocean shores, in Florida and in the Galápagos. There is the red mangrove, the yellow, the button, and the black. They are all short, messy trees, waxy-leaved, laced all over with aerial roots, woody arching buttresses, and weird leathery berry pods. All this tangles from a black muck soil, a black muck matted like a mud-sopped rag, a muck without any other plants, shaded, cold to the touch, tracked at the water's edge by herons and nosed by sharks.

It is these shoreline trees which, by a fairly common accident, can become floating islands. A hurricane flood or a riptide can wrest a tree from the shore, or from the mouth of a tidal river, and hurl it into the ocean. It floats. It is a mangrove island, blown.

There are floating islands on the planet; it amazes me. Credulous

Pliny described some islands thought to be mangrove islands floating on a river. The people called these river islands *the dancers,* "because in any consort of musicians singing, they stir and move at the stroke of the feet, keeping time and measure."

Trees floating on rivers are less amazing than trees floating on the poisonous sea. A tree cannot live in salt. Mangrove trees exude salt from their leaves; you can see it, even on shoreline black mangroves, as a thin white crust. Lick a leaf and your tongue curls and coils; your mouth's a heap of salt.

Nor can a tree live without soil. A hurricane-born mangrove island may bring its own soil to the sea. But other mangrove trees make their own soil—and their own islands—from scratch. These are the ones which interest me. The seeds germinate in the fruit on the tree. The germinated embryo can drop anywhere—say, onto a dab of floating muck. The heavy root end sinks; a leafy plumule unfurls. The tiny seedling, afloat, is on its way. Soon aerial roots shooting out in all directions trap debris. The sapling's networks twine, the interstices narrow, and water calms in the lee. Bacteria thrive on organic broth; amphipods swarm. These creatures grow and die at the trees' wet feet. The soil thickens, accumulating rainwater, leaf rot, seashells, and guano; the island spreads.

More seeds and more muck yield more trees on the new island. A society grows, interlocked in a tangle of dependencies. The island rocks less in the swells. Fish throng to the backwaters stilled in snarled roots. Soon, Asian mudskippers—little four-inch fish—clamber up the mangrove roots into the air and peer about from periscope eyes on stalks, like snails. Oysters clamp to submersed roots, as do starfish, dog whelk, and the creatures that live among tangled kelp. Shrimp seek shelter there, limpets a holdfast, pelagic birds a rest.

And the mangrove island wanders on, afloat and adrift. It walks teetering and wanton before the wind. Its fate and direction are random. It may bob across an ocean and catch on another mainland's shores. It may starve or dry while it is still a sapling. It may topple in a storm, or pitchpole. By the rarest of chances, it may stave into another mangrove island in a crash of clacking roots, and mesh. What it is most likely to do is drift anywhere in the alien ocean, feeding on death and growing, netting a makeshift soil as it goes, shrimp in its toes and terns in its hair.

We could do worse.

I alternate between thinking of the planet as home—dear and familiar stone hearth and garden—and as a hard land of exile in which we are all sojourners. Today I favor the latter view. The word "so-journer" occurs often in the English Old Testament. It invokes a no-madic people's sense of vagrancy, a praying people's knowledge of estrangement, a thinking people's intuition of sharp loss: "For we are strangers before thee, and sojourners, as were all our fathers: our days on the earth are as a shadow, and there is none abiding."

We don't know where we belong, but in times of sorrow it doesn't seem to be here, here with these silly pansies and witless mountains, here with sponges and hard-eyed birds. In times of sorrow the inno-cence of the other creatures—from whom and with whom we evolved—seems a mockery. Their ways are not our ways. We seem set among them as among lifelike props for a tragedy—or a broad lampoon—on a thrust rock stage.

It doesn't seem to be here that we belong, here where space is curved, the earth is round, we're all going to die, and it seems as wise to stay in bed as budge. It is strange here, not quite warm enough, or too warm, too leafy, or inedible, or windy, or dead. It is not, frankly, the sort of home for people one would have thought of—although I lack the fancy to imagine another.

The planet itself is a sojourner in airless space, a wet ball flung across nowhere. The few objects in the universe scatter. The coher-ence of matter dwindles and crumbles toward stillness. I have read, and repeated, that our solar system as a whole is careering through space toward a point east of Hercules. Now I wonder: what could that possibly mean, east of Hercules? Isn't space curved? When we get "there," how will our course change, and why? Will we slide down the universe's inside arc like mud slung at a wall? Or what sort of welcoming shore is this east of Hercules? Surely we don't anchor there, and disembark, and sweep into dinner with our host. Does someone cry, "Last stop, last stop"? At any rate, east of Hercules, like east of Eden, isn't a place to call home. It is a course without di-rection; it is "out." And we are cast.

These are enervating thoughts, the thoughts of despair. They crowd back, unbidden, when human life as it unrolls goes ill, when we lose control of our lives or the illusion of control, and it seems that we are not moving toward any end but merely blown. Our life seems cursed to be a wiggle merely, and a wandering without end. Even nature is hostile and poisonous, as though it were impossible for our vulnerability to survive on these acrid stones.

Whether these thoughts are true or not I find less interesting than the possibilities for beauty they may hold. We are down here in time, where beauty grows. Even if things are as bad as they could possibly be, and as meaningless, then matters of truth are themselves indifferent; we may as well please our sensibilities and, with as much spirit as we can muster, go out with a buck and wing.

The planet is less like an enclosed spaceship—spaceship earth—than it is like an exposed mangrove island beautiful and loose. We the people started small and have since accumulated a great and solacing muck of soil, of human culture. We are rooted in it; we are bearing it with us across nowhere. The word "nowhere" is our cue: the consort of musicians strikes up, and we in the chorus stir and move and start twirling our hats. A mangrove island turns drift to dance. It creates its own soil as it goes, rocking over the salt sea at random, rocking day and night and round the sun, rocking round the sun and out toward east of Hercules.

■ CONSIDERATIONS OF MEANING AND METHOD

1. To what extent is this an essay about mangrove islands? Is Dillard really interested in mangrove islands? Is she an expert on the subject?

2. At what point does Dillard begin to develop her analogy between mangrove islands and the planet Earth? Is her analogy implicit or explicit? Where is it stated? How does her use of descriptive language establish and clarify the analogy? Find specific examples of such language in the text.

3. What does Dillard see as the point of existence?

■ POSSIBILITIES FOR WRITING

1. Analogy can make abstract ideas more concrete and easier for the reader to understand and relate to. And yet successful analogies are difficult to develop. Try your hand at analogy in an essay that, as "Sojourner" does, relates a relatively familiar, concrete process to a relatively unfamiliar and abstract one.

■ GRETEL EHRLICH
Rules of the Game: Rodeo

Gretel Ehrlich was born in Santa Barbara, California, in 1946. She attended Bennington College, the University of California, the Los Angeles Film School, and the New School for Social Research. She lives and writes in Shell, Wyoming, where she is a ranch hand and sheepherder. She is a poet, fiction writer, and essayist. Her books include The Solace of Open Spaces *(1985),* Heart Mountain *(1988), and* Islands, the Universe, Home *(1991).*

Ehrlich had been a documentary filmmaker working in New York for the Public Broadcasting System, but in 1976, while she was in Wyoming filming a documentary about sheepherders, she decided to leave her job and New York. Ehrlich traveled for two years, ultimately returning to Wyoming to take up sheepherding herself in an isolated but beautiful landscape, among a quiet, close-knit though far-flung community of ranchers and sheepherders. "For the first time," Ehrlich says, "I was able to take up residence on earth with no alibis, no self-promoting schemes."

Countering the myth of the American cowboy as rough-riding and crude, Ehrlich has written in several essays about the ranch hands, sheepherders, and rodeo riders she has known in Wyoming, about the ways in which a rugged landscape and physically challenging, lonely occupations have shaped and cultivated a special code of manners, especially among men in these professions. In "Rules of the Game: Rodeo," she describes the skills of rodeo riders as well as their civility, and in the end proposes that she and her husband, honeymooning at the National Finals Rodeo in Oklahoma City, have a lot to learn from these "rules of the game" as they begin their marriage.

Instead of honeymooning in Paris, Patagonia, or the Sahara as we had planned, my new husband and I drove through a series of blizzards to Oklahoma City. Each December the National Finals Rodeo is held in a modern, multistoried colosseum next to buildings that house banks and petroleum companies in a state whose flatness resembles a swimming pool filled not with water but with oil.

The National Finals is the "World Series of Professional Rodeo," where not only the best cowboys but also the most athletic horses and bucking stock compete. All year, rodeo cowboys have been vying for the honor to ride here. They've been to Houston, Las Vegas, Pendleton, Tucson, Cheyenne, San Francisco, Calgary; to as many as eighty rodeos in one season, sometimes making two or three on a day like the Fourth of July, and when the results are tallied up (in money won, not points) the top fifteen riders in each event are invited to Oklahoma City.

We climbed to our peanut gallery seats just as Miss Rodeo America, a lanky brunette swaddled in a lavender pantsuit, gloves, and cowboy hat, loped across the arena. There was a hush in the audience; all the hats swimming down in front of us, like buoys, steadied and turned toward the chutes. The agile, oiled voice of the announcer boomed: "Out of chute number three, Pat Linger, a young cowboy from Miles City, Montana, making his first appearance here on a little horse named Dillinger." And as fast as these words sailed across the colosseum, the first bareback horse bumped into the lights.

There's a traditional order to the four timed and three rough stock events that make up a rodeo program. Bareback riders are first, then steer wrestlers, team ropers, saddle bronc riders, barrel racers, and finally, the bull riders.

After Pat Linger came Steve Dunham, J. C. Trujillo, Mickey Young, and the defending champ, Bruce Ford on a horse named Denver. Bareback riders do just that: they ride a horse with no saddle, no halter, no rein, clutching only a handhold riveted into a girth that goes around the horse's belly. A bareback rider's loose style suggests a drunken, comic bout of lovemaking: he lies back on the horse and, with each jump and jolt, flops delightfully, like a libidinous Raggedy Andy, toes turned out, knees flexed, legs spread and pumping, back arched, the back of his hat bumping the horse's rump as if nodding, "Yes, let's do 'er again." My husband, who rode saddle broncs in amateur rodeos, explains it differently: "It's like riding a runaway bicycle down a steep hill and lying on your back; you can't see where you're going or what's going to happen next."

Now the steer wrestlers shoot out of the box on their own well-trained horses: there is a hazer on the right to keep the steer running straight, the wrestler on the left, and the steer between them. When the wrestler is neck and neck with the animal, he slides sideways out of his saddle as if he'd been stabbed in the ribs and reaches for the horns. He's airborne for a second; then his heels swing into the dirt, and with his arms around the horns, he skids to a stop, twisting the steer's head to one side so the animal loses his balance and falls to the ground. It's a fast-paced game of catch with a thousand-pound ball of horned flesh.

The team ropers are next. Most of them hail from the hilly, oak-strewn valleys of California where dally roping originated.[1] Ropers are the graceful technicians, performing their pas de deux (plus steer) with a precision that begins to resemble a larger clarity—an erudi-

---

[1]The word dally is a corruption of the Spanish da la vuelta, meaning to take a turn, as with a rope around the saddle horn.

tion. Header and heeler come out of the box at the same time, steer between them, but the header acts first: he ropes the horns of the steer, dallies up, turns off, and tries to position the steer for the heeler who's been tagging behind this duo, loop clasped in his armpit as if it were a hen. Then the heeler sets his generous, unsweeping loop free and double-hocks the steer. It's a complicated act which takes about six seconds. Concomitant with this speed and skill is a feminine grace: they don't clutch their stiff loop or throw it at the steer like a bag of dirty laundry the way I do, but hold it gently, delicately, as if it were a hoop of silk. One or two cranks and both arm and loop vault forward, one becoming an appendage of the other, as if the tendons and pulse that travel through the wrist had lengthened and spun forward like fishing line until the loop sails down on the twin horns, then up under the hocks like a repeated embrace that tightens at the end before it releases.

The classic event at rodeo is saddle bronc riding. The young men look as serious as academicians: they perch spryly on their high-kicking mounts, their legs flicking forward and back, "charging the point," "going back to the cantle" in a rapid, staccato rhythm. When the horse is at the high point of his buck and the cowboy is stretched out, legs spurring above the horse's shoulder, rein-holding arm straight as a board in front, and free hand lifted behind, horse and man look like a propeller. Even their dismounts can look aeronautical: springing off the back of the horse, they land on their feet with a flourish—hat still on—as if they had been ejected mechanically from a burning plane long before the crash.

Barrel racing is the one women's event. Where the men are tender in their movements, as elegant as if Balanchine had been their coach, the women are prodigies of Wayne Gretsky, all speed, bully, and grit. When they charge into the arena, their hats fly off; they ride brazenly, elbows, knees, feet fluttering, and by the time they've careened around the second of three barrels, the whip they've had clenched between their teeth is passed to a hand, and on the home stretch they urge the horse to the finish line.

Calf ropers are the whiz kids of rodeo: they're expert on the horse and on the ground, and their horses are as quick-witted. The cowboy emerges from the box with a loop in his hand, a piggin' string in his mouth, coils and reins in the other, and a network of slack line strewn so thickly over horse and rider, they look as if they'd run through a tangle of kudzu before arriving in the arena. After roping the calf and jerking the slack in the rope, he jumps off the horse, sprints down the length of nylon, which the horse keeps taut, throws the calf down, and ties three legs together with the piggin' string. It's said of Roy Cooper, the defending calf-roping champion, that "even with pins and metal plates in his arm, he's known for the fastest groundwork in the business; when he springs down his rope to flank the calf, the resulting action is pure rodeo poetry." The six or seven separate movements he makes are so fluid they look like one continual unfolding.

Bull riding is last, and of all the events it's the only one truly dangerous. Bulls are difficult to ride: they're broad-backed, loose-skinned, and powerful. They don't jump balletically the way a horse does; they jerk and spin, and if you fall off, they'll try to gore you with a horn, kick, or trample you. Bull riders are built like the animals they ride: low to the ground and hefty. They're the tough men on the rodeo circuit, and the flirts. Two of the current champs are city men: Charlie Samson is a small, shy black from Watts, and Bobby Del Vecchio, a brash Italian from the Bronx who always throws the audience a kiss after a ride with a Catskill-like showmanship not usually seen here. What a bull rider lacks in technical virtuosity—you won't see the fast spurring action of a saddle bronc rider in this event—he makes up for in personal flamboyance, and because it's a deadlier game they're playing, you can see the belligerence rise up their necks and settle into their faces as the bull starts his first spin. Besides the bull and the cowboy, there are three other men in the ring—the rodeo clowns—who aren't there to make children laugh but to divert the bull from some of his deadlier tricks, and, when the rider bucks off, jump between the two—like secret service men—to save the cowboy's life.

Rodeo, like baseball, is an American sport and has been around almost as long. While Henry Chadwick was writing his first book of rules for the fledgling ball clubs in 1858, ranch hands were paying $25 a dare to a kid who would ride five outlaw horses from the rough string in a makeshift arena of wagons and cars. The first commercial rodeo in Wyoming was held in Lander in 1895, just nineteen years after the National League was formed. Baseball was just as popular as bucking and roping contests in the West, but no one in Cooperstown, New York, was riding broncs. And that's been part of the problem. After 124 years, rodeo is still misunderstood. Unlike baseball, it's a regional sport (although they do have rodeos in New Jersey, Florida, and other eastern states); it's derived from and stands for the western way of life and the western spirit. It doesn't have the universal appeal of a sport contrived solely for the competition and winning; there is no ball bandied about between opposing players.

Rodeo is the wild child of ranch work and embodies some of what ranching is all about. Horsemanship—not gunslinging—was the pride of western men, and the chivalrous ethics they formulated, known as the western code, became the ground rules for every human game. Two great partnerships are celebrated in this Oklahoma arena: the indispensable one between man and animal that any rancher or cowboy takes on, enduring the joys and punishments of the alliance; and the one between man and man, cowboy and cowboy.

Though rodeo is an individualist's sport, it has everything to do with teamwork. The cowboy who "covers" his bronc (stays on the full eight seconds) has become a team with that animal. The cowboys' competitive feelings amongst each other are so mixed with western tact as to appear ambivalent. When Bruce Ford, the bareback rider, won a go-round he said, "The hardest part of winning this year was taking it away from one of my best friends, Mickey Young, after he'd worked so hard all year." Stan Williamson, who'd just won the steer wrestling, said, "I just drew a better steer. I didn't want Butch to get a bad one. I just got lucky, I guess."

Ranchers, when working together, can be just as diplomatic. They'll apologize if they cut in front of someone while cutting out a calf, and their thanks to each other at the end of the day has a formal sound. Like those westerners who still help each other out during branding and roundup, rodeo cowboys help each other in the chutes. A bull rider will steady the saddle bronc rider's horse, help measure out the rein or set the saddle, and a bareback rider might help the bull rider set his rigging and pull his rope. Ropers lend each other horses, as do barrel racers and steer wrestlers. This isn't a show they put on; they offer their help with the utmost goodwill and good-naturedness. Once, when a bucking horse fell over backward in the chute with my husband, his friend H.A., who rode bulls, jumped into the chute and pulled him out safely.

Another part of the "westernness" rodeo represents is the drifting cowboys do. They're on the road much of their lives the way turn-of-the-century cowboys were on the trail, but these cowboys travel in style if they can—driving pink Lincolns and new pickups with a dozen fresh shirts hanging behind the driver, and the radio on.

Some ranchers look down on the sport of rodeo; they don't want these "drugstore cowboys" getting all the attention and glory. Besides, rodeo seems to have less and less to do with real ranch work. Who ever heard of gathering cows on a bareback horse with no bridle, or climbing on a herd bull? Ranchers are generalists—they have to know how to do many things—from juggling the futures market to overhauling a tractor or curing viral scours (diarrhea) in calves—while rodeo athletes are specialists. Deep down, they probably feel envious of each other: the rancher for the praise and big money; the rodeo cowboy for the stay-at-home life among animals to which their sport only alludes.

People with no ranching background have even more difficulty with the sport. Every ride goes so fast, it's hard to see just what happened, and perhaps because of the Hollywood mythologizing of the West which distorted rather than distilled western rituals, rodeo is often considered corny, anachronistic, and cruel to animals. Quite the opposite is true. Rodeo cowboys are as sophisticated athletically as Bjorn Borg or Fernando Valenzuela. That's why they don't need to be from a ranch anymore, or to have grown up riding horses. And to undo another myth, rodeo is not cruel to animals. Compared to the arduous life of any "using horse" on a cattle or dude ranch, a bucking horse leads the life of Riley. His actual work load for an entire year, i.e., the amount of time he spends in the arena, totals approximately 4.6 minutes, and nothing done to him in the arena or out could in any way be called cruel. These animals aren't bludgeoned into bucking; they love to buck. They're bred to behave this way, they're athletes whose ability has been nurtured and encouraged. Like the cowboys who compete at the National Finals, the best bulls and horses from all the bucking strings in the country are nominated to appear in Oklahoma, winning money along with their riders to pay their own way.

The National Finals run ten nights. Every contestant rides every night, so it is easy to follow their progress and setbacks. One evening we abandoned our rooftop seats and sat behind the chutes to watch the saddle broncs ride. Behind the chutes two cowboys are rubbing rosin—part of their staying power—behind the saddle swells and on their Easter-egg-colored chaps which are pink, blue, and light green with white fringe. Up above, standing on the chute rungs, the stock contractors direct horse traffic: "Velvet Drums" in chute #3, "Angel Sings" in #5, "Rusty" in #1. Rick Smith, Monty Henson, Bobby Berger, Brad Gjermudson, Mel Coleman, and friends climb the chutes. From where I'm sitting, it looks like a field hospital with five separate operating theaters, the cowboys, like surgeons, bent over their patients with sweaty brows and looks of concern. Horses are being haltered; cowboys are measuring out the long, braided reins, saddles are set: one cowboy pulls up on the swells again and again, repositioning his hornless saddle until it sits just right. When the chute boss nods to him and says, "Pull 'em up, boys," the ground crew tightens front and back cinches on the first horse to go, but very slowly so he won't panic in the chute as the cowboy eases himself down over the saddle, not sitting on it, just hovering there. "Okay, you're on." The chute boss nods to him again. Now he sits on the saddle, taking the rein in one hand, holding the top of the chute with the other. He flips the loose bottoms of his chaps over his shins, puts a foot in each stirrup, takes a breath, and nods. The chute gate swings open releasing a flood—not of water, but of flesh, groans, legs kicking. The horse lunges up and out in the first big jump like a wave breaking whose crest the cowboy rides, "marking out the horse," spurs well above the bronc's shoulders. In that first second under the lights, he finds what will be the rhythm of the ride. Once again he "charges the point," his legs pumping forward, then so far back his heels touch behind the cantle. For a moment he looks as though he were kneeling on air, then he's stretched out again, his whole body taut but released, free hand waving in back of his head like a palm frond, rein-holding hand thrust forward: *En garde!* he seems to be saying, but he's airborne; he looks like a wing that has sprouted suddenly from the horse's broad back. Eight seconds. The whistle blows. He's covered the horse. Now two gentlemen dressed in white chaps and satin shirts gallop beside the bucking horse. The cowboy hands the rein to one and grabs the waist of the other—the flank strap on the bronc has been undone, so all three horses move at a run—and the pickup man from whom the cowboy is now dangling slows almost to a stop, letting him slide to his feet on the ground.

Rick Smith from Wyoming rides, looking pale and nervous in his white shirt. He's bucked off and so are the brash Monty "Hawkeye" Henson, and Butch Knowles, and Bud Pauley, but with such grace and aplomb, there is no shame. Bobby Berger, an Oklahoma cowboy, wins the go-round with a score of 83.

By the end of the evening we're tired, but in no way as exhausted as these young men who have ridden night after night. "I've never been so sore and had so much fun in my life," one first-time bull rider exclaims breathlessly. When the performance is over we walk across the street to the chic lobby of a hotel chock full of cowboys. Wives hurry through the crowd with freshly ironed shirts for tomorrow's ride, ropers carry their rope bags with them into the coffee shop, which is now filled with contestants, eating mild midnight suppers of scrambled eggs, their numbers hanging crookedly on their backs, their faces powdered with dust, and looking at this late hour prematurely old.

We drive back to the motel, where, the first night, they'd "never heard of us" even though we'd had reservations for a month. "Hey, it's our honeymoon," I told the night clerk and showed him the white ribbons my mother had tied around our duffel bag. He looked embarrassed, then surrendered another latecomer's room.

The rodeo finals in Oklahoma may be a better place to honeymoon than Paris. All week, we've observed some important rules of the game. A good rodeo, like a good marriage, or a musical instrument when played to the pitch of perfection, becomes more than what it started out to be. It is effort transformed into effortlessness; a balance becomes grace, the way love goes deep into friendship.

In the rough stock events such as the one we watched tonight, there is no victory over the horse or bull. The point of the match is not conquest but communion: the rhythm of two beings becoming one. Rodeo is not a sport of opposition; there is no scrimmage line here. No one bears malice—neither the animals, the stock contractors, nor the contestants; no one wants to get hurt. In this match of equal talents, it is only acceptance, surrender, respect, and spiritedness that make for the midair union of cowboy and horse. Not a bad thought when starting out fresh in a marriage.

■ CONSIDERATIONS OF MEANING AND METHOD

1. Does Ehrlich offer any information or profess any views in this essay that you found surprising? What information was new to you? Which of her views run contrary to popular belief or to views you yourself have held? Did the essay change your perceptions about anything? If so, how?

2. What is Ehrlich's point of view in the essay? Is she an insider or an outsider? How does she come by her expertise?

3. At what point does Ehrlich draw her analogy? How explicit is it? Did you find it effective? This is an essay about rodeo and marriage. Is it ultimately more about one thing than the other? What do you think Ehrlich's primary purpose was in writing?

4. To what extent is this a process essay? What other strategies of development does Ehrlich employ? How does she organize her essay? Illustrate with examples from the text.

■ **POSSIBILITIES FOR WRITING**

1. In an essay for newlyweds, develop an analogy in which you compare a sport (other than rodeo) to a marriage—either a good marriage or a bad one. Keep in mind the differences between analogy and comparison and contrast.

2. Describe a process from the point of view of an outsider or a critical observer, as someone who does not have direct experience with or expertise related to the process described. For example, if you have never played football, describe how the game works and analyze it from an outsider's point of view. Or, although you are not a botanist or a biologist, describe the life cycle of a plant or animal. You may have to consult outside sources to fill your gaps of understanding of the workings of a process with which you are not very familiar. Firsthand observation will probably be key, however. Choose as your reader someone who, like you, is an outsider or unfamiliar with the process you describe, *or* someone who is an insider, intimately familiar with the process. Your choice of reader will greatly impact the approach you take in writing, as well as your ultimate purpose.

■ **MAXINE KUMIN**
Building Fence

Poet, children's author, fiction writer, and essayist Maxine Kumin (1925–) is originally from Philadelphia, Pennsylvania. She received her A.B. and A.M. degrees from Radcliffe College. She has taught at colleges, universities, and writers' conferences throughout the United States and has served as poetry consultant to the Library of Congress and Poet Laureate of New Hampshire. Best known as a poet, in 1973 Kumin won the Pulitzer Prize for poetry for Up Country: Poems of New England *(1972). Some of her many other volumes include* House, Bridge, Fountain, Gate *(1975),* Closing the Ring: Selected Poems *(1984), and* The Long Approach *(1985). Many of her children's books were written in collaboration with her friend, poet Anne Sexton, including* Eggs and Things *(1964) and* The Wizard's Tears *(1975). "Building*

Fence" is from In Deep: Country Essays *(1987). Kumin lives and writes on her farm in New Hampshire.*

*"I'm usually described as a pastoral, or a New England poet,"
Kumin says. "I have been twitted with the epithet 'Roberta Frost,'
which is not a bad thing to be." As is Frost's, Kumin's writing is
rooted in nature, the seasons, family relationships, and life in rural
New England. Writer Joyce Carol Oates has called her "a poet of
nature," but one who "insists on showing the natural world as it
really is, and not as a benign fantasy." In "Building Fence," Kumin
describes the arduous and tedious process of (and the motivations
behind) staking out well-defined pastures in the rocky woodlands
of her New Hampshire farm.*

Making fences presupposes not only pastures but a storehouse of
diligence. When you start from a tangle of sumac and blackberry,
every reclaimed square yard seems more precious than an acre of
riverbottom land. For a dozen years we've been pushing back the
forest, clearing, seeding, and sustaining what now adds up to fourteen up-and-down acres of the once two hundred-odd that nurtured
a dairy herd between the two world wars.

Building the fence itself is an imperfect science. Despite actual
measurements, you have to yield to the contours of the land. Post
holes are soul destroyers. Technology hasn't done much for the fence
line on a hill farm. Even if you hire a neighbor's tractor with auger
attachment, at least half the holes will have to be hand crafted as you
ease them this side or that of expectation. Stones annoy, rocks im-
pede, boulders break your heart as you tunnel down at a slant, hunting in vain for the earth bottom. If obdurate ledge or obstinate pud-
ding stone does not require acts of faith and leaps of imagination,
here and there you can count on a slope too steep for machinery to
navigate. The gasoline-powered two-man auger is more adaptable,
but even that ingenious tool will not maneuver between stump and
bedrock with the same agility as the old manual clamshell tool.

Setting the posts exacts more faith from the dogged fence-pilgrim.
Somehow there is never enough dirt in the pile you took out, even
after you've placed a ring of stones in the bottom of the hole to brace
the post. Even with a ring of stones stomped in nearly at the top for
further support, your supply of loose dirt has vanished. You end up
digging part of a second hole to make enough friable earth to hold
the first pole solid. Clearly, you do not come out even.

You've set 225 posts, roughly ten feet apart. From an appropriate distance, if you squint, it's merely a toothpick stockade, inconclusive and raw-looking. You long to get on with it, to establish the feeling of fence, the ethos of enclosure.

The best part of building the fence is tacking up the string that denotes where the line of top boards means to be. You go around importantly to do this light work, trailing your ball of twine, wearing your apron of nails. You measure with your fold-up rule fifty-two inches from the ground—but where exactly *is* the ground? This mound, this declivity, this solitary flat patch? You tap in a nail, pull the string taut from the previous post, catch it with a few easy twists around, and so on. String stands in for wood, a notion, a suggestion of what's to come. Foreshadowing, you could call it.

Because this is New England, the fence travels uphill and down; only little bits of it are on the level. Although string lightheartedly imitates the contours of the land, boards have to be held in place, the angle of cut defined by pencil. Invariably, both ends of the boards want cutting. The eye wants readjustments despite the ruler. Sometimes bottom boards catch on hummocks, outcroppings, or earth bulges which must be shoveled out or the board rearranged. But let's say you've tacked up your whole top line for the day, you've stepped back, eyeballed and readjusted it. Oh, the hammering home! The joy and vigor of sending nails through hemlock into the treated four-by-four uprights. Such satisfying whacks, such permanence, such vengeance against the mass bustications of horses and heifers through the puny electric wire of yore. Visions of acres and acres of fences, field after field tamed, groomed, boarded in; that is the meaning of gluttony.

Finishing the fence—painting, staining, or applying preservative—requires the same constancy as the slow crafting of it. You put in your two hours a day, rejoice when rain interrupts the schedule and your Calvinist soul is permitted to tackle some other chore. Cleaning tack, for example, provides a pleasurable monotony compared to the servitude of the four-inch roller and the can of Noxious Mixture. In our case, it's composed of one-third diesel oil, one-third used crankcase oil, and one-third creosote. You are properly garbed to apply this Grade C syrup, wearing cast-off overalls, a battered felt hat, decayed boots, and thick neoprene gloves. You stand almost an arm's length away from the fence in order to get enough leverage so the mixture will penetrate wood grain—here tough, there smooth, here cracked and warty, there slick as a duck's feather. You invent methods for relieving the dreary sameness of the job. On one course you begin left to right, top to bottom, back to front. On the next you reverse the order. Sometimes you do all the undersides first, or all the backs. Sometimes you spring ahead, lavishly staining all the front-facing boards just to admire the dark wood lines dancing against the hummocky terrain of these young—yea, virginal—fields. The process gets you in the shoulder blades, later in the knees. You spatter freckles of the stuff on your protected body. Your protective eyeglasses are now freckled with iridescent dots. The stench of the mix permeates your hair, your gloved hands, becomes a way of life. You can no longer gain a new day without putting in your two hours staining board fences. More compelling than tobacco or alcohol, that addictive odor of char, of disinfectant, of grease pits. The horses follow you along the fence line, curious, but even the fresh-faced filly keeps a respectful distance from you and your repellent mixture.

A year later you sit atop the remnants of a six-foot-wide stone wall unearthed along the perimeter of number two field and look across to the remarkable pear tree that stands alone in the third and newest field. Behind you, the first field; behind it, the barn. Between fields, hedgerow and hickory trees, red pine and hemlock. An intermittent brook further defines the boundary between number one and number two. A tributary meanders at the foot of number three. Beyond, a life-time of second-growth woodland awaits. In your mind's eye, an infinity of fenced fields recedes but never vanishes. And all the livestock of a lifetime safely graze.

■ CONSIDERATIONS OF MEANING AND METHOD

1. Is "Building Fence" an inductive or deductive essay? How do the points Kumin makes in the opening and closing paragraphs differ? How do they relate?

2. Kumin wrote "Building Fence" in the present tense, and in the second person. Choose a couple of paragraphs from the essay and rewrite them in your journal, substituting past tense for present and first person for second. Compare the paragraphs, and consider Kumin's reasons for choosing to write in the tense and voice she did.

3. What does Kumin mean by "the feeling of fence, the ethos of enclosure" in the fourth paragraph? How does this phrase predict her conclusion?

4. Kumin is best known as a poet. Do any particular elements of her

use of language in this essay strike you as "poetic"? Give examples, and explain.

■ POSSIBILITIES FOR WRITING

1. In a description of process essay, explain an especially tedious process, but one with a reward at the end. Is the reward enough to make the process worthwhile?

2. In an essay in which you use comparison and contrast to help develop your ideas, relate the aspects of country living, small town living, suburban living, or city living that are most or least satisfying to you, explaining to your reader why.

■ LIZABETH CLABAUGH
Journal (Explorations and Draft)
Belay On? On Belay

Here Liz Clabaugh introduces herself, then goes on to describe how her essay, "Belay On? On Belay," came about and her goals in writing it. "Belay On? On Belay," she says, is "an account of over-energetic college students," and the old caution applies: Do not attempt this trick at home, boys and girls!

Believe it or not, I am now an avid rock climber and have, since writing this essay, rappelled off cliffs much higher than my dorm's balcony.

I am from Vashon, Washington, an island accessible only by ferry, where everyone knows everything about everybody. I am studying human biology, focusing specifically on the psychological effects of physical and mental disability. My future plans include physical therapy school, a master's degree in psychology, and the Peace Corps.

I have found that I enjoy writing most when I can write about my own experiences. I began this assignment writing about the sea and the cycle of waves crashing on the sand. The writing is descriptive and flowery, but the experience is not uniquely mine, and so it seemed distant. Years from now I will not reread that journal writing and be flooded by memories. But as fate would have it, in the middle of writing about the ocean, I decided to take a break and discovered my three friends planning their quest on the balcony. I begged to be included, and as soon as my feet hit the floor, I ran off to plan and draft my essay. I had found my subject.

In this essay I am describing both a process that can be repeated (rappelling) and a unique event (rappelling off the balcony in Toyon Hall). In writing the essay, I found it very helpful to work from an outline. That way I was certain of including each of the steps in correct order. The first draft is more descriptive and has more of a sense of danger about it than the revision, but I opted to leave some of this out of the final version in order to develop the characters further. I excluded myself from the scene because I wanted to write as an observer rather than as a participant.

Note: In the following journal selection, the crossed-out words and phrases were deleted during and after drafting. Words and phrases in bold type were added, and in some places also deleted, in later stages of drafting.

Journal (Explorations and Draft)

The rocks loomed ahead in the distance, jutting skyward from the sandy shore. The roar of the waves as they broke into ~~foamy~~ surf echoed ~~between the two cliffs, carved into a for centuries by the water amplifying~~ off the ~~cliff~~ walls, ~~rounded~~ carved and smooth from the centuries of pounding water. Up the narrow valley raced the

The rocks loomed in the distance, their dampened surfaces reflecting moonlight gently, their edges softened by the darkness. Between the cliffs, a river swelled and receded with each wave, its bed carved ~~by~~ in the rocks by the neverending surge of water. Thick white foam—California snow, rode in and out, trailing its bubbles with each new rush of tide. ~~In the no sound a silence prevailed~~ sound was erased in the narrow valley ~~as~~, the foam ~~acted as~~ insulated the frosty air from the ~~gurgling of the~~ **gurgle** ~~of the waters.~~ ~~a~~ cushioned by the _____ foam.

Beyond the rocky outcrop, the ~~pale, sand beach lay changing absorbed the tremendous form of the crashing waves. Moonlight~~ waves crashed upon the glistening shoreline, hurtling waters with tremendous force to the sand below. Moonlight glinted off their steep sides and diffused as the crested barrels broke into foam, reaching far up the beach.

As each wave ~~broke against~~ crashed into the shore, a new ~~one~~ force of water slowly gained power and momentum as it crept ~~inland~~ towards the land from the unknown depths ~~beyond~~ of the sea. like an awakening monster. it grew in ~~height as the sheer~~ volume, ~~soon~~ towering above choppy ~~sea~~ waters. ~~But then gravity pulled the beast~~

~~Gravity~~ a terrific struggle ~~between~~ **ensued** between ~~the~~ gravity and the ~~swell~~ **tremendous** surge of ~~of water~~, but in the end, the giant crumpled, losing the battle as it folded back towards earth with one last roar, ~~spreading~~ **defiantly** spreading its remains across the sugar-fine ~~sands~~ sand.

New Process!!

> repelling off the balcony in Toyon lounge.
> steps: 1. tying ropes to pillars
>   -knots.
>   2.   tying ropes to harness
>   -carabeeners
>   3.   putting on harness
>   4.   testing knots
>   -leaning against pillars
>   -safety rope test
>   5.   up on ledge
>   talking through it
>   -initial step≠fall
>   -laugh, relief at not dying.

=sweat on face
=smell
=ropes creaking
=spectators
fear > relief

Jan. 25

Repel! The wall grows closer

The three men ~~kneeled~~ knelt in the lounge chairs, usually occupied by ~~snoring~~ students ~~snoring~~ , ~~with books~~ snoring softly texts open on their laps, ~~But at 11:00 on Sunday night the balcony was unusually quiet~~, peering over the edge of the balcony to the lounge below. Their whispering voices tense with excitement, they discussed the feasibility of their next ~~spontaneous~~ adventure. Spontaneous camping on the Santa Cruz beach one Saturday night and **exploring** the steam tunnels ~~lying around~~ under the campus **before** had both proven highly successful. **but** Could they repel off the balcony **of Toyon** to the tiled floor of the lounge below? Hamish, Alex and Craig decided ~~to give it a tr~~ try the impossible.

~~Carefully th~~ the three separated to collect the equipment from their rooms ~~around~~ in ~~Toyon Hall~~ **about the dorm.** Ropes—one ~~for safety~~ to repel against, the other a safety precaution, the waist harness, and carabeeners to hold ~~the ropes to the harness~~ everything together materialized from their closets and drawers. Memories of the previous summer's climbs came rushing back, ~~an~~ conversation flew back and forth as the young men feverishly checked the ropes for ~~weak spots~~ frayinged spots. Each looked up and caught the other's eye, **that** one glance revealing ~~the one common thought~~ everything. ~~I'm terrified too, but let's we've got to do it!~~ They were terrified, **but there was no turning back. It simply had to be done.**

Skillfully Hamish ~~wrapped~~ tied the ropes around supporting pillars, ~~tying~~ knotting the cords ~~into knots~~ upon ~~upon~~ which ~~momentarily~~ their lives would ~~momentarily~~ precariously hang (?). One false ~~mo~~ turn of the rope **in the knot,** and the first steps would also be their last. Alex jerked the lifelines hard, checking to make sure that there was no slippage on the **complicated** ~~twisted co~~ twists.

~~Everything set~~ Craig looked on, occasionally peering over the edge of the wall, as if to ~~check that the floor below was still~~ make sure that they

Everything was set to go, Hamish climbed into the waist harness, strapped the belt tightly. Alex and Craig clicked the ropes and carabeeners into place. The ~~metalic~~ click of the metal **as the carabeeners** snapped shut ~~had~~ ~~had an air of finality in its sound~~ echoed loudly throughout the deserted lounge, ~~adding~~ **creating** a ~~sense~~ an air of finality. As Hamish climbed onto the ledge, Alex firmly wrapped the safety rope around his waist, his knuckles ~~turni~~ whitening as his body anticipated the ensuing climb—teetering on the edge, Hamish turned inward. ~~The look of concentration grew His~~ eyebrows tensed downwards and ~~his~~ lips tightened, the ~~look of~~ concentration spread visibly across his face. ~~One~~ A single drop of sweat trickled from his blonde sideburn and slowly slid downwards, (its trail ending at his jawbone,) **as** the liquid hung waiting to fall into oblivion. "Belay on? On belay. ———————

Their voices went quietly back and forth, checking readiness but also calming inwardly the men as they followed the ritual of thousands of climbers. ~~was~~ Hamish leaned slowly backwards, the slack tightening in the ropes. A student wandered into the lounge below, ~~and looking~~ and looked up curiously. His voice, like the crack of ~~the~~ a whip, broke into the heavy silence, shattering the concentration of the climber and his friends. "What's that you're doing?"

~~Ham Hamish~~ Pulling himself upright, ~~Ham the conten~~ concentration fading from his features, Hamish answered back casually. "just repelling," as if it were done every day in the lounge. "Oh," came the reply, ~~as~~ and the intruder ~~left in search of more excitement~~ retreated back into silence.

~~Hamish once again te~~ Muscles tense, Hamish once again ~~started~~ invoked the ritual. Belay on? Alex glanced up, the casual smile turning serious once again. On Belay ——————

Out into ~~the~~ freedom Hamish leaned.

Belay On? On Belay

The three men kneel on the lounge chairs usually occupied by students snoring with textbooks open on their laps, and peer over the edge of the balcony to the lobby below. Their whispering voices are tense with excitement as they discuss the feasibility of their next adventure. Spontaneous camping on the Santa Cruz beach and exploring the steam tunnels beneath the campus had proven highly successful, but rappelling off of the balcony of Toyon Hall will be a precarious feat.

Hamish eyes Craig and Alex expectantly, waiting for their replies. Alex, who has climbed a few times before, readily nods his consent. Craig glances towards the lobby, hesitating before answering. Unlike the other two, he has never climbed before. The balcony seems especially high now that they are planning to rappel off of it. But not wanting to disappoint his friends, Craig shrugs his shoulders in compliance.

Hamish bounds off to collect his equipment. Ropes—one to rappel against, the other belayed out by a person on the balcony as a safety precaution, a waist harness, and carabineers, to attach the ropes to the harness—materialize from his closets and drawers. Memories of his previous summer's climbs come rushing back. Hamish paints pictures of rugged mountains, pinnacled rocks, and loose handholds as the young men carefully check the ropes for frayed spots. Each looks up and catches the others' eyes, those small glances revealing their innermost feelings. Hamish can hardly wait to begin, but the other two are a little more nervous. But even Craig knows that he is going to make the descent down the wall; there is no turning back now.

Hamish ties the ropes around supporting pillars, skillfully knotting the cords upon which their entire weight will be suspended during the rappel. One false turn in the knot and their first step might also be their last. Alex jerks hard on the lifelines, checking to make sure that there is no slippage in the complicated twists. Craig looks on, occasionally gazing over the edge of the wall, as if to confirm his fears. But he smiles when Alex catches his eye.

Once all the ropes are adjusted Hamish climbs into the harness and straps the belt tightly about his waist, doubling the band over about the buckle. Alex and Craig snap the ropes into the carabineers; the clicking metal echoes loudly throughout the deserted lounge. Set and ready to go, Hamish deftly creeps onto the ledge as Alex takes up the safety rope, wrapping it around his waist for extra traction, knuckles whitening as he anticipates the ensuing climb. Teetering on the edge, Hamish's body tenses and an intense concentration overtakes his face. His eyebrows tighten downwards and his lips draw together into a thin, white line. One drop of sweat trickles from his blonde sideburn and slides downwards toward his jawline, leaving a glistening trail on his cheek. All three are sweating, and the smell of their fear pervades the air as Hamish nervously wipes his palms on his khaki shorts.

"Belay on?" Hamish questions.

"On belay," Alex replies, tightening his grip on the rope.

"Climbing?"

"Climb on."

Their voices go quietly back and forth, checking readiness, but also calming them as they repeat words used by climbers for decades. Hamish leans slowly backwards, tightening the slack in the ropes. Craig anxiously clicks the metal closure of an extra carabineer as he surveys the scene, apprehensive about Hamish's safety.

Just then a student wanders into the lounge below and looks up curiously. His voice, like the crack of a whip, breaks the silence, shattering the concentration of the climber and his safety man: "What's that you're doing?"

Pulling himself upright, the concentration fading from his features, Hamish answers back casually, "Just rappelling," as if it were an everyday occurrence in the lounge.

"Oh," comes the reply, and the intruder retreats, leaving the lounge deserted once more.

Muscles tense, Hamish once again asks for concentration and readiness: "Belay on?"

Alex glances up, the relaxed smile turning serious again. "On belay."

"Climbing?"

"Climb on."

One more time Hamish leans out over the edge of the balcony, his whole body focused on the transitional step to the face below. Nimbly, he transfers his weight to support a perpendicular stance against the surface of the wall, controlling downward momentum by pulling on the rope gripped tightly in his right hand. Perched against the stone, Hamish experiments with a few steps, checking the traction of his hiking boots on the smooth siding. The textured rubber does not slide.

The awkward part over, a grinning Hamish yells to Alex to cut him some slack on the safety line. He ricochets down the wall, jumping out backwards, then catching himself against the stone with his feet, glancing up every few seconds to his friends as if to reassure them. Reaching the open doorway of the lounge, he swings through triumphantly, lowering himself by bouncing up and down on the ropes. Craig looks incredulously at Alex, questioning the sanity of their suspended friend. Touching ground, his face triumphant, Hamish whoops loudly, "I did it! Who's next?" He unbuckles himself from the harness and peers intensely at Alex and Craig, awaiting the reply.

Craig turns pale, not certain if he is ready, but Alex volunteers as they pull the harness back up to the balcony. Craig relaxes visibly, glad to delay his turn a few more minutes.

Hamish bounds up the stairs and returns, beaming, to where his friends wait. Balancing on Craig's arm, Alex steps into the harness, and begins to strap himself in, beginning the process again.

■ CONSIDERATIONS OF MEANING AND METHOD

1. In what ways might the focus and effect of this essay have been different had Clabaugh written in the first rather than the third person, including herself in the scene?

2. Why does Clabaugh switch from past to present tense in her revision of the essay?

3. How similar or different is Clabaugh's writing process from yours?

4. This essay has characteristics of both narration and description of process. What is the difference between narration and process writing? What characterizes this essay as a narrative? What indications do you have in language and references that Clabaugh is describing a process?

■ **POSSIBILITIES FOR WRITING**

1. In a process essay for other student writers, describe and explain your own writing process. How does the way in which you go about writing affect the quality of your writing?

MAKING CRITICAL CONNECTIONS: QUESTIONS FOR DISCUSSION, RESEARCH, AND WRITING

Note: The readings of this chapter lend themselves particularly well to comparisons of the writers' purposes and their rhetorical strategies. The following questions might suggest good topics for class discussions and/or comparison and contrast essays. Remember that effective comparisons and contrasts will require support in the form of specific illustrations and concrete examples from the texts.

1. In this text, there are two readings by Noel Perrin: "Falling for Apples" in this chapter and another essay in Chapter 6, "Forever Virgin· The American View of America" (page 369). Read the second essay, and discuss the similarities and differences you perceive in these essays in (a) Perrin's purposes in writing, (b) the modes of development he uses to explain his ideas, and (c) his writing style.

2. Maxine Kumin in "Building Fence" and Noel Perrin in "Falling for Apples" characterize rural life in New England. Compare and contrast their apparent attitudes about life on their New Hampshire farms. As a second possibility, read "The Northeast Kingdom," an essay in Chapter 6 (page 352), in which Wallace and Page Stegner describe New England lifestyles in personal as well as historical terms. Discuss Kumin's or Perrin's essay, or both, in light of what you learn from the Stegners' essay.

3. Compare and contrast the use of analogy as a strategy of development in Annie Dillard's "Sojourner" and in Gretel Ehrlich's "Rules of the Game: Rodeo."

4. Compare your writing process and that of other students in your class. How widely do they differ? What factors contribute to these differences? Does one approach produce better results than another? If you use these questions as the basis for a writing topic, try comparing your writing style with that of one or two other students (whom you will have to interview carefully). Keep in mind that your essay in response to these questions will, by nature, require your use of both description of process and comparison and contrast as modes of development.

Ⅲ
NARRATIONS

Human Encounters
with the Natural World

*"I would ask you to remember only this one thing," said Badger.
"These stories people tell have a way of taking care of them. If stories come to you, care for them. And learn to give them away where
they are needed. Sometimes a person needs a story more than food to
stay alive. That is why we put these stories in each other's memory.
This is how people care for themselves."*

Badger speaks to Crow and Weasel
from *Crow and Weasel* by Barry Lopez

We are compelled to share our stories: from what happened yesterday at the bus stop to the stories of our parents' and grandparents' or
earlier ancestors' lives to the stories of our cultures; from human history
to planetary history; from stories of creation to stories of apocalypse.
Narrations come in many forms: true stories, imagined stories, histories, myths, and conjectures. The storyteller is a traditionally powerful
person—the guardian of history, the purveyor of insight, the teller of
futures. He or she is the entertainer, sometimes the humorist, and always the cultural analyst.

We delight in listening to stories as much as we do in telling them. In
the face of a good story, we are all children—and all the better if we are
read to. The voice of a story entrances us; the words proliferate an array
of internal imagery, engaging the imagination, bringing to life alternate

realities. We witness, we empathize, we participate; we learn as we relate others' experiences to our own. Stories, whether on an intimate or a grand scale, allow us to feel connected, part of a common life, a common experience and history, a common heart and mind.

In ancient cultures, as in some "primitive" cultures which survive today, storytelling as an oral art had practical, historical, and artistic functions. It was the way in which information, culture, and wisdom were passed from one generation to the next, evolving as they went. Instead of listening to stories around a campfire, most of us receive our first stories in cozy chairs at bedtime from our elders, and later in institutions, like schools and libraries, that are designed in part for this purpose, or in our peer groups and social gatherings, or even at the comedy club. And, really, these are not so different from the ancient ways.

But storytelling is no longer a primarily oral art. A good many of the stories we "hear" come to us through books, magazines, and newspapers. Print, as a means of relating stories of all kinds, affects the storyteller's art, as well as the role of the listener/reader, in significant ways. Reading is, generally, a solitary and silent activity. The written story may be vivid, but it is disembodied from the storyteller; it has a life and history of its own. The storyteller and the reader do not meet, except symbolically, through the story itself. For many decades, more and more of our stories, true or imagined, have come to us through television, film, and video. For many Americans who do not read or who rarely read, being at the receiving end of a story is an almost entirely passive experience.

With recent developments in computing and electronic networking technologies, we are at the same time more distant and more present in storytelling or story-reading/listening. In multimedia, a story can be offered to you in print and in audio-visual forms simultaneously. With interactive media, you can place yourself within a story, affecting its direction and outcome through your participation. With electronic networking you can send, or receive, written communications to virtually any number of readers all over the globe in seconds. Whether these developments bring us closer to or lead us further away from the oral tradition in storytelling is difficult to tell.

Whatever form they take, though, stories captivate us. Whether we receive them in nonfiction or fiction forms, we want to know what other humans' experiences have been; we also want to know what sense these people have made of their experiences, as individuals and as members of a larger society. We share our stories in order to make sense of our lives, of our existence on the planet, our existence in history. Our stories—whether they are individual or collective, true or fictionalized, historical or speculative, and whether they come from experts or from ordinary people—help us reconcile the past, find meaning in the present, and project and shape our future.

CHAPTER 4

Contemplation, © Joel Gordon, 1990

PERSONAL NARRATIVES

RHETORIC:
WRITING ABOUT
PERSONAL EXPERIENCE

WRITING THE PERSONAL NARRATIVE

The personal narrative is among the most creative and flexible of essay forms, offering writer and reader the joy of entering into a good story as well as the occasion to learn and to analyze and reflect. The personal narrative springs from real life and real events, and the subject of a personal narrative is as limitless as experience itself. Writing a strong personal narrative requires that the writer pay attention to the events of his or her life (whether these be small or large events, ordinary or extraordinary), understand their possible relationship and significance to a reader, and go about telling his or her story in an interesting way, asking interesting questions and suggesting interesting conclusions.

The writer of a personal narrative can be anyone, since we are all experts when it comes to telling the stories of our own lives. All of us, no matter who we are—young or old, students or professionals—possess areas of expertise that others may well relate or even aspire to. You may have come to be something of an expert on the special problems and issues of children of divorced parents by virtue of your experience and your considerable reflection on the subject. You may have been playing back-lot baseball for ten years and know a good deal more about the game than the average TV fan. You may have thought long and hard about sexual harassment, maybe even talked to others about it and been compelled to do some reading on the subject, if you experienced it in

193

your summer job. In a personal narrative, you can share an experience that may resemble one that the reader has had, or provide a reader with something new and enlightening to feel and think about, to experience vicariously. And in the process, of course, you may clarify your own experience for yourself.

In many respects, the structure and technique of personal narration are much like the structure and technique of fiction. Writers in both forms need to consider point of view, plot, characterization, and thematic coherence and depth. The short fiction writer invents reality, though, while the writer of the personal narrative records it. And although both interpret the events they relate in some fashion, in most cases the essayist does so a bit more frankly. The writer of the personal narrative is often working simultaneously with many rhetorical modes. He or she is telling a story, reflecting upon and often comparing it to others, and possibly even actively trying to persuade the reader to accept a particular conclusion or point of view.

Choosing a Subject
for the Personal Narrative

Choosing a good subject for a personal narrative is, as in other forms of writing, largely a matter of the writer recognizing his or her own interests. A promising subject for a personal narrative is an experience that has moved the writer, one that keeps returning in memory and that the writer has thought about a good deal. It is an experience that resonates for the writer; it means something to him or her. It will likely, too, mean something to the reader, if the writer is able to recreate the experience effectively in language. The job of the writer of a personal narrative, then, is to recreate an experience vividly and to provide the reader with a context in which to understand its significance and how it relates to the reader's own life and perhaps to our collective lives.

Student writers often claim that nothing of real interest ever happens to them, so they don't have anything to write about. An interesting, provocative experience does not have to be exotic or profound-with-a-capital-"P" to make a good subject for personal narrative. We don't have to be travelers or adventurers, old, or even uncommonly wise to recognize that in our daily lives significant things—events which further personal growth and self-understanding and our understanding of nature (human or otherwise)—happen all the time. Many of the most interesting personal narratives describe events that are quite ordinary, and these, in fact, supply the reader with important, familiar points of reference. What raises these narratives above the ordinary is that the writer has reflected upon these events deeply or from a unique point of view, clarifying events for writer and reader alike.

Events Past: Perspective in Personal Narration

Since writers of personal narratives are describing events that have already occurred, the action of most personal narratives is related in the past tense. Sometimes, however, when the writer is describing ongoing events or reflecting upon the significance of past events from a current perspective, he or she will write in the present tense. A few writers of essays in this chapter's readings use the present tense as an effective way of drawing the reader into the immediacy of the events they describe. Even though writers of personal narrative sometimes use present tense for effect, the reality is that the writer is looking back on events, whether distant or relatively recently past.

Powerful recent events may seem like promising subjects for personal narratives, since these events are vivid and fresh in our minds. But sometimes they are not the best choices for the writer of personal narrative. The events may be vivid, but we may have not yet had a chance to understand them fully, to relate them to other events, to place them within a broader context in our experience or our thinking. There is a reflective element to the personal narrative that asks us not only to tell a good story, but also to interpret it to some degree, and this is usually best accomplished with a little bit of distance. It is true that often the very act of writing can help clarify an event for the writer—he or she can achieve a better understanding in the process of writing about it. But often, in writing of recent events, the writer (and the reader) may get caught up in the story but feel somewhat at a loss when it comes to understanding its significance. All aspects of the event may seem equally important when the event is too immediate (or perhaps when events have not even finished unfolding), and the writer may need a little time in order to gain enough perspective to write clearly about it.

Personal narratives, then, draw upon memory. Some time will have lapsed between the experience and the writing about it, but the writer will have to recall the event precisely and with immediacy in order to recreate it vividly for the reader. As you prepare to write a personal narrative, it might be useful to you to review the prewriting techniques for writing from recollection described in Chapter 2 (page 79).

Organizing the Personal Narrative

In order to capture your reader's interest, how should you begin a personal narrative? In order to sustain that interest and make your point, how should you proceed? The personal narrative is less likely than many other kinds of essays to open with an introductory paragraph in which the author states an overt thesis. Very often, a personal narrative will open with action, as most short stories do. The reasons for this are perhaps obvious: the writer wants to involve the reader in the events being described right away, and readers whose wandering concentration has yet to be snagged as they begin to read are more likely to be captivated by a story than by an abstraction or a premature conclusion. Writers working in other nonfiction forms are aware of this as well; in a more overt argument or analysis, the writer may relate his or her own experience as an effective way to begin, thereby capturing the reader's attention, giving him or her the opportunity to relate to the essay's situation or themes in a personal way.

Although the opening paragraph or paragraphs of a personal narrative may not contain a one- or two-sentence statement that you could underline and refer to as *the thesis,* the initial paragraphs should give the reader an indication of the essay's subject and direction. Early paragraphs should suggest the question, the dilemma, or the theme that the writer will explore.

If you begin a personal narrative with action, you should think carefully about *what* action to begin with. The action should relate to the entire narrative and to the conclusions you draw. You may, in fact, want to open with the climax, placing the reader directly into the event in which the essay's central question is most clearly posed but which has yet to be resolved. You might then want to organize the body of the essay around building a context of understanding, by filling in narrative details, offering background and reflection, and then resolving the dilemma in your conclusion. This approach may be more dramatic and more interesting in some respects, but you will be challenged in moving back and forth in time, weaving immediate events with flashback, action with reflection and analysis.

On the other hand, you may want to take a more straightforward chronological approach, beginning your narrative at the beginning. In this case, you might begin by providing the reader with a context for the essay by providing background information or a vivid description of setting in order to place the reader within the scene.

Whichever method you use in posing the theme of your personal narrative in its early paragraphs and developing this theme in the body of the essay, the conclusions you reach by the end of the essay need to be earned. Personal essays generally involve action, and the reader should feel like a participant in these events, rather than a removed observer. The reader should understand what happened to you and be ready to understand the conclusions you draw from your experience.

In many cases, the closing paragraphs of a personal narrative are a better place for a thesis than the opening paragraphs: the writer has earned a conclusion by the end of the essay through describing and reflecting upon the experience throughout. By drawing the conclusion in the closing paragraph, the writer offers the reader the opportunity to participate both in the events described and in the process of drawing conclusions. An inductive pattern of development, in which an essay moves from particulars to a general statement that presents the writer's conclusion, is often more effective in the personal narrative than a deductive pattern of development, in which the essay moves from a thesis statement to particulars that illustrate or prove the thesis.

Unity and Coherence in the Narrative

In relating events in narrative writing, it may seem that in order to achieve coherence all the writer has to do is simply transcribe the chain of events: *this happened, then this happened, then this happened.* This is the style in which children tend to tell stories—with run-on enthusiasm but a lack of selectivity when it comes to determining the relative importance of the particulars. In a personal narrative, each paragraph should have a thematic and not merely a chronological thrust. If narrative paragraphs have no overt paragraph thesis, they should nonetheless be unified by a central idea and convey a dominant impression. Achieving paragraph unity necessitates a certain degree of interpretation of events described. The writer needs to decide which parts of the chain of events are important and which are extraneous, and among the relevant details, which need to be emphasized to support the theme clearly.

For example, when the writer begins to describe a particular moment within a larger event—say, the point at which two people begin to lose patience with one another in a conversation, or the turning point in a race—there will probably be a paragraph break, and this moment will probably be narrated within one paragraph. Not only has there been a shift in action (that is, an interaction between two people has shifted dramatically, or the runner suddenly realizes at the final turn that she has a chance of winning a race for the first time in her life), there has also been a shift in thought or mood. The two people who are deep in conversation suddenly feel angry or threatened, or the runner is ecstatic and energized. These qualities of emotion or mood should provide the dominant impression of a narrative paragraph, and all the narrative and descriptive details should contribute to this effect.

The writer should leave himself or herself open to surprises and to learning something new and interesting through the act of writing itself. At the same time, the writer should know in advance of relating the narrative what central idea he or she wants the narrative, or individual paragraphs in it, to support. This can be a delicate balancing act. Saving a concluding statement for the closing paragraph does not mean that the writer will have no sense during the writing of the essay what that conclusion might be. Having an idea of the conclusion in advance will certainly help the writer shape a unified and coherent essay during the process of writing. However, if the writer lets specific conclusions take shape throughout the process of writing a personal narrative, these conclusions will feel more honest and better-earned. It is always a good idea for the writer of personal narrative, as well as other essay forms, to return to the beginning after finishing the first draft and revise the beginning with special attention to unity and coherence, taking into account where the essay has traveled and what conclusions the writer has reached.

Dialogue

Dialogue is a means of both furthering action and enriching characterization in a personal narrative. When characters speak for themselves, we can sometimes learn a great deal about them, about events, and about the points the writer wishes to draw attention to. Dialogue can add texture and variety to a piece of writing, helping to sustain the reader's interest and enriching the prose. It is an effective way of drawing the reader into the immediacy of both character and action in a narrative, as well as a way of enlivening a story, whether fictional or true.

Dialogue often seems easier to write than it actually is. The writer will need to have a firm understanding of the narrative situation, of the character and style of the person speaking, and of the personal dynamics illustrated in a verbal exchange. Dialogue often sounds stilted. When we speak written dialogue aloud, we may find that this stiltedness comes from the fact that the words sound written rather than spoken. The reader's internal ear will probably pick up this awkwardness even in silent reading. The writer should therefore read dialogue aloud, testing it to make sure it sounds right to the ear, since this is much more important than whether it looks correct on the page.

The following excerpt is from student writer Amelia Hughart's personal narrative, "Looking Out":

> Even the tamed, predictable natural world could scare me if I stopped taking it for granted for a second and doubted the control that humans had over it. Part of domination is complete knowledge of the controlled. One spring evening, after dinner, I stared at the dogwood tree cut into white-edged squares by the window frame. I asked my grandmother if I could ever know everything about everything in the world.
>
> "No," she replied.
> "Everything about trees?"
> "No."
> "Everything about dogwoods?"
> "No."
> "Well, could I at least know everything about that dogwood?"
> "No."
> "Everything about one leaf of that dogwood?"
> "No," she replied.
>
> This shook my confidence in the sturdiness of the world my parents had presented to me. If no one could know everything about it, how could I know that it was safe?

In bringing this conversation with her grandmother to life with dialogue, rather than reporting it expositorily, Hughart has accomplished several things. She has articulated a complex and abstract idea effectively in simple, concrete, and personal terms. She has demonstrated her grandmother's wisdom and her role as Hughart's mentor in childhood. Through the rhythm of the exchange, her questions and her grandmother's repeated "no's," she has emphasized the impossibility of knowing and controlling even the smallest part of nature. And, in an essay in which this is the only dialogue, she has varied her writing style as one means of sustaining her reader's interest.

Integrating Action and Reflection

One personal narrative may emphasize the narrative more than reflection or analysis, and another may emphasize reflection, analysis, or even argument more than the narrative itself. Whichever kind of personal narrative you write, it is probable that your purpose will be, to some degree, both to tell a good story and to make a point. In fact, it is one of the appeals of the personal narrative, for writer and reader alike, that the writer can present an interesting idea by means of telling a good story.

Writers of personal narrative generally have to ask themselves, in writing about their experiences, the same question their readers will most likely ask: *Yes, but so what?* If the writer does not have a clear sense of why he or she is writing the narrative, the essay is likely to lack direction and coherence and may collapse into an aimless jumble of narrative detail. Although a story may be fun to read for its detail, unless readers have a clear sense of why they are reading it, it will probably be soon forgotten.

The reflective nature of the personal narrative poses specific challenges for the writer. Many student writers, aware that they want not only to tell their stories but to draw conclusions from them, find themselves trying to do so in two distinct stages: first they tell the story, then they reflect upon it, analyze it, or attempt to base an argument upon it. This approach often leads to an awkward transition toward the end of the essay where the writer switches from narrative to reflective, analytic, or argumentative modes. Writers may feel at this juncture as though they are taping a "moral-to-the-story" onto the narrative. Possibly because so many of us have been taught that analysis or argumentation in writing must be accomplished in a formal style, whereas our natural inclination in narrating a personal event is to write in a casual style, this transition may result not only in an abrupt shift from one mode of writing to another, but also from one style to another. Therefore, the transition may feel awkward, and as a result the essay may feel disjointed, like two different essays rather than one that is unified.

In anticipating or resolving this writing dilemma, it may be helpful for you to realize that in any experience you describe from a personal point of view, there are really two stories developing simultaneously: one involving external events and the other internal events. If your purpose in writing is not only to describe an experience but to reflect upon or analyze it, part of your narration should include an account of what you were feeling and thinking at the moment. If you take care to describe both events and your own awareness of them as they unfold, you will have reflective points of reference throughout the essay. In the conclusion, you can build upon these, and your analysis will not feel as though it is coming out of the blue. Your conclusions will be within easier reach of the reader's understanding and empathy, and both you and your reader will feel that these conclusions are a more natural outcome of the experience itself.

DRAWING GENERAL CONCLUSIONS FROM PERSONAL EXPERIENCE

How broad can conclusions be when they are based on personal experience? The degree to which a writer can generalize from personal experience depends upon (a) the kind of experience it is; (b) the writer's level of familiarity, knowledge and expertise beyond the experience itself; and (c) the purpose the writer hopes to achieve in writing, or the effect he or she wants to have on the reader.

Levels of Generalization

A generalization is a conclusion, and in order to arrive at and support a conclusion credibly, the writer must provide evidence in the form of particulars. Evidence may range from descriptive and narrative details and illustrations drawn from personal experience to references to outside sources. *Low-level generalizations* are conclusions that are limited and fairly intimate in scope; *high-level generalizations* apply much more broadly to situations and people. The thesis of any given piece of writing, including the personal narrative, is likely to provide that writing's highest level of generalization.

In personal narrative, assuming that the writer's experience is directly related to the point he or she ultimately makes and that he or she has thought carefully about both the experience and the point, the writer's experience alone will probably be enough to support a low-level generalization. The higher the level of generalization, however, the more likely it will be that the writer will have to cite other evidence in addition to personal experience in order to support the generalization adequately.

Of course, generalizations don't come at just two levels—low and high. There are many gradients on the scale. Consider the following four thesis statements. Each generalizes, on an ascending scale.

> 1. *I decided to become a vegetarian because eating animal flesh made me feel physically unhealthy, environmentally irresponsible, and morally culpable.*

Although in this sentence the speaker makes a strong statement, it is a low-level generalization. The speaker draws a general conclusion that is based solely on her own experience and applies only to herself. Her vegetarianism, and the thoughtfulness with which she has approached her decision to become vegetarian, provide her with authority in writing about the subject from a personal perspective. In order to support this low-level generalization adequately, the author will probably not need to cite evidence beyond her personal experience and the progress of her own thinking that led to her decision, although her experience will probably include persuasive information she has encountered in favor of vegetarianism. Because she has cited three reasons central to her decision—personal health, environmental considerations, and moral questions—she will need to explain her decision as it relates to all three areas.

The speaker's purpose in writing an essay based on this thesis, beyond self-clarification, might be to offer her own experience as an example to the reader. Although the speaker believes strongly that her decision was the right one for her, she may not want or feel qualified to lecture the nonvegetarian reader, urging him or her to abandon a nonvegetarian lifestyle. The speaker will naturally want to present the reasons for her choice in a positive light, and the reader, whether vegetarian or not, will naturally compare his or her experience to the speaker's. The reader is likely to feel contemplative in reading this essay, but not pressured to accept the speaker's conclusion as his or her own.

2. *Like many of my friends, I believe that a vegetarian diet makes for physically and spiritually healthy individuals as well as a healthier environment.*

This statement generalizes at a higher level than the first. The speaker allies herself with a group—although an intimate one consisting of her vegetarian friends—and the statement of her belief encompasses what is good for "individuals," which may include her readers. Her statement implies that if readers make the choice she and her friends have made, they will be healthier as well as more responsible people.

The speaker's own experience with vegetarianism may allow her to write about the subject with knowledge and insight, but the higher level of generalization—her reference to the experience of others and her direct involvement of the reader through her use of the general term "individuals"—will probably require more than personal experience in the way of credible proof. She will have to draw upon the experiences of her friends as well as her own as examples; since her purpose is more overtly persuasive, the reader will probably feel the need for more information from outside sources in order to be convinced that we will be healthier and more responsible people if we choose not to eat meat. The reader, especially the nonvegetarian, is likely to feel personally challenged by this speaker's essay, and his or her need for tangible proof will increase accordingly. Personal experience, the speaker's own and that of her friends, will still serve as crucial elements of the essay, an effective way for the author to illustrate the personal dimensions of a complex issue.

3. *Vegetarianism is on the rise in the United States because more Americans are questioning not only the health and environmental effects of meat consumption, but its morality as well.*

In this statement, the speaker generalizes at an even higher level. Her own experience may have motivated her to research and write the essay, and she may or may not refer to her personal experience as one way of illustrating and supporting her assertion. But personal experience alone (whether her own or others') will certainly not be enough to support this high-level generalization. Because her statement refers to trends toward vegetarianism and to reasons held by a great many people, the bulk of her evidence must address the scope of these generalized references. She will cite information from outside sources that quantitatively supports her assertion that Americans are becoming vegetarians at an increasing rate. She could cite both statistical and *anecdotal* (pertaining to personal experience, whether her own or others') evidence that more Americans are questioning meat consumption for the three reasons cited. She may cite evidence from sources that include people with a great deal more professional expertise in the subject than she has, supporting her assertions that eating meat is bad for health, morally questionable, and damaging to the environment.

This generalization would make a strong thesis for an extensive research essay. The purpose of this essay would be to inform and, finally, to persuade the reader that vegetarianism is a well-established trend and a sound personal choice. The scope of the generalization encompasses us all, whether we are vegetarians or not. In fact, the generalization perhaps encourages readers to see vegetarians and nonvegetarians as members of opposing camps, and asks the nonvegetarian to cross over. Readers, if they are vegetarians, are likely to feel supported by such an essay, part of an important trend. Nonvegetarians may feel challenged, but possibly not in a very personal way, since they will see themselves as part of a large group. The main advantage of including personal experience in an essay to support a high-level generalization is that the personal dimension makes it difficult for the reader to disappear within the numbers and the abstractions needed to support a high-level generalization.

> 4. *Nonvegetarians have no self-respect, no commitment to environmental principles, and no reverence for life.*

This statement reflects an extremely high level of generalization and is impossible to support with any kind of evidence. There is no way, through personal experience or statistical evidence, to prove that "nonvegetarians have no self-respect, no commitment to environmental principles, and no reverence for life" because it simply isn't true. This is a vast overgeneralization, and, like all inflammatory rhetoric, it says a great deal about the speaker's prejudices but sheds no light on the real complexity of the subject at hand. A reader of an essay which "supports" this statement, whether vegetarian or nonvegetarian, would be right in feeling embarrassed for, or hostile toward, the speaker.

If, in revising an essay in which you use personal experience in support of a generalization, you find that your generalization is too high to be adequately supported by your experience alone, you have two choices. You will either need to adjust your generalization, taking it down a notch or two from higher to lower, so that your experience supports it reasonably, or you will need to expand your evidence to support the high level of generalization you are aiming for.

The personal narrative provides an opportunity for the exchange of both ideas and experience between writers and readers. It helps reinforce the common bond between individuals, providing a way of understanding individual experience within a larger social context. In writing and reading personal narratives, we understand better not only the nature of our own experience, but how our experiences relate to the experiences of others, and how, taken together, individual experience applies in a much broader world of ideas and interactions on a grand scale.

PEER REVIEW

Student writers often struggle with the concept of audience. Although they may be asked to imagine a reader other than their instructor, the reality is that in most college writing, the instructor will be the only person who reads what students write. This is a one-way interaction, and often the grade the essay receives will feel like the only important consequence of this communication.

In an exchange of work in peer review, the student writer expands his or her readership and has the chance to test the effectiveness of his or her writing on a reader whose role is constructive more than evaluative. As a peer reviewer, you can help your classmates develop their thinking and writing as well as hone your own revision and editing skills. You can also compare your approach to an assignment with someone else's, and learn in the process.

To do a peer review, exchange your work at the draft stage with someone in your class who is at work on the same assignment. Make sure you both understand the objectives and criteria of the assignment as well as each other's individual purposes and goals in writing. There are several kinds of comments that your peer review partner may find helpful, and that you will find helpful in his or her review of your work.

In *reader-based comments,* the reviewer will offer a personal response. For example, "I am confused by this paragraph. Is there some action missing here?" or "This description makes me feel as if I'm there!" are reader-based comments. These kinds of comments may come in the form of observations and questions. The advantages of reader-based comments are that they provide the writer with an immediate, uncluttered response, and the reviewer does not pretend to be the final authority. Reader-based comments are easy to give and easy to receive because they are nonjudgmental.

In *criterion-based comments,* the reviewer will note successes or problems in accordance with criteria determined by the instructor, by the specifications of the assignment, or by widely accepted writing conventions. For example, "You have two comma splices in this paragraph" or "This generalization is well-supported by your evidence" are criterion-based comments. Criterion-based comments take more time and consideration to write because the reviewer must not only respond on a personal level, but also analyze the reason for the effectiveness or lack of effectiveness of the writing based on an understanding of the criteria. Responding in this way is good exercise for the reviewer because it requires his or her understanding of criteria. Since these kinds of comments are more pointed, and may feel to the writer to be more critical, it is important to remember that the reviewer is not the person who invented the criteria.

Directive comments offer the writer constructive solutions. In offering a directive comment, the reviewer will not only identify a specific problem ("You have a comma splice here") but will offer a suggestion to fix it ("Try a semicolon to separate two independent clauses that are related"). Directive comments require both an understanding of criteria and an understanding of how to fix a problem when criteria are not being met. A student reviewer will sometimes, but by no means always, feel qualified to offer a solution to a writing problem. If as a reviewer you have some doubt as to whether your solution is correct, it is best to stick to reader- or criteria-based comments or to phrase your suggestion tentatively ("Isn't this a direct quotation? I think you need to put this sentence in quotation marks, but you'd better check with the instructor to make sure").

The purpose in reviewing another student's work is not merely to catch obvious shortcomings. Be honest. Be constructive. Give the writer the kind of feedback you yourself would find most helpful. Don't forget to let the writer know what he or she is doing right as well as what could be improved. If you think something in the essay you are reviewing is not working well, say so, but be sure to support your criticisms with clear reasons, specific examples, and, if possible, suggestions for improvement. Try to meet in person with your peer review partner to discuss your comments, even when they are written.

The peer review questions that follow are designed to focus your review of a classmate's personal narrative. The questions can be adapted to your specific assignment.

Peer Review of the Personal Narrative[*]

1. Does the author forecast the direction of the essay clearly enough early on? Is there a thesis statement? Does there need to be one? Write what <u>you</u> think the author's main point is.

2. Has the author provided an effective context for the essay? Does it feel natural? Forced?

3. Does the essay draw a conclusion, and does this conclusion feel earned? Do the introduction and conclusion relate effectively without repeating?

4. How high or low is the author's highest level of generalization? Is the level of generalization adequately supported by the right kinds and amount of evidence? Is either the level of generalization or the evidence supporting it in need of adjustment?

---

[*]Thanks to Clifford Barnett, Department of Anthropology, Stanford University, for the format and some of the wording of this peer review form.

5. Do you feel the author has observed carefully enough? Have his or her description and narration created a vivid and compelling picture in your mind?

6. Do narration and reflection or analysis seem well-balanced? Do transitions between action and reflection/analysis feel smooth?

7. Does each paragraph (excluding dialogue) have a distinct central idea, a paragraph thesis, or a dominant impression? Are the author's statements in each paragraph well-supported, illustrated, explained? Are details within each paragraph arranged in a logical sequence?

8. Do you feel the author has emphasized the "right" things? Does the essay touch on anything you would like to see developed further? Is there needless material that should be omitted?

9. Are there any grammatical or mechanical errors (including problems with punctuation) that appear more than a couple of times that the author will need to focus attention on in revising? Are there any consistent problems with diction, usage, or any misused words that you can point out to the author?

10. Beyond mechanical and grammatical errors, comment on the author's writing style. Does he or she vary sentence structure? Are there too many short, choppy sentences or ones that are overly complex and need to be broken up? Does the author choose precise words? Is there any wordiness?

11. What would you say are the essay's major strengths and why?

12. What do you think the author needs to focus on most in order to improve this essay?

READINGS:
FLIGHTS OF FACT

Much of the most popular, interesting, and beautiful writing about nature—both past and present—exists in the form of the personal narrative. The theme of human relationships to the natural world has connections with many kinds of experience, with nearly every conceivable area of study, and with many professions. Among the authors who write about nature in the form of personal narrative are poets, novelists, journalists, memoirists, social or natural historians, biologists, archaeologists, medical doctors, lawyers, activists, transcendentalists, explorers and adventurers, gardeners, geologists, anthropologists, physicists, feminists, and others of myriad professions and points of view. What this diversity may begin to suggest is that effective writing evolves and works according to its audience and purpose and that nature, like many great themes and important social issues, has implications that cross disciplinary boundaries and relate our fields of study, our professional interests, and our personal, social, and political concerns.

Much of the writing in other chapters of this book also qualifies as personal narrative, or has strong personal narrative elements. All of the journal selections of Chapter 1, for example, involve personal narration to one extent or another. The personal narrative, though it may be written looking back in time rather than in the moment, is, like most journal writing, a chronicling of personal events. In many of the essays of Chapters 2 and 3, the writers' firsthand experiences feature strongly, although their subjects are generally more external than internal, and in these essays the writers tend to look at nature more than at themselves. For example, N. Scott Momaday's introduction to *The Way to Rainy*

Mountain, Noel Perrin's "Falling for Apples," Gretel Ehrlich's "Rules of the Game: Rodeo," and Maxine Kumin's "Building Fence" are written from a personal point of view, in the first person, and in each the writer's experience is important to the point the essay makes. The reader may, in fact, be able to relate better to the larger, more general points because they are offered in personal terms. In the histories in Chapter 6, Wallace and Page Stegner see their family's experience as part of a larger regional history. In the conceptual writings of Chapter 7, Joyce Carol Oates, in her essay "Against Nature," uses her personal experiences with nature as the tool of exploration and the occasion for analysis.

The readings in this chapter have been selected because the writer's *main* task here is to tell a personal story, to relate a significant encounter with the natural world and to draw conclusions from it. The subject of each of these essays tends to be the writer him- or herself, though the conclusion may have broader implications: in focusing on moments of encounter with the natural world, each of these writings is about the writer in the process of revelation or change and the role the natural world plays in bringing about this change.

In their encounters with and contemplations of the natural world, the writers of essays included in this chapter see nature as serving various functions and as meaning various things. For Henry Bibb, in Section XI from his slave narrative, nature is wilderness, and wilderness is both a barrier and the necessary first step toward freedom. Confronting the wilderness, for Bibb, is a metaphor for trusting in God. For John Muir, communing with nature is tantamount to communing with God; nature is the source of both joy and adventure in "A Wind-Storm in the Forests." Other writers are instructed by nature, and their conclusions relate broadly to human relationships to the natural world as in David Quammen's "The Face of a Spider" and Alice Walker's "Am I Blue?"

As part of our experience, we may see nature as a physical force or as an image that sparks our imaginations. For us, nature may be reality or metaphor, obstacle or adventure, teacher or victim. How do you regard your relationship to nature? Is nature for you real and tangible or is it a romantic idea? Do you see yourself, along with human life and culture, as part of nature or separate from it? These are some of the fundamental thematic questions that arise when we consider, in reading and writing, what our most memorable encounters with nature mean—the ways in which nature forms and informs us and what effects we have on the natural world.

■ HENRY BIBB

Section XI from *Narrative of the Life and Adventures of Henry Bibb, an American Slave*

Henry Bibb was born to a slave mother by a white father in eastern Kentucky in 1815. His determination to escape the degradation and toil of slavery began when he was young. At eighteen he married, and his reluctance to leave his wife, Malinda, and their child, Frances, or to subject them to the dangers of escaping together caused him to delay his attempts. In 1838, though, he attempted and succeeded in escaping alone. After living briefly in Ohio and Michigan, he disguised himself as a peddler, passing as white, and prepared to return to Kentucky to free his family. In Cincinnati, he was detected by black slave catchers, posing themselves as abolitionists, and was returned to Kentucky. This and other attempts to escape earned him the reputation as a runaway and, ultimately, a more difficult slave life on a Louisiana plantation, although miraculously he had not yet been separated from his family. The section of Bibb's narrative included here tells of a disastrous attempt to escape with his wife and daughter and of their eventual recapture. As a consequence, Bibb was finally separated from his wife and child and sold first to a group of gamblers, who took him with them west into the prairie, and then to an Indian. Bibb's narrative ends with his final, successful escape—across the prairie and to solitary freedom. Bibb settled in Ontario, Canada, around 1850 and there he published The Voice of the Fugitive, *an antislavery paper.*

By the time Henry Bibb published his autobiography in 1849, the slave narrative was a popular form. Many slave narratives preceded Bibb's; the Autobiography of Frederick Douglass *(1845) and the* Narrative of William Wells Brown *(1847) were probably the most widely read by Northern abolitionists. Slave narratives, including Bibb's, provided "an effective weapon in the abolitionist arsenal," according to Maxwell Whiteman, editor of a reprinted edition of Bibb's narrative. In his essay "We'll Stand the Storm: Slave Songs and Narratives" from his book* Ride Out the Wilderness: Geography and Identity in Afro-American Literature, *Melvin Dixon observes that Henry Bibb and others who sang and wrote about the slave experience saw the American wilderness for what it was: a fearsome obstacle and a test, but also, since entering it was a step toward freedom, a symbol of freedom itself. In the wilderness, Dixon says, American slaves saw loathsomeness, but God and deliverance as well.*

I attend a prayer meeting.—Punishment therefor threatened.—I attempt to escape alone.—My return to take my family.—Our sufferings.—Dreadful attack of wolves.—Our recapture.

Some months after Malinda had recovered from her sickness, I got permission from the Deacon, on one Sabbath day, to attend a prayer meeting, on a neighboring plantation, with a few old super-annuated slaves, although this was contrary to the custom of the country—for slaves were not allowed to assemble for religious worship. Being more numerous than the whites there was fear of rebellion, and the overpowering of their oppressors in order to obtain freedom.

But this gentleman on whose plantation I attended the meeting was not a Deacon nor a professor of religion. He was not afraid of a few old Christian slaves rising up to kill their master because he allowed them to worship God on the Sabbath day.

We had a very good meeting, although our exercises were not conducted in accordance with an enlightened Christianity; for we had no Bible—no intelligent leader—but a conscience, prompted by our own reason, constrained us to worship God the Creator of all things.

When I returned home from meeting I told the other slaves what a good time we had at our meeting, and requested them to go with me to meeting there on the next Sabbath. As no slave was allowed to go from the plantation on a visit without a written pass from his master, on the next Sabbath several of us went to the Deacon, to get permission to attend that prayer meeting; but he refused to let any go. I thought I would slip off and attend the meeting and get back before he would miss me, and would not know that I had been to the meeting.

When I returned home from the meeting as I approached the house I saw Malinda, standing out at the fence looking in the direction in which I was expected to return. She hailed my approach, not with joy, but with grief. She was weeping under great distress of mind, but it was hard for me to extort from her the reason why she wept. She finally informed me that her master had found out that I had violated his law, and I should suffer the penalty, which was five hundred lashes, on my naked back.

I asked her how he knew that I was gone?

She said I had not long been gone before he called for me and I was not to be found. He then sent the overseer on horseback to the place where we were to meet to see if I was there. But when the overseer got to the place, the meeting was over and I had gone back home, but had gone a nearer route through the woods and the overseer happened not to meet me. He heard that I had been there and hurried back home before me and told the Deacon, who ordered him to take me on the next morning, strip off my clothes, drive down four stakes in the ground and fasten my limbs to them; then strike me five hundred lashes for going to the prayer meeting. This was what distressed my poor companion. She thought it was more than I could bear, and that it would be the death of me. I concluded then to run away—but she thought they would catch me with the blood hounds by their taking my track. But to avoid them I thought I would ride off on one of the Deacon's mules. She thought if I did, they would sell me.

"No matter, I will try it," said I, "let the consequences be what they may. The matter can be no worse than it now is." So I tackled up the Deacon's best mule with his saddle, &c., and started that night and went off eight or ten miles from home. But I found the mule to be rather troublesome, and was like to betray me by braying, especially when he would see cattle, horses, or any thing of the kind in the woods.

The second night from home I camped in a cane break down in the Red River swamp not a great way off from the road, perhaps not twenty rods, exposed to wild ferocious beasts which were numerous in that section of country. On that night about the middle of the night the mule heard the sound of horses feet on the road, and he commenced stamping and trying to break away. As the horses seemed to come nearer, the mule commenced trying to bray, and it was all that I could do to prevent him from making a loud bray there in the woods, which would have betrayed me.

I supposed that it was the overseer out with the dogs looking for me, and I found afterwards that I was not mistaken. As soon as the people had passed by, I mounted the mule and took him home to prevent his betraying me. When I got near by home I stripped off the tackling and turned the mule loose. I then slipt up to the cabin wherein my wife laid and found her awake, much distressed about me. She informed me that they were then out looking for me, and that the Deacon was bent on flogging me nearly to death, and then selling me off from my family. This was truly heart-rending to my poor wife; the thought of our being torn apart in a strange land after having been sold away from all her friends and relations, was more than she could bear.

The Deacon had declared that I should not only suffer for the crime of attending a prayer meeting without his permission, and for running away, but for the awful crime of stealing a jackass, which was death by the law when committed by a negro.

But I well knew that I was regarded as property, and so was the ass; and I thought if one piece of property took off another, there could be no law violated in the act; no more sin committed in this than if one jackass had rode off another.

But after consultation with my wife I concluded to take her and my little daughter with me and they would be guilty of the same crime that I was, so far as running away was concerned; and if the Deacon sold one he might sell us all, and perhaps to the same person.

So we started off with our child that night, and made our way down to the Red River swamps among the buzzing insects and wild beasts of the forest. We wandered about in the wilderness for eight or ten days before we were apprehended, striving to make our way from slavery; but it was all in vain. Our food was parched corn, with wild fruit such as pawpaws, percimmons, grapes, &c. We did at one time chance to find a sweet potato patch where we got a few potatoes; but most of the time, while we were out, we were lost. We wanted to cross the Red River but could find no conveyance to cross in.

I recollect one day of finding a crooked tree which bent over the river and over one fork of the river, where it was divided by an island. I should think that the tree was at least twenty feet from the surface of the water. I picked up my little child, and my wife followed me, saying, "if we perish let us all perish together in the stream." We succeeded in crossing over. I often look back to that dangerous event even now with astonishment, and wonder how I could have run such a risk. What would induce me to run the same risk now? What could induce me now to leave home and friends and go to the wild forest and lay out on the cold ground night after night without covering, and live on parched corn?

What would induce me to take my family and go into the Red River swamps of Louisiana among the snakes and alligators, with all the liabilities of being destroyed by them, hunted down with blood hounds, or lay myself liable to be shot down like the wild beasts of the forest? Nothing I say, nothing but the strongest love of liberty, humanity, and justice to myself and family, would induce me to run such a risk again.

When we crossed over on the tree we supposed that we had crossed over the main body of the river, but we had not proceeded far on our journey before we found that we were on an Island surrounded by water on either side. We made our bed that night in a pile of dry leaves which had fallen from off the trees. We were much rest-broken, wearied from hunger and travelling through briers, swamps and cane brakes—consequently we soon feel asleep after lying down. About the dead hour of the night I was aroused by the awful howling of a gang of blood-thirsty wolves, which had found us out and surrounded us as their prey, there in the dark wilderness many miles from any house or settlement.

My dear little child was so dreadfully alarmed that she screamed loudly with fear—my wife trembling like a leaf on a tree, at the thought of being devoured there in the wilderness by ferocious wolves.

The wolves kept howling, and were near enough for us to see their glaring eyes, and hear their chattering teeth. I then thought that the hour of death for us was at hand; that we should not live to see the light of another day; for there was no way for our escape. My little family were looking up to me for protection, but I could afford them none. And while I was offering up my prayers to that God who never forsakes those in the hour of danger who trust in him, I thought of Deacon Whitfield; I thought of his profession, and doubted his piety. I thought of his hand-cuffs, of his whips, of his chains, of his stocks, of his thumb-screws, of his slave driver and overseer, and of his religion; I also thought of his opposition to prayer meetings, and of his five hundred lashes promised me for attending a prayer meeting. I thought of God, I thought of the devil, I thought of hell; and I thought of heaven, and wondered whether I should ever see the Deacon there. And I calculated that if heaven was made up of such Deacons, or such persons, it could not be filled with love to all mankind, and with glory and eternal happiness, as we know it is from the truth of the Bible.

The reader may perhaps think me tedious on this topic, but indeed it is one of so much interest to me, that I find myself entirely unable to describe what my own feelings were at that time. I was so much excited by the fierce howling of the savage wolves, and the frightful screams of my little family, that I thought of the future; I thought of the past; I thought the time of my departure had come at last.

My impression is, that all these thoughts and thousands of others, flashed through my mind, while I was surrounded by these wolves. But it seemed to be the will of a merciful providence, that our lives should be spared, and that we should not be destroyed by them.

I had no weapon of defence but a long bowie knife which I had slipped from the Deacon. It was a very splendid blade, about two feet in length, and about two inches in width. This used to be a part of his armor of defence while walking about the plantation among his slaves.

The plan which I took to expel the wolves was a very dangerous one, but it proved effectual. While they were advancing to me, prancing and accumulating in number, apparently of all sizes and grades, who had come to the feast, I thought just at this time, that there was no alternative left but for me to make a charge with my bowie knife. I well knew from the action of the wolves, that if I made no farther resistance, they would soon destroy us, and if I made a break at them, the matter could be no worse. I thought if I must die, I would die striving to protect my little family from destruction, die striving to escape from slavery. My wife took a club in one hand, and her child in the other, while I rushed forth with my bowie knife in hand, to fight off the savage wolves. I made one desperate charge at them, and at the same time making a loud yell at the top of my voice, that caused them to retreat and scatter, which was equivalent to a victory on our part. Our prayers were answered, and our lives spared through the night. We slept no more that night, and the next morning there were no wolves to be seen or heard, and we resolved not to stay on that island another night.

We travelled up and down the river side trying to find a place where we could cross. Finally we found a lot of drift wood clogged together, extending across the stream at a narrow place in the river, upon which we crossed over. But we had not yet surmounted our greatest difficulty. We had to meet one which was far more formidable than the first. Not many days after I had to face the Deacon.

We had been wandering about through the cane brakes, bushes, and briers, for several days, when we heard the yelping of blood hounds, a great way off, but they seemed to come nearer and nearer to us. We thought after awhile that they must be on our track; we listened attentively at the approach. We knew it was no use for us to undertake to escape from them, and as they drew nigh, we heard the voice of a man hissing on the dogs.

After awhile we saw the hounds coming in full speed on our track, and the soul drivers close after them on horse back, yelling like tigers, as they came in sight. The shrill yelling of the savage blood hounds as they drew nigh made the woods echo.

The first impulse was to run to escape the approaching danger of ferocious dogs, and blood-thirsty slave hunters, who were so rapidly approaching me with loaded muskets and bowie knives, with a determination to kill or capture me and my family. I started to run with my little daughter in my arms, but stumbled and fell down and scratched the arm of Little Frances with a brier, so that it bled very much; but the dear child never cried, for she seemed to know the danger to which we were exposed.

But we soon found that it was no use for us to run. The dogs were soon at our heels, and we were compelled to stop, or be torn to pieces by them. By this time, the soul drivers came charging up on their horses, commanding us to stand still or they would shoot us down.

Of course I surrendered up for the sake of my family. The most abusive terms to be found in the English language were poured forth on us with bitter oaths. They tied my hands behind me, and drove us home before them, to suffer the penalty of a slaveholder's broken law.

As we drew nigh the plantation my heart grew faint. I was aware that we should have to suffer almost death for running off. I was filled with dreadful apprehensions at the thought of meeting a professed follower of Christ, whom I knew to be a hypocrite! No tongue, no pen can ever describe what my feelings were at that time.

■ CONSIDERATIONS OF MEANING AND METHOD

1. Bibb explains, quite logically: "I should not only suffer for the crime of attending a prayer meeting . . . but for the awful crime of stealing a jackass. . . . But I well knew that I was regarded as property, and so was the ass; and I thought if one piece of property took off another, there could be no law violated in the act; no more sin committed in this than if one jackass had rode off another." Bearing in mind Bibb's audience of abolitionists and his purpose in writing, describe the tone of this passage. Which of Bibb's specific word choices and phrasings convey his tone most strongly?

2. Point out the specific places in the narrative where Bibb steps back from the story and offers reflection or commentary. His

story is certainly exciting and compelling enough to make vivid reading without commentary. Why does he include it?

3. How does Bibb characterize the Deacon? What makes the Deacon perhaps even more contemptible than the "average" slave owner?

4. How does Bibb convey his feelings about the wilderness? What words and images, specifically, does he use to describe it?

■ **POSSIBILITIES FOR WRITING**

1. In a short essay, describe a frightening chase. In your first draft, write for yourself, simply recording the event in as vivid detail as you can without attempting to introduce your essay to a reader in any way or to reflect upon your experience. When you are finished, read back over what you've written and reflect upon what it was that made this event, whether it was reality or a dream, so frightening to you. In your revision of the essay, provide a context for the narrative by adding an opening and closing paragraph or paragraphs. Revise the narrative itself with its effect on your reader in mind, emphasizing the elements which best contribute to the point you want to make in relating it.

2. Our experience of wilderness is largely determined by the circumstances of our lives. Describe an incident in which a particular set of circumstances caused you to be fearful in a natural setting or in a wild place. How did this experience affect you after the event was over? Did your fear pass, or did it sink in, and does it affect you still? Were there other emotional dimensions to your response besides fear?

■ **JOHN MUIR**
A Wind-Storm in the Forests

See the headnote for John Muir's writing in Chapter 1 (page 28) for biographical information.

John Muir was more than a careful observer of nature; he was a participant in wilderness adventure. His accounts in Chapter 1 describe his experience of nearly getting swept from the face of Yosemite Falls after crawling out on a ledge in the middle of the night. This account describes his experience riding the top of a tree during a wind-storm in California's Sierra range. In this essay, from The Mountains of California *(1894), Muir conveys both information about, and his appreciation of, the mountain forests of California, but it is his wild ride that makes us wonder at this man and his drive for connection with things wild and beautiful in nature.*

The mountain winds, like the dew and rain, sunshine and snow, are measured and bestowed with love on the forests to develop their strength and beauty. However restricted the scope of other forest influences, that of the winds is universal. The snow bends and trims the upper forests every winter, the lightning strikes a single tree here and there, while avalanches mow down thousands at a swoop as a gardener trims out a bed of flowers. But the winds go to every tree, fingering every leaf and branch and furrowed bole; not one is forgotten; the Mountain Pine towering with outstretched arms on the rugged buttresses of the icy peaks, the lowliest and most retiring tenant of the dells; they seek and find them all, caressing them tenderly, bending them in lusty exercise, stimulating their growth, plucking off a leaf or limb as required, or removing an entire tree or grove, now whispering and cooing through the branches like a sleepy child, now roaring like the ocean; the winds blessing the forests, the forests the winds, with ineffable beauty and harmony as the sure result.

After one has seen pines six feet in diameter bending like grasses before a mountain gale, and ever and anon some giant falling with a crash that shakes the hills, it seems astonishing that any, save the lowest thickset trees, could ever have found a period sufficiently stormless to establish themselves; or, once established, that they should not, sooner or later, have been blown down. But when the storm is over, and we behold the same forests tranquil again, towering fresh and unscathed in erect majesty, and consider what centuries of storms have fallen upon them since they were first planted,—hail, to break the tender seedlings; lightning, to scorch and shatter; snow, winds, and avalanches, to crush and overwhelm,—while the manifest result of all this wild storm-culture is the glorious perfection we behold; then faith in Nature's forestry is established, and we cease to deplore the violence of her most destructive gales, or of any other storm-implement whatsoever.

There are two trees in the Sierra forests that are never blown down, so long as they continue in sound health. These are the Juniper and the Dwarf Pine of the summit peaks. Their stiff, crooked roots grip the storm-beaten ledges like eagles' claws, while their lithe, cordlike branches bend round compliantly, offering but slight holds for winds, however violent. The other alpine conifers—the Needle Pine, Mountain Pine, Two-leaved Pine, and Hemlock Spruce—are never thinned out by this agent to any destructive extent, on account of their admirable toughness and the closeness of their growth. In general the same is true of the giants of the lower zones. The kingly Sugar Pine, towering aloft to a height of more than 200 feet, offers a fine mark to storm-winds; but it is not densely foliaged, and its long, horizontal arms swing round compliantly in the blast, like tresses of green, fluent algae in a brook; while the Silver Firs in most places keep their ranks well together in united strength. The Yellow or Silver Pine is more frequently overturned than any other tree on the Sierra, because its leaves and branches form a larger mass in proportion to its height, while in many places it is planted sparsely, leaving open lanes through which storms may enter with full force. Furthermore, because it is distributed along the lower portion of the range, which was the first to be left bare on the breaking up of the ice-sheet at the close of the glacial winter, the soil it is growing upon has been longer exposed to post-glacial weathering, and consequently is in a more crumbling, decayed condition than the fresher soils farther up the range, and therefore offers a less secure anchorage for the roots.

While exploring the forest zones of Mount Shasta, I discovered the path of a hurricane strewn with thousands of pines of this species. Great and small had been uprooted or wrenched off by sheer force, making a clean gap, like that made by a snow avalanche. But hurricanes capable of doing this class of work are rare in the Sierra, and when we have explored the forests from one extremity of the range to the other, we are compelled to believe that they are the most beautiful on the face of the earth, however we may regard the agents that have made them so.

There is always something deeply exciting, not only in the sounds of winds in the woods, which exert more or less influence over every mind, but in their varied waterlike flow as manifested by the movements of the trees, especially those of the conifers. By no other trees are they rendered so extensively and impressively visible, not even by the lordly tropic palms or tree-ferns responsive to the gentlest breeze. The waving of a forest of the giant Sequoias is indescribably impressive and sublime, but the pines seem to me the best interpreters of winds. They are mighty waving goldenrods, ever in tune, singing and writing wind-music all their long century lives. Little, however, of this noble tree-waving and tree-music will you see or hear in the strictly alpine portion of the forests. The burly Juniper, whose girth sometimes more than equals its height, is about as rigid as the rocks on which it grows. The slender lash-like sprays of the Dwarf Pine stream out in wavering ripples, but the tallest and slenderest are far too unyielding to wave even in the heaviest gales. They only shake in quick, short vibrations. The Hemlock Spruce, however, and the Mountain Pine, and some of the tallest thickets of the Two-leaved species bow in storms with considerable scope and gracefulness. But it is only in the lower and middle zones that the meeting of winds and woods is to be seen in all its grandeur.

One of the most beautiful and exhilarating storms I ever enjoyed in the Sierra occurred in December, 1874, when I happened to be exploring one of the tributary valleys of the Yuba River. The sky and the ground and the trees had been thoroughly rain-washed and were dry again. The day was intensely pure, one of those incomparable bits of California winter, warm and balmy and full of white sparkling sunshine, redolent of all the purest influences of the spring, and at the same time enlivened with one of the most bracing wind-storms conceivable. Instead of camping out, as I usually do, I then chanced to be stopping at the house of a friend. But when the storm began to sound, I lost no time in pushing out into the woods to enjoy it. For on such occasions Nature has always something rare to show us, and the danger to life and limb is hardly greater than one would experience crouching deprecatingly beneath a roof.

It was still early morning when I found myself fairly adrift. Delicious sunshine came pouring over the hills, lighting the tops of the pines, and setting free a stream of summery fragrance that contrasted strangely with the wild tones of the storm. The air was mottled with pine-tassels and bright green plumes, that went flashing past in the sunlight like birds pursued. But there was not the slightest dustiness, nothing less pure than leaves, and ripe pollen, and flecks of withered bracken and moss. I heard trees falling for hours at the rate of one every two or three minutes; some uprooted, partly on account of the loose, water-soaked condition of the ground; others broken straight across, where some weakness caused by fire had determined the spot. The gestures of the various trees made a delightful study. Young Sugar Pines, light and feathery as squirrel-tails, were bowing almost to the ground; while the grand old patriarchs, whose massive boles had been tried in a hundred storms, waved solemnly above them, their long, arching branches streaming fluently on the gale, and every needle thrilling and ringing and shedding off keen lances of light like a diamond. The Douglas Spruces, with long sprays drawn out in level tresses, and needles massed in a gray, shimmery glow, presented a most striking appearance as they stood in bold relief along the hill-tops. The madroños in the dells, with their red bark and large glossy leaves tilted every way, reflected the sunshine in throbbing spangles like those one so often sees on the rippled surface of a glacier lake. But the Silver Pines were now the most impressively beautiful of all. Colossal spires 200 feet in height waved like supple goldenrods chanting and bowing low as if in worship, while the whole mass of their long, tremulous foliage was kindled into one continuous blaze of white sun-fire. The force of the gale was such that the most stead-fast monarch of them all rocked down to its roots with a motion plainly perceptible when one leaned against it. Nature was holding high festival, and every fiber of the most rigid giants thrilled with glad excitement.

I drifted on through the midst of this passionate music and mo-tion, across many a glen, from ridge to ridge, often halting in the lee of a rock for shelter, or to gaze and listen. Even when the grand an-them had swelled to its highest pitch, I could distinctly hear the vary-ing tones of individual trees,—Spruce, and Fir, and Pine, and leafless Oak,—and even the infinitely gentle rustle of the withered grasses at my feet. Each was expressing itself in its own way,—singing its own song, and making its own peculiar gestures,—manifesting a richness of variety to be found in no other forest I have yet seen. The conifer-ous woods of Canada, and the Carolinas, and Florida, are made up of trees that resemble one another about as nearly as blades of grass, and grow close together in much the same way. Coniferous trees, in gen-eral, seldom possess individual character, such as is manifest among Oaks and Elms. But the California forests are made up of a greater number of distinct species than any other in the world. And in them we find, not only a marked differentiation into special groups, but also a marked individuality in almost every tree, giving rise to storm effects indescribably glorious.

Toward midday, after a long, tingling scramble through copses of hazel and ceanothus, I gained the summit of the highest ridge in the neighborhood; and then it occurred to me that it would be a fine thing to climb one of the trees to obtain a wider outlook and get my ear close to the Aeolian music of its topmost needles. But under the circumstances the choice of a tree was a serious matter. One whose instep was not very strong seemed in danger of being blown down, or of being struck by others in case they should fall; another was branchless to a considerable height above the ground, and at the same time too large to be grasped with arms and legs in climbing; while others were not favorably situated for clear views. After cautiously casting about, I made choice of the tallest of a group of Douglas Spruces that were growing close together like a tuft of grass, no one of which seemed likely to fall unless all the rest fell with it. Though comparatively young, they were about 100 feet high, and their lithe, brushy tops were rocking and swirling in wild ecstasy. Being accustomed to climb trees in making botanical studies, I experienced no difficulty in reaching the top of this one, and never before did I enjoy so noble an exhilaration of motion. The slender tops fairly flapped and swished in the passionate torrent, bending and swirling backward and forward, round and round, tracing indescribable combinations of vertical and horizontal curves, while I clung with muscles firm braced, like a bobolink on a reed.

In its widest sweeps my tree-top described an arc of from twenty to thirty degrees, but I felt sure of its elastic temper, having seen others of the same species still more severely tried—bent almost to the ground indeed, in heavy snows—without breaking a fiber. I was therefore safe, and free to take the wind into my pulses and enjoy the excited forest from my superb outlook. The view from here must be extremely beautiful in any weather. Now my eye roved over the piney hills and dales as over fields of waving grain, and felt the light running in ripples and broad swelling undulations across the valleys from ridge to ridge, as the shining foliage was stirred by corresponding waves of air. Oftentimes these waves of reflected light would break up suddenly into a kind of beaten foam, and again, after chasing one another in regular order, they would seem to bend forward in concentric curves, and disappear on some hillside, like sea-waves on a shelving shore. The quantity of light reflected from the bent needles was so great as to make whole groves appear as if covered with snow, while the black shadows beneath the trees greatly enhanced the effect of the silvery splendor.

Excepting only the shadows there was nothing somber in all this wild sea of pines. On the contrary, notwithstanding this was the winter season, the colors were remarkably beautiful. The shafts of the pine and libocedrus were brown and purple, and most of the foliage was well tinged with yellow; the laurel groves, with the pale undersides of their leaves turned upward, made masses of gray; and then there was many a dash of chocolate color from clumps of manzanita, and jet of vivid crimson from the bark of the madroños, while the ground on the hillsides, appearing here and there through openings between the groves, displayed masses of pale purple and brown.

The sounds of the storm corresponded gloriously with this wild exuberance of light and motion. The profound bass of the naked branches and boles booming like waterfalls; the quick, tense vibrations of the pine-needles, now rising to a shrill, whistling hiss, now falling to a silky murmur; the rustling of laurel groves in the dells, and the keen metallic click of leaf on leaf—all this was heard in easy analysis when the attention was calmly bent.

The varied gestures of the multitude were seen to fine advantage, so that one could recognize the different species at a distance of several miles by this means alone, as well as by their forms and colors, and the way they reflected the light. All seemed strong and comfortable, as if really enjoying the storm, while responding to its most enthusiastic greetings. We hear much nowadays concerning the universal struggle for existence, but no struggle in the common meaning of the word was manifest here; no recognition of danger by any tree; no deprecation; but rather an invincible gladness as remote from exultation as from fear.

I kept my lofty perch for hours, frequently closing my eyes to enjoy the music by itself, or to feast quietly on the delicious fragrance that was streaming past. The fragrance of the woods was less marked than that produced during warm rain, when so many balsamic buds and leaves are steeped like tea; but, from the chafing of resiny branches against each other, and the incessant attrition of myriads of needles, the gale was spiced to a very tonic degree. And besides the fragrance from these local sources there were traces of scents brought from afar. For this wind came first from the sea, rubbing against its fresh, briny waves, then distilled through the redwoods, threading rich ferny gulches, and spreading itself in broad undulating currents over many a flower-enameled ridge of the coast mountains, then across the golden plains, up the purple foot-hills, and into these piny woods with the varied incense gathered by the way.

Winds are advertisements of all they touch, however much or little we may be able to read them; telling their wanderings even by their scents alone. Mariners detect the flowery perfume of land-winds far at sea, and sea-winds carry the fragrance of dulse and tangle far inland, where it is quickly recognized, though mingled with the scents of a thousand landflowers. As an illustration of this, I may tell here that I breathed sea-air on the Firth of Forth, in Scotland, while a boy;

then was taken to Wisconsin, where I remained nineteen years; then, without in all this time having breathed one breath of the sea, I walked quietly, alone, from the middle of the Mississippi Valley to the Gulf of Mexico, on a botanical excursion, and while in Florida, far from the coast, my attention wholly bent on the splendid tropical vegetation about me, I suddenly recognized a sea-breeze, as it came sifting through the palmettos and blooming vine-tangles, which at once awakened and set free a thousand dormant associations, and made me a boy again in Scotland, as if all the intervening years had been annihilated.

Most people like to look at mountain rivers, and bear them in mind; but few care to look at the winds, though far more beautiful and sublime, and though they become at times about as visible as flowing water. When the north winds in winter are making upward sweeps over the curving summits of the High Sierra, the fact is sometimes published with flying snow-banners a mile long. Those portions of the winds thus embodied can scarce be wholly invisible, even to the darkest imagination. And when we look around over an agitated forest, we may see something of the wind that stirs it, by its effects upon the trees. Yonder it descends in a rush of water-like ripples, and sweeps over the bending pines from hill to hill. Nearer, we see detached plumes and leaves, now speeding by on level currents, now whirling in eddies, or, escaping over the edges of the whirls, soaring aloft on grand, upswelling domes of air, or tossing on flame-like crests. Smooth, deep currents, cascades, falls, and swirling eddies, sing around every tree and leaf, and over all the varied topography of the region with telling changes of form, like mountain rivers conforming to the features of their channels.

After tracing the Sierra streams from their fountains to the plains, marking where they bloom white in falls, glide in crystal plumes, surge gray and foam-filled in boulder-choked gorges, and slip through the woods in long, tranquil reaches—after thus learning their language and forms in detail, we may at length hear them chanting all together in one grand anthem, and comprehend them all in clear inner vision, covering the range like lace. But even this spectacle is far less sublime and not a whit more substantial than what we may behold of these storm-streams of air in the mountain woods.

We all travel the milky way together, trees and men; but it never occurred to me until this stormday, while swinging in the wind, that trees are travelers, in the ordinary sense. They make many journeys, not extensive ones, it is true; but our own little journeys, away and back again, are only little more than tree-wavings—many of them not so much.

When the storm began to abate, I dismounted and sauntered down through the calming woods. The storm-tones died away, and, turning toward the east, I beheld the countless hosts of the forests hushed and tranquil, towering above one another on the slopes of the hills like a devout audience. The setting sun filled them with amber light, and seemed to say, while they listened, "My peace I give unto you."

As I gazed on the impressive scene, all the so-called ruin of the storm was forgotten, and never before did these noble woods appear so fresh, so joyous, so immortal.

■ CONSIDERATION OF MEANING AND METHOD

1. How does Muir introduce his narrative in the opening paragraph of "A Wind-Storm in the Forests"? What is his main point in that paragraph? What state of mind does he want his reader to have before reading on? How does he create this state of mind through the language he uses?

2. Muir's introduction to this narrative is not limited to his opening paragraph. What else does he provide in the way of introduction? Is this information essential preparation for the narrative itself?

3. What makes Muir's description of this event vivid for the readers? Point to specific examples in the text.

4. What new and fundamental lesson does Muir take from his tree-riding adventure? Where does he express it? Is this the essay's thesis? If so, what is the advantage of placing it where he does?

5. Make a list of Muir's highest-level generalizations from "A Wind-Storm in the Forests." How does he support them? Do you think they are adequately supported?

6. Compare Bibb's and Muir's attitudes toward wilderness. Are there any similarities?

■ POSSIBILITIES FOR WRITING

1. Write a personal narrative in which you focus on one encounter with the natural world and intersperse information and/or other experiences within the main narrative in order to enrich your story. For example, if you were to write about the experience of watching a sea otter feeding (assuming that you are not an expert on sea otter behavior) you might look up something in the library about sea otters' feeding habits to supplement your experi-

ence in observing. Or if you are writing about a specific hike in the woods, you might recall other hikes as well, to add more dimension to your narration of this particular hike.

2. If you have ever put yourself knowingly in a dangerous situation, write about the incident and its outcome, as well as your motivations in doing what you did. Was the situation less or even more dangerous than it appeared? Why? Would you do it again?

■ SUE HUBBELL
Becoming Feral

Sue Hubbell (1935–) lives with eighteen million honeybees in the Ozark Mountains of Missouri. She has worked as a bookstore manager and as a librarian but has supported herself for nearly the past twenty-five years as a commercial beekeeper. Born in Kalamazoo, Michigan, Hubbell attended Swarthmore College and, for graduate study, the University of Michigan, the University of Southern California, and Drexel Institute. She has been a contributor to many magazines and newspapers, and her books include A Country Year: Living with the Questions *(1986), from which the essay "Becoming Feral" is taken, and* A Book of Bees *(1988), which is about her experience in keeping bees.*

Her farm on a hilltop in southern Missouri is the scene and subject of much of her writing. Hubbell is a careful observer of nature, its cycles and seasons, and, like many nature writers, she sees reflected in the external landscape, in natural processes, much about her own internal landscape and about human nature. In a review in the Washington Post Book World, *author Ivan Doig noted that Hubbell "watches language as sagaciously as she eyes nature, and the combination makes* A Country Year *steadily eloquent not just of her life but all life."*

Hoohoo-hoohoo . . . hoohoo-hoohooaww. My neighbor across the river is doing his barred owl imitation in hopes of rousing a turkey from the roost. It is turkey-hunting season, and at dawn the hunters are trying to outwit wild turkeys and I listen to them as I drink my coffee under the oak trees.

Hoohoo-hoohoo . . . hoohoo-hoohooawww.

GahgahGAHgah replies an imitation turkey from another direction. I know that neighbor, too. Yesterday he showed me the hand-held wooden box with which he made the noise that is supposed to sound like a turkey cock gobbling. It doesn't. After the turkey cocks are down from their roosts, the hunters, by imitating hen turkeys, try to call them close enough to shoot them. The barred owl across the river once showed me his turkey caller. He held it in his mouth and made a soft clucking noise with it.

"Now this is the really sexy one," he said, arching one eyebrow, "*Putput . . . putterputput.*"

It is past dawn now, and I imagine both men are exasperated. I have not heard one real turkey yet this morning. The hunting season is set by the calendar but the turkeys breed by the weather, and the spring has been so wet and cold that their mating has been delayed this year. In the last few mornings I have started hearing turkeys gobbling occasionally, and it will be another week or two before a wise and wary turkey cock could be fooled by a man with a caller.

There are other birds out there this morning. The indigo buntings, who will be the first birds to sing in the dawn later on, have not yet returned to the Ozarks, but I can hear cardinals and Carolina chickadees. They wintered here, but today their songs are of springtime. There are chipping sparrows above me in the oak trees and field sparrows nearby. There are warblers, too; some of their songs are familiar, and others, those of the migrators, are not. I hear one of the most beautiful of birdsongs, that of the white-throated sparrow. He is supposed to sing "Old Sam Peabody, Peabody, Peabody." This is the cadence, to be sure, but it gives no hint of the lyrical clarity and sweetness of the descending notes of his song.

I slept outdoors last night because I could not bear to go in. The cabin, which only last winter seemed cozy and inviting, has begun to seem stuffy and limiting, so I spread a piece of plastic on the ground to keep off the damp, put my sleeping bag on it and dropped off to sleep watching the stars. Tazzle likes to be near me, and with me on the ground she could press right up to my back. But Andy is a conservative dog who worries a lot, and he thought it was unsound to sleep outside where there might be snakes and beetles. He whined uneasily as I settled in, and once during the night he woke me up, nuzzling me and whimpering, begging to be allowed to go inside to his rug. I think he may be more domesticated than I am. I wonder if I am becoming feral. Wild things and wild places pull me more strongly than they did a few years ago, and domesticity, dusting and cookery interest me not at all.

Sometimes I wonder where we older women fit into the social

scheme of things once nest building has lost its charm. A generation ago Margaret Mead, who had a good enough personal answer to this question, wondered the same thing, and pointed out that in other times and other cultures we have had a role.

There are so many of us that it is tempting to think of us as a class. We are past our reproductive years. Men don't want us; they prefer younger women. It makes good biological sense for males to be attracted to females who are at an earlier point in their breeding years and who still want to build nests, and if that leaves us no longer able to lose ourselves in the pleasures and closeness of pairing, well, we have gained our Selves. We have another valuable thing, too. We have Time, or at least the awareness of it. We have lived long enough and seen enough to understand in a more than intellectual way that we will die, and so we have learned to live as though we are mortal, making our decisions with care and thought because we will not be able to make them again. Time for us will have an end; it is precious, and we have learned its value.

Yes, there are many of us, but we are all so different that I am uncomfortable with a sociobiological analysis, and I suspect that, as with Margaret Mead, the solution is a personal and individual one. Because our culture has assigned us no real role, we can make up our own. It is a good time to be a grown-up woman with individuality, strength and crotchets. We are wonderfully free. We live long. Our children are the independent adults we helped them to become, and though they may still want our love they do not need our care. Social rules are so flexible today that nothing we do is shocking. There are no political barriers to us anymore. Provided we stay healthy and can support ourselves, we can do anything, have anything and spend our talents any way that we please.

Hoohoo-hoohoo . . . hoohoo-hooaww.

The sun is up now, and it is too late for a barred owl. I know that man across the river, and I know he must be getting cross. He is probably sitting on a damp log, his feet and legs cold and cramped from keeping still. I also know the other hunter, the one with the wooden turkey caller. This week what both men want is a dead turkey.

I want a turkey too, but I want mine alive, and in a week I'll have my wish, hearing them gobbling at dawn. I want more, however. I want indigo buntings singing their couplets when I wake in the morning. I want to read *Joseph and His Brothers* again. I want oak leaves and dogwood blossoms and fireflies. I want to know how the land lies up Coon Hollow. I want Asher to find out what happens to moth-ear mites in the winter. I want to show Liddy and Brian the big rocks down in the creek hollow. I want to know much more about grand-daddy-longlegs. I want to write a novel. I want to go swimming naked in the hot sun down at the river.

That is why I have stopped sleeping inside. A house is too small, too confining. I want the whole world, and the stars too.

■ CONSIDERATIONS OF MEANING AND METHOD

1. How does Hubbell's narrative about the turkey hunters relate to her reflections about being an older woman? Why does she include these two elements in the same essay?

2. How high are the generalizations Hubbell makes about the nature of men and the nature of women? Are her generalizations about one gender higher than about the other? How does she develop and support these generalizations? Are they adequately supported? Are they convincing to you? Why or why not?

3. In what ways does Hubbell contradict the stereotyped image we tend to have of older women in our culture? Are there any ways in which you think she reinforces stereotypes?

4. How would you characterize Hubbell's tone in this essay? Point to specific examples in the text which illustrate tone.

■ POSSIBILITIES FOR WRITING

1. Write an essay, drawing upon personal experience, in which you make observations about the nature of men and women. How high can your generalizations be when you are referring to your experience alone? If you add the experiences of other people to your own in order to illustrate and support your generalizations, does this allow you to generalize more widely? If you cite outside sources, in the form of information and the observations of experts, can you generalize more widely still?

2. In an essay whose primary reader might be someone of your gender and approximate age, write about an older person of your gender who is a role model for you. In describing this person to your reader you will want to convey the qualities he or she possesses that you find admirable. You may want to include physical description, description of setting, information about this person's history, and/or narrative episodes that best illustrate these qualities.

■ **NANCY MAIRS**
On Being a Scientific Booby

*Essayist and poet Nancy Mairs has said of herself: "As a radical
feminist, pacifist, and cripple . . . [in] my writing I aim to speak the
'unspeakable,' in defiance of polite discourse, so as to expose ways
in which my personal experiences inscribe cultural values
dangerous to women and other creatures worth preserving."*

*Mairs's autobiographical essays, in particular, have been highly
acclaimed. Her collection of essays* Plaintext: Deciphering a
Woman's Life *(1986), from which "On Being a Scientific Booby" is
taken, is a triumph "of will, style, candor, thought and . . . form,"
according to reviewer Art Seidenbaum, a work of "sensitivity
tempered by toughness." Mairs suffers from multiple sclerosis as
well as depression and agoraphobia (a fear of open spaces). In*
Plaintext *and in her other collections of essays, including*
Remembering the Bone-House *(1989) and* Carnal Acts *(1990), she
has written frankly about the challenges of her personal life and
challenging social subjects, ranging from madness and suicide to
marital sex and sexism in the literary world. Mairs has also
published poems, including* In All the Rooms of the Yellow House
(1984), and has written "Hers" columns in the New York Times
Magazine.

*Born in Long Beach, California in 1943, Mairs currently lives
with her family in Tucson, Arizona. She attended Wheaton College
as an undergraduate and earned graduate degrees at the
University of Arizona. She has worked as a technical writer and
editor, and as a high school and college teacher. In "On Being a
Scientific Booby," Mairs recalls her "failure" to do well in science
in college, attributing it to the perception of her biology teacher
that she was good at something else—writing—and so could not be
good at science. In her daughter she sees someone who has been encouraged to believe that she can do both, and all.*

My daughter is dissecting a chicken. Her first. Her father, whose
job this usually is, has been derelict in his duties, and my hands are
now too weak to dissect much more than a zucchini. If she wants
dinner (and she does), she will make this pale, flabby carcass into
eight pieces I can fit into the skillet. I act as coach. To encourage her,
I tell her that her great-great-grandfather was a butcher. This is true,
not something I have made up to con her into doing a nasty job.

Now that she's gotten going, she is having a wonderful time. She has made the chicken crow and flap and dance all over the cutting board, and now it lies quiet under her short, strong fingers as she slices the length of its breastbone. She pries back the ribs and peers into the cavity. "Oh, look at its mesenteries!" she cries. I tell her I thought mesentery was something you got from drinking the water in Mexico. She pokes at some filmy white webs. Mesenteries, she informs me, are the membranes that hold the chicken's organs in place. My organs too. She flips the chicken over and begins to cut along its spine. As her fingers search out joints and the knife severs wing from breast, leg from thigh, she gives me a lesson in the comparative anatomy of this chicken and the frog she and her friend Emily have recently dissected at school.

I am charmed by her enthusiasm and self-assurance. Since she was quite small, she has talked of becoming a veterinarian, and now that she is approaching adulthood, her purpose is growing firmer. During this, her junior year in a special high school, she is taking a college-level introductory course in biology. I took much the same course when I was a freshman in college. But if I entered that course with Anne's self-confidence, and I may very well have done so, I certainly had none of it by the time I wrote the last word of my final examination in my blue book and turned it in the following spring. As the result of Miss White and the quadrat report, I am daunted to the point of dysfunction by the notion of thinking or writing "scientifically."

That woman—damn that woman!—turned me into a scientific cripple, and did so in the name of science at a prestigious women's college that promised to school me in the liberal arts that I might "have life and have it abundantly." And really, I have had it abundantly, so I suppose I oughtn't to complain if it's been a little short in *Paramecia* and *Amanita phalloides* and *Drosophila melanogaster*, whose eyes I have never seen.

Still, Miss White should not have been allowed to teach freshman biology because she had a fatal idiosyncracy (fatal, that is, to the courage of students, not to herself, though I believe she is dead now of some unrelated cause): She could not bear a well-written report. One could be either a writer or a scientist but not both, she told me one November afternoon, the grey light from a tall window sinking into the grain of the dark woodwork in her cramped office in the old Science Building, her fingers flicking the sheets of my latest lab write-up. She was washing her hands of me, I could tell by the weariness of her tone. She didn't even try to make me a scientist. For that matter, she didn't even point to a spot where I'd gone wrong and show me what she wanted instead. She simply wrinkled her nose at the odor of my writing, handed me the sheets, and sent me away. We never had another conference. At the end of the semester, I wrote my quadrat report, and Miss White failed it. She allowed me to rewrite it. I wrote it again, and she failed it again. Neither of us went for a third try.

All the same, I liked my quadrat, which was a twenty-by-twenty plot in the College Woods behind the Library. Mine was drab compared to some others: Pam Weprin's, I remember, had a brook running through it, in which she discovered goldfish. It turned out that her magical discovery had a drab explanation: In a heavy rain the water from Peacock Pond backed up and spilled its resident carp into the brook. Even so, her quadrat briefly held an excitement mine never did. Mine was, in fact, as familiar as a living room, since I had spent large portions of my youth tramping another such woods sixty miles north. The lichen grew on the north side of the trees. In the rain the humus turned black and rank. Afterwards, a fallen log across one corner would sprout ears of tough, pale fungus.

Each freshman biology student received a quadrat. There were enough of us that we had to double up, but I never met my quadrat-mate or even knew her name. It occurs to me now that I ought to have found out, ought to have asked her what she got on her quadrat report, but I was new to failure and knew no ways to profit from it. I simply did as I was told—visited my quadrat to observe its progress through the seasons and wrote up my observations—and then discovered that I had somehow seen and spoken wrong. I wish now that I had kept the report. I wonder exactly what I said in it. Probably something about ears of fungus. Good God.

With a D+ for the first semester I continued, perversely, to like biology, but I also feared it more and more. Not the discipline itself. I pinned and opened a long earthworm, marveling at the delicately tinted organs. I dissected a beef heart, carefully, so as not to spoil it for stuffing and roasting at the biology department's annual beef-heart feast. For weeks I explored the interior of my rat, which I had opened neatly, like the shutters over a window. He was a homely thing, stiff, his fur yellow and matted from formaldehyde, and because he was male, not very interesting. Several students got pregnant females, and I envied them the intricate organs, the chains of bluish-pink fetuses. At the end of each lab, I would reluctantly close the shutters, swaddle my rat in his plastic bag, and slip him back into the crock.

No, biology itself held more fascination and delight than fear. But with each report I grew more terrified of my own insidious poetic nature, which Miss White sniffed out in the simplest statement about planaria or left ventricles. Years later, when I became a technical editor and made my living translating the garbled outbursts of scientists, I learned that I had done nothing much wrong. My understanding was limited, to be sure, but Miss White would have forgiven me ignorance, even stupidity I think, if I had sufficiently muddled the language. As it was, I finished biology with a C–, and lucky I was to get it, since the next year the college raised the passing grade from C– to C. I have always thought, indeed, that the biology department awarded me a passing grade simply so that they wouldn't have to deal with me another year.

And they didn't. Nor did anyone else. I never took another science course, although I surprised myself long afterward by becoming, perforce and precipitously, a competent amateur herpetologist. My husband arrived home one afternoon with a shoebox containing a young bull snake, or gopher snake as this desert variety is called, which he had bought for a quarter from some of his students at a school for emotionally disturbed boys so that they wouldn't try to find out how long a snake keeps wriggling without its head. This was Ferdinand, who was followed by two more bull snakes, Squeeze and Beowulf, and by a checkered garter snake named Winslow J. Tweed, a black racer named Jesse Owens, a Yuma king snake named Hrothgar, and numerous nameless and short-lived blind snakes, tiny and translucent, brought to us by our cats Freya, Burton Rustle, and Vanessa Bell. I grew so knowledgeable that when my baby boa constrictor, Crictor, contracted a respiratory ailment, I found that I was more capable of caring for him than were any of the veterinarians in the city. In fact, I learned, veterinarians do not do snakes; I could find only one to give Crictor the shot of a broad-spectrum antibiotic he needed.

So I do do snakes. I have read scientific treatises on them. I know that the Latin name for the timber rattlesnake is *Crotalus horridus horridus.* I know that Australia has more varieties of venomous snakes than any other continent, among them the lethal sea snakes and the willfully aggressive tiger snake. I know how long one is likely to live after being bitten by a mamba (not long). I read the treatises; but I don't, of course, write them. Although as a technical editor I grew proficient at unraveling snarls in the writing of scientists, I have never, since Miss White, attempted scientific experimentation or utterance.

Aside from my venture into herpetology, I remain a scientific booby. I mind my stupidity. I feel diminished by it. And I know now that it is unnecessary, the consequence of whatever quirk of fate brought me into Miss White's laboratory instead of Miss Chidsey's or Dr. McCoy's. Miss White, who once represented the whole of scientific endeavor to me, was merely a woman with a hobbyhorse. I see through her. Twenty years later, I am now cynical enough to write a quadrat report badly enough to pass her scrutiny, whereas when I had just turned seventeen I didn't even know that cynicism was an option—knowledge that comes, I suppose, from having life abundantly. I've learned, too, that Miss White's bias, though unusually strong, was not peculiar to herself but arose from a cultural rift between the humanities and the sciences resulting in the assumption that scientists will naturally write badly, that they are, in fact, rhetorical boobies. Today I teach technical writing. My students come to me terrified of the word-world from which they feel debarred, and I teach them to breach the boundaries in a few places, to step with bravado at least a little way inside. Linguistic courage is the gift I can give them.

In return, they give me gifts that I delight in—explanations of vortex centrifuges, evaluations of copper-smelting processes, plans for extracting gums from paloverde beans. These help me compensate for my deficiencies, as do the works of the popularizers of science. Carl Sagan. Loren Eiseley. Lewis Thomas and his reverential reflections subtitled *Notes of a Biology Watcher*. Stephen Jay Gould, James Burke and Jacob Bronowski. Pierre Teilhard de Chardin. John McPhee, who has made me love rocks. Isaac Asimov. Elaine Morgan. I watch television too. *Nova. Odyssey. The Undersea World of Jacques Cousteau. The Body in Question.* But always I am aware that I am having translated for me the concepts of worlds I will never now explore for myself. I stand with my toes on the boundaries, peering, listening.

Anne has done a valiant job with the chicken. She's had a little trouble keeping its pajamas on, and one of the thighs has a peculiar trapezoidal shape, but she's reduced it to a workable condition. I brown it in butter and olive oil. I press in several cloves of garlic and then splash in some white wine. As I work, I think of the worlds Anne is going to explore. Some of them are listed in the college catalogues she's begun to collect: "Genetics, Energetics, and Evolution"; "Histology of Animals"; "Vertebrate Endocrinology"; "Electron Microscopy"; "Organic Synthesis"; "Animal Morphogenesis."

Anne can write. No one has yet told her that she can be a scientist or a writer but not both, and I trust that no one ever will. The complicated world can ill afford such lies to its children. As she plunges from my view into the thickets of calculus, embryology, and chemical thermodynamics, I will wait here for her to send me back messages. I love messages.

■ CONSIDERATIONS OF MEANING AND METHOD

1. What is it that Miss White resented in "a well-written report"? What do you think Miss White fears is being compromised in "a well-written report"?

2. Mairs writes, "I've learned . . . that Miss White's bias, though unusually strong, was not peculiar to herself but arose from a cultural rift between the humanities and the sciences resulting in the assumption that scientists will naturally write badly, that they are, in fact, rhetorical boobies." This is probably her highest generalization in the essay. How does she support it? Do you find it credible?

3. Is it your experience that girls and boys or women and men are treated differently in science education?

4. In her closing paragraph, Mairs writes, "No one has yet told [Anne] that she can be a scientist or a writer but not both, and I trust that no one ever will. The complicated world can ill afford such lies to its children." What does she mean?

5. Are you offended at Mairs's use of the word "cripple" in paragraph 4, or in her statement quoted in the headnote? Why or why not?

■ POSSIBILITIES FOR WRITING

1. In an essay for your peers, explain what in your experience supports or refutes Mairs's perception of "a . . . rift between the humanities and the sciences." Is your own experience more aligned with that of Mairs or with that of her daughter?

■ **DAVID QUAMMEN**
The Face of a Spider

A writer of remarkable versatility, essayist and fiction writer David Quammen is not a professional scientist, although much of his most noted writing is on scientific subjects, specifically subjects in nature. His natural history essays have been praised for their scientific accuracy and their intelligence, as well as their "funky

New Journalistic" style, as reviewer James Kaufmann termed it, which have made them accessible and appealing to a wide readership. In fact, Quammen is a journalist, the author of a popular monthly column, "Natural Acts," in Outside *magazine, where the following essay, "The Face of a Spider," first appeared. Although Quammen is not a professional scientist, he is, says critic Bil Gilbert, "a man of scientific curiosity as well as a writer who does not need nor is inclined to substitute pious . . . clichés for real words or thoughts."*

Quammen's natural history writings include Natural Acts: A Sidelong View of Science and Nature *(1985), in which "The Face of a Spider" was collected along with other of his writings for* Outside *magazine, and* The Flight of the Iguana: A Sidelong View of Science and Nature *(1988). His earlier work includes two well-received novels,* To Walk a Line *(1970), published when he was only 22, and the political thriller* The Zolta Configuration *(1983). With his most recent novel,* The Soul of Viktor Tronko *(1987), Quammen "has leaped to the head of the pack of American thriller writers," asserted reviewer Alan Cheuse.*

David Quammen was born in 1948 in Cincinnati, Ohio. He earned his B.A. from Yale University (where he was a Rhodes Scholar) and his B.Litt. from Oxford University, England. He currently lives and writes in Montana.

One evening a few years ago I walked back into my office after dinner and found roughly a hundred black widow spiders frolicking on my desk. I am not speaking metaphorically and I am not making this up: a hundred black widows. It was a vision of ghastly, breathtaking beauty, and it brought on me a wave of nausea. It also brought on a small moral crisis—one that I dealt with briskly, maybe rashly, in the dizziness of the moment, and that I've been turning back over in my mind ever since. I won't say I'm *haunted* by those hundred black widows, but I do remember them vividly. To me, they stand for something. They stand, in their small synecdochical way, for a large and important question.

The question is, How should a human behave toward the members of other living species?

A hundred black widows probably sounds like a lot. It is—even for Tucson, Arizona, where I was living then, a habitat in which black widows breed like rabbits and prosper like cockroaches, the females of the species growing plump as huckleberries and stringing their ragged webs in every free corner of every old shed and basement window. In Tucson, during the height of the season, a person can always on short notice round up eight or ten big, robust black widows, if that's what a person wants to do. But a hundred in one room? So all right, yes, there was a catch: These in my office were newborn babies.

A hundred scuttering bambinos, each one no bigger than a poppyseed. Too small still for red hourglasses, too small even for red egg timers. They had the aesthetic virtue of being so tiny that even a person of good eyesight and patient disposition could not make out their hideous little faces.

Their mother had sneaked in when the rains began and set up a web in the corner beside my desk. I knew she was there—I got a reminder every time I dropped a pencil and went groping for it, jerking my hand back at the first touch of that distinctive, dry, high-strength web. But I hadn't made the necessary decision about dealing with her. I knew she would have to be either murdered or else captured adroitly in a pickle jar for relocation to the wild, and I didn't especially want to do either. (I had already squashed scores of black widows during those Tucson years but by this time, I guess, I was going soft.) In the meantime, she had gotten pregnant. She had laid her eggs into a silken egg sac the size of a Milk Dud and then protected that sac vigilantly, keeping it warm, fending off any threats, as black widow mothers do. While she was waiting for the eggs to come to term, she would have been particularly edgy, particularly unforgiving, and my hand would have been in particular danger each time I reached for a fallen pencil. Then the great day arrived. The spiderlings hatched from their individual eggs, chewed their way out of the sac, and started crawling, brothers and sisters together, up toward the orange tensor lamp that was giving off heat and light on the desk of the nitwit who was their landlord.

By the time I stumbled in, fifty or sixty of them had reached the lampshade and rappelled back down on dainty silk lines, leaving a net of gossamer rigging between the lamp and the Darwin book (it happened to be an old edition of *Insectivorous Plants*, with marbled endpapers) that sat on the desk. Some dozen others had already managed dispersal flights, letting out strands of buoyant silk and ballooning away on rising air, as spiderlings do—in this case dispersing as far as the bookshelves. It was too late for one man to face one spider with just a pickle jar and an index card and his two shaky hands. By now I was proprietor of a highly successful black widow hatchery.

And the question was, How should a human behave toward the members of other living species?

The Jain religion of India has a strong teaching on that question. The Sanskrit word is *ahimsa,* generally rendered in English as "non-injury" or the imperative "do no harm." *Ahimsa* is the ethical center-piece of Jainism, an absolute stricture against the killing of living beings—*any* living beings—and it led the traditional Jains to some extreme forms of observance. A rigorously devout Jain would burn no candles or lights, for instance, if there was danger a moth might fly into them. The Jain would light no fire for heating or cooking, again because it might cause the death of insects. He would cover his mouth and nose with a cloth mask, so as not to inhale any gnats. He would refrain from cutting his hair, on grounds that the lice hiding in there might be gruesomely injured by the scissors. He could not plow a field, for fear of mutilating worms. He could not work as a carpenter or a mason, with all that dangerous sawing and crunching, nor could he engage in most types of industrial production. Consequently the traditional Jains formed a distinct socioeconomic class, composed almost entirely of monks and merchants. Their ethical canon was not without what you and I might take to be glaring contradictions (vegetarianism was sanctioned, plants as usual getting dismissive treatment in the matter of rights to life), but at least they took it seriously. They lived by it. They tried their best to do no harm.

And this in a country, remember, where 10,000 humans died every year from snakebite, almost a million more from malaria carried in the bites of mosquitoes. The black widow spider, compared to those fellow creatures, seems a harmless and innocent beast.

But personally I hold no brief for *ahimsa,* because I don't delude myself that it's even theoretically (let alone practically) possible. The basic processes of animal life, human or otherwise, do necessarily entail a fair bit of ruthless squashing and gobbling. Plants can sustain themselves on no more than sunlight and beauty and a hydroponic diet—but not we animals. I've only mentioned this Jainist ideal to suggest the range of possible viewpoints.

Modern philosophers of the "animal liberation" movement, most notably Peter Singer and Tom Regan, have proposed some other interesting answers to the same question. So have writers like Barry Lopez and Eugene Linden, and (by their example, as well as by their work) scientists like Jane Goodall and John Lilly and Dian Fossey. Most of the attention of each of these thinkers, though, has been devoted to what is popularly (but not necessarily by the thinkers themselves) considered the "upper" end of the "ladder" of life. To my mind, the question of appropriate relations is more tricky and intriguing—also more crucial in the long run, since this group accounts for most of the planet's species—as applied to the "lower" end, down there among the mosquitoes and worms and black widow spiders.

These are the extreme test cases. These are the alien species who experience human malice, or indifference, or tolerance, at its most automatic and elemental. To squash or not to squash? Mohandas Gandhi, whose own ethic of nonviolence owed much to *ahimsa,* was once asked about the propriety of an antimalaria campaign that involved killing mosquitoes with DDT, and he was careful to give no simple, presumptuous answer. These are the creatures whose treatment, by each of us, illuminates not just the strength of emotional affinity but the strength, if any, of principle.

But what is the principle? Pure *ahimsa,* as even Gandhi admitted, is unworkable. Vegetarianism is invidious. Anthropocentrism, conscious or otherwise, is smug and ruinously myopic. What else? Well, I have my own little notion of one measure that might usefully be applied in our relations with other species, and I offer it here seriously despite the fact that it will probably sound godawful stupid.

Eye contact.

Make eye contact with the beast, the Other, before you decide upon action. No kidding, now, I mean get down on your hands and knees right there in the vegetable garden, and look that snail in the face. Lock eyes with that bull snake. Trade stares with the carp. Gaze for a moment into the many-faceted eyes—the windows to its soul—of the house fly, as it licks its way innocently across your kitchen counter. Look for signs of embarrassment or rancor or guilt. Repeat the following formula silently, like a mantra: "This is some mother's darling, this is some mother's child." *Then* kill if you will, or if it seems you must.

I've been experimenting with the eye-contact approach for some time myself. I don't claim that it has made me gentle or holy or put me in tune with the cosmic hum, but definitely it has been interesting. The hardest cases—and therefore I think the most telling—are the spiders.

The face of a spider is unlike anything else a human will ever see. The word "ugly" doesn't even begin to serve. "Grotesque" and "menacing" are too mild. The only adequate way of communicating the effect of a spiderly countenance is to warn that it is "very different," and then offer a photograph. This trick should not be pulled on loved ones just before bedtime or when trying to persuade them to accompany you to the Amazon.

The special repugnant power of the spider physiognomy derives, I think, from fangs and eyes. The former are too big and the latter are too many. But the fangs (actually the fangs are only terminal barbs on the *chelicerae*, as the real jaw limbs are called) need to be large, because all spiders are predators yet they have no pincers like a lobster or a scorpion, no talons like an eagle, no social behavior like a pack of wolves. Large clasping fangs armed with poison glands are just their required equipment for earning a living. And what about those eight eyes—big ones and little ones, arranged in two rows, all bugged-out and pointing everywhichway? (My wife the biologist offers a theory here: "They have an eye for each leg, like us—so they don't *step* in anything.") Well, a predator does need good eyesight, binocular focus, peripheral vision. Sensory perception is crucial to any animal that lives by the hunt and, unlike insects, arachnids possess no antennae. Beyond that, I don't know. I don't *know* why a spider has eight eyes.

I only know that, when I make eye contact with one, I feel a deep physical shudder of revulsion, and of fear, and of fascination; and I am reminded that the human style of face is only one accidental pattern among many, some of the others being quite drastically different. I remember that we aren't alone. I remember that we are the norm of goodness and comeliness only to ourselves. I wonder about how ugly I look to the spider.

The hundred baby black widows on my desk were too tiny for eye contact. They were too numerous, it seemed, to be gathered one by one into a pickle jar and carried to freedom in the backyard. I killed them all with a can of Raid. I confess to that slaughter with more resignation than shame, the jostling struggle for life and space being what it is. I can't swear I would do differently today. But there is this lingering suspicion that I squandered an opportunity for some sort of moral growth.

I still keep their dead and dried mother, and their vacated egg sac, in a plastic vial on an office shelf. It is supposed to remind me of something or other.

And the question continues to puzzle me: How should a human behave toward the members of other living species?

Last week I tried to make eye contact with a tarantula. This was a huge specimen, all hairy and handsomely colored, with a body as big as a hamster and legs the size of Bic pens. I ogled it through a sheet of plate glass. I smiled and winked. But the animal hid its face in distrust.

■ CONSIDERATIONS OF MEANING AND METHOD

1. What is Quammen's thesis? How definitive is it? Where does he state it, and what is the purpose and significance of its placement in the essay?

2. Take note of the way in which Quammen structures his essay. How does his question, "How should a human behave toward the members of another species?" and its variations function in the development of the essay? How do his divisions between the essay's four sections function, and what is the purpose of each section? How do these sections work together?

3. In the second section of the essay, Quammen discusses the Jain practice of *ahimsa,* cites statistics of deaths resulting from snakebite, and refers to philosophers and writers who have, directly or indirectly, addressed the question that interests him. Why, in a personal essay, does he draw upon these broader references outside his experience?

4. How would you characterize Quammen's tone and writing style? Point to specific examples in the essay that demonstrate tone. Who is his audience, and how does he fit his writing to his audience? How serious is he in proposing "eye contact" as "one measure" of assessing our appropriate behavior toward animals? Why the eyes?

■ POSSIBILITIES FOR WRITING

1. If you have ever established what might be called a "relationship" with an undomesticated animal (an individual animal, not a species), describe the experience in a narrative essay, noting how the relationship or familiarity developed over time. Your reader might be someone for whom the idea of a "relationship" with an undomesticated animal might seem strange at first. What did you begin to notice about this individual animal over time? Did it "teach" you anything new? How did your relationship with it differ from your relationship with a domesticated animal?

■ ALICE WALKER
Am I Blue?

Alice Walker was born in 1944 in Georgia, the youngest of eight children. Her father, a sharecropper and dairy farmer, was the first black man to vote in Eatonville, Georgia. At eight years old, Walker was blinded in one eye when one of her brothers shot her with a BB gun, and this, she says, turned her inward. Valedictorian of her senior class, Walker remembers receiving three important gifts from her mother during high school: a sewing machine, which meant independence; a typewriter, the writer's tool; and for a graduation present, a suitcase, which was "permission to travel." Walker attended Spelman and Sarah Lawrence Colleges, and following her junior year she traveled to Africa. After college, she became deeply involved in the civil rights movement in New York, Georgia, and Mississippi. In 1967 she married a civil rights lawyer, Melvyn Rosenman Leventhal, and they were the first legally married interracial couple to live in the state of Mississippi.

Alice Walker's many influential books include her first novel, The Third Life of Grange Copeland *(1970); an early collection of short stories,* In Love and Trouble *(1973), which won the American Academy and Institute of Arts and Letters Rosenthal Award;* Petunias and Other Poems *(1973), which was nominated for the National Book Award;* Meridian *(1976), hailed as one of the best novels to come out of the civil rights movement; and her best-known novel,* The Color Purple *(1982), which won both the American Book Award and the Pulitzer Prize for Fiction. More recently published are her two novels* In the Temple of My Familiar *(1989) and* Possessing the Secret of Joy *(1992). Her collections of essays, which have also been highly influential, especially in feminist circles, include* In Search of Our Mother's Gardens *(1983) and* Living by the Word *(1988), from which the essay "Am I Blue?" is taken. Particularly in her more recent writing, Walker's themes frequently relate women's experience to nature and the land.*

Alice Walker refers to herself as a "womanist" rather than a feminist, and in the enormous body of her work she has captured an essence of African American life, and of African American women's lives in particular. Walker currently lives in San Francisco and teaches at the University of California at Berkeley.

"Ain't these tears in these eyes tellin' you?"*

For about three years my companion and I rented a small house in the country that stood on the edge of a large meadow that appeared to run from the end of our deck straight into the mountains. The mountains, however, were quite far away, and between us and them there was, in fact, a town. It was one of the many pleasant aspects of the house that you never really were aware of this.

It was a house of many windows, low, wide, nearly floor to ceiling in the living room, which faced the meadow, and it was from one of these that i first saw our closest neighbor, a large white horse, cropping grass, flipping its mane, and ambling about—not over the entire meadow, which stretched well out of sight of the house, but over the five or so fenced-in acres that were next to the twenty-odd that we had rented. I soon learned that the horse, whose name was Blue, belonged to a man who lived in another town, but was boarded by our neighbors next door. Occasionally, one of the children, usually a stocky teen-ager, but sometimes a much younger girl or boy, could be seen riding Blue. They would appear in the meadow, climb up on his back, ride furiously for ten or fifteen minutes, then get off, slap Blue on the flanks, and not be seen again for a month or more.

There were many apple trees in our yard, and one by the fence that Blue could almost reach. We were soon in the habit of feeding him apples, which he relished, especially because by the middle of summer the meadow grasses—so green and succulent since January—had dried out from lack of rain, and Blue stumbled about munching the dried stalks half-heartedly. Sometimes he would stand very still just by the apple tree, and when one of us came out he would whinny, snort loudly, or stamp the ground. This meant, of course: I want an apple.

It was quite wonderful to pick a few apples, or collect those that had fallen to the ground overnight, and patiently hold them, one by one, up to his large, toothy mouth. I remained as thrilled as a child by his flexible dark lips, huge, cubelike teeth that crunched the apples, core and all, with such finality, and his high, broad-breasted *enormity;* beside which, I felt small indeed. When I was a child, I used to ride horses, and was especially friendly with one named Nan until the day I was riding and my brother deliberately spooked her and I was thrown, head first, against the trunk of a tree. When I came to, I was in bed and my mother was bending worriedly over me; we silently agreed that perhaps horseback riding was not the safest sport for me. Since then I have walked, and prefer walking to horseback riding—but I had forgotten the depth of feeling one could see in horses' eyes.

I was therefore unprepared for the expression in Blue's. Blue was lonely. Blue was horribly lonely and bored. I was not shocked that this should be the case; five acres to tramp by yourself, endlessly, even in the most beautiful of meadows—and his was—cannot provide many interesting events, and once rainy season turned to dry that was about it. No, I was shocked that I had forgotten that human animals and nonhuman animals can communicate quite well; if we are brought up around animals as children we take this for granted. By the time we are adults we no longer remember. However, the animals have not changed. They are in fact *completed* creations (at least they seem to be, so much more than we) who are not likely *to* change; it is their nature to express themselves. What else are they going to express? And they do. And, generally speaking, they are ignored.

After giving Blue the apples, I would wander back to the house, aware that he was observing me. Were more apples not forthcoming then? Was that to be his sole entertainment for the day? My partner's small son had decided he wanted to learn how to piece a quilt; we worked in silence on our respective squares as I thought . . .

Well, about slavery: about white children, who were raised by black people, who knew their first all-accepting love from black women, and then, when they were twelve or so, were told they must "forget" the deep levels of communication between themselves and "mammy" that they knew. Later they would be able to relate quite calmly, "My old mammy was sold to another good family." "My old mammy was ———— ————." Fill in the blank. Many more years later a white woman would say: "I can't understand these Negroes, these blacks. What do they want? They're so different from us."

And about the Indians, considered to be "like animals" by the "settlers" (a very benign euphemism for what they actually were), who did not understand their description as a compliment.

And about the thousands of American men who marry Japanese, Korean, Filipina, and other non-English-speaking women and of how happy they report they are, "*blissfully,*" until their brides learn to speak English, at which point the marriages tend to fall apart. What then did the men see, when they looked into the eyes of the women they married, before they could speak English? Apparently only their own reflections.

I thought of society's impatience with the young. "Why are they playing the music so loud?" Perhaps the children have listened to much of the music of oppressed people their parents danced to before they were born, with its passionate but soft cries for acceptance and love, and they have wondered why their parents failed to hear.

I do not know how long Blue had inhabited his five beautiful, boring acres before we moved into our house; a year after we had arrived—and had also traveled to other valleys, other cities, other worlds—he was still there.

But then, in our second year at the house, something happened in Blue's life. One morning, looking out the window at the fog that lay like a ribbon over the meadow, I saw another horse, a brown one, at the other end of Blue's field. Blue appeared to be afraid of it, and for several days made no attempt to go near. We went away for a week. When we returned, Blue had decided to make friends and the two horses ambled or galloped along together, and Blue did not come nearly as often to the fence underneath the apple tree.

When he did, bringing his new friend with him, there was a different look in his eyes. A look of independence, of self-possession, of inalienable *horse*ness. His friend eventually became pregnant. For months and months there was, it seemed to me, a mutual feeling between me and the horses of justice, of peace. I fed apples to them both. The look in Blue's eyes was one of unabashed "this is *it*ness."

It did not, however, last forever. One day, after a visit to the city, I went out to give Blue some apples. He stood waiting, or so I thought, though not beneath the tree. When I shook the tree and jumped back from the shower of apples, he made no move. I carried some over to him. He managed to half-crunch one. The rest he let fall to the ground. I dreaded looking into his eyes—because I had of course noticed that Brown, his partner, had gone—but I did look. If I had been born into slavery, and my partner had been sold or killed, my eyes would have looked like that. The children next door explained that Blue's partner had been "put with him" (the same expression that old people used, I had noticed, when speaking of an ancestor during slavery who had been impregnated by her owner) so that they could mate and she conceive. Since that was accomplished, she had been taken back by her owner, who lived somewhere else.

Will she be back? I asked.

They didn't know.

Blue was like a crazed person. Blue *was,* to me, a crazed person. He galloped furiously, as if he were being ridden, around and around his five beautiful acres. He whinnied until he couldn't. He tore at the ground with his hooves. He butted himself against his single shade tree. He looked always and always toward the road down which his partner had gone. And then, occasionally, when he came up for apples, or I took apples to him, he looked at me. It was a look so piercing, so full of grief, a look so *human,* I almost laughed (I felt too sad to cry) to think there are people who do not know that animals suffer. People like me who have forgotten, and daily forget, all that animals try to tell us. "Everything you do to us will happen to you; we are your teachers, as you are ours. We are one lesson" is essentially it, I think. There are those who never once have even considered animals' rights: those who have been taught that animals actually want to be used and abused by us, as small children "love" to be frightened, or women "love" to be mutilated and raped. . . . They are the great-grandchildren of those who honestly thought, because someone taught them this: "Women can't think," and "niggers can't faint." But most disturbing of all, in Blue's large brown eyes was a new look, more painful than the look of despair: the look of disgust with human beings, with life; the look of hatred. And it was odd what the look of hatred did. It gave him, for the first time, the look of a beast. And what that meant was that he had put up a barrier within to protect himself from further violence; all the apples in the world wouldn't change that fact.

And so Blue remained, a beautiful part of our landscape, very peaceful to look at from the window, white against the grass. Once a friend came to visit and said, looking out on the soothing view: "And it *would* have to be a *white* horse; the very image of freedom." And I thought, yes, the animals are forced to become for us merely "images" of what they once so beautifully expressed. And we are used to drinking milk from containers showing "contented" cows, whose real lives we want to hear nothing about, eating eggs and drumsticks from "happy" hens, and munching hamburgers advertised by bulls of integrity who seem to command their fate.

As we talked of freedom and justice one day for all, we sat down to steaks. I am eating misery, I thought, as I took the first bite. And spit it out.

■ CONSIDERATIONS OF MEANING AND METHOD

1. Walker says that as children, if we have grown up with animals, we understand instinctively that animals can and do communicate with human beings, but as adults we tend to forget this. Do you agree with Walker? What might account for this forgetfulness?

2. Walker focuses, as does David Quammen in "The Face of a Spider," on an animal's eyes as the source of communication. What do Blue's eyes communicate to Walker over the course of the essay, and what accounts for the changes in their expression? Do you think she is anthropomorphizing Blue (projecting human characteristics onto him), or is she reading what is really there?

3. How does Walker establish a parallel between the perception and treatment of animals and the perception and treatment of slaves, Native Americans, non-English-speaking women, and even the young by society? Do these seem to you to be reasonable comparisons? Why or why not?

4. Toward the end of the essay, Walker says that the look in Blue's eyes "gave him, for the first time, the look of a beast." What does Walker mean by "beast"? To what or whom, and in what situations, might you apply this term according to Walker's definition?

5. To what extent is "Am I Blue?" an argument against eating meat? What effect does Walker want to have on her reader?

■ POSSIBILITIES FOR WRITING

1. Walker says that animals are our "teachers." In an analytical essay, first explain what Walker thinks we can we learn about ourselves and about our relationships with others—especially others who may be different from us—through our relationships with animals. Then explain your reasons for agreeing or disagreeing with her view.

2. Write an essay in which you describe and illustrate your relationship with a domesticated animal—or perhaps more than one, comparing them—conveying to your reader the unique character of the animal, the quality of your interaction with it, and the ways in which you communicated. Make it your goal to introduce this animal to your reader as a distinct individual, and to portray your relationship with it as unique.

■ AMELIA HUGHART
Looking Out

In introducing herself and her essay, "Looking Out," student Amelia Hughart writes:

The images that I used in this essay were collected from my experiences growing up in Washington, D.C. I spent much of my childhood in the backyards of the suburb of Bethesda, moved out of the country for four years, and then moved into the city of D.C. itself. I have always loved to read, talk, and tell stories. After graduating from high school, I convinced myself that I would major in either biology or economics, but after a year of college I am completely undecided. I hope that whatever I choose to do allows me to travel extensively, play with math and statistics, read, and write.

I wrote this essay to examine the way that I learned to look at nature. I wanted to consider my fear of nature in particular. Writing this essay gave form and shape to thoughts and fears that had been floating in the back of my head. I knew that they existed, but I had no idea what they looked like before I started to write. My writing is contemplative and loosely structured. It follows my train of thought and poses questions. I hope that it invites readers to go on their own contemplative journeys and discover their own questions.

The major boundary of my natural world as a child was the wooden split rail fence around the yard. Within its bounds, I felt safe and secure. Everything followed a plan and worked as it was supposed to. In the context of an environment almost completely controlled by man, I learned to fear the wild. For me, safety was always first. Natural beauty was only a gorgeous afterthought.

Much of the natural world seemed alien to me. I discovered mountains in picture books and on vacation, where they seemed about as real as Disney World. On weekends my father and I took an exhaust-stained metro bus into the core of the city to visit museums, libraries, and other repositories of artifacts from exciting faraway worlds. I watched gibbons swinging behind bars at the zoo and studied panoramas of stuffed ostriches with glazed stares at the Museum of Natural History.

I was certain that nothing could harm me inside of my fenced-in yard, because I knew my environment intimately. I tasted specks of dirt and crushed leaves of plants to inhale their sharp or bland odors. I knew which sort of liquid oozed out when the stem broke and which plants sheltered worms and other wiggling creatures. The yard was tame. Trees, flowers, and grass grew where they were supposed to. My mother planned her garden the way a painter visualizes a picture. In the fall, we trekked to the nursery and bought shiny white paper bags of bulbs, covered with picture promises for the spring to come. All was planned and calculated. The garden was artfully arranged to appear natural, like a still life. To my eyes, it was more beautiful than a natural landscape because my mother designed it to look balanced and appealing, just as the juicy red hybrid strawberries draped over the side of their frame tasted and looked better than the small, seedy, bland ones that grew between blades of grass.

Within the yard, I felt safe enough to let my imagination go without fear of bumping into any truly frightening thoughts about nature. Gaping holes full of writhing snakes never opened beneath my feet. I was the grand master of potato bug life, the snow princess in a burrowed igloo, a sorcerer casting spells with leafy wands, and a chemist grinding mud, leaves, and seeds into beauty compounds and cures for cancer. Perched in the boughs of a dogwood tree above deceptively soft ground cover, I could lose myself in cloud races and dream about life in a fluffy soft meringue cloud castle. The worst things that I imagined couldn't hurt me. Make-believe tigers rarely bite. Even when they do, it never hurts for very long.

The garden was not without real dangers. Several yew bushes with dark green spiky leaves produced soft red poisonous berries that I liked to squeeze between my fingers. Their pulpy interiors stained my finger tips and scared my mother. The dangerous things in the yard did not scare me because they were well-known and well-marked. I knew where they were and how to avoid them if I chose to.

All that was truly dangerous lay outside the split rail border. The area across the back fence along the alley was especially frightening and exciting because it was inhabited by raccoons, squirrels, and wandering pets. Chunks of concrete and broken glass hid under a soft blanket of decaying leaves. Poison ivy lurked among tangles of honeysuckle and other weeds. Trash cans full of mysterious material and lingering odors presided over the forbidding area where I dared not venture.

The natural world outside of the fence was messy. Plump purple mulberries, fallen from their trees onto the sidewalk, stuck between my toes and bled into the sidewalk during humid summer strolls around the block. Their crushed bodies covered the ground with a sticky film that filled the air with a pungent odor. I enjoyed the lack of order as long as I was not too far from a neat, predictable home base. I loved dancing on the sidewalk in warm pouring summer rain. I let the rain soak through to my skin while I spun in circles, secure in the knowledge that a warm bath, dry clothing, and steamy hot chocolate were within easy reach.

Even the tamed, predictable natural world could scare me if I stopped taking it for granted for a second and doubted the control that humans had over it. Part of domination is complete knowledge of the controlled. One spring evening, after dinner, I stared at the dogwood tree cut into white squares by the window frame. I asked my grandmother if I could ever know everything about everything in the world.

"No," she replied.

"Everything about trees?"

"No."

"Everything about dogwoods?"

"No."

"Well, could I at least know everything about that dogwood?"

"No."

"Everything about one leaf of that dogwood?"

"No," she replied.

This shook my confidence in the sturdiness of the world that my parents had presented to me. If no one could know everything about it, how could I know that it was safe?

In the spring, I watched brilliant orange and green aphids swarm over the opening buds of peonies. The tiny dots scurried over leaves and traveled past each other on the stiff, dark green stems. Their whole world seemed to be contained in one plant, which was such a small part of my universe. What if my world was just a tiny part of someone else's, and I but a small scurrying dot? I was shocked by the possible unimportance of my own existence and shoved the thought away, saving it for later. The sheer size of nature inspires awe. How can humans hope to control vast stretches of ocean, or a sky that reaches into infinity, when they cannot truly control their own back-yards?

This summer, I lost my father in a mountain forest. He wandered off of the trail alone, without water, food, or good boots. Sitting on a sunny rock in the middle of a meadow full of flowers, I imagined him lying unconscious somewhere, his skull oozing blood. I felt completely helpless. There was no way for me to find him and nothing I could do that would possibly help. When he finally came into view, I started to cry. He laughed at me for being so silly and asked if it had been that bad to wait by myself for a couple of hours in a picture-perfect landscape. I mumbled "No," but didn't mean it. I couldn't tell him that, if I could have, I would have paved the trail and bordered it with guide ropes to make sure that he was safe. The thick white clouds drifting above my head and the swaying sticks of lupine did not filter into my thoughts until I felt secure. Without the illusion of safety and control, the beauty of nature meant little to me.

■ CONSIDERATIONS OF MEANING AND METHOD

1. In many places and in many ways in her essay, Amelia Hughart describes nature in terms of its enclosure and containment by humans. Find examples of this imagery in the essay. How is it important to Hughart's development of her theme?

2. What is the significance of Hughart's title?

3. How does Hughart organize her essay? What is its pattern of development? Take note of the first sentence in each paragraph to help you track the pattern. What does Hughart mean when she says in her statement preceding the essay that it is "loosely structured"?

4. Does Hughart make any high-level generalizations in her narrative? If so, what are they? Are they adequately supported? Is her thesis a high-level generalization? Where does she state it?

5. Does Hughart's purpose in writing go beyond the personal?

■ POSSIBILITIES FOR WRITING

1. If you had a backyard when you were growing up, in a personal narrative describe it from your point of view as a child. How does it—or would it, if you had a chance to see it again—look to you now?

2. How did your parents' attitudes and values about the natural world affect the development of your own, then and now? Are your attitudes and values different from or similar to those of your parents? How typical are your parents' and your own atti-

tudes and values compared to those of others—such as people of a different generation or from a different place? In an essay, address these questions and illustrate your response with remembered episodes from your childhood (determine before you write whether you would like to include your family among your readers).

3. Use the peer review form at the end of the rhetorical introduction to this chapter to evaluate Amelia Hughart's essay.

Making Critical Connections:
Questions for Discussion, Research, and Writing

1. Find out more about slave narratives. In your library, locate a slave narrative by another writer—perhaps Frederick Douglass, William Wells Brown, or Solomon Northup. Compare the section from the *Narrative of the Life and Adventures of Henry Bibb, an American Slave* with a selection from one of these other works. What are the similarities between them in subject, theme, writing style, or apparent purpose? How do they differ?

2. Many of the writers—the "popularizers of science"—whom Mairs refers to toward the end of "On Being a Scientific Booby" as being inspirational or, at the least, important sources of information for her are writers whose work you will have read in this chapter or will read in other chapters of this book. In writing or in discussion, compare the effect that several of these writers have had in popularizing scientific subjects for you.

3. Compare the attitudes of David Quammen in "The Face of a Spider" and Alice Walker in "Am I Blue?" about the animals with whom they share intimate living and work spaces. In conversation in class or in writing, discuss the similarities and the differences you detect. Support your observations with examples from the text.

4. Are there characteristically American ways of relating to nature? If you think there are, what are they? Have they changed over time? How, and due to what factors? Whether in writing or discussion, use references to several of this chapter's readings to illustrate and support your views on this subject.

5. In his book *Second Nature*, writer Michael Pollan observes that "One of the things childhood is is a process of learning about the various paths that lead out of nature and into culture. . . ." Relating nature and culture is a learning process that can begin in childhood and extend into adulthood. In the personal narratives in this chapter, how do the writers relate nature and culture? Choose two of the readings that provide for interesting comparisons and/or contrasts in light of this question, and explore the question in writing or discussion.

CHAPTER 5

Navajo Hopscotch, © Joel Gordon, 1991

FICTIONAL ACCOUNTS

RHETORIC:
WRITING ABOUT
LITERATURE

RESPONDING TO LITERATURE

Most of us enjoy reading literature in some or many of its forms because it informs and entertains us, extending the boundaries of our immediate lives. Literature allows us to participate in lives and events, whether imagined or actual, that may be foreign to our experience and that we might not otherwise have come to know. And when the real or imagined lives and events we read about in literature bear a clearer resemblance to our own lives and experiences, we learn more about ourselves and others in comparing them.

Reading, as we've learned, is not a passive act. Good writing of any kind will invite you to participate, engaging your senses, emotions, imagination, and intellect. It will trigger your own memories and associations, and it will stimulate your thinking. When you read, you absorb, evaluate, and extend what the writer has articulated, interpreting it in light of who you are and what you know. In this sense, when you read a work of literature, you recreate it.

Imaginative literature, especially, will engage you on multiple levels simultaneously. A good short story will involve you both viscerally and critically. The story itself will captivate you, drawing you into the events and the lives of its characters, while at the same time exciting your intellect, suggesting certain associations and meanings that apply well beyond the story itself. And if you read with a writer's eye, you will gain a deeper understanding of how the writer has created the effect he or she has had on you.

WRITING ABOUT LITERATURE

When you respond to works of literature in your own writing, you are attempting to explain to your reader what it is about a particular work that you find especially interesting, whether this interest stems from your excitement or your frustration. You are also contributing to an ongoing dialogue with your classmates, your instructor, and others interested in the work you are discussing. A dialogue about literary topics is much broader than the literature itself: it relates our reading of literature to the events of our lives, to our broader areas of interest, and to our common social and intellectual activity. This dialogue, like all dialogues, includes both commonalities and differences in the views and the voices of the people participating in it. We learn by exploring our own interpretations and comparing them with those of others.

In writing about literature, your primary goal may be to explain a personal response to the work and how the work relates to your own life, or it may be to analyze a key element of the work itself without direct reference to your own experience. Often, of course, you will be doing both things at once. An extended and focused essay exploring your personal response to a short story, for example, will require you to analyze the sources of, and reasons for, that response, which will be rooted in the story itself. And an essay in which you analyze a key thematic or structural element of a short story will be mechanical indeed if you have not been personally affected by the story.

Personal Responses

When you respond personally to a work of literature in your writing, you are making connections between your own life and the ideas or situations presented in the work you have read. These connections often come in the form of comparisons. For example, you may compare yourself with the characters of a story, or incidents you have experienced with those experienced by these characters. A work of literature may challenge or confirm certain of your values, beliefs, or ways of thinking, and you might want to explain, in a personal response, the specific ways in which it has done so. Since literature exposes us to new worlds of ideas and experience, much of your personal response to works of literature is rooted in what you learn from them, whether in the form of information or ideas. In writing about your personal responses to a work of literature, you may want to reflect on what new information or insight the work gave you, how this new information and insight has affected you, and how it applies to your own life.

You may be attempting to explain, in writing about your personal responses to a work of literature, your likes and dislikes—what it is in a work that attracts or repels you, pleases or disturbs you. These responses will be largely subjective; they are more explanations than arguments. Although in a written personal response to a work of literature you will certainly want to persuade your reader of the integrity of your perceptions, your most useful tool in accomplishing this will be to explain your response as clearly as possible. Your reader may accept or reject your response as being more or less aligned with his or her own. Personal responses to literature are not definitive, but they add a crucial dimension to an ongoing discussion about literature. Whether or not your own reader "agrees" with your response, your writing will extend and enhance his or her experience of the literature, and he or she may see the work in a new light. Instructors often assign essays calling for a personal response to a work of literature precisely because they want you to relate literature to your own life, to understand literature's relevance in personal terms.

Analytical Responses

Your analysis of a work of literature often grows from your personal response to it, but in a formal analysis the emphasis shifts from you and your personal relationship to the work to the content and structure of the work itself. Your goal in an analysis is to explore what the work means in a more universal sense than a personal sense, and how the form and structure of the work contribute to its meaning.

When we analyze something we break it down into parts, examine each part carefully, establish relationships between the parts, and then put them back together with a better understanding of the whole. We analyze all the time, in our attempts to explain others' behavior or our own, to understand how mechanisms work, or to arrive at the answers to mathematical equations. In analyzing a fictional work, our goal may be to understand a complex thematic element, what motivates a certain character's behavior, the function of time or location in a story, the implications of the writer's choice of point of view, or stylistic elements unique to the author's voice.

Works of literature—even short works, such as poems and short stories—are complex, and there is no single way of understanding them.

There are many doors which will open a work of literature to a richer comprehension. A strong analysis of a work of literature will focus on one important aspect of that work, exploring in depth the crucial elements which contribute to its function. In explaining and illustrating your analysis in an essay, and in drawing conclusions from it, you are interpreting the work.

Because a literary analysis focuses on the content and form of the work itself as well as on the reader's personal response to them, analytic essays are more clearly arguments. In developing a literary analysis, you will need to strive to reason clearly and to support your thesis with convincing evidence that goes beyond the personal. (For more on reasoning and argumentation, see Chapters 7 and 8.)

Your primary purpose in writing one essay about literature may be to explain a personal response to it; your primary purpose in writing another may be to argue for a particular interpretation of it based on analysis. But in reading literature and in writing about it, personal and analytic responses are interwoven; you can hardly have one without the other. Both contribute, in the early as well the late stages of writing, to the process of understanding.

DEVELOPING AN INTERPRETATION

Active reading is an essential part of the analytical process, and an important tool in directing analysis is the writing process itself. Through writing, we develop, test, revise, and extend our analyses, building our understanding of literary (and other) subjects. Although an analytical essay about a work of literature may be the end goal in writing, developing an analysis of it through the writing process happens in stages.

You might want to review the introduction to Chapter 1 (pages 8–17) in which stages of both the writing and reading processes are discussed in general terms. Here, however, we'll take a closer look at how these two processes are interwoven in the development of an analysis of literature.

Note Taking and Journal Writing

The early stages of exploring and articulating your responses to a work of literature will probably take the form of notes and journal explorations. In these writings, the only audience that matters is yourself.

Your purpose is to identify your responses to a work of literature and to explore the sources of these responses as you begin to articulate them to yourself.

Your style in notes and early journal explorations is informal. You may find that many of your responses are highly subjective, asserting themselves as likes and dislikes. Your coverage will be incomplete, and your observations may seem largely unrelated, even random, since you may not yet have defined your writing topic and you certainly will not have made all the connections you will make in later stages of your analysis and writing. It is natural to have more questions than answers at this point; questioning is the necessary first step, motivating and focusing the analytical process and shaping the more coherent, audience-specific writing to come. Sometimes your instructor or your textbook will provide questions to focus your reading of works of literature; you may even have been assigned your writing topic in advance of reading. These questions will provide a clear context for critical reading.

In analyzing a work of literature, you should plan to read it more than once. Try to allow yourself an initial reading in which you don't feel pressured to organize your response. Your primary goal in an initial reading is to gather a first reaction to the work and an impression of the work as a whole. Read the work straight through, letting it affect you on a subjective level. If you take notes at all, you might try keeping them to shorthand: Insert exclamation points or question marks to highlight portions of the work that affected you strongly, whether positively or negatively, or that puzzled you. An initial reading of long works, such as novels, is not always possible. However, if your task is to analyze a short work, such as a short story, a first reading in which you are relatively unburdened by the analytical task will give you a better sense of the work, in terms of the author's point, purpose, and style, and the writing's effect on you.

In your next and closer reading, but still in the early stages of your writing about the work, you will probably compose notes within the text itself, underlining and commenting upon words, phrases, or passages that strike you as especially interesting, either because of what the writer is saying or how he or she is saying it. You might highlight passages that remind you of other works you have read or related ideas or events—either events in your own life or, more broadly, current or historical ones. You will probably elaborate to some extent with notes in the margins, whether you phrase them in simple words or phrases, complete thoughts, or questions. These notes will accomplish two purposes. First, they will help you fix your thinking about specific portions of the text. Second, as you build your notes during the course of close reading, they will begin to unify your response to the text. You should begin to see how portions of the text relate to each other and how some elements affect and unify your responses to the work.

After you have taken notes within the text itself, try reading over your notes in an attempt to identify what seem to you to be the most important points. These points may begin to suggest possible essay topics. Before you actually choose a topic and begin drafting an essay, try exploring, developing, and relating important ideas in informal journal writing. This writing could take the form of a focused freewrite around one particular idea or theme. You might want to do several freewrites, then read them together, looking for ways in which they might relate. Then try another freewrite in which you explore the relationship between the previous ones. Although some instructors assign and read such journal explorations, the primary audience for journal explorations is generally yourself, and the primary purpose is to provide you with an unpressured place for free exploration of ideas.

Defining a Topic: Posing a Key Question

What makes a good writing topic for an essay about literature? As you begin to consider this question, you will need to keep two fundamental factors in mind: (1) your readers' expectations and (2) your own interests. Sometimes instructors will assign specific writing topics that will require you to analyze a work of literature in a particular way, but more often they will not be that specific. In fact, your choice of an interesting writing topic is important to the analytical process because when you make this choice, you are determining for yourself what is most significant about a work.

An understanding of who your reader is and what your purpose is in writing is crucial to the selection of a good topic. Although your instructor is an important reader, you should not consider him or her your only reader. Your readers include *all* members of the community that provides the occasion for your writing—your instructor, your classmates, and yourself. These readers will want you to pose, explore, and attempt to answer a significant question about the work. They will expect you to have read and thought about the work carefully, but they will not expect you to be an expert in literary analysis. In your essay, you will certainly want to try to convince your readers that your motivating question is one worth asking and that your analysis is sound. Remember, though, that you are also writing for yourself, to clarify your own responses to the work.

Key questions about works of literature may arise from the work itself or from the circumstances that surrounded its creation. Questions about the work itself may relate to theme (what does the work mean?) or structure and style (how is the work constructed to convey meaning or effect?). Questions about the context of the work may have to do with events in the author's life or times and how these influenced the work. Since most analyses of works of literature you write in college will be relatively short, perhaps as short as a few pages, a good topic in writing about literature will be one that attempts to answer a specific, rather than a broad, question.

Many good ideas for writing topics begin as general or free-floating ideas. These ideas are good to begin with because they have provoked your thought, although they are often too vague to serve as finished writing topics. They will need to be further defined, through questioning, before you attempt to write about them. Here is an example, using one of this chapter's readings, of how you might get from a general idea to a key question in selecting a topic for an analysis of a literary work:

- *The general idea.* Because you have wondered about point of view in Ursula K. Le Guin's story "May's Lion," you suspect that a good writing topic for an analytic essay about the work might involve "the role of the narrator in 'May's Lion.'"
- *The specific idea.* To help you focus this topic more carefully, you might ask yourself, "What *about* the role of the narrator in 'May's Lion'?" In thinking this over—perhaps through reexamining the story, looking over your notes, or exploring possible answers to that question in your journal freewrites—you may realize that you are not entirely sure why Le Guin's narrator relates two versions of May's story, one "true," the other an "invention."
- *The key question.* In defining your topic in more concrete terms, you pose the key question that your essay will attempt to answer: "Why does Le Guin's narrator in 'May's Lion' reinvent May's story?"

When you pose a key question about a work of literature, you are defining your subject. When you answer that question, you are asserting your thesis. Between the formulation of the question and the answering of it you will need to identify and investigate the points which best illuminate the question and lead you toward your conclusions. Your journal is perhaps the best place to explore these points experimentally before you begin to strategize more explicitly in an outline or articulate more carefully in a draft.

Outlining and Drafting

In developing an analytical essay, outlining can be extremely useful as you map out ideas, plan organizational and rhetorical strategies, and establish support for your thesis. Useful outlines range widely between rough and formal. A rough outline can be a sequence of words and phrases scribbled on a napkin in a coffee house. Even in a rough outline, however, you can (1) pose your key question, (2) indicate the main points that contribute to an answer to that question, (3) establish the primary support of these main points, and (4) state a tentative conclusion (that is, assert a tentative thesis). A formal outline can be many pages long and quite detailed, illustrating not only general but specific organization and not only general but specific use of evidence (refer to the appendix, page 625, for an example of a formal outline). There are, of course, many options between rough and formal outlines. The following outline, using the example of "May's Lion," might fall in the middle range.

Tentative Title: Reinventing May's Story:
The Role of the Narrator in "May's Lion"

Introduction

    Key question: Why does Le Guin's narrator in "May's Lion" reinvent May's story?

Body

    Point #1: In the original story, May is alienated from nature.

    Support #1: May is afraid of the lion, and shuts herself in the house.

    Support #2: When she can't think of anything else to do ("it might have rabies" and "I did need to get Rosie"), May calls the police, and they come shoot the lion.

    Point #2: The narrator recognizes that in the original story May's intentions are good but her options are limited.

Support #1: May thinks the lion has come to her for help or company; she just doesn't know how to help.

Support #2: May doesn't like that it was shot; she just can't imagine an alternative.

Point #3: In the reinvented story, Rains End is attuned to nature.

Support #1: Although Rains End has a healthy respect for the lion, she is not afraid of it and does not shut herself away from it.

Support #2: Because Rains End understands nature and why the lion has come to her, what were insurmountable obstacles in the original story (milking Rosie) become manageable.

Point #4: Rains End can act on her good intentions in the reinvented story because she has an understanding of nature, her place in it, and the tools to act.

Support #1: The lion has "come for company in dying." Rains End accepts her responsibility (a "gift") and sings the lion from this world to the next.

Support #2: Native American tradition accepts that nature is harmonious and balanced, and that humans are part of, but not in control of, it. Rains End and the lion are equals, spiritually linked.

Conclusion

Tentative thesis: In reinventing the story of May's lion, the narrator shows that if May had seen herself as part of nature rather than apart from it, the balance of nature would have been preserved and May would have been spiritually more at peace. (*Loose ends:* The narrator reinvents the story for May, but May is dead. So it's Le Guin who invents and reinvents the story for all her readers. What's the difference between the narrator and the author?)

This outline would give you, as the writer of the essay that grows from it, a solid sense of direction in drafting your essay: the key question is clear, as are the main points and their fundamental support, and the conclusion, or thesis, although not fully developed, grows logically from the question and the exploration of it. There is still plenty of room, as you move from outline to draft, for addition of detail, for experimentation and adjustment, and for further development in the conclusion.

Through outlining, you may understand better in advance of drafting what rhetorical approach you will take in developing your ideas. In composing the outline, you may have already instinctively realized that your analysis of "May's Lion" will require a comparison of the two versions of May's story contained within Le Guin's story. In mapping out this comparison in outline form, you can easily check to make sure that you have observed the main principle of organization in comparison and contrast writing, namely, that your points in analyzing each story are comparable.

As you write and review an outline before drafting, you will have more perspective in considering whether you want to take a deductive or inductive approach in writing—that is, whether your thesis will appear early on and the body of the essay will prove it, or whether your thesis will appear in the conclusion as a natural consequence of your analysis in the essay. Many writers (and instructors) prefer deduction, especially in analytical writing. They want to encounter thesis statements rather than key questions early on, since thesis statements provide more forceful guidance in an essay's development.

If you take an inductive approach in an analytical essay because your thesis is the natural outcome of analysis, you might add a "because" statement to your key question in the essay's introduction. For example, the key question "Why does Le Guin's narrator in 'May's Lion' reinvent May's story?" could be changed to the following "because" statement: "Le Guin's narrator in 'May's Lion' reinvents May's story because Le Guin wants to show that there is a more spiritually satisfying alternative to May's feelings of alienation from nature." This statement does not answer the question fully, but it does answer it enough to provide a clear direction for the essay.

A good outline for an analytical essay will make the drafting of that essay easier and somewhat more relaxed. An outline provides you with a structure to work within that can keep you from getting hopelessly lost in a tangent as you draft your essay: you can always refer back to your outline and get yourself back on track. You can also revise an outline as you go if you discover that it is flawed or unrealistic. The structure of an outline gives you the freedom to take risks in drafting that you might not otherwise take, and it allows you to concentrate primarily on writing rather than planning when you get to the drafting stage.

Drafting without an outline can be a little like taking a long trip by car through unfamiliar country without a road map. If you have all the time in the world and no particular destination in mind, who needs a map? Some kinds of writing, especially personal writing, are like this, and it can be a great pleasure to indulge in them. But the more particularly defined your purpose is in writing, and the more complex your ideas are, the more you will need some kind of structure. An outline, like a map, will define the boundaries and guide your journey. You will know your general route, and if you want to explore off the main route, you can do this without getting lost. You will also know when you've arrived because you will know where you are going.

Revising and Editing

You will see, by now, how the analytical process and the writing process are interrelated. You may also see that both processes are *recursive:* as you move through each stage of analysis or writing, you will from time to time refer back or jump forward between stages. For example, as you take notes, you might be searching for a writing topic; as you outline, you might try drafting an opening paragraph; as you draft, you may go back and rework a section of your outline, or you may revise portions of your first draft as you go.

Revising and editing can also be recursive, but it is important to realize that revising and editing are not the same activity (see "Revising," p. 13). Revising (or re-visioning) involves making changes on a large scale as opposed to editing, which involves making changes on a small scale. The most profitable revisions grow out of carefully conceived and well-articulated drafts, where you have confidence in your ideas and have explained and supported them to your own satisfaction. A good revision requires that you gain some distance from your own work since you will have to approach it as your reader would. If you can spare the time, let your draft sit for a day or so before you attempt to revise it. A lapse of time will allow you to see your draft in a fresh light and it will help you identify yourself more strongly with your reader.

In your first reading after drafting and before beginning to revise, jot down questions and revision ideas as they occur to you. (*Rephrase thesis in one or two sentences. Why is this important? Provide more context for this idea. I don't need to give a plot summary—reader knows the plot, so what's my point? Is this relevant? More evidence from text in support here? Revise paragraph transition to explain how these ideas relate. Tie ideas in conclusion more clearly to questions raised by introduction.*) This first reading between drafting and revising can offer an opportunity for critical reading, especially if you are able to detach yourself from your draft and are able to assume the frame of mind of the reader.

Since you will not be able to distance yourself entirely from your own work, try asking another student from your class to read and review your draft before revising, and offer to return the favor. (Your instructor may have already allowed for review of drafts in some form, through conferences or peer reviews, or through his or her written comments on drafts.) Keep in mind, though, that your peer reader, no matter how perceptive, is only one reader among many, and his or her word is not the last word.

To edit successfully, you will also have to assume your reader's perspective. Grammatical and typographical errors interfere with a smooth reading and, no matter how insightful you are in your analysis, these kinds of errors will distract your reader and detract from the quality of your writing. At best, such errors leave a bad impression, and at worst, they make for confused reading. Have someone else proofread your work after you have done a thorough job of it yourself, pointing out any errors you might have missed.

More difficult to catch than grammatical or typographical errors is awkwardness in word choice, phrasing, and sentence structure. These problems are sometimes hard for writers themselves to catch because they arise out of habits of speech and writing that may be second nature to writers. Sometimes, however, if you read your writing out loud, your ear will catch awkward phrasing or constructions that seem invisible on the page. It can also be especially helpful to have someone else read your work aloud to you; you will hear your reader stumble over certain words and phrases, and even if neither you nor your reader can put your finger on the reason at the time, you can mark these spots in your draft, returning to figure them out later.

THE "CORRECT" ANALYSIS

Students who otherwise enjoy reading literature may dislike reducing its pleasurable aspects to what feels like a test in writing analyses of it. A student may fear that his or her response to a work is wrong. It is important to remember that there is no categorically right or wrong interpretation of any given literary text. There are, however, analyses and interpretations that are well-considered, well-developed, and well articulated and others that are less so. Most instructors, in reading student writing about literature, are not looking for *the* correct answer. They are looking for a sound explanation or argument in support of an interesting response or analysis. You will find that writing such an essay is certainly challenging work, but if you have chosen to explore in your writing an important question (one of real interest to you and of consequence to your reader), have analyzed the text carefully and thoroughly, and have drawn conclusions that are well-earned, you need not worry about making a "wrong" interpretation.

CHALLENGES OF STYLE AND VOICE

Any writer—especially a beginning writer—is challenged by questions of style and voice. Voice is the quality in writing that most strongly reflects the personality of the writer, but it can also reflect the nature and purpose of the writing task. In the personal narrative, for example, because such writing tends to be subjective, the writer generally feels more freedom to write informally in a voice that fits his or her personality. But when we write about specialized subjects and for specialized audiences, it is often necessary to conform to the standard of writing in the field, and we may feel a certain pressure to sound "professional." To an extent, this is a necessary accommodation to audience.

Sometimes, however, when we are not yet fully versed or entirely comfortable in a field of study, our attempts to assume a "professional voice" can result in a strained, stilted, and sometimes pompous prose style. In our attempts to please our readers and to write with authority, we may sacrifice clarity and uniqueness of voice. Perceptions and patterns of thought that may be marvelous in their simplicity and straightforwardness may become burdened or obscured by inflated language or overly complex sentence structure—all as a result of our attempts to sound intelligent to our readers. Analytical essays about literature are, quite often, more formally constructed and articulated than personal essays. But in attempting to write intelligently, take care not to sacrifice the clarity of your thinking and your unique way of "speaking" on the page. The best advice, perhaps, is that you should pay more attention to developing an intelligent analysis than to trying to *sound* intelligent.

THE ELEMENTS OF FICTION

As you head into this chapter's readings, which include short stories and chapters from novels, a brief explanation of the major elements of fiction will provide you with useful points of reference in speaking or writing about fiction. Understanding the elements of fiction will help you understand how and why works of fiction have the effect upon readers that they have, and this understanding will provide contexts for writing about fiction in analytical and interpretive essays.

Plot

Plot, quite simply, is what happens in a story or novel. Usually, plot is more than incident; it is the whole structure of action. Keep in mind when reading excerpts from novels (as you will in some of this chapter's readings) that you are glimpsing only portions of plots. An effective excerpt may feel self-contained like a short story, but it is not: its full impact can be gathered only within its proper context of the entire novel.

The pattern of action in a traditional plot may include certain predictable elements. The story may begin with explanatory writing or *exposition*, revealing an unstable situation; a series of causally related events contributes to rising action; there is a climax in which the critical problem comes to a head; and, finally, falling action leads to the story's conclusion and relative stability.

One of the essential characteristics of plot in fiction is conflict. Nearly all stories are built around conflict, whether *external* (demonstrated by action) or *internal* (taking place within the minds of the characters).

The *protagonist* of a story is generally the story's main character, the person who struggles most directly with conflict. The *antagonist* is the character or force that works most powerfully against the protagonist, generating or intensifying the conflict. Although the protagonist of a story is usually human, this is not always the case. Neither will the antagonist necessarily be human; in fact, quite often it will be an internal force (such as guilt, which may drive the main character) or an external force (such as nature).

Character and Characterization

Characters are the people (and, sometimes, other creatures) who participate in the action of a story. When characters are not human beings, the writer will usually identify or invest in them human qualities or characteristics or assign them roles in the sphere of human events. There are *main characters* and *minor characters,* as well as *flat* (one-dimensional) characters and *round* (complex) characters.

Characterization refers to the way in which the writer develops the characters of a story or novel, and how he or she presents them to the reader. Readers come to know characters through exposition (in which the writer explains a character's motivation or internal qualities), description (in which the writer describes external details, such as a character's physical appearance, letting the reader draw inferences from them), and narration (in which the writer, in describing events involving the character, lets the character's actions speak for themselves).

Setting

The setting of a story or novel may involve more than the place in which the action occurs; it may involve time (the story's period in history and the span of time it covers), social environment (often related to time and place, the cultural context of a story, including manners and mores), and atmosphere (the feel of place, time, and social environment). Not all of these elements of setting will be of equal importance in every story or novel; sometimes one or more will be irrelevant. When one or more of these elements of setting is highly significant, however, an understanding of the way it functions in a story or novel can produce an intriguing analysis.

Point of View

Point of view is conveyed through a narrator, who may or may not be a character in the story. It is also the means by which the writer expresses most directly his or her fundamental ideas and attitudes. Thus, point of view tends to be intimately related to theme.

Four points of view—or perspectives from which the story is told—are most common in fiction. In some fiction (more often in novels than in short stories), point of view shifts from one perspective to another, but usually point of view is consistent.

1. *Omniscient point of view.* In assuming the omniscient, or all-knowing, point of view, the writer him- or herself narrates the story in the third person. The omniscient narrator has full knowledge of the characters' histories, motives, actions, and even their futures and can be anywhere at any time in the story, occupying first one character's mind, then another's. From the omniscient point of view, the writer may even speak directly to the reader, injecting commentary into the narrative.

2. *Limited omniscient point of view.* With the limited omniscient point of view, the writer narrates the story in the third person, as with the omniscient point of view, but his or her knowledge is limited to that of one character, through whose perceptions, emotions, and thoughts we grasp the writer's fictional world. The narrator, and therefore the

reader, has full knowledge and understanding of this character (often more than the character him- or herself does), but no special knowledge or understanding of other characters or situations as they develop. Although this character may be a minor character, more often he or she is the main character, and often the story will focus upon this character's self-discovery.

3. *First-person point of view (character narrator).*   In a work of fiction in which the writer employs first-person narration, the main character, or sometimes a minor character, narrates the story from his or her point of view. This character may be naive or relatively self-aware, but generally the reader will have more insight into what motivates this character, or what may befall him or her, than the character him- or herself does. To let a character tell his or her story with limited understanding, while simultaneously providing the information necessary for the reader to deduce the truth, requires special skill of a writer employing this point of view. The consequences of the character narrator's limited understanding, or his or her growing self-awareness, may be an important thematic element in the story.

4. *Objective (or dramatic) point of view.*   Writers who employ the objective point of view refuse to enter any character's mind, declining any special knowledge or insight. They do not interpret; they simply witness and report, in the third person. Through the writer, we as readers encounter characters and fictional situations as we would strangers on the street and unfamiliar events in real life, with no point of reference beyond our subjective experience and what we take note of as the description and narration unfold. What we come to know and understand about these characters and situations is cumulative, and self-contained within the story. This point of view is sometimes also referred to as the dramatic point of view, because characters and events speak for themselves, as in a play.

Theme

In fiction, as in other forms of writing, there is a difference between subject (what the work is about) and theme (what it says about its subject). Theme is what makes a work of fiction meaningful, usually on a universal rather than a particular level. A work's subject may have to do specifically with its characters and what happens to them, but its theme will generalize, drawing universal significance from the particulars of the story, commenting upon human nature or experience in general. Usually, writers intend to convey universally applicable themes through their stories, and some works have multiple themes. Many writers of fiction are content to raise their themes as complicated questions, ones without pat answers. Thus, in interpreting themes in works of fiction, you may be confronted with a puzzle of meaning that is difficult—sometimes impossible—to solve neatly.

READINGS:
FLIGHTS OF FANCY

INVENTING EXPERIENCE

In fiction, how much is truth and how much is invention? Or put another way, what *is* truth, and what *is* invention?

It is not always easy to tell the difference between fact and fiction, history and story, for they have many qualities in common. Both facts and fictions are concrete, particular. Both stories and histories are narratives, and they can tell us fundamental truths about ourselves and others—who we were, who we are, and what we may become. The fiction writers represented in this chapter have invented characters and dramatic situations in which the characters learn something about nature and about themselves through encounters with the natural world. The plots, characters, and details surrounding them are particular; they are inventions. The themes, generalized from what the stories' main characters learn, are universal, and have the ring of truth about them.

In inventing their stories, fiction writers draw upon a plethora of actual experience, both their own and that of others, and their points of reference, like our own, are rooted in the physical world, in society, and in history itself. Like Dr. Frankenstein, a fiction writer may assemble his or her story from materials recycled from real lives and real events, suturing them with invention and with vision. Some fictions are elaborate patchworks, like Aldous Huxley's futuristic novel *Brave New World* (1932), in which, working from certain familiar and somewhat plausible scientific and social principles, the author imagines the existence and the implications of the genetic engineering of human beings—long before this was even a remote possibility. Other works of fiction are comparatively simple creations, cut from real life, and lightly embroidered: in her introduction to "The Wind-Chill Factor," M. F. K.

Fisher wonders why she "wrote in the third person, because [the story] is one of the most directly personal accounts I have ever given of something that has happened to me."

Casting a truth in fictional form allows certain freedoms. This freedom may come in gaining enough distance from personal events to lend them perspective, to allow them to be written about (perhaps the case for Fisher). In Huxley's case, the freedom may have come in being able to speculate about *possibilities,* rather than being confined to a world of so-called certainties. Fiction not only allows us to invent stories, but to *reinvent* realities. Through her narrator in the story "May's Lion," Ursula K. Le Guin invents the story of May's encounter with the dying mountain lion, and, when it does not satisfy, she reinvents the story to illustrate a better alternative to May's distance from the natural world and from her self, offering this alternative to her reader like a gift.

Good fiction is discovery, for both the writer and the reader. Although grounded in worlds that are fundamentally familiar, fiction allows us immediacies of perspective and experience, sometimes in the extreme, that we could not, or would not, have otherwise. Fiction allows us to explore, with the author, dimensions of the question *What if?*

LANDSCAPE AS CHARACTER IN FICTION

Novelist and literary theorist Henry James wrote that in fiction, "landscape is character." Indeed, for many writers of fiction, including all of those whose work is represented in this chapter's readings, nature is considerably more than setting, more than pastoral backdrop and more, even, than atmosphere. It is a force fundamental to these stories' plots and themes, a primary catalyst of change for the characters. Although in many of these stories, nature can be seen as the antagonist—a source of conflict for the protagonist—in most, the more important antagonistic element is the main character's resistance to the forces of nature, and the resolution of conflict comes when the character achieves a degree of harmony with nature. This achievement of harmony often comes at considerable cost, including the character's loss of some fundamental aspect of human identity—such as human relationships, reason and sanity, or moral standards—that characterizes our special place in the natural order.

Yet the problem that many of these stories pose has to do with questioning the position that humans occupy in the natural order. As the reasoning animal, the civilized animal, we have set ourselves apart, or have been set apart, from the rest of nature; many of us feel the loss, yearning to be part, once again, of an apparently simpler world of nature rather than of civilization. Some characters in these stories seek out situations in which they must choose between nature and civilization, but for many, the choice is forced upon them by circumstance: nature imposes itself upon them and asks them to choose. For all of these writers, and all of their characters, the ultimate goal may be to achieve a balance between human identity and affinity with nature, a harmonious relationship; but the writers see nature as a force in various ways, and their characters respond to its force variously as well.

For many writers in this chapter, nature is a fundamental and primeval force, drawing forth from their characters an older, less rational self than the characters, or the reader, may be comfortable with. Loren Eiseley's story "The Dance of the Frogs" and M. F. K. Fisher's "The Wind-Chill Factor" can be seen as being about madness—or at least the loss of human rationality—in the face of nature's primeval presence. There is a terror in this: in our daily lives we may feel far removed, because of our capacity for reason, from natural law and the simple, relentless struggle for survival; but we are close enough in evolutionary terms to our primitive, instinctive selves to recognize, and to fear, the primordial darkness when we see it.

Some writers in this chapter find, rather than terror, promise, wisdom, and a spiritual solace in the prospect of letting go of our sense of separateness from nature, of achieving a better harmony with it. Although Loren Eiseley's character in "The Dance of the Frogs," Dr. Dreyer, is badly shaken by his encounter with the supernatural in nature, its presence not only haunts him, but has also made him wise. In Ursula K. Le Guin's story "May's Lion" and in the excerpt from Barry Lopez's fable *Crow and Weasel,* nature is our ultimate teacher—or can be, if we manage not to get too distracted by our apparent success in putting ourselves above and beyond its reach.

■ ALDOUS HUXLEY
Chapter 1 from *Brave New World*

Novelist, poet, playwright, and essayist Aldous Huxley, grandson of famous naturalist T. H. Huxley, was born in 1894 in Godalming, Surrey, England, and died in California in 1963. He was educated at Oxford University and was employed briefly as a schoolmaster at Eaton College and, between 1919 and 1924, as a newspaperman. Huxley was probably most renowned for his utopian novel Brave New World *(1932), the first chapter of which is included here. His early novels, including* Chrome Yellow *(1921) and* Antic Hay *(1923), as well as* Brave New World, *are works of social satire; his later writing, including the novels* Eyeless in Gaza *(1936) and* Island *(1962), and his infamous* The Doors of Perception *(1954), where he describes his experiences with hallucinogenic drugs, are essentially mystical works in which he explores personal and perceptual transformation. His novel* Point Counter Point *(1928), considered by many critics to be his best, unites characteristics of both his early and later work.*

Huxley had been determined to pursue a career in medicine, but when he was stricken by a corneal disease at the age of sixteen and temporarily blinded, he altered his plans. His interests in science, however, as well as his early scientific training, strongly influenced the subjects of his writing and his ways of looking at and interpreting them. In the 1965 Memorial Volume, *Huxley's brother Julian explains that Aldous was fascinated in equal degrees by the facts of science and by mystical experience; both for Huxley were means of discovery, but "the more comprehension [science] gives us of the mechanisms of existence, the more clearly does the mystery of existence stand out."*

In the opening chapter of Brave New World, *Huxley, through the character of the Director, takes us on a tour of the Central London Hatchery and Conditioning Centre, where human clones are manufactured according to castes: the intelligent Alphas and Betas are destined to be society's governors and managers; the Deltas, Gammas, and Epsilons, engineered to be less intelligent, will unquestioningly undertake society's menial tasks. Although it is a comfortable society, the dystopia that Huxley depicts is one in which "community, identity, stability" are preserved at the cost of creativity, individuality, and liberty. Huxley's depiction of this "brave new world" takes on a greater resonance today since we are much closer—closer than perhaps even Huxley could have imagined—to the reality of creating, through genetic engineering, "improved" human beings (see the readings on genetic engineering in Chapter 8).*

A squat grey building of only thirty-four stories. Over the main entrance the words, CENTRAL LONDON HATCHERY AND CONDITIONING CENTRE, and, in a shield, the World State's motto, COMMUNITY, IDENTITY, STABILITY.

The enormous room on the ground floor faced towards the north. Cold for all the summer beyond the panes, for all the tropical heat of the room itself, a harsh thin light glared through the windows, hungrily seeking some draped lay figure, some pallid shape of academic goose-flesh, but finding only the glass and nickel and bleakly shining porcelain of a laboratory. Wintriness responded to wintriness. The overalls of the workers were white, their hands gloved with a pale corpse-coloured rubber. The light was frozen, dead, a ghost. Only from the yellow barrels of the microscopes did it borrow a certain rich and living substance, lying along the polished tubes like butter, streak after luscious streak in long recession down the work tables.

"And this," said the Director opening the door, "is the Fertilizing Room."

Bent over their instruments, three hundred Fertilizers were plunged, as the Director of Hatcheries and Conditioning entered the room, in the scarcely breathing silence, the absent-minded, soliloquizing hum or whistle, of absorbed concentration. A troop of newly arrived students, very young, pink and callow, followed nervously, rather abjectly, at the Director's heels. Each of them carried a notebook, in which, whenever the great man spoke, he desperately scribbled. Straight from the horse's mouth. It was a rare privilege. The D.H.C. for Central London always made a point of personally conducting his new students round the various departments.

"Just to give you a general idea," he would explain to them. For of course some sort of general idea they must have, if they were to do their work intelligently—though as little of one, if they were to be good and happy members of society, as possible. For particulars, as every one knows, make for virtue and happiness; generalities are intellectually necessary evils. Not philosophers but fret-sawyers and stamp collectors compose the backbone of society.

"To-morrow," he would add, smiling at them with a slightly menacing geniality, "you'll be settling down to serious work. You won't have time for generalities. Meanwhile. . . "

Meanwhile, it was a privilege. Straight from the horse's mouth into the notebook. The boys scribbled like mad.

Tall and rather thin but upright, the Director advanced into the room. He had a long chin and big, rather prominent teeth, just covered, when he was not talking, by his full, floridly curved lips. Old, young? Thirty? Fifty? Fifty-five? It was hard to say. And anyhow the question didn't arise; in this year of stability, A.F. 632, it didn't occur to you to ask it.

"I shall begin at the beginning," said the D.H.C. and the more zealous students recorded his intention in their notebooks: *Begin at the beginning.* "These," he waved his hand, "are the incubators."

And opening an insulated door he showed them racks upon racks of numbered test-tubes. "The week's supply of ova. Kept," he explained, "at blood heat; whereas the male gametes," and here he opened another door, "they have to be kept at thirty-five instead of thirty-seven. Full blood heat sterilizes." Rams wrapped in theremogene beget no lambs.

Still leaning against the incubators he gave them, while the pencils scurried illegibly across the pages, a brief description of the modern fertilizing process; spoke first, of course, of its surgical introduction—"the operation undergone voluntarily for the good of Society, not to mention the fact that it carries a bonus amounting to six months' salary"; continued with some account of the technique for preserving the excised ovary alive and actively developing; passed on to a consideration of optimum temperature, salinity, viscosity; referred to the liquor in which the detached and ripened eggs were kept; and, leading his charges to the work tables, actually showed them how this liquor was drawn off from the test-tubes; how it was let out drop by drop onto the specially warmed slides of the microscopes; how the eggs which it contained were inspected for abnormalities, counted and transferred to a porous receptacle; how (and he now took them to watch the operation) this receptacle was immersed in a warm bouillon containing free-swimming spermatozoa—at a minimum concentration of one hundred thousand per cubic centimetre, he insisted; and how, after ten minutes, the container was lifted out of the liquor and its contents re-examined; how, if any of the eggs remained unfertilized, it was again immersed, and, if necessary, yet again; how the fertilized ova went back to the incubators; where the Alphas and Betas remained until definitely bottled; while the Gammas, Deltas and Epsilons were brought out again, after only thirty-six hours, to undergo Bokanovsky's Process.

"Bokanovsky's Process," repeated the Director, and the students underlined the words in their little notebooks.

One egg, one embryo, one adult—normality. But a bokanovskified egg will bud, will proliferate, will divide. From eight to ninety-six buds, and every bud will grow into a perfectly formed embryo, and every embryo into a full-sized adult. Making ninety-six human beings grow where only one grew before. Progress.

"Essentially," the D.H.C. concluded, "bokanovskification consists of a series of arrests of development. We check the normal growth and, paradoxically enough, the egg responds by budding."

Responds by budding. The pencils were busy.

He pointed. On a very slowly moving band a rack-full of test-tubes was entering a large metal box, another rack-full was emerging. Machinery faintly purred. It took eight minutes for the tubes to go through, he told them. Eight minutes of hard X-rays being about as much as an egg can stand. A few died; of the rest, the least susceptible divided into two; most put out four buds; some eight; all were returned to the incubators, where the buds began to develop; then after two days, were suddenly chilled, chilled and checked. Two, four, eight, the buds in their turn budded; and having budded were dosed almost to death with alcohol; consequently burgeoned again and having budded—bud out of bud out of bud—were thereafter—further arrest being generally fatal—left to develop in peace. By which time the original egg was in a fair way to becoming anything from eight to ninety-six embryos—a prodigious improvement, you will agree, on nature. Identical twins—but not in piddling twos and threes as in the old viviparous days, when an egg would sometimes accidentally divide; actually by dozens, by scores at a time.

"Scores," the Director repeated and flung out his arms, as though he were distributing largesse. "Scores."

But one of the students was fool enough to ask where the advantage lay.

"My good boy!" The Director wheeled sharply round on him. "Can't you see? Can't you *see*?" He raised a hand; his expression was solemn. "Bokanovsky's Process is one of the major instruments of social stability!"

Major instruments of social stability.

Standard men and women; in uniform batches. The whole of a small factory staffed with the products of a single bokanovskified egg.

"Ninety-six identical twins working ninety-six identical machines!" The voice was almost tremulous with enthusiasm. "You really know where you are. For the first time in history." He quoted the planetary motto. "Community, Identity, Stability." Grand words. "If we could bokanovskify indefinitely the whole problem would be solved."

Solved by standard Gammas, unvarying Deltas, uniform Epsilons. Millions of identical twins. The principle of mass production at last applied to biology.

"But, alas," the Director shook his head, "we *can't* bokanovskify indefinitely."

Ninety-six seemed to be the limit; seventy-two a good average. From the same ovary and with gametes of the same male to manufacture as many batches of identical twins as possible—that was the best (sadly a second best) that they could do. And even that was difficult.

"For in nature it takes thirty years for two hundred eggs to reach maturity. But our business is to stabilize the population at this moment, here and now. Dribbling out twins over a quarter of a century—what would be the use of that?"

Obviously, no use at all. But Podsnap's Technique had immensely accelerated the process of ripening. They could make sure of at least a hundred and fifty mature eggs within two years. Fertilize and bokanovskify—in other words, multiply by seventy-two—and you get an average of nearly eleven thousand brothers and sisters in a hundred and fifty batches of identical twins, all within two years of the same age.

"And in exceptional cases we can make one ovary yield us over fifteen thousand adult individuals."

Beckoning to a fair-haired, ruddy young man who happened to be passing at the moment, "Mr. Foster," he called. The ruddy young man approached. "Can you tell us the record for a single ovary, Mr. Foster?"

"Sixteen thousand and twelve in this Centre," Mr. Foster replied without hesitation. He spoke very quickly, had a vivacious blue eye, and took an evident pleasure in quoting figures. "Sixteen thousand and twelve; in one hundred and eighty-nine batches of identicals. But of course they've done much better," he rattled on, "in some of the tropical Centres. Singapore had often produced over sixteen thousand five hundred; and Mombasa has actually touched the seventeen thousand mark. But then they have unfair advantages. You should see the way a negro ovary responds to pituitary! It's quite astonishing, when you're used to working with European material. Still," he added, with a laugh (but the light of combat was in his eyes and the lift of his chin was challenging), "still, we mean to beat them if we can. I'm working on a wonderful Delta-Minus ovary at this moment. Only just eighteen months old. Over twelve thousand seven hundred children already, either decanted or in embryo. And still going strong. We'll beat them yet."

"That's the spirit I like!" cried the Director, and clapped Mr. Foster on the shoulder. "Come along with us and give these boys the benefit of your expert knowledge."

Mr. Foster smiled modestly. "With pleasure." They went.

In the Bottling Room all was harmonious bustle and ordered activity. Flaps of fresh sow's peritoneum ready cut to the proper size came shooting up in little lifts from the Organ Store in the subbasement. Whizz and then, click! the lift-hatches flew open; the bottle-liner had only to reach out a hand, take the flap, insert, smooth-down, and before the lined bottle had had time to travel out of reach along the endless band, whizz, click! another flap of peritoneum had shot up from the depths, ready to be slipped into yet another bottle, the next of that slow interminable procession on the band.

Next to the Liners stood the Matriculators. The procession advanced; one by one the eggs were transferred from their test-tubes to the large containers; deftly the peritoneal lining was slit, the morula dropped into place, the saline solution poured in . . . and already the bottle had passed, and it was the turn of the labellers. Heredity, date of fertilization, membership of Bokanovsky Group—details were transferred from test-tube to bottle. No longer anonymous, but named, identified, the procession marched slowly on; on through an opening in the wall, slowly on into the Social Predestination Room.

"Eighty-eight cubic metres of card-index," said Mr. Foster with relish, as they entered.

"Containing *all* the relevant information," added the Director.

"Brought up to date every morning."

"And co-ordinated every afternoon."

"On the basis of which they make their calculations."

"So many individuals, of such and such quality," said Mr. Foster.

"Distributed in such and such quantities."

"The optimum Decanting Rate at any given moment."

"Unforeseen wastages promptly made good."

"Promptly," repeated Mr. Foster. "If you knew the amount of overtime I had to put in after the last Japanese earthquake!" He laughed good-humouredly and shook his head.

"The Predestinators send in their figures to the Fertilizers."

"Who give them the embryos they ask for."

"And the bottles come in here to be predestinated in detail."

"After which they are sent down to the Embryo Store."

"Where we now proceed ourselves."

And opening a door Mr. Foster led the way down a staircase into the basement.

The temperature was still tropical. They descended into a thickening twilight. Two doors and a passage with a double turn insured the cellar against any possible infiltration of the day.

"Embryos are like photograph film," said Mr. Foster waggishly, as he pushed open the second door. "They can only stand red light."

And in effect the sultry darkness into which the students now followed him was visible and crimson, like the darkness of closed eyes on a summer's afternoon. The bulging flanks of row on receding row and tier above tier of bottles glinted with innumerable rubies, and among the rubies moved the dim red spectres of men and women with purple eyes and all the symptoms of lupus. The hum and rattle of machinery faintly stirred the air.

"Give them a few figures, Mr. Foster," said the Director, who was tired of talking.

Mr. Foster was only too happy to give them a few figures.

Two hundred and twenty metres long, two hundred wide, ten high. He pointed upwards. Like chickens drinking, the students lifted their eyes towards the distant ceiling.

Three tiers of racks: ground floor level, first gallery, second gallery.

The spidery steel-work of gallery above gallery faded away in all directions into the dark. Near them three red ghosts were busily unloading demijohns from a moving staircase.

The escalator from the Social Predestination Room.

Each bottle could be placed on one of fifteen racks, each rack, though you couldn't see it, was a conveyor travelling at the rate of thirty-three and a third centimetres an hour. Two hundred and sixty-seven days at eight metres a day. Two thousand one hundred and thirty-six metres in all. One circuit of the cellar at ground level, one on the first gallery, half on the second, and on the two hundred and sixty-seventh morning, daylight in the Decanting Room. Independent existence—so called.

"But in the interval," Mr. Foster concluded, "we've managed to do a lot to them. Oh, a very great deal." His laugh was knowing and triumphant.

"That's the spirit I like," said the Director once more. "Let's walk round. You tell them everything, Mr. Foster."

Mr. Foster duly told them.

Told them of the growing embryo on its bed of peritoneum. Made them taste the rich blood surrogate on which it fed. Explained why it had to be stimulated with placentin and thyroxin. Told them of the *corpus luteum* extract. Showed them the jets through which at every twelfth metre from zero to 2040 it was automatically injected. Spoke of those gradually increasing doses of pituitary administered during the final ninety-six metres of their course. Described the artificial maternal circulation installed on every bottle at Metre 112; showed them the reservoir of blood-surrogate, the centrifugal pump that kept the liquid moving over the placenta and drove it through the synthetic lung and waste-product filter. Referred to the embryo's troublesome tendency to anaemia, to the massive doses of hog's stomach extract and fetal foal's liver with which, in consequence, it had to be supplied.

Showed them, the simple mechanism by means of which, during the last two metres out of every eight, all the embryos were simultaneously shaken into familiarity with movement. Hinted at the gravity of the so-called "trauma of decanting," and enumerated the precautions taken to minimize, by a suitable training of the bottled embryo, that dangerous shock. Told them of the tests for sex carried out in the neighbourhood of metre 200. Explained the system of labelling—a T for the males, a circle for the females and for those who were destined to become freemartins a question mark, black on a white ground.

"For of course," said Mr. Foster, "in the vast majority of cases, fertility is merely a nuisance. One fertile ovary in twelve hundred—that would really be quite sufficient for our purposes. But we want to have a good choice. And of course one must always leave an enormous margin of safety. So we allow as many as thirty per cent of the female embryos to develop normally. The others get a dose of male sex-hormone every twenty-four metres for the rest of the course. Result: they're decanted as freemartins—structurally quite normal ("except," he had to admit, "that they *do* have just the slightest tendency to grow beards"), but sterile. Guaranteed sterile. Which brings us at last," continued Mr. Foster, "out of the realm of mere slavish imitation of nature into the much more interesting world of human invention."

He rubbed his hands. For of course, they didn't content themselves with merely hatching out embryos: any cow could do that.

"We also predestine and condition. We decant our babies as socialized human beings, as Alphas or Epsilons, as future sewage workers or future. . ." He was going to say "future World controllers," but correcting himself, said "future Directors of Hatcheries," instead.

The D.H.C. acknowledged the compliment with a smile.

They were passing Metre 320 on rack 11. A young Beta-Minus mechanic was busy with screwdriver and spanner on the blood-surrogate pump of a passing bottle. The hum of the electric motor deepened by fractions of a tone as he turned the nuts. Down, down. . . A final twist, a glance at the revolution counter, and he was done. He moved two paces down the line and began the same process on the next pump.

"Reducing the number of revolutions per minute," Mr. Foster explained. "The surrogate goes round slower; therefore passes through the lung at longer intervals; therefore gives the embryo less oxygen. Nothing like oxygen-shortage for keeping an embryo below par." Again he rubbed his hands.

"But why do you want to keep the embryo below par?" asked an ingenuous student.

"Ass!" said the Director, breaking a long silence. "Hasn't it occurred to you that an Epsilon embryo must have an Epsilon environment as well as an Epsilon heredity?"

It evidently hadn't occurred to him. He was covered with confusion.

"The lower the caste," said Mr. Foster, "the shorter the oxygen." The first organ affected was the brain. After that the skeleton. At seventy per cent of normal oxygen you got dwarfs. At less than seventy eyeless monsters.

"Who are no use at all," concluded Mr. Foster.

Whereas (his voice became confidential and eager), if they could discover a technique for shortening the period of maturation what a triumph, what a benefaction to Society!

"Consider the horse."

They considered it.

Mature at six; the elephant at ten. While at thirteen a man is not yet sexually mature; and is only full-grown at twenty. Hence, of course, that fruit of delayed development, the human intelligence.

"But in Epsilons," said Mr. Foster very justly, "we don't need human intelligence."

Didn't need and didn't get it. But though the Epsilon mind was mature at ten, the Epsilon body was not fit to work till eighteen. Long years of superfluous and wasted immaturity. If the physical development could be speeded up till it was as quick, say, as a cow's what an enormous saving to the Community!

"Enormous!" murmured the students. Mr. Foster's enthusiasm was infectious.

He became rather technical; spoke of the abnormal endocrine coordination which made men grow so slowly; postulated a germinal mutation to account for it. Could the effects of this germinal mutation be undone? Could the individual Epsilon embryo be made a revert, by a suitable technique, to the normality of dogs and cows? That was the problem. And it was all but solved.

Pilkington, at Mombasa, had produced individuals who were sexually mature at four and full-grown at six and a half. A scientific triumph. But socially useless. Six-year-old men and women were too stupid to do even Epsilon work. And the process was an all-or-nothing one; either you failed to modify at all, or else you modified the whole way. They were still trying to find the ideal compromise between adults of twenty and adults of six. So far without success. Mr. Foster sighed and shook his head.

Their wanderings through the crimson twilight had brought them to the neighbourhood of Metre 170 on Rack 9. From this point onwards Rack 9 was enclosed and the bottles performed the remainder of their journey in a kind of tunnel, interrupted here and there by openings two or three metres wide.

"Heat conditioning," said Mr. Foster.

Hot tunnels alternated with cool tunnels. Coolness was wedded to discomfort in the form of hard X-rays. By the time they were decanted the embryos had a horror of cold. They were predestined to emigrate to the tropics, to be miners and acetate silk spinners and steel workers. Later on their minds would be made to endorse the judgment of their bodies. "We condition them to thrive on heat," concluded Mr. Foster. "Our colleagues upstairs will teach them to love it."

"And that," put in the Director sententiously, "that is the secret of happiness and virtue—liking what you've *got* to do. All conditioning aims at that: making people like their unescapable social destiny."

In a gap between two tunnels, a nurse was delicately probing with a long fine syringe into the gelatinous contents of a passing bottle. The students and their guides stood watching her for a few moments in silence.

"Well, Lenina," said Mr. Foster, when at last she withdrew the syringe and straightened herself up.

The girl turned with a start. One could see that, for all the lupus and the purple eyes, she was uncommonly pretty.

"Henry!" Her smile flashed redly at him—a row of coral teeth.

"Charming, charming," murmured the Director and, giving her two or three little pats, received in exchange a rather deferential smile for himself.

"What are you giving them?" asked Mr. Foster, making his tone very professional.

"Oh, the usual typhoid and sleeping sickness."

"Tropical workers start being inoculated at Metre 150," Mr. Foster explained to the students. "The embryos still have gills. We immunize the fish against the future man's diseases." Then, turning back to Lenina, "Ten to five on the roof this afternoon," he said, "as usual."

"Charming," said the Director once more, and, with a final pat, moved away after the others.

On Rack 10 rows of next generation's chemical workers were being trained in the toleration of lead, caustic soda, tar, chlorine. The first of a batch of two hundred and fifty embryonic rocket-plane engineers was just passing the eleven hundred metre mark on Rack 3. A special mechanism kept their containers in constant rotation. "To improve their sense of balance," Mr. Foster explained. "Doing repairs on the outside of a rocket in mid-air is a ticklish job. We slacken off the circulation when they're right way up, so that they're half starved, and double the flow of surrogate when they're upside down. They learn to associate topsy-turvydom with well-being; in fact, they're only truly happy when they're standing on their heads.

"And now," Mr. Foster went on, "I'd like to show you some very interesting conditioning for Alpha Plus Intellectuals. We have a big batch of them on Rack 5. First Gallery level," he called to two boys who had started to go down to the ground floor.

"They're round about Metre 900," he explained. "You can't really do any useful intellectual conditioning till the fetuses have lost their tails. Follow me."

But the Director had looked at his watch. "Ten to three," he said. "No time for the intellectual embryos, I'm afraid. We must go up to the Nurseries before the children have finished their afternoon sleep."

Mr. Foster was disappointed. "At least one glance at the Decanting Room," he pleaded.

"Very well then." The Director smiled indulgently. "Just one glance."

■ CONSIDERATIONS OF MEANING AND METHOD

1. How does the language Huxley uses to describe the Central London Hatchery and Conditioning Centre in the first two paragraphs establish the tone of the chapter? That is, what does it reveal about Huxley's attitude toward his subject? Point to specific words, phrases, and images which most effectively convey tone.

2. How do the students respond to the Director? What does the pattern of their response emphasize about the nature of their re-

sponse? Does Mr. Foster respond to the Director in the same way?

3. How are differences between Alphas, Betas, Deltas, Epsilons, and Gammas enhanced by variations in incubation and conditioning processes? Once they are "decanted," how do these differences lend themselves to fulfillment of "the World State's motto, 'Community, Identity, Stability'"?

4. What in this chapter suggests that this society is not only strictly delineated according to caste, but may be, at least among the intelligent elite, racist and sexist as well?

5. Huxley adapts his writing style in some interesting ways throughout this chapter to help illustrate and reinforce his theme. For example, he sometimes writes in sentence fragments. Why? Can you find other examples in which sentence structure or rhetorical patterns enhance theme?

6. What technological problems involving fertilization and maturation have scientists yet to solve in this "brave new world"? How does the Director hope society will change once these problems are solved?

■ POSSIBILITIES FOR WRITING

1. In writing *Brave New World,* Huxley wanted more than to entertain us or to tickle our imaginations; he wanted us to see a reflection of our own society in his fictional one. In giving the students "a general idea" of how and why the Central London Hatchery and Conditioning Centre works, the Director reflects that "some sort of general idea they must have, if they were to do their work intelligently—though as little of one, if they were to be good and happy members of society, as possible. For particulars, as every one knows, make for virtue and happiness; generalities are intellectually necessary evils. Not philosophers but fretsawyers [craftspeople who use fret-saws for fine, detailed woodwork] and stamp collectors compose the backbone of society." In an analytical essay, discuss and illustrate with examples the extent to which you think this statement applies in our own society, perhaps comparing it to Huxley's.

2. In your library, locate one or two recent articles in magazines (look for relatively popular magazines that will nevertheless offer a reasonably in-depth look at the subject) that describe recent breakthroughs or the current state of technology as it relates to human cloning or artificial wombs. In an essay for readers familiar with *Brave New World,* address the question of how close we are to the reality—in part or whole—of cloning human beings or

growing them outside the human body. What do you think and how do you feel about what you've learned?

■ LOREN EISELEY
The Dance of the Frogs

Loren Eiseley was born in 1907 in Lincoln, Nebraska, and died of cancer in 1977 in Philadelphia, Pennsylvania. He is best known for his essays about anthropology, archaeology, natural history, and the history of science. Educated at the University of Nebraska and the University of Pennsylvania, Eiseley was a prominent sociologist and anthropologist who taught anthropology and the history and philosophy of science for many years at the University of Pennsylvania. Between 1966 and 1968, Eiseley hosted a television program called "Animal Secrets" and was a member of the presidential task force on preservation of natural beauty from 1964 to 1965. He also served for many years as a member of the advisory board of the National Parks Division of the Department of the Interior.

Eiseley's many collections of essays for popular and literary audiences on subjects of natural and human history include The Immense Journey *(1957),* The Firmament of Time *(1960), and* The Unexpected Universe *(1969). His volumes of poetry include* Notes of an Alchemist *(1972),* The Innocent Assasins *(1973), and* Another Kind of Autumn *(1977). The following story, "The Dance of the Frogs," was located among his unpublished manuscripts after his death and was included in* The Star Thrower *(1978), a selection of works published posthumously.*

In addition to their scientific thrust, many of Eiseley's nonfiction works have a mythical or mystical quality about them. "The Dance of the Frogs" is an unusual example of Eiseley's writing because it is a fictional work in which he indulges wholeheartedly in his view of nature as the source of inexplicable mysteries—mysteries of which human beings may occasionally catch a glimpse, if they risk leaving reason behind them.

I

He was a member of the Explorers Club, and he had never been outside the state of Pennsylvania. Some of us who were world travelers used to smile a little about that, even though we knew his scientific reputation had been, at one time, great. It is always the way of youth to smile. I used to think of myself as something of an adventurer, but the time came when I realized that old Albert Dreyer, huddling with his drink in the shadows close to the fire, had journeyed farther into the Country of Terror than any of us would ever go, God willing, and emerge alive.

He was a morose and aging man, without family and without intimates. His membership in the club dated back into the decades when he was a zoologist famous for his remarkable experiments upon amphibians—he had recovered and actually produced the adult stage of the Mexican axolotl, as well as achieving remarkable tissue transplants in salamanders. The club had been flattered to have him then, travel or no travel, but the end was not fortunate. The brilliant scientist had become the misanthrope; the achievement lay all in the past, and Albert Dreyer kept to his solitary room, his solitary drink, and his accustomed spot by the fire.

The reason I came to hear his story was an odd one. I had been north that year, and the club had asked me to give a little talk on the religious beliefs of the Indians of the northern forest, the Naskapi of Labrador. I had long been a student of the strange mélange of superstition and woodland wisdom that makes up the religious life of the nature peoples. Moreover, I had come to know something of the strange similarities of the "shaking tent rite" to the phenomena of the modern medium's cabinet.

"The special tent with its entranced occupant is no different from the cabinet," I contended. "The only difference is the type of voices that emerge. Many of the physical phenomena are identical—the movement of powerful forces shaking the conical hut, objects thrown, all this is familiar to Western psychical science. What is different are the voices projected. Here they are the cries of animals, the voices from the swamp and the mountain—the solitary elementals before whom the primitive man stands in awe, and from whom he begs sustenance. Here the game lords reign supreme; man himself is voiceless."

A low, halting query reached me from the back of the room. I was startled, even in the midst of my discussion, to note that it was Dreyer.

"And the game lords, what are they?"

"Each species of animal is supposed to have gigantic leaders of more than normal size," I explained. "These beings are the immaterial controllers of that particular type of animal. Legend about them is confused. Sometimes they partake of human qualities, will and intelligence, but they are of animal shape. They control the movements of game, and thus their favor may mean life or death to man."

"Are they visible?" Again Dreyer's low, troubled voice came from the back of the room.

"Native belief has it that they can be seen on rare occasions," I answered. "In a sense they remind one of the concept of the archetypes, the originals behind the petty show of our small, transitory existence. They are the immortal renewers of substance—the force behind and above animate nature."

"Do they dance?" persisted Dreyer.

At this I grew nettled. Old Dreyer in a heckling mood was something new. "I cannot answer that question," I said acidly. "My informants failed to elaborate upon it. But they believe implicitly in these monstrous beings, talk to and propitiate them. It is their voices that emerge from the shaking tent."

"The Indians believe it," pursued old Dreyer relentlessly, "but do *you* believe it?"

"My dear fellow—I shrugged and glanced at the smiling audience—"I have seen many strange things, many puzzling things, but I am a scientist." Dreyer made a contemptuous sound in his throat and went back to the shadow out of which he had crept in his interest. The talk was over. I headed for the bar.

II

The evening passed. Men drifted homeward or went to their rooms. I had been a year in the woods and hungered for voices and companionship. Finally, however, I sat alone with my glass, a little mellow, perhaps, enjoying the warmth of the fire and remembering the blue snowfields of the North as they should be remembered—in the comfort of warm rooms.

I think an hour must have passed. The club was silent except for the ticking of an antiquated clock on the mantel and small night noises from the street. I must have drowsed. At all events it was some time before I grew aware that a chair had been drawn up opposite me. I started.

"A damp night," I said.

"Foggy," said the man in the shadow musingly. "But not too foggy. They like it that way."

"Eh?" I said. I knew immediately it was Dreyer speaking. Maybe I had missed something; on second thought, maybe not.

"And spring," he said. "Spring. That's part of it. God knows why, of course, but we feel it, why shouldn't they? And more intensely."

"Look—" I said. "I guess—" The old man was more human than I thought. He reached out and touched my knee with the hand that he always kept a glove over—burn, we used to speculate—and smiled softly.

"You don't know what I'm talking about," he finished for me. "And, besides, I ruffled your feelings earlier in the evening. You must forgive me. You touched on an interest of mine, and I was perhaps overeager. I did not intend to give the appearance of heckling. It was only that . . . "

"Of course," I said. "Of course." Such a confession from Dreyer was astounding. The man might be ill. I rang for a drink and decided to shift the conversation to a safer topic, more appropriate to a scholar.

"Frogs," I said desperately, like any young ass in a china shop. "Always admired your experiments. Frogs. Yes."

I give the old man credit. He took the drink and held it up and looked at me across the rim. There was a faint stir of sardonic humor in his eyes.

"Frogs, no," he said, "or maybe yes. I've never been quite sure. Maybe yes. But there was no time to decide properly." The humor faded out of his eyes. "Maybe I should have let go," he said. "It was what they wanted. There's no doubting that at all, but it came too quick for me. What would you have done?"

"I don't know," I said honestly enough and pinched myself.

"You had better know," said Albert Dreyer severely, "if you're planning to become an investigator of primitive religions. Or even not. I wasn't, you know, and the things came to me just when I least suspected—But I forget, you don't believe in them."

He shrugged and half rose, and for the first time, really, I saw the black-gloved hand and the haunted face of Albert Dreyer and knew in my heart the things he had stood for in science. I got up then, as a young man in the presence of his betters should get up, and I said, and I meant it, every word: "Please, Dr. Dreyer, sit down and tell me. I'm too young to be saying what I believe or don't believe in at all. I'd be obliged if you'd tell me."

Just at that moment a strange, wonderful dignity shone out of the countenance of Albert Dreyer, and I knew the man he was. He bowed and sat down, and there were no longer the barriers of age and youthful ego between us. There were just two men under a lamp, and around them a great waiting silence. Out to the ends of the universe,

I thought fleetingly, that's the way with man and his lamps. One has to huddle in, there's so little light and so much space. One——

III

"It could happen to anyone," said Albert Dreyer. "And especially in the spring. Remember that. And all I did was to skip. Just a few feet, mark you, but I skipped. Remember that, too.

"You wouldn't remember the place at all. At least not as it was then." He paused and shook the ice in his glass and spoke more easily.

"It was a road that came out finally in a marsh along the Schuylkill River. Probably all industrial now. But I had a little house out there with a laboratory thrown in. It was convenient to the marsh, and that helped me with my studies of amphibia. Moreover, it was a wild, lonely road, and I wanted solitude. It is always the demand of the naturalist. You understand that?"

"Of course," I said. I knew he had gone there, after the death of his young wife, in grief and loneliness and despair. He was not a man to mention such things. "It is best for the naturalist," I agreed.

"Exactly. My best work was done there." He held up his black-gloved hand and glanced at it meditatively. "The work on the axolotl, newt neoteny. I worked hard. I had—" he hesitated—"things to forget. There were times when I worked all night. Or diverted myself, while waiting the result of an experiment, by midnight walks. It was a strange road. Wild all right, but paved and close enough to the city that there were occasional street lamps. All uphill and downhill, with bits of forest leaning in over it, till you walked in a tunnel of trees. Then suddenly you were in the marsh, and the road ended at an old, unused wharf.

"A place to be alone. A place to walk and think. A place for shadows to stretch ahead of you from one dim lamp to another and spring back as you reached the next. I have seen them get tall, tall, but never like that night. It was like a road into space."

"Cold?" I asked.

"No. I shouldn't have said 'space.' It gives the wrong effect. Not cold. Spring. Frog time. The first warmth, and the leaves coming. A little fog in the hollows. The way they like it then in the wet leaves and bogs. No moon, though; secretive and dark, with just those street lamps wandered out from the town. I often wondered what graft had brought them there. They shone on nothing—except my walks at midnight and the journeys of toads, but still . . . "

"Yes?" I prompted, as he paused.

"I was just thinking. The web of things. A politician in town gets a rake-off for selling useless lights on a useless road. If it hadn't been for that, I might not have seen them. I might not even have skipped. Or, if I had, the effect—How can you tell about such things afterwards? Was the effect heightened? Did it magnify their power? Who is to say?"

"The skip?" I said, trying to keep things casual. "I don't understand. You mean, just skipping? Jumping?"

Something like a twinkle came into his eyes for a moment. "Just that," he said. "No more. You are a young man. Impulsive? You should understand."

"I'm afraid—" I began to counter.

"But of course," he cried pleasantly. "I forget. You were not there. So how could I expect you to feel or know about this skipping. Look, look at me now. A sober man, eh?"

I nodded. "Dignified," I said cautiously.

"Very well. But, young man, there is a time to skip. On country roads in the spring. It is not necessary that there be girls. You will skip without them. You will skip because something within you knows the time—frog time. Then you will skip."

"Then I will skip," I repeated, hypnotized. Mad or not, there was a force in Albert Dreyer. Even there under the club lights, the night damp of an unused road began to gather.

IV

"It was a late spring," he said. "Fog and mist in those hollows in a way I had never seen before. And frogs, of course. Thousands of them, and twenty species, trilling, gurgling, and grunting in as many keys. The beautiful keen silver piping of spring peepers arousing as the last ice leaves the ponds—if you have heard that after a long winter alone, you will never forget it." He paused and leaned forward, listening with such an intent inner ear that one could almost hear that far-off silver piping from the wet meadows of the man's forgotten years.

I rattled my glass uneasily, and his eyes came back to me.

"They come out then," he said more calmly. "All amphibia have to return to the water for mating and egg laying. Even toads will hop miles across country to streams and waterways. You don't see them unless you go out at night in the right places as I did, but that night——

"Well, it was unusual, put it that way, as an understatement. It was late, and the creatures seemed to know it. You could feel the forces of mighty and archaic life welling up from the very ground. The water was pulling them—not water as we know it, but the mother, the ancient life force, the thing that made us in the days of creation, and that lurks around us still, unnoticed in our sterile cities.

"I was no different from any other young fool coming home on a spring night, except that as a student of life, and of amphibia in particular, I was, shall we say, more aware of the creatures. I had performed experiments"—the black glove gestured before my eyes. "I was, as it proved, susceptible.

"It began on that lost stretch of roadway leading to the river, and it began simply enough. All around, under the street lamps, I saw little frogs and big frogs hopping steadily toward the river. They were going in my direction.

"At that time I had my whimsies, and I was spry enough to feel the tug of that great movement. I joined them. There was no mystery about it. I simply began to skip, to skip gaily, and enjoy the great bobbing shadow I created as I passed onward with that leaping host all headed for the river.

"Now skipping along a wet pavement in spring is infectious, particularly going downhill, as we were. The impulse to take mightier leaps, to soar farther, increases progressively. The madness worked into me. I bounded till my lungs labored, and my shadow, at first my own shadow, bounded and labored with me.

"It was only midway in my flight that I began to grow conscious that I was not alone. The feeling was not strong at first. Normally a sober pedestrian, I was ecstatically preoccupied with the discovery of latent stores of energy and agility which I had not suspected in my subdued existence.

"It was only as we passed under a street lamp that I noticed, beside my own bobbing shadow, another great, leaping grotesquerie that had an uncanny suggestion of the frog world about it. The shocking aspect of the thing lay in its size, and the fact that, judging from the shadow, it was soaring higher and more gaily than myself.

"'Very well,' you will say"—and here Dreyer paused and looked at me tolerantly—"'Why didn't you turn around? That would be the scientific thing to do.'

"It would be the scientific thing to do, young man, but let me tell you it is not done—not on an empty road at midnight—not when the shadow is already beside your shadow and is joined by another, and then another.

"No, you do not pause. You look neither to left nor right, for fear of what you might see there. Instead, you dance on madly, hopelessly. Plunging higher, higher, in the hope the shadows will be left behind, or prove to be only leaves dancing, when you reach the next street light. Or that whatever had joined you in this midnight bacchanal will take some other pathway and depart.

"You do not look—you cannot look—because to do so is to destroy the universe in which we move and exist and have our transient being. You dare not look, because, beside the shadows, there now comes to your ears the loose-limbed slap of giant batrachian feet, not loud, not loud at all, but there, definitely there, behind you at your shoulder, plunging with the utter madness of spring, their rhythm entering your bones until you too are hurtling upward in some gigantic ecstasy that it is not given to mere flesh and blood to long endure.

"I was part of it, part of some mad dance of the elementals behind the show of things. Perhaps in that night of archaic and elemental passion, that festival of the wetlands, my careless hopping passage under the street lights had called them, attracted their attention, brought them leaping down some fourth-dimensional roadway into the world of time.

"Do not suppose for a single moment I thought so coherently then. My lungs were bursting, my physical self exhausted, but I sprang, I hurtled, I flung myself onward in a company I could not see, that never outpaced me, but that swept me with the mighty ecstasies of a thousand springs, and that bore me onward exultantly past my own doorstep, toward the river, toward some pathway long forgotten, toward some unforgettable destination in the wetlands and the spring.

"Even as I leaped, I was changing. It was this, I think, that stirred the last remnants of human fear and human caution that I still possessed. My will was in abeyance; I could not stop. Furthermore, certain sensations, hypnotic or otherwise, suggested to me that my own physical shape was modifying, or about to change. I was leaping with a growing ease. I was——

"It was just then that the wharf lights began to show. We were approaching the end of the road, and the road, as I have said, ended in the river. It was this, I suppose, that startled me back into some semblance of human terror. Man is a land animal. He does not willingly plunge off wharfs at midnight in the monstrous company of amphibious shadows.

"Nevertheless their power held me. We pounded madly toward

the wharf, and under the light that hung above it, and the beam that made a cross. Part of me struggled to stop, and part of me hurtled on. But in that final frenzy of terror before the water below engulfed me I shrieked, '*Help! In the name of God, help me! In the name of Jesus, stop!*'"

Dreyer paused and drew in his chair a little closer under the light. Then he went on steadily.

"I was not, I suppose, a particularly religious man, and the cries merely revealed the extremity of my terror. Nevertheless this is a strange thing, and whether it involves the crossed beam, or the appeal to a Christian deity, I will not attempt to answer.

"In one electric instant, however, I was free. It was like the release from demoniac possession. One moment I was leaping in an inhuman company of elder things, and the next moment I was a badly shaken human being on a wharf. Strangest of all, perhaps, was the sudden silence of that midnight hour. I looked down in the circle of the arc light, and there by my feet hopped feebly some tiny froglets of the great migration. There was nothing impressive about them, but you will understand that I drew back in revulsion. I have never been able to handle them for research since. My work is in the past."

He paused and drank, and then, seeing perhaps some lingering doubt and confusion in my eyes, held up his black-gloved hand and deliberately pinched off the glove.

A man should not do that to another man without warning, but I suppose he felt I demanded some proof. I turned my eyes away. One does not like a webbed batrachian hand on a human being.

As I rose embarrassedly, his voice came up to me from the depths of the chair.

"It is not the hand," Dreyer said. "It is the question of choice. Perhaps I was a coward, and ill prepared. Perhaps"—his voice searched uneasily among his memories—"perhaps I should have taken them and that springtime without question. Perhaps I should have trusted them and hopped onward. Who knows? They were gay enough, at least."

He sighed and set down his glass and stared so intently into empty space that, seeing I was forgotten, I tiptoed quietly away.

■ CONSIDERATIONS OF MEANING AND METHOD

1. Of what significance is it that Albert Dreyer's odd encounter occurs on "a strange road. Wild all right, but paved and close enough to the city that there were occasional street lamps"?

2. In this story, there are many references to light and dark and shadow. What does the narrator mean when he reflects that "there's so little light and so much space"?

3. What terrified Dreyer so deeply about his experience on the road that spring night? Why does he question his choice not to "[trust] them and [hop] onward"? Why did this experience mean an end to his research?

4. How might Eiseley's specific scientific expertise have helped him not only to write but to conceive this story? How do you imagine his colleagues—other scientists—might have responded and might continue to respond to it?

■ POSSIBILITIES FOR WRITING

1. Science, possibly more than any other field of study, puts its practitioners in close proximity to life's most fundamental mysteries. And yet, perhaps paradoxically, the success of scientific inquiry is generally measured by the degree of its objectivity and the irrefutability of its proof. Interview several professional scientists—perhaps people who teach or conduct research at your school—in order to get a sense of what motivated them to pursue careers in science, their attitudes about what we are capable of knowing and not knowing, and how they approach their daily work. Report and interpret what you learn from these interviews in an analytical essay. Consider whom you would like your primary audience to be: scientists, nonscientists, or both?

2. In an analytical essay for readers as familiar as you are with Eiseley's work, compare his short story "The Dance of the Frogs" to one of his many essays that explore comparable themes in a nonfiction form. Many of the essays in *The Star Thrower* would be likely candidates for comparison.

■ M. F. K. (MARY FRANCES KENNEDY) FISHER
The Wind-Chill Factor

M. F. K. Fisher was born in Albion, Michigan, in 1908 and died in the northern California wine country in 1992. Her special niche in American literature is an unusual one: she wrote most frequently, and most eloquently, about food. Her books are about both the pleasures of cooking and the pleasures of eating, and many of them include recipes. Fisher wrote about food as more than a source of physical sustenance. For Fisher, food provided aesthetic and spiritual nourishment as well. Her essays are frequently as much about place—the kitchens or countries in which food is prepared and eaten—as about food itself. Some of her many books are Consider the Oyster *(1941),* How to Cook a Wolf *(1942),* The Gastronomical Me *(1943),* An Alphabet for Gourmets *(1949),* The Story of Wine in California *(1962),* Maps of Another Town: A Memoir of Provence *(1964), and* Among Friends *(1971). Later in her career, Fisher wrote about the problems of aging but continued to, as she said, "enjoy the practice and contemplation of adapting the need to eat to the need to be properly nourished."*

The story "The Wind-Chill Factor" is taken from her collection of essays, As They Were, *published in 1982, and it is not altogether typical of Fisher's best-known writing: it is not about food (although perhaps it is in some respects about nourishment), and it is written in the third, not the first, person. We must wonder, along with Fisher in her preface to the "story," why, since she is describing an event that actually happened to her, she chose to narrate it through Mrs. Thayer and whether this makes the piece more a work of fiction than of fact.*

Preface

And here is the story or rather the report I wrote about a few days and nights on the dunes of Long Island, when I learned that I could survive, at least something like Sound and at least for a time longer than was really needed.

It seems odd, by now, that I wrote in the third person, because it is one of the most directly personal accounts I have ever given of something that has happened to me. I think that I probably felt I should detach myself as deliberately in the report as I had done while the winds blew.

Certainly it was no longer a question of professional timidity, as it was when I wrote my first article for publication and sent it off to the house organ of the Southern California Automobile Association, as I have described in the preface to "Pacific Village."

I still believe in both kindliness and justice, but have no patience with self-deception. When I filled out the notes I had forced myself to make during the winds, I was like a pale invalid, unable to identify with the immediate past. At least, that is how it now seems. Unless I look at the story I do not even remember what name I gave myself. And while the winds blew, I knew that I had no name at all.

In Sag Harbor, though, when I confronted the emphatic discipline of telling a straight story of the far past, it was much harder to write without prettifying, smudging. I had made no notes as things progressed on Painter Avenue in Whittier. Perhaps it is fortunate for older people that children seldom keep hour-by-hour reports of their own storms. They do not yet know how to deceive themselves.

There was doubt in the woman's mind about whether it would be wise of her to try to make some notes about her experience at once, or let the long blizzard go through its sixth noisy night. Perhaps putting onto paper what had happened to her could make things worse, invite another such experience, and she was not sure how well she would handle it, or more truthfully if she could survive it.

Her name was Mrs. Thayer, and she was living alone in a friend's cottage, ideally installed for a solitary good few months on wild dunes toward the tip of Long Island. The house faced the ocean, and except for the earth's rounding she could have looked east to Portugal and south to Cuba. In the rooms heated by electricity things were cozy and fine, until an uncommonly sustained blizzard moved onto that part of the planet, and onto the tiny spit of sand, like a bull covering and possessing the cow, the warm shelter.

Mrs. Thayer finally had, or went through, or lived past, a most astonishing experience in her life, on the fifth night of the storm.

By then she was used to adjusting the thermostats in each of the five heated rooms, and turning them up in the bathroom when she could no longer put off a shower, and then down in her bedroom once the electric pad had warmed her guts. The house had a kind of private weather station on one wall, and the barometer and thermometer worked among all the other gadgets that did not: the meters for wind velocity and wind direction, the tide clock, something called a durotherm hygrometer. The ship's bells sounded later and later, and finally went silent. Now and then a delicate needle spun meaninglessly in one of the brass puddings with their crystal crusts, as the blizzard yowled above and around. Mrs. Thayer found that she looked at them fairly often, as if to keep track of what might really be happening, and noticing blandly when the barometer dropped in a few hours from 30.15 to 28.60, whatever that might mean.

She also accustomed herself to listen through the static on the kitchen radio to mysteriously progressing reports about ice conditions on New York and Boston streets, and how much garbage lay on their sidewalks. She herself had no such problems, for the little car in her friend's garage would not start, even if she had wanted to hold it on the road into the nearest village and, because she lived alone, she made so little rubbish that it was all right to put it tidily in an unheated corridor until the wind stopped. Another problem in the cities was animals, who must of course befoul the snow, since few four-legged people have adapted themselves to flush plumbing. Mrs. Thayer was, for the first time in most of her lives, without such a friend, which may have added to the severity of her experience on the fifth night.

The wind, which had during the first two days shifted capriciously this way and that, finally settled into a northwest blow, steady but fiercely insistent. It bent the grasses almost flat on the dunes, and when occasional dry snow piled up in corners, it soon soiled the sculptured drifts with yellowish sand from the implacable surf. Waves changed from long piling rollers to mighty beasts wearing spume four times their height. The sound of them, and of the gale that pushed them sideways, took possession of the house.

Mrs. Thayer found, after the third night, that as she slipped into good sleep she would feel for a few minutes as if she were being rocked, moved, gently tipped, by what was happening outside the tight little shelter. She knew that she did not actually feel this, but she accepted it as a part of being so intimately close to the majesty she lay beside.

The air grew steadily colder, and the woman alone there in the dunes (the natives knew better than to build anywhere but inland in such brutal country) closed off rooms she did not need, and limited herself to the kitchen, the bedroom, the toilet. Everything stayed cozy for her, with no apprehensions: if the electricity went off, she would wait for people who knew she was there to get to her somehow, before the place grew too cold. . . . Almost nonchalantly she did not think about such things, even when the telephone went dead for a couple of days. It would ring clearly, and there would be only a wild squawk on the line. She suspected that her own voice might be heard, and would say in a high firm way, "This is Mrs. Thayer. Everything is all right. I am all right. Thank you." It was childish to feel rather pleased and excited about the game, but she did.

The night of the fourth day she ate a nice supper at the table in the warm kitchen, and adjusted thermostats here and there and tidied herself for sleep, with parts of at least six books to read first. In bed she turned on the electric warmer, and succumbed late but easily to sleep, perhaps at one o'clock in the morning. She felt well fed, warm, and serene.

A little after four an extraordinary thing happened to her. From deep and sweet-dreaming sleep she was wrenched into the conscious world, as cruelly as if she had been grabbed by the long hairs of her head. Her heart had changed its slow quiet beat, and bumped in her rib cage like a rabbit's. Her breath was caught in a kind of net in her throat, not going in and down fast enough. She touched her body and it was hot, but her palms felt clammy, and stuck to her.

Within a few seconds she knew that she was in a state, perhaps dangerous, of pure panic.

It had nothing to do with physical fear, as far as she could tell. She was not afraid of being alone, nor of being on the dunes in a storm. She was not afraid of bodily attack, rape, all that. She was simply in panic, or what Frenchmen home from the Sahara used to call *le cafard affolé*.

This is amazing, she said. This is indescribable. It is here. I shall survive it, or else run out howling across the dunes and die soon in the waves and the wind. Such a choice seemed very close and sweet, for her feeling was almost intolerably wishful of escape from the noise. It was above and against and around her, and she felt that it was invading her spirit. This is dangerous indeed, she said, and I must try not to run outside. That is a suicide wish, and weak. I must try to breathe more slowly, and perhaps swallow something to get back my more familiar rhythms. She was speaking slowly to herself, with silent but precise enunciation.

She waited for some minutes to see if she could manage the breathing in bed, but her heart and lungs were almost out of control when she got unsteadily to her feet, tied her night robe around her, and went into the little toilet. There, it took a minute to get her hand to turn on the light, for she was wracked with a kind of chill, which made her lower back and thighs ache as if she were in labor, and her jaws click together like bare bones. She remembered that in her friend's mirror-cabinet was a bottle of some variety of aspirin, and with real difficulty, almost as if she were spastic, she managed to run water into a mug and swallow the pills down her throat. If you cannot swallow, she said flatly, you are afraid of your enemy. She felt sick, and won this tiny battle of holding down the medicine at great

moral cost, for by now in the astonishing onslaught she was as determined as an apparently insensate animal not to submit to the steady
roaring all around her.

She dared not look at herself for a time, but walked in a staggering
way about the warmer parts of the cottage, recalling methods she had
studied, and even practiced, for self-preservation. There was one,
taught to her during a period of deep stress, in which one takes three
slow small sips of almost any liquid, and then waits a set period, from
five to fifteen minutes, and takes three more, and so on. She devoted
her whole strength to this project, as if life depended on it, which it
may well have. She carefully heated some milk, and when she could
not open the bottle of Angostura which might have taken the curse
off its insipidity, and she sensed that she might break the little bottle
with her almost uncontrollable hands, she poured in two big spoon-
fuls of sugar. It was a revolting brew, but she drank about half the
mugful of it over the next period of carefully repulsed frenzy.

The wind had become different. Its steady pressure of sound had
changed to a spasmodic violence. Snow was stinging against the
northern and western storm windows, and Mrs. Thayer already
knew that the doors on those sides were frozen shut. It did not matter. A door to the outside place where people changed bathing suits
in the summer began to bang hard, in irregular patterns. It is un-
hinged, she said with a sly grin. It did not matter either. The whole
thing she must work on was to keep herself inside her own skin, and
she was the only one there to do it, and with real sweat she did.

She pulled every trick out of the bag over her long life with neu-
rotics. She brushed her hair firmly, and all the while her heart kept
kicking against her ribs, and she felt so sick that she could scarcely lift
her arm. She tried to say some nursery rhymes and the Twenty-Third
Psalm, but with no better result than an impatient titter. She sipped
the dreadful sweet milk. She prayed to those two pills, called Quick
Relief for Nervous Tension on the radio, to help, to help fast, never
to cure of course of *course*, see your physician for persistent muscular
discomfort. . . .

If I permit myself to think in my present terms I am done for, she
said in rounded words and clearly punctuated sentences, in a silent
voice that rang like Teacher's in her head, like Father Joseph's, like
Dr. Rab's. It is a question of moral energy, she said. Subconsciously I
am admitting that the storm is great and I am small, and for a time or
possibly forever I have lost the balance that human beings must

maintain between their own inner force and that of Nature. I was un-aware of what the wind and the ocean were doing to me. I have been respectful and awed, but too bland. Now I am being told. Told off. Yes, she said, I am admitting it. But do I have to bow any deeper, cry Uncle, lose everything?

She went on playing several canny games like this as she moved feebly about the rooms. Heavy curtains moved in the fierce air, and she gradually added long woolen socks and a leather coat to her strange coverings, but managed as part of her dogged rescue work to focus enough on a mirror to arrange her hair nicely and put on firm eyebrows and a mouth that looked poutish instead of as hard as she had hoped. This is simply going on too long, she said like a woman on the delivery table, and added more lipstick.

For a time, as the aspirin and the warm milk seemed to slow down her limitless dread (Dread of what? Not that the roof would fly off, that she was alone, that she might die . . .), she made herself talk rea-sonably to what was puking and trembling and flickering in her spirit. She was a doctor, or rather an unwitting bystander caught in some kind of disaster, forced to be cool and wise with one of the vic-tims, perhaps a child bleeding toward death or an old man pinned under a truck wheel. She talked quietly to this helpless shocked soul fluttering in its poor body. She was strong and calm. All the time she knew cynically that she was nonexistent except in the need thrust upon her, and that soon the patient would either die or recover and forget her dramatic saintliness when the real ambulance came.

"Listen to your breathing," she said coolly. "You are not badly hurt. Soon you will feel all right. Sip this. It will make the pain go away. Lift your head now, and breathe slowly. You are not really in trouble." And so on. Whenever the other part of Mrs. Thayer, the threatened one, let her mind slip back to the horror of an imminent breaking with all reason, all lucidity, and then out the door it would be final, the kindly stranger seemed to see it in the eyeballs and the pulse as she bent over the body, and spoke more firmly: "Now hold the cup. You can. I know you can. You will be all right."

This got monotonous, and in fact it was embarrassing, to have the two things floating inside her, as she tried consciously to go with the sounds of the gale instead of letting her consciousness accept them weakly and undermine her. Finally she said rudely to the kind crea-ture (a fellow passenger?) who had been trying to give her some help, "Go away. I *will* be all right." And the other part of her shrugged and withdrew, knowing there was nothing more to do, knowing that she would not have been dismissed if Mrs. Thayer depended on her any further.

The next step was to try to read. But the poor soul found it hard to focus her eyes on the print, and when she did it was on sentences picked hit-or-miss from this page or that. There was one from an anonymous book called *Streetwalker:* " . . . to admit fear and weakness to any living soul . . . would be to reveal my unfitness for the life I have chosen, and, since no other is now possible for me, to reach the limits of despair—and God knows what would happen then."

I am being played with, Mrs. Thayer said angrily, and with great care put the book back in its shelf-place and then was reading, in a controlled way, while her head thugged along and she felt wambly all over, "This is the day for each of us to assess our own strength, in utter silence to plumb the depth of our own spirit." What in God's name was she looking at? She saw coldly the title, *Second Thoughts* by old man Mauriac, and all her admiration of a lot of things in him turned into fuming jelly, and instead of putting back the book neatly she tossed it on the floor, and started to walk about the little house again.

Its secret balance, the stuff like the fluid of the inner ear, was centered now a little below her diaphragm, and she walked with special care, in order to keep the whole place from crushing like an egg as the giant thrashed.

Her father had talked often about a couple of years he'd once spent as a reporter in North Dakota. He said that farm women went stark mad there for one good reason, and that was because in their lonely cabins, when they could see out the window, the snow would always be blowing horizontally. Always. It sent them mad, that sideways snow on and on. It was not the wind, for them. The sideways snow did it.

Mrs. Thayer knew. The sound of the wind, for her, was going sideways, exactly on a line with the far horizon of the Atlantic, for days, nights, perhaps five or a week or anyway much too long. It was in her bowels, and suddenly they were loosened and then later, also to her surprise, she threw up. She told herself dizzily that the rhythm of the wind had bound her around, and that now she was defying it, but it kept on howling.

The pills worked, helped by the warm drink. The human parts of her body helped. The mind did not fail her, and she knew all the time, or at least brought herself gradually to believe so, that she would never have run out like a beast, to die quickly on the dunes. Once she stopped roaming and lay down, feeling purged and calmer, but the minute she was flat on the bed she heard the wind pressing against the wall beyond her head, and it was as if she were locked in a cell and in the next one a giant lay in his last agony, breathing with a terrible rage and roar. She got up and brushed at her hair again, and then walked with a decreasing stagger about the little rooms.

In a couple more hours everything was all right inwardly with her, except that she was languid, as if she had lain two weeks in a fever. The peculiar panic which had seized her bones and spirit faded fast, once routed. She was left wan and bemused. Never had she been afraid, that is, of tangibles like cold and sand and wind. She was not afraid, as far as she knew, of dying either fast or slowly. It was, she decided precisely, a question of sound. If the storm had not lasted so long, with its noise so much into her, into her brain and muscles . . . If this had been a kind of mating, it was without joy.

Gradually she was breathing with deep but not worried rhythm as she lay under a cover on her bed. The wind still thrust at her, but she sensed that the giant was in that state of merciful lull that rewards old scoundrels in their final throes: he was not choking and hitting out at her. She got up carefully, and did several small things like polishing her fingernails, and then poached an egg in some beef broth and ate it. She felt as hollow as an old shell, and surprisingly trembly. She slept for two hours, out like a drunk.

The whole peculiar experience was still in her mind when she awakened. Why did it happen? Was it a question of decibels, of atmospheric pressure? Had her ears, which like every other living human ears in the world were different from any other living human ears, simply been too long assaulted by the pullulations of the violently moving air about her? Where was *she*, then? Could she survive such an obvious dare again? Why must she? All of this puzzled her, and she found herself hoping like a child that the air would be calmer, and soon.

She permitted herself the weakness of one gentle tap on the barometer, and felt no real dismay when its thin fluttering indicator went down a little more. If there was any message in it, perhaps it said that since Mrs. Thayer had lived through the past hours, she would never know them again. It is probable, she said, that if I must, I shall bow, succumb, admit greater strength.

There was no point in thinking much about this, in her weak lackadaisical state, so she wrote a few notes to herself, not caring if they might bring on more wind or not, and went to bed. And during the late afternoon, while she dozed with a deep soft detachment, the sound abated and then died, and she was lost in the sweet dream-life of a delivered woman.

—Bridgehampton, 1973

■ CONSIDERATIONS OF MEANING AND METHOD

1. What exactly happens to Mrs. Thayer during the storm? Why does she respond to the storm, its relentless noise, in the way that she does? Can you diagnose what is wrong with her from the description she gives of her symptoms?

2. Fisher speculates in her preface to "The Wind-Chill Factor" about her reasons for telling this story in the third person rather than in a first-person account. Do her reasons make sense to you? Can you think of any other reasons? Do you think "The Wind-Chill Factor" is correctly placed in Chapter 5 of this book rather than Chapter 4?

3. People are capable of responding with extreme anxiety in all kinds of situations. What do you think it was about this particular situation that brought about Mrs. Thayer's response? What is she afraid of? Why is she taken by surprise by her own panic?

4. Did the fact that Fisher recorded details of the experience at the time, in the form of writing notes to herself, in any way influence the experience itself? Why do you think Fisher was compelled later to write this "story or rather . . . report" of her experience to share with readers whom she didn't know?

■ POSSIBILITIES FOR WRITING

1. In your journal, rewrite a portion of Fisher's story—a few paragraphs at least—in the first person, imagining that you are M. F. K. Fisher. Then write in your journal about how the change in person seemed to change the writing. Are there differences in the impact of the writing? Did the change of person lead you to make any other changes as well? If so, what kind, and why? Based on your experiment, do you think Fisher made the right choice in writing in the third person?

2. If you have ever experienced a psychological, emotional, and/or physical response in any way like Fisher's, compare your experience with hers. What was the situation that produced your re-

sponse? What were you panicked about? How did it feel, and how did you react? To what degree was your response irrational or reasonable? Have time or distance lent perspective to the experience? Your reader may be someone unfamiliar, except through your and Fisher's writing, with this kind of experience, so your goal in writing is to promote understanding and perhaps empathy.

■ URSULA K. LE GUIN
May's Lion

See the headnote for Ursula K. Le Guin's "A Very Warm Mountain" in Chapter 2 (page 117) for biographical information.

Ursula K. Le Guin's short story, "May's Lion," is taken from Buffalo Gals and Other Animal Presences *(1987). She tells us in the introduction to the book that "By climbing up into his head and shutting out every voice but his own, 'Civilized Man' has gone deaf. He can't hear the wolf calling him brother—not Master, but brother. He can't hear the earth calling him child—not Father, but son. He hears only his own words making up the world.... But still there will be stories, there will always be stories, in which the lion's mother scolds the lion, and the fish cries out to the fisherman, and the cat talks; because it is true that all creatures talk to one another, if only one listens."*

Jim remembers it as a bobcat, and he was May's nephew, and ought to know. It probably was a bobcat. I don't think May would have changed her story, though you can't trust a good story-teller not to make the story suit herself, or get the facts to fit the story better. Anyhow she told it to us more than once, because my mother and I would ask for it; and the way I remember it, it was a mountain lion. And the way I remember May telling it is sitting on the edge of the irrigation tank we used to swim in, cement rough as a lava flow and hot in the sun, the long cracks tarred over. She was an old lady then with a long Irish upper lip, kind and wary and balky. She liked to come sit and talk with my mother while I swam; she didn't have all that many people to talk to. She always had chickens, in the chicken-house very near the back door of the farmhouse, so the whole place smelled pretty strong of chickens, and as long as she could she kept a cow or two down in the old barn by the creek. The first of May's cows I remember was Pearl, a big handsome Holstein who gave four-teen or twenty-four or forty gallons or quarts of milk at a milking, whichever is right for a prize milker. Pearl was beautiful in my eyes when I was four or five years old; I loved and admired her. I remem-ber how excited I was, how I reached upward to them, when Pearl or the workhorse Prince, for whom my love amounted to worship, would put an immense and sensitive muzzle through the three-strand fence to whisk a cornhusk from my fearful hand; and then the munching and the sweet breath and the big nose would be at the barbed wire again: the offering is acceptable. . . . After Pearl there was Rosie, a purebred Jersey. May got her either cheap or free because she was a runt calf, so tiny that May brought her home on her lap in the back of the car, like a fawn. And Rosie always looked like she had some deer in her. She was a lovely, clever little cow and even more willful than old May. She often chose not to come in to be milked. We would hear May calling and then see her trudging across our lower pasture with the bucket, going to find Rosie wherever Rosie had decided to be milked today on the wild hills she had to roam in, a hundred acres of our and Old Jim's land. Then May had a fox terrier named Pinky, who yipped and nipped and turned me against fox ter-riers for life, but he was long gone when the mountain lion came; and the black cats who lived in the barn kept discreetly out of the story. As a matter of fact now I think of it the chickens weren't in it either. It might have been quite different if they had been. May had quit keeping chickens after old Mrs. Walter died. It was just her all alone there, and Rosie and the cats down in the barn, and nobody else within sight or sound of the old farm. We were in our house up the hill only in the summer, and Jim lived in town, those years. What time of year it was I don't know, but I imagine the grass still green or just turning gold. And May was in the house, in the kitchen, where she lived entirely unless she was asleep or outdoors, when she heard this noise.

Now you need May herself, sitting skinny on the edge of the irri-gation tank, seventy or eighty or ninety years old, nobody knew how old May was and she had made sure they couldn't find out, opening her pleated lips and letting out this noise—a huge, awful yowl, start-ing soft with a nasal hum and rising slowly into a snarling gargle that sank away into a sobbing purr. . . . It got better every time she told the story.

"It was some meow," she said.

So she went to the kitchen door, opened it, and looked out. Then she shut the kitchen door and went to the kitchen window to look out, because there was a mountain lion under the fig tree.

Puma, cougar, catamount; *Felis concolor,* the shy, secret, shadowy lion of the New World, four or five feet long plus a yard of black-tipped tail, weighs about what a woman weighs, lives where the deer live from Canada to Chile, but always shyer, always fewer, the color of dry leaves, dry grass.

There were plenty of deer in the Valley in the forties, but no mountain lion had been seen for decades anywhere near where people lived. Maybe way back up in the canyons; but Jim, who hunted, and knew every deer-trail in the hills, had never seen a lion. Nobody had, except May, now, alone in her kitchen.

"I thought maybe it was sick," she told us. "It wasn't acting right. I don't think a lion would walk right into the yard like that if it was feeling well. If I'd still had the chickens it'd be a different story maybe! But it just walked around some, and then it lay down there," and she points between the fig tree and the decrepit garage. "And then after a while it kind of meowed again, and got up and come into the shade right there." The fig tree, planted when the house was built, about the time May was born, makes a great, green, sweet-smelling shade. "It just laid there looking around. It wasn't well," says May.

She had lived with and looked after animals all her life; she had also earned her living for years as a nurse.

"Well, I didn't know exactly what to do for it. So I put out some water for it. It didn't even get up when I come out the door. I put the water down there, not so close to it that we'd scare each other, see, and it kept watching me, but it didn't move. After I went back in it did get up and tried to drink some water. Then it made that kind of meowowow. I do believe it come here because it was looking for help. Or just for company, maybe."

The afternoon went on, May in the kitchen, the lion under the fig tree.

But down in the barnyard by the creek was Rosie the cow. Fortunately the gate was shut, so she could not come wandering up to the house and meet the lion; but she would be needing to be milked, come six or seven o'clock, and that got to worrying May. She also worried how long a sick mountain lion might hang around, keeping her shut in the house. May didn't like being shut in.

"I went out a time or two, and went shoo!"

Eyes shining amidst fine wrinkles, she flaps her thin arms at the lion. "Shoo! Go on home now!"

But the silent wild creature watches her with yellow eyes and does not stir.

"So when I was talking to Miss Macy on the telephone, she said it might have rabies, and I ought to call the sheriff. I was uneasy then. So finally I did that, and they come out, those county police, you know. Two carloads."

Her voice is dry and quiet.

"I guess there was nothing else they knew how to do. So they shot it."

She looks off across the field Old Jim, her brother, used to plow with Prince the horse and irrigate with the water from this tank. Now wild oats and blackberry grow there. In another thirty years it will be a rich man's vineyard, a tax write-off.

"He was seven feet long, all stretched out, before they took him off. And so thin! They all said, 'Well, Aunt May, I guess you were scared there! I guess you were some scared!' But I wasn't. I didn't want him shot. But I didn't know what to do for him. And I did need to get to Rosie."

I have told this true story which May gave to us as truly as I could, and now I want to tell it as fiction, yet without taking it from her: rather to give it back to her, if I can do so. It is a tiny part of the history of the Valley, and I want to make it part of the Valley outside history. Now the field that the poor man plowed and the rich man harvested lies on the edge of a little town, houses and workshops of timber and fieldstone standing among almond, oak, and eucalyptus trees; and now May is an old woman with a name that means the month of May: Rains End. An old woman with a long, wrinkled-pleated upper lip, she is living alone for the summer in her summer place, a meadow a mile or so up in the hills above the little town. Sinshan. She took her cow Rose with her, and since Rose tends to wander she keeps her on a long tether down by the tiny creek, and moves her into fresh grass now and then. The summerhouse is what they call a nine-pole house, a mere frame of poles stuck in the ground—one of them is a live digger-pine sapling—with stick and matting walls, and mat roof and floors. It doesn't rain in the dry season, and the roof is just for shade. But the house and its little front yard where Rains End has her camp stove and clay oven and matting loom are well shaded by a fig tree that was planted there a hundred years or so ago by her grandmother.

Rains End herself has no grandchildren; she never bore a child, and her one or two marriages were brief and very long ago. She has a nephew and two grandnieces, and feels herself an aunt to all children, even when they are afraid of her and rude to her because she has got so ugly with old age, smelling as musty as a chickenhouse. She considers it natural for children to shrink away from somebody part way dead, and knows that when they're a little older and have got used to her they'll ask her for stories. She was for sixty years a member of the Doctors Lodge, and though she doesn't do curing any more people still ask her to help with nursing sick children, and the children come to long for the kind, authoritative touch of her hands when she bathes them to bring a fever down, or changes a dressing, or combs out bed-tangled hair with witch hazel and great patience.

So Rains End was just waking up from an early afternoon nap in the heat of the day, under the matting roof, when she heard a noise, a huge, awful yowl that started soft with a nasal hum and rose slowly into a snarling gargle that sank away into a sobbing purr. . . . And she got up and looked out from the open side of the house of sticks and matting, and saw a mountain lion under the fig tree. She looked at him from her house; he looked at her from his.

And this part of the story is much the same: the old woman; the lion; and, down by the creek, the cow.

It was hot. Crickets sang shrill in the yellow grass on all the hills and canyons, in all the chaparral. Rains End filled a bowl with water from an unglazed jug and came slowly out of the house. Halfway between the house and the lion she set the bowl down on the dirt. She turned and went back to the house.

The lion got up after a while and came and sniffed at the water. He lay down again with a soft, querulous groan, almost like a sick child, and looked at Rains End with the yellow eyes that saw her in a different way than she had ever been seen before.

She sat on the matting in the shade of the open part of her house and did some mending. When she looked up at the lion she sang under her breath, tunelessly; she wanted to remember the Puma Dance Song but could only remember bits of it, so she made a song for the occasion:

You are there, lion.
You are there, lion. . . .

As the afternoon wore on she began to worry about going down to milk Rose. Unmilked, the cow would start tugging at her tether and making a commotion. That was likely to upset the lion. He lay so close to the house now that if she came out that too might upset him, and she did not want to frighten him or to become frightened of him. He had evidently come for some reason, and it behoved her to find out what the reason was. Probably he was sick; his coming so close to a human person was strange, and people who behave strangely are usually sick or in some kind of pain. Sometimes, though, they are spiritually moved to act strangely. The lion might be a messenger, or might have some message of his own for her or her townspeople. She was more used to seeing birds as messengers; the four-footed people go about their own business. But the lion, dweller in the Seventh House, comes from the place dreams come from. Maybe she did not understand. Maybe someone else would understand. She could go over and tell Valiant and her family, whose summerhouse was in Gahheya meadow, farther up the creek; or she could go over to Buck's, on Baldy Knoll. But there were four or five adolescents there, and one of them might come and shoot the lion, to boast that he'd saved old Rains End from getting clawed to bits and eaten.

Mooooooo! said Rose, down by the creek, reproachfully.

The sun was still above the southwest ridge, but the branches of pines were across it and the heavy heat was out of it, and shadows were welling up in the low fields of wild oats and blackberry.

Moooooo! said Rose again, louder.

The lion lifted up his square, heavy head, the color of dry wild oats, and gazed down across the pastures. Rains End knew from that weary movement that he was very ill. He had come for company in dying, that was all.

"I'll come back, lion," Rains End sang tunelessly. "Lie still. Be quiet. I'll come back soon." Moving softly and easily, as she would move in a room with a sick child, she got her milking pail and stool, slung the stool on her back with a woven strap so as to leave a hand free, and came out of the house. The lion watched her at first very tense, the yellow eyes firing up for a moment, but then put his head down again with that little grudging, groaning sound. "I'll come back, lion," Rains End said. She went down to the creekside and milked a nervous and indignant cow. Rose could smell lion, and demanded in several ways, all eloquent, just what Rains End intended to *do*? Rains End ignored her questions and sang milking songs to her: "Su bonny, su bonny, be still my grand cow . . ." Once she had to slap her hard on the hip. "Quit that, you old fool! Get over! I am *not* going to untie you and have you walking into trouble! I won't let him come down this way."

She did not say how she planned to stop him.

She retethered Rose where she could stand down in the creek if she liked. When she came back up the rise with the pail of milk in hand, the lion had not moved. The sun was down, the air above the ridges turning clear gold. The yellow eyes watched her, no light in them. She came to pour milk into the lion's bowl. As she did so, he all at once half rose up. Rains End started, and spilled some of the milk she was pouring. "Shoo! Stop that!" she whispered fiercely, waving her skinny arm at the lion. "Lie down now! I'm afraid of you when you get up, can't you see that, stupid? Lie down now, lion. There you are. Here I am. It's all right. You know what you're doing." Talking softly as she went, she returned to her house of stick and matting. There she sat down as before, in the open porch, on the grass mats.

The mountain lion made the grumbling sound, ending with a long sigh, and let his head sink back down on his paws.

Rains End got some cornbread and a tomato from the pantry box while there was still daylight left to see by, and ate slowly and neatly. She did not offer the lion food. He had not touched the milk, and she thought he would eat no more in the House of Earth.

From time to time as the quiet evening darkened and stars gathered thicker overhead she sang to the lion. She sang the five songs of *Going Westward to the Sunrise,* which are sung to human beings dying. She did not know if it was proper and appropriate to sing these songs to a dying mountain lion, but she did not know his songs.

Twice he also sang: once a quavering moan, like a house cat challenging another tom to battle, and once a long, sighing purr.

Before the Scorpion had swung clear of Sinshan Mountain, Rains End had pulled her heavy shawl around herself in case the fog came in, and had gone sound asleep in the porch of her house.

She woke with the grey light before sunrise. The lion was a motionless shadow, a little farther from the trunk of the fig tree than he had been the night before. As the light grew, she saw that he had stretched himself out full length. She knew he had finished his dying, and sang the fifth song, the last song, in a whisper, for him:

The doors of the Four Houses
are open.
Surely they are open.

Near sunrise she went to milk Rose, and to wash in the creek. When she came back up to the house she went closer to the lion, though not so close as to crowd him, and stood for a long time looking at him stretched out in the long, tawny, delicate light. "As thin as I am!" she said to Valiant, when she went up to Gahheya later in the morning to tell the story and to ask help carrying the body of the lion off where the buzzards and coyotes could clean it.

It's still your story, Aunt May; it was your lion. He came to you. He brought his death to you, a gift; but the men with the guns won't take gifts, they think they own death already. And so they took from you the honor he did you, and you felt that loss. I wanted to restore it. But you don't need it. You followed the lion where he went, years ago now.

■ CONSIDERATIONS OF MEANING AND METHOD

1. The story "May's Lion" is told from the point of view of a first-person narrator. Who is this narrator? Can you tell what her relationship to May is? Why is the narrator compelled to tell May's story, and to retell it?

2. In the opening paragraph, the narrator says that some of the facts of the story are unclear, a matter of interpretation. She says, ". . . you can't trust a good storyteller not to make the story suit herself, or get the facts to fit the story better." How does this prepare us for what is to come?

3. In the first account, the "true" account, of May's encounter with the mountain lion, how does she interpret his presence and how does she respond to it? Does she have any regrets? In the revised account, the "fiction," how is Rains End's reaction to the animal different from May's, and why? How does she interpret his presence and her role in his dying in this version?

4. What point does Le Guin ultimately wish to make in this story?

■ POSSIBILITIES FOR WRITING

1. In a chart, map out every parallel you can detect between the two versions of the story, whether large or small. These parallels will reveal both similarities and differences. For example, the houses in the two stories are similar in some basic respects and crucially different in others: one is closed and the other is open, for example. May's and Rains End's names mean the same thing, but they

come from different cultural reference points. May says, "Shoo! Go home now!" while Rains End sings to the lion, "You are there, lion." When you have charted these parallels, review your chart and try to determine what fundamental factors account for the differences, and how they lend purpose to the variations in the second story. Write an analytical essay in which you articulate your view, using the details you have charted to support and illustrate it.

2.   The fictional location for this story is probably based on a real location, near the Napa Valley in northern California. Pomo, Miwok, and Wappo Indians inhabited this area before the Spanish came—and still do, although they are widely dispersed and their numbers and cultures have long been decimated. In your library, look up one or more of these tribes, and read about their religion and culture. Note, in particular, any references you might run across to the mountain lion. For other students in your class, report on what you discover. Is there anything recognizable in Le Guin's fictional portrayal of Native American culture and beliefs in the story of Rains End and the lion?

■ BARRY LOPEZ
from *Crow and Weasel*

Barry Lopez (1945–) was born in New York and raised, for part of his life, in New York City, but he has strong ties with the West Coast, having lived during his early childhood in rural California and for most of his life since his early twenties in the western United States. He received his A.B. and M.A.T. degrees from Notre Dame University and did post-graduate work at the University of Oregon. He is one of the country's best-known natural history writers, in nonfiction and fiction forms. He has written for Smithsonian *and* National Geographic, *among many other magazines. His fiction includes* Desert Notes: Reflections in the Eye of a Raven *(1976) and* River Notes: The Dance of Herons *(1979). His nonfiction works include* Of Wolves and Men *(1978), winner of the John Burroughs Medal for distinguished natural history writing;* Arctic Dreams: Imagination and Desire in a Northern Landscape *(1986), winner of the National Book Award in nonfiction;* Crossing Open Ground *(1988); and* Crow and Weasel *(1990), from which the following excerpt is taken.*

Lopez has spoken articulately of his role as a writer. "I'm often trying to act as an intermediary in my work between particular situations and the reader . . . ," he says. "I'm conscious of trying to clarify, to make the language work beautifully, and of the reader's needs—how easy is it going to be for the reader to follow, or how can the reader be brought into the scene . . . ?" He thinks of writing as "an extraordinary act of self-assertion. You put down on paper the way you understand the world. But, for me, there must be a point where the reader loses sight of the writer, where he gains another understanding, a vision of what lies before the writer; so by the time the reader finishes a book or an essay, he's really think-ing about his own thoughts with regard to that subject, or that place, or that set of events. . . . The initial step is an act of ego, the next step a loss of ego, a sort of disappearance." In the process of learning about his subject, whether it is wolves or Inuit Indian myths, Lopez says, "I'm always aware of having to put myself in a position of someone who knows very little. If I begin to think I know a lot about what's going on, then I won't hear half of what I need to hear."

Crow and Weasel is a fable in which, as in traditional Native American mythology, the boundary between human and animal identity is blurred, as is the distinction between nature and deity. In Lopez's story, Crow and Weasel set out on a quest, to discover new lands, new peoples, and their own wisdom. Badger, whom they encounter on their long trek back home to the plains from the Eskimo lands of the far north, offers them some lessons in the craft of storytelling; these lessons may, in some ways, feel familiar to you as a student of writing that is constantly subjected to the criticism of well-meaning teachers.

Half the cycle of the moon found them past the lake country, back on a path that bore their tracks. They rode for some days toward the forest. One evening before they stopped to camp they were hailed by someone in the fading light. They saw it was Badger when they rode up. She bid them enter her lodge, which was underground.

"I heard you coming toward me all day," said Badger with plea-sure and excitement. "I hear everything, through the ground. Where have you come from?"

"We have been far to the north, but we live far away to the south and are headed home," said Crow.

"Well, you must stay here the night, and tell me of where you have been. There is good grass here for your horses, and no one around to bother them. We will have a good dinner and you will leave refreshed in the morning."

Crow and Weasel had never seen a lodge quite like Badger's. Quivers and parfleches, all beautifully decorated, hung from the walls, along with painted robes, birdbone breastplates, and many pieces of quillwork—leggings and moccasins, elktooth dresses, awl cases, and pipe bags. Lances decorated with strips of fur and small colored stones stood in the corners, and painted shields were hung on the walls beside medicine bundles. Other bundles were suspended from tripods.

Badger made up a good meal, and after they ate, Crow offered the pipe. In the silence that followed, Crow and Weasel felt a strange obligation to speak of what they had seen.

"Now tell me, my friends, what did you see up north? I have always wanted to know what it is like up there."

Weasel began to speak.

"My friend," said Badger. "Stand up, stand up here so you can express more fully what you have seen."

Weasel stood up, though he felt somewhat self-conscious in doing so. He began to speak about the people called Inuit and their habit of hunting an unusual white bear.

"Wait, my friend," said Badger. "Where were you when this happened?"

"We were in their camp. They told us."

"Well, tell me something about their camp."

Weasel described their camp, and then returned again to the story of hunting the bear.

"But, my friend," interrupted Badger, "tell me a little first of who these people are. What did they look like?"

Badger's words were beginning to annoy Weasel, but Crow could see what Badger was doing, and he smiled to himself. Weasel began again, but each time he would get only a little way in his story before Badger would ask for some point of clarification. Weasel was getting very irritated.

Finally Crow spoke up.

"Badger," he said, "my friend is trying very hard to tell his story. And I can see that you are only trying to help him, by teaching him to put the parts together in a good pattern, to speak with a pleasing rhythm, and to call on all the details of memory. But let us now see if he gets your meaning, for my friend is very smart."

"That is well put," said Badger, curious.

"Weasel," continued Crow, "do you remember what that man said before he began to tell us stories about Sedna and those other beings? He said, 'I have put my poem in order on the threshold of my tongue.' That's what this person Badger, who has taken us into her lodge, is saying. Pretend Badger and I are the people waiting back in our village. Speak to us with that kind of care."

Badger looked at Crow with admiration. Weasel, who had been standing uneasily before them, found his footing and his voice. He began to speak with a measured, fetching rhythm, painting a picture of the countryside where they had been, and then drawing the Inuit people and the others, the caribou, up into life, drawing them up out of the ground.

When Weasel finished, Badger nodded with gratitude, as though she had heard something profound.

"You know," she said to Weasel, "I have heard wondrous rumors of these Inuit people, but you are the first person I've heard tell a story about them who had himself been among them. You make me marvel at the strangeness of the world. That strangeness, the intriguing life of another people, it is a crucial thing, I think, to know."

"Now Crow," said Weasel, taking his seat, "tell Badger of our people and of our village. Tell her about this journey of ours."

Crow took his place in front of the other two. He also felt awkward, but with the help of Badger, a few pointed questions to sharpen his delivery, he began to speak strongly, with deliberation and care, about all that Weasel had asked him to say.

"You are fine young men," said Badger when Crow had finished. "I can see that. But you are beginning to sense your responsibilities, too, and the journey you have chosen is a hard one. If you keep going, one day you will be men. You will have families."

"We are very grateful for your hospitality, Badger," said Crow. "Each place we go, we learn something, and your wisdom here has helped us."

"I would ask you to remember only this one thing," said Badger. "The stories people tell have a way of taking care of them. If stories come to you, care for them. And learn to give them away where they are needed. Sometimes a person needs a story more than food to stay alive. That is why we put these stories in each other's memory. This is how people care for themselves. One day you will be good storytellers. Never forget these obligations."

No one since Mountain Lion had spoken so directly to them of their obligations, but this time Crow and Weasel were not made uncomfortable. Each could understand what Badger was talking about, and each one knew that if his life went on he would one day know fully what Badger meant. For now, all it meant was that it was good to remember and to say well what happened, if someone asked to hear.

In the morning when they left, Badger told them a way to get through the forest that was not quite so difficult as the way they had come. "It is an open trail," she said, "and there are not so many trees. You will be able to go more quickly. But, still, it is a long way to your country. And soon it will be the first Snow Moon."

She gave them each a winter robe of buffalo. They gave her a beaded bag from home, which she accepted with wonder and humility. And they said goodbye.

■ CONSIDERATIONS OF MEANING AND METHOD

1. For Badger, what specific qualities make for a good story? Badger is instructing Weasel in storytelling as an oral art. Would these qualities of good storytelling be any different for stories that are written down?

2. Why is good storytelling so important, according to Badger?

3. You may recognize in Badger certain qualities of your own teachers. Describe Badger's "teaching style," her approach in instructing Weasel. How does Weasel respond, initially, to Badger's instruction? Would you have responded similarly or differently?

4. In what ways is this fable similar to, and in what ways is it different from, the popular and traditional fables you may be familiar with—Aesop's fables, for example?

5. What is the difference between a myth and a fable?

■ POSSIBILITIES FOR WRITING

1. Using the qualities of a good story that Badger mentions as a starting point, write your own set of guidelines for storytelling. You might refer to the "Elements of Fiction" section in the introduction to this chapter (page 267) and the peer review form in the introduction to Chapter 4 (page 206) for more ideas. Consider, too, which stories in this chapter have affected you most strongly and why. Share these guidelines with your instructor and with

other students in your class. They should be useful not only to writers of fiction but to readers of fiction as well, as they assess the qualities of fiction that contribute to its effectiveness.

■ JENNIFER DONALDSON
Silent Sufferers: A Response to Alice Walker's "Am I Blue?"

In the following statement, student Jennifer Donaldson describes how she approached and organized her analysis of Alice Walker's essay, which can be found in Chapter 4 (page 242).

This essay was written as both an analysis of Walker's style and as a salute to the opinions Walker expresses in "Am I Blue?" I chose to respond to this essay for two reasons. First, "Am I Blue?" concerns itself with an often-debated issue, one my reader is likely to be familiar with, which makes refutation or confirmation of the views Walker expresses relatively easy. Second, the subject of Walker's essay is something that I, personally, care about a great deal. I agree with Walker, and therefore support her opinions, because I believe in animal equality, especially vegetarianism. I think that it is often easier to analyze a work that embodies what one believes in and feels strongly for (or against).

I wanted to show how Walker's style contributes to the effectiveness of her point. In the opening paragraph, I state which three elements of style I will analyze in my essay. In the body of my essay, I discuss each point in detail and offer examples and illustrations from Walker's essay. In the conclusion, I acknowledge that I agree with Walker's position. It is important that this acknowledgment be clearly stated, even though phrases such as "this compelling personal narrative" throughout my essay imply my partiality toward Walker's essay. Since I strongly agree with the ideas she expresses in "Am I Blue?" I felt that some sort of homage needed to be paid to both Walker's style and the points she makes in her essay. "Silent Sufferers" is an attempt to do so.

In "Am I Blue?" writer Alice Walker takes an anecdotal approach to convey her feelings on the subject of animal rights. In her essay, Walker touches the heart of the animal lover by telling the story of an ignored horse living in a pasture next to her house. The effectiveness of this essay lies in three main areas, all contributing to her main point—that all beings are entitled to freedom and justice. First, by using a personal account to make her points, Walker personalizes animal-rights issues for her readers. Second, Walker's use of anthropomorphic language underscores the equality she perceives between humans and nonhumans. And last, several analogous segments extend the essay's theme, as Walker compares the plights of oppressed peoples to those of oppressed animals.

In this compelling personal narrative, one learns of the three years during which a lonesome horse named Blue lives in a meadow next to Walker's house. Seldom does anyone visit Blue; Walker is the only one to pay steady attention to him, feeding him apples from a tree in her yard. Something of a friendship ensues as Walker recalls from childhood reading the emotions in a horse's eyes. After two years, another horse is brought to mate with Blue. Only then does Walker see liveliness and respite from boredom in his eyes. Then, sadly, his love is taken away, the goal accomplished. After the separation, Walker sees an immense change in the saddened Blue. With his love torn from him, "Blue was . . . a crazed person. . . . He galloped furiously, as if he were being ridden, around and around his five beautiful acres. He whinnied until he couldn't. He tore at the ground with his hooves. He butted himself against his single shade tree." Blue's heart is broken, and Walker sees in his "large brown eyes . . . a new look, more painful than the look of despair: the look of disgust with human beings, with life; the look of hatred. . . . It gave him, for the first time, the look of a beast." The experience transforms Walker, who, at the end of the essay, sits down to a dinner of steak: "I am eating misery, I thought, as I took the first bite. And I spit it out." The experience may transform Walker's readers as well, since they have lived the story of Blue along with Walker. Walker's own experience, recounted in a moving, personal narrative, may be more effective than a lecture on animal rights.

Through her effective use of anthropomorphic language throughout the essay, Walker emphasizes her point that animals, as people do, deserve respect and humane treatment. To stress the traits that animals share with humans and to establish that equality should exist between humans and nonhumans, Walker uses phrases to describe her horse friend such as "our closest neighbor," his "look of independence, of self-possession," and "Blue was . . . a crazed person." When readers encounter these anthropomorphic descriptions, they are more likely to understand that animals, in actuality, do possess human qualities.

Aided by her use of analogy, Walker not only adds a creative flair to the essay but also extends the essay's central theme, asking readers to relate animal rights to human rights. Walker compares "Japanese, Korean, Filipina, and other non-English-speaking women" to the silent companions we find in nonhumans. American husbands report that these marriages are often "blissfully" happy "until their brides learn to speak English, at which point the marriages tend to fall apart." Walker also compares the strife and prejudice that black slaves and Indians have experienced to the plight of nonhumans. Many people convince themselves that because others are different from them, they can be treated like objects rather than, as living beings, with respect. These people tend to believe myths such as "women 'love' to be mutilated" and "niggers can't faint." By using such strong phrases to express her point, Walker grabs the reader, shaking him or her until the point sinks in. In "Am I Blue?" Blue comes to represent the silent or silenced victims of oppression found the world over. At the close of the essay, Walker points out the irony that horses represent freedom when, actually, they and other animals are slaves to humans. They exist as property, landscape, or mere burdens to humankind.

In "Am I Blue?" Walker reminds us of what "animals try to tell us": "Everything you do to us will happen to you; we are your teachers, as you are ours. We are one lesson." She also leaves us with an important question. How can one eat the flesh of someone he or she acknowledges as equal? Walker asks us in this essay to look into the eyes of those who, although they may not speak our language, have a lot to say, to see the silent suffering there, and to empathize. Some readers may not be able to bridge the communication gap between humans and nonhumans, but for those who understand that fundamental equality exists among all animals, "Am I Blue?" is both an immensely touching account of the physical and emotional massacre of these nonhumans and a public call-to-arms in the fight for animal rights.

■ CONSIDERATIONS OF MEANING AND METHOD

1. What is the thesis of Donaldson's essay? Where does she state it? Is her approach in supporting her thesis deductive or inductive? Can you infer from her thesis what the question might have been that motivated her analysis?

2. Donaldson cites three elements of style which contribute to the effectiveness of Walker's essay and devotes a paragraph to an analysis of each. Locate the thesis of each of these paragraphs. Does Donaldson offer adequate support of each paragraph the-

sis? Can you find additional illustrations and examples from the text of "Am I Blue?" that would support the thesis of each paragraph?

3. In paragraph 2, Donaldson offers a plot summary. What might her reasons have been for doing so? Do you think this plot summary is necessary?

4. Identify elements of Walker's writing strategies and style in "Am I Blue?" that Donaldson does not mention that contribute to the effectiveness of Walker's essay. What examples from the text illustrate them? If you disagree with Donaldson's estimation of Walker's essay, what elements of Walker's writing strategies and style are, to your mind, liabilities? What examples from the text would you cite in support of your critique?

5. If Donaldson had written a personal, rather than an analytical, response to Walker's essay, in what ways might her essay have been different?

■ POSSIBILITIES FOR WRITING

1. In an analytical essay for readers familiar with the work, demonstrate how specific elements of style contribute to or detract from the effectiveness of one of the works of fiction in this chapter or one of the personal narratives of Chapter 4.

2. In an essay articulating your personal response to one of the works of fiction in this chapter or one of the personal narratives of Chapter 4, explain how the work affected you on a personal level, drawing upon your own experience, the experience of people you know, and/or your knowledge of public events, past or current.

MAKING CRITICAL CONNECTIONS:
QUESTIONS FOR DISCUSSION, RESEARCH, AND WRITING

1. In several of this chapter's readings, including Eiseley's "The Dance of the Frogs" and Fisher's "The Wind-Chill Factor," the characters must give something up in order to achieve harmony with or even simply to survive in the natural world. These sacrifices include qualities that we think of as being essential to human identity and experience: reason, civilized behavior, human relationships, and so forth. Comparing two selections in this chapter, analyze their differences and similarities in light of this important theme.

2. The narrator in Loren Eiseley's "The Dance of the Frogs" declares early in the story, "I have seen many strange things, many puzzling things, but I am a scientist." What are the implications of this comment? To what extent do science and scientists defy or embrace life's mysteries in attempts to explain them? Several readings in this chapter, as well as readings in other chapters, approach this question from various angles. In an analytical essay, compare several authors' treatments of this question, drawing upon readings from this chapter and/or others in this text.

3. Loren Eiseley's "The Dance of the Frogs," Ursula K. LeGuin's "May's Lion," and the excerpt from Barry Lopez's *Crow and Weasel* depict indigenous people's views of nature which provide a sharp contrast to the views and attitudes assumed by the dominant culture. What accounts for the differences in these views and attitudes? Find out more about the role of nature, particularly the role of animals, in Native American religion, myth, and culture. In your library, do a little research into the legends and the cultural and religious practices of one particular Indian tribe—perhaps one from the area in which you live or grew up—particularly as they relate to animals, and report orally or in writing to your class on what you find.

4. Explain the function of point of view in two of this chapter's readings. Select two works narrated from different points of view—for example, one from first-person point of view and one from omniscient or limited-omniscient point of view—and explain how point of view contributes in each story to characterization and/or theme.

5. One excellent way to learn more about the structure of fiction, the elements that contribute to the creation of a work of literary imagination, is to try your hand at writing a short story. Let this chapter's readings suggest possible themes to you. It might help,

in your search for a theme that intrigues you, to review the intro-duction to this chapter's readings in which prevalent themes are discussed. In reviewing the "Elements of Fiction" section in the rhetorical introduction to this chapter (pages 267–71), consider potential plots for your story, where and when it might be set, what characters would further the story's action, and how these elements could work together to elucidate your theme. From what point of view would the story be most effectively narrated? You might consider setting your story in the future, as Aldous Huxley did in *Brave New World,* in order to explore the kinds of situations our attitudes about and relationships to nature, science, or technology may eventually lead us into.

CHAPTER 6

Cliff Palace Ruin, Mesa Verde National Park, Colo. © Alex
Lowry, 1989. (Photo Researchers)

HISTORIES

RHETORIC:
WRITING ABOUT
HISTORICAL EVENTS

CAUSES AND EFFECTS OF EVENTS

Analysis of causes and effects is a crucial tool in thinking and writing about historical topics. We analyze causes and effects on a personal level all the time. *(Will skipping one class affect my grade? My parents want me to major in business, but I want to major in political science; how will I convince them that this is a good choice for me?)* We automatically sort out major contributing factors from less significant ones. We anticipate consequences. We recognize the complexity of both influences and possible outcomes. We base many of our decisions upon cause and effect analyses.

We also analyze the causes and effects of collective events, both current and past, although sometimes we may question the relevance of doing so. We may ask why we should go to the effort of understanding events and trends that apparently have nothing to do with us. There are several good reasons. Sometimes events that seem to have nothing to do with us directly have significant indirect effects on us, since events tend to evolve in complicated chains and webs of cause and effect. For example, Americans are still dealing with the effects of Manifest Destiny which drove the settlement and development of the West in the 1800s. Although the first and last atomic bombs used in warfare were dropped on Japan in 1945, the balance of nuclear power still has a critical effect on foreign policy and international relations as well as on individual citizens' sense of relative security and well-being. Another reason for ana-

327

lyzing the causes and effects of events, especially those of the past, is that we learn from events by using them as models. For example, analyzing the failure of Lyndon Johnson's "War on Poverty" may help us establish more effective social programs in the future. Understanding the causes and effects of collective or historical events helps us understand the society and culture to which we belong and in which we must live out our lives.

When you confront questions such as *What happened?*, *How and why did it happen?*, and *What will the consequences be?*, your objective is to discover the answers because they are both personally and socially relevant. While keeping this objective in sight, you must maintain relative objectivity in gathering the facts that provide the foundation for cause and effect analysis.

ESTABLISHING FACTS: *WHAT HAPPENED?*

The first step in cause and effect analysis is to understand what happened. Your understanding of what happened will depend upon your accurate understanding of the facts. Facts are easier to gather when you trace the causes and effects of personal events, since personal events are firsthand experiences. The larger the number of people involved in an event, or the further it exists outside your immediate experience, the harder you will have to work to ascertain facts not readily available to you.

Very often a report of facts and events will lay the foundation for analysis and interpretation. Someone reading the facts of an event in the newspaper will analyze and interpret these facts, adding them to what he or she already knows. In some kinds of journalistic writing, *how* and *why* are added to the questions *who, what, where,* and *when,* and the journalist offers the reader both facts and analysis of them. In a lab report, the Results section, in which the outcome of an experiment is objectively described, will be followed by a Discussion section, in which these results are interpreted by the researcher-writer.

What Is a Fact?

The police report reads:

> *The victim is Margaret Draper, 59 years old. The coroner estimates the time of death was between midnight and 2:00 A.M. on the morning of March 16, 1994. The victim died of strangulation. The murder weapon was a cord from a living room blind, which investigating officers first dis-*

covered missing and later found stuffed inside the piano bench. Lab analysis revealed particles of the victim's skin and hair adhered to the cord. Patrons of the Blue Swallow Bar say that Sam Stillwater, the butler and only other resident of the house, arrived at the establishment at 9:00 P.M. that night and drank beer and played darts until the bar closed at 2:00 A.M. Mr. Stillwater says that he arrived home at approximately 2:30 A.M., after walking the 1.2 kilometers from the Blue Swallow to his and the victim's residence, and went straight to bed. He says that he discovered the body at approximately 8:00 A.M. as he passed the living room on his way to the kitchen. He called police and informed them of the death at 8:04 A.M. The first officer arrived on the scene at 8:22 A.M.

These are the facts—or some of the facts. A fact is not an opinion; it doesn't depend upon the personal preferences or biases of the person who maintains it. A fact is not an assertion or an arguable statement; a fact can't be true to a degree, and since it has no value attached to it, we can't assemble reasons for or against it. A fact, unlike an opinion or an assertion, is a statement of truth that is verifiable. There is a crucial qualifier here, however: a fact is a statement of truth that is verifiable, *if we agree on the means of its verification.*

That Sam Stillwater called the police at 8:04 A.M. on March 16, 1994, is a fact, if we accept Greenwich standard time and the Christian calendar as reasonable means of labeling time and dates, and if we trust the local police to record them correctly. That the victim died of strangulation between midnight and 2:00 A.M., and that the murder weapon was the cord from the living room blind, are facts, if we accept the coroner as a reliable expert and the lab analysis as a reliable procedure. It is also a fact that Sam Stillwater *said* he went straight to bed that night and discovered the body at approximately 8:00 A.M. the next morning, although it is not an established fact that this is actually what occurred. If we are suspicious types—and it is proper that we should be—we might wonder, of course, if the butler really did do it.

Once we have agreed that something is a fact (that is, that we can agree on the means of measuring and verifying it), it is pointless to argue over it. However, there can be, and often is, a great deal of debate over demonstration of facts, and, therefore, over what can be labeled as fact. In the sciences, for example, the evaluation of facts begins with hypotheses and proceeds to demonstrations of facts. What may be for one expert an adequate demonstration of fact may be inadequate for another expert. Sam Stillwater, if accused of the murder of Margaret Draper, will be acquitted or convicted according to the facts of the case; if he has a decent lawyer, however, we trust that he or she will argue convincingly for an interpretation of the facts that will best serve Sam's interests.

Sources of Factual Information

We come by facts in various forms:

- through personal experience and direct observation;
- through primary sources, in speaking with other people with experience and expertise in the subjects we're interested in or in examining original, perhaps historical, documents; and
- through secondary sources, in reading what others have written about our subjects.

Generally speaking, the closer we get to the event itself, using observation and primary source material, the more confidence we will have in the facts; the further removed we are from the event, when we gather facts from secondary source material, the more difficult it may be to verify facts and to distinguish them from interpretations.

Investigators in the Margaret Draper murder case have gathered facts from a variety of sources. They have observed and recorded facts first-hand at the scene of the crime. They have collected facts from primary sources, by consulting experts, such as the coroner, and by interviewing others directly involved in the case, such as Sam Stillwater and the patrons at the Blue Swallow. They have found relevant facts in primary documents, such as the report from the forensic lab. (You might recommend that they consult other primary documents, including Margaret Draper's will and her life insurance policy.) Your investigations of events and analyses of causes and effects in college writing are likely to be less dramatic and less immediate than a murder investigation. Although you will use direct observation, personal experience, and primary sources as research tools, you will probably often rely more upon secondary sources in gathering facts. In whatever form you gather facts, however, it is important to know not only how to recognize them but also how to verify them.

We verify facts by seeking a reasonable authority, and, depending upon the subject at hand, a reasonable authority can exist in any number of forms. If you find yourself guessing at how to spell *anthropomorphism,* you look it up in the dictionary. If you and your sister disagree about the date of your parents' wedding anniversary, you ask them. If you're not sure how photosynthesis works, you consult an encyclopedia or botany textbook.

Sometimes, however, verification of facts can be tricky, and will require not only common sense but also critical evaluation of sources.

What if, for example, two sources provide two different sets of national population statistics? Perhaps the disparity between the two sources can be attributed to a reasonable margin of error. But perhaps one source is more credible than the other: for example, you would rely with more confidence on a firsthand report of results of the federal census than on a casual reference to population statistics in *Reader's Digest.* Or perhaps, given equal credibility, one source was published more recently than the other and draws upon more recent data. When there is disagreement about facts between sources, it is a good idea to consider the relative credibility of your sources, trusting expert and original sources over popular and secondhand sources. It is also a good idea to check on how current your sources are, since many facts change over time, and to corroborate your sources—that is, to confirm the facts with a third or fourth source.

EXPLAINING CAUSES:
HOW AND WHY DID IT HAPPEN?

We probe the hows and whys of an event, its causes, by looking backward in time, attempting to establish causal relationships between relevant facts. Explaining causes involves a good deal more than explaining the sequence of events.

In examining causes, we begin, of course, by contemplating an event. Let's say that you are sitting at dusk in a suburban backyard watching (with mixed feelings) as a doe and her fawn munch the pansies in the neighbor's garden. It's wonderful, you think, to be able to watch these animals up close, although you doubt your neighbor will much appreciate the sacrifice of his flowers for your intimate encounter with these wild creatures. You remember that lately you've had several encounters with deer in this suburban neighborhood; you've seen them from a distance on the fringes of other yards, and in the past few weeks, driving, you've come close to hitting a couple when they've darted across the road at night. There seem to be more and more deer every season, but this year they seem to be everywhere.

THE EVENT:

- The booming deer population in this suburban neighborhood.

You may simply take note of the event and go on to something else. But if you are the curious type, you will wonder *why*. Out of your contemplation of this event questions will arise: Why are there so many deer in the area lately? How has this situation developed? What causes have contributed to this effect?

When we look carefully at an event, even an apparently simple one, in order to analyze its causes, we begin to realize that there are multiple causes, though some are more significant than others. Some possible causes may occur to us immediately, arising from what we already know or can logically infer about a situation.

As you sit in the backyard, two possible causes of the booming deer population come to mind. For three years, there has been higher than average rainfall in this area, and winter rains have extended into the usually dry summer season. In normal years, grass would be sparser and drier, but for the past several years, the land has been green and lush well into the summer. Perhaps, you think, the increase in food supply has resulted in a higher survival rate among deer. You are also aware that this neighborhood is bordered by state park land, where hunting of deer is prohibited. Some of the suburban population of deer may be spillover from the state park.

This is good thinking and these causes are certainly plausible, but you suspect there's more to it than this. You have reached the limits of your own knowledge and understanding. If you are a *very* curious type, you might decide to dig more deeply into the possible causes of this event, to undertake some research beyond observation, personal experience, and your existing understanding of the situation. What you need now are new facts and information, and the observations and insights of people who have studied the subject carefully.

Who or what, you wonder, is in a position to provide information and expertise in this subject? You decide to consult a primary source, a living expert. The next day, you drop in at the headquarters of the state park, and you ask the ranger-naturalist on duty your driving question: why are there so many deer in the area lately? It is a question that she and the entire park administration have considered carefully, because the growing deer population presents them with certain problems.

The ranger confirms that recent rainy winters and the protected status of deer on state park land are, indeed, factors contributing to the rise in population. You add to your list some additional factors as a result of your conversation with the park ranger. As the suburban area has grown and local agriculture has dwindled, the state has been buying up more land for public use, in a race with suburban land developers. The increase in public lands, and the parallel increase in suburban development, helps explain the increase in deer population because (a) the deer are even more widely protected by hunting prohibitions on public land, and (b) most suburban landowners are not interested in hunting deer on their own land, whereas traditionally, local farmers had been. You also learn from the park ranger that deer in this area no longer have any natural predators. Originally, wolves, grizzly bears, mountain lions, and coyotes preyed on deer in the area, helping to keep populations in check. Wolves and grizzly bears have been extinct in the area for a hundred years. The last mountain lion was shot nearly fifty years ago, and no coyotes have been seen in the area for about a decade.

The park ranger lends you a book—a history of the area—that she thinks may be of further interest to you. Later, at home, as you peruse this secondary source, you discover an additional fact. In 1924, a wealthy landowner imported a species of deer from Europe for hunting purposes. Its major attributes were that it was shy, and therefore made for good sport, and it was also of very light coloring and therefore made an excellent target once sighted. This species of deer is also growing in numbers along with the indigenous deer, but it is rarely seen outside the most remote areas of the park. You speculate that, as numbers of both species grow, the indigenous deer are being pushed toward the park's outlying areas by the exotic species.

You make a chart to see what these causes add up to in a possible explanation of the event:

CAUSES:

- Decline of farming
- Increase of public land
- Increase of suburban development
- Decline of predator populations
- Introduction of nonnative species of deer
- Recent rainy winters

EFFECT:

- Booming deer population in this suburban neighborhood

You are beginning to understand the complexity of causal analysis. There are clearly multiple causes that have contributed to this single effect; you realize, in looking at your list of causes, that some contribute more dramatically or directly to the current situation than others, and that not all of them are the same type of cause.

Main, Contributory, and Precipitating Causes

A *main cause* is, as the term suggests, the most important cause of an event. *Contributory causes* are the less important causes of an event. Sometimes a main cause is easy to recognize: you caught a bad cold during exam week because someone sneezed in your face. It hadn't helped, though, that your resistance to infection was low since you'd gone several nights in a row with only a few hours of sleep and had been living on root beer and potato chips for days as you studied for exams. The fact that you were physically run-down is a contributory cause, especially as it affected how severe your cold was.

In considering the dramatic increase in deer population in your suburban neighborhood, you may recognize that the gradual extinction of the deer's natural predators, as well as the introduction of an exotic species of deer in the 1920s, are contributory, not main, causes. These factors may have contributed to population increase over time, but the extinction of predators does not account for the recent surge in the deer population, and the introduction of an exotic species, though it may help explain why indigenous deer are overreaching into the suburbs, does not explain why the deer population in general is increasing.

The main cause of the steady increase in numbers of deer over the past five or ten years appears to be that there is more land on which these animals can thrive, including state park land, where they are protected, and privately owned suburban land, where they are not in direct competition with commercial farming. But you are interested in more than a trend in considering the question of why there are so many deer in this area lately. You want to know, specifically, why there has been such a dramatic increase in the last few years, and especially in this current season. This question will lead you to look for a precipitating cause, which, in this case, is a main cause of the most immediate effect.

A *precipitating cause* will force an event to happen. The precipitating cause of the recent dramatic increase in deer population in your suburban area is the higher-than-average rainfall of the past three years, extending late into the season. Food has been abundant, and more deer have survived. This year, in fact, the many fawns who were born in that first rainy season, most of which survived to adulthood, are for the first time giving birth to young of their own. Without heavy and extended rainfall as a precipitating cause, we would have had a population trend; because of it, we have a population explosion.

Here is how your chart looks now:

MAIN CAUSES:

- Decline of farming
- Increase of public land
- Increase of suburban development

EFFECT:

- Booming deer population in this suburban neighborhood

PRECIPITATING CAUSE:

- Recent rainy winters

CONTRIBUTORY CAUSES:

- Decline of predator populations
- Introduction of non-native species of deer

DESCRIBING EFFECTS: *WHAT WILL THE CONSEQUENCES BE?*

When we analyze the consequences of an event, we look forward in time, describing its effects. If the event we are analyzing has occurred in the past, we can analyze not only its causes but also its effects, since many or all of these effects may have already come about. How has the atomic bombing of Japan influenced the international balance of power in the past fifty years? What changes did the *Challenger* accident in 1986 bring about in the Space Shuttle program? What were the immediate environmental effects of the Exxon Valdez oil spill? Much of the work of cause and effect analysis involves putting together the pieces of the puzzle of history, making sense of events that have already occurred.

The event we are analyzing may have happened very recently or may even exist currently, as with the booming deer population; when this is the case, our descriptions of its effects, or its consequences, will require us to make projections, based on patterns and trends already in place, into the future. In projecting the consequences of events that have yet to unfold fully, we may sometimes recommend a course of action based on our predictions. Where the event you are analyzing is located in time—in the past or the present—will determine the way in which you go about analyzing it, and your reasons for doing so.

Clearly, an effect in one instance may be a cause in another: our booming deer population is both the cause of various effects and the effect of various causes. Looking ahead, as you sit in your backyard watching the deer decimate your neighbor's flower garden, you may wonder not only why there are so many deer in the area lately, but also what the consequences of so many deer will be in the short and/or long term. Adding a consideration of future consequences to causal analysis is a natural step in analyzing current events or existing situations.

As was the case in your analysis of causes, some possible effects of the population explosion among deer in your area spring to mind. You imagine that when your neighbor returns home and finds that deer have eaten all his flowers, he will be compelled to take some steps to prevent this from happening in the future. You doubt that he'll bring out his shotgun to address the problem, but he may decide to invest in a large dog or build a high fence around his property (which would be a shame, since you enjoy looking at his flowers as much as he does). Remembering the occasions this year when you nearly hit deer while driving, you speculate that many people *have* probably hit deer on the highways this year. You also speculate that, since the unusually heavy rainfall of the past three seasons will not continue indefinitely, sooner or later the currently abundant food supply will dwindle, and this will leave an inflated population of deer competing for an inadequate food supply.

You recall that the park ranger with whom you spoke previously had mentioned that the booming deer population presented the state park administration with certain problems, and you decide to go back and talk with her again, since these problems will suggest the effects of a booming deer population. The park ranger confirms that a seemingly inevitable consequence of an overpopulation of deer will be starvation in drier years, possibly mass starvation. She also confirms that there has been an increase in traffic accidents involving deer, both within the park and countywide. In fact, such accidents have doubled this year over last year and have tripled over the last four years. Human injuries and fatalities have risen in proportion to the increase in numbers of accidents. Both the state park and the county have exceeded their budgets in disposing of road-killed deer.

She notes other effects that you had not or could not have anticipated, and you add them to your list. She reports that there has been an increase in disease among deer living in too close proximity, so the population is increasingly unhealthy. Furthermore, a rise in the tick population, which has grown in proportion to the deer population, has resulted in more cases of Lyme disease (for humans, a potentially serious disease contracted through tick bites) reported by park visitors and county residents. She says that the park administration is concerned that ultimately the indigenous species of deer may actually die out in this area, since it seems that the species imported in the 1920s is hardier, more resistant to diseases plaguing the indigenous population, and able to subsist on a sparser food supply. She observes that the imported species are rarely hit by cars, since they prefer secluded areas of the park.

The state park and the county have a problem on their hands, and a number of solutions to the problem have been proposed and are currently being debated. Some citizens have proposed that the prohibition against hunting on public land be lifted in the case of deer, at least in the short term. Some people believe that through hunting or other means, the nonnative deer should be eradicated entirely. The state park administration is considering other means of reducing both native and nonnative deer populations: rangers may begin shooting deer or the park may hire professional hunters for this purpose. People who oppose the killing of deer have proposed various birth control measures. Still others have suggested that relocation of some deer to other areas might be a solution. A few people have even suggested that natural predators be reintroduced in the park, although objections to this have been loud in view of public safety in a populated area. There are arguments in favor of and against each of these suggestions, and it is possible that a combination of methods might eventually be employed in an attempt to control or reduce the local deer population.

When you get home, you chart the existing effects along with the potential effects caused by the current population explosion among deer in your area:

CAUSE:	CURRENT EFFECTS:
• Booming deer population in this suburban neighborhood	• Gardeners must defend their gardens
	• Citizens get to experience wildlife up close
	• More traffic accidents
	• More disease among deer

- More Lyme disease in humans

PROJECTED EFFECTS:

- More of the above in the short term
- Starvation among deer in the longer term
- Indigenous deer could die out eventually

POSSIBLE EFFECTS IN THE FORM OF SOLUTIONS:

- Private hunting on public land?
- Eradication of nonnative deer?
- Culling of deer on public land by rangers or professional hunters?
- Birth control?
- Relocation?
- Reintroduction of predators?

It is easy to see how cause and effect analyses, especially when they project consequences, can evolve into arguments. In analyzing effects, both existing and projected, in our example above, you will weigh positive effects against negative effects. Although you enjoy watching deer close up, and you imagine that many other people do as well, the negative effects of the deer population boom in the area far outweigh the positive ones, so it's clear that something should be done to control the population in order to minimize future negative effects. The question, of course, is what should be done.

Often in an essay based on cause and effect analysis, the writer proposes a solution to a problem, recommending a course of action in the form of a specific policy or what the writer sees as the most productive way of thinking about a problem. Which of the possible solutions in our example is most feasible? Which is least cruel? Which is most economical? At this point in a cause and effect analysis, in order to arrive at a personal decision or to be in a position to recommend a course of action, the principles of fair argumentation take over. You will need to investigate further, then weigh the advantages and disadvantages of all possible solutions according to the criteria you consider to be most important. For more on techniques of investigation and argumentation, see the introduction to Chapter 8.

ORGANIZING CAUSE AND EFFECT ESSAYS

The structure of cause and effect essays varies, depending upon whether the writer emphasizes causes, effects, or both. The choice of which to emphasize has a great deal to do with the purpose of the writing.

In tracing the causes of an event, your primary purpose may be to report. If this is the case, you may want to organize your writing chronologically, describing causes and effects in the order of their occurrence. If you take this approach, you will have to be especially careful to avoid *post hoc reasoning*. Post hoc reasoning is an error in logic based on the mistaken assumption that simply because one event follows another in time, the second event was caused by the first. For example, if, as you watched a full solar eclipse, a tree were to fall across the road in front of your house, you would not assume that the eclipse had caused the tree to fall. This may be an interesting coincidence, but it is not indicative of cause and effect. To avoid post hoc reasoning you must be able to distinguish coincidence from logical causes and effects.

More than simply reporting the causes of an event in an essay, your purpose will very likely involve an interpretation of causes. If this is the case, there are approaches to structuring a cause and effect analysis that would allow you to emphasize the conclusions you draw through analysis more clearly than in a chronological approach. You will probably want to emphasize main causes over contributory causes. Some writers, after establishing a context in which the event has taken place and identifying precipitating causes, prefer to discuss main causes first, because of their importance, before moving on to a consideration of contributory causes; other writers prefer to discuss contributory causes first and main causes closer to the conclusion of the essay, for emphasis.

These are simply two approaches that accomplish the same thing in different ways: in both cases, the writer intends to stress main causes over contributory causes in his or her analysis.

If your purpose is to analyze the effects of an event, or both its causes and its effects, you will want to consider effects in terms of their positive and their negative impacts. In some cases, positive effects will outweigh negative ones, and in other cases, the opposite will be true. The way in which you structure your essay should allow you to stress which kinds of effects—positive or negative—are most important. As is the case in discussing main and contributory causes, you have two basic options in achieving this emphasis: you could stress the more important effects (whether positive or negative) first and foremost, then more briefly discuss the less important effects (again, whether positive or negative) before drawing a conclusion. Or you could save discussion of the most important effects (whether positive or negative) for nearer the end of your essay.

If your ultimate purpose in a cause and effect essay is to urge a course of action, your essay will include characteristics of an argument, and the way in which you go about structuring it should help convince your reader that your position or recommendation is sensible. After establishing causes and analyzing effects according to one of the approaches described above, you will want to discuss possible solutions, explaining why the solution you stand behind makes the most sense of all the possible solutions. (See the introduction to Chapter 8 for more on structuring an effective argument.)

Whether your primary purpose in writing a cause and effect essay is to report, to explain, or to argue, you should provide your reader with a clear idea of your subject, its relevance, and your intention in writing about it in the opening paragraph or two. The reader will want to know early on in the essay whether you are considering causes, effects, or both, and why such consideration is worthwhile. If a problem exists, your reader will want to know what that problem is. If you take a deductive approach in writing a cause and effect analysis, your thesis statement—which will appear early in the essay—will state the most fundamental conclusion you have drawn through your analysis, or it will state your solution to the problem; if you take an inductive approach, your reader will encounter this thesis in your closing paragraphs.

READINGS:
PERSPECTIVES ON
COLLECTIVE EXPERIENCE

The process of biological evolution is built upon complicated chains and webs of cause and effect. Plants and animals, entire ecological systems, change over time in order to survive and proliferate. The survival of any species, including the human species, depends upon its ability to adapt to changing conditions, conditions that until relatively recently have developed slowly and have been determined by the forces of nature rather than by human activity. Over history, some species have succeeded in adapting and have therefore survived, and many, lacking an essential flexibility, have died out.

Human cultures evolve as well, and they evolve differently under varying circumstances, just as biological systems do. From one culture to another, different attitudes about human relationships with nature—about the degree to which human beings are part of or separate from the rest of nature—prevail, and different assumptions arise concerning the roles human beings play in the natural order. In Western culture, we tend to see ourselves as existing in large part outside the natural order, in a class of our own, and as having priority over other species. These attitudes about our relationship to nature are expressed in our religious and moral beliefs, and they forge the nature and direction of our scientific and technological advancements.

It is important to remember that the widely held belief in human superiority within the natural order is a cultural assumption, not an absolute truth. Traditional Native American cultures have tended to see human beings as having an equal rather than a dominant role in the balance of nature. These cultures have long appreciated that life on this planet is interrelated, and that when one part of the system disappears or dominates, the entire system suffers an imbalance.

Noel Perrin, in his essay in this chapter, "Forever Virgin: The American View of America," maintains that somewhere in the middle of this century, the balance of power between nature and human beings shifted: "We really are [now] what our ancestors only claimed to be: the masters of nature—or at least we're the dominant partner in the collaboration." Our accelerating technologies, developed from the intelligence and facility with tools that sets us apart from (and seemingly above) other species, have for the first time in history put us in direct control of our destiny, along with the destinies of many species and of entire ecological systems. We may wonder, along with Perrin, where our technological achievements, our immediate evolutionary success, will lead. The ultimate cause and effect question may be whether or not the human species will survive, and if it does, what the cost will be to life on this planet.

We are beginning to realize the truth of what many other cultures— and now ecologists—tell us: that no species exists independently within an ecological system. When we look at ecological or social systems in broad terms, the question *What will happen to me?* becomes a larger question: *What will happen to us?* And it's a good question, since our fates are intertwined.

Perrin warns us that environmentally, "The green light has turned yellow, and there is a real possibility that it will go red." If learning is a key component of adaptation, and adaptation is fundamental to survival, then understanding the roots and consequences of our assumptions about ourselves and nature, as well as something about cultures that differ from our own, can hardly hurt. This understanding, along with the adjustments in prevailing attitudes about our role in nature that so many environmental writers urge, may better prepare us to confront the environmental problems that our success as a species has spawned, problems which press upon us with increasing urgency.

The readings in this chapter describe the experiences of groups of people rather than of individuals. The readings illustrate and explain attitudes about human relationships with the natural world that have arisen under a variety of circumstances and within different cultural contexts. The two creation stories—the excerpt from the book of Genesis in the Bible and the Pomo Indian myth "Marumda and Kuksu Make the World"—illustrate two vastly different interpretations of creation, deity, and human roles in the natural order. The excerpt from Genesis provides a context in which we might better understand the evolution of the prevailing attitudes about nature that Perrin describes in "Forever Virgin: The American View of America." Although they arise from different Native American cultures, the Pomo creation myth may provide a point of reference as we read Leslie Marmon Silko's essay "Landscape, History, and the Pueblo Imagination," in which Silko explains how history, thought, and language among the Pueblo people of New Mexico are tied inextricably to landscape.

Although the readings of this chapter are related to nature and the environment, they are less about nature, ultimately, than about culture. In describing the land's reversion to wilderness in parts of northern New England, Wallace and Page Stegner, in their essay "The Northeast Kingdom," describe the character of people who continue to live there, on nature's terms. The student work in this chapter, Kevin Cunningham's "Gentrification," describes the negative consequences of an urban phenomenon, the expensive and exclusive upscaling of declining city neighborhoods.

There are many kinds of writing represented in this chapter's readings, reflecting a wide range of perspectives and purposes. The Pomo creation story was intended to entertain or move listeners, not readers. Some of the writing is formal; some is informal. The primary purpose of some selections is to report and explain; the primary purpose of other pieces is to analyze and persuade. What these works have in common is that in looking at causes and effects, they address the questions *What happened?*, *How and why?*, and *What will the consequences be?* from a collective point of view.

■ TWO CREATION STORIES

Genesis 1–3
Marumda and Kuksu Make the World

In the following selections, creation is explained from two very different cultural viewpoints. One can understand, given such different religious perspectives, how cultures clashed when Europeans arrived in North America. The familiar Genesis story from the biblical Old Testament outlines what might be seen as the hierarchy of creation: God creates and has dominion over all creation and over all creatures, including man, made in his image; woman is created from man's rib; man and woman together have dominion over the other creatures of the earth and over all its bounty. The Pomo creation story depicts the creation of the world as, if not accidental, to some degree the consequence of a whim of the gods. These gods are powerful but very human, and the world is created from humble materials indeed, suggesting the sacred potential of all things. Despite the differences between the two stories, there are some striking similarities between them as well, in their content, their symbols, and even in their style.

The Pomo Indians are a tribe native to northern California. Much of Pomo history, extending back thousands of years, has been lost as a consequence of the conquest and settlement of Pomo lands (begun by the Russians and the Spanish in the early 1800s), the decimation of Pomo populations by diseases imported by white settlers, and the general indifference of whites to Indian culture. Yet some legends, such as this one, survive, part of an oral tradition.

Genesis 1–3

One

In the beginning God created the heavens and the earth. ²The earth was without form and void, and darkness was upon the face of the deep; and the Spirit of God was moving over the face of the waters.

³And God said, "Let there be light"; and there was light. ⁴And God saw that the light was good; and God separated the light from the darkness. ⁵God called the light Day, and the darkness he called Night. And there was evening and there was morning, one day.

⁶And God said, "Let there be a firmament in the midst of the waters, and let it separate the waters from the waters." ⁷And God made the firmament and separated the waters which were under the firmament from the waters which were above the firmament. And it was so. ⁸And God called the firmament Heaven. And there was evening and there was morning, a second day.

⁹And God said, "Let the waters under the heavens be gathered together into one place, and let the dry land appear." And it was so. ¹⁰God called the dry land Earth, and the waters that were gathered together he called Seas. And God saw that it was good. ¹¹And God said, "Let the earth put forth vegetation, plants yielding seed, and fruit trees bearing fruit in which is their seed, each according to its kind, upon the earth." And it was so. ¹²The earth brought forth vegetation, plants yielding seed according to their own kinds, and trees

bearing fruit in which is their seed, each according to its kind. And God saw that it was good. [13]And there was evening and there was morning, a third day.

[14]And God said, "Let there be lights in the firmament of the heavens to separate the day from the night; and let them be for signs and for seasons and for days and years, [15]and let them be lights in the firmament of the heavens to give light upon the earth." And it was so. [16]And God made the two great lights, the greater light to rule the day, and the lesser light to rule the night; he made the stars also. [17]And God set them in the firmament of the heavens to give light upon the earth, [18]to rule over the day and over the night, and to separate the light from the darkness. And God saw that it was good. [19]And there was evening and there was morning, a fourth day.

[20]And God said, "Let the waters bring forth swarms of living creatures, and let birds fly above the earth across the firmament of the heavens." [21]So God created the great sea monsters and every living creature that moves, with which the waters swarm, according to their kinds, and every winged bird according to its kind. And God saw that it was good. [22]And God blessed them, saying, "Be fruitful and multiply and fill the waters in the seas, and let birds multiply on the earth." [23]And there was evening and there was morning, a fifth day.

[24]And God said, "Let the earth bring forth living creatures according to their kinds: cattle and creeping things and beasts of the earth according to their kinds." And it was so. [25]And God made the beasts of the earth according to their kinds and the cattle according to their kinds, and everything that creeps upon the ground according to its kind. And God saw that it was good.

[26]Then God said, "Let us make man in our image, after our likeness; and let them have dominion over the fish of the sea, and over the birds of the air, and over the cattle, and over all the earth, and over every creeping thing that creeps upon the earth." [27]So God created man in his own image, in the image of God he created him; male and female he created them. [28]And God blessed them, and God said to them, "Be fruitful and multiply, and fill the earth and subdue it; and have dominion over the fish of the sea and over the birds of the air and over every living thing that moves upon the earth." [29]And God said, "Behold, I have given you every plant yielding seed which is upon the face of all the earth, and every tree with seed in its fruit; you shall have them for food. [30]And to every beast of the earth, and to every bird of the air, and to everything that creeps on the earth, everything that has the breath of life, I have given every green plant

for food." And it was so. [31]And God saw everything that he had made, and behold, it was very good. And there was evening and there was morning, a sixth day.

Two

Thus the heavens and the earth were finished, and all the host of them. [2]And on the seventh day God finished his work which he had done, and he rested on the seventh day from all his work which he had done. [3]So God blessed the seventh day and hallowed it, because on it God rested from all his work which he had done in creation.

[4]These are the generations of the heavens and the earth when they were created.

In the day that the Lord God made the earth and the heavens, [5]when no plant of the field was yet in the earth and no herb of the field had yet sprung up—for the Lord God had not caused it to rain upon the earth, and there was no man to till the ground; [6]but a mist went up from the earth and watered the whole face of the ground— [7]then the Lord God formed man of dust from the ground, and breathed into his nostrils the breath of life; and man became a living being. [8]And the Lord God planted a garden in Eden, in the east; and there he put the man whom he had formed. [9]And out of the ground the Lord God made to grow every tree that is pleasant to the sight and good for food, the tree of life also in the midst of the garden, and the tree of the knowledge of good and evil.

[10]A river flowed out of Eden to water the garden, and there it divided and became four rivers. [11]The name of the first is Pishon; it is the one which flows around the whole land of Hav'ilah, where there is gold; [12]and the gold of that land is good; bdellium and onyx stone are there. [13]The name of the second river is Gihon; it is the one which flows around the whole land of Cush. [14]And the name of the third river is Hid'dekel, which flows east of Assyria. And the fourth river is the Euphra'tes.

[15]The Lord God took the man and put him in the garden of Eden to till it and keep it. [16]And the Lord God commanded the man, saying, "You may freely eat of every tree of the garden; [17]but of the tree of the knowledge of good and evil you shall not eat, for in the day that you eat of it you shall die."

[18]Then the Lord God said, "It is not good that the man should be alone; I will make him a helper fit for him." [19]So out of the ground the Lord God formed every beast of the field and every bird of the

air, and brought them to the man to see what he would call them; and whatever the man called every living creature, that was its name. ²⁰The man gave names to all cattle, and to the birds of the air, and to every beast of the field; but for the man there was not found a helper fit for him. ²¹So the Lord God caused a deep sleep to fall upon the man, and while he slept took one of his ribs and closed up its place with flesh; ²²and the rib which the Lord God had taken from the man he made into a woman and brought her to the man. ²³Then the man said,

> "This at last is bone of my bones
>   and flesh of my flesh;
> she shall be called Woman,
>   because she was taken out of Man."

²⁴Therefore a man leaves his father and his mother and cleaves to his wife, and they become one flesh. ²⁵And the man and his wife were both naked, and were not ashamed.

Three

Now the serpent was more subtle than any other wild creature that the Lord God had made. He said to the woman, "Did God say, 'You shall not eat of any tree of the garden'?" ²And the woman said to the serpent, "We may eat of the fruit of the trees of the garden; ³but God said, 'You shall not eat of the fruit of the tree which is in the midst of the garden, neither shall you touch it, lest you die.'" ⁴But the serpent said to the woman, "You will not die. ⁵For God knows that when you eat of it your eyes will be opened, and you will be like God, knowing good and evil." ⁶So when the woman saw that the tree was good for food, and that it was a delight to the eyes, and that the tree was to be desired to make one wise, she took of its fruit and ate; and she also gave some to her husband, and he ate. ⁷Then the eyes of both were opened, and they knew that they were naked; and they sewed fig leaves together and made themselves aprons.

⁸And they heard the sound of the Lord God walking in the garden in the cool of the day, and the man and his wife hid themselves from the presence of the Lord God among the trees of the garden. ⁹But the Lord God called to the man, and said to him, "Where are you?" ¹⁰And he said, "I heard the sound of thee in the garden, and I was afraid, because I was naked; and I hid myself." ¹¹He said, "Who told you that you were naked? Have you eaten of the tree of which I

commanded you not to eat?" ¹²The man said, "The woman whom thou gavest to be with me, she gave me fruit of the tree, and I ate." ¹³Then the Lord God said to the woman, "What is this that you have done?" The woman said, "The serpent beguiled me, and I ate."

¹⁴The Lord God said to the serpent,
"Because you have done this,
cursed are you above all cattle,
and above all wild animals;
upon your belly you shall go,
and dust you shall eat
all the days of your life.
¹⁵I will put enmity between you and the woman,
and between your seed and her seed;
he shall bruise your head,
and you shall bruise his heel."
¹⁶To the woman he said,
"I will greatly multiply your pain in childbearing;
in pain you shall bring forth children,
yet your desire shall be for your husband,
and he shall rule over you."
¹⁷And to Adam he said,
"Because you have listened to the voice of your wife,
and have eaten of the tree
of which I commanded you,
'You shall not eat of it,'
cursed is the ground because of you;
in toil you shall eat of it all the days of your life;
¹⁸thorns and thistles it shall bring forth to you;
and you shall eat the plants of the field.
¹⁹In the sweat of your face
you shall eat bread
till you return to the ground,
for out of it you were taken;
you are dust,
and to dust you shall return."

²⁰The man called his wife's name Eve, because she was the mother of all living. ²¹And the Lord God made for Adam and for his wife garments of skins, and clothed them.

²²Then the Lord God said, "Behold, the man has become like one of us, knowing good and evil; and now, lest he put forth his hand and take also of the tree of life, and eat, and live for ever"—²³therefore the Lord God sent him forth from the garden of Eden, to till the

ground from which he was taken. [24]He drove out the man; and at the east of the garden of Eden he placed the cherubim, and a flaming sword which turned every way, to guard the way to the tree of life.

Marumda and Kuksu Make the World

He lived in the north, the Old Man, his name was Marumda. He lived in a cloud-house, a house that looked like snow, like ice. And he thought of making the world. "I will ask my older brother who lives in the south," thus he said, the Old Man Marumda. "Wah! What shall I do?" thus he said. "Eh!" thus he said.

Then he pulled out four of his hairs. He held out the hairs. "Lead me to my brother!" thus he said, Marumda the Old Man. Then he held the hairs to the east; after that he held the hairs to the north; after that he held them to the west; after that he held them to the south, and he watched.

Then the hairs started to float around, they floated around, and floated toward the south, and left a streak of fire behind, they left a streak of fire, and following it floated the cloud-house, and Marumda rode in it.

He sat smoking. He quit smoking. And then he went to sleep. He was lying asleep, sleeping . . . , sleeping . . . , sleeping . . . , sleeping . . . Then he awoke. He got up and put tobacco into his pipe. He smoked, and smoked, and smoked, and then he put the pipe back into the sack.

That was his first camp, they say, and then he lay down to sleep. Four times he lay down to sleep, and then he floated to his elder brother's house. His name was Kuksu. This Kuksu was the elder brother of Marumda.

The Kuksu, his house was like a cloud, like snow, like ice, his house. Around it they floated, four times they floated around it the hairs, and then through a hole they floated into the house, and following them the Marumda entered the house.

"Around the east side!" said the Kuksu. Then around the east side he entered the house, and he sat down, he sat, and he took off the little sack hung around his neck. He took out his pipe and filled it with tobacco, he laid a coal on it, and he blew, he blew, and then he blew it afire. Then he removed the coal and put it back into his little sack. After that he smoked, four times he put the pipe to his mouth. After that he offered it to his older brother the Kuksu.

Then Kuksu received it. "Hyoh!" he said, the Kuksu. "Hyoh!

Good will be our knowledge, good will end our speech! Hyoh! May it happen! Our knowledge will not be interfered with! May it happen! Our knowledge will go smoothly. May it happen! Our speech will not hesitate. May it happen! Our speech will stretch out well. The knowledge we have planned, the knowledge we have laid, it will succeed, it will go smoothly, our knowledge! Yoh ooo, hee ooo, hee ooo, hee oo, hee ooo! May it happen!" Thus he said, the Kuksu, and now he quit smoking. . . .

Then Kuksu poked Marumda with the pipe, and Marumda received the pipe, he received it and put it back in his little dried-up sack. Then the Marumda scraped himself in the armpits, he scraped himself and got out some of the armpit wax. He gave the armpit wax to the Kuksu. Then Kuksu received it, he received it, and stuck it between his big toe and the next. And then he also scraped himself in the armpits, he scraped himself, and rolled the armpit wax into a ball. His own armpit wax he then stuck between Marumda's toes.

Then Marumda removed it and blew on it, four times he blew on it. Then Kuksu also removed the armpit wax and blew on it four times, and after that he sat down. Then Marumda went around the Kuksu four times, and then he sat down. And then the Kuksu, he got up, he got up, and four times around the Marumda he went. Then they both stood still.

Now they mixed together their balls of armpit wax. And Kuksu mixed some of his hair with it. And then Marumda also mixed some of his hair with the armpit wax.

After that they stood up; facing south, and then facing east, and then facing north, and then facing west, and then facing the zenith, and then facing the nadir: "These words are to be right and thus everything will be. People are going to be according to this plan. There is going to be food according to this plan. There will be food from the water. There will be food from the land. There will be food from under the ground. There will be food from the air. There will be all kinds of food whereby the people will be healthy. These people will have good intentions. Their villages will be good. They will plan many things. They will be full of knowledge. There will be many of them on this earth, and their intentions will be good.

"We are going to make in the sky the traveling-fire. With it they will ripen their food. We are going to make that with which they will cook their food overnight. The traveling-fires in the sky, their name will be Sun. The one who is Fire, his name will be Daytime-Sun. The one who gives light in the night, her name will be Night-Sun. These words are right. This plan is sound. Everything according to this plan is going to be right!" Thus he spoke, the Kuksu.

And now the Marumda made a speech. Holding the armpit wax, holding it to the south, he made a wish: "These words are right!" Thus he said, the Marumda. And then he held it to the east, and then he held it to the north, and then he held it to the west, and then he held it to the zenith, and then he held it to the nadir: "According to this plan, people are going to be. There are going to be people on this earth. On this earth there will be plenty of food for the people! According to this plan there will be many different kinds of food for the people! Clover in plenty will grow, grain, acorns, nuts!" Thus he spoke, the Marumda.

And then he blew tobacco-smoke in the four directions. Then he turned around to the left four times. Then he put the armpit-wax into his little dried-up sack. After that he informed the Kuksu: "I guess I'll go back, now!" Thus he said, and then he asked the Kuksu: "Sing your song, brother!" And then the Kuksu sang [in an archaic language]: "Hoya, hoha, yuginwe, hoya, . . . etc. . . . etc."

After that Marumda floated away to the north, singing the while a wishing song [also in an archaic language]: "Hinaa ma hani ma . . . etc. . . . etc. . . . " Thus he sang, the Marumda.

With this song he traveled north, the Marumda, riding in his house, in his cloud-house. He was singing along, holding the armpit-wax in his hand and singing the song. Then he tied a string to the ball of armpit-wax, passed the string through his own ear-hole and made it fast. Then he went to sleep.

He was lying asleep, when suddenly the string jerked his ear. He sat up and looked around but he did not see anything, and he lay down again to sleep. It went on like that for eight days, it went on for eight days, and then it became the earth. The armpit-wax grew large while Marumda was sound asleep, and the string jerked his ear. At last Marumda sat up, he sits up, and he untied the string from his ear-hole. Then he threw the earth out into space.

■ CONSIDERATIONS OF MEANING AND METHOD

1. How, specifically, do the creators, and their acts of creation, differ in the stories? In what ways are they similar?

2. What is the relationship between human beings and knowledge in each creation story? Do you think "knowledge" means the same thing in both accounts?

3. Do either or both of these creation stories describe a cause and effect relationship of events? Explain, pointing to examples in the texts. What implications arise when you compare the two myths in light of this question?

4. The Pomo myth of creation was meant to be heard. Here it is not only written but translated. Although it would be impossible for you to tell exactly what may have been lost in the translation, can you speculate about what, if anything, may be missing in this transcription?

5. Locate another creation myth, from a different culture or religion, and share it with your class, comparing it to Genesis and "Marumda and Kuksu Make the World." In comparing these two versions of creation with others, what similarities and what differences arise?

6. Certain assumptions about the place human beings are meant to occupy in the natural order are evident in Genesis and deeply rooted in the Judeo-Christian tradition. Can you think of specific examples in which our personal priorities and/or public policies reflect these assumptions?

■ POSSIBILITIES FOR WRITING

1. Write an analytical essay in which you compare the role of human beings in the natural order as described in these two accounts of creation. You might also consider the relationship between human beings and deities.

2. Analyze these two works closely, not only in terms of meaning, but also in terms of their rhetoric. Read the works aloud. Consider carefully the patterns and rhythms of language. Write an essay in which you compare these two stories rhetorically. How does rhetoric relate to purpose and to meaning?

3. In an essay, elaborate on your response to question 3, question 5, or question 6 above.

■ WALLACE AND PAGE STEGNER
The Northeast Kingdom

In their book American Places, *from which the following regional portrait is taken, Wallace Stegner and his son, Page, along with photographer Eliot Porter, explore local people and regional settings in words and pictures, creating a mosaic of American places* and lives. *"Their characters are rich examples of American life—of individuals and of the settings they've adjusted to—or altered,"* writes critic Richard Lillard. *The Stegners believe that environment is "as much the ambiance created by a community of human beings as it is the flora and the fauna, the topography and the climate." The relationship between people and the land "is their great theme, just as it is the basic theme of today's environmental movement and all of American history."*

Wallace Stegner, renowned novelist, scholar, and nonfiction author, was born in 1909 in Lake Mills, Iowa. As a boy, Stegner lived in the western United States and Saskatchewan in Canada. He attended the University of Iowa as an undergraduate and earned M.A. and Ph.D. degrees from the State University of Iowa. Having taught at the University of Utah, the University of Wisconsin, and Harvard University, Stegner took a position at Stanford University in 1945, teaching there for 26 years. In 1961, Stegner served as Assistant to the Secretary of the Interior, and from 1962 to 1966 he was a member and, in his last year, chairman of the National Parks Advisory Board. He died in 1993 in Los Altos Hills, California.

Page Stegner, born in Salt Lake City, Utah, in 1937, earned his undergraduate and graduate degrees at Stanford University, and has taught at the University of California at Santa Cruz since 1968. His novels include The Edge *(1968),* Hawks and Harriers *(1971), and* Sportscar Menopause *(1978). He has written extensively about writer Vladimir Nabokov and has edited many collections of his works.*

Wallace Stegner's many novels include Remembering Laughter *(1937),* The Big Rock Candy Mountain *(1943),* All the Little Live Things *(1967),* Angle of Repose *(1971), for which he won the Pulitzer Prize in 1972, and* The Spectator Bird *(1976), winner of the National Book Award in 1977. One of the most highly praised of his nonfiction works is* Beyond the Hundredth Meridian: John Wesley Powell and the Second Opening of the West, *a biography of the nineteenth-century western explorer whose expeditions on the Green and Colorado Rivers yielded some of the earliest geological surveys of the West.*

Stegner wrote primarily of the American West and often about historical subjects. He was, according to reviewer James Houston, "a regional writer in the richest sense of the word." But another critic, Richard Simpson, believes that his "main region is the human spirit. . . . Each [novel] explores a question central in Stegner's life and in American culture: How does one achieve a sense of identity, permanence, and civilization—a sense of home— in a place where rootlessness and discontinuity dominate?" Stegner himself explained to an interviewer with the Southwest Review *why he was drawn to write about history: "I think to become aware of your life, to examine your life in the best Socratic way, is to become aware of history and of how little history is written, formed, and shaped. I also think that writers in a new tradition, in a new country, invariably, by a kind of reverse irony, become hooked on the past, which in effect doesn't exist and therefore has to be created even more than the present needs to be created."*

The first of our procession of four cars turns left at the one-room school beyond Shatney's, and eases out on the track to Long Pond. The second and third cars follow it into the woods, but I stop for a minute to look down the road that continues past the school. It is a road I know; it runs through years of my life. For a half dozen summers in the 1940s we lived in the last inhabited house on it. I follow it in my mind past the next farm—the last operative one, whose housewife used to scuttle for the house when our approaching car caught her at the mailbox; past the abandoned black-silver shell just beyond, across whose windows our late lights used to slide with a furtive, greasy gleam; past two more abandoned places, in our time briefly inhabited by families who stuffed the broken windows with rags, and whose Indian-wild boys prowled the woods carrying an old broken-stocked .22 mended with friction tape; past the entrance to our own place, now surely overgrown; over the hill past another dead farmhouse among gnarled and weather-broken apple trees, and so on down to join Highway 16 at the head of Runaway Pond.

It is a road of failed effort, of lonely, hard, stubborn labor defeated and beaten back. They first cut this track through the timber at the end of the eighteenth century. In 1810 it saw one of the spectacular events of Vermont history, when Aaron Wilson's attempt to improve his millrace by deepening the outlet of Long Pond (not the one we are headed for now, but another of the same name) struck quicksand, and the whole pond emptied itself in one roaring rush through the village of Glover.

Hardly anyone uses the road now. Beyond this point, farms that produced wool and mutton during the Civil War, and wheat during World War I, and milk after that, have been quietly returning to woods since the 1930s. The last time I visited our own place, I could hardly get to the old foundations for the rose bushes, heliotrope, goldenglow, lilacs, and Virginia creeper, all gone rank and wild; and in the raspberry patch where the barn used to be I came upon bear dung still smoking.

The day is balmy, the breeze fitful and soft; shadows of fair-weather clouds darken me and pass on. It is the kind of day I remember best from our summers here, the high blue weather full of earth smells and grass smells, the dew still glittering off daisies and paintbrush and buttercups and bending grass, the sweet tang of wild strawberries on the tongue, and the expansive sense of work to be done, things to be built. I remember the nights, too: how we used to squirt a flashlight beam out our gable window and pan it slowly around the blackness of surrounding woods, and pick up the eyes—a pair here, a pair there, green, golden, waiting. There never was a darkness more impenetrable, a wildness more patient.

I see that Shatney has planted hybrid corn and built a silo, and has supplemented his big herd of Ayrshires with some red, shaggy, fierce-horned Highland cattle. But his farm lies as it used to lie under the light fingering wind, one of those rocky hill farms of which it is said the Devil emptied his apron into their pastures.

Shatney makes it because of the hard diligence, the capacity for work, that he shares with his whole culture. His cattle are prize cattle, despite the Highlanders' look of belonging outside a Cro-Magnon cave. The pile of pulp along the Long Pond road tells me that the year-round routines go on: haying in summer (I can hear the tractor down in the field that slopes toward the Lamoille), plowing and liming and manuring and seeding in late summer, pulp-making and wood-making in the fall and winter, sugaring in March, fence-mending on odd days or when the heifers break out, the milking of up to a hundred cows night and morning throughout the year. He lives close to the earth, uses it, understands it, is bound to it. He looks after his land and makes it yield him hay, fodder, garden stuff, milk, maple sugar, sawlogs, and pulp. Like all his neighbors he is an implacable hunter and trapper, hard on the wildlife, but he keeps his land healthy. It is the people in the last stages of unsuccess who are hard on the land, who log off their sugarbush and skin off the softwood down to the last six-inch balsam and then disappear, abandoning the wreckage to the bank, which will eventually dispose of it to some paper company willing to wait thirty years for a return, or to a summer person who asks no usufruct from his acres and lets them grow up in brush, or, more recently, to a speculator who will hold his open space against the inevitable rise in value.

I cramp the wheels and turn in along Carroll Shatney's pulp pile and follow the others into the woods. A mile or so in, I come up with them where they have been stopped by an impassable bog hole. We string out along the trail under the broken shade, the women and children bright as butterflies, the men camouflaged in khaki and green.

A generation ago a group like this would have been less likely, though not impossible. There are Hub Vogelman, professor of botany at the University of Vermont and the state representative of Nature Conservancy, and his wife Marie. There are Lewis Hill and his wife Nancy, native Vermonters who run a nursery specializing in plants and trees adapted to this northern climate. There are a half dozen of us, both Vermonters and summer people, who are interested in the purpose of this excursion, which is to see if Nature Conservancy may want to start a preserve in the Gray family's property on Long Pond. And there is a considerable delegation of Grays, two generations of them, who have already given one of Vermont's two Conservancy preserves, that on Barr Hill above the town of Greensboro.

The road runs deep in trees, brush, and ferns. Shatney's logging has left stumps and slash, but his cutting has been selective, and in this climate the slash will quickly rot and the clearings will spring up in dense hardwood seedlings. This country *wants* to be trees; it is clearings that are hard to maintain. Lewis Hill tells us that when his great-grandparents came here in 1791 the land was all deep woods. Ninety years later, in his grandparents' time, 80 percent of it was cleared and growing crops, and the wildlife had been cleaned out so thoroughly that they saw nothing but an occasional woodchuck. Deer in the 1880s were extinct in Vermont, and only a planting and a long closed season brought them back. Now, ninety-odd years later, 80 percent of this land is woods, not fields, and deer, bear, foxes, coyotes, porcupines, beaver, fishers, skunks, and raccoons have come back to inherit the restored wild. A few years ago a moose came down from somewhere and grazed among the cows at the edge of East Hardwick. As for the deer, Lewis has given up on them. He grows such succulent goodies in his nursery that ten-foot fences, all-night vigils, dogs, and the enlistment of neighbors hungry for doe-burgers are all unavailing. He plants an extra share for the wildlife.

We walk in dappled greenish forest shade. The air smells of mold, damp, fungi. Except for the rutted road, which once led to the Rut-ledge farm, the woods might be primeval, though in the virgin forest the trees were surely bigger, and included white pine, now almost eliminated by cutting and blister rust. Once, those white pines would have matched well with western trees. In one of Robert Frost's Ver-mont houses, the one in Concord Corner, there used to be a wainscot made of a single pine board nearly four feet wide. There are no such trees any more. The biggest I see are some yellow birch perhaps six-teen inches in diameter.

Nevertheless, the *feel* of this wood is wilderness. There is no sound of chain saw, tractor, car, or airplane, nothing but the buzzing of flies in sunny openings, the quick light voices of children, the murmur of Hub Vogelman or Lewis Hill identifying plants we ask about. And far off in the woods, the pipe of a white-throated spar-row advising his farmer friend to "Sow wheat, Peabody, Peabody, Peabody . . . "

The trees of this mixed northern forest we all know—sugar and swamp maple, yellow and gray and white birch, beech, wild cherry, elm (the old ones all dead), white ash; and white and black spruce, balsam fir, hemlock, hackmatack, aspen, basswood, white cedar in the swampy places. A rich variety, each with its own color and smell and way of growing. You can tell what you are walking under by the shape of the flakes of sun the leaves let through.

We know the commonest ferns—Christmas, cinnamon, inter-rupted, hay-scented, sensitive, but we need the experts to identify New York fern with its evenly diminishing fronds down the stem, Long Beach fern with its walrus mustaches at the base, polypodies that grow only around or on granite boulders dropped by the ice sheet. We know raspberry, gooseberry, wood sorrel, trillium; but we have to be instructed in bunchberry, with its small red clusters; and Indian pipe, whose white fleshy pipes turn black after being picked; and creeping snowberry with its tiny laddered leaves and tiny white berries and its smell like wintergreen; and baneberry, whose poiso-nous white berries, Vogelman says, the Indians used to mash up with jack-in-the-pulpit and throw into lakes to stun the fish. All around the Blueberry Rocks, on the east shore of the pond but not within the Gray land, we find mountain holly hanging its red berries over the granite.

From Blueberry Rocks we see only wildness. Not a human habita-tion, not a road or pole line, not a mark of man's passing. Sunk in its pocket among the hills, this warm, shallow lake, lightly riffling from our cedar shore to the spruce-and-fir shore opposite, has watched humanity go by, and recovered from the visit.

Once a carriage road ran through Skunk Hollow, on the other side. It is overwhelmed by trees now; the only way to walk it is to walk with an aerial photograph in hand, guiding oneself by the slight streak that the air view shows, and by the stone walls that appear and disappear in thick woods. Once the hayfields of the Rutledge place sloped to the water's edge on the north shore. Now, Clive Gray tells me, the Rutledge place is swallowed up like Tikal, and so is the shack that a local minister used to maintain on the northwest shore. Clive is not sure he could find the site of either any more.

This is hard to believe. Thirty-five years ago, when we brought a friend here, hunting a summer place, the Rutledge farm was a big, well-built farmhouse on hewn granite foundations, its windows unbroken, its rooms as clean as if the Rutledges had moved out only the week before. But it was remote, at the end of a road that could not be kept open in winter, and our friend did not buy it. Some years later someone else did, and turned it into the Tamarack Ranch, a resort camp which failed. Now, neglected for more than a decade, it is gone. Its stone walls are hedgerows of chokecherry and mountain ash, and its hayfields are full of Christmas trees.

For years there has been hardly any human activity on Long Pond except some summer camping permitted by the principal landowners, the Igleheart-Merrill-Freeman family. The special spot on the south shore where many of us have taken first our children and then our grandchildren to camp out and catch a boatload of perch and sunfish, is a precarious beachhead only. Left unvisited even for a year or two, that campsite would disappear in the woods, and the road in would become like the Skunk Hollow road, detectible only from the air. What we look out at from Blueberry Rocks is a home for loon and beaver, as lonely a pond as Rogers' Rangers ever camped by on their desperate return from the St. Francis villages in 1759.

Less than two hundred years from wilderness to wilderness. And this is Orleans County, where farming is still a solid way of life, one of the highest milk-producing counties in the state. In Caledonia County there are places wilder than this. In Essex County nearly everything is as wild as this. In Essex County, much of which was never farmed, but only logged, the population after two centuries of settlement is still less than ten to the square mile. Essex County contains towns like Averill, chartered as early as 1762, which have never been organized as towns, and have fewer than two dozen residents. It contains towns like Brunswick and Ferdinand, with neither church nor store. It contains towns like Avery's Gore and Lewis, with no public roads and no known residents. Opened only after the ending of the French and Indian War made it safe, and settled only after the Revolution, this Northeast Kingdom was born of our post-revolutionary frontiering, contemporary with the migration into Kentucky. Manifest Destiny came north as early as it went west. History touched these wild woods early, struggled for a time against weather and loneliness and hardship, and eventually either hung on in stalemate or withdrew.

As ontogeny repeats phylogeny, our family experience reproduced the history of the generations before us. We put a lot of work into our backwoods place, and in the end were forced closer in, to a friendlier location. What was once a farm is now a woodlot, what was once a house is an overgrown cellar, what was once a meadow is a plantation of red pines, many of them killed or deformed by the hedgehogs. The memories of our summers on the back road are lost with the memories of Orange King, the previous owner, whoever he was. We heard that he once grew wheat there, and in his spare time manufactured out of cedar or white pine the sap buckets and butter firkins that have since been replaced by metal.

Once, prowling the dense woods a half mile back from the house, we came upon the old sugarhouse, collapsing, dim, a cathedral for chipmunks and white-footed mice. Stacked beyond the rusting pan and scattered woodpile were six or seven dozen wooden sap buckets bound with wythes, the kind that now excites women on the lawns of country churches where antiques are auctioned off. They go with hand-hewn beams and hand-wrought square-headed nails to give a touch of authenticity to electrically heated, wall-to-wall-carpeted summer homes. We took out four, all we could conveniently carry, to use as wastebaskets. That summer we didn't get back to that secret silvery high-roofed cathedral in the woods. When we tried the next summer, we couldn't find it.

So much for Orange King, whoever he. So much for Mary and Page and Wallace Stegner, whoever they. As for our own Mud Pond, one of at least a dozen Vermont ponds by that name, a hushed and hidden patch of water where Page and I went a few times to fish for chubs and watch the great blue herons wade the shallows with their spears poised—Mud Pond is going too. It is eutrophic, a body of water on its way to becoming a swamp and then a meadow. Below it the returning beaver have dammed the brook and killed several acres of timber, creating such an impassable bog that you would have to be a mink to get through it.

This reclamation, unlike the human kind that kills rivers to create reservoirs, does not assert human purposes; it restores natural processes. All through the three northeastern counties of Vermont, through our forty years' acquaintance with them and our many summers of living in one of them, we have watched the north woods working quietly and inexorably to reclaim themselves, or part of themselves.

History and culture are artifacts of different kinds. One does not necessarily imply the other. The culture may survive and flourish while history is all but lost. Verbalized as stories and ballads, people and their actions become legend, epic, and folklore. Frozen as records, they become history. Either way, if they happen to matter enough to a people, they may last as long as the language itself. But if they are never memorialized in language or monuments, they die with the heads that remembered them, they rot like a birch in wet woods, they sink into the ground. Vermont knows the history of its few great events, and has its folk heroes such as Ethan Allen and his Green Mountain Boys, and treasures its brief period as an independent republic. But the long stalemate with the woods that produced the Vermont culture has been largely taken for granted by the people who have inherited it, and its history is known only to the few.

Lewis and Nancy Hill, members of the county historical society, are among the few. They have an unending curiosity about their country and its life. They know, though many who live on it probably do not, that the road we came out from Greensboro on was once the Norton Road, the main thoroughfare north. They know that the land now belonging to Shatney was granted in 1790 to the first child born in Greensboro. They know when people first came into these woods—about the Bayley-Hazen Road that during the Revolution was cut from Newbury, Vermont, to just beyond Hazens Notch, under Jay Peak, to facilitate an invasion of Canada that never took place. They can trace the road, on the map or on the ground, up the Connecticut Valley to Barnet, across through Peacham, Danville, Walden, Hardwick, Greensboro, Craftsbury, and Albany. Their kind of people, with their kind of cultural self-consciousness, erected the monument on Hardwick Street, opposite the old Stage House whose secret chamber concealed refugees during the War of 1812 and runaway slaves before the Civil War; and the other monument on the west shore of Caspian Lake where Indians killed two young soldiers in 1781. The Hills can tell you how, when peace came in 1783, settlers found their way up the Bayley-Hazen Road and began the daunting job of hacking farms out of the forest. It is a source of pride to them that like the Wilderness Road across the Cumberland Gap into Kentucky, and like the Santa Fe and Oregon and California trails later, their ninety-two miles of forest track were a road of empire.

But even the Hills can tell us little about Orange King. Memory and hearsay take them back as far as their parents' or grandparents' generation, and then blur out. Human history in the Northeast Kingdom is largely lost because it attaches to no great name or great event. It is the collective history of nameless people who took more territory than they could hold and then gradually, generation by generation, had to give it back to the wilderness.

The process built the Vermont character and the Vermont countryside, both justly celebrated. It also left along the back roads, on the dying hill farms, back in the woods, a fringe of people living below the poverty level, people with many skills and the toughness of badgers, but without the capital, luck, or ambition to get a start and hold it. They are not unlike the people whom the California Gold Rush knew as Pikes, whom Bayard Taylor defined as "Anglo-Saxons relapsed into barbarism." They live by odd jobs, logging, hunting. Sometimes they are on the town, or on the state and federal welfare programs that, against the will of a lot of Vermonters, have replaced the town. Many of them, coming toward the end of a life-long losing battle, are dignified, unself-pitying, as enduring as old roots. Some are defective or retarded, many are made lumpish by a bad diet. Some are simply independent, asserting what Frost called their God-given right to be good for nothing.

They are sly, ironic, humorous, watchful around summer people, at ease only among themselves, sometimes violent, never servile. The necessity for making do has created a race as ingenious as Eskimos. They can toggle up anything, they know machinery, animals, tools, the woods. At their worst they can be Tobacco Road hoodlums like those who threw dead coons on the porch of a black stranger in Irasburg. At their best, among those they know and trust, they are neighborly, helpful, and quite astonishingly tolerant of difference and eccentricity. They judge a man primarily by how he works. And all of them know who they are. The social commentators, usually outsiders, who point out that the whole Northeast Kingdom is well below the state and national averages in income, and that in Orleans County actual hunger exists, should probably work to improve the statistics but spare their alarm. This is poverty which has lost neither its independence nor its self-respect, poverty that half the time doesn't even know it's poor.

Years ago, in company with Phil and Peg Gray, the parents of the present generation of Grays, we used to take annual walking trips with a packhorse, choosing the remotest back roads we could find. In the Lowell Mountains, on the northernmost reach of the Hazen Road, we took refuge one rainy night in 1939 in a farmer's haymow, and next morning had breakfast with the farmer and his wife. Both were past eighty. Their eight children had one by one gone down-country to find work. They now had no help, hired or otherwise. The old man still milked twenty cows, by hand. The old woman kept up a big garden, a flock of hens, a few geese and turkeys. Her cellar was full of Mason jars of peas, beans, beets, corn, and applesauce, its bins stocked with potatoes just dug and put down. They were some-what flustered to have company. The woman reminded us of Mrs. Shatney, Carroll's mother, who used to ambush us at the mailbox when she heard our car coming, and hold us in talk for half an hour with her hands tucked in her armpits.

We could detect no self-pity in what this old couple told us, though we could see that their farm was the last kept-up place on the road. Everything on the way in was ramshackle, beyond them there was nothing but woods. Another year or two, until the winters got too hard, and then they would have to sell if they could, or simply move out if they couldn't. An auction to dispose of the cows and the usable machinery, furniture, and tools, and they would be in some home for the aged. The farm had been their life, they had made it with their bare hands. But no one would have known from their talk that they found it hard to have no sons or daughters who wanted it. They accepted and endured as they had always done.

That was one kind. Very different was the cracked old cackler who visited our camp on Zack Woods Pond and told us, among other things, that the fish were all drownding. So many camper women going in swimming nekkid that the fish got too stiff to swim.

The next year we walked from the valley of the Lamoille past South Maid Hill and around Wheelock Mountain. The road we walked had been a carriage road in 1911, when our USGS quadrangle was printed, but in places we had to hack a path for the packhorse with machetes. It was three days before we met a living soul, and he was an old man with cataract-blue eyes who was living in his milk shed, his house and barn having burned, and getting into Lyndon every week or two by horse and buggy. He sold us—tried his best to give us—a mess of snap beans and sweet corn, and told us that in his boyhood it was common for people to drive the way we had come, and that in the fall parties used to go out by buggy or car to see the color.

About noon of the next day we had our second human contact, a man plowing with oxen and a bulltongue plow. He turned the plow on its side, left the oxen standing, and came hopping across the furrows, a man with a whiskery face and no teeth, his mouth a delighted black hole. "I God," he said, "I thought for sure you was a camel! I thought you was comin' right out of the Bible, God if I didn't!"

Now a woman came striding down from the house along the drive. She waved her arms as she came; she was saying something loud and unintelligible. The farmer stopped talking, an expression knowing and weary crossed his face, he sucked in his cheeks and closed his toothless gums together, wizening his whiskered jaws. On the other side from the approaching woman, his finger made a brief twirling gesture at his temple.

Then the woman was before us, vigorous, brown-legged, considerably younger than he. She had eyes as quick as mice and as big as millwheels, and she too was fascinated by our horse, a superannuated Irish hunter seventeen hands high without his pack. The woman walked all around him twice, popping her lips like a fish. She spoke in poetry and parable. "What is in the pack, a lifeless form? You will be left all forlorn. The French will show no mercy. What did they do in Twenty-two? Who'll be alive in Forty-five?"

She said a good deal more before the man took her by the elbow, and with a hand as firm as a tow-bar led her back to the house. He had offered us camping space in his lower meadow, by the brook, but we did not like the thought of being visited by that Cassandra, and though it was a hot, smothery day, and our legs were dead, we walked another three miles before we stopped.

As for the road we had walked over to make that contact, it was a road even further gone than the Norton Road. We had passed dead farms in clearings that were closing in from all sides. We had snooped through an abandoned one-room school and an abandoned church. We had come upon stone walls that appeared and disappeared in deep woods, with trees a foot in diameter growing out of the piled stones. We had paused in a lost cemetery, still surrounded by sagging barbed wire, its slate and granite and marble stones buried in black-berry vines, mullein, goldenrod, and milkweed. The earliest grave we found was 1812, the latest 1931. Only nine years ago the last burial had taken place there, the last farm had been closed up and left empty.

In August 1978, a friend and I took a walk in the first few miles of that same obliterated road. It is not as obliterated as it was forty years ago. A half mile off Highway 16 we passed a planting of red pine, planted since that trip in 1940 and now all dead of *Sclerorerris* canker: proof that man-made pure-stand forests are more vulnerable than the mixed forest nature developed for this country. One of the formerly abandoned farms was lived in by a family that gave off mixed signals. The mother sounded like pure backroads Vermont, the daughter in tight jeans and T-shirt might have been one of the city dropouts that have been flocking to these woods since the sixties. They said that grandpa and grandma were cutting and skidding tie-logs another mile in: that at least established them as Vermonters and not city folks.

We found grandpa and grandma logging—he riding the tractor, she walking behind to unhook the log chain and carry it, a seventy-pound iron python, back along their rutted skin road. They told us where the cemetery was, and we found it after struggling through a creation raspberry patch. Its feeling had not changed. The stones were even more overrun by brambles, milkweed, mullein, and gold-enrod, and some cedars and firs had taken root and grown to ten or twelve feet. But the sky was blue overhead, the wind was hushed there in God's acre. My skin itched with spiderwebs and pollen, my hands smelled of raspberries. Off in the woods a wood thrush and a hermit thrush were competing, the wood thrush always beginning on the same note, the hermit starting anywhere on the scale he pleased. It seemed one of the pleasantest and most restful of all places in the world to be laid away, and it seemed to say what now we hear Long Pond saying—that people had come, and struggled for a while, and gone for good.

But the graveyard did not tell a completely true story, and Long Pond may not either. The insistent *memento mori,* the tale of human intrusion quietly leafed over, is not quite accurate. For one thing, that salty, well-matched, friendly pair snaking out poplar logs represented an activity that is going to go on indefinitely. Trees are what the country produces naturally, and trees are a cash crop. For another, look what had happened to the abandoned schoolhouse after forty or fifty years of abandonment. Its inside was now equipped with four double-decker bunks, a kitchen range, and a table. A sign on the door said "Island Pond Rest Center." What was that? A hippie pad? Mystery. Island Pond was miles away. And rest center for whom? Furthermore, there was the music we heard in the woods, music that did not come from thrushes either wood or hermit, or from Peabody birds, but from the Grateful Dead. Following it, we came to a geodesic dome half finished in a clearing, and near it a van parked under some trimmed-up spruces, with laundry inert on a length of wire.

Nature abhors a vacuum. Land relinquished to the wild, especially at a time when the wild is being overwhelmed in most parts of the continent, inevitably attracts seekers, as Orange King's abandoned farm attracted us in 1938. There is hardly an empty farmhouse in the Northeast Kingdom that has not been taken over and to some extent patched up and renovated. Up in Glover a whole community of Bread-and-Puppet young people create summer Happenings in a meadow for thousands of the bare-backed, barefooted, and long-haired, plus hundreds of the local curious. Their meadow during a performance is as colorful as the Field of the Cloth of Gold. And up at Norton, on the Canadian line in Essex County, is the Earth People's Park, eyed with suspicion by the local people and gingerly avoided by both American and Canadian authorities. By some variant of the Second Law of Thermodynamics, Vermont's returning wilderness is moved in on, even as it returns, by the restless energies of outsiders at odds with what the United States has become elsewhere. What has been happening throughout the emptier quarters of the West has been happening even more swiftly in Vermont—perhaps because Vermont is close to the great concentrations of people in the East Coast megalopolis, perhaps in part because it is convenient to an imperfectly patrolled international border.

Local people cannot say much good for the Earth People's Park except that it probably *started* all right, with draft evaders and flower children and somewhat dewy idealists—committed, it is true, to the drug culture, but as consumers, not pushers. Shortly, however, the park was moved in on by other kinds. That border has from its earliest beginnings had its share of illegal activities. Smugglers' Notch was not named out of mere whim; and during Prohibition Bernard De-Voto, who summered for a couple of years on Lake Seymour, near Morgan Center, made a reputation as a host at Harvard because he happened to know a Vermont farmer with a sugarbush that merged with the Canadian woods. The officials at the Derby Line port of entry now report a considerable monthly haul of drugs and illegal aliens, and they assume that their haul is only a fraction of what gets away.

But the Earth People's Park has shown signs of growing ugly. In the 1960s a literary friend saw signs clear down in Mexico: "Trouble with the law? Draft Board after you? Being hassled by the old lady? Come to Earth People's Park, Norton, Vermont." Some saw in that invitation exactly what they were looking for, and in recent years the People's Park has got a reputation as a dangerous place. Some of its residents are reputed to go armed. There have been confrontations and clashes between Earth People and the farmers of Norton. Increases in crime in the region are commonly laid to that dropout heaven. It is the Missouri Breaks of the Northeast Kingdom, and though there are surely some perfectly ordinary and harmless people there, there seem to be enough hard cases to damage the reputation of the whole place.

The usual back-road immigrants, however, the young people whom Lewis and Nancy Hill call "homesteaders," are another matter. A lot of them are well educated, many of them have trust funds, or families who will supply what Vermont's niggardly woods and fields fail to. They often work their heads off, they are full of idealism and enthusiasm, they are readers and students of history, they make good winter company. Being year-round residents, they instantly acquire a respectability in Vermont eyes that no summer person can expect: it is people who are up to staying past Labor Day who get inside a Vermonter's wariness. As year-round residents, too, they can vote in town meetings in March, and many a town meeting has recently been stirred up in ways it has not known for generations.

Finally, they are Earth People, at least as authentic as any in Norton's park. They are children of the sixties and the first Earth Year. They care about the environment, and know something about it, and they are becoming a force behind Vermont's increasingly enlightened land-use laws. They are against billboards, shopping centers, motorboats, unselective logging, and the smoke and rats of unsanitary landfills. They make the shut-in winters livelier, they reintroduce the notes of hope and growth.

And it is easy to tell the real ones from the imitations. The imitations run around all summer in their vans, undressing on the public beaches and offending the godly with their promiscuity and idleness. The real ones probably live by couples, whether legally married or not, and work, and listen, and learn. The real ones are not caught, some early October morning, with cracks in their houses, no storm doors or windows, no insulation, no bank of brush or tarpaper around their foundations, and a winter woodpile that will last till Thanksgiving. The real ones don't appear barefooted, bare-assed, and shivering in Willeys' store on the morning after the first freeze, frantically looking for shoes and socks and long underwear. The real ones are not grasshoppers but ants, and they are likely to have a part in the future of the state. The real ones don't buy steaks with food stamps, or sell food stamps at a discount to buy beer.

Vermont is a great character mill, and it grinds exceeding fine. It is too rough a country for pretenders, but it will make room for anyone, however odd, if he doesn't put on airs or show himself incompetent or think himself above the homespun and the calluses and the hard-mouthed virtues that Vermonters have come to the hard way, and don't intend to lose.

As for Long Pond, which we have all but forgotten, it may or may not remain dedicated to its natural processes as quasi-wilderness. There are boundary problems; other landowners have differing aspirations for their pieces of shoreline. The next generation may find the pond's future still hanging in the balance.

But I take it as a good omen that many people of many kinds want to see the pond preserved as a natural treasure. The Igleheart clan, "immigrants" of some twenty-five years' standing, successively dairy farmers and then builders, have large holdings on or near the pond as the result of a generation's hard work. They have shown a reluctance to develop in any way that will damage the pond. The lots they offer for sale are removed a healthy distance from the shoreline, and one of their principal attractions is the assurance of a preserved and natural lake. The Grays, who also favor a "natural" as opposed to a "developed" pond, represent the best of the summer people—academics most of them, with four generations of Vermont summers behind them. The Hills just as clearly represent the most thoughtful and informed native Vermonters, active in every socializing aspect of their town's life: 4-H leaders, officers of the historical society, authors of books on horticulture under the St. Lawrence storm track, people who are solidly traditional but open to the new, and friendly up down and across the various layers of the town's population.

Walking out, we have a feeling that we are closing Long Pond for the winter. Nobody is going to be in there much, now that summer is ending, unless it is some farm boy trapping muskrats. Through the winter it will lie locked under four or five feet of snow, its water frozen clear to the bottom in many places, its fish driven into the deeper parts to wait for spring. When spring finally comes, every twig of every tree, every uncoiling fiddlehead of fern, is going to come on with one idea in mind: to hide that woods-bound lake even deeper in green.

Up to now, it is the pond that has saved itself. But against speculators with money—Florida money, California money, Venezuelan money, Kuwaiti money, Mafia money, whatever kind of money—it is going to need help. To a certain kind of eye, Long Pond's hushed remoteness might be transformed into a vision of a thousand shore-front summer cottages, each with dock and boathouse; and an inn with a bar, tennis courts, perhaps a nine-hole golf course where the Rutledge meadow used to slope down to the water's edge.

If Long Pond were in California, that vision would almost certainly come true. Since it is in Vermont, there is a chance that something better may happen. For there is something in Vermont—in its climate, people, history, laws—that wins people to it in love and loyalty, and does not welcome speculation and the unearned increment and the treatment of land and water as commodities. Here, if anywhere in the United States, land is a heritage as well as a resource, and ownership suggests stewardship, not exploitation.

■ CONSIDERATIONS OF MEANING AND METHOD

1. How, in the opening paragraphs, do the Stegners set the tone and establish the theme of the essay?

2. Why are the farmer Shatney's efforts at making a go of his farm apparently successful? Why do many other farmers fail, and what happens to the land when they do?

3. The Stegners write that it's been "Less than two hundred years from wilderness to wilderness" in Orleans County. How has the land functioned as the key agent in patterns of settlement and retreat in this part of northern Vermont?

4. The Northeast Kingdom, write the Stegners, was settled by "people who took more territory than they could hold and then gradually, generation by generation, had to give it back to the wilderness. The process built the Vermont character and the Vermont countryside, both justly celebrated." How is this "Vermont character" manifested in the people who have, over generations, remained there? How is it manifested in some of Vermont's newcomers? What qualities, according to the Stegners, does it take to endure in this part of Vermont?

5. What possibilities for the future do the Stegners envision for this area? What is their hope for it? Do you think their hope is warranted?

6. Compare the Stegners' descriptions of farming in Northern Vermont (where "the Devil emptied his apron into their pastures") with the descriptions of New Hampshire farming that Noel Perrin, in "Falling for Apples," and Maxine Kumin, in "Building Fence" (in Chapter 3), provide in their essays. Does it sound as if they are describing farming in the same part of the country? In what way do you think the Stegners might see Perrin or Kumin as contributing to the future of northern New England?

■ POSSIBILITIES FOR WRITING

1. In a cause and effect essay, describe how the land has shaped the history, the professions, or the character of people in the part of the country, or the world, that you are from. If you are from a place where the land has been more dominated than dominating, describe causes and effects from a different point of view: how have people shaped and affected the land, and according to what needs?

2. As population grows and demographics (the patterns in which populations are distributed) shift in this country, many communities are experiencing an influx of newcomers. In an essay, explain the causes and effects of population growth and shifting demographics in your community. What attracted long-time residents to your community? What attracts newcomers? Are long-time residents and newcomers different in significant ways? How? Is there any conflict or mistrust among them? Why? What do they have in common? How is the character of your community evolving as a consequence of these changes?

■ NOEL PERRIN
Forever Virgin:
The American View of America

See the headnote for Noel Perrin's "Falling for Apples" in Chapter 3 (page 156) for biographical information.

"Forever Virgin: The American View of America" is an example of Noel Perrin's more scholarly writing, as opposed to his essays for popular readers, such as "Falling for Apples" in Chapter 3. Even in

*writing on scholarly and historical subjects, however, Perrin's style
is relaxed and straightforward, clear and accessible to the general
reader. In this essay, he explains the causes and effects of most
Americans' persistent belief (despite the fact that often, at least
intellectually, we know better) that somehow nature can absorb indefinitely all our manipulations of it.*

If there is one novel that nearly all educated Americans have read,
it's F. Scott Fitzgerald's *The Great Gatsby*. If there's a single most famous passage in that novel, it's the one on the last page where
Fitzgerald talks about Gatsby's belief in the green light ahead. He has
in mind two or three kinds of green light at once. There's the literal
green dock-identification light that Gatsby can see from his Long Island mansion, glimmering across the bay where Daisy lives. There's
the metaphorical green traffic light: the future is open, the future is
GO. And finally there's the green light that nature produces: the reflection from trees, and especially from a whole forest, a forest
crowding right up to the shore of Long Island Sound.

In that famous last passage, the narrator of the book is standing in
front of Gatsby's mansion at night—a summer night. He is looking
across the bay, just as Gatsby used to do. There is a bright moon. As
he looks, "the inessential houses began to melt away until gradually I
became aware of the old island here that flowered once for Dutch
sailors' eyes—a fresh, green breast of the new world. Its vanished
trees, the trees that had made way for Gatsby's house, had once pan-
dered in whispers to the last and greatest of all human dreams; for a
transitory enchanted moment man must have held his breath in the
presence of this continent . . . face to face for the last time in history
with something commensurate to his capacity for wonder."

Fitzgerald says in this passage that it was just for a moment that
men and women beheld the new world as a fresh, untouched place, a
virgin world, a place where the future is open and green. But, of
course, it wasn't. We still see it that way—or most of us do most of
the time. Certainly that was how Jay Gatsby saw it sixty years ago. In
the narrator's vision, there on the last page, that is how he, too, sees
it: Long Island with the houses invisible in the moonlight, the island
like a green breast, the breast of Mother Nature, inexhaustibly nour-
ishing. As I am going to try to show in a little while, that is how most
Americans still perceive the country now: morning in America, a
green light ahead, nature glad and strong and free. Or at least we do
in our dominant mood, and that's why the majority of us don't really

worry much about acid rain, or recycling, or any of that. We have a consciousness below knowledge that the big country can handle all that.

But there are two things I want to do before I come to the relationship between human beings and nature in America in the 1980s: a short thing and a long thing. The short one is simply to make clear what I mean by nature. And the long one is to give some of the history of the encounter between us and nature since we got here. Because of course I am not claiming we feel exactly the same as Henry Hudson's sailors did in 1609. We have changed, and the country has changed since then a lot. All I'm claiming is that we still see the green light.

First, what nature is. Among other things, it's a word that if you look it up turns out to have twelve meanings, plus eight more submeanings. They vary so widely that Robert Frost could and did once write a poem on the subject. In the poem, he and an anonymous college official are arguing about what the word means in the epitaph that the Victorian poet Walter Savage Landor wrote for himself. Landor summed up his life thus:

> I strove with none, for none was worth my strife.
> Nature I loved, and next to Nature, Art.
> I warm'd both hands before the fire of life;
> It sinks, and I am ready to depart.

Frost and the administrator can't agree on what it was that Landor loved, and the result is a mocking little poem that begins

> Dean, adult education may seem silly.
> What of it, though? I got some willy-nilly
> The other evening at your college deanery.
> And grateful for it (let's not be facetious!)
> For I thought Epicurus and Lucretius
> By Nature meant the Whole Goddam Machinery
> But you say that in college nomenclature
> The only meaning possible for Nature
> In Landor's quatrain would be Pretty Scenery.

Well, what I mean by nature is more than pretty scenery, but slightly less than the whole goddam machinery. I mean everything that exists on this planet (or elsewhere) that was not made by man. It's what most people mean. Only the minute you look closely, it turns out to be very hard to decide what was made by man and what wasn't. A plastic bag or a beer can is easy: Both were made by man—though of course out of natural materials, since that's all there are. But what about a garden? Nature made the carrot, but man modified it, planted it, grew it. There are two wills in collaboration here—the will of the carrot to be orange and to taste carroty and so forth—and the will of human beings to have it be a large carrot that travels well, keeps in cold storage, and so forth. What about a lake that exists because someone has built a dam, a so-called man-made or artificial lake? What about a tree? Only God—or nature—can make them, as Joyce Kilmer pointed out. But then, there are hybrid poplars: designed, planted, shaped by human beings. Again, a collaboration. Almost the entire surface of England is such a collaboration, and most of the United States, too. Only a wilderness area is not at least partly a collaboration. Lots of the prettiest scenery *is*.

So what I'm going to call nature is everything on this planet that is at least partially under the control of some other will than ours. Pure nature is of course what exists entirely without our will. In terms of landscape, there isn't much of it.

That still leaves one big question unanswered. Is man himself part of nature? Our remote ancestors certainly were: They evolved without planning to. But we ourselves? Well, I think we're partly in and partly out of nature—and the balance varies from age to age. But for the moment I'm going to say we're outside of nature. Certainly we thought of ourselves that way when we came to America. The Dutch sailors did, the pioneer settlers did. The authors of the Bible did.

Now let me drop back a little, and talk history. Not as far back as 1609—the Dutch sailors didn't leave much record of what they thought when they saw Long Island—but back to the eighteenth century and to a book called *Letters From an American Farmer,* which was written in the 1770s (though not published until 1782), and which was one of the very early American best-sellers. Basically, it's a report to Europeans on conditions in America just before the Revolution. Most of it is about what it's like to come be a farmer in one of the thirteen colonies, though there is one long section on what it's like to live on Nantucket and be a sailor.

At that time "America" was a strip of land about 300 miles wide, going south from Maine to Georgia. In the absence of airplanes, satellites, and so forth, no one knew exactly how much more land there was west of the frontier.

But the general feeling was that for all practical purposes this continent was infinite. As Hector St. John de Crevecoeur says in *Letters From an American Farmer*, "Many ages will not see the shores of our great lakes replenished with inland nations, nor the unknown bounds of North America entirely peopled. Who can tell how far it extends?"

St. John was wrong, of course. It did not take many ages to start inland nations on the shores of our Great Lakes. It took about two generations. Fifty years after he wrote the book, the inland nation of Illinois came into being. Another fifty years and Chicago was a large city, another forty and it had two million people. But he couldn't know that. He and everyone else in 1770 thought we would still have a frontier in, say, the twenty-fifth century, and that the still-growing country could absorb all the immigrants who might ever wish to come, that it, in fact, would always *need* more. "There is room for everybody in America," he wrote. And, remember, America had already existed for a century and a half when he wrote that: The image was firmly fixed that this was an infinite country.

The other thing that St. John took for granted was that pure nature is an appalling thing. He saw no beauty in wilderness whatsoever. Trackless forests did not appeal to him, and he considered frontiersmen corrupt and degenerate barbarians. What he liked, what he thought beautiful was the collaboration between man and nature that a farm is, and he considered that the best possible use of a person's time lay in taming wild nature.

> To examine how the world is gradually settled, how the howling swamp is converted into a pleasing meadow, the rough ridge into a fine field; and to hear the cheerful whistling, the rural song, where there was no sound heard before save . . . the screech of the owl or the hissing of the snake—

that, says St. John, gives him enormous pleasure. He explains to his European audience how the first thing an American does when he comes into a new piece of wilderness is to build a bridge over whatever creek or little river runs through it, and the second is to take his axe and chop down as many acres of trees as he has energy to do that year, and the third is to start draining swamps and other wetlands. And perfectly reasonable, too, since the woods, the swamps, and the rivers are infinite. But St. John's assumptions are that nature is not in any way sacred, or precious, or to be treasured just because it exists; on the contrary it is badly in need of collaboration with man, and only under our governance can it become the beautiful thing it should be. And he also assumes, as the Bible told him to, that nature has no other important function than to serve us. He even thinks that God intended the wolves, the bears, the snakes, and the Indians themselves to give way before us. He doesn't worry about their becoming extinct, because the continent is infinite—but I think if you pressed him, he'd say that had to be their eventual fate.

One other observation of St. John's demands mention, even though it has little to do with nature, only nurture. I mentioned that one long section of the book is about Nantucket, a place St. John greatly admired. It was a Quaker community, and already deep into whaling—the people St. John met there were the great-grandfathers of the people Melville wrote about in *Moby Dick*. St. John also admired the women of Nantucket, who ran the farms while their husbands were off whaling—and whom he regarded as the most spirited, independent, and, incidentally, good-looking women in America—which for him means they were the most spirited, independent, and good-looking women in the world. But, he says, "a singular custom prevails here among the women, at which I was greatly surprised. . . . They have adopted these many years the Asiatic custom of taking a dose of opium every morning, and so deeply rooted is it that they would be at a loss how to live without this indulgence; they would rather be deprived of any necessary than forego their favorite luxury." Nantucket men, St. John says, didn't touch opium.

Now I want to move ahead to 1804, which was the year that President Jefferson sent Captains Meriwether Lewis and William Clark of the U.S. Army across the continent on foot, the first human beings, so far as I know, to make that entire trip across what is now the United States. It took them and their party of twenty-five enlisted men and a couple of guides two years to get to the Pacific Ocean and back again. Plus, as usual, rather more money than the government had anticipated. President Jefferson budgeted the two-year trip for thirty people, including boats, a newly invented airgun to impress the Indians, all supplies, at $2,500. The actual cost of the expedition was nearly $5,000. But it did reach the Pacific.

After Lewis and Clark, no one could think that North America was infinite. They returned with maps and mileage estimates. The shrinking process had begun. But it was still huge—a place that takes you a year to cross in each direction—and it was still largely pure nature.

Lewis and Clark did not see the wilderness quite the way St. John did—partly because the region he knew was all woods, and a great deal of their time was spent crossing the Great Plains, the grassy open plains with herds of antelope and buffalo. What struck them was that nature had already made the center of America into a garden, just waiting for the settlers to come cultivate it. In fact, some of it God or nature had already cultivated for us. On July 10, 1804, going up the Missouri River, they passed a piece of bottom-land: 2,000 acres covered with wild potatoes. At any time, there were hordes of deer, wild turkeys, elk, just waiting to be killed. Lewis gave it as his professional army captain's opinion that two hunters could keep a regiment supplied with meat. On August 5, 1804, Captain Clark noticed how abundant the fresh fruit was. "Great quantities of grapes on the banks. I observe three kinds, at this time ripe." On August 16, 1804, Captain Lewis and twelve men spent the morning fishing. Here's the report: "Caught upwards of 800 fine fish: 79 pike, 8 salmon resembling trout, 1 rock, 1 flat back, 127 buffalo and red horse, 4 bass, 490 cats, with many small silver fish and shrimp."

Sometimes, when the captains climbed a hill for the view, a whole section of what is now Iowa or Nebraska would remind them of a giant stock farm back in Virginia. Lewis described one view in which there was a forest of wild plum trees on one side—"loaded with fruit and now ripe"—and on the other twenty miles of open grassland, smooth as a bowling green. "This scenery," he says, "already rich, pleasing, and beautiful, was still further heightened by immense herds of buffalo, deer, elk, and antelopes, which we saw in every direction. . . . I do not think I exaggerate when I estimate the number of buffalo which could be comprehended at one view to be 3,000." The wolves prowling around the edge of each herd even reminded him of the sheepdogs back in Virginia.

Again, the sense is that nature is so bounteous that we could never possibly run short of anything. Nor was this some special white prejudice. The Indians felt the same. Lewis and Clark watched several times while a small tribe of Plains Indians drove a whole herd of buffalo over a cliff, took the tongues and humps of a couple of dozen to eat, and left all the rest to rot. Why not? There was no more need to be frugal with buffalo than we feel the need to be frugal with, say, ice cubes. Don't think I'm blaming either Lewis and Clark or the Indians. Their behavior made perfect sense at the time.

Nature wasn't all bounty, though. For example, the whole region was swarming with grizzly bears: eating plums, waiting at the bottoms of cliffs for someone to drive a herd of buffalo over, and just generally enjoying life. They were not a bit afraid of American soldiers. And in fact a soldier with a single-shot rifle was in no way a match for a grizzly. By experience, Lewis and Clark found that about six soldiers equaled one grizzly. If all six shot, they were pretty likely to kill the bear with no one being hurt or chased up a tree. If fewer shot, there was apt to be trouble.

There was other trouble, too. When the expedition reached the Rocky Mountains, they found the peaks terrifying. Not beautiful (except snow-capped from a distance), not fun to be in. Instead, a place where you were very apt to starve to death, freeze to death, fall off a cliff. A typical campsite was by the mountain stream they called Hungry Creek—"at that place we had nothing to eat"—where they spent the night of September 18, 1805. A typical adventure occurred the next morning when Private Robert Frazer's packhorse, bought from the Indians, lost its footing and rolled a hundred yards down a precipice.

Most of the year, the only food you were going to find in the Rockies was what you carried in on your back, and when you ran out of that, there was no store to buy more at, nor could you decide to quit and hitch a ride back to Virginia, much less catch a plane to Denver. In short, not only was nature huge, but man was weak. Clever—clever enough to have invented axes and to drive stupid buffalo off cliffs—but weak. Nature, Mother Nature, was a worthy opponent as well as a worthy partner. In fact, let me make a sort of metaphor out of the grizzly and the buffalo, the two of them standing for wild nature. Both are physically stronger than men, and can run faster. One, the grizzly, is untameable, and more or less useless to us. So the thing to do is kill them, and that's a heroic and dangerous task: one part of subduing the wilderness. The other, the buffalo, is partially tameable, and very useful to us. Kill them, too, but not all of them, because we want them around to eat. Or else replace them with cattle, which are completely tameable. That's another part of subduing the wilderness—less heroic, maybe, but still a big job, and still nature offers plenty of resistance to the changes we make. The collaboration is not entirely on our terms, but partly on hers.

In sum, for the first two centuries that Europeans lived in North America, they saw the continent as a giant wilderness or desert—they used the two words interchangeably—the motto of Dartmouth College, *Vox clamantis in deserto*, translates to "A voice crying in the wilderness." They saw a vast, powerful, and immensely rich wilderness, which it would be the bounden duty of their descendants to turn into farms and gardens and alabaster cities, but which we would never entirely do, because the country was so damned big and the power of the axe and plow so limited.

All that began to change in the nineteenth century with the growth of technology. Railroads and steamboats were, of course, the first major manifestations. They made the wilderness accessible and the continent (relatively) small. In so doing, they produced the first few converts to a new point of view. Henry David Thoreau was one. Thoreau lived right next to the Fitchburg Railroad. He saw quite clearly the threat steam posed to untamed nature. Steam engines are bigger and faster than grizzlies. Steam saws can cut trees up far more quickly than forests can grow them. Steam shovels can drain an everglade.

Wilderness threatened became wilderness desirable—for the handful of converts. Thoreau was, as far as I know, the first American who publicly concluded that wilderness as wilderness—that is, pure nature—was a good thing to have around. In the 1850s he made a proposal that each town in Massachusetts save a 500-acre piece of woods which would be forever wild: no lumbering, no changes at all. Needless to say, he got nowhere, not even in Concord itself. It was still too much like going down to McDonald's and suggesting to the manager that he put 500 ice cubes in permanent deep freeze, against the time when ice may be scarce.

John Muir was a slightly later convert. It's a coincidence, but a nice coincidence, that the year in which he began to describe the western mountains as wonderful places, sacred ground, God's outdoor temples, was the same year in which the transcontinental railroad was completed. That was 1869. Henceforth the Lewis and Clark journey of a year could be done in a few days. Muir, like Thoreau before him, sensed the growth of man's power against nature, though in 1869 nature was still stronger. And, of course, Muir could be romantic about mountains in part because by now the country had been so much tamed that within one day's walk of most of his camping places in the Sierras he could borrow or buy flour to make bread with, sometimes even go to a regular store. He could even be worried about the ecological harm that overgrazing by sheep was doing in the Sierras, and eventually have some success in banning sheep from portions.

Ever since then, human power has grown at an almost geometric rate, while the forces of nature have remained static. The ascending line was bound eventually to cross the level one. It's not possible to pinpoint the year in which this happened, but it *is* possible to suggest a decade. I think the 1950s represent the swing point in man's relationship to nature, certainly in the United States, and probably in the whole world. During that decade we became stronger than our surroundings. Certainly not in all ways—such physical phenomena as earthquakes and hurricanes and volcanoes remain quite beyond our power to control. But in most ways. The biggest river isn't even difficult for us to bridge, or to dam. No other living creature can seriously dispute us, certainly not on a one-to-one basis. In Melville's day, six men in a whaleboat were generally a match for one whale—but not always; sometimes the whale won. By the 1950s, one man with a harpoon gun could do in any number of whales. There's not even any thrill to it.

More important than any of this, by the 1950s our science and our engineering enabled us to produce new substances and to distribute old substances on a scale equal to nature's own. For example, we can put sulfur dioxide in the air at a rate faster than the volcanoes do. One single refinery in Sudbury, Ontario, became the source of 5 percent of all the sulfur dioxide that entered the air of the entire planet, there to become sulfuric acid and to come down again as acid rain and snow. One fleet of jet airplanes could seriously affect the ozone layer.

We have earth-moving machinery that can rearrange a whole landscape. We have new chemical compounds that can affect the whole chain of life. Nature cannot easily absorb the effect of DDT or of Sevin; nature is no longer resilient. We can nearly eliminate whales, sort of half-meaning to, and we can all but extinguish peregrine falcons as an unintended by-product of raising crops. We really are what our ancestors only claimed to be: the masters of nature—or at least we're the dominant partner in the collaboration. To use one more metaphor, we are like goldfish who have been living in an aquarium for as long as we can remember; and being clever goldfish, we have discovered how to manipulate the controls of the aquarium: put more oxygen in the water, get rid of the pesky turtle we never liked anyway, triple the supply of goldfish food. Only once we realize we're partly running the aquarium, it scares some of us. What if we make a mistake, and wreck the aquarium entirely? We couldn't live outside it.

That has been the actual position since the 1950s, and it is what our rational minds clearly report. The green light has turned yellow, and there is a real possibility it will go to red. But it is not what our emotions tell us. Emotionally, almost all of us still believe what the Dutch sailors thought: that here is an inexhaustible new world, with plenty of everything for everybody.

And because of that emotion, which I, too, share, we have had a double response since the 1950s. One is to do our damndest to keep part of our continent still virgin—pure nature, wilderness. That's the nature-lover's response, the Sierra Club response, and sometimes the environmentalist's response. It's almost uniquely American. I have a friend, for example, who is a Spanish environmentalist, and I know from him that there is exactly one national park in Spain, the former hunting forest of the dukes of Medina, and even that is by no means a wilderness area. Spain is not virgin country. At the moment, about 2 percent of the United States is official wilderness, just about the same amount that is paved. And in a country this big, 2 percent is quite a lot: something like 60,000 square miles, twelve times as big as the state of Connecticut.

In terms of our whole population, to be sure, it's less impressive: If you put all of us in the wilderness at once, we'd each have a fifth of an acre. But it's enough to give a comforting illusion that pure nature is still going, independent of us. And most people who seek that illusion also want to downplay their separateness from nature, and to say that we have no right to meddle, our collaboration is deadly. We goldfish should stand back and let the aquarium run itself as it always has.

The other response involves a much greater illusion—or I think it does, anyway. And that is simply to deny that anything has changed significantly since the days of Hector St. John de Crevecoeur and Lewis and Clark. This is the response, for example, of the present United States government. We're still just collaborators with nature, people who hold this view say, more effective collaborators than we used to be, certainly; and if we do our part, nature will do its. Nature is still resilient; it can still absorb anything we do. Besides, we were meant to rule the planet—this aquarium was designed specially for us—and what we do was pretty much all allowed for in the original design.

One group wants to re-create the world the Dutch sailors saw, and the other denies that it has ever ceased to exist. If I have to choose, of course I choose to be one of the re-creators—to try to protect as much wilderness as possible. I'd like to get the proportion of untouched land up to 3 percent. I've even dreamt of 4 percent.

But neither group, I think, is right. Neither has really dealt with the fact that a generation ago the green light turned to yellow. If there is anything that is really, really worth doing in the rest of this century, I think, it's to find a third and better way of dealing with the relationship between man and nature.

■ CONSIDERATIONS OF MEANING AND METHOD

1. In "Forever Virgin," Noel Perrin uses cause and effect analysis as his primary mode of development. What other modes of development does he use in expressing his ideas in this essay?

2. Perrin says that Hector St. John de Crevecoeur and other European-Americans of the eighteenth century made two fundamental assumptions about nature. What were they? To what extent does Perrin think these assumptions among Americans have changed, and to what extent do they persist? To what extent do you think they have changed or persisted?

3. What events does Perrin identify as turning points in American history and the evolution of Americans' thinking about nature? How are these events related in cause and effect?

4. Perrin maintains that there is a difference now between what we know and what we feel about nature. He writes, "Emotionally, almost all of us still believe what the Dutch sailors thought: that here is an inexhaustible new world. . . . " Do you agree or disagree with Perrin? Think of examples from the worlds of American politics, industry, or lifestyle to illustrate your view.

5. What, as a consequence of "that emotion," does Perrin identify as our "double response since the 1950s"? And why has "neither . . . dealt with the fact that a generation ago the green light turned to yellow"? Perrin leaves the "third and better way of dealing with the relationship between man and nature" up to his readers. Do you have any ideas about what that way might be?

6. Look back at Perrin's other essay in this text, "Falling for Apples" in Chapter 3 (page 156). What similarities and differences do you detect in his writing style when you compare his two essays, and what do you think accounts for them? Do you find his style in "Forever Virgin" effective? Why or why not?

■ POSSIBILITIES FOR WRITING

1. In an essay for readers familiar with Perrin's essay, extend the discussion of some of the fundamental points he raises. Offer your own definition of nature, illustrating it with examples, and compare your definition with his. Also compare your answer and Perrin's to the question "Is man himself part of nature?"

2. Perrin says that "the authors of the Bible" thought of human beings as "outside of nature." Explain in an essay for readers who may or may not have more than a passing familiarity with the Bible what Perrin means by this statement. Referring to Genesis, support your explanations with specific examples from the biblical text.

■ LESLIE MARMON SILKO
Landscape, History, and the Pueblo Imagination

In her often-anthologized essay "Landscape, History, and the Pueblo Imagination," Leslie Marmon Silko writes of the deep connection between New Mexico's Pueblo Indian people and the land, and about how daily experience, the spoken record of Pueblo history, and the people themselves are inextricably tied to landscape. Silko, of Laguna Pueblo, Mexican, and Anglo descent, was born in 1948 in Albuquerque, New Mexico, and grew up at Laguna Pueblo, steeped in the stories and rituals of her people. She both attended and has taught at the University of New Mexico, and she has also taught at the University of Arizona. Her works include her celebrated novel Ceremony *(1977); collections of short stories and poems, including* Laguna Woman *(1974) and* Storyteller *(1981); and, most recently, her novel* Almanac of the Dead *(1991). Silko received the Pushcart Prize for Fiction in 1977 and a five-year MacArthur Foundation grant in 1983.*

In her poems as well as her short and long fiction, Silko writes of Indian experience and uses traditional storytelling techniques, providing both the theme and the structure of her work. New York Times Book Review *critic Frank McShane has called her "without question . . . the most accomplished Indian writer of her generation." Of Indian history, and perhaps of her own work, Silko tells us in "Landscape, History, and the Pueblo Imagination,"*

"The ancient people perceived the world and themselves within that world as part of an ancient continuous story composed of innumerable bundles of other stories."

From a High Arid Plateau
in New Mexico

You see that after a thing is dead, it dries up. It might take weeks or years, but eventually if you touch the thing, it crumbles under your fingers. It goes back to dust. The soul of the thing has long since departed. With the plants and wild game the soul may have already been borne back into bones and blood or thick green stalk and leaves. Nothing is wasted. What cannot be eaten by people or in some way used must then be left where other living creatures may benefit. What domestic animals or wild scavengers can't eat will be fed to the plants. The plants feed on the dust of these few remains.

The ancient Pueblo people buried the dead in vacant rooms or partially collapsed rooms adjacent to the main living quarters. Sand and clay used to construct the roof make layers many inches deep once the roof has collapsed. The layers of sand and clay make for easy grave-digging. The vacant room fills with cast-off objects and debris. When a vacant room has filled deep enough, a shallow but adequate grave can be scooped in a far corner. Archaeologists have remarked over formal burials complete with elaborate funerary objects excavated in trash middens of abandoned rooms. But the rocks and adobe mortar of collapsed walls were valued by the ancient people. Because each rock had been carefully selected for size and shape, then chiseled to an even face. Even the pink clay adobe melting with each rainstorm had to be prayed over, then dug and carried some distance. Corn cobs and husks, the rinds and stalks and animal bones were not regarded by the ancient people as filth or garbage. The remains were merely resting at a mid-point in their journey back to dust. Human remains are not so different. They should rest with the bones and rinds where they all may benefit living creatures—small rodents and insects—until their return is completed. The remains of things—animals and plants, the clay and the stones—were treated with respect. Because for the ancient people all these things had spirit and being.

The antelope merely consents to return home with the hunter. All phases of the hunt are conducted with love. The love the hunter and the people have for the Antelope People. And the love of the antelope who agree to give up their meat and blood so that human beings will not starve. Waste of meat or even the thoughtless handling of bones cooked bare will offend the antelope spirits. Next year the hunters will vainly search the dry plains for antelope. Thus it is necessary to return carefully the bones and hair, and the stalks and leaves to the earth who first created them. The spirits remain close by. They do not leave us.

The dead become dust, and in this becoming they are once more joined with the Mother. The ancient Pueblo people called the earth the Mother Creator of all things in this world. Her sister, the Corn Mother, occasionally merges with her because all succulent green life rises out of the depths of the earth.

Rocks and clay are part of the Mother. They emerge in various forms, but at some time before, they were smaller particles or great boulders. At a later time they may again become what they once were. Dust.

A rock shares this fate with us and with animals and plants as well. A rock has being or spirit, although we may not understand it. The spirit may differ from the spirit we know in animals or plants or in ourselves. In the end we all originate from the depths of the earth. Perhaps this is how all beings share in the spirit of the Creator. We do not know.

From the Emergence Place

Pueblo potters, the creators of petroglyphs and oral narratives, never conceived of removing themselves from the earth and sky. So long as the human consciousness remains *within* the hills, canyons, cliffs, and the plants, clouds, and sky, the term *landscape,* as it has entered the English language, is misleading. "A portion of territory the eye can comprehend in a single view" does not correctly describe the relationship between the human being and his or her surroundings. This assumes the viewer is somehow *outside* or *separate from* the territory he or she surveys. Viewers are as much a part of the landscape as the boulders they stand on. There is no high mesa edge or mountain peak where one can stand and not immediately be part of all that surrounds. Human identity is linked with all the elements of Creation through the clan: you might belong to the Sun Clan or the Lizard Clan or the Corn Clan or the Clay Clan. Standing deep within the natural world, the ancient Pueblo understood the thing as it was—the squash blossom, grasshopper, or rabbit itself could never be created by the human hand. Ancient Pueblos took the modest view that the thing itself (the landscape) could not be improved upon. The ancients did not presume to tamper with what had already been created. Thus *realism,* as we now recognize it in painting and sculpture, did not catch the imaginations of Pueblo people until recently.

The squash blossom itself is *one thing:* itself. So the ancient Pueblo potter abstracted what she saw to be the key elements of the squash blossom—the four symmetrical petals, with four symmetrical stamens in the center. These key elements, while suggesting the squash flower, also link it with the four cardinal directions. By representing only its intrinsic form, the squash flower is released from a limited meaning or restricted identity. Even in the most sophisticated abstract form, a squash flower or a cloud or a lightning bolt became intricately connected with a complex system of relationships which the ancient Pueblo people maintained with each other, and with the populous natural world they lived within. A bolt of lightning is itself, but at the same time it may mean much more. It may be a messenger of good fortune when summer rains are needed. It may deliver death, perhaps the result of manipulations by the Gunnadeyahs, destructive necromancers. Lightning may strike down an evil-doer. Or lightning may strike a person of good will. If the person survives, lightning endows him or her with heightened power.

Pictographs and petroglyphs of constellations or elk or antelope draw their magic in part from the process wherein the focus of all prayer and concentration is upon the thing itself, which, in its turn, guides the hunter's hand. Connection with the spirit dimensions requires a figure or form which is all-inclusive. A "lifelike" rendering of an elk is too restrictive. Only the elk *is* itself. A *realistic* rendering of an elk would be only one particular elk anyway. The purpose of the hunt rituals and magic is to make contact with *all* the spirits of the Elk.

The land, the sky, and all that is within them—the landscape—includes human beings. Interrelationships in the Pueblo landscape are complex and fragile. The unpredictability of the weather, the aridity and harshness of much of the terrain in the high plateau country explain in large part the relentless attention the ancient Pueblo people gave the sky and the earth around them. Survival depended upon harmony and cooperation not only among human beings, but among all things—the animate and the less animate, since rocks and mountains were known to move, to travel occasionally.

The ancient Pueblos believed the Earth and the Sky were sisters (or sister and brother in the post-Christian version). As long as good family relations are maintained, then the Sky will continue to bless her sister, the Earth, with rain, and the Earth's children will continue to survive. But the old stories recall incidents in which troublesome spirits or beings threaten the earth. In one story, a malicious ka'tsina, called the Gambler, seizes the Shiwana, or Rainclouds, the Sun's beloved children. The Shiwana are snared in magical power late one afternoon on a high mountain top. The Gambler takes the Rainclouds to his mountain stronghold where he locks them in the north room of his house. What was his idea? The Shiwana were beyond value. They brought life to all things on earth. The Gambler wanted a big stake to wager in his games of chance. But such greed, even on the part of only one being, had the effect of threatening the survival of all life on earth. Sun Youth, aided by old Grandmother Spider, outsmarts the Gambler and the rigged game, and the Rainclouds are set free. The drought ends, and once more life thrives on earth.

Through the Stories
We Hear Who We Are

All summer the people watch the west horizon, scanning the sky from south to north for rain clouds. Corn must have moisture at the time the tassels form. Otherwise pollination will be incomplete, and the ears will be stunted and shriveled. An inadequate harvest may bring disaster. Stories told at Hopi, Zuni, and at Acoma and Laguna describe drought and starvation as recently as 1900. Precipitation in west-central New Mexico averages fourteen inches annually. The western pueblos are located at altitudes over 5,600 feet above sea level, where winter temperatures at night fall below freezing. Yet evidence of their presence in the high desert plateau country goes back ten thousand years. The ancient Pueblo people not only survived in this environment, but many years they thrived. In A.D. 1100 the people at Chaco Canyon had built cities with apartment buildings of stone five stories high. Their sophistication as sky-watchers was surpassed only by Mayan and Inca astronomers. Yet this vast complex of knowledge and belief, amassed for thousands of years, was never recorded in writing.

Instead, the ancient Pueblo people depended upon collective memory through successive generations to maintain and transmit an entire culture, a world view complete with proven strategies for survival. The oral narrative, or "story," became the medium in which the complex of Pueblo knowledge and belief was maintained. Whatever the event or the subject, the ancient people perceived the world and themselves within that world as part of an ancient continuous story composed of innumerable bundles of other stories.

The ancient Pueblo vision of the world was inclusive. The impulse was to leave nothing out. Pueblo oral tradition necessarily embraced all levels of human experience. Otherwise, the collective knowledge and beliefs comprising ancient Pueblo culture would have been incomplete. Thus stories about the Creation and Emergence of human beings and animals into this World continue to be retold each year for four days and four nights during the winter solstice. The "humma-hah" stories related events from the time long ago when human beings were still able to communicate with animals and other living things. But, beyond these two preceding categories, the Pueblo oral tradition knew no boundaries. Accounts of the appearance of the first Europeans in Pueblo country or of the tragic encounters between Pueblo people and Apache raiders were no more and no less important than stories about the biggest mule deer ever taken or adulterous couples surprised in cornfields and chicken coops. Whatever happened, the ancient people instinctively sorted events and details into a loose narrative structure. Everything became a story.

Traditionally everyone, from the youngest child to the oldest person, was expected to listen and to be able to recall or tell a portion, if only a small detail, from a narrative account or story. Thus the remembering and retelling were a communal process. Even if a key figure, an elder who knew much more than others, were to die unexpectedly, the system would remain intact. Through the efforts of a great many people, the community was able to piece together valuable accounts and crucial information that might otherwise have died with an individual.

Communal storytelling was a self-correcting process in which listeners were encouraged to speak up if they noted an important fact or detail omitted. The people were happy to listen to two or three different versions of the same event or the same humma-hah story. Even conflicting versions of an incident were welcomed for the entertainment they provided. Defenders of each version might joke and tease one another, but seldom were there any direct confrontations. Implicit in the Pueblo oral tradition was the awareness that loyalties, grudges, and kinship must always influence the narrator's choices as she emphasizes to listeners this is the way *she* has always heard the story told. The ancient Pueblo people sought a communal truth, not an absolute. For them this truth lived somewhere within the web of differing versions, disputes over minor points, outright contradictions tangling with old feuds and village rivalries.

A dinner-table conversation, recalling a deer hunt forty years ago when the largest mule deer ever was taken, inevitably stimulates similar memories in listeners. But hunting stories were not merely after-dinner entertainment. These accounts contained information of critical importance about behavior and migration patterns of mule deer. Hunting stories carefully described key landmarks and locations of fresh water. Thus a deer-hunt story might also serve as a "map." Lost travelers, and lost piñon-nut gatherers, have been saved by sighting a rock formation they recognize only because they once heard a hunting story describing this rock formation.

The importance of cliff formations and water holes does not end with hunting stories. As offspring of the Mother Earth, the ancient Pueblo people could not conceive of themselves within a specific landscape. Location, or "place," nearly always plays a central role in the Pueblo oral narratives. Indeed, stories are most frequently recalled as people are passing by a specific geographical feature or the exact place where a story takes place. The precise date of the incident often is less important than the place or location of the happening. "Long, long ago," "a long time ago," "not too long ago," and "recently" are usually how stories are classified in terms of time. But the places where the stories occur are precisely located, and prominent geographical details recalled, even if the landscape is well-known to listeners. Often because the turning point in the narrative involved a peculiarity or special quality of a rock or tree or plant found only at that place. Thus, in the case of many of the Pueblo narratives, it is impossible to determine which came first: the incident or the geographical feature which begs to be brought alive in a story that features some unusual aspect of this location.

There is a giant sandstone boulder about a mile north of Old Laguna, on the road to Paguate. It is ten feet tall and twenty feet in circumference. When I was a child, and we would pass this boulder driving to Paguate village, someone usually made reference to the story about Kochininako, Yellow Woman, and the Estrucuyo, a monstrous giant who nearly ate her. The Twin Hero Brothers saved Kochininako, who had been out hunting rabbits to take home to feed her mother and sisters. The Hero Brothers had heard her cries just in time. The Estrucuyo had cornered her in a cave too small to fit its monstrous head. Kochininako had already thrown to the Estrucuyo all her rabbits, as well as her moccasins and most of her clothing. Still the creature had not been satisfied. After killing the Estrucuyo with their bows and arrows, the Twin Hero Brothers slit open the Estrucuyo and cut out its heart. They threw the heart as far as they could. The monster's heart landed there, beside the old trail to Paguate village, where the sandstone boulder rests now.

It may be argued that the existence of the boulder precipitated the creation of a story to explain it. But sandstone boulders and sandstone formations of strange shapes abound in the Laguna Pueblo area. Yet most of them do not have stories. Often the crucial element in a narrative is the terrain—some specific detail of the setting.

A high dark mesa rises dramatically from a grassy plain fifteen miles southeast of Laguna, in an area known as Swanee. On the grassy plain one hundred and forty years ago, my great-grandmother's uncle and his brother-in-law were grazing their herd of sheep. Because visibility on the plain extends for over twenty miles, it wasn't until the two sheepherders came near the high dark mesa that the Apaches were able to stalk them. Using the mesa to obscure their approach, the raiders swept around from both ends of the mesa. My great-grandmother's relatives were killed, and the herd lost. The high dark mesa played a critical role: the mesa had compromised the safety which the openness of the plains had seemed to assure. Pueblo and Apache alike relied upon the terrain, the very earth herself, to give them protection and aid. Human activities or needs were maneuvered to fit the existing surroundings and conditions. I imagine the last afternoon of my distant ancestors as warm and sunny for late September. They might have been traveling slowly, bringing the sheep closer to Laguna in preparation for the approach of colder weather. The grass was tall and only beginning to change from green to a yellow which matched the late-afternoon sun shining off it. There might have been comfort in the warmth and the sight of the sheep fattening on good pasture which lulled my ancestors into their fatal inattention. They might have had a rifle whereas the Apaches had only bows and arrows. But there would have been four or five Apache raiders, and the surprise attack would have canceled any advantage the rifles gave them.

Survival in any landscape comes down to making the best use of all available resources. On that particular September afternoon, the raiders made better use of the Swanee terrain than my poor ancestors did. Thus the high dark mesa and the story of the two lost Laguna herders became inextricably linked. The memory of them and their story resides in part with the high black mesa. For as long as the mesa stands, people within the family and clan will be reminded of the story of that afternoon long ago. Thus the continuity and accuracy of the oral narratives are reinforced by the landscape—and the Pueblo interpretation of that landscape is *maintained.*

The Migration Story: An Interior Journey

The Laguna Pueblo migration stories refer to specific places— mesas, springs, or cottonwood trees—not only locations which can be visited still, but also locations which lie directly on the state highway route linking Paguate village with Laguna village. In traveling this road as a child with older Laguna people I first heard a few of the stories from that much larger body of stories linked with the Emergence and Migration. It may be coincidental that Laguna people continue to follow the same route which, according to the Migration story, the ancestors followed south from the Emergence Place. It may be that the route is merely the shortest and best route for car, horse, or foot traffic between Laguna and Paguate villages. But if the stories about boulders, springs, and hills are actually remnants from a ritual that retraces the creation and emergence of the Laguna Pueblo people as a culture, as the people they became, then continued use of that route creates a unique relationship between the ritual-mythic world and the actual, everyday world. A journey from Paguate to Laguna down the long incline of Paguate Hill retraces the original journey from the Emergence Place which is located slightly north of the Paguate village. Thus the landscape between Paguate and Laguna takes on a deeper significance: the landscape resonates the spiritual or mythic dimension of the Pueblo world even today.

Although each Pueblo culture designates a specific Emergence Place—usually a small natural spring edged with mossy sandstone and full of cattails and wild watercress—it is clear that they do not agree on any single location or natural spring as the one and only true Emergence Place. Each Pueblo group recounts its own stories about Creation, Emergence, and Migration, although they all believe that all human beings, with all the animals and plants, emerged at the same place and at the same time.

Natural springs are crucial sources of water for all life in the high desert plateau country. So the small spring near Paguate village is literally the source and continuance of life for the people in the area.

The spring also functions on a spiritual level, recalling the original Emergence Place and linking the people and the spring water to all other people and to that moment when the Pueblo people became aware of themselves as they are even now. The Emergence was an emergence into a precise cultural identity. Thus the Pueblo stories about the Emergence and Migration are not to be taken as literally as the anthropologists might wish. Prominent geographical features and landmarks which are mentioned in the narratives exist for ritual purposes, not because the Laguna people actually journeyed south for hundreds of years from Chaco Canyon or Mesa Verde, as the archaeologists say, or eight miles from the site of the natural springs at Paguate to the sandstone hilltop at Laguna.

The eight miles, marked with boulders, mesas, springs, and river crossings, are actually a ritual circuit or path which marks the interior journey the Laguna people made: a journey of awareness and imagination in which they emerged from being within the earth and from everything included in earth to the culture and people they became, differentiating themselves for the first time from all that had surrounded them, always aware that interior distances cannot be reckoned in physical miles or in calendar years.

The narratives linked with prominent features of the landscape between Paguate and Laguna delineate the complexities of the relationship which human beings must maintain with the surrounding natural world if they hope to survive in this place. Thus the journey was an interior process of the imagination, a growing awareness that being human is somehow different from all other life—animal, plant, and inanimate. Yet we are all from the same source: the awareness never deteriorated into Cartesian duality, cutting off the human from the natural world.

The people found the opening into the Fifth World too small to allow them or any of the animals to escape. They had sent a fly out through the small hole to tell them if it was the world which the Mother Creator had promised. It was, but there was the problem of getting out. The antelope tried to butt the opening to enlarge it, but the antelope enlarged it only a little. It was necessary for the badger with her long claws to assist the antelope, and at last the opening was enlarged enough so that all the people and animals were able to emerge up into the Fifth World. The human beings could not have emerged without the aid of antelope and badger. The human beings depended upon the aid and charity of the animals. Only through interdependence could the human beings survive. Families belonged to clans, and it was by clan that the human being joined with the animal and plant world. Life on the high arid plateau became viable when the human beings were able to imagine themselves as sisters and brothers to the badger, antelope, clay, yucca, and sun. Not until they could find a viable relationship to the terrain, the landscape they found themselves in, could they *emerge*. Only at the moment the requisite balance between human and *other* was realized could the Pueblo people become a culture, a distinct group whose population and survival remained stable despite the vicissitudes of climate and terrain.

Landscape thus has similarities with dreams. Both have the power to seize terrifying feelings and deep instincts and translate them into images—visual, aural, tactile—into the concrete where human beings may more readily confront and channel the terrifying instincts or powerful emotions into rituals and narratives which reassure the individual while reaffirming cherished values of the group. The identity of the individual as a part of the group and the greater Whole is strengthened, and the terror of facing the world alone is extinguished.

Even now, the people of Laguna Pueblo spend the greater portion of social occasions recounting recent incidents or events which have occurred in the Laguna area. Nearly always, the discussion will precipitate the retelling of older stories about similar incidents or other stories connected with a specific place. The stories often contain disturbing or provocative material, but are nonetheless told in the presence of children and women. The effect of these inter-family or inter-clan exchanges is the reassurance for each person that she or he will never be separated or apart from the clan, no matter what might happen. Neither the worst blunders or disasters nor the greatest financial prosperity and joy will ever be permitted to isolate anyone from the rest of the group. In the ancient times, cohesiveness was all that stood between extinction and survival, and, while the individual certainly was recognized, it was always as an individual simultaneously bonded to family and clan by a complex bundle of custom and ritual. You are never the first to suffer a grave loss or profound humiliation. You are never the first, and you understand that you will probably not be the last to commit or be victimized by a repugnant act. Your family and clan are able to go on at length about others now passed on, others older or more experienced than you who suffered similar losses.

The wide deep arroyo near the Kings Bar (located across the reservation borderline) has over the years claimed many vehicles. A few years ago, when a Viet Nam veteran's new red Volkswagen rolled backwards into the arroyo while he was inside buying a six-pack of beer, the story of his loss joined the lively and large collection of stories already connected with that big arroyo. I do not know whether the Viet Nam veteran was consoled when he was told the stories about the other cars claimed by the ravenous arroyo. All his savings of combat pay had gone for the red Volkswagen. But this man could not have felt any worse than the man who, some years before, had left his children and mother-in-law in his station wagon with the engine running. When he came out of the liquor store his station wagon was gone. He found it and its passengers upside down in the big arroyo. Broken bones, cuts and bruises, and a total wreck of the car. The big arroyo has a wide mouth. Its existence needs no explanation. People in the area regard the arroyo much as they might regard a living being, which has a certain character and personality. I seldom drive past that wide deep arroyo without feeling a familiarity with and even a strange affection for this arroyo. Because as treacherous as it may be, the arroyo maintains a strong connection between human beings and the earth. The arroyo demands from us the caution and attention that constitute respect. It is this sort of respect the old believers have in mind when they tell us we must respect and love the earth.

Hopi Pueblo elders have said that the austere and, to some eyes, barren plains and hills surrounding their mesa-top villages actually help to nurture the spirituality of the Hope *way*. The Hopi elders say the Hopi people might have settled in locations far more lush where daily life would not have been so grueling. But there on the high silent sandstone mesas that overlook the sandy arid expanses stretching to all horizons, the Hopi elders say the Hopi people must "live by their prayers" if they are to survive. The Hopi way cherishes the intangible: the riches realized from interaction and interrelationships with all beings above all else. Great abundances of material things, even food, the Hopi elders believe, tend to lure human attention away from what is most valuable and important. The views of the Hopi elders are not much different from those elders in all the Pueblos.

The bare vastness of the Hopi landscape emphasizes the visual impact of every plant, every rock, every arroyo. Nothing is overlooked or taken for granted. Each ant, each lizard, each lark is imbued with great value simply because the creature is there, simply because the creature is alive in a place where any life at all is precious. Stand on the mesa edge at Walpai and look west over the bare distances toward the pale blue outlines of the San Francisco peaks where the ka'tsina spirits reside. So little lies between you and the sky. So little lies between you and the earth. One look and you know that simply to survive is a great triumph, that every possible resource is needed, every possible ally—even the most humble insect or reptile. You realize you will be speaking with all of them if you intend to last out the year. Thus it is that the Hopi elders are grateful to the landscape for aiding them in their quest as spiritual people.

CONSIDERATIONS OF MEANING AND METHOD

1. Can you explain the Pueblo people's view of their relationship with the land in terms of cause and effect?

2. Why do you think Silko uses separately titled sections to both divide and unite her essay?

3. This essay was originally published in 1986 in *Antaeus,* a prominent literary journal. What do you think Silko's purpose was in writing it? In what ways might audience and purpose have influenced her writing style?

4. What functions do story-making and storytelling serve in Pueblo culture? In what ways do these functions differ from those of story-making and storytelling in other cultures you know well?

5. How does Silko explain the assumptions behind the creation of art, in the form of painting and sculpture, in Pueblo culture?

POSSIBILITIES FOR WRITING

1. In her essay, Silko tells several stories that serve to fix important information, both practical and spiritual, about the land and its inhabitants in the people's memories. In popular American culture such stories exist as well, although they may take a different form as folklore. Stories abound about lovers' lanes and lovers' leaps, for example, or about dangerous or frightening or magical places. In an essay to share with others in your class, relate a story that has grown up around a place with which you are familiar—perhaps one you grew up near—and analyze this story in terms of the cultural function it seems to serve.

■ **KEVIN CUNNINGHAM**

Gentrification

Kevin Cunningham was born in Brooklyn, New York, and raised in Flemington, New Jersey. While attending college, majoring in mechanical engineering, he lived in an apartment with several other students in a waterfront neighborhood in Burlington, Vermont—a neighborhood that, like many others in cities all over the country, is on the brink of gentrification. Cunningham realized that he and many of his neighbors might not be able to afford to live in their "improved" neighborhood. Here Cunningham comments on researching, writing, and revising "Gentrification," a cause and effect essay.

I don't mind writing at all, but I hate doing rewrites. Actually, I always have trouble getting started, and I can spend a lot of time trying to get the first couple of paragraphs or the first page down, but once I get started I can roar right along to the end. In fact, I need to, because if I stop to think too much about any part I can lose the thread. After I've finished a draft I let it sit and then go back to it, and that's when I can see what works and what doesn't. I enjoy the second draft, because I can see the paper as a whole, but the third draft is just torture. I guess I don't have the patience—it's like I've done this twice already. But I see that it has to be done again.

In my first draft of this essay, I strung things together almost on a geographical basis, as if I were walking down Lakeview Terrace talking with my neighbors—which is actually one of the things I did. For my second draft, to show my professor, I was just polishing the writing. Then he showed me that the logic wasn't quite there—it jumped around from one idea to another, and also I took some stuff for granted that needed explaining.

I used to think of a cause and effect paper as just an explanation of why something happens; but in this essay, I was writing about a subject that affects me, so part of me wanted to keep it objective and part of me was trying to say what I feel. My professor said, "Look, if you want to say something, just use this as your vehicle for saying it." So I felt much freer when I went back to revise again, because I could say what I wanted to say.

In cause and effect writing you have to know your subject, and you have to be honest. For example, my downstairs neighbors moved out last month because the rent was raised. Somebody who didn't know the situation might say, "See? Gentrification." But that wasn't the reason—it's that heating costs also went up. This is New England, and we have had a cold winter; gentrification had nothing to do with it. It's something that is just beginning to happen and it's going to have a big effect, but we haven't actually felt many of its effects here yet.

I went back to Ohio, and my city was gone . . . "

—Chrissie Hynde, of the Pretenders

My city is in Vermont, not Ohio, but soon my neighborhood will probably be gone, too. Or maybe it's I that will be gone. My street, Lakeview Terrace, lies unobtrusively in the old northwest part of Burlington and is notable, as its name suggests, for spectacular views of Lake Champlain framed by the Adirondacks. It's not that the neighborhood is going to seed—no, quite the contrary. Recently it has been Discovered, and now it is on the verge of being Gentrified. For some of us who live here, that's bad.

Cities are often assigned human characteristics, one of which is a life cycle: they have a birth, a youth, a middle age, and an old age. A neighborhood is built and settled by young, vibrant people, proud of their sturdy new homes. Together, residents and houses mature, as families grow larger and extensions get built on. Eventually, though, the neighborhood begins to show its age. Buildings sag a little, houses aren't repainted as quickly, and maintenance slips. The neighborhood may grow poorer, as the young and upwardly mobile find new jobs and move away, while the older and less successful inhabitants remain.

One of three fates awaits the aging neighborhood. Decay may continue until the neighborhood becomes a slum. It may face urban renewal, with old buildings being razed and ugly, new apartment houses taking their place. Or it may undergo redevelopment, in which government encourages the upgrading of existing housing stock by offering low-interest loans or outright grants; thus, the original character of the neighborhood may be retained or restored, allowing the city to keep part of its identity.

An example of redevelopment at its best is Hoboken, New Jersey. In the early 1970s Hoboken was a dying city, with rundown housing and many abandoned buildings. However, low-interest loans enabled some younger residents to begin to refurbish their homes, and soon the area began to show signs of renewed vigor. Even outsiders moved in and rebuilt some of the abandoned houses. Today, whole blocks have been restored, and neighborhood life is active again. The city does well too, because property values are higher and so are property taxes. And there, at least for my neighborhood, is the rub.

Lakeview Terrace is a demographic potpourri of students and families, young professionals and elderly retirees, home-owners and renters. It's a quiet street where kids can play safely and the neighbors know each other. Most of the houses are fairly old and look it, but already some redevelopment has begun. Recently, several old houses were bought by a real estate company, rebuilt, and sold as condominiums; the new residents drive BMWs and keep to themselves. The house where I live is owned by a Young Urban Professional couple—he's an architect—and they have renovated the place to what it must have looked like when it was new. They did a nice job, too. These two kinds of development are the main forms of gentrification, and so far they have done no real harm.

But the city is about to start a major property tax reappraisal. Because of the renovations, the houses on Lakeview Terrace are currently worth more than they used to be; soon there will be a big jump in property taxes. And then a lot of people will be hurt—even dispossessed from their own neighborhood.

Clem is a retired General Electric employee who has lived on Lakeview for over thirty years and who owns his home. About three years ago some condos were built on the lot next door, which didn't please Clem—he says they just don't fit in. But with higher property taxes, it may be Clem that no longer fits in. At the very least, since he's on a fixed income, he will have to make sacrifices in order to stay. Ryan works as a mailman and also owns his Lakeview Terrace home, which is across the street from the houses that were converted into condos: same cause, same effect.

Then there are those of us who rent. As our landlords have to pay higher property taxes, they will naturally raise rents at least as much (and maybe more, if they've spent money on renovations of their own). Some of us won't be able to afford the increase and will have to leave. "Some of us" almost certainly includes me, as well as others who have lived on Lakeview Terrace much longer than I have. In fact, the exodus has already begun, with the people who were displaced by the condo conversions.

Of course, many people would consider what's happening on

Lakeview Terrace a genuine improvement in every way, resulting not only in better-looking houses but also in a better class of people. I dispute that. The new people may be more affluent than those they displace, but certainly not "better," not by any standard that counts with me. Gentrification may do wonders for a neighborhood's aesthetics, but it certainly can be hard on its soul.

■ CONSIDERATIONS OF MEANING AND METHOD

1. Why, in the first paragraph, does Cunningham capitalize "Discovered" and "Gentrified"?

2. How does Cunningham describe the life cycle of a city neighborhood in terms of cause and effect? Do you take Cunningham's description of a city neighborhood's life cycle to be an analogy, or is it literal?

3. What three possible futures does Cunningham forecast as a consequence of a neighborhood's aging? Can you foresee any additional possibilities?

4. Cunningham writes that in gentrification "the original character of the neighborhood may be retained or restored, allowing the city to keep part of its identity." He also writes that "Gentrification may do wonders for a neighborhood's aesthetics, but it certainly can be hard on its soul." Is there a contradiction here? Why or why not? What are the sources of a city's "character," "identity," or "soul"?

5. Gentrified neighborhoods pose very real problems for long-time residents who may no longer be able to afford living in them. It also holds promise for new residents as well as economic advantages for cities in which these neighborhoods exist. Make a two-column list of the costs and benefits of gentrification to individuals and to cities, building upon the points Cunningham makes in his essay. Weighing costs and benefits, do you think gentrification is a positive or a negative trend? What, finally, is Cunningham's position on gentrification? What is yours?

■ POSSIBILITIES FOR WRITING

1. In an essay for readers unfamiliar with it, describe the neighborhood in which you live (this "neighborhood" might be the one in which you grew up, or in which your family now lives, or even your college dormitory) in terms of the homogeneity or the diversity of its population. How is the character of your neighborhood defined by the people who live in it?

2. If you have lived in a neighborhood for a long enough period of time to notice that it has undergone specific changes in terms of development or demographics, write an essay explaining these changes. What was your neighborhood like when you were younger, or even before you were born? How would you describe it now? In what specific ways has it changed? What factors have contributed to these changes? Where do you think these changes will lead in the future?

MAKING CRITICAL CONNECTIONS: QUESTIONS FOR DISCUSSION, RESEARCH, AND WRITING

1. This chapter's readings should provide you with a sense of how vastly white Europeans' and Native Americans' religious views differ in defining the relationship between human beings and the natural world. Consider exploring this relationship from another religious perspective—for example, in learning and writing about Buddhist or about Islamic views, comparing them to Judeo-Christian or Native American perspectives, or in comparing the perspectives of two different native cultures.

2. Research, through primary and secondary sources, a history of your home county, your home town, or, if you grew up in a large city, your home neighborhood. In your research and in your writing, look beyond a "this happened, then this happened, then this happened" approach to reporting history; look for opportunities to explain the cause and effect relationships of events, as Wallace and Page Stegner and Kevin Cunningham do in their essays. How and why has your county, town, or neighborhood developed in the ways that it has? Local libraries will be excellent sources of primary documents and secondary source information, as will local historical societies. Look for opportunities to get history or experience firsthand through interviewing elderly residents or residents involved in professions that are key to the identity or economy of the community. Your local historical society will almost certainly be interested in receiving a copy of what you write, especially if it involves primary research. Consider illustrating your history with photographs of landscape, architecture, or people, including those you interview.

3. In "Landscape, History, and the Pueblo Imagination," Leslie Marmon Silko writes that "Ancient Pueblos took a modest view that the thing itself (the landscape) could not be improved upon. The ancients did not presume to tamper with what had already been created. Thus *realism*, as we now recognize it in painting and sculpture, did not catch the imaginations of Pueblo people until recently." American landscape painters of the nineteenth century, whose subjects were often the American frontier (and sometimes Indians themselves), had a very different aesthetic view of nature that arose from a very different set of cultural assumptions. Their paintings did attempt realism, but they were also infused with emotion. In your library, locate some examples of American landscape painting from the Romantic period, around the mid-1800s, and compare these interpretations of nature and landscape with examples of American Indian art of the

same period. In what ways does the art demonstrate differing cultural assumptions about human beings and the natural world?

4. Of the many environmental problems we face, which do you find to be the most pressing or worrisome, and why? Of recent efforts by government or nongovernmental agencies to address these problems, which do you find most promising or most discouraging, and why? Address these questions in discussion and/or in writing.

IV
INVESTIGATIONS

Environmental Challenges, Social Dilemmas

We live in a crowded and complex world, fraught with environmental and social problems. The manifestations of these problems are sometimes clear and immediate—for example, mass starvation is occurring among many human populations worldwide. Sometimes they are more subtle, though pervasive. So many of our technological advances—for example, automobiles, which have granted us so much freedom, leisure, and prosperity—are now instruments which threaten the ecological health of the planet that sustains us. Technology and mass communication have also made the planet a smaller place. There are few truly isolated human populations today. We live in a global community, and increasingly, the problems of one part of the world are the problems of other parts of the world. Our actions, and our fates, are increasingly intertwined.

We can easily identify many of the environmental problems we face. Environmental pollutants threaten our health, our food and water supplies, the air we breathe. The disappearance of wilderness and open space—as well as the alarming rate at which species are becoming extinct—not only negatively affect the quality of our lives, but also, in reducing biodiversity, disrupt the planet's ecology, permanently sever opportunities for learning, and quite possibly threaten our own survival. We may recognize, correctly, that the practical impossibility of sustaining current rates of human population growth poses perhaps the ultimate environmental challenge.

401

Many social and ethical dilemmas, especially those born from advances in science and technology, can also be understood, broadly, as environmental—or ecological—problems, arising from our attitudes about our species' relationship to, and often conflict with, the rest of nature. In considering the question of animal rights, we wonder what our moral obligation is to other species. In confronting the abortion question, we wonder about the sanctity of life. And, in understanding the prospects of genetic engineering of life—of plants, of other animals, and of human beings themselves—we may wonder if we have the right to play God, and whether, in playing God, we might be playing with fire.

It is increasingly difficult to separate our personal issues and individual fates from the issues and fates of others, and, indeed, from the fate of the planet. Our personal explorations, in living and in writing about our lives, often evolve into investigations of matters of public concern and public debate. We find that the broader our frame of reference is, the more we need to know, and that the more complex the issues we confront are, the more our understanding of them will depend upon sources outside our immediate experience. We must draw on information that extends what we already know and on experiences and points of view that help us define our own.

In the arena of public debate, there is always disagreement and some degree of discord. Most issues worth debating, including environmental issues and those involving the ethics of science and technology, are hotly debated because there is something important at stake, both personally and collectively. Because no single individual, institution, or nation can be categorically correct, the dialogue inherent in debate is what moves us, in degrees, forward as we attempt to find answers to complicated questions and workable solutions to complex problems. Therefore, as individuals, institutions, or nations, it is our responsibility in participating in the ongoing human dialogue to not only speak, but listen. In doing so, we may surprise ourselves in what we come to learn.

CHAPTER 7

Wind Generators, Tehachapi Pass, Calif. © Peter Menzel, 1990. (Stock, Boston)

CONCEPTS OF NATURE, SCIENCE, AND TECHNOLOGY

RHETORIC:
REASONING

Sound reasoning is fundamental to any kind of persuasive writing, including the many forms of analysis that we've explored in earlier chapters—interpretations of works of literature, writing that explains causes and effects, writing that compares and contrasts. Reasoning is key in any writing in which the writer attempts to make general statements with the expectation that his or her reader will accept them as valid. It is especially crucial in argumentative writing, where the writer's goal is to justify a position on a complex issue or to recommend to the reader a course of action. The more directly persuasive the writing is intended to be, the more careful a writer will have to be in his or her reasoning.

In earlier chapters of this book, we have already encountered many of the important components of sound reasoning. In this chapter introduction, we'll take a closer look at *logic,* the study of the principles of reason. Logic in writing applies both widely, to the most fundamental assertion made and supported in an essay or longer work, and particularly, to individual paragraphs and sentences. The effect of logic (or a lack of logic) in sentences, in paragraphs, and in an entire essay adds up, determining the degree to which your reader will judge your argument as valid or invalid.

THE LOGIC OF ARGUMENT

In the introduction to Chapter 8, we'll learn more about the purposes, applications, and strategies of argument. Here we'll begin by defining argument and looking at its logical components. First let's consider why we argue and the sorts of things we argue over.

Why Argue?

Some motives for argument are more constructive than others. Opposing viewpoints, especially those that are exaggerated or extreme, may irritate us and compel us to respond in kind, with arguments of our own that are just as exaggerated and extreme. If someone says to you that vegetarians are better human beings than people who eat meat, you might be inclined to respond with "Oh, yeah? Well, vegetarians are wimps!" Although defensiveness is perhaps an understandable emotional response, it does not provide a very sound basis for logical and effective argumentation, and it does nothing to further a reasonable exchange of ideas on a complex issue.

Other motives for argument are more reasonable and more productive, though we may sometimes wonder about how practical they are. Often, in both conversation and writing, we find ourselves arguing over the answers to hypothetical questions or over matters of value to which no tangible consequences are attached. (*Did dinosaurs become extinct as a result of a huge comet colliding with the earth or as a consequence of the Ice Age? Why do homeowners in southern California tend to fence their yards while those in New England tend not to?*) Sometimes we engage in heated arguments over the answers to these kinds of questions, in part because it's fun: there's an intellectual challenge inherent in the activity. But the answers to these kinds of questions, and the arguments that grow out of them, no matter how well-supported and convincing, will change nothing—neither the fate of the dinosaurs nor, most likely, homeowners' decisions in various parts of the country to fence or not fence their yards.

Are arguments over such matters pointless then? No. Such arguments may lack *apparent* or immediate consequences, but they are not inconsequential. Understanding the motivations and consequences of people's choices of whether or not to fence their yards may help us to understand better some aspect of our culture, our personal and collective values and beliefs. Furthermore, arguments without apparent or immediate consequences can have hidden or ultimate consequences. What we learn about the circumstances that led to the extinction of the dinosaurs may help us answer broader questions about the evolution of life on earth or provide us with information that, though we may not have a practical application for it now, might eventually prove useful in our attempts to save other species (perhaps even our own) threatened by extinction.

Many arguments, however—perhaps most arguments—are motivated by immediate practical consequences: something is at stake, whether on a personal, community, national, or even global scale. Say your school is considering a hike in student fees to expand its recycling program, or your town is debating whether or not to close off the downtown area to automobile traffic, or the President has proposed to Congress important amendments to the Endangered Species Act, or the United Nations is urging that countries that generate airborne pollutants damaging to neighboring countries be held financially responsible for that damage. Because there is something tangible at stake—policies that have specific and direct effects upon people's lives, including your own—such arguments are usually heated, and always complex, matters of public debate.

Intelligent people disagree over complicated issues. The real motivation for argument should not be to one-up the opposition, or even necessarily to "win." There are generally many more than two sides to any issue or argument, and solutions to problems usually involve compromise. In argumentative writing, the higher goal is to promote discussion and an exchange of views and creative ideas, in an attempt to resolve the complex questions and difficult issues that we face personally and collectively.

What We Do—and Do Not—Argue Over:
Facts, Personal Preferences,
and Arguable Statements

In our discussion of cause and effect analysis in the introduction to Chapter 6, we learned that it is pointless to argue over facts and personal preferences. Facts (*The train leaves at 6:02 a.m.*) are verifiable by reasonable authority. Accurate facts are true, and erroneous facts are untrue. Personal preferences have to do with individual tastes, likes and dislikes. Reasons exist for them, but these reasons are subjective. A personal preference can be explained, but it cannot be proven with evidence and we cannot expect to persuade others to accept our personal preferences on the basis of logic.

I love my pitt bull terrier is a statement of preference; *Pitt bull terriers make great pets* is an arguable statement. Arguable statements (also called assertions), unlike personal preferences, can be supported by reasons and evidence that exist outside a personal frame of reference. Reasons and evidence that support an arguable statement do not depend upon the individual making the statement, and readers or listeners who are presented with reasons in support of an arguable statement can agree or disagree with, accept or reject the assertion, in part or entirely.

Statements of personal preference are sometimes confused with arguable statements because statements of preference can easily be phrased as arguable statements, and arguable statements can be similarly disguised as statements of preference. *Insects are disgusting,* no matter how emphatically stated, is a statement of preference, not an arguable statement. On the other hand, *It's my feeling that the survival of the logging industry in the Northwest is more important than the survival of the spotted owl,* no matter how tentatively stated, is an arguable statement.

Developing a Logical Argument: The Simplified Toulmin Method

In a persuasive essay, you will probably develop support for an arguable statement by making a series of claims—some of them claims of fact and some of them claims of value (see page 409)—which themselves will be supported by evidence, and from which you will draw a series of smaller conclusions that will contribute to your larger conclusion.

In his book *The Uses of Argument,* British philosopher Stephen Toulmin proposes a useful method for analyzing and working with the logical structure of argument, based on patterns of *claims, evidence,* and *warrants.* The simplified Toulmin model for analyzing or creating logical argument follows a fundamental pattern:

A claim *(an assertion)*⟶

is supported or illustrated by evidence⟶

which gives rise to a warrant *(a statement that clarifies the relationship between claim and evidence).*

This pattern can be applied to entire essays in which the goal is to propose an idea, develop support for it, and reach a logical conclusion in the form of a thesis. It can also be applied to parts of essays—to individual paragraphs, for instance—in which the goal is to illustrate or prove one particular assertion that will lead logically to the next, related assertion. In the following example, we can see this pattern at work:

Claim: *In Robert Frost's poem "Stopping by Woods on a Snowy Evening," the depth of the narrator's isolation is underscored by his horse's nervous responses.*

Evidence:

> *My little horse must think it queer*
> *To stop without a farmhouse near*
> *Between the woods and frozen lake*
> *The darkest evening of the year.*
>
> *He gives his harness bells a shake*
> *To ask if there is some mistake.*

Warrant: *The horse's nervousness calls to mind the anxiety one has alone in a strange and wild place.**

One of the important things to notice about this pattern in argument is that in using it the writer is not only stating his or her claim and supporting it with concrete evidence (in this case, with an illustration from the text); in stating the warrant, the writer is also drawing from the relationship between the claim and the evidence a larger idea—an idea that places claim and evidence within a broader context and may help the writer make a transition into the next idea, lending coherence to the argument.

In the example above, there is only one piece of evidence offered in support of the claim, and it is a specific type: an illustration from the text. Writers can—and sometimes should—offer more than one piece of evidence in support of the claim; in support of other claims, writers might draw upon other kinds of evidence, including facts, the observations of experts, or even personal experience. Similarly, a writer might offer more than one warrant to justify or clarify the relationship of evidence to claim.

Claims of Fact and Claims of Value

The two kinds of claims—*claims of fact* and *claims of value*—serve different purposes in the development of logical argument. Strategies for applying the Toulmin model in argument differ depending upon the kind of claim the writer wants to make.

Claims of fact are assertions that have no value attached to them, but that do require proof in the form of factual evidence. In some cases, this factual evidence will be relatively obvious and simple to come by: *Many people enjoy picnicking at the city park on Sundays* is a claim of fact and can be easily supported by statistics, and these statistics will be relatively easy to acquire through the Department of Parks and Public

---

*Thanks to the Program in Writing and Critical Thinking at Stanford University for providing this example.

Works or even through direct observation. *Public lands in the Southwest are suffering from the effects of overgrazing* is also a claim of fact—it has no value attached to it—but it is a more complicated claim of fact than the first example. It will require support in the form of more complicated factual evidence. When a reader encounters a claim of fact, any doubt he or she has about its validity will likely be focused on the question of whether or not the facts exist to support it.

Private ranching on public lands is a heated issue that gives rise to heated debate, and there are certainly many claims of value that could be made about it. *Private use of public lands by ranchers should not be allowed* is a claim of value. So is the statement *Urban Americans benefit from time spent outdoors.* The arguer's values, which may or may not be values we are inclined to share, are implicit in the statement. Factual evidence, though certainly not irrelevant in supporting claims of value, is not where the reader's (or listener's) primary attention is likely to be focused. What we are really interested in are the underlying assumptions of value behind the claim.

Interpretations and Assumptions

Hidden assumptions often lie behind warrants and claims of value. When there is a chance that your reader will not share these assumptions, you must address them first before going on to argue your specific point. Sometimes, in recognizing the assumptions hidden within your argument, you will realize that you are basing the logic of your argument on assumptions that not only your reader, but you yourself may question.

Assumptions are not necessarily false. Many assumptions simply require explanation and support—arguments on their own behalf. Uncovering and addressing the assumptions behind arguments is really just one way of accomplishing one of the necessities of effective and fair argumentation: anticipating opposing views and refuting them to a reasonable degree. The following example illustrates hidden assumptions that, unless they are addressed, might undercut an entire argument:

Claim of value: *The ban on motorboats should continue at Jewel Lake.*

Evidence #1: *Motorboats disturb wildlife.*

Evidence #2: *Motorboats pollute the water.*

Warrant: *Our children deserve to experience Jewel Lake in its current pristine state.*

A writer could base the development of an entire essay upon an elaboration of the example above. It has the makings of a reasonable argument. But in the warrant, there are hidden assumptions. The writer is assuming several things: first, that the reader or listener cares about "our" children and their future experience; second, that the lake is currently pristine; and third, that even if the reader or listener does care about the future experience of "our" children, the experience of a pristine lake (as opposed to, say, a ride in a motorboat) is the kind of experience he or she values. If the writer fails to address the hidden assumptions inherent in the warrant, and to argue for them as well as for the motorboat ban, the argument might easily be dismissed by readers or listeners who do not share the writer's values or interpret the facts the way the writer does.

Accepting and basing arguments upon hidden assumptions can lead you quickly into errors in reasoning.

LOGICAL FALLACIES AND RELATED ERRORS IN REASONING

Logical fallacies are errors in reasoning that create flaws in argumentation. At best, they weaken arguments, and at worst, they invalidate them completely. Fallacies arise when writers oversimplify complex issues and when they avoid real issues altogether. Sometimes writers generate fallacies intentionally because they think that in argumentation it is good strategy. But such motives reflect a lack of respect for the reader and do not promote real thinking, real dialogue, or real solutions to the difficult issues we often debate.

Oversimplification

Many logical fallacies arise from oversimplification of complex issues, a tendency arising from ignorance, bias, the search for easy answers, or an attempt on the writer's part to manipulate emotion. Although there are others, here are some of the most obvious and most common forms of oversimplification:

No choice: This fallacy occurs when a writer claims that the only valid choice is his or her own choice: *We must agree that . . .* or *We have no choice but to accept/reject. . . .* There is always more than one choice; choices are precisely that—choices among several possibilities. Choices are not absolute, though we may and frequently do develop reasonable arguments for the wisdom of one choice over another.

Either/or: This fallacy, instead of limiting choices to one, offers only two choices—one (the writer's) reasonable and the other unfairly exaggerated to seem ridiculous or unrealistically threatening. *You're either part of the problem or part of the solution* is a classic example of such a fallacy. We can be simultaneously parts of problems and solutions: for instance, as American consumers, we generate a terrific amount of waste and we may, at the same time, be trying to contribute something to a solution through recycling.

No costs: "No cost" fallacies suggest that a given solution to a problem has no drawbacks, only positive effects. This is rarely, if ever, true. Acknowledging that with virtually any solution there will inevitably be negative side effects, or costs, will not change the fact, if it is warranted, that the positive effects outweigh the negative effects. Your reader will feel deceived if you try to fool him or her into thinking otherwise. If a drug manufacturer were licensed to sell a drug to the public because overall it offered effective treatment, and that company did not list potentially harmful side effects on the package, that manufacturer would be held liable.

The end justifies the means: This fallacy claims that because the result is positive, we can ignore the moral costs or negative consequences in achieving it. Terrorists draw on this fallacy in rationalizing the deaths of innocent people in order to achieve a "higher good"—that is, the objectives of their cause.

The reason: "The reason" fallacies maintain that one reason can explain a complex problem or justify a solution. *Kids who watch violence on television exhibit violent behavior* is an example of such a fallacy. It is possible that violence on television is associated with violent behavior in children, but it is certainly not the only cause. Many different factors, both personal and cultural, contribute to such behavior.

Hasty generalizations: Hasty generalizations (or overgeneralizations) occur when we leap to conclusions on the basis of insufficient evidence. Stereotyping is a form of hasty generalization, as in *Environmentalists are out of touch with economic realities.* One solution may be to qualify a statement to the appropriate degree by adding "most," "many," "some," or "a few"; but this may be a superficial solution. What may really be necessary is more evidence.

Non sequitur: Non sequitur in Latin means "It does not follow." The reader of a non sequitur is likely to respond with reasonable confusion, because no apparent connection exists between the argument's conclusion and the evidence and/or claim. Any connection that *might* exist is buried in a subjective jumble in the arguer's mind and is unclear to the reader. *I'm considering a career in environmental protection. I think I'll volunteer for Senator Martinez's reelection campaign* is a non sequitur.

It will remain a *non sequitur* unless the writer provides the logical link between these two apparently unrelated statements by establishing that Senator Martinez's bid for reelection hinges, in large part, on his strong advocacy of environmental protection measures and that working for Martinez's reelection campaign would provide the writer with insight and worthwhile professional experience.

False analogy: Analogies can easily stretch the limits of logic since in analogy we are comparing what we perceive as similar qualities of two essentially dissimilar things. When writers imply in analogy that the two things being compared are similar in ways in which they are not, they are making false analogies. As an example, consider the statement *Homosexuality is a virus that is sweeping the country in epidemic proportions.* The rate at which homosexuals are making their sexual preference public may be on the increase, but homosexuality is not a disease and is not, as the analogy suggests, contagious.

Post hoc reasoning: Cause and effect analyses often suffer from this logical fallacy. *Post hoc ergo propter hoc* ("after that, therefore because of that") fallacies assume, or in some cases argue, that because X occurred before Y, X caused Y. *After I changed to a toothpaste with special whiteners, two different men asked me out on dates. That stuff really works!* No doubt, the manufacturer of this brand of toothpaste would appreciate your falling into this fallacy.

Slippery slope or *ad absurdum*: Slippery slope or *ad absurdum* ("to absurdity") arguments are vastly overstated, attempting to dismiss opposing positions by stretching them to absurd extremes. The statement *If we elect a woman president, we will have to be prepared for the vice president to take charge of the nation for several days of every month* is an example of a slippery slope argument.

Undocumented assertions or *forced hypothesis:* This fallacy is so common that it can be considered more fundamental than a simple fallacy. When you do not support general statements with sufficient evidence or when you draw premature conclusions, conclusions for which sufficient evidence does not exist, you are indulging in undocumented assertions or a forced hypothesis.

Avoiding the Issue

In oversimplifying a complex issue, a writer or speaker may offer weak arguments supported by inadequate proof. But in avoiding the issue altogether, he or she offers no argument at all because the so-called proof, no matter how aggressively stated, is irrelevant to the issue at hand. Logical fallacies that result when writers dodge real issues make for desperate "arguments" indeed. Often these fallacies are intentional; the writer wants to divert attention away from the center of the matter and to provoke an emotional rather than a reasoned response in the reader. The following fallacies result from avoiding the issue:

Ipse dixit: *Ipse dixit* ("he himself said it") fallacies appeal to unqualified authority. These fallacies can be unintentional. For example, I may make the error of thinking that because my sister is a lawyer, her opinion that criminals are mentally ill is an expert rather than a personal opinion. Yet it is a personal opinion, since she has no expertise in psychology. On the other hand, this fallacy is often intentionally committed when writers and speakers scramble for support of weak positions. In doing so they hope we as readers will accept authority at face value and that we will not scrutinize the qualifications of that authority very carefully, when it is exactly our job to do so.

Ad hominem: *Ad hominem* ("against the man") fallacies are name-calling, pure and simple. They are shoddy attempts to discredit opposing viewpoints by making personal attacks instead of engaging in real discussion of the issues. (*Senator Mitchell supports socialized medicine. And you thought we'd defeated the Communists!*) These attacks may backfire, however, since most of us recognize unfair and irrelevant personal attacks when we see them, and our disdain for the creator of the fallacy may far exceed our disdain for the person or group being attacked.

Bandwagon: Bandwagon "logic" says that if everybody's doing it, it must be good, or at least okay. It is a cornerstone of advertising strategy. *Four out of five housewives recommend Brand X for those extra-tough jobs* (or at least four out of the five Company X preselected for the survey)—so, obviously, we should buy brand X too. But bandwagon "logic" can be even more insidious: it can be rationalization, not to mention cynicism, on a grand scale. *Nobody pays attention to the legal drinking age any more; all teenagers drink, so what's the big deal?* There are two things wrong with the logic here: first, the statement is exaggerated—plenty of people still abide by the legal drinking age; second, the fact that many people don't does not make underage drinking right or particularly smart.

Ad populem: These fallacies appeal "to the people" and to our desire to be considered part of a group—identified with its values and beliefs—rather than being on the outside. *If you care about family values, you won't support sex education in the public schools.* Reasonable arguments can be presented both for and against sex education in the schools, but to imply that anyone who does support distribution of such information in public schools does not care about family values is fallacious, an unfair appeal to emotion that avoids the real issues that are up for debate.

Circular reasoning: This fallacy involves begging the question in circular form. It is a tactic by which the arguer attempts to prove a point by simply restating it. *Every American consumer must accept responsibility for recycling the waste he or she generates because it is our obligation to recycle.* Here the only reason the arguer has offered in support of his or her point is the point itself.

Intentional obscurity: Sometimes, when wording is so vague as to obscure meaning or to deny us important information while at the same time giving the *appearance* of imparting meaning or information, there are ulterior motives. Our tendency toward *euphemism* (using "polite" language to discuss uncomfortable subjects) can distance us from subjects that demand to be more closely examined (consider the term "ethnic cleansing," which means the mass murders of people of an ethnic minority). Such terms allow us to make oblique reference to something we'd rather not think about. In its aggressive forms in propaganda, deception in the form of intentional obscurity allows governments to hide truths from their citizens as they pursue their own agendas. In World War II Germany, instead of being told that the Nazis were slaughtering millions of Jews, the people were "informed" that their government was pursuing "the final solution."

Straw man: "Straw man" arguments are intentional misrepresentations of opposing views. In an attempt to make his or her own position look stronger, the writer or speaker attributes untrue and absurd arguments to the opposing side because these arguments can be easily knocked down: *Environmentalists want to put every logging operation in Washington, Oregon, and northern California out of business.*

Rationalization: Most of us rationalize fairly often, whether intentionally or unintentionally, in attempts to deceive ourselves and/or others. When we rationalize, we justify our own actions with plausible-sounding explanations for our motives, behavior, or positions because these explanations are more palatable than the truth, or because they cast us in a better light. Rationalizations that we use to justify our own actions are simply self-deceptions: *If I go to the party tonight instead of studying, I'll be more relaxed for the exam tomorrow morning* (the truth is probably that you simply don't feel like studying any more). Rationalizations that we use to convince others are lies, or partial lies. Consider the statement *The only reason I am applying for this job is for the opportunity to help others.* Having the opportunity to help others may, in fact, be one of the reasons you are applying for this job, but in all likelihood you also need the paycheck and the job experience.

In many instances, the fallacies that result when writers or speakers dodge the real issues are intentional. They are attempts to divert the reader's or listener's attention or to manipulate his or her emotions. When they are intentional, these fallacies are symptomatic of more than poor reasoning; they signal the writer's lack of respect for the reader, as well as a refusal to engage in open and fair discussion. Such intentional fallacies are ethical breaches, abuses rather than legitimate uses of persuasive rhetoric.

READINGS:
POINTS OF REFERENCE

Readings within each individual chapter of this text (with the exception of Chapter 8) have been presented chronologically in the hope that a sense of history will emerge, and with it a growing understanding of the ways in which attitudes about the natural world have evolved over time. The readings in this chapter include conceptual essays, often arguments, which convey the evolution of thought about nature and environment, science and technology in this country over the past one hundred or so years. The readings suggest, perhaps, where our attitudes may lead us as we grapple with environmental problems and questions about ethical uses of technology that press upon us with increasing urgency. These readings are not comprehensive, but they may serve as important points of reference as we consider the role nature plays in human lives, and, increasingly, the role human beings play in the evolution of life on the planet.

In our attitudes about nature, we are products of both history and culture. Many of those who have written most articulately about nature's role in the lives of human beings, or about human beings' impact upon the natural world, have expressed ideas that differ from the popular attitudes of their time, though they may still have held some of the common assumptions of that time. Henry David Thoreau was one of the first Americans of European descent to propose that wilderness deserved protection because it had an intrinsic value (beyond its economic value); yet for Thoreau and other transcendentalists, including Ralph Waldo Emerson, nature was still at the service of human beings, in a moral or spiritual sense if not in an economic or even a scientific one. For these thinkers, nature existed not only in and for itself, but also as an extension and reflection of human experience. Today, many of us retain a romanticized view of nature, given to us by Emerson, Thoreau and others, that Joyce Carol Oates criticizes in her essay, "Against Nature": an appreciation not of *"Nature-in-itself* but *Nature-as-experience."* Inherent in the tendency to romanticize nature, to see it as "the self's (flattering) mirror" are assumptions of human superiority, or of *anthrocentrism.* How different are these assumptions from those that compelled people in the past, and continue to compel many powerful people today, to see nature as an object to be conquered, subdued, and rendered economically profitable?

Although most of us feel a real fondness for nature—whether for "Nature-in-itself" or "Nature-as-experience"—we can less afford now simply to let nature be. There are too many of us, and the technologies that we have developed both as a reason for and a consequence of our species' evolutionary success have created a multitude of environmental problems and ethical dilemmas that demand practical solutions. Our romanticization of nature is tempered by the realities of survival. The new pragmatism in our attitudes about nature is largely determined by what we know now about ecology: that within ecosystems, life forms are interrelated, and the survival of one form of life (including the human species) may depend upon the survival of others. Environmentalists and conservationists as Aldo Leopold pointed out quite early on in "The Land Ethic" (1949) have learned that arguments for the conservation of "Nature-as-itself" are less readily accepted than arguments that demonstrate how a healthy environment can directly benefit human beings.

In "The Land Ethic," Leopold argues that we must accept our role as responsible members of the biotic community, not because we have an economic stake in it, but because it is ethically correct. Stewardship of the land is a relatively recent and unique concept to human experience, both connecting us to and emphasizing our separation from the rest of nature. Development of an ethical relationship to the land, Leopold argues, requires that we put long-range consequences of our actions before short-range profit, and that we put community interests (including those of *other* species) before personal interests. This, he suggests, calls for a fundamental shift in our attitudes about nature: "No important change in ethics," he says, "was ever accomplished without an internal change in our intellectual emphasis, loyalties, affections, and convictions." As "the moral animal," we watch dramatic shifts in the balance of nature that we ourselves have caused, and we wonder about both survival and its costs. We may wonder, too, whether the role of stewards of nature that many of us are prepared to accept might ultimately involve delusions of grandeur.

■ RALPH WALDO EMERSON
from "Nature"

One of the founders of American transcendentalism, preacher, writer, poet, and lecturer Ralph Waldo Emerson was born in 1803 in Boston and died in 1882 in Concord, Massachusetts. Emerson graduated from Harvard in 1821. He attended Harvard Divinity School in 1825 and 1827, and although he did not graduate, he was approved as a preacher in 1826 by the Middlesex association of ministers—probably more as a consequence of family connections than of distinction as a divinity student. After teaching school and preaching in various locations in New England, Emerson took a position as pastor at the Second Church in Boston in 1829. Emerson and his church hosted antislavery speakers, and he was active in various philanthropic movements and in city and state affairs, serving on the Boston school committee and as chaplain of the state senate. Emerson resigned his pastorate in 1833.

In 1836, Emerson published his first and highly influential book, Nature, which is more a philosophical work than a theological one. Contained in this seminal work, some critics maintain, are all the themes Emerson elaborated upon in his subsequent lectures and writings. According to scholar Donald Avery, Nature speaks of "the universe consisting of nature and the soul. According to Emerson, everything in nature corresponds to some state of mind. Natural laws in the scheme of things always become moral laws and teach the worship of God, the idea of the absolute, that God cannot be described, and, indeed, that nature is but one form of God." This book gave voice to transcendentalism.

In 1836, the Transcendental Club was founded in Concord, and Emerson was probably its leader from the start. Members of the group also founded the Dial, a magazine that served as a literary forum for the movement; Emerson's friend and protégé Henry David Thoreau contributed writing to virtually every issue of the Dial. When the magazine ceased publication in 1844, Emerson turned his attention to writing and speaking on important issues, including slavery and women's suffrage, and his home in Concord became a gathering place for leading writers and thinkers of his time.

Some of Emerson's major works are Nature *(1836),* Essays *(1841),* Essays: Second Series *(1844), from which the following selection, "Nature," is taken,* Poems *(1847),* Representative Men: Seven Lectures *(1850),* The Conduct of Life *(1860),* Society and Solitude *(1870), and* Miscellanies *(1884).*

There are days which occur in this climate, at almost any season of the year, wherein the world reaches its perfection; when the air, the heavenly bodies and the earth, make a harmony, as if nature would indulge her offspring; when, in these bleak upper sides of the planet, nothing is to desire that we have heard of the happiest latitudes, and we bask in the shining hours of Florida and Cuba; when everything that has life gives sign of satisfaction, and the cattle that lie on the ground seem to have great and tranquil thoughts. These halcyons may be looked for with a little more assurance in that pure October weather which we distinguish by the name of the Indian summer. The day, immeasurably long, sleeps over the broad hills and warm wide fields. To have lived through all its sunny hours, seems longevity enough. The solitary places do not seem quite lonely. At the gates of the forest, the surprised man of the world is forced to leave his city estimates of great and small, wise and foolish. The knapsack of custom falls off his back with the first step he takes into these precincts. Here is sanctity which shames our religions, and reality that discredits our heroes. Here we find nature to be the circumstance which dwarfs every other circumstance, and judges like a god all men that come to her. We have crept out of our close and crowded houses into the night and morning, and we see what majestic beauties daily wrap us in their bosom. How willingly we would escape the barriers which render them comparatively impotent, escape the sophistication and second thought, and suffer nature to intrance us. The tempered light of the woods is like a perpetual morning, and is stimulating and heroic. The anciently-reported spells of these places creep on us. The stems of the pines, hemlocks and oaks almost gleam like iron on the excited eye. The incommunicable trees begin to persuade us to live with them, and quit our life of solemn trifles. Here no history, or church, or state, is interpolated on the divine sky and the immortal year. How easily we might walk onward into the opening landscape, absorbed by new pictures and by thoughts fast succeeding each other, until by degrees the recollection of home was crowded out of the mind, all memory obliterated by the tyranny of the present, and we were led in triumph by nature.

These enchantments are medicinal, they sober and heal us. These are plain pleasures, kindly and native to us. We come to our own, and make friends with matter, which the ambitious chatter of the school would persuade us to despise. We never can part with it; the mind loves its old home: as water to our thirst, so is the rock, the ground, to our eyes and hands and feet. It is firm water; it is cold flame; what health, what affinity! Ever an old friend, even like a dear friend and brother when we chat affectedly with strangers, comes in this honest face, and takes a grave liberty with us, and shames us out of our nonsense. Cities give not the human senses room enough. We go out daily and nightly to feed the eyes on the horizon, and require so much scope, just as we need water for our bath. There are all degrees of natural influence, from these quarantine powers of nature, up to her dearest and gravest ministrations to the imagination and the soul. There is the bucket of cold water from the spring, the wood-fire to which the chilled traveller rushes for safety,—and there is the sublime moral of autumn and of noon. We nestle in nature, and draw our living as parasites from her roots and grains, and we receive glances from the heavenly bodies, which call us to solitude and foretell the remotest future. The blue zenith is the point in which romance and reality meet. I think if we should be rapt away into all that and dream of heaven, and should converse with Gabriel and Uriel, the upper sky would be all that would remain of our furniture.

It seems to me as if the day was not wholly profane in which we have given heed to some natural object. The fall of snowflakes in a still air, preserving to each crystal its perfect form; the blowing of sleet over a wide sheet of water, and over plains; the waving rye-field; the mimic waving of acres of houstonia, whose innumerable florets whiten and ripple before the eye; the reflections of trees and flowers in glassy lakes; the musical, streaming, odorous south wind, which converts all trees to wind-harps; the crackling and spurting of hemlock in the flames, or of pine logs, which yield glory to the walls and faces in the sitting-room,—these are the music and pictures of the most ancient religion. My house stands in low land, with limited outlook and on the skirt of the village. But I go with my friend to the shore of our little river, and with one stroke of the paddle I leave the village politics and personalities, yes, and the world of villages and personalities, behind, and pass into a delicate realm of sunset and moonlight, too bright almost for spotted man to enter without novitiate and probation. We penetrate bodily this incredible beauty; we dip our hands in this painted element; our eyes are bathed in these lights and forms. A holiday, a *villeggiatura*, a royal revel, the proudest, most heart-rejoicing festival that valor and beauty, power and taste, ever decked and enjoyed, establishes itself on the instant. These sunset clouds, these delicately emerging stars, with their private and ineffable glances, signify it and proffer it. I am taught the poorness of our invention, the ugliness of towns and palaces. Art and luxury have early learned that they must work as enchantment and sequel to this original beauty. I am over-instructed for my return. Henceforth I shall be hard to please. I cannot go back to toys. I am grown expensive and sophisticated. I can no longer live without elegance, but a countryman shall be my master of revels. He who knows the most, he who knows what sweets and virtues are in the ground, the waters, the plants, the heavens, and how to come at these enchantments,—is the rich and royal man. Only as far as the masters of the world have called in nature to their aid, can they reach the height of magnificence. . . .

But it is very easy to outrun the sympathy of readers on this topic, which schoolmen called *natura naturata*, or nature passive. One can hardly speak directly of it without excess. It is as easy to broach in mixed companies what is called "the subject of religion." A susceptible person does not like to indulge his tastes in this kind without the apology of some trivial necessity: he goes to see a wood-lot, or to look at the crops, or to fetch a plant or a mineral from a remote locality, or he carries a fowling-piece or a fishing-rod. I suppose this shame must have a good reason. A dilettantism in nature is barren and unworthy. The fop of the fields is no better than his brother of Broadway. Men are natural hunters and inquisitive of wood-craft, and I suppose that such a gazetteer as woodcutters and Indians would furnish facts for, would take place in the most sumptuous drawing rooms of all the "Wreaths" and "Flora's chaplets" of the bookshops; yet ordinarily, whether we are too clumsy for so subtle a topic, or from whatever cause, as soon as men begin to write on nature, they fall into euphuism. Frivolity is a most unfit tribute to Pan, who ought to be represented in the mythology as the most continent of the gods. I would not be frivolous before the admirable reserve and prudence of time, yet I cannot renounce the right of returning often to this one topic. The multitude of false churches accredits the true religion. Literature, poetry, science are the homage of man to this unfathomed secret, concerning which no sane man can effect an indifference or incuriosity. . . .

Nature is always consistent, though she feigns to contravene her own laws. She keeps her laws, and seems to transcend them. She arms and equips an animal to find its place and living in the earth, and at the same time she arms and equips another animal to destroy it. . . . If we look at her work, we seem to catch a glimpse of a system in transition. Plants are the young of the world, vessels of health and vigor; but they grope ever upward towards consciousness; the trees are imperfect men, and seem to bemoan their imprisonment, rooted in the ground. The animal is the novice and probationer of a more advanced order. The men, though young, having tasted the first drop from the cup of thought, are already dissipated; the maples and ferns are still uncorrupt; yet no doubt when they come to consciousness they too will curse and swear. Flowers so strictly belong to youth that we adult men soon come to feel that their beautiful generations concern not us: we have had our day; now let the children have theirs. The flowers jilt us, and we are old bachelors with our ridiculous tenderness. . . .

If we consider how much we are nature's, we need not be superstitious about towns, as if that terrific or benefic force did not find us there also, and fashion cities. Nature, who made the mason, made the house. We may easily hear too much of rural influences. The cool disengaged air of natural objects makes them enviable to us, chafed and irritable creatures with red faces, and we shall be as grand as they if we camp out and eat roots; but let men be men instead of woodchucks and the oak and the elm shall gladly serve us, though we sit in chairs of ivory on carpets of silk.

This guiding identity runs through all the surprises and contrasts of the piece, and characterizes every law. Man carries the world in his head, the whole astronomy and chemistry suspended in a thought. Because the history of nature is characterized in his brain, therefore is he the prophet and discoverer of her secrets.

■ CONSIDERATIONS OF MEANING AND METHOD

1. How, in the opening paragraph of this excerpt from "Nature," does Emerson draw his reader in to the "enchantments" of nature, which, he says in the second paragraph, are "medicinal"?

What is the central idea of the opening paragraph? Is it the central idea of the entire piece?

2. What does Emerson mean when he writes that in knowing the "plain pleasures" of nature, "We come to our own, and make friends with matter, which the ambitious chatter of school would persuade us to despise"?

3. Emerson writes at the beginning of paragraph 4 of this excerpt that "it is very easy to outrun the sympathy of readers on this topic, which schoolmen called *natura naturata,* or nature passive. One can hardly speak directly of it without excess." Did he outrun your sympathies in these opening paragraphs? Why or why not? From a contemporary perspective, does the writing seem antiquated to you, in its ideas or its style?

4. When Emerson accuses "the fop of the fields" as being "no better than his brother of Broadway," whom and what is he criticizing? He concludes this paragraph with the observation that "The multitude of false churches accredits the true religion." To what religion is he referring?

5. In the fifth paragraph, Emerson describes nature as "a system in transition," in which "plants . . . grope ever upward toward consciousness; the trees are imperfect men. . . . The animal is the novice and probationer of a more advanced order." This is an extremely anthrocentric view of nature (and certainly, fifteen years before publication of Darwin's *On the Origin of the Species* in 1859, of evolution). Do you find any contradiction in Emerson's simultaneous worship of nature and his use of man as its measure?

6. What is Emerson's final point in this excerpt? To what extent do you agree or disagree with his thesis?

■ **POSSIBILITIES FOR WRITING**

1. Through research in your library, find out more about the history and philosophy of the transcendental movement. In an essay for your class, explain how Emerson's essay illuminates some of transcendentalism's key precepts. To what extent do you yourself share a belief in these precepts?

2. Do you think that transcendentalism provides any ongoing legacy that informs popular attitudes about nature in the United States today, particularly in Americans' relationships with the outdoors or in the conservation and environmental movements?

Explain and illustrate your response to this question in an essay for your class.

■ JOHN BURROUGHS
from "In the Noon of Science"

John Burroughs was a leading voice in American nature writing in the era of Henry David Thoreau and John Muir. He was not an activist, as was Thoreau, and not a wilderness adventurer, as was Muir. His early essays were so much in the style of Ralph Waldo Emerson that a few were erroneously attributed to Emerson. Burroughs was very widely read in his day, "first," as scholar Thomas J. Lyon writes, "as a writer of pleasant rambles, and later as nothing less than an American country sage, a man who could make the new universe seem an accessible, friendly place. He did this by telling and showing people how to look."

Burroughs was born in 1837 near Roxbury, New York, in the Catskill Mountains. His father was a farmer, and Burroughs was from early on a lover of nature. He alternated his own studies, including terms at Ashland Collegiate Institute and Cooperstown Seminary, with teaching. In 1864, he traveled to Washington, D.C., and served until 1873 as a clerk in the Treasury Department. While in Washington, Burroughs began publishing his essays on nature, some of his first in the Atlantic *magazine. He also met the poet Walt Whitman, who was tending the Civil War sick and wounded in Washington hospitals, and the two became close friends. Some of Burroughs's other important and long-standing friendships were with John Muir, Thomas Edison, Theodore Roosevelt, and Henry Ford. From 1873 to 1884, Burroughs served as U.S. Bank Examiner for New York State. He purchased a fruit farm near Esopus, New York, and eventually bought back his family's old property in the Catskills. Burroughs died of an abscess in his chest during a train trip home from a winter in southern California in 1921, just short of his eighty-fourth birthday.*

Some of Burroughs's many works include Notes on Walt Whitman, As Poet and Person *(1867), his first book;* Ways of Nature *(1905);* Camping and Tramping With Roosevelt *(1907);* The Summit of the Years *(1913), from which "In the Noon of Science" is taken; and* Accepting the Universe *(1920).*

Burroughs was strongly affected by the work of evolutionist

Charles Darwin. "Everything about [him]," wrote Burroughs, "indicates the master. In reading him you breathe the air of the largest and most serene mind." Thomas J. Lyon explains that "To Burroughs, the largest minds saw beyond the usual categories of good and evil, predator and prey, life and death, and perceived that all terms that seemed to be polar opposites were essentially complementary, as was the great system that gave birth to them. This penetration is what 'accepting the universe' means." Burroughs had a great disdain for certain nature writers whom he referred to as "nature-fakers." He accused these writers of skewing reality through anthropomorphism, attributing human qualities and characteristics to subjects in nature, and thus playing upon readers' sentimentalities and perpetuating their lack of understanding of the natural world. Burroughs was critical as well, however, as "In the Noon of Science" demonstrates, of a purely mechanized view of nature through science. "We cannot find God by thinking," he wrote.

I

How surely the race is working away from the attitude of mind toward life and nature begotten by an age of faith, into an attitude of mind toward these things begotten by an age of science! However the loss and gain may finally foot up, the movement to which I refer seems as inevitable as fate; it is along the line of the mental evolution of the race, and it can be no more checked or thwarted than can the winds or the tides. The disturbance of our mental and spiritual equilibrium consequent upon the change is natural enough.

The culture of the race has so long been of a nonscientific character; we have so long looked upon nature in the twilight of our feelings, of our hopes and our fears, and our religious emotions, that the clear midday light of science shocks and repels us. Our mental eyesight has not yet got used to the noonday glare. Our anthropomorphic views of creation die hard, and when they are dead we feel orphaned. The consolations which science offers do not move our hearts. At first, the scientific explanation of the universe seems to shut us into a narrower and lower world. The heaven of the ideal seems suddenly clouded over, and we feel the oppression of the physical. The sacred mysteries vanish, and in their place we have difficult or unsolvable problems.

Physical science magnifies physical things. The universe of matter with its irrefragable laws looms upon our mental horizon larger than ever before, to some minds blotting out the very heavens. There are no more material things in the world than there always have been, and we are no more dependent upon them than has always been the case, but we are more intently and exclusively occupied with them, subduing them to our ever-growing physical and mental needs.

I am always inclined to defend physical science against the charge of materialism, and that it is the enemy of those who would live in the spirit; but when I do so I find I am unconsciously arguing with myself against the same half-defined imputation. I too at times feel the weary weight of the material universe as it presses upon us in a hundred ways in our mechanical and scientific age. I well understand what one of our women writers meant the other day when she spoke of the "blank wall of material things" to which modern science leads us. The feminine temperament—and the literary and artistic temperament generally—is quite likely, I think, to feel something like a blank wall shutting it in, in the results of modern physical sciences. We feel it in Herbert Spencer and Ernest Haeckel, and now and then in such lambent spirits as Huxley and W. K. Clifford. Matter, and the laws of matter, and the irrefragable chain of cause and effect, press hard upon us.

We feel this oppression in the whole fabric of our civilization—a civilization which, with all its manifold privileges and advantages, is probably to a large class of people the most crushing and soul-killing the race has ever seen. It practically abolishes time and space, while it fills the land with noise and hurry. It arms us with the forces of earth, air, and water, while it weakens our hold upon the sources of personal power; it lengthens life while it curtails leisure; it multiplies our wants while it lessens our capacity for simple enjoyments; it opens up the heights and depths, while it makes the life of the masses shallow; it vastly increases the machinery of education, while it does so little for real culture. "Knowledge comes but wisdom lingers," because wisdom cannot or will not come by railroad, or automobile, or aeroplane, or be hurried up by telegraph or telephone. She is more likely to come on foot, or riding on an ass, or to be drawn in a one-horse shay, than to appear in any of our chariots of fire and thunder.

With the rise of the scientific habit of mind has come the decline in great creative literature and art. With the spread of education based upon scientific principles, originality in mind and in character fades. Science tends to eliminate the local, the individual; it favors the gen-

eral, the universal. It makes our minds and characters all alike; it uni-
fies the nations, but it tames and, in a measure, denatures them. The
more we live in the scientific spirit, the spirit of material knowledge,
the farther we are from the spirit of true literature. The more we live
upon the breath of the newspaper, the more will the mental and spiritual condition out of which come real literature and art be barred to
us. The more we live in the hard, calculating business spirit, the farther are we from the spirit of the master productions; the more we
surrender ourselves to the feverish haste and competition of the industrial spirit, the more the doors of the heaven of the great poems
and works of art are closed to us.

Beyond a certain point in our culture, exact knowledge counts for
so much less than sympathy, love, appreciation. We may know
Shakespeare to an analysis of his last word or allusion, and yet miss
Shakespeare entirely. We may know an animal in the light of all the
many tests that laboratory experimentation throws upon it, and yet
not really know it at all. We are not content to know what the animal
knows naturally, we want to know what it knows unnaturally. We
put it through a sort of inquisitorial torment in the laboratory, we
starve it, we electrocute it, we freeze it, we burn it, we incarcerate it,
we vivisect it, we press it on all sides and in all ways, to find out
something about its habits or its mental processes that is usually not
worth knowing.

Well, we can gain a lot of facts, such as they are, but we may lose
our own souls. This spirit has invaded school and college. Our young
people go to the woods with pencil and note-book in hand; they
drive sharp bargains with every flower and bird and tree they meet;
they want tangible assets that can be put down in black and white.
Nature as a living joy, something to love, to live with, to brood over,
is now, I fear, seldom thought of. It is only a mine to be worked and
to be through with, a stream to be fished, a tree to be shaken, a field
to be gleaned. With what desperate thoroughness the new men study
the birds; and about all their studies yield is a mass of dry, unrelated
facts.

In school and college our methods are more and more thorough
and businesslike, more and more searching and systematic: we would
go to the roots of the tree of knowledge, even if we find a dead tree
on our hands. We fairly vivisect Shakespeare and Milton and Virgil.
We study a dead language as if it were a fossil to be classified, and
forget that the language has a live literature, which is the main concern. We study botany so hard that we miss the charm of the flower

entirely; we pursue the bird with such a spirit of gain and exactitude that a stuffed specimen in the museum would do as well. Biology in the college class means dissecting cats and rats and turtles and frogs; psychology means analogous experimental work in the laboratory. Well, we know a lot that our fathers did not know; our schools and colleges are turning out young men and women with more and more facts, but, so it often seems to me, with less and less manners, less and less reverence, less and less humility, less and less steadfastness of character.

In this age of science we have heaped up great intellectual riches of the pure scientific kind. Our mental coffers are fairly bursting with our stores of knowledge of material things. But what will it profit us if we gain the whole world and lose our own souls? Must our finer spiritual faculties, whence come our love, our reverence, our humility, and our appreciation of the beauty of the world, atrophy? "Where there is no vision, the people perish." Perish for want of a clear perception of the higher values of life. Where there is no vision, no intuitive perception of the great fundamental truths of the inner spiritual world, science will not save us. In such a case our civilization is like an engine running without a headlight. Spiritual truths are spiritually discerned, material and logical truths—all the truths of the objective world—are intellectually discerned. The latter give us the keys of power and the conquest of the earth, but the former alone can save us—save us from the materialism of a scientific age.

The scientific temperament, unrelieved by a touch of the creative imagination, is undoubtedly too prone to deny the existence of everything beyond its ken. But science has its limitations, which its greatest exponents like Tyndall and Huxley are frank to acknowledge.

All questions that pertain to the world within us are beyond the reach of science. Science is the commerce of the intellect with the physical or objective world; the commerce of the soul with the subjective and invisible world is entirely beyond its sphere. The very word "soul" belongs to literature and religion, and not to science. Science has no use for such a word because it stands for something which transcends its categories. Professor Tyndall confessed himself utterly unable to find any logical connection between the molecular activities of the brain-substance and the phenomenon of consciousness.

In trying to deal with such a question, he says, we are on the boundary line of the intellect where the canons of science fail us. Science denies all influence of subjective phenomena over physical processes. In the absence of the empirical fact, science would be bound to deny that a man could raise his arm by an act of volition; only "the phenomena of matter and force come within our intellectual range." There are questions of mind and there are questions of matter; philosophy deals with the former, science with the latter. The world of the unverifiable is the world of the soul, the world of the verifiable is the world of the senses. We have our spiritual being in the one and our physical being in the other, and science is utterly unable to bridge the gulf that separates them.

■ CONSIDERATIONS OF METHOD AND MEANING

1. Burroughs writes that in an age of science, our "anthropomorphic views of creation die hard, and when they are dead we feel orphaned." Considering where science has led us since 1913, to what extent do you consider this statement to be true—more true or less true—today? Have our "anthropomorphic views of creation" died, and do "we feel orphaned"?

2. Do you agree with Burroughs that "with the rise of the scientific habit of mind has come the decline in great creative literature and art"?

3. In this essay, Burroughs offers a powerful critique of education in an age of science, maintaining that education, whether in literature (where, Burroughs says, "we fairly vivisect Shakespeare") or the sciences (where "we study botany so hard we miss the charm of the flower entirely"), dwells too much in imparting facts and not enough in imparting a sense of spirituality. Have you found this to be true in your years of education?

4. Burroughs writes that "Professor Tyndall confessed himself utterly unable to find any logical connection between the molecular activities of the brain-substance and the phenomenon of consciousness." Since 1913, how much further do you think we have come in resolving such mysteries, in bridging the gap between "the world of the unverifiable" and "the world of the verifiable"?

■ POSSIBILITIES FOR WRITING

1. Burroughs writes, "Spiritual truths are spiritually discerned, material and logical truths—all the truths of the objective world—are intellectually discerned. The latter give us the keys of power and the conquest of the earth, but the former alone can save us—save us from the materialism of a scientific age." Write an essay

for your class in which you discuss the extent to which you believe Burroughs's assertion has proved true or untrue. How do you think the statement might apply in the future? Support your discussion with concrete examples.

2. Many people believe that what Burroughs wrote in 1913 is still true (or that if it was not true more than eighty years ago, it is definitely true today): " . . . our schools and colleges are turning out young men and women with more and more facts, but, so it often seems to me, with less and less manners, less and less reverence, less and less humility, less and less steadfastness of character." In an essay for educators, parents, or fellow students, based on your own experience and that of other students you know, refute or support Burroughs's observation, in reference to education and to young men and women today.

■ ALDO LEOPOLD
The Land Ethic

Widely acknowledged as the father of the wildlife conservation movement in this country, Aldo Leopold was born in 1887 in Burlington, Iowa. His early and continuing interest in natural history led him to attend the Sheffield Scientific School at Yale University and, as a graduate student, the School of Forestry at Yale, the first graduate program of its kind in the country. In 1909, after his graduation, he joined the U.S. Forestry Service, which had been established only three years earlier, and went to the Southwest as a forest ranger; he soon became supervisor of the immense Carson National Forest. During his time in the Southwest, Leopold's ideas about land management evolved. Initially, his approach to wildlife management was traditional and production-oriented, geared, for example, toward reducing the numbers of large predators that seemed to pose a threat to livestock; gradually, however, he came to believe that wildlife and land management could not be looked at in fragments, and that a fundamental understanding of larger ecological systems was essential if healthy lands and habitats were to be maintained. In 1924, he took the position of Associate Director of the U.S. Forest Products Laboratory in Madison, Wisconsin, and in 1933 he became chair in Game Management at the University of Wisconsin. Leopold died of a heart attack, helping neighbors fight a grass fire, in 1948.

Leopold's "The Land Ethic" is a seminal document of the Amer-

ican conservation movement. *Although some of Leopold's premises are more generally familiar today than they were in 1949, when* A Sand County Almanac *(from which "The Land Ethic" is taken) was published, many of Leopold's points have still not fully penetrated popular American thinking or official management policies. In "The Land Ethic" Leopold argues that stewardship of the land is both an ethical and a practical necessity; he urges us to look at the complex and related interests of the entire "biotic community" and beyond short-term self-interest in our attitudes about the land and our use of its resources.*

A widely respected scientist, Leopold wrote about conservation for both specialized and more popular audiences. In addition to A Sand County Almanac, *he wrote* Game Management, *a classic text still used today, as well as hundreds of articles about the science and policies of land and wildlife management. He served the United Nations as an advisor on conservation issues, and has been named to the National Wildlife Federation's Conservation Hall of Fame. In 1978, thirty years after his death, Leopold won the John Burroughs Medal for his life's work.*

When god-like Odysseus returned from the wars in Troy, he hanged all on one rope a dozen slave-girls of his household whom he suspected of misbehavior during his absence.

This hanging involved no question of propriety. The girls were property. The disposal of property was then, as now, a matter of expediency, not of right and wrong.

Concepts of right and wrong were not lacking from Odysseus' Greece: witness the fidelity of his wife through the long years before at last his black-prowed galleys clove the wine-dark seas for home. The ethical structure of that day covered wives, but had not yet been extended to human chattels. During the three thousand years which have since elapsed, ethical criteria have been extended to many fields of conduct, with corresponding shrinkages in those judged by expediency only.

The Ethical Sequence

This extension of ethics, so far studied only by philosophers, is actually a process in ecological evolution. Its sequences may be described in ecological as well as in philosophical terms. An ethic, ecologically, is a limitation on freedom of action in the struggle for existence. An ethic, philosophically, is a differentiation of social from anti-social conduct. These are two definitions of one thing. The thing has its origin in the tendency of interdependent individuals or groups to evolve modes of co-operation. The ecologist calls these symbioses. Politics and economics are advanced symbioses in which the original free-for-all competition has been replaced, in part, by co-operative mechanisms with an ethical content.

The complexity of co-operative mechanisms has increased with population density, and with the efficiency of tools. It was simpler, for example, to define the anti-social uses of sticks and stones in the days of the mastodons than of bullets and billboards in the age of motors.

The first ethics dealt with the relation between individuals; the Mosaic Decalogue is an example. Later accretions dealt with the relation between the individual and society. The Golden Rule tries to integrate the individual to society; democracy to integrate social organization to the individual.

There is as yet no ethic dealing with man's relation to land and to the animals and plants which grow upon it. Land, like Odysseus' slave-girls, is still property. The land-relation is still strictly economic, entailing privileges but not obligations.

The extension of ethics to this third element in human environment is, if I read the evidence correctly, an evolutionary possibility and an ecological necessity. It is the third step in a sequence. The first two have already been taken. Individual thinkers since the days of Ezekiel and Isaiah have asserted that the despoliation of land is not only inexpedient but wrong. Society, however, has not yet affirmed their belief. I regard the present conservation movement as the embryo of such an affirmation.

An ethic may be regarded as a mode of guidance for meeting ecological situations so new or intricate, or involving such deferred reactions, that the path of social expediency is not discernible to the average individual. Animal instincts are modes of guidance for the individual in meeting such situations. Ethics are possibly a kind of community instinct in-the-making.

The Community Concept

All ethics so far evolved rest upon a single premise: that the individual is a member of a community of interdependent parts. His instincts prompt him to compete for his place in that community, but his ethics prompt him also to co-operate (perhaps in order that there may be a place to compete for).

The land ethic simply enlarges the boundaries of the community to include soils, waters, plants, and animals, or collectively: the land.

This sounds simple: do we not already sing our love for and obligation to the land of the free and the home of the brave? Yes, but just what and whom do we love? Certainly not the soil, which we are sending helter-skelter downriver. Certainly not the waters, which we assume have no function except to turn turbines, float barges, and carry off sewage. Certainly not the plants, of which we exterminate whole communities without batting an eye. Certainly not the animals, of which we have already extirpated many of the largest and most beautiful species. A land ethic of course cannot prevent the alteration, management, and use of these 'resources,' but it does affirm their right to continued existence, and, at least in spots, their continued existence in a natural state.

In short, a land ethic changes the role of *Homo sapiens* from conqueror of the land-community to plain member and citizen of it. It implies respect for his fellow-members, and also respect for the community as such.

In human history, we have learned (I hope) that the conqueror role is eventually self-defeating. Why? Because it is implicit in such a role that the conqueror knows, *ex cathedra,* just what makes the community clock tick, and just what and who is valuable, and what and who is worthless, in community life. It always turns out that he knows neither, and this is why his conquests eventually defeat themselves.

In the biotic community, a parallel situation exists. Abraham knew exactly what the land was for: it was to drip milk and honey into Abraham's mouth. At the present moment, the assurance with which we regard this assumption is inverse to the degree of our education.

The ordinary citizen today assumes that science knows what makes the community clock tick; the scientist is equally sure that he does not. He knows that the biotic mechanism is so complex that its workings may never be fully understood.

That man is, in fact, only a member of a biotic team is shown by an ecological interpretation of history. Many historical events, hitherto explained solely in terms of human enterprise, were actually biotic interactions between people and land. The characteristics of the land determined the facts quite as potently as the characteristics of the men who lived on it.

Consider, for example, the settlement of the Mississippi valley. In the years following the Revolution, three groups were contending for its control: the native Indian, the French and English traders, and the American settlers. Historians wonder what would have happened if the English at Detroit had thrown a little more weight into the Indian side of those tipsy scales which decided the outcome of the colonial migration into the cane-lands of Kentucky. It is time now to ponder the fact that the cane-lands, when subjected to the particular mixture of forces represented by the cow, plow, fire, and axe of the pioneer, became bluegrass. What if the plant succession inherent in this dark and bloody ground had, under the impact of these forces, given us some worthless sedge, shrub, or weed? Would Boone and Kenton have held out? Would there have been any overflow into Ohio, Indiana, Illinois, and Missouri? Any Louisiana Purchase? Any transcontinental union of new states? Any Civil War?

Kentucky was one sentence in the drama of history. We are commonly told what the human actors in this drama tried to do, but we are seldom told that their success, or the lack of it, hung in large degree on the reaction of particular soils to the impact of the particular forces exerted by their occupancy. In the case of Kentucky, we do not even know where the bluegrass came from—whether it is a native species, or a stowaway from Europe.

Contrast the cane-lands with what hindsight tells us about the Southwest, where the pioneers were equally brave, resourceful, and persevering. The impact of occupancy here brought no bluegrass, or other plant fitted to withstand the bumps and buffetings of hard use. This region, when grazed by livestock, reverted through a series of more and more worthless grasses, shrubs, and weeds to a condition of unstable equilibrium. Each recession of plant types bred erosion; each increment to erosion bred a further recession of plants. The result today is a progressive and mutual deterioration, not only of plants and soils, but of the animal community subsisting thereon. The early settlers did not expect this: on the ciénegas of New Mexico some even cut ditches to hasten it. So subtle has been its progress that few residents of the region are aware of it. It is quite invisible to the tourist who finds this wrecked landscape colorful and charming (as indeed it is, but it bears scant resemblance to what it was in 1848).

This same landscape was 'developed' once before, but with quite different results. The Pueblo Indians settled the Southwest in pre-Columbian times, but they happened *not* to be equipped with range livestock. Their civilization expired, but not because their land expired.

In India, regions devoid of any sod-forming grass have been settled, apparently without wrecking the land, by the simple expedient
of carrying the grass to the cow, rather than vice versa. (Was this the
result of some deep wisdom, or was it just good luck? I do not
know.)

In short, the plant succession steered the course of history; the pioneer simply demonstrated, for good or ill, what successions inhered
in the land. Is history taught in this spirit? It will be, once the concept
of land as a community really penetrates our intellectual life.

The Ecological Conscience

Conservation is a state of harmony between men and land. Despite
nearly a century of propaganda, conservation still proceeds at a
snail's pace; progress still consists largely of letterhead pieties and
convention oratory. On the back forty we still slip two steps backward for each forward stride.

The usual answer to this dilemma is 'more conservation education.' No one will debate this, but is it certain that only the *volume* of
education needs stepping up? Is something lacking in the *content* as
well?

It is difficult to give a fair summary of its content in brief form,
but, as I understand it, the content is substantially this: obey the law,
vote right, join some organizations, and practice what conservation is
profitable on your own land; the government will do the rest.

Is not this formula too easy to accomplish anything worth-while?
It defines no right or wrong, assigns no obligation, calls for no sacrifice, implies no change in the current philosophy of values. In respect
of land-use, it urges only enlightened self-interest. Just how far will
such education take us? An example will perhaps yield a partial answer.

By 1930 it had become clear to all except the ecologically blind
that southwestern Wisconsin's topsoil was slipping seaward. In 1933
the farmers were told that if they would adopt certain remedial practices for five years, the public would donate CCC labor to install
them, plus the necessary machinery and materials. The offer was
widely accepted, but the practices were widely forgotten when the
five-year contract period was up. The farmers continued only those
practices that yielded an immediate and visible economic gain for
themselves.

This led to the idea that maybe farmers would learn more quickly if they themselves wrote the rules. Accordingly the Wisconsin Legislature in 1937 passed the Soil Conservation District Law. This said to farmers, in effect: *We, the public, will furnish you free technical service and loan you specialized machinery, if you will write your own rules for land-use. Each county may write its own rules, and these will have the force of law.* Nearly all the counties promptly organized to accept the proffered help, but after a decade of operation, *no county has yet written a single rule.* There has been visible progress in such practices as strip-cropping, pasture renovation, and soil liming, but none in fencing woodlots against grazing, and none in excluding plow and cow from steep slopes. The farmers, in short, have selected these remedial practices which were profitable anyhow, and ignored those which were profitable to the community, but not clearly profitable to themselves.

When one asks why no rules have been written, one is told that the community is not yet ready to support them; education must precede rules. But the education actually in progress makes no mention of obligations to land over and above those dictated by self-interest. The net result is that we have more education but less soil, fewer healthy woods, and as many floods as in 1937.

The puzzling aspect of such situations is that the existence of obligations over and above self-interest is taken for granted in such rural community enterprises as the betterment of roads, schools, churches, and baseball teams. Their existence is not taken for granted, nor as yet seriously discussed, in bettering the behavior of the water that falls on the land, or in the preserving of the beauty or diversity of the farm landscape. Land-use ethics are still governed wholly by economic self-interest, just as social ethics were a century ago.

To sum up: we asked the farmer to do what he conveniently could to save his soil, and he has done just that, and only that. The farmer who clears the woods off a 75 per cent slope, turns his cows into the clearing, and dumps its rainfall, rocks, and soil into the community creek, is still (if otherwise decent) a respected member of society. If he puts lime on his fields and plants his crops on contour, he is still entitled to all the privileges and emoluments of his Soil Conservation District. The District is a beautiful piece of social machinery, but it is coughing along on two cylinders because we have been too timid, and too anxious for quick success, to tell the farmer the true magnitude of his obligations. Obligations have no meaning without conscience, and the problem we face is the extension of the social conscience from people to land.

No important change in ethics was ever accomplished without an internal change in our intellectual emphasis, loyalties, affections, and convictions. The proof that conservation has not yet touched these foundations of conduct lies in the fact that philosophy and religion have not yet heard of it. In our attempt to make conservation easy, we have made it trivial.

Substitutes for a Land Ethic

When the logic of history hungers for bread and we hand out a stone, we are at pains to explain how much the stone resembles bread. I now describe some of the stones which serve in lieu of a land ethic.

One basic weakness in a conservation system based wholly on economic motives is that most members of the land community have no economic value. Wildflowers and songbirds are examples. Of the 22,000 higher plants and animals native to Wisconsin, it is doubtful whether more than 5 per cent can be sold, fed, eaten, or otherwise put to economic use. Yet these creatures are members of the biotic community, and if (as I believe) its stability depends on its integrity, they are entitled to continuance.

When one of these non-economic categories is threatened, and if we happen to love it, we invent subterfuges to give it economic importance. At the beginning of the century songbirds were supposed to be disappearing. Ornithologists jumped to the rescue with some distinctly shaky evidence to the effect that insects would eat us up if birds failed to control them. The evidence had to be economic in order to be valid.

It is painful to read these circumlocutions today. We have no land ethic yet, but we have at least drawn nearer the point of admitting that birds should continue as a matter of biotic right, regardless of the presence or absence of economic advantage to us.

A parallel situation exists in respect of predatory mammals, raptorial birds, and fish-eating birds. Time was when biologists somewhat overworked the evidence that these creatures preserve the health of game by killing weaklings, or that they control rodents for the farmer, or that they prey only on 'worthless' species. Here again, the evidence had to be economic in order to be valid. It is only in recent years that we hear the more honest argument that predators are members of the community, and that no special interest has the right to exterminate them for the sake of a benefit, real or fancied, to itself.

Unfortunately this enlightened view is still in the talk stage. In the field the extermination of predators goes merrily on: witness the impending erasure of the timber wolf by fiat of Congress, the Conservation Bureaus, and many state legislatures.

Some species of trees have been 'read out of the party' by economics-minded foresters because they grow too slowly, or have too low a sale value to pay as timber crops: white cedar, tamarack, cypress, beech, and hemlock are examples. In Europe, where forestry is ecologically more advanced, the non-commercial tree species are recognized as members of the native forest community, to be preserved as such, within reason. Moreover some (like beech) have been found to have a valuable function building up soil fertility. The interdependence of the forest and its constituent tree species, ground flora, and fauna is taken for granted.

Lack of economic value is sometimes a character not only of species or groups, but of entire biotic communities: marshes, bogs, dunes, and 'deserts' are examples. Our formula in such cases is to relegate their conservation to government as refuges, monuments, or parks. The difficulty is that these communities are usually interspersed with more valuable private lands; the government cannot possibly own or control such scattered parcels. The net effect is that we have relegated some of them to ultimate extinction over large areas. If the private owner were ecologically minded, he would be proud to be the custodian of a reasonable proportion of such areas, which add diversity and beauty to his farm and to his community.

In some instances, the assumed lack of profit in these 'waste' areas has proved to be wrong, but only after most of them had been done away with. The present scramble to reflood muskrat marshes is a case in point.

There is a clear tendency in American conservation to relegate to government all necessary jobs that private landowners fail to perform. Government ownership, operation, subsidy, or regulation is now widely prevalent in forestry, range management, soil and watershed management, park and wilderness conservation, fisheries management, and migratory bird management, with more to come. Most of this growth in governmental conservation is proper and logical, some of it is inevitable. That I imply no disapproval of it is implicit in the fact that I have spent most of my life working for it. Nevertheless the question arises: What is the ultimate magnitude of the enterprise? Will the tax base carry its eventual ramifications? At what point will governmental conservation, like the mastodon, become handicapped by its own dimensions? The answer, if there is any, seems to be in a land ethic, or some other force which assigns more obligation to the private landowner.

Industrial landowners and users, especially lumbermen and stockmen, are inclined to wail long and loudly about the extension of government ownership and regulation to land, but (with notable exceptions) they show little disposition to develop the only visible alternative: the voluntary practice of conservation on their own lands.

When the private landowner is asked to perform some unprofitable act for the good of the community, he today assents only with outstretched palm. If the act costs him cash this is fair and proper, but when it costs only forethought, open-mindedness, or time, the issue is at least debatable. The overwhelming growth of land-use subsidies in recent years must be ascribed, in large part, to the government's own agencies for conservation education: the land bureaus, the agricultural colleges, and the extension services. As far as I can detect, no ethical obligation toward land is taught in these institutions.

To sum up: a system of conservation based solely on economic self-interest is hopelessly lopsided. It tends to ignore, and thus eventually to eliminate, many elements in the land community that lack commercial value, but that are (as far as we know) essential to its healthy functioning. It assumes, falsely, I think, that the economic parts of the biotic clock will function without the uneconomic parts. It tends to relegate to government many functions eventually too large, too complex, or too widely dispersed to be performed by government.

An ethical obligation on the part of the private owner is the only visible remedy for these situations.

The Land Pyramid

An ethic to supplement and guide the economic relation to land presupposes the existence of some mental image of land as a biotic mechanism. We can be ethical only in relation to something we can see, feel, understand, love, or otherwise have faith in.

The image commonly employed in conservation education is 'the balance of nature.' For reasons too lengthy to detail here, this figure of speech fails to describe accurately what little we know about the land mechanism. A much truer image is the one employed in ecology: the biotic pyramid. I shall first sketch the pyramid as a symbol of land, and later develop some of its implications in terms of land-use.

Plants absorb energy from the sun. This energy flows through a circuit called the biota, which may be represented by a pyramid consisting of layers. The bottom layer is the soil. A plant layer rests on the soil, an insect layer on the plants, a bird and rodent layer on the insects, and so on up through various animal groups to the apex layer, which consists of the larger carnivores.

The species of a layer are alike not in where they came from, or in what they look like, but rather in what they eat. Each successive layer depends on those below it for food and often for other services, and each in turn furnishes food and services to those above. Proceeding upward, each successive layer decreases in numerical abundance. Thus, for every carnivore there are hundreds of his prey, thousands of their prey, millions of insects, uncountable plants. The pyramidal form of the system reflects this numerical progression from apex to base. Man shares an intermediate layer with the bears, raccoons, and squirrels which eat both meat and vegetables.

The lines of dependency for food and other services are called food chains. Thus soil-oak-deer-Indian is a chain that has now been largely converted to soil-corn-cow-farmer. Each species, including ourselves, is a link in many chains. The deer eats a hundred plants other than oak, and the cow a hundred plants other than corn. Both, then, are links in a hundred chains. The pyramid is a tangle of chains so complex as to seem disorderly, yet the stability of the system proves it to be a highly organized structure. Its functioning depends on the co-operation and competition of its diverse parts.

In the beginning, the pyramid of life was low and squat; the food chains short and simple. Evolution has added layer after layer, link after link. Man is one of thousands of accretions to the height and complexity of the pyramid. Science has given us many doubts, but it has given us at least one certainty: the trend of evolution is to elaborate and diversify the biota.

Land, then, is not merely soil; it is a fountain of energy flowing through a circuit of soils, plants, and animals. Food chains are the living channels which conduct energy upward; death and decay return it to the soil. The circuit is not closed; some energy is dissipated in decay, some is added by absorption from the air, some is stored in soils, peats, and long-lived forests; but it is a sustained circuit, like a slowly augmented revolving fund of life. There is always a net loss by downhill wash, but this is normally small and offset by the decay of rocks. It is deposited in the ocean and, in the course of geological time, raised to form new lands and new pyramids.

The velocity and character of the upward flow of energy depend on the complex structure of the plant and animal community, much as the upward flow of sap in a tree depends on its complex cellular organization. Without this complexity, normal circulation would presumably not occur. Structure means the characteristic numbers, as well as the characteristic kinds and functions, of the component species. This interdependence between the complex structure of the land and its smooth functioning as an energy unit is one of its basic attributes.

When a change occurs in one part of the circuit, many other parts must adjust themselves to it. Change does not necessarily obstruct or divert the flow of energy; evolution is a long series of self-induced changes, the net result of which has been to elaborate the flow mechanism and to lengthen the circuit. Evolutionary changes, however, are usually slow and local. Man's invention of tools has enabled him to make changes of unprecedented violence, rapidity, and scope.

One change is in the composition of floras and faunas. The larger predators are lopped off the apex of the pyramid; food chains, for the first time in history, become shorter rather than longer. Domesticated species from other lands are substituted for wild ones, and wild ones are moved to new habitats. In this world-wide pooling of faunas and floras, some species get out of bounds as pests and diseases, others are extinguished. Such effects are seldom intended or foreseen; they represent unpredicted and often untraceable readjustments in the structure. Agricultural science is largely a race between the emergence of new pests and the emergence of new techniques for their control.

Another change touches the flow of energy through plants and animals and its return to the soil. Fertility is the ability of soil to receive, store, and release energy. Agriculture, by overdrafts on the soil, or by too radical a substitution of domestic for native species in the superstructure, may derange the channels of flow or deplete storage. Soils depleted of their storage, or of the organic matter which anchors it, wash away faster than they form. This is erosion.

Waters, like soil, are part of the energy circuit. Industry, by polluting waters or obstructing them with dams, may exclude the plants and animals necessary to keep energy in circulation.

Transportation brings about another basic change: the plants or animals grown in one region are now consumed and returned to the soil in another. Transportation taps the energy stored in rocks, and in the air, and uses it elsewhere; thus we fertilize the garden with nitrogen gleaned by the guano birds from the fishes of seas on the other side of the Equator. Thus the formerly localized and self-contained circuits are pooled on a world-wide scale.

The process of altering the pyramid for human occupation releases stored energy, and this often gives rise, during the pioneering period, to a deceptive exuberance of plant and animal life, both wild and tame. These releases of biotic capital tend to becloud or postpone the penalties of violence.

This thumbnail sketch of land as an energy circuit conveys three basic ideas:

(1) That land is not merely soil.

(2) That the native plants and animals kept the energy circuit open; others may or may not.

(3) That man-made changes are of a different order than evolutionary changes, and have effects more comprehensive than is intended or foreseen.

These ideas, collectively, raise two basic issues: Can the land adjust itself to the new order? Can the desired alterations be accomplished with less violence?

Biotas seem to differ in their capacity to sustain violent conversion. Western Europe, for example, carries a far different pyramid than Caesar found there. Some large animals are lost; swampy forests have become meadows or plowland; many new plants and animals are introduced, some of which escape as pests; the remaining natives are greatly changed in distribution and abundance. Yet the soil is still there and, with the help of imported nutrients, still fertile; the waters flow normally; the new structure seems to function and to persist. There is no visible stoppage or derangement of the circuit.

Western Europe, then, has a resistant biota. Its inner processes are tough, elastic, resistant to strain. No matter how violent the alterations, the pyramid, so far, has developed some new *modus vivendi* which preserves its habitability for man, and for most of the other natives.

Japan seems to present another instance of radical conversion without disorganization.

Most other civilized regions, and some as yet barely touched by civilization, display various stages of disorganization, varying from initial symptoms to advanced wastage. In Asia Minor and North Africa diagnosis is confused by climatic changes, which may have been either the cause or the effect of advanced wastage. In the United States the degree of disorganization varies locally; it is worst in the Southwest, the Ozarks, and parts of the South, and least in New England and the Northwest. Better land-uses may still arrest it in the less advanced regions. In parts of Mexico, South America, South Africa, and Australia a violent and accelerating wastage is in progress, but I cannot assess the prospects.

This almost world-wide display of disorganization in the land seems to be similar to disease in an animal, except that it never culminates in complete disorganization or death. The land recovers, but at some reduced level of complexity, and with a reduced carrying capacity for people, plants, and animals. Many biotas currently regarded as 'lands of opportunity' are in fact already subsisting on exploitative agriculture, i.e. they have already exceeded their sustained carrying capacity. Most of South America is overpopulated in this sense.

In arid regions we attempt to offset the process of wastage by reclamation, but it is only too evident that the prospective longevity of reclamation projects is often short. In our own West, the best of them may not last a century.

The combined evidence of history and ecology seems to support one general deduction: the less violent the manmade changes, the greater the probability of successful readjustment in the pyramid. Violence, in turn, varies with human population density; a dense population requires a more violent conversion. In this respect, North America has a better chance for permanence than Europe, if she can contrive to limit her density.

This deduction runs counter to our current philosophy, which assumes that because a small increase in density enriched human life, that an indefinite increase will enrich it indefinitely. Ecology knows of no density relationship that holds for indefinitely wide limits. All gains from density are subject to a law of diminishing returns.

Whatever may be the equation for men and land, it is improbable that we as yet know all its terms. Recent discoveries in mineral and vitamin nutrition reveal unsuspected dependencies in the up-circuit: incredibly minute quantities of certain substances determine the value of soils to plants, of plants to animals. What of the down-circuit? What of the vanishing species, the preservation of which we now regard as an esthetic luxury? They helped build the soil; in what unsuspected ways may they be essential to its maintenance? Professor Weaver proposes that we use prairie flowers to reflocculate the wasting soils of the dust bowl; who knows for what purpose cranes and condors, otters and grizzlies may some day be used?

Land Health and the A-B Cleavage

A land ethic, then, reflects the existence of an ecological conscience, and this in turn reflects a conviction of individual responsibility for the health of the land. Health is the capacity of the land for self-renewal. Conservation is our effort to understand and preserve this capacity.

Conservationists are notorious for their dissensions. Superficially these seem to add up to mere confusion, but a more careful scrutiny reveals a single plane of cleavage common to many specialized fields. In each field one group (A) regards the land as soil, and its function as commodity-production; another group (B) regards the land as a biota, and its function as something broader. How much broader is admittedly in a state of doubt and confusion.

In my own field, forestry, group A is quite content to grow trees like cabbages, with cellulose as the basic forest commodity. It feels no inhibition against violence; its ideology is agronomic. Group B, on the other hand, sees forestry as fundamentally different from agronomy because it employs natural species, and manages a natural environment rather than creating an artificial one. Group B prefers natural reproduction on principle. It worries on biotic as well as economic grounds about the loss of species like chestnut, and the threatened loss of the white pines. It worries about whole series of secondary forest functions: wildlife, recreation, watersheds, wilderness areas. To my mind, Group B feels the stirrings of an ecological conscience.

In the wildlife field, a parallel cleavage exists. For Group A the basic commodities are sport and meat; the yardstick of production are ciphers of take in pheasants and trout. Artificial propagation is acceptable as a permanent as well as a temporary recourse—if its unit costs permit. Group B, on the other hand, worries about a whole series of biotic side-issues. What is the cost in predators of producing a game crop? Should we have further recourse to exotics? How can management restore the shrinking species, like prairie grouse, already hopeless as shootable game? How can management restore the threatened rarities, like trumpeter swan and whooping crane? Can management principles be extended to wildflowers? Here again it is clear to me that we have the same A-B cleavage as in forestry.

In the larger field of agriculture I am less competent to speak, but there seem to be somewhat parallel cleavages. Scientific agriculture was actively developing before ecology was born, hence a slower penetration of ecological concepts might be expected. Moreover the farmer, by the very nature of his techniques, must modify the biota more radically than the forester or the wildlife manager. Nevertheless, there are many discontents in agriculture which seem to add up to a new vision of "biotic farming."

Perhaps the most important of these is the new evidence that poundage or tonnage is no measure of the food-value of farm crops; the products of fertile soil may be qualitatively as well as quantitatively superior. We can bolster poundage from depleted soils by pouring on imported fertility, but we are not necessarily bolstering food-value. The possible ultimate ramifications of this idea are so immense that I must leave their exposition to abler pens.

The discontent that labels itself 'organic farming,' while bearing some of the earmarks of a cult, is nevertheless biotic in its direction, particularly in its insistence on the importance of soil flora and fauna.

The ecological fundamentals of agriculture are just as poorly known to the public as in other fields of land-use. For example, few educated people realize that the marvelous advances in technique made during recent decades are improvements in the pump, rather than the well. Acre for acre, they have barely sufficed to offset the sinking level of fertility.

In all of these cleavages, we see repeated the same basic paradoxes: man the conqueror *versus* man the biotic citizen; science the sharpener of his sword *versus* science the searchlight on his universe; land the slave and servant *versus* land the collective organism. Robinson's injunction to Tristram may well be applied, at this juncture, to *Homo sapiens* as a species in geological time:

> Whether you will or not
> You are a King, Tristram, for you are one
> Of the time-tested few that leave the world,
> When they are gone, not the same place it was.
> Mark what you leave.

The Outlook

It is inconceivable to me that an ethical relation to land can exist without love, respect, and admiration for land and a high regard for its value. By value, I of course mean something far broader than mere economic value; I mean value in the philosophical sense.

Perhaps the most serious obstacle impeding the evolution of a land ethic is the fact that our educational and economic system is headed away from, rather than toward, an intense consciousness of land. Your true modern is separated from the land by many middlemen, and by innumerable physical gadgets. He has no vital relation to it; to him it is the space between cities on which crops grow. Turn him loose for a day on the land, and if the spot does not happen to be a golf links or a 'scenic' area, he is bored stiff. If crops could be raised by hydroponics instead of farming, it would suit him very well. Synthetic substitutes for wood, leather, wool, and other natural land products suit him better than the originals. In short, land is something he has 'outgrown.'

Almost equally serious as an obstacle to a land ethic is the attitude of the farmer for whom the land is still an adversary, or a taskmaster that keeps him in slavery. Theoretically, the mechanization of farming ought to cut the farmer's chains, but whether it really does is debatable.

One of the requisites for an ecological comprehension of land is an understanding of ecology, and this is by no means co-extensive with 'education'; in fact, much higher education seems deliberately to avoid ecological concepts. An understanding of ecology does not necessarily originate in courses bearing ecological labels; it is quite as likely to be labeled geography, botany, agronomy, history, or economics. This is as it should be, but whatever the label, ecological training is scarce.

The case for a land ethic would appear hopeless but for the minority which is in obvious revolt against these 'modern' trends.

The 'key-log' which must be moved to release the evolutionary process for an ethic is simply this: quit thinking about decent land-use as solely an economic problem. Examine each question in terms of what is ethically and esthetically right, as well as what is economically expedient. A thing is right when it tends to preserve the integrity, stability, and beauty of the biotic community. It is wrong when it tends otherwise.

It of course goes without saying that economic feasibility limits the tether of what can or cannot be done for land. It always has and it always will. The fallacy the economic determinists have tied around our collective neck, and which we now need to cast off, is the belief that economics determines *all* land-use. This is simply not true. An innumerable host of actions and attitudes, comprising perhaps the bulk of all land relations, is determined by the land-users' tastes and predilections, rather than by his purse. The bulk of all land relations hinges on investments of time, forethought, skill, and faith rather than on investments of cash. As a land-user thinketh, so is he.

I have purposely presented the land ethic as a product of social evolution because nothing so important as an ethic is ever 'written.' Only the most superficial student of history supposes that Moses 'wrote' the Decalogue; it evolved in the minds of a thinking community, and Moses wrote a tentative summary of it for a 'seminar.' I say tentative because evolution never stops.

The evolution of a land ethic is an intellectual as well as emotional process. Conservation is paved with good intentions which prove to be futile, or even dangerous, because they are devoid of critical understanding either of the land, or of economic land-use. I think it is a truism that as the ethical frontier advances from the individual to the community, its intellectual content increases.

The mechanism of operation is the same for any ethic: social approbation for right actions; social disapproval for wrong actions.

By and large, our present problem is one of attitudes and implements. We are remodeling the Alhambra with a steam-shovel, and we are proud of our yardage. We shall hardly relinquish the shovel, which after all has many good points, but we are in need of gentler and more objective criteria for its successful use.

■ CONSIDERATIONS OF MEANING AND METHOD

1. Why does Leopold open "The Land Ethic" with his reference to Odysseus hanging the slave girls? What function does the reference serve? Does he make any subsequent reference to it in the essay?

2. How does Leopold define an ecological ethic, and how does he define a philosophical ethic? How does he support his assertion, through reasoning, that they "are two definitions of the same thing"?

3. How would you characterize Leopold's writing style in this essay? How do you think his style is adapted to audience and purpose? If he were writing for an audience of land or wildlife management specialists, or an audience of farmers, in what ways might his persuasive strategies and his writing style be different?

4. How does Leopold explain the land—or biotic—pyramid? Why is the pyramid a "truer image" than "the balance of nature" or even the food chain? In the ongoing process of evolution, how has the pyramid changed? In what ways specifically does the human species threaten the stability of the land pyramid?

5. What is the A-B cleavage? To what specific fields does Leopold

apply the A-B paradigm? Can you think of any other conservation or environmental fields or enterprises to which the A-B cleavage might apply? With which group (A or B) does Leopold identify himself?

6. "The Land Ethic" is an explanatory essay, but it is also a persuasive essay. Its effectiveness depends first upon Leopold's ability to explain complex ecological relationships in clear and straightforward terms; its ultimate success as a persuasive essay depends upon a kind of pyramid of reasoning. What arguments form the base of this logical pyramid? What, ultimately, is Leopold asking of you as a reader? Is the essay successful, for you, in both explaining and persuading? Why or why not?

7. This essay was published in 1949. To what extent do you think Leopold's ideas about sound land use policy, practice, and prevailing attitudes about a land ethic have sunk in since then? How much have things changed?

■ POSSIBILITIES FOR WRITING

1. In "The Land Ethic," Leopold describes relatively "resistant biotas" (such as New England, the northwestern United States, and Western Europe) and ones that are more fragile, less resistant (such as the southwestern United States, the Ozarks, and parts of the southern United States). How relatively resistant or fragile is the biota in the part of the country or world you are from? How has the biota there undergone change as a consequence of human settlement and activity? Research, report, and explain the answers to these questions in an essay. Can you project likely future developments? What direction or changes in land use, environmental practices, or citizens' attitudes might you recommend? If you address these last two questions, your essay will take on persuasive dimensions. Beyond your instructor and classmates, what other audiences might appreciate reading your essay? Consider sending a copy to organizations or agencies such as your county farm bureau, the local historical society, city or county planning agencies, local environmental groups, or, in abbreviated form, as a letter to the editor to a local newspaper.

2. "In parts of Mexico, South America, South Africa, and Australia," writes Leopold, "a violent and accelerating wastage [disorganization in the land pyramid] is in progress, but I cannot assess the prospects." From a current perspective, we may be in a better position to assess some of these prospects that eluded Leopold in 1949. Focusing upon a specific region within one of

the broad geographical areas Leopold mentions (a region at environmental risk, such as Brazilian rainforests), research the extent to which "wastage" has progressed since 1949. To what specific factors can it be attributed? Write an essay for your class, reporting what you discover.

3. Leopold writes, "Your true modern is separated from the land by many middlemen and by innumerable physical gadgets. He has no vital relation to it; to him it is the space between cities on which crops grow. . . . In short, land is something he has 'outgrown.'" Do you think that this statement aptly describes most Americans' relationships to and attitudes about the land today? To what extent does it describe your own attitudes? Where are these attitudes, or our changes in attitude, leading us? Explain and support your conclusions in an essay for your class.

■ **LEWIS THOMAS**
Making Science Work

See the headnote for Lewis Thomas's "Ponds" in Chapter 2 (page 107) for biographical information.

Thomas's essay "Making Science Work" is from his book Late Night Thoughts on Listening to Mahler's Ninth Symphony *(1984). Although this essay has a much more serious theme than that of "Ponds," it is, like "Ponds," aimed more at the general than the specialized reader. Here, Thomas argues on behalf of science for readers who may not fully understand science and who may even mistrust it. He acknowledges that the applications of science in the form of technology have gotten us into many of the environmental and societal messes in which we now find ourselves; still, Thomas maintains, science is also our only hope for the future. Thomas's attitude seems to be guardedly optimistic as he urges us to monitor technology carefully but to give science "its head" as we confront the challenges that the next century will bring.*

For about three centuries we have been doing science, trying science out, using science for the construction of what we call modern civilization. Every dispensable item of contemporary technology, from canal locks to dial telephones to penicillin to the Mars Lander, was pieced together from the analysis of data provided by one or another series of scientific experiments—also the technologies we fear the most for the threat they pose to civilization: radioactivity from the stored, stacked bombs or from leaking, flawed power plants, acid rain, pesticides, leached soil, depleted ozone, and increased carbon dioxide in the outer atmosphere.

Three hundred years seems a long time for testing a new approach to human interliving, long enough to settle back for critical appraisal of the scientific method, maybe even long enough to vote on whether to go on with it or not. There is an argument. Voices have been raised in protest since the beginning, rising in pitch and violence in the nineteenth century during the early stages of the industrial revolution, summoning urgent crowds into the streets any day these days on the issue of nuclear energy. Give it back, say some of the voices, it doesn't really work, we've tried it and it doesn't work, go back three hundred years and start again on something else less chancy for the race of man.

The scientists disagree, of course, partly out of occupational bias, but also from a different way of viewing the course and progress of science in the past fifty years. As they see it, science is just at its beginning. The principal discoveries in this century, taking all in all, are the glimpses of the depth of our ignorance about nature. Things that used to seem clear and rational, matters of absolute certainty—Newtonian mechanics, for example—have slipped through our fingers, and we are left with a new set of gigantic puzzles, cosmic uncertainties, ambiguities; some of the laws of physics are amended every few years, some are canceled outright, some undergo revised versions of legislative intent as if they were acts of Congress.

In biology, it is one stupefaction after another. Just thirty years ago we called it a biological revolution when the fantastic geometry of the DNA molecule was exposed to public view and the linear language of genetics was decoded. For a while things seemed simple and clear; the cell was a neat little machine, a mechanical device ready for taking to pieces and reassembling, like a tiny watch. But just in the last few years it has become almost imponderably complex, filled with strange parts whose functions are beyond today's imagining. DNA is itself no longer a straightforward set of instructions on a tape. There are long strips of what seem nonsense in between the genes, edited out for the assembly of proteins but essential nonetheless for the process of assembly; some genes are called jumping genes, moving from one segment of DNA to another, rearranging the messages, achieving instantly a degree of variability that we once thought would require eons of evolution. The cell membrane is no longer a simple skin for the cell; it is a fluid mosaic, a sea of essential mobile signals; an organ in itself. Cells communicate with one another, exchange messages like bees in a hive, regulate one another. Genes are switched on, switched off, by molecules from the outside whose nature is a mystery; somewhere inside are switches which, when thrown one way or the other, can transform any normal cell into a cancer cell, and sometimes back again.

It is not just that there is more to do, there is everything to do. Biological science, with medicine bobbing somewhere in its wake, is under way, but only just under way. What lies ahead, or what *can* lie ahead if the efforts in basic research are continued, is much more than the conquest of human disease or the amplification of agricultural technology or the cultivation of nutrients in the sea. As we learn more about the fundamental processes of living things in general we will learn more about ourselves, including perhaps the ways in which our brains, unmatched by any other neural structures on the planet, achieve the earth's awareness of itself. It may be too much to say that we will become wise through such endeavors, but we can at least come into possession of a level of information upon which a new kind of wisdom might be based. At the moment we are an ignorant species, flummoxed by the puzzles of who we are, where we came from, and what we are for. It is a gamble to bet on science for moving ahead, but it is, in my view, the only game in town.

The near views in our instruments of the dead soil of Mars, the bizarre rings of Saturn, and the strange surfaces of Saturn, Jupiter, Venus, and the rest, literally unearthly, are only brief glances at what is ahead for mankind in the exploration of our own solar system. In theory, there is no reason why human beings cannot make the same journeys in person, or out beyond into the galaxy.

We will solve our energy problems by the use of science, and in no other way. The sun is there, to be sure, ready for tapping, but we cannot sit back in the lounges of political lobbies and make guesses and wishes; it will take years, probably many years, of research. Meanwhile, there are other possibilities needing deeper exploration. Nuclear fission power, for all its present disadvantages, including where on earth to put the waste, can be made safer and more reliable by better research, while hydrogen fusion, inexhaustibly fueled from the oceans and much safer than fission, lies somewhere ahead. We may learn to produce vast amounts of hydrogen itself, alcohol or methane, when we have learned more about the changeable genes of single-celled microorganisms. If we are to continue to burn coal in large amounts, we will need research models for predicting how much more carbon dioxide we can inject into the planet's atmosphere before we run into the danger of melting the ice shelves of western Antarctica and flooding all our coasts. We will need science to protect us against ourselves.

It has become the fashion to express fear of computers—the machines will do our thinking, quicker and better than human thought, construct and replicate themselves, take over and eventually replace us—that sort of thing. I confess to apprehensions of my own, but I have a hunch that those are on my mind because I do not know enough about computers. Nor, perhaps, does anyone yet, not even the computer scientists themselves. For my comfort, I know for sure only one thing about the computer networks now being meshed together like interconnected ganglia around the earth: what they contain on their microchips are bits of information put there by human minds; perhaps they will do something like thinking on their own, but it will still be a cousin of human thought once removed and, because of newness, potentially of immense usefulness.

The relatively new term "earth science" is itself an encouragement. It is nice to know that our own dear planet has become an object of as much obsessive interest to large bodies of professional researchers as a living cell, and almost as approachable for discovering the details of how it works. Satellites scrutinize it all day and night, recording the patterns of its clouds, the temperatures at all parts of its surface, the distribution and condition of its forests, crops, waterways, cities, and barren places. Seismologists and geologists have already surprised themselves over and over again, probing the movement of crustal plates afloat on something or other, maybe methane, deep below the surface, meditating the evidences now coming in for the reality and continuing of continental drift, and calculating with increasing precision the data that describe the mechanisms involved in earthquakes. Their instruments are becoming as neat and informative as medicine's CAT scanners; the earth has deep secrets still, but they are there for penetrating.

The astronomers have long since become physicists, the physicists are astronomers; both are, as well, what we used to call chemists, examining the levels of ammonia or formaldehyde in clouds drifting billions of light-years away, measuring the concentrations of methane in the nearby atmosphere of Pluto, running into paradoxes. Contemporary physics lives off paradox. Niels Bohr said that a great truth is one for which the opposite is also a great truth. There are not so many neutrinos coming from our sun as there ought to be; something has gone wrong, not with the sun but with our knowledge. There are radioastronomical instruments for listening to the leftover sounds of the creation of the universe; the astronomers are dumbstruck, they can hardly hear themselves think.

The social scientists have a long way to go to catch up, but they may be up to the most important scientific business of all, if and when they finally get down to the right questions. Our behavior toward each other is the strangest, most unpredictable, and almost entirely unaccountable of all the phenomena with which we are obliged to live. In all of nature there is nothing so threatening to humanity as humanity itself. We need, for this most worrying of puzzles, the brightest and youngest of our most agile minds, capable of dreaming up ideas not dreamed before, ready to carry the imagination to great depths and, I should hope, handy with big computers but skeptical about long questionnaires and big numbers.

Fundamental science did not become a national endeavor in this country until the time of World War II, when it was pointed out by some influential and sagacious advisers to the government that whatever we needed for the technology of warfare could be achieved only after the laying of a solid foundation of basic research. During the Eisenhower administration a formal mechanism was created in the White House for the explicit purpose of furnishing scientific advice to the President, the President's Science Advisory Committee (PSAC), chaired by a new administration officer, the Science Adviser. The National Institutes of Health, which had existed before the war as a relatively small set of laboratories for research on cancer and infectious disease, expanded rapidly in the postwar period to encompass all disciplines of biomedical science. The National Science Foundation was organized specifically for the sponsorship of basic science. Each of the federal departments and agencies developed its own research capacity, relevant to its mission; the programs of largest scale were those in defense, agriculture, space, and atomic energy.

Most of the country's basic research has been carried out by the universities, which have as a result become increasingly dependent on the federal government for their sustenance, even their existence, to a degree now causing alarm signals from the whole academic community. The ever-rising costs of doing modern science, especially the prices of today's sophisticated and complex instruments, combined with the federal efforts to reduce all expenditures, are placing the universities in deep trouble. Meanwhile, the philanthropic foundations, which were the principal source of funds for university research before the war, are no longer capable of more than a minor contribution to science.

Besides the government's own national laboratories and the academic institutions there is a third resource for the country's scientific enterprise—industry. Up to very recently, industrial research has been conducted in relative isolation, unconnected with the other two. There are signs that this is beginning to change, and the change should be a source of encouragement for the future. Some of the corporations responsible for high technology, especially those involved in energy, have formed solid linkages with a few research universities—MIT and Cal Tech, for example—and are investing substantial sums in long-range research in physics and chemistry. Several pharmaceutical companies have been investing in fundamental biomedical research in association with medical schools and private research institutions.

There needs to be much more of this kind of partnership. The nation's future may well depend on whether we can set up within the private sector a new system for collaborative research. Although there are some promising partnership ventures now in operation, they are few in number; within industry the tendency remains to concentrate on applied research and development, excluding any consideration of basic science. The academic community tends, for its part, to stay out of fields closely related to the development of new products. Each side maintains adversarial and largely bogus images of the other, money-makers on one side and impractical academics on the other. Meanwhile, our competitors in Europe and Japan have long since found effective ways to link industrial research to government and academic science, and they may be outclassing this country before long. In some fields, most conspicuously the devising and production of new scientific instruments, they have already moved to the front.

There are obvious difficulties in the behavior of the traditional worlds of research in the United States. Corporate research is obliged by its nature to concentrate on profitable products and to maintain a high degree of secrecy during the process; academic science, by its nature, must be carried out in the open and depends for its progress on the free exchange of new information almost at the moment of finding. But these are not impossible barriers to collaboration. Industry already has a life-or-death stake in what will emerge from basic research in the years ahead; there can be no more prudent investment for the corporate world, and the immediate benefit for any corporation in simply having the "first look" at a piece of basic science would be benefit enough in the long run. The university science community, for all the talk of ivory towers, hankers day and night for its work to turn out useful; a close working connection with industrial researchers might well lead to an earlier perception of potential applicability than is now the case.

The age of science did not really begin three hundred years ago. That was simply the time when it was realized that human curiosity about the world represented a deep wish, perhaps embedded somewhere in the chromosomes of human beings, to learn more about nature by experiment and the confirmation of experiment. The doing of science on a scale appropriate to the problems at hand was launched only in the twentieth century and has been moving into high gear only within the last fifty years. We have not lacked explanations at any time in our recorded history, but now we must live and think with the new habit of requiring reproducible observations and solid facts for the explanations. It is not as easy a time for us as it used to be: we are raised through childhood in skepticism and disbelief; we feel the need of proofs all around, even for matters as deep as the working of our own consciousness, where there is as yet no clear prospect of proof about anything. Uncertainty, disillusion, and despair are prices to be paid for living in an age of science. Illumination is the product sought, but it comes in small bits, only from time to time, not ever in broad, bright flashes of public comprehension, and there can be no promise that we will ever emerge from the great depths of the mystery of being.

Nevertheless, we have started to do science on a world scale, and to rely on it, and hope for it. Not just the scientists, everyone, and not for the hope of illumination, but for the sure predictable prospect of new technologies, which have always come along, like spray in the wake of science. We need better ways of predicting how a piece of new technology is likely to turn out, better measures available on an international level to shut off the ones that carry hazard to the life on the planet (including, but perhaps not always so much *first of all,* as is usually the only consideration, our own species' life). We will have to go more warily with technology in the future, for the demands will be increasing and the stakes will be very high. Instead of coping, or trying to cope, with the wants of four billion people, we will very soon be facing the needs, probably desperate, of double that number and, soon thereafter, double again. The real challenge to human ingenuity, and to science, lies in the century to come.

I cannot guess at the things we will need to know from science to get through the time ahead, but I am willing to make one prediction about the method: we will not be able to call the shots in advance. We cannot say to ourselves, we need this or that sort of technology, therefore we should be doing this or that sort of science. It does not work that way. We will have to rely, as we have in the past, on science in general, and on basic, undifferentiated science at that, for the new insights that will open up the new opportunities for technological development. Science is useful, indispensable sometimes, but whenever it moves forward it does so by producing a surprise; you cannot specify the surprise you'd like. Technology should be watched closely, monitored, criticized, even voted in or out by the electorate, but science itself must be given its head if we want it to work.

■ CONSIDERATIONS OF MEANING AND METHOD

1. How does Thomas establish the urgency of his argument? How does his argument apply to each of the particular branches of science he mentions?

2. What important distinctions does Thomas make between sciences (or basic science) and technology (or applied science)? How effectively can the two be differentiated?

3. About halfway through his essay, Thomas moves into a discussion of the history of scientific research and development in the United States. What function does this discussion serve in constructing the essay's overall argument?

4. Thomas maintains that academic researchers can rely less on government funding than in the past. Why? Thomas argues that we need more research partnerships between academic institutions and private industry. Why has there been a traditional resistance to such partnerships? What reasons does Thomas cite in arguing that there should be more of these kinds of partnerships? What counterarguments—arguments *against* collaborative research ventures between industry and academic institutions—can you think of? Do you think other research partnerships, such as those between government and industry or between government and universities, should be limited in any way?

5. Examine the specific arguments Thomas provides in paragraphs 12 to 17 of "Making Science Work." Outline the relationship between claim, evidence, and warrant in each of these paragraphs, according to the simplified Toulmin method (see the introduction to this chapter). According to the Toulmin method, is Thomas constructing a logical argument? Does he provide ade-

quate evidence in support of claims? Does he draw logical conclusions, or warrants?

6. In this essay, Thomas argues for this thesis: "Technology should be watched closely, monitored, criticized, even voted in or out by the electorate, but science itself must be given its head if we want it to work (page 457)." To what extent do you agree or disagree with him? If you agree, what in Thomas's arguments did you find most convincing? How much were you inclined to agree with him before you read this essay? If you disagree with him, what in his argument did you find unconvincing? How much were you inclined toward disagreement before reading the essay?

■ POSSIBILITIES FOR WRITING

1. Consider instances in which basic scientific research (atomic or genetic research are just two of many examples) has yielded, or promises to yield, complicated and controversial technologies, ones with both positive and negative consequences and potentials—in other words, problems as well as solutions. In an analytical and argumentative essay, examine one such example, weighing the positive and the negative consequences of the research and evaluating how worthwhile it is. In your example, how can we tell the difference between the basic scientific research and the technologies that evolve from it? In what ways have the technological applications been "watched closely, monitored, criticized, even voted in or out by the electorate," or how might this happen in the future?

Before writing your argument, identify your audience and clarify your purpose. Are you addressing relatively neutral readers, or readers with wide-ranging views? Are you writing to readers whose views are relatively set, whether in agreement with or opposition to your own position? Consider how audience and purpose will affect your argumentative strategies and the tone of your essay.

■ JOYCE CAROL OATES
Against Nature

Joyce Carol Oates is one of the most prolific writers of our age. Since 1963, when her first book, By the North Gate *(a collection of short stories), appeared (when Oates was only twenty-five), she has*

*published an average of two books a year and has written countless
essays and reviews for newspapers, popular magazines, and literary
journals. Oates has written acclaimed novels, short fiction, poetry,
plays, and criticism; she has written realistic fiction and Gothic
novels, as well as nonfiction works on topics ranging from the
poetry of D. H. Lawrence to boxing. Although she certainly cannot
be called a nature writer, she defies labeling in general. "I am
concerned with only one thing," she told a* Chicago Tribune Book
World *interviewer, "the moral and social conditions of my
generation."*

*Oates has been criticized by some critics for the violence that
dominates much of her work, even though much of this violence is
implied, and often psychological rather than physical in nature.
Oates points out that the violence in her writing comes from the
violence that is so pervasive in our culture, not from her. In a* New
York Times Book Review *article, Oates writes, "Uplifting endings
and resolutely cheery world views are appropriate to television commercials but insulting elsewhere." In another essay, entitled "Why
Is Your Writing So Violent?" and published in the* New York
Times Book Review, *Oates writes, "It was once put to me directly,
and no doubt has often been suggested by indirection, that I should
focus my writing on 'aesthetic' and 'subjective' material, in a
manner (for instance) of Jane Austen and Virginia Woolf, that I
should leave the social-psychological issues to men. . . . The question
is always insulting. The question is always ignorant. The question is
always sexist. . . . The serious writer, after all, bears witness."*

*Oates was born in Lockport, New York, in 1938 and raised on
her grandparents' farm in Erie County. Her father was a tool-and-
die designer and her mother was a homemaker. Her parents
recognized early on that their daughter possessed extraordinary
gifts, and they supported her in developing them. Oates graduated
from Syracuse University in 1960 and earned her M.A. at the
University of Wisconsin. She has taught writing and literature at
Princeton University since 1978. Oates lives a disciplined life,
devoting several hours every day to writing. Although the scope is
different, perhaps the thrust of what Oates describes as her process
in writing a novel will strike you as familiar: "The first six weeks is
always a very hard time for me, when I don't have the voice; I
have a lot of notes and I have ideas, and I'm waiting for some sort
of organizing principle or catalyst, some process of crystallization.
. . . Later on, when . . . [I am] really in the process of writing, and*

particularly near the end, when things have coalesced, then it's quite hypnotic. . . . I do a lot of rewriting, revision, though, and I find that very satisfying too. I've come to consider revising a dialogue of sorts with an earlier self; at times, almost, a 'dialogue' with language itself."

A partial list of Oates's works includes the novels A Garden of Earthly Delights *(1967),* Expensive People *(1967),* Them *(1969),* Bellefleur *(1980),* A Bloodsmoor Romance *(1982),* Marya: A Life *(1986), and* You Must Remember This *(1987); the short story collections* Marriages and Infidelities *(1972) and* Where Are You Going, Where Have You Been? *(1974); and the nonfiction works* The Profane Art: Essays and Reviews *(1983),* On Boxing *(1987), and* (Woman) Writer: Occasions and Opportunities *(1988). In the following essay, Oates criticizes what she sees as an overly romanticized view of nature in both prevailing cultural attitudes and popular writing about nature.*

We soon get through with Nature. She excites an expectation which she cannot satisfy.

—*Thoreau,* Journal, *1854*

Sir, if a man has experienced the inexpressible, he is under no obligation to attempt to express it.

—*Samuel Johnson*

The writer's resistance to Nature.

It has no sense of humor: in its beauty, as in its ugliness, or its neutrality, there is no laughter.

It lacks a moral purpose.

It lacks a satiric dimension, registers no irony.

Its pleasures lack resonance, being accidental; its horrors, even when premeditated, are equally perfunctory, "red in tooth and claw" et cetera.

It lacks a symbolic subtext—excepting that provided by man.

It has no (verbal) language.

It has no interest in ours.

It inspires a painfully limited set of responses in "nature-writers"

—REVERENCE, AWE, PIETY, MYSTICAL ONENESS.
It eludes us even as it prepares to swallow us up, books and all.

*   *   *

I was lying on my back in the dirt-gravel of the towpath beside the
Delaware-Raritan Canal, Titusville, New Jersey, staring up at the sky
and trying, with no success, to overcome a sudden attack of tachycardia that had come upon me out of nowhere—such attacks are always
"out of nowhere," that's their charm—and all around me Nature
thrummed with life, the air smelling of moisture and sunlight, the
canal reflecting the sky, red-winged blackbirds testing their spring
calls—the usual. I'd become the jar in Tennessee, a fictitious center,
or parenthesis, aware beyond my erratic heartbeat of the numberless
heartbeats of the earth, its pulsing pumping life, sheer life, incalcula-
ble. Struck down in the midst of motion—I'd been jogging a minute
before—I was "out of time" like a fallen, stunned boxer, privileged
(in an abstract manner of speaking) to be an involuntary witness to
the random, wayward, nameless motion on all sides of me.

Paroxysmal tachycardia is rarely fatal, but if the heartbeat acceler-
ates to 250–270 beats a minute you're in trouble. The average attack
is about 100–150 beats and mine seemed so far to be about average;
the trick now was to prevent it from getting worse. Brainy people try
brainy strategies, such as thinking calming thoughts, pseudo-mystic
thoughts, *If I die now it's a good death,* that sort of thing, *if I die this
is a good place and a good time,* the idea is to deceive the frenzied
heartbeat that, really, you don't care: you hadn't any other plans for
the afternoon. The important thing with tachycardia is to prevent
panic! you must prevent panic! otherwise you'll have to be taken by
ambulance to the closest emergency room, which is not so very nice a
way to spend the afternoon, really. So I contemplated the blue sky
overhead. The earth beneath my head. Nature surrounding me on all
sides, I couldn't quite see it but I could hear it, smell it, sense it—
there is something *there,* no mistake about it. Completely oblivious
to the predicament of the individual but that's only "natural" after
all, one hardly expects otherwise.

When you discover yourself lying on the ground, limp and unre-
sisting, head in the dirt, and helpless, the earth seems to shift forward
as a presence; hard, emphatic, not mere surface but a genuine force—
there is no other word for it but *presence.* To keep in motion is to
keep in time and to be stopped, stilled, is to be abruptly out of time,

in another time-dimension perhaps, an alien one, where human language has no resonance. Nothing to be said about it expresses it, nothing touches it, it's an absolute against which nothing human can be measured. . . . Moving through space and time by way of your own volition you inhabit an interior consciousness, a hallucinatory consciousness, it might be said, so long as breath, heartbeat, the body's autonomy hold; when motion is stopped you are jarred out of it. The interior is invaded by the exterior. The outside wants to come in, and only the self's fragile membrane prevents it.

The fly buzzing at Emily's death.

Still, the earth *is* your place. A tidy grave-site measured to your size. Or, from another angle of vision, one vast democratic grave.

Let's contemplate the sky. Forget the crazy hammering heartbeat, don't listen to it, don't start counting, remember that there is a clever way of breathing that conserves oxygen as if you're lying below the surface of a body of water breathing through a very thin straw but you *can* breathe through it if you're careful, if you don't panic, one breath and then another and then another, isn't that the story of all lives? careers? Just a matter of breathing. Of course it is. But contemplate the sky, it's there to be contemplated. A mild shock to see it so blank, blue, a thin airy ghostly blue, no clouds to disguise its emptiness. You are beginning to feel not only weightless but near-bodiless, lying on the earth like a scrap of paper about to be blown off. Two dimensions and you'd imagined you were three! And there's the sky rolling away forever, into infinity—if "infinity" can be "rolled into"—and the forlorn truth is, that's where you're going too. And the lovely blue isn't even blue, is it? isn't even there, is it? a mere optical illusion, isn't it? no matter what art has urged you to believe.

＊　　＊　　＊

Early Nature memories. Which it's best not to suppress.

. . . Wading, as a small child, in Tonawanda Creek near our house, and afterward trying to tear off, in a frenzy of terror and revulsion, the sticky fat black bloodsuckers that had attached themselves to my feet, particularly between my toes.

. . . Coming upon a friend's dog in a drainage ditch, dead for several days, evidently the poor creature had been shot by a hunter and left to die, bleeding to death, and we're stupefied with grief and horror but can't resist sliding down to where he's lying on his belly, and we can't resist squatting over him, turning the body over . . .

... The raccoon, mad with rabies, frothing at the mouth and tearing at his own belly with his teeth, so that his intestines spilled out onto the ground ... a sight I seem to remember though in fact I did not see. I've been told I did not see.

❊   ❊   ❊

Consequently, my chronic uneasiness with Nature-mysticism; Nature-adoration; Nature-as-(moral)-instruction-for-mankind. My doubt that one can, with philosophical validity, address "Nature" as a single coherent noun, anything other than a Platonic, hence discredited, is-ness. My resistance to "Nature-writing" as a genre, except when it is brilliantly fictionalized in the service of a writer's individual vision—Thoreau's books and *Journal,* of course—but also, less known in this country, the miniaturist prose-poems of Colette (*Flowers and Fruit*) and Ponge (*Taking the Side of Things*)—in which case it becomes yet another, and ingenious, form of storytelling. The subject is *there* only by the grace of the author's language.

Nature has no instructions for mankind except that our poor beleaguered humanist-democratic way of life, our fantasies of the individual's high worth, our sense that the weak, no less than the strong, have a right to survive, are absurd.

In any case, where *is* Nature? one might (skeptically) inquire. Who has looked upon her/its face and survived?

❊   ❊   ❊

But isn't this all exaggeration, in the spirit of rhetorical contentiousness? Surely Nature is, for you, as for most reasonably intelligent people, a "perennial" source of beauty, comfort, peace, escape from the delirium of civilized life; a respite from the ego's ever-frantic strategies of self-promotion, as a way of insuring (at least in fantasy) some small measure of immortality? Surely Nature, as it is understood in the usual slapdash way, as human, if not dilettante, *experience* (hiking in a national park, jogging on the beach at dawn, even tending, with the usual comical frustrations, a suburban garden), is wonderfully consoling; a place where, when you go there, it has to take you in?—a palimpsest of sorts you choose to read, layer by layer, always with care, always cautiously, in proportion to your psychological strength?

Nature: as in Thoreau's upbeat Transcendentalist mode ("The indescribable innocence and beneficence of Nature,—such health, such cheer, they afford forever! and such sympathy have they ever with our race, that all Nature would be affected . . . if any man should ever for a just cause grieve"), and not in Thoreau's grim mode ("Nature is hard to be overcome but she must be overcome").

Another way of saying, not *Nature-in-itself* but *Nature-as-experience.*

The former, Nature-in-itself, is, to allude slantwise to Melville, a blankness ten times blank; the latter is what we commonly, or perhaps always, mean when we speak of Nature as a noun, a single entity—something of *ours.* Most of the time it's just an activity, a sort of hobby, a weekend, a few days, perhaps a few hours, staring out the window at the mind-dazzling autumn foliage of, say, Northern Michigan, being rendered speechless—temporarily—at the sight of Mt. Shasta, the Grand Canyon, Ansel Adams's West. Or Nature writ small, contained in the back yard. Nature filtered through our optical nerves, our "senses," our fiercely romantic expectations. Nature that pleases us because it mirrors our souls, or gives the comforting illusion of doing so. As in our first mother's awakening to the self's fatal beauty—

> I thither went
> With unexperienc't thought, and laid me down
> On the green bank, to look into the clear
> Smooth Lake, that to me seem'd another Sky.
> As I bent down to look, just opposite,
> A Shape within the watr'y gleam appear'd
> Bending to look on me, I started back,
> It started back, but pleas'd I soon return'd,
> Pleas'd it return'd as soon with answering looks
> Of sympathy and love; there I had fixt
> Mine eyes till now, and pin'd with vain desire.

—in these surpassingly beautiful lines from Book IV of Milton's *Paradise Lost.*

Nature as the self's (flattering) mirror, but not ever, no, never, Nature-in-itself.

＊　　＊　　＊

Nature is mouths, or maybe a single mouth. Why glamorize it, romanticize it, well yes but we must, we're writers, poets, mystics (of a sort) aren't we, precisely what else are we to do but glamorize and romanticize and generally exaggerate the significance of anything we focus the white heat of our "creativity" upon . . . ? And why not Nature, since it's there, common property, mute, can't talk back, allows us the possibility of transcending the human condition for a while, writing prettily of mountain ranges, white-tailed deer, the purple crocuses outside this very window, the thrumming dazzling "life-force" we imagine we all support. Why not.

Nature *is* more than a mouth—it's a dazzling variety of mouths. And it pleases the senses, in any case, as the physicists' chill universe of numbers certainly does not.

*   *   *

Oscar Wilde, on our subject: "Nature is no great mother who has borne us. She is our creation. It is in our brain that she quickens to life. Things are because we see them, and what we see, and how we see it, depends on the Arts that have influenced us. To look at a thing is very different from seeing a thing. . . . At present, people see fogs, not because there are fogs, but because poets and painters have taught them the mysterious loveliness of such effects. There may have been fogs for centuries in London. I dare say there were. But no one saw them. They did not exist until Art had invented them. . . . Yesterday evening Mrs. Arundel insisted on my going to the window and looking at the glorious sky, as she called it. And so I had to look at it. . . . And what was it? It was simply a very second-rate Turner, a Turner of a bad period, with all the painter's worst faults exaggerated and over-emphasized."

(If we were to put it to Oscar Wilde that he exaggerates, his reply might well be: "Exaggeration? I don't know the meaning of the word.")

*   *   *

Walden, that most artfully composed of prose fictions, concludes, in the rhapsodic chapter "Spring," with Henry David Thoreau's contemplation of death, decay, and regeneration as it is suggested to him, or to his protagonist, by the spectacle of vultures feeding off carrion. There is a dead horse close by his cabin and the stench of its decomposition, in certain winds, is daunting. Yet: " . . . the assurance it gave me of the strong appetite and inviolable health of Nature was my compensation. I love to see that Nature is so rife with life that myriads can be afforded to be sacrificed and suffered to prey upon one another; that tender organizations can be so serenely squashed out of existence like pulp,—tadpoles which herons gobble up, and tortoises and toads run over in the road; and that sometimes it has rained flesh and blood! . . . The impression made on a wise man is that of universal innocence."

Come off it, Henry David. You've grieved these many years for your elder brother John, who died a ghastly death of lockjaw; you've never wholly recovered from the experience of watching him die. And you know, or must know, that you're fated too to die young of consumption. . . . But this doctrinaire Transcendentalist passage ends *Walden* on just the right note. It's as impersonal, as coolly detached, as the Oversoul itself: a "wise man" filters his emotions through his brain.

Or through his prose.

*   *   *

Nietzsche: "We all pretend to ourselves that we are more simple-minded than we are: that is how we get a rest from our fellow men."

*   *   *

Once out of nature I shall never take
My bodily form from any natural thing,
But such a form as Grecian goldsmiths make
Of hammered gold and gold enamelling
To keep a drowsy Emperor awake;
Or set upon a golden bough to sing
To lords and ladies of Byzantium
Of what is past, or passing, or to come.

> —*William Butler Yeats*
> *"Sailing to Byzantium"*

Yet even the golden bird is a "bodily form taken from (a) natural thing." No, it's impossible to escape!

*   *   *

The writer's resistance to Nature.

Wallace Stevens: "In the presence of extraordinary actuality, consciousness takes the place of imagination."

*   *   *

Once, years ago, in 1972 to be precise, when I seemed to have been another person, related to the person I am now as one is related, tangentially, sometimes embarrassingly, to cousins not seen for decades,—once, when we were living in London, and I was very sick,

I had a mystical vision. That is, I "had" a "mystical vision"—the heart sinks: such pretension—or something resembling one. A fever-dream, let's call it. It impressed me enormously and impresses me still, though I've long since lost the capacity to see it with my mind's eye, or even, I suppose, to believe in it. There is a statute of limitations on "mystical visions" as on romantic love.

I was very sick, and I imagined my life as a thread, a thread of breath, or heartbeat, or pulse, or light, yes it was light, radiant light, I was burning with fever and I ascended to that plane of serenity that might be mistaken for (or *is*, in fact) Nirvana, where I had a waking dream of uncanny lucidity—

My body is a tall column of light and heat.

My body is not "I" but "it."

My body is not one but many.

My body, which "I" inhabit, is inhabited as well by other creatures, unknown to me, imperceptible—the smallest of them mere sparks of light.

My body, which I perceive as substance, is in fact an organization of infinitely complex, overlapping, imbricated structures, radiant light their manifestation, the "body" a tall column of light and blood-heat, a temporary agreement among atoms, like a high-rise building with numberless rooms, corridors, corners, elevator shafts, windows. . . . In this fantastical structure the "I" is deluded as to its sovereignty, let alone its autonomy in the (outside) world; the most astonishing secret is that the "I" doesn't exist!—but it behaves as if it does, as if it were one and not many.

In any case, without the "I" the tall column of light and heat would die, and the microscopic life-particles would die with it . . . will die with it. The "I," which doesn't exist, is everything.

But Dr. Johnson is right, the inexpressible need not be expressed. And what resistance, finally? There is none.

✻   ✻   ✻

This morning, an invasion of tiny black ants. One by one they appear out of nowhere—that's their charm too!—moving single file across the white Parsons table where I am sitting, trying without much success to write a poem. A poem of only three or four lines is what I want, something short, tight, mean, I want it to hurt like a white-hot wire up the nostrils, small and compact and turned in upon itself with the density of a hunk of rock from the planet Jupiter. . . .

But here come the black ants: harbingers, you might say, of spring. One by one by one they appear on the dazzling white table and one by one I kill them with a forefinger, my deft right forefinger, mashing each against the surface of the table and then dropping it into a wastebasket at my side. Idle labor, mesmerizing, effortless, and I'm curious as to how long I can do it, sit here in the brilliant March sunshine killing ants with my right forefinger, how long I, and the ants, can keep it up.

After a while I realize that I can do it a long time. And that I've written my poem.

■ CONSIDERATIONS OF MEANING AND METHOD

1. What was your initial response to this essay's title? Do you think the title was an effective choice on Oates's part?

2. Do you agree with Oates's characterization of nature in the opening section of her essay? What accounts for "the writer's resistance to Nature," according to Oates?

3. In terms of style, in what ways might this essay be considered untraditional, and in what respects traditional? Do you think Oates's style in "Against Nature" has anything to do with the essay's subject? Did you find her style effective? Why or why not? (After you have considered your response to this question, you might compare this essay to others Oates has written.)

4. How would you describe Oates's tone in this essay? Cite specific words, phrases, sentences, or passages that illustrate tone. How does tone relate to Oates's subject and purpose?

5. In the second and third sections of her essay and again in the concluding two sections, Oates recounts personal experiences with nature, one relating a series of childhood memories; one an adult experience, many years old; one a recent experience; and one an immediate experience that coincides with her writing the essay you have just read. How do Oates's experiences of nature change over time? How are they related? In an essay about writing about nature, what does this personal dimension add?

6. Oates classifies Thoreau's books and his *Journal* as "fictionalized in the service of a writer's individual vision," and she calls *Walden* "that most artfully composed of prose fictions." These might be considered back-handed compliments, since these writings by Thoreau are nonfiction works. What does Oates mean? Although Oates does not mention Emerson in her essay, she

might well have done so. What do you think her view would be of Emerson's "Nature"?

7. What is your personal response to the essay's closing passage?

■ **POSSIBILITIES FOR WRITING**

1. Consider what Oates has to say about the human tendency to understand "Nature-as-experience," "Nature as the self's (flattering) mirror, but not ever, no, never, Nature-in-itself" (page 464). In a reasoned argument, contemplate the old philosophical question, "If a tree falls in the woods, and no one is around to hear it, does it make a sound?" Speculate in your essay upon the implications of the question as well as its possible answers. Share your essay with other students in your class who have written on the same subject.

■ **BENJAMIN JUN**

Consciousness

In the following statement, student writer Benjamin Jun introduces his essay, "Consciousness." In the essay he refers to several other essays, including David Quammen's "Animal Rights and Beyond" in Chapter 8 (page 548); John Burroughs's "In the Noon of Science," excerpted in this chapter (page 425); and an essay by Francis Krick and Christof Koch, "The Problem of Consciousness," which Jun located in his university library in his attempt to answer some questions left unanswered by the other readings.

I was born in Ohio and raised in the suburbs of Washington, D.C. As an aspiring electrical engineer and "techie" at heart, I often feel more at home near computers and small electronic boxes than in situations requiring creativity. My mind enjoys asking questions and helping others do the same, which is one reason I am assisting in teaching high school students and am considering teaching high school, at least for a while, after graduation.

The essays I refer to in my paper taught me about some of the touchier, subjective issues in science, technology, and ethics. Many writers who write about these subjects don't use the language of scientific analysis. I chose this topic after wondering how attempting a scientific definition of "consciousness" would affect my understanding of Tom Regan's and David Quammen's arguments about animal experimentation. In searching for additional sources, I think I was secretly hoping to find someone in a lab coat who would give a stringent definition of consciousness and list the implications.

After I began this essay, I realized my sources discussed radically different parts of the issue. Science is not ready to address the problem of consciousness, let alone make judgments based on its definition. In earlier drafts, I found myself wavering between perspectives that left too big a question mark about the nature of consciousness and perspectives that treated scientific theory as something entirely separate from moral questions. I settled on a conclusion that confronts the issues that fall between the cracks of "objective" science and morality.

What is consciousness? *Webster's Dictionary* defines it as the state of awareness of one's own existence, sensations, thoughts, and surroundings. To be conscious is to have the essence of soul and spirit; it is a defining characteristic of human nature. Most would agree that it is a process residing in the brain. And yet, it seems self-defeating to explain a foundation for humanity with a chemical process. What beings qualify as having consciousness, and how does it operate? Can a scientific evaluation of consciousness be used to classify sentient life?

In human society, a person's degree of consciousness is a factor in measuring his or her value of life. The process of aging is feared because the brain (and consciousness) diminishes in capability. People who are alive but have no consciousness are classified as brain-dead. For a human being, consciousness is required to live a significant life. In "Animal Rights and Beyond," David Quammen tells us that animal rights activists try to protect "significant" animals with the same criteria. Quammen reports that animal rights advocate Tom Regan defines animals with inherent value as those who can "perceive and remember . . . have beliefs, desires, and preferences . . . [and those who] are sentient and have an emotional life." Regan looks for "boundaries of consciousness" to determine if it is ethically appropriate to use an animal for testing.

Scientists have been searching for these boundaries. In "The Problem of Consciousness," Francis Crick and Christof Koch report their studies of consciousness in which they collected data on the human visual system. The visual system reads images from the optic nerve and sends signals based on the information to portions of the brain. The distant goal of Crick and Koch is to find "an all-embracing theory" of consciousness. Scientists believe that most computations carried out by the brain are unconscious, and only the later, active processes of interpretation are the fundamental element of consciousness. This is consistent with Regan's usage of consciousness; while "lower" organisms might have the first stage of unconscious reflexes, "higher" organisms will have the second-stage capacity to interpret these reflexes.

Crick and Koch conclude that the neocortex of the brain plays a central role in conscious thought. The neocortex interprets sensory information which has been processed and filtered by unconscious, reflexive computations inside the brain. It identifies incoming sensory information by matching the information with categories it has learned, and sends signals once a match has been made. Consciousness, therefore, involves the incorporation of past memories. Because visual and auditory interpretation are vitally important to conscious thought, Crick and Koch believe the human neocortex has evolved to use sophisticated techniques to "track" multiple concepts and squeeze high-speed performance from relatively slow neurons. Crick and Koch cite an experiment which clocked impressive neocortex reaction times of 0.06 second when the human brain was exposed to new visual scenes.

Thus, the essence of consciousness appears to be the analytical process connecting memory and new information, which uses a highly developed part of the brain. With this scientific definition of consciousness, we can support animal activists and classify the animal species which possess "inherent value." Quammen mocks animal rights activist Peter Singer's "damning stare" at the oyster, but it does seem that an oyster might only have unconscious thought. It is conceivable that scientists may some day be able to devise a test—perhaps by monitoring brain activity—to determine if an animal is capable of conscious thought. It is still, however, likely to be a long time until science narrows the broad line between conscious and unconscious beings. Until then, more subjective judgments about the gray areas of sentient life will further the debate on animal rights.

A more important question might be whether or not any scientific definition of inherent value absolves humans from responsibility in their treatment of lower beings. Quammen points out the absurdity of suggesting experiments on "lesser" retarded or brain-dead patients. Any conclusive definition which judges the inherent value of beings spurs many new questions. Do human beings have a responsibility to protect lower creatures? Could the true basis of consciousness be beyond the grasp of science—is there a consciousness of God, or a collective human consciousness? Perhaps Regan and Singer should look for a new definition of "inherent value," or find another way to face the human responsibility question.

The possibility that cognition may one day be scientifically defined does not assist either argument, for or against animal experimentation. With current research, a definition of consciousness exists which disputes Quammen's universally equalizing conclusion that "Life is life." However, if scientists can quantify a thought process on a chemical and cellular level, will we "lose our souls," as Burroughs writes in "In the Noon of Science"? Does locating the "all-embracing theory" cheapen (and therefore justify testing and eating) the lesser animals, and might it reduce humankind to the same level? When consciousness becomes a precise, predictable, and programmed science, it will introduce many more questions than it answers.

Additional Source

Crick, Francis, and Christof Koch. "The Problem of Consciousness." *Scientific American*, July 1992: 152–9.

■ CONSIDERATIONS OF MEANING AND METHOD

1. After you have read Jun's essay all the way through, look at it paragraph by paragraph and in your journal or notebook, outline it in list form, articulating the main idea of each paragraph in one sentence, phrase, or question. Is the essay well-organized? Is the progression of ideas clear and logical? Are the individual paragraphs unified?

2. Jun opens his essay with a dictionary definition of "consciousness." Does this definition provide a helpful point of reference? How does Jun elaborate upon this definition?

3. What does Jun's use of Crick and Koch's essay as a source contribute to his discussion of consciousness? How does he relate this source to David Quammen's essay "Animal Rights and Beyond" (Chapter 8) and to Peter Singer's and Tom Regan's views, to which Quammen refers in his essay? Why and how does Jun use John Burroughs's "In the Noon of Science" as a source?

4. This is an essay in which many more questions are asked than answers given. Does this weaken the essay? Does the essay have an identifiable thesis? If so, what is it, where does Jun state it, and does it justify Jun's question-driven approach?

5. How would you define consciousness? Has your definition of consciousness become more or less certain as a consequence of reading and thinking more about it?

6. Jun suggests that the presence or absence of consciousness—assuming that it can be satisfactorily defined and identified—may not be the real point in ascertaining our moral obligations to "lower beings." Do you think consciousness should be the determining factor in directing our treatment of other living things? If not, what should guide our behavior?

■ POSSIBILITIES FOR WRITING

1. Many essays in this chapter's readings are, implicitly if not explicitly, about human consciousness, in its practical, ethical, and spiritual dimensions. Select two or three readings from this chapter for comparison, and in an analytical essay discuss human consciousness as a theme in each. How does consciousness define our position in nature, according to each writer? What dilemmas does consciousness pose? How similar or dissimilar, finally, are the views of the writers whose works you are comparing? How do their views compare to your own?

MAKING CRITICAL CONNECTIONS:
QUESTIONS FOR DISCUSSION, RESEARCH, AND WRITING

1. In his essay, "In the Noon of Science" (1913), John Burroughs maintains that "Spiritual truths . . . alone can save us—save us from the materialism of science." Lewis Thomas in "Making Science Work" (1983) maintains that although "it is a gamble to bet on science for moving ahead . . . it is . . . the only game in town." To what extent are the two writers in opposition? After all these years, does Burroughs still have something to teach us about "spiritual truths" in an age of science? Does the fact that Thomas is writing so recently give his argument more credibility? In discussion or in an analytical essay, compare and evaluate Burroughs's and Thomas's arguments about how far and where science can and should take us. To your mind, what, if anything, is required to temper or to balance our scientific understanding and endeavors?

2. Ralph Waldo Emerson writes at the conclusion of the excerpt from "Nature," "Man carries the world in his head, the whole astronomy and chemistry suspended in a thought. Because the history of nature is characterized in his brain, therefore is he the prophet and discoverer of her secrets." Lewis Thomas writes in "Making Science Work," "As we learn more about the fundamental processes of living things in general we will learn more about ourselves, including perhaps the ways in which our brains, unmatched by any other neural structures on the planet, achieve the earth's awareness of itself." To what extent are Emerson and Thomas expressing the same, or different, ideas about the nature and consequences of human consciousness and the role human consciousness assigns to us in the natural order? How do their perspectives differ?

3. In discussion or writing, compare Aldo Leopold's land ethic—which, he says, requires us to make not only superficial changes in our practices but "an internal change in our intellectual emphasis, loyalties, affections, and convictions"— with what you have learned through readings in this text about various Native American people's views about human beings' relationships to the land.

4. In an analytical essay, discuss the work of one or more writer represented in this text in light of Joyce Carol Oates's critique in "Against Nature," her claim that nature "inspires a painfully limited set of responses in 'nature-writers'— REVERENCE, AWE, PIETY, MYSTICAL ONENESS." If you tend to agree with

Oates's view, at least as it applies to the work (or works) you are analyzing, explain and illustrate why and how the writing demonstrates this "painfully limited set of responses." If you tend to disagree with her, show how the writer's (or writers') response (or responses) in the writing you are analyzing is not "painfully limited." Early in your analysis, you might consider how you would define or classify "nature-writing." In the conclusion of your argument, consider to what extent you can generalize about the genre of writing about nature and about writers who work in this genre.

CHAPTER 8

(*Greig Crana*, The Picture Cube)

ISSUE BY ISSUE:
THREE READING CYCLES

RHETORIC: INVESTIGATING AND ARGUING

DIFFERENCES BETWEEN INVESTIGATING AND ARGUING

The difference between writing that investigates and writing that argues is really a difference in the intent of the writer. A writer's intent may be to a large extent determined by an assignment. A teacher may ask you, for example, to write an argument as opposed to a report, or an employer may ask you to write a report as opposed to an argument. Your intent and the purposes of your writing will be adapted to other circumstances as well, namely to what you discover in learning about your subject. The kinds of conclusions you draw, and how emphatically you state them, will depend upon how well your conclusions are warranted by the evidence. In order to draw honest conclusions in writing, you must approach investigation, and even argumentation, with flexibility and an open mind.

Investigations do not necessarily produce arguments. If you are assigned the job of writing a report, you are being asked to educate yourself about a subject and to report to your reader what you have learned. Generally you are not being asked to argue for one interpretation or position over another. Report writing requires careful research, in one or a combination of its many forms, and the expression of what you learn in coherent writing.

Although investigations do not necessitate arguments, arguments *do* require investigation; in fact, arguments are built upon investigations. How can writers reasonably defend positions or recommend policies if they have not first educated themselves carefully about the subject at hand by considering and analyzing a range of other interpretations or options? Effective argumentation requires investigation first and foremost.

Investigations and arguments both demand evidence. You will remember, from the introduction to Chapter 7 ("Reasoning"), that *claims of fact* require support in the form of evidence just as *claims of value* do. You will also recall, from earlier chapters, that evidence can come in various forms or in a combination of forms. Evidence may arise from personal experience, and from your own memory. It can take the form of direct observation and analysis of a phenomenon (a scientific experiment, a sunset, the behavior of people or animals, for instance), an event (a film, a ballet, or an ice hockey game), or primary texts (the short story you are writing about or the text of the Emancipation Proclamation, if that is your subject).

When you need more than your existing knowledge, direct observation, and/or your own perspective in building a stable platform from which to report, to argue, or to report and then argue, you will seek out primary sources and/or secondary source material. Primary sources include original research that you yourself conduct. You may decide to interview people, either because they are uniquely qualified experts on your subject, or because they are *not* unique, but instead are representative of many of us. Primary sources may also include questionnaires (including polls or surveys) of your own design in which you ask a large number of people the same questions in order to find any trend or consensus among their answers.

Whether your intent is to investigate and report or to investigate and argue, you will probably begin with a motivating question that will direct your research. This question, whether it is relatively simple (*What is the sea otter's range?*) or relatively complex (*What is eugenics?*), might be answered by facts alone. Often, however, the questions that motivate our investigations through research begin simply enough, but, in the process of discovering their answers, we learn that there are more pertinent or more crucial questions we might ask, questions that involve judgments: *What more can we do to protect the sea otter, an endangered species? Is genetic therapy just another form of eugenics?* Often, if we are given the leeway in an investigative writing assignment, we begin with investigative questions which will evolve into interpretive or argumentative questions. Answering investigative questions will require assembling a body of factual information from research.

INVESTIGATING

In investigative writing, your job is to learn as much about your subject as you can. Your primary purpose in writing will be to inform your reader. In the academic world, as well as in the larger world, there are many forms and many specific applications of investigative writing. Not only journalists, but scientists, doctors, professionals in business, law, and government, and many others, investigate and report the results of their investigations to readers who need to be informed, whether they are specialized or general readers. In this chapter's readings, Sharman Apt Russell's "Range War" and Amy Virshup's "Perfect People?" are investigative essays. Russell's essay explores a range of views about the controversial issue of private grazing rights on public land, and Virshup's piece arose from an assignment from *New York* magazine to investigate the choices people make about genetic testing and, consequently, abortion. Neither writer argues for one position over another in these essays; both writers' jobs are to expose general readers, as they themselves were exposed, to a range of experience and a range of views, letting readers draw their own conclusions. What readers expect from an investigation is a clear and accurate accounting of the facts from a researcher-writer whose objectivity they can trust.

In investigating, it may be hard to keep an open mind and to suspend your judgments when it is appropriate to do so, but these are essential to the fundamental purpose of investigative writing, which is to inform, not to persuade. When you investigate and report, recognizing your biases and suspending your judgments is easier said than done, of course. While recognizing that pure objectivity is impossible, we must not excuse ourselves from the obligation to retain as much objectivity as possible. The degree to which we succeed or fail to maintain relative objectivity in investigating and reporting will be evident in the sources of information we choose and the ways in which we use these sources in our writing.

Allowing Your Motivating Question to Direct Your Investigation

If your motivating question were *What is the sea otter's range?*, the information you would need to answer it would be fairly easy to come by in secondary sources such as a handbook to marine mammals. If your motivating question were *What more can we do to protect the sea otter, an endangered species?*, you would probably have a wider range of options in the kinds of sources you could go to for relevant information. The same handbook to marine mammals would be useful here, as well as other secondary source material, such as books and articles in magazines and newspapers that would describe what steps have already been taken to protect this species and, perhaps, what additional steps have been proposed, and by whom. Some sources might offer arguments for or against taking further steps, or for or against one method of protection over another. Primary documents might also be useful, even essential, to your investigation since you would need to learn, and to report to your reader, under what laws this species is currently protected. Primary sources in the form of interviews with experts would provide useful information and perspectives as well.

If you were to adjust your specific interest (and thus your motivating question) so that it leaned more toward gauging popular attitudes, your new question might be, *How important do college students think the protection of endangered species is?* Although the kinds of sources mentioned above might still be useful in providing background information, the emphasis in research for this motivating question will revolve around other kinds of primary research, probably in the form of interviews of a cross-section of college students or a survey or poll of many students. You would want to ask them questions that would reveal their attitudes on the subject of protection of endangered species.

In investigating, you are obliged to keep an open mind, but your sources will not necessarily feel the same obligation. Very often, strong views, arguments, and biases exist in primary sources and in secondary sources as well. It can be difficult indeed to absorb and analyze information while resisting the temptation to draw premature conclusions. However, in investigation this is exactly your job: to learn and to confirm the facts, and to consult sources that represent a fair range of views.

Planning and Conducting Interviews

Interviews can provide extraordinarily useful sources of information that may simply not be available, in written and other forms of record, in libraries. The kinds of people you might choose to talk with about your subject, and your reasons for selecting them, will depend upon the kinds of information you are looking for. You will want to interview people with a particular area of expertise that is directly relevant to your subject, especially if you want information that is perhaps even too current to be in print or an expert's individual perspective. But you may also interview nonexperts, if you want to discover their personal habits or their beliefs and attitudes about your subject. You will have to be careful, even in interviewing experts, not to draw broader conclusions than are warranted by your sources. One opinion—even an expert opinion—is not the final word on a subject, and interviews with experts generally need to be balanced with other sources, including information from other experts, either through further interviews or through secondary sources.

Interviewing generally involves a good deal more than sitting down for a spontaneous chat. You will first need to decide whom you want to interview. In locating experts to interview, look first within your college community (where a large number of experts in a number of areas of specialty will probably be available). Your college catalogue and directory will give you names, office telephone numbers, and specific areas of expertise of faculty, researchers, and administrators at your school. If, for example, you are investigating a question of anthropology (say your motivating question is *What Indian tribes inhabited this area before it was colonized by Europeans?*), you will be able to tell which professors in the anthropology department are likely to have expertise in this area by noting what courses they teach.

In your residential community, depending on the subject you are investigating, there may be many kinds of experts who would be glad to share their experience and knowledge with you. If your motivating question were *Among women, who supported the suffragist movement in this country and who opposed it, and why?*, you might interview several elderly women in your community. If your motivating question were *How expensive is it to run an environmentally responsible business?*, you might find several business people—those who do and those who do not operate "green" businesses—who would be willing to talk with you.

In arranging an interview, whether with a person with professional expertise or with a carefully selected representative person, be knowledgeable, be polite, and be confident. You will want to know enough about your subject and your interviewee in advance to know what questions you want to ask; especially with experts, you should not ask the kinds of basic questions for which you could easily find answers in an introductory book or a simple article on the subject. This would be a waste of the interviewee's time, and he or she would know and probably resent it.

First, call your potential subject, state your name, your purpose for calling, and your request ("Hello, this is James Tate from Southern State

University. I'm writing a paper about local Indian cultures, and I wonder if you might have a half hour some time this week to sit down with me and answer a few specific questions I have."). Generally, people are happy, if their time permits, to discuss subjects that fascinate them, even with strangers. It is important, though, to conduct an interview on the interviewee's terms as much as possible. Meet your interviewee on his or her ground, or at a place of his or her choice. Remember to confirm the date, time, and place of your meeting, and get directions in advance.

Think carefully before the interview about the specific questions you would like to ask. Write them down legibly so that you will have no trouble reading them. By the time the interview rolls around, however, you should be so familiar with your questions that you will need make only passing reference to them.

It is an excellent idea to tape-record interviews, especially if there is the possibility that you will want to quote your source or if the material covered in the interview is at all complex. Virtually no one can accurately recall direct quotations from memory or even transcribe quotations perfectly, word-for-word, on the spot. If you plan to tape-record the interview, make sure to ask your interviewee's permission in advance. One disadvantage of taping is that it may make some subjects nervous. But it will aid both your interviewee's and your own confidence if you take the time to familiarize yourself with your equipment in advance in order to avoid fumbling or technical problems. Usually, after a few minutes, neither you nor your subject will remember that a recording is being made. (If you do record, be sure to take notes as a back-up in case of technical failures.)

Show up, appropriately dressed, a few minutes early for your interview, if possible, so that you will be relaxed and focused when you begin. You will probably want to begin by getting additional information about your interviewee and confirming the information you already have, including the spelling of your subject's name, his or her position and title, and any degrees, licences, or personal experience that qualify him or her as an expert on the subject you are investigating. Also make note of the date, time, and location of the interview; this information will be relevant in your writing when you acknowledge and cite your source. You might also note any details about the location of the meeting (especially if it is home turf for the interviewee), as well as details of appearance and personality that could be useful in your writing.

If, during the course of the interview, the interviewee says something that is not quite clear to you, or that you would like to have him or her

confirm or rephrase, ask for clarification. A phrase like "So, you're saying that ..." should produce the desired result. If your interviewee gets
off on a tangent, look for an opportunity to bring him or her back to
the subject by asking one of your prepared questions. On the other
hand, tangents can sometimes be very productive, especially if you
know enough about the subject to help guide them by asking spontaneous but relevant questions. If the opportunity arises to learn something new and unexpected, be prepared to seize it.

Limit your interview to the length of time you agreed upon in advance with your interviewee. Try not to run overtime; no doubt your
interviewee has other things to do as well. When you are finished, thank
your interviewee for the time and help, shake hands, and leave. It is a
good idea to follow up the interview with a thank-you note. Your interviewee might also appreciate your sending a copy of your paper when it
is finished.

If you have taken notes as a way of keeping a record of your interview, go over them immediately following the interview. At this point
they will be fresh in your mind, while within a day or so they will probably become somewhat obscure. Many investigative writers who do a
lot of interviewing will transcribe their written notes immediately following an interview, either on their computers or on note cards that can
be easily coordinated with other note cards from other primary or secondary source material. If you have tape-recorded the interview, it is a
good idea to transcribe the tape—or at least the most relevant parts—
and then make note cards from your transcription.

If you locate a good interview subject who lives too far away for you
to arrange a personal meeting, you may have to conduct your interview
by phone, mail, fax, or electronic mail. Most of the basic guidelines for
successful interviewing above will apply to interviews conducted in
these other forms as well, but with some additions. If you are interviewing over the telephone, you will want, in your initial call, to set up with
your interviewee a convenient date and time (specifying length of time)
to call back, when both you and your interviewee will be prepared to
talk at length. If you would like to tape-record your phone interview, it
is essential that you ask permission since your taping will not be obvious to your interviewee. As your interviewee is doing you a favor in
giving you his or her time, you should plan to pay any long-distance
charges.

If you are conducting your interview by mail, fax, or electronic mail,
you will need to write out a list of questions, keeping them as well-
focused and as brief as possible. Be careful to phrase your questions

well, and make sure that they are neatly typed. In a cover letter, provide any relevant information about your project, along with the date by which you need your interviewee's answers, allowing him or her a reasonable length of time to respond. Remember that a written response is likely to take your interviewee more time and effort than a spoken response. Be prepared to follow up with a telephone or written inquiry if you have not received your interviewee's response within the time promised. When you interview by mail, always enclose with your questions a self-addressed stamped envelope so that your interviewee can simply drop his or her response into the nearest mailbox.

Sometimes, as you proceed with your investigation, other specific questions will arise, and you might realize that you would like to ask one or more of your interviewees a few follow-up questions. Usually, since you have established a relationship with your interviewee, this can be accomplished over the phone. Give your interviewee a call and ask if you can pose your follow-up questions then and there, if convenient, or at a future time that would be more convenient for him or her. Discovering that you have follow-up questions is not a sign that you have failed in your investigation in any way; it simply indicates that, as your own understanding of your subject grows, you are recognizing what specific gaps need to be filled so that you can answer your motivating question well.

Designing Questionnaires

When you need to gather specific information from groups of people in order to ascertain and compare their habits, behavior, attitudes, values, or beliefs, a questionnaire of your own design can provide you with exactly the kind of information you need. If you are careful not to generalize too broadly from your limited sampling, the results of a survey you conduct may be extremely valuable in indicating both the range of, and trends in, people's behavior and thought, whether these people are randomly selected or identified with a particular group.

Your purpose in surveying is to learn about people's habits or attitudes in relation to a subject. If you wanted to learn more about how recycling works, you might interview an expert such as the manager of a recycling company. If, on the other hand, you wanted to learn something about people's recycling habits or their attitudes about recycling, you might survey a cross-section of the population, asking them a series of questions about their habits and/or attitudes.

Some surveys are *random;* in conducting a random survey, you would select people to respond to your survey on a random basis, your goal being to find respondents of a wide range of ages, professions, beliefs, and affiliations. For example, if you were conducting a random survey of people's habits and attitudes about recycling, you might position yourself, at different times of day over several days, at several different locations in your town, asking people at random if they would briefly respond to the questions of your survey. Other surveys target people who are identified with particular groups. For example, if you wanted to know, specifically, about the recycling habits and attitudes of students at your school, you would want to station yourself at various locations on your campus, at various times of day and night, over several days, to pose your questions to students. You are targeting a specific group, but within your sampling, you will select your subjects randomly.

If your questions are very brief and can be answered "yes" or "no" or nearly as simply, you could ask these questions orally and tally your respondents' oral answers on the spot. Often, however, a written questionnaire is more reliable, and through it you can gather more information. Whether the questions or the answers to them are oral or written, you must pose the same questions to everyone.

In designing your questionnaire, you will need to consider carefully what, if any, background information you need. Is it important that respondents give their names, or is anonymity better? Do you need to know where your respondents live, and if so how precisely? Is information about gender, race, or ethnicity relevant? Do you need to know anything about your respondents' professions or academic majors, their hobbies, or their political affiliations? Do not ask more questions than are absolutely necessary; necessity is determined, of course, by the direct relevance that questions and answers have to your subject.

There are several kinds of questions you might ask in your questionnaire. *Two-way questions* ask the respondent to choose one of two answers:

> *Is curbside recycling provided where you live?*
>   __ *yes* __ *no*
> *If curbside recycling is provided in your community, is it*
>   __ *a municipal service or* __ *a private service?*
> *Do you recycle?*
>   __ *yes* __ *no*

The answers to two-way questions can be extremely useful, and they are certainly easy enough to analyze, but since they limit the range of answers, they can, under some circumstances, be of limited use.

Complex questions are often better answered with a range of possible answers. *Multiple choice questions* provide for this range, while at the same time directing responses into categories that lend themselves to relatively simple analysis:

> *What materials do you recycle?*
> __ *glass*   __ *plastics*   __ *aluminum*   __ *newspaper*
> __ *cardboard*   __ *toxic material*   __ *other (please specify)*
> *Where do you recycle?*
> __*curbside*   __ *city landfill*   __*private landfill*
> __ *other (please specify)*
> *If you have curbside recycling, which materials does your recycling service pick up?*
> __ *glass*   __ *plastics*   __ *aluminum*   __ *newspaper*
> __ *cardboard*   __ *toxic material*   __ *other (please specify)*

A third kind of question, the *open-ended question*, provides the widest leeway in individual responses as well as the greatest challenge in analyzing and categorizing answers:

> *Why do you, or do you not, recycle?*
>
> *Where do you think the money should come from to pay for recycling programs?*
>
> *What kinds of recycling services, if any, do you think your city should provide?*

Such questions are complicated, and the answers to them are highly subjective. In some cases, you might not want to limit your respondents' answers in any way, especially if you are looking for their own ideas rather than a confirmation of your own. Answers to open-ended questions are obviously difficult to report statistically, but they may offer information and ideas that are hard to come by through more limited kinds of questioning.

Possibilities for Structuring
the Investigative Essay

In Chapter 3 of this text, we learned about description of process, as well as about comparison and contrast, and in Chapter 6 about cause-and-effect analysis. Any of these modes of development may offer an effective structural framework to an investigative essay. Whichever rhetorical approach you take in the overall structure of your investigative writing, you are likely to employ—in the process of developing your ideas—other modes of development as well, including definition, classification, description, and narration. Illustrations and examples will be essential in providing evidence with which you will support your claims.

In writing an investigative essay, you will want to convince your reader that you yourself are a reliable source of information, that you know the facts and have investigated the important implications of your subject. You will want to feel, along with your reader, that you have answered your motivating question carefully and thoroughly. An investigative essay may be an end in itself, when your purpose in writing is to report or to explain. But your investigation may also be part of a larger picture, a different purpose: investigation is essential to effective argumentation, and the purpose of argumentative writing, beyond reporting and explaining, is to persuade.

ARGUING

The argument is probably the most widely practiced form of college writing. Arguments arise quite naturally out of any writing assignment that asks us to think carefully about a text, an idea, or an issue and to draw a strong conclusion from it. You want to persuade your reader that your line of reasoning is logical and that your conclusion is not only sound but worth confirming or adopting.

"Winning" an argument may not always be possible; indeed, it is not always desirable. The ideal purpose of argumentative writing, on a personal level, is to allow the writer to learn and think about a complex and often controversial subject in depth, and, on the basis of his or her new-found expertise, to draw a conclusion warranted by the evidence. At the level of public discourse, the ideal purpose of argumentation is to promote dialogue about complicated ideas and issues to which there is not one right answer or one correct solution. Generally, as we wrestle with these ideas and issues in the academic and social arenas, our public thought and public policies are shaped slowly, and formed by the ongoing debate. The solutions we arrive at inevitably involve compromise.

It is important, in argumentative writing, to avoid arguments that arise from preconceived notions, knee-jerk reactions, or ignorance of the facts or the range of possible viewpoints or solutions. It is also important to realize that a strong conclusion in argument does not have to be absolute. The argumentative writer may argue a definitive "yes" or "no" answer quite convincingly if such a conclusion is warranted. However, he or she may also argue for the necessity to question or reevaluate our actions or assumptions in complicated situations, or for caution in moving forward. If the writer has investigated carefully and worked hard to reach an honest conclusion, this is not a weak conclusion.

The Audience for Argument

When you write an argument, you may assume, as many writers do, that your reader is someone of the opposing camp; this assumption often produces arguments that are defensive and even hostile. In coming to terms with your purpose in writing argumentatively and in determining your approach and your tone in argumentative writing, remember that although someone with a diametrically opposed view may be among your readers, more of your readers will very likely be undecided or even sympathetic. It is unlikely that anyone's argument will cause someone whose mind is already made up to abruptly change his or her views; it is much more likely that our reasonable and articulate arguments will persuade neutral readers to lean in our direction, or motivate readers who are already inclined to sympathize with our position to take some concrete action.

With a more realistic picture of the reader to whom you are addressing your argument and of your purpose in writing, you may be able to avoid one of the pitfalls of argumentation: defensiveness and hostility. The following long-accepted rules of fair play apply to argumentation:

- Appeal to logic in order to persuade your reader.
- You may appeal to your readers' emotions as well, but only if in doing so you do not distort the issue or unfairly represent people who hold opposing views.

- Acknowledge the complexity of the issue and the strengths of opposing views.
- Support your claims with convincing evidence.

If you have a strong and logical position and have arrived at a conclusion that is based on an understanding of the issue and is warranted by convincing evidence, you have nothing to lose and everything to gain in acknowledging complexity, including opposing views, and in adopting a reasonable instead of a hostile or inflammatory tone. Such an argument will persuade those who, like you, respect the process of open inquiry and fair debate.

Building upon Investigation: Evaluating Others' Views

Rarely is it the case that there are only two sides to an issue. Generally, there are degrees of adherence to a complicated proposition. A more accurate representation than simply pro and con on a complex issue might look like this:

Yes!   Yes, if . . .   Yes, but . . .   Maybe so . . .   I don't know
Maybe not . . .   No, but . . .   No, if . . .   No!

In investigating your subject and evaluating others' arguments relating to it, you will certainly want to read arguments that occupy both extreme ends of the spectrum; exposing yourself to one extreme without exposing yourself to the other will hardly produce a balanced view of your own. An argument could be made, however, that the most productive source within this range is the one that draws the "I don't know" conclusion. This source is likely to be more of an investigation than an argument itself. If the writer has done his or her homework, has carefully examined the facts and the range of views him- or herself, and still arrived at an "I don't know" conclusion, it is likely that the writer will give you a fairly objective overview of the subject and a good sense of its complexity. This kind of source can provide, in investigation, an excellent counterpoint, at the very least, to more extreme views and biased arguments.

Almost by definition, the more categorical an argument is, the more likely the source is to be biased. A biased source is not by any means an invalid source; it is crucial, however, in your investigation of sources, that you recognize bias when you see it and scrutinize it carefully. Bias is reflected not only in the intensity and extremity of the argument, but often in the qualifications of the source itself. For example, a source may have strong political or other affiliations that will signal bias. Sometimes a writer will confess his or her own bias. Edward Abbey, for instance, in his speech in this chapter's readings, "Even the Bad Guys Wear White Hats," freely admits that he has a strong prejudice against ranchers who use public lands for private grazing of their cattle. In other cases, the critical reader must search out bias in its more subtle forms. For example, Cynthia Riggs does not state in her essay, "Access to Public Lands: A National Necessity," that the Exxon Corporation holds the copyright to her writing, a fact that indicates bias. Thus, in investigating your sources, it is extremely important to learn as much as possible about your sources themselves. There are many works in the reference section of your library that provide valuable biographical information about authors whose writing you may encounter in your investigations of a wide range of subjects. One such work is *Contemporary Authors,* a comprehensive and current biographical dictionary, indexed and published in many volumes by Gale Research, Incorporated.

Where a piece of writing is published can also sometimes indicate bias, especially in the case of articles appearing in magazines and journals. Just as many periodical publications have an area of speciality, some magazines have strong political agendas. An article about the spotted owl controversy and its effect on the logging industry in the Northwest in *The New Republic* (a politically conservative magazine) will cover the same subject quite differently than an article on the same subject in *Mother Jones* (a politically liberal publication). Another very useful source in the reference section of your library, *Magazines for Libraries* by Bill Katz and Linda Sternberg, will provide descriptions of a wide range of periodical publications, including their specialized interests and political and other affiliations.

Although the existence of bias, reflected in the individual writer or in the publication in which the writing appears, does not invalidate the source, it does mean that in your investigation you must search out viewpoints which balance that source and contribute to a fair range of views.

Developing an Effective and Fair Argument

The writer of argument may harbor a deep and secret fear. A writer who has begun with a preconceived notion of what the conclusion should be may dread running across convincing evidence that will raise doubts about his or her governing assumptions or preconceptions. This will require that the writer examine the real complexity of the issue, unfamiliar facts relating to it, and unfamiliar points of view. If this happens to you, know that you have your work cut out for you. But know, as well, that you are on the road to developing a truly worthwhile argument, one that is the consequence of real learning on your part, as well as a potential source of it for your reader.

In investigating your subject and developing a fair, honest, and effective argument, you might use the following points as a checklist:

- *Know the facts.* Do you have an accurate understanding of the facts that provide the foundation for effective argumentation? Test yourself by asking the journalist's questions: do you know *who? what? where? when? how?* and *why?* as they apply to your subject?

- *Know the range of views.* Are you acknowledging the real complexity of the issue? Do you understand the full spectrum of views that relate to the position for which you are arguing? Do these views include not only the positions at the extremes, but more moderate voices as well? Are you in a position to acknowledge the strengths of opposing views and to refute those you disagree with while emphasizing your position?

- *Be logical.* Does your position make sense? Do you have sufficient evidence to support it, or are you relying on oversimplifications or unfair appeals to your reader's emotions in attempting to "prove" your assertions? Are you confronting the real issues head-on?

- *Be honest.* Are your conclusions warranted by the evidence? Are you generalizing too broadly or being too absolute? Are you forcing conclusions in an attempt to make a strong argument? If you are, adjust your conclusion so that it is fairly supported by the evidence, or try to find more, or more convincing, evidence in support of your conclusion.

What Every Argument Needs

Every argument needs four things: a claim to be supported; an audience to be persuaded; exigence, that is, a reason for the argument to be made; and reasons in support of the claim.

A claim. Your claim is the position that you will support in your argument, and it will be stated in your thesis. Let's use the proposal for continuation of the ban on motorboats on Jewel Lake, from the previous chapter's introduction, as a working example of the various ways in which you might arrive at your thesis.

The existing ban on motorboats on Jewel Lake is being challenged by developers of a new condominium complex under construction at Jewel Lake. The developers think that suspension of the motorboat ban would make their condominiums more valuable; they'd like to feature a marina in their community plan. They've made a formal proposal for lifting the ban to the local planning commission, and there are plenty of residents who also support lifting the ban.

Let's say you have grown up on Jewel Lake, and since childhood you have valued the serenity of the lake. You enjoy quiet canoeing on the lake and the opportunities it provides you for observing wildlife. The idea of motorboats zigzagging noisily about the lake is abhorrent to you. Your thesis might arise from your gut reaction to the situation, an immediate response based upon personal experience: *The ban on motorboats on Jewel Lake should be maintained.*

You might, however, arrive at this same thesis through a process of investigation. If you are undecided about whether or not the ban should be lifted or maintained, you might investigate the pros and cons of the issue, allowing yourself to arrive at a conclusion as a consequence of what you learn. After looking into the issue, you decide that the reasons to maintain the ban outweigh those for lifting it: *The ban on motorboats on Jewel Lake should be maintained.*

However you arrive at your thesis, you will need more than this claim to mount an argument. In targeting an audience for your argument, establishing exigence for it and assembling reasons in support of your claim, you will have the choice of structuring your argument deductively or inductively. With a deductive strategy, you would state your thesis early on, and then go about proving its merits with evidence. If you use an inductive strategy, you would probably pose the motivating question (*Should the ban on motorboats at Jewel Lake be lifted?*) early on, then guide the reader through an analysis of the issue, building your evidence and your argument toward the conclusion, in which you state your thesis.

An audience. Your strategy in argumentation depends a great deal on who your audience is. Whom are you trying to persuade in arguing your claim? Are you trying to convince the condominium developers to withdraw their proposal for lifting the ban? This would be an ambitious goal indeed, and probably not a very realistic one. This audience is too diametrically opposed to your position to be convinced. Would you like to try to convince other residents of the community who currently support lifting the ban that it would not be in their best interest to do so? This is probably a more realistic goal, since you might be able to persuade this audience, or some of it, with convincing evidence that the adverse effects of motorboating on the lake will affect their quality of life. Perhaps the most effective audience to be targeted are people who have not yet made up their minds on the issue, people who need information and a convincing argument to be urged in the direction of the position you support. A fourth possible audience would be people who, like you, do not want the ban to be lifted and whom you might call upon to take action to defeat this proposal.

The tone of your argument and the way in which you structure it will vary, depending upon audience and purpose.

Exigence. Exigence is the need for an argument to be made at a particular time and place, its reason for being. In establishing exigence, you must consider who your audience is and be prepared to convince the audience of the relevance of the issue in their lives.

If you were to attend a meeting of the planning commission to which interested community members were invited to discuss the question of whether or not the motorboat ban should be lifted, you would not have to work at all toward establishing exigence. Everyone attending the meeting, no matter what their stand on the issue, would be there exactly because they realized the importance of the debate. If you stood up at this meeting and spoke, you would have to state your claim clearly; you would have to take into consideration whom you were speaking to and what, exactly, you wanted to convince them to do; and you would have to provide convincing reasons in support of your claim. But exigence, in this case, is a given.

In written arguments, however, you will need to work harder to establish exigence, explaining to uninformed, distracted, or neutral readers why the issue you consider important should be important to them. The first step is to get your reader to consider your argument; the second is to argue persuasively. If, for example, your argument took the form of a letter to the editor of the *Jewel Lake Daily News*, you would need to inform your reader of the debate and convince him or her early on that something significant was at stake; otherwise, your reader might move on to the comic page or the crossword puzzle instead of reading your argument. In your opening paragraph, then, you might describe the future unpleasant sights and sounds of Jewel Lake if the motorboat ban is lifted, and through this image create a vivid picture of how the life of community members, including your reader, might be affected.

Reasons. No matter how strong your thesis, how clear your under-standing of audience and purpose in writing, and how well you have es-tablished exigence, your argument will not be an argument unless you provide convincing reasons in support of your claim and back these rea-sons up with strong evidence.

Before you begin to assemble reasons in support of your claim, you should examine that claim for underlying assumptions. When you claim that the ban on motorboats should be maintained, for example, you are assuming that one kind of experience of Jewel Lake is more valuable than another—that a quiet, undisturbed lake without gasoline slicks provides for a more rewarding experience than a day of water-skiing. This may seem obvious to you, but it will not necessarily be obvious to your reader. In order to provide a convincing foundation for your argu-ment, you will have to explain your reasons for believing that your un-derlying assumption is valid.

Your two most fundamental reasons for opposing the lifting of the motorboat ban on Jewel Lake are that (a) motorboat activity, including noise, will disrupt wildlife, and (b) motorboats will pollute the lake. You may have arrived at these reasons through common sense, or they may have become evident to you through your investigation of the issue. In either case, you will need to supply your reader with concrete evidence in support of these claims of fact through observation and ex-perience, primary sources, and/or secondary source material. Simply as-serting that motorboat traffic will disrupt wildlife and pollute the lake will not do. To what extent is wildlife likely to be disturbed? Which an-imals stand to be most affected, and in what specific ways will they be affected? What form would water pollution take? How widespread would it be? How exactly would this pollution affect wildlife and human beings? Concrete evidence detailing and supporting these asser-tions may come from observations and reports of what has occurred in and around other, similar lakes on which motorboat traffic is permitted.

In the process of assembling reasons in support of your claims, you may discover additional reasons that will bolster your argument. For example, you may discover statistics on motorboat accidents that con-vince you, and that may convince your reader, that heavy motorboat traffic on a small lake can be more than a noisy inconvenience to those who are not enthusiasts; it can pose a public danger.

You may also discover, as you learn more about the issue, that your argument is not as cut and dried as you imagined it to be. You may dis-cover articulate arguments made by motorboat enthusiasts who main-tain that they, too, have a fundamental right to enjoy public waterways in their own fashion. These are responsible people who obey the law and who, like you, enjoy the outdoors. You may discover that in resolving this issue, other communities have reached what, for most of their citizens, have been satisfactory compromises. In one lake community, for example, motorboats are allowed in certain areas but forbidden in others, where waterfowl nest and where public swimming areas are located.

If, after considering all the evidence, you are still convinced that motorboat traffic should continue to be banned at Jewel Lake, you will need to anticipate opposing views and refute them in your argument. If some opposing views seem reasonable to you, you will need to grant them credit. In the process of investigating an issue, of weighing costs and considering reasonable solutions to complex problems, you may find that you change your mind. You may, having started convinced that a total ban on motorboat traffic was the only solution, come to believe that a compromise is workable. Be prepared to argue strongly for your position, but be prepared, too, to shift your position if this is where the most convincing evidence leads you.

Structuring the Argumentative Essay

In classical rhetoric, a formal argument contains six parts in the following order:

- In the *introduction*, the writer will announce the subject of the argument and find an interesting way to capture the reader's attention. In classic argumentation, the writer will also advertise his or her own good character in the introduction.

- In the next part, the *narration*, the writer will provide a context for the argument, including background information; a clear statement of the problem at hand; definition of key terms; and/or an examination of assumptions that provide a foundation for the argument.

- In the *partition*, the writer will state his or her claim and outline the key points of the argument to follow.

- The *argument* itself will enumerate the writer's reasons, and the writer will provide concrete evidence to support them.

- In the *refutation*, the writer will state key opposing arguments and respond to them with counterarguments, crediting opposing views where warranted.

- The *conclusion* will summarize the positive arguments in support of the thesis, and here the writer will propose a solution, if the subject involves a problem to which a solution is possible. The conclusion will generally bring the argument full circle, referring back to the introduction.

The structure of classical argumentation may provide a useful model, a point of reference as you plan effective strategy in writing your own arguments, but it is not a sure-fire formula for effective argumentation. Although strong arguments will tend to share fundamental characteristics, writers of effective arguments will adapt their specific strategies to the contexts in which their arguments exist. In tailoring contemporary arguments to specific audiences and specific purposes, experiment with variations on this classical approach.

For example, in the introduction, although you will certainly want to grab the reader's attention, it may not seem necessary or relevant to you to advertise your own good character; you may want the logic of your argument to accomplish this effect. You may decide to take an inductive rather than a deductive approach in writing, stating your thesis in the conclusion rather than early in the essay. It might be more effective, in your mind, to refute opposing arguments openly, using refutation as a platform upon which to build your further, positive arguments, or you may want to interweave refutation and confirmation in point-counterpoint fashion. In your conclusion, you may feel that it is redundant to summarize points that you have already made, so you might instead end with a particularly poignant example, or with a provocative question that will leave your reader to ponder what you see as the most essential point.

The form of classical argumentation should remind you of the four essential components of argument—claim, audience, exigence, and reasons. It should also remind you of the necessity, as you develop and advance your arguments, of being well-informed, both of the relevant facts and of the range of views in addressing complex issues. If you are able to convince your reader that you yourself are a credible and reasonable source, you will have come a long way toward convincing him or her that your claim is valid.

READINGS:
CONFLICTS OF INTEREST

ISSUE BY ISSUE

The three cycles of investigation and argumentation that comprise this chapter's readings give a sample of the range of possible subjects and controversies that arise as we consider the most fundamental theme this book addresses: the place human beings occupy in this planet's ecology. Subjects relevant to this theme draw on virtually all of our fields of academic study: history, literature, philosophy, religion, and education in the humanities; sociology, psychology, anthropology, political science, and economics in the social sciences; biology, zoology, geology, astronomy, physics, and mathematics in the sciences. And, on a very practical level, subjects arising from this theme are often related to our work in a wide range of professions, including medicine, law, business, agriculture, social service, urban and environmental planning, international relations, communications, and education, among many others.

We are bombarded by the media and in our daily lives by specific controversies that have much to do with the broad subject of our relationship to nature, and with the related subjects of science and technology. Many of us are concerned about an overwhelming array of environmental issues: about the effects of expanding urban and suburban development and of shrinking wilderness; about the disappearance of plant and animal species and of indigenous cultures; about the hole in the ozone layer and the greenhouse effect; about toxic waste and the fact that so many of our toxic dumps are located in minority communities; about the danger of pesticides in our food; about air and water pollution and waning energy reserves; about our overburdened and leaking landfills; about widespread famine among a world population of nearly six billion human beings (a population that, were the current rate of growth of 2 percent per year to continue, would be 50 billion by the year 2100).

We may find a glimmer of hope for resolving many of our environmental problems in the fact that some of the long-held attitudes about human beings' relationships to the natural world are changing in response to environmental crises. We may see promise in sustainable agriculture; in the expanding "green" consumer markets; in the growing number of grassroots environmental organizations in this country and worldwide; in the environmental justice movement; in environmental education campaigns; and in increasing awareness of what the consequences will be if we do not radically curtail human population growth. We may believe, as Lewis Thomas asserts in "Making Science Work" in Chapter 7, that our best hope in solving many of our environmental problems lies with science and in new technologies. Through science and technology, we may develop alternative energy sources; more efficiently designed, environmentally sound communities; more productive agricultural practices; and healthier people as well as healthier ecosystems.

In the past, paying attention to environmental issues, including issues involving the direction of scientific research and the uses of technology, seemed optional; we could get away with avoiding such issues since they didn't seem to have much relevance to our daily lives. But this is less and less the case. Environmental issues press us on all sides and in many ways—in our personal lives, in our communities, as a nation, and within the global community—and we can no longer afford to ignore them. These problems demand solutions. In the information age, an educated public is an essential component in the ongoing debate about environment and technology. We vote on environmental policy and, increasingly, on issues involving ethical uses of technology; we fund these endeavors through our tax monies and even our tuition payments. And, ultimately, we bear the consequences of our decisions.

The issues raised when we consider what our role is, or should be, in the natural order are not theoretical. They affect us, both personally and publicly. When we learn how large, seemingly theoretical ideas apply on a practical level, we begin to appreciate that our own individual lives exist within a larger social and historical context. The issues explored in this chapter's readings may reflect conflicts of interest within areas of controversy, but the controversies themselves reveal the extent to which our interests are held in common.

THE READING CYCLES

The readings of this chapter explore three specific controversies. Each of the three cycles in investigation and argumentation addresses one subject, exploring a specific controversy from various perspectives. Each of the three reading cycles includes a student essay, written in response to a question that the student writer considered unanswered by the cycle of readings. Some of the readings of Chapter 7 are intended to serve as specific points of reference for this chapter's reading cycles as well.

The first reading cycle concerns use of public lands. The readings raise the question of whether or not, or to what extent, our public lands should be open to private commercial use. Sharman Apt Russell and Edward Abbey address ranchers' traditional rights to graze cattle on public lands in the Southwest (as in some other parts of the country). One of the reasons this particular issue is so complex is that the individual's "right" to make a livelihood comes into direct conflict with sound land use policy. Cynthia Riggs, in her essay, points out that pressure to develop commercial interests on public lands comes from big business as well, particularly from oil and timber companies. She argues that more public lands should be opened to commercial development. The student essay in this cycle, By Pham's "Public Lands Should Remain Public," offers a counterargument to Riggs's essay. Aldo Leopold's essay in Chapter 7, "The Land Ethic" (page 431), will serve as a particularly valuable point of reference as you consider this cycle of readings.

The second reading cycle concerns the question of animal rights and, specifically, the ethics of animal research. Most medical research involves animal experimentation. In weighing the rights of animals and the rights of human beings, can we justify animal experimentation? Some people argue that animals have no inherent rights and that animal experimentation is not only morally justifiable but is, in fact, the scientist's obligation in striving to improve the human condition. Others, among them Peter Singer in "When Are Experiments on Animals Justifiable?," argue that human beings have no rights that supersede animals' rights and that animal experimentation is morally reprehensible under virtually any circumstance. Many people, including David Quammen in "Animal Rights and Beyond," recognize the troubling inconsistencies that arise when we assign moral consideration to some forms of life and not to others. In her essay, "Animal Rights: Alternative Approaches," student writer Anne Pollock investigates the middle ground in the animal rights debate. In this reading cycle, two readings from Chapter 7 serve as especially interesting points of reference: the excerpt from John Burroughs's "In the Noon of Science" (page 425)—but bear in mind that "noon" for Burroughs was 1913—and student writer Benjamin Jun's essay, "Consciousness" (page 469).

The last of the three reading cycles probes the complex subject of human genetic engineering, posing difficult questions. In screening for genetic abnormalities, and (as is often the consequence) in aborting fetuses because of them, are we playing God? Do we have the right to preselect offspring according to their genetic make-up? How will we define "defect"? Our future capacity to alter human genes will allow us to "cure" certain genetic diseases before children are born, but how do we avoid—or do we wish to avoid—designing a "superrace" in the process? Genetic engineering poses moral and ethical questions that are complex and difficult to resolve since what benefits one individual may conflict with another individual's rights or with the good of society. Amy Virshup's investigative essay "Perfect People?" explores the difficult choices that individuals make as a consequence of genetic screening. The selection from Jeremy Rifkin's book *Algeny*, "A Heretic's View on the New Bioethics," offers an argument against genetic engineering, human or otherwise, and Stephen Jay Gould's essay, "On the Origin of Specious Critics," is a refutation of Rifkin's arguments. In her essay "American Eugenics Society II?," student writer Jennifer Harris investigates and reports on a subject referred to but not explored in enough depth to satisfy her in Rifkin's essay, the history of eugenics. As you read this cycle of readings, consider Lewis Thomas's "Making Science Work" in Chapter 7 (page 450) as a point of reference; you might also, in this case, consider the excerpt from Aldous Huxley's *Brave New World* in Chapter 5 (page 274) as a point-of-reference reading.

Land Use

■ SHARMAN APT RUSSELL
Range War

Sharman Apt Russell was born in 1954 in California. She holds a B.S. degree in conservation and natural resources from the University of California at Berkeley and an M.F.A. degree in English and creative writing from the University of Montana. She lives and writes, for both adult and young readers, in Mimbres, New Mexico. Some of her books include Songs of the Fluteplayer *(1993),* Kill the Cowboy: A Battle of Mythology in the West

(1993), The Humpbacked Fluteplayer *(1993), and* Frederick Douglass *(1987). She received the* Mountains and Plains Regional Book Award *and the* New Mexico Press Women's Award, *both in 1992.*

"Range War" is taken from Songs of the Fluteplayer *(1993), a collection of essays about the Southwest, Russell's most frequent writing subject. In this investigative essay, she sets out to explore the public and personal dimensions of a divisive political issue among her own neighbors: the use of public lands in the Southwest by private ranchers for cattle grazing.*

The room is full of ranchers. The young ones look traditionally lean, while on the older men the tight-fitting Western shirt and jeans mercilessly reveal every sign of aging, from the slumped shoulder to the hanging belly. Everyone in the room is deeply tanned. Many are angry. They sit on metal folding chairs, arms across their chests, not bending to chat with a neighbor or friend, but waiting silently for the meeting to begin. As I sign the register, a bullish-looking man also waits for me to identify myself, to write under the appropriate space Silver City *Daily Press* or Diamond D Bar or Audubon Society. He stares at me intently. I leave that part blank.

This meeting is for us, the public, to express our views to a task force of ten men ranged in a semicircle at the front of the room. What draws us here is the growing competition between elk and livestock in the Gila National Forest. Exterminated in the 1900s, reintroduced elk can now be seen in herds of fifty to two hundred, their big angular bodies flashing across a meadow or retreating ghostlike into the shadows of pine. Goaded by a recent drought, these herds are coming down from the high mountains to eat on pastures where ranchers who lease the public lands traditionally graze cows. By the end of this meeting, one rancher will be pounding the table in front of him, shouting "All we get is the runaround! There are people going broke here!" At the same time, today marks the end of a hunt in which twenty elk, most of them pregnant, were legally killed out of season. The untimely death of these animals did not please local hunters and outfitters. Environmentalists, too, are asking the question they believe is rhetorical: who has first right on our wilderness areas and national forests? Meanwhile, land shared by cattle and elk is becoming daily, perhaps seriously, overgrazed.

It is the Forest Service who organized this task group and this meeting. They have hired a facilitating firm to field questions and summarize our statements onto big sheets of paper which are taped up hurriedly all over the room. At first I am amused by these New Age professionals: a studiously friendly man in slacks and loose shirt and a well-dressed woman assistant. Rather soon, I see how necessary they are. The comments begin with direct, undisguised hostility. The ranchers feel that both the Forest Service and the Game and Fish Department should have prevented the increase in elk and are not doing enough about the problem now.

"It's one lousy job of management," a man scolds the District Range and Wildlife Supervisor. "If we manage cows, we should be managing wildlife!"

"In 1905, 1906, we made an agreement with you guys," an elderly man, whose painful body movements speak of a life falling off horses and getting back on, uses his wife's arm for support as he speaks. "The Forest Service was charged to protect the habitat, the land, and the local economy, our local industries of timber and ranching from outside, unfair interests," he pauses and then restates, quite firmly, this last phrase. "To protect our local industries of timber and ranching from outside, unfair interests."

His statement confuses me—elk? outside interests?—until a woman in the audience rises to explain. Womanlike, she tries to defuse the confrontation.

"Our fight is not with the Forest Service," she says. "It's with these ego-environmentalists who want this country returned to wilderness. They're the ones putting pressure on Congress. These people are ridiculous! They're ridiculous! And they're trying to get rid of us. This is a well thought-out plan."

The facilitator intervenes to talk about the need not to "label" people or name-call.

A spokesman from the National Rifle Association picks up the woman's point and enlarges on it. "Gentlemen," he begins, "I want to warn you about something. There is an unseen presence in this room. There is a third force here today, and I know of what I speak, for we in the National Rifle Association have been driven to our knees by the environmentalists. Gentlemen, these people command millions and millions of dollars, of TV and advertising time! They are looking over your shoulder! Gentlemen, the genie is out of the bottle! You can't win an argument on an environmental issue. If it comes down between cows and elk, you are going to lose!"

I look about the room of thirty men and five women, some sitting forward, drinking in these words, others with their arms still crossed, their faces blank. I look at the few "environmentalists" here; I know them by name and would know them anyway by their hairstyles and clothing. I understand why they have not spoken up in this last hour of comment. There is too much passion swirling through this room, too much fear behind these blank faces.

The fear, and the discussion this morning, goes beyond the problem of elk. There are many people in this country, some associated with the far-left environmental group Earthfirst! and some not, who don't want cows grazing on the public lands. There are slogans in the political wind like "Cattle free by '93" or the more silly "No more moo by '92." Every rancher here can quote these slogans, and nearly every one has cattle on the Gila National Forest or the Gila Wilderness or the nearby Aldo Leopold Wilderness. Although these ranchers refuse to admit it, their real fight is not with Earthfirst!ers but with the heartless and compelling logic of numbers.

The West produces 20 percent of the country's beef. Less than 5 percent of the nation's cattle graze on the public lands. (Sheep graze too, but most of the forage is consumed by cows.) Only 31,000 ranchers or corporations lease grazing permits from the federal government, but they proceed to crop 268 million acres: 89 percent of our Bureau of Land Management land and 69 percent of national forest. The majority of wildlife refuges, many wilderness areas, and some national parks and monuments are also grazed.

The health of these lands is unclear. In 1988, the United States General Accounting Office surveyed range managers who estimated, conservatively, that 27 percent of grazing allotments are threatened with damage or actually declining "because authorized livestock grazing levels were higher than the land could support." The managers also felt that conditions and trends were simply unknown for another quarter of the public lands. In 1986 the BLM issued its report that 59 percent of its land was in fair or poor condition, the lower two of four categories. The Forest Service surveyed fifty million acres and decided that 54 percent of its land showed 0–50 percent of its potential natural community—in other words, of the native plants and animals it once supported. The numbers are worse depending on who is computing them. They are far worse when one just considers riparian or streamside areas. They are usually worse in the Southwest. In 1989 the National Wildlife Federation considered 72 percent of New Mexico's public land to be ecologically unsatisfactory.

Ironically, the repeated statement that the American range is in its best condition ever in this century is probably true, given the extreme destruction of the nineteenth century on through World War I and the 1930s. The truth is that most of the West is simply too dry for sustained, heavy grazing—even the buffalo knew that and stayed out of places like Arizona. The best lands for ranching were snapped up by private citizens. What remained—the public land—is the most rugged, the most fragile, and the least suited for cattle. Still, these lands are our watersheds. They are our recreation areas. They are a refuge for wildlife and a gift to our grandchildren. Should we be risking them for beef grown more easily and at less cost in Missouri?

It's no wonder that public lands ranchers feel threatened! Organizations like the Cattlemen's Association, uniting both public and private lands ranchers, were once strong and effective lobbyists. Reagan was a part-time rancher, and for eight years men wearing cowboy hats determined land use policy. All this served to hide what is becoming more obvious to politicians and resource managers. Public lands ranchers are not only outnumbered. They are outnumbered by men and women equally passionate about the subject of bunchgrass or the placement of water tanks. The Sierra Club has nearly fifteen times as many members as there are public lands grazers. The National Wildlife Federation has a membership of five million.

At this meeting, and across the West, it is not only ranchers who feel threatened. Many of the people here came down from small towns and one-store stops nestled against the shoulder of the Gila National Forest or tucked within its very heart. Recently, Forest Service guidelines that protect the Mexican spotted owl and its associated old growth forest have meant reductions in the local timber for sale. For this, and other reasons, mill operations are cutting back.

"Our timber industry is about lost," says the man who will later pound the table. "And just about everyone in our county uses public lands or depends on their revenue. We don't have enough private property for a tax base to support our schools and our county government. We just passed a school bond bill. Who's going to pay for that, for our kids' education?"

"The environmental movement has gone beyond Homo-sapiens," another rancher agrees. "It's human beings damned and be damned! If we don't do something about it, we're going to lose our rural communities. We're just going to disappear."

"You're going to lose anyway," intones the man from the National Rifle Association. "The environmentalists will get you!"

"Well," drawls a voice from the far back of the room. "They'll have spur marks on them if they try."

A number of people smile. I am not sure how I feel. In part, I feel bullied. I resent all this hard masculine anger. I resent the ease of these violent metaphors. At the same time, I like ranchers and want them to like me. The analysis of this goes beyond the romance of films and cigarette commercials. I have watched my son—not my daughter—yearn to be a cowboy ever since he was eleven months old. I have watched him collect a sizeable herd of toy horses. I have made innumerable halters out of yarn and string. As my son grows older, I have had to make rules as to how and when ropes can be swung in the house and which pieces of furniture can double as calves. I have been impressed and appalled by his obsession to dominate his rocking horse. This is, I think, more primal than cultural; this is biology. This is an embrace of power and competence and, yes, joy in the physical world. When I admire this physicality, I am admiring those very ranchers who set their spur marks so firmly on the land.

The facilitator is smiling, perhaps with relief, as he announces a lunch break. The meeting will reconvene in one hour. As I walk out into the windy spring afternoon, dry as the leaves on the dying trees, dry as the yellow hills in this year of drought—we all know that the problem is weather as much as elk—I am struck by how much ranchers and environmentalists have in common. Both believe the other side is powerful, wealthy, ignorant, and ruthless. Both believe the government is their adversary. Both believe they need to educate the public about range management. Both believe they are concerned with the protection of natural resources.

On the sidewalk, next to my parked car, the meeting has spilled out into a voluable group who stand talking among themselves. They look at me warily. Some of them know that my husband is an outfitter in the Gila Wilderness. They all know, by my hair and clothing and because New Mexico is that small a state, that I am not a rancher. A woman from the Mimbres Valley finally greets me: "Well, Sharman, are you for us or against us?"

In half an hour I have driven thirty miles east and am at the place where Highway 90 enters a mountain pass and the Mimbres Valley comes into view. The Black Range, named for its dark fur of trees, defines the horizon with bold calligraphy. Below these mountains, the hills lump and fold like shaggy beasts descending into the valley bottom. Seventy percent of the West is grazed, and in the Mimbres I would guess that number to be more like ninety. If the land is not someone's backyard or garden, then a cow is probably on it. I am so used to this dry and rocky country—I am so used to fence lines grazed brown on one side but still grassy on the other—that like ranchers themselves I hardly see anymore what is healthy and what is not. Now, from the car, I can tell that some of these private pastures have more dirt than forage. The presence of plants like snakeweed, beargrass, and buckhorn cholla also suggest overgrazing, although at this time of year it's easy to blame cattle for what too many clear blue skies have done. Later I will go to the Forest Service and be told that on the nearby public lands there are, indeed, allotments that look pretty bad, that there are, basically, too many cows in the forest.

Here in the Mimbres Valley most of the ranchers are what a local economist calls "heartbreak operations." North, near the headwaters of the river, are a few big places like the Ponderosa, which has a lease to run eight hundred cows on the Gila National Forest. At the lower end is the Nan Ranch, with fifteen hundred cows, over one hundred thousand private acres, and a bare sliver of BLM land. Typically, both these large ranches have absentee owners. In the middle of the valley are the small homesteads. A few of these have long, irrigated, emerald fields upon which black Angus and white Charolais look pleasantly pastoral. The majority also have grazing leases on public forest in the Black Range or on the lower BLM land. How many of these ranchers make a living from their cows is hard to say. Often enough, a rancher's wife is a nurse or schoolteacher. The rancher himself may have a part-time job or work as a truck driver at the copper mines.

Socially, the ranching community is going strong. The night lights of the Mimbres Valley Arena Rodeo come on around the Fourth of July and from our house, on many Sundays, we can hear the tinny voice of the announcer. The Cowbelles can boast over fifty members; as a way of promoting beef, these women give chunks of meat to high school home-ec classes and distribute gift certificates to senior citizens. There are, of course, the usual number of feuds between neighbors and within families in which the children must split up a one income ranch. A fair handful of these ranchers are second and third generation; their grandmothers were promoting beef when the Gila National Forest was still a twinkle in some administrator's eye. Ethnically, most of the ranchers are Anglo. (It is Hispanics who keep to the tradition of farming, patterning the valley floor with apple orchards and corn fields.) After living here for ten years, my own contact with ranchers is still friendly and still minimal. The ones I know well tend to be black sheep: Bob Jacobsen practices Ai-kido, Frankie Hudson is both a woman and a vegetarian.

Cows and apples and corn. Twenty years ago, that about summed up the Mimbres Valley. Since then the population has probably quadrupled, with the newcomers a mix of retirees and people like me who work in Silver City or Deming. Most days, when I come home from Silver City, that moment of revelation—through the mountain pass—confirms in me my decision to move here. The pastel colors seem exactly right; the hills in proportion to the lift of Cooke's Peak. Now, in the fallout of this meeting, I see a pall over the land, a division, and a paranoia.

Are you for us or against us?

August is our true spring. The summer afternoon rains have had a chance to green the hills. Penstemon, lupine, and scarlet beardstongue bloom in the pastures along the road. This morning my husband has coaxed me into riding with him to Bob Jacobsen's ranch, just behind our house and ten miles through pink rock canyon, a jump to the ridge, a gallop over the mesa, then descent again, sliding the slope. I understand that I am nervous riding because I am not yet competent. I am not in control, and I don't know why. As a younger woman, I had my share of physical courage. I felt stronger than the world around me. Now, although I see clearly the power of horsemanship, some layer of fear has grown up over the years. Something undermines me. Still, I want that centaur magic. I want that leap into animalism, and so I keep riding, irregularly, not enough to get better, just enough to hone my fear and desire.

Bob and Norma Jean Jacobsen are new friends. We met them at the local hot springs, where people bathe nude and ranchers don't go. Bob is forty years old and has been cowboying and ranching for over twenty years. For twelve of those years, he was content to just cowboy, riding the ranges of western New Mexico, bunking with the boys, and working his way up to foreman. Eventually he got married and stood at the highest rung of the cowboy's career ladder: he bought himself a ranch.

The economics of this are instructive. What Bob really bought was eighty acres of deeded land, with an attached Forest Service permit to graze 280 cows on sixty sections in the Gila National Forest. One section is 640 acres. This means that the Forest Service felt that five cows could feed themselves per 640 acres of Bob's lease. That amounts to land that is pretty marginal although, as Bob points out, not unusual in the West. Also on Bob's deeded property was a one-room shack that had no electricity, telephone, or running water. For all this, he went into debt for half a million dollars. For the grazing permit alone, he paid to the previous owner $1,000 per animal unit or $280,000. This did not include the cows themselves, which he had to buy.

Each year Bob and Norma also pay a grazing fee to the Forest Service. The fee fluctuates with politics and cattle prices and in 1990 was $1.81 per cow per month. To lease non-irrigated private land would be three or four times more. Some environmentalists object to the low cost of the public lands fee, and out of this comes the phrase "welfare ranching." But Bob points out that the government subsidizes almost every public lands user; each year, for example, the Forest Service operates its recreation program at a loss of millions of dollars. He also refutes the claim that low grazing fees give public lands ranchers a competitive edge. In his mind, the expense of managing cows in rugged terrain and the initial price tag of the grazing permit offset any advantage. In addition, ranchers on public lands bear some costs in maintaining improvements like fences and water tanks.

Like most ranchers here, Bob and Norma Jean run a cow and calf operation, caring for cattle year-round, selling off 90 percent of calves and 10 percent of older cows each fall. The previous owner of their ranch had tried to raise steers which are bought young, fattened, and then sold. This rancher overstocked the range by running a thousand yearlings (considered the equivalent of five hundred mature cows) only six months. When the Jacobsens got here, the land was already overgrazed. A dry winter and spring meant an increase in predator loss, and that first year one bear alone killed twenty calves. Norma spent a lot of time alone with the two kids. The water in the tanks dropped low. The cows grew painfully thin.

In their second year at the ranch, Bob met with the Forest Service and agreed to reduce his herd by forty-five head. The Forest Service, in turn, promised to do a range study in seven years to see if the number of cows could go back up. This agreement was strictly verbal, and Bob made sure that his original allotment of 280 cows was still "on the books." Although the Forest Service doesn't consider a grazing permit to be property, it is treated as such—banks lend money on that 280 number, the value of Bob's deeded land is based on it, and the IRS will tax it as part of his estate. Such "temporary non-use agreements" are not uncommon on the Gila Forest. The forest ranger can also permanently reduce an allotment, but for now this is considered a draconian measure.

To me, to my husband, and probably to Norma Jean, Bob's workday is enviable. He's independent. He's outside. He is connected, in a way that we are not, to the natural world and the passing of seasons.

Spring is the time to ride the high pastures and gather cows, perhaps as many as thirty in one morning. The days are so clear that sometimes he can see all the way to Mexico. As the weeks go by, only the stragglers, the wild ones, are left, hidden in the sculpted rock of back canyons or staring down defiantly from a scrub oak ridge. Pushing his horse through thickets of brush or charging across a mesa, Bob is lucky now to get three or four cows in a full day. When they are finally corralled, the cattle are branded, vaccinated, dehorned, and castrated. Then they're moved to summer pasture, and Bob begins the labor of fixing dams, digging postholes, stringing fences, and repairing windmills. In the fall, he gathers again, sells, and takes the remaining herd to their winter home. Winter is slow. Maybe he'll ride up to break ice in a tank or pack in some salt. In part because his land is so mountainous, Bob does almost all his work on a horse. Also, instead of a modern squeeze-chute and branding table, he ropes his cows, pinning them to the ground like they do at the rodeo. Like many ranchers, he relishes tradition.

The rewards of this are Zen-like, immediate, limited to the working day. After twelve years of ranching, Bob has managed to upgrade his house to include a living room and flush toilet, but it hasn't been easy. Overall, he guesses that he averages $40,000 a year. This keeps him well in debt, what with his interest payments. What keeps him going are his low costs (horse feed and horse shoes) and a love of the lifestyle.

Recently Bob has been borrowing books from us, subscribing to new magazines, seeking a window on an outside world of backpackers and deep ecologists, a world of five billion people. This is not his first psychic rumbling. A few years ago, he jettisoned the cowboy image. "For a long time, I thought is was the wildest, most wonderful life a person could lead," he once told me. "But a cowboy has to dress a certain way. He has to talk a certain way. He has to think a certain way. It's a dead end. Finally, I didn't want to be that confined. I didn't want to be just what a cowboy is supposed to be."

It was sometime later that Bob went into ungrazed parts of the Gila Wilderness for the first time. He was "bowled over" by its beauty—not, he says, the approved cowboy reaction. The next year he and his family attended a three-day celebration of the 1964 Wilderness Act, sponsored here by the Forest Service. Other local ranchers boycotted the event, and the New Mexico Farm and Livestock Bureau demanded an audit of expenses. These protests were both vehement and deeply rooted. Historically, the rancher's role has been to tame wilderness, not celebrate it.

"Ranchers look at wilderness on the map and see it as another place for cows," Bob says. "I don't always like what we have to do in order to survive. Maybe we see erosion. Maybe we know we should pull out some cattle because it hasn't rained much and the land is suffering. Maybe we read that killing predators isn't good in the long run. But we have to bury those things. We have to repress all that if we want to survive."

Survival. When we reach Bob and Norma's ranch that day, I am relieved that, once again, my horse (who is twenty years old) has not pitched me down a mountain or thrown me into a cactus. We are barely on the ground before Bob tells us that he and Norma Jean have found a buyer for their ranch.

I am amazed. I didn't know they were looking for one.

Inside the house, Bob is a little manic. He is a big man, and I have wondered before if half his charisma didn't come from that, from plain bigness. Now he seems to fill up the living room. I can't help but think of all the bears he has shot. He is much like a bear now, pacing, shambling, cornered.

"We could have gone on," he says. "I think ranching is viable if you're smart and a good manager. But I got tired of all the worrying. Worrying about the weather, worrying about interest rates, worrying about what the government was going to do. I could hardly enjoy it anymore. I couldn't ride up a canyon without counting how many fence posts I might get from the juniper trees. I couldn't enjoy the spring because I knew how damned dry it was. I couldn't enjoy the summer for wondering when it was going to rain or the fall for wondering if it would rain too much and I wouldn't get the cattle in."

Norma Jean is setting out food and drink and tending to her children at the same time. These things, not the ranch, have always been her center of power. Bob turns suddenly and asks the question we have not dared ask him. His voice is a well-mannered Western monotone, still soft, still unwilling to scale new ranges of grief and hope and giddy excitement. He has never gone to college. He knows one thing only and knows it well. "What am I going to do now?" he asks Norma.

A few miles from here lives a woman named Sherri who doesn't much care for Bob. They have never met, but for Sherri, a divorced mother with two sons, it is enough that Bob is a public lands rancher.

When Sherri came to the Mimbres Valley, she too had a dream. With money she saved working as a secretary, she bought five acres of irrigated land, thinking to farm intensively and solar-dry her products. Sherri is a smart woman. But her dream couldn't withstand two dry summers followed by a flood and plague of grasshoppers. Rather soon, she had to get a job in town to support her life in the country. Last year, she let her fields be taken over by Johnson grass. She has begun to brood in her adobe house on the hill, and part of her brooding concerns cows.

Unlike environmentalists who don't live near cows, Sherri's grudge is personal as well as political. She believes that overgrazing in the upstream watershed was in part responsible for the "hundred-year flood" that destroyed her raspberries and swept away my car a few winters ago. She maintains that if it weren't for cows, I would still own that Volkswagen. She believes the reason our friends, Jack and Roberta Greene, sold their land was because, for two years in a row, steers broke in and ravished their garden. It broke her heart to see it, and she is certain that it broke theirs. (Since the entire Mimbres Valley is still open range, there is little any of us can do when cattle come bumbling through our orchards and fields. Legally, it is our job to fence them out, and although damages can be claimed, the channels are tortuous and we have to collect the money ourselves—from the very rancher who couldn't or wouldn't put money into his own fences. At any rate, the value of a garden or a favorite peach tree is not really claimable.)

With a passion that seems disproportionate (unless you, too, work indoors in town all day) Sherri will recount some of the hikes she has taken with her sons. "We were walking up a narrow canyon, up to Cooke's Peak, and these cows are preceding me, dropping shit everywhere, drooling shit, immediate and *fresh*, all the way up. We had to watch where we put our feet every step! Yesterday we went down the East Fork of the Gila River, and there were cows everywhere! This is in the wilderness itself! This is supposed to be pristine!"

Sherri is among those who would like to see ranchers off the public lands. She notes that the current grazing fees, as low as they are, pay only one-third of the cost of the BLM and Forest Service grazing management programs. In 1986, that cost was $63 million. Sherri, to be sure, is a storehouse of facts and figures. She can tell you how many coyotes, bear, and mountain lions were killed in New Mexico last year by the Department of Agriculture at the request of ranchers. She can tell you at what rate riparian cottonwood habitat is disappearing in Arizona, which bird and animal species are endangered by overgrazing, and the percent of water taken from the Colorado River to grow hay for cattle.

"What about the people themselves?" I ask her. "The men and women who have worked years on a ranch, who love the lifestyle, who know nothing else?"

"What about *me*?" Sherri snaps. "I would love to have an agricultural lifestyle. I'd love to get up at sunrise and work hard in the garden, in the earth all day. But it's not possible. I can't afford it, and no one has offered to subsidize me. I'm a secretary instead, and if I don't want to be a secretary, then I have to find, all on my own, something else to do."

She hears herself and doesn't like it. She is vice-president of the Native Plants Society, she has a degree in botany, she has gone to jail to protest a nuclear power plant. She does not need to base her dislike of public lands ranching on envy.

"We are becoming a desert," Sherri says. "It's been progressive since the cattle came. A third of North America has undergone severe to very severe desertification, and some people think this is what the West *is*, a desert, and it's *not*. Just read about what was here, before the 1880s, and you know: we're choosing this. We'll never see the land the way it once was. We'll never regain what we lost. But we can't afford to lose any more!"

The next day Sherri telephones me. She has been thinking about the rancher's point of view, and now she has a plan. She points out that Silver City could use an adobe industry, that people are looking for adobes and shipping them in from as far away as Albuquerque. She suggests that local ranchers trade in their four-wheel drive pickups to invest in adobe machines. "It's hard work," she enthuses. "It's outside. It's physical. It's what they are used to."

There is a long silence on the phone. I can not imagine the ranchers I know making adobes. I tell her that, realistically, they would rather be on a horse.

"They can ride on the weekend," Sherri says, "like the rest of us."

She is implacable.

John Forgue is different from me or Sherri or Bob Jacobsen in that John's grandfather came here in 1908. Alongside his dad, John began riding up to the Black Range, where his ranch has a national forest lease of seventy sections, before he began first grade. When he finished high school, he stayed right here, working for ranches up and down the valley. When his father died unexpectedly, John took over the family ranch. He runs 237 cows on his leased land (five years ago he took a temporary reduction) and another hundred on his eight sections of private land. He is a third generation rancher who married the daughter of a nearby rancher and who hopes that his only child, a boy, will be a rancher too. Long before I met him, I had heard about John: the best cowboy in the Mimbres Valley, a man admired by other men for his roping, his endurance, his way with horses. John and his wife live in a trailer down five miles of dirt road and beautiful scenery. I do not expect to ever learn that they have just found a buyer.

John's cramped living room is dominated by a mountain lion's skin on the wall and a gleaming wood cabinet full of trophies with brass horses on top. His wife is out catching a straying bull. Sitting on the edge of a fake-leather armchair, John carefully removes his hat. He is willing to talk to me because he thinks that the rancher's side of the story is not being told.

"The legitimate rancher isn't about to abuse the land or overgraze it because that's his livelihood," John explains. "If we abuse the land, what will we have ten years from now? I'm looking down the road here. I'm looking out for the future."

I have heard ranchers say this before, that taking care of the land was "just good business," and like other things I've heard—"If it weren't for ranchers, there wouldn't be wildlife" or "The rancher was the first environmentalist"—it hasn't always rung true. It simply isn't true for many ranches that are absentee owned, bought for the tax write off, bought as a second income, bought as a form of semi-retirement, or bought as a kind of Western playground.

On the table beside me are pictures of the Forgue son. Framed and obviously taken by a professional, they show the boy first as a baby, a toddler, and then a sturdy third-grader with freckles and slicked down hair. When John Forgue says he's working for the future, I believe him. When he says he's not getting rich off his cows, I believe him too. So I ask him why he keeps on ranching. I ask him why he doesn't sell his land to developers, invest the money, and take his wife to Hawaii.

John sits back in his armchair.

"Gosh," he says. "That's a good question."

At first, suspiciously, I can't believe he has not thought of it himself. But his answer has all the pauses and circles of a heartfelt belief never before articulated.

"I can't explain it," he tries. "It's my home, I guess. Even that old Forest Service land, which we don't own, which we only lease, it's home to me. I can go up there and be working cattle, just off out there by myself, and that's where I'm the happiest. That's just what I am."

This is, I suppose, the answer I was fishing for. I know a few other people who are "happiest in nature" but for various reasons none of them followed that happiness. It is not a daily affair. It is not so imbued in their life as to be unnamed, unexamined, or uncorrupted.

For various reasons, I am personally glad that John is at home in the Black Range. It gives me hope.

John and I are strangers and of different gender, and having shared a moment of intimacy, we both react against it. For a while, we talk about easier things, about changes in the valley and how it saddens him to see more lights at night, more trash on the forest from overnight campers, more four-wheelers tearing up the grass. He is polite: "I know it's progress. You all live in one of those subdivisions, don't you? But I hate to see the river being cut up like it is." We talk about beef prices, which are good now, $1.20 per pound for a four-hundred-pound calf. John is quick to say that as the supply builds up, the prices will go down again. His family survives by putting money aside for leaner years. We talk about the weather—a ritual we missed before—until finally I return to the disagreeable subject I have come to talk about.

And John says that, no, he does not think the public lands are in bad shape or that we need less grazing or more wilderness. He thinks the land needs to be productive. This is his main point: you can't eat scenery. He believes that if "we take more and more land out of production the American people will ultimately suffer. We've got to have food. We've got to have our timber and our ranching. We've got to have houses and paper to write on. I'm afraid we'll wake up some day and not have these things and there won't be anyone around who still knows how to do it."

John also thinks that as the government starts interfering more with public and private lands, "us and Russia are kind of reversing roles." He's heard about how environmentalists sabotage ranchers. He has read that in northern New Mexico they poison salt blocks. He thinks these people should be caught and prosecuted. He thinks his own land, public and private, is pretty healthy. He thinks that ranching is a full time job and says that a rancher has to get out and keep the cows scattered, keep them away from streams, keep them moving. He comes back, as ranchers do now, to fear.

"All they have to do is raise those grazing fees," he says. "People like me, the family ranch, the small ranch, we'd be out of business."

John Forgue is ready to listen as well as talk. "We can't deal with those radical groups like Earthfirst! That 'Cattle-free by '93' stuff. But people in the Sierra Club or the Audubon Society, they're the type we could work with and should work with. That's what it's going to come down to. Ranchers and non-ranchers. We have to sit down and work out our differences."

I am reminded of another conversation with another rancher. "It's changing, changing every day," he told me, and I could see him seeing it. "That train is coming."

I remember talking to a young Forest Service official, off the record, after the elk and livestock meeting. "These ranchers will have to change the way they do business." His voice, too, was serene and implacable. "They'll have to reduce and manage more. Whether they stay is up to them."

An hour later, when I leave the Forgue place, I shut their gate tight, in the momentary conviction that there is a place for their son on our public lands. In the same way that we need Mexican spotted owls, we need ranchers like John Forgue. We need a width and breadth of human experience.

When I get home, my husband tells me that a herd of elk are jumping fences to eat alfalfa on a neighbor's irrigated field—just a mile from our own. We have never heard of elk coming down so low. I have never heard of an elk in this valley.

In the coming week, the Arizona Cattle Growers' Association will demand that over 60 percent of Arizona's twenty thousand elk be reduced and that the government pay damages to public lands ranchers. This is hardly the spirit of compromise, in a state where ranchers number less than four thousand (about fifteen hundred on public lands) out of over three million people. In New Mexico, too, some ranchers are claiming that their grazing rights have, ipso facto, become property rights which the government is obliged to protect against the encroachment of wildlife. Through usage and tradition, they say, the public land is now theirs.

When I asked John Forgue why he didn't go to the elk and livestock meeting, he told me that he prefers to stay at home and mind his own business. "But maybe I'm at fault," he mused, "for not getting out there more to give my views. Maybe the time is past for staying at home."

Maybe he's right, I think.

Changing, changing every day. And not all the changes are for the worst. I like the wildness implied in having elk behind my hill.

I also like living in a community of ranchers.

I am not sure they will both be here in twenty years time.

■ CONSIDERATIONS OF MEANING AND METHOD

1. What implicit promise does Russell make to her readers in the opening paragraph? How does it reflect her purpose in writing? Who is her audience? How does she establish exigence early in the essay?

2. In her account of the meeting, whom does Russell identify as major participants in the debate? How does she characterize them? What are their argumentative stances or strategies? Specifically, how do the meeting's facilitators monitor and guide the debate?

3. Russell cites quite a lot of factual information in her essay, some of it attributed to secondary sources. What are some of these sources? Do you consider them to be objective or biased sources?

4. Although they are not necessarily Russell's own, "Range War" does contain arguments. What major claims are offered, and what reasons are given to support them?

5. Russell's research methods in investigating her subject include direct observation and interviewing. Why do you think she chose the three particular interview subjects she did? How does she characterize each of her interviewees? Do her choices of interview subjects reflect a fair range of views on the issue of private ranching on public lands, and do her characterizations fairly represent these views?

6. Overall, do you consider Russell herself to be a credible source? Why or why not? Does she provide a fair and objective overview of this complicated issue? Does she reveal any bias of her own in the essay? If you think she does reveal bias, where and how is it revealed?

7. What final conclusion does Russell draw? Does it seem to be a reasonable conclusion?

8. In "Range War," Russell takes a personal approach, both in in-

vestigating the personal dimensions of the public lands issue and in writing about it. As one of her readers, did you find her relatively informal styles of investigating and writing effective? Why or why not?

9. After reading "Range War," what questions remain unanswered for you? What further information do you need to understand the issue of private grazing on public lands? What aspects of the issue would you like to know more about?

■ POSSIBILITIES FOR WRITING

1. In policy matters, it is sometimes the case that individuals will suffer certain immediate costs as the larger system strives to achieve a general fairness. For example, some white males claim that affirmative action policies amount to reverse discrimination against them. As another example, the expense of conforming to increasingly strict environmental regulations has forced some small businesses, including family farms, out of business. It is difficult to argue against the ultimate goals of affirmative action or an improved environment; on the other hand, we may have considerable sympathy for individuals who pay a heavy price for a "greater good."

What are some current and perhaps hotly debated policies on your campus, in your community, in your state or in the nation at large—policies in which certain individuals stand to lose as the greater society stands to gain? Focus upon one such issue that captures your interest. Research the issue carefully, first by finding the facts that will provide you with full understanding of the issue—the history surrounding it, the policy in question, its ultimate goals. Ask yourself the journalist's questions: *who? what? where? when? how?* and *why?* Now consider more carefully the *who* involved. Who is responsible for forming or implementing the policy? Who stands to be most directly affected by it? Select several interview subjects who represent a range of roles and views relative to this issue, and interview them. In an essay for your class, report the results of your investigation. Consider carefully the kind of essay you want to write, and your audience and purpose in writing. Would it be more appropriate and effective to put yourself into the essay, as Russell did in "Range War," or to leave direct reference to yourself and your investigative process out of it? Based on the conclusions you draw through your investigation, will your essay be a report or an argument?

■ EDWARD ABBEY
Even the Bad Guys Wear White Hats

*One of the most vocal advocates for wilderness protection,
particularly in the Southwest, was Edward Abbey. Born in 1927 in
Home, Pennsylvania, Abbey died in 1989 in Oracle, New Mexico,
and is buried in a Southwest desert. Politically, Abbey claimed to
be an "agrarian anarchist," and his religion as "Piute." Following
service in the army from 1945 to 1946, Abbey hitchhiked west and
was so enthralled by the desert and mountain landscapes of
Arizona, New Mexico, and Utah that he stayed there. He attended
the University of New Mexico, studying philosophy and literature,
and he worked for many years as a fire lookout and seasonal park
ranger for the National Park Service, teaching part-time at the
University of Arizona.*

In perhaps his best-known book, Desert Solitaire *(1968), Abbey
describes one season (from April through September) at Arches National Monument where he served, largely in isolation, as a park
ranger in the late 1950s. In a review, Pulitzer Prize-winning
nature writer Edwin Way Teale called* Desert Solitaire *"a voice
crying in the wilderness,* for *the wilderness." Abbey's love and his
impassioned advocacy for desert and other wildernesses were fierce,
and his disdain for politicians, developers, and even tourists who
were bent on its destruction (in other words, his disdain for
"progress") was just as fierce, even bitter. Edwin Way Teale notes
that* Desert Solitaire *is "rather than a balanced book, judicially
examining in turn all sides, . . . a forceful presentation of one side.
And that side needs presenting. It is a side too rarely presented.
There will always be others to voice the other side, the side of
pressure and power and profit."*

*Abbey was convinced that peaceful protest on behalf of
environmental protection is not always enough. If* Desert Solitaire
*inspired a budding environmental movement in the late 1960s with
its lyrical fierceness, his 1975 novel,* The Monkeywrench Gang,
*incited action. In this entertaining and humorous novel, Abbey
tells the story of an unlikely group of environmental guerrillas
intent on blowing up the Glen Canyon Dam of the Colorado
River. The book is said to have encouraged the birth of the radical
environmental organization Earth First!, whose tactics of
environmental protest include sabotaging bulldozers (as in the*

novel) and spiking trees to deter loggers from risking cutting them
with chainsaws. The term "monkeywrenching," derived from
Abbey's book, means sabotage on behalf of the environment.

Some of Abbey's other novels include The Brave Cowboy *(1958)*
upon which the film Lonely Are the Brave *(1962) was based;* Fire
on the Mountain *(1962), winner of the Western Heritage Award*
for Best Novel in 1963; and The Fool's Progress *(1988). Others of*
his nonfiction works (or "personal histories," as Abbey called them)
are Abbey's Road: Take the Other *(1979),* Down the River *(1982),*
and Slumgullion Stew: An Edward Abbey Reader *(1984). Abbey*
wrote introductions for several books, including Ecodefense: A
Field Guide to Monkeywrenching, *edited by Dave Foreman*
(1987). Abbey won, but declined, an American Academy of Arts
and Letters Award in 1987.

"Abbey," acknowledged reviewer Kerry Luft, "is not for
everybody. He's about as subtle as a wrecking ball." Another
reviewer, Grace Lichtenstein, writes that "Abbey's polemic essays
on such subjects as cattle subsidies . . . scattered through a half-
dozen volumes, remain so angry, so infuriating yet so relevant that
they still provoke arguments among his followers." You might con-
sider, as you read "Even the Bad Guys Wear White Hats," what
Abbey's purposes are in writing. It might help you to know that
Abbey delivered the original version as a speech at the University
of Montana in 1985, though it was later published in Harper's.

When I first came West in 1948, a student at the University of
New Mexico, I was only twenty years old and just out of the Army. I
thought, like most simple-minded Easterners, that a cowboy was a
kind of mythic hero. I idolized those scrawny little red-nosed hired
hands in their tight jeans, funny boots, and comical hats.

Like other new arrivals in the West, I could imagine nothing more
romantic than becoming a cowboy. Nothing more glorious than
owning my own little genuine working cattle outfit. About the only
thing better, I thought, was to be a big league baseball player. I never
dreamed that I'd eventually sink to writing books for a living. Un-
luckily for me—coming from an Appalachian hillbilly background
and with a poor choice of parents—I didn't have much money. My
father was a small-time logger. He ran a one-man sawmill and a sub-
marginal side-hill farm. There wasn't any money in our family, no inheritance you could run 10,000 cattle on. I had no trust fund to back

me up. No Hollywood movie deals to finance a land acquisition program. I lived on what in those days was called the G.I. Bill, which paid about $150 a month while I went to school. I made that last as long as I could—five or six years. I couldn't afford a horse. The best I could do in 1947 and '48 was buy a thirdhand Chevy sedan and roam the West, mostly the Southwest, on holidays and weekends.

I had a roommate at the University of New Mexico. I'll just call him Mac. I don't want him to come looking for me. Mac came from a little town in southwest New Mexico where his father ran a feed store. Mackie was a fair bronc rider, eager to get into the cattle-growing business. And he had some money, enough to buy a little cinder-block house and about forty acres in the Sandia Mountains east of Albuquerque, near a town we called Landfill. Mackie fenced those forty acres, built a corral, and kept a few horses there, including an occasional genuine bronco for fun and practice.

I don't remember exactly how Mackie and I became friends in the first place. I was majoring in classical philosophy. He was majoring in screwworm management. But we got to know each other through the mutual pursuit of a pair of nearly inseparable Kappa Kappa Gamma girls. I lived with him in his little cinder-block house. Helped him meet the mortgage payments. Helped him meet the girls. We were both crude, shy, ugly, obnoxious—like most college boys.

My friend Mac also owned a 1947 black Lincoln convertible, the kind with the big grille in front, like a cowcatcher on a locomotive, chrome plated. We used to race to classes in the morning, driving the twenty miles from his house to the campus in never more than fifteen minutes. Usually Mac was too hung over to drive, so I'd operate the car, clutching the wheel while Mac sat beside me waving his big .44, taking potshots at jackrabbits and road signs and billboards and beer bottles. Trying to wake up in time for his ten o'clock class in brand inspection.

I'm sorry to say that my friend Mac was a little bit gun-happy. Most of his forty acres was in tumbleweed. He fenced in about half an acre with chicken wire and stocked that little pasture with white rabbits. He used it as a target range. Not what you'd call sporting, I suppose, but we did eat the rabbits. Sometimes we even went deer hunting with handguns. Mackie with his revolver, and me with a chrome-plated Colt .45 automatic I had liberated from the U.S. Army over in Italy. Surplus government property.

On one of our deer hunting expeditions, I was sitting on a log in a big clearing in the woods, thinking about Plato and Aristotle and the

Kappa Kappa Gamma girls. I didn't really care whether we got a deer that day or not. It was a couple of days before opening, anyway. The whole procedure was probably illegal as hell. Mac was out in the woods somewhere looking for deer around the clearing. I was sitting on the log, thinking, when I saw a chip of bark fly away from the log all by itself, about a foot from my left hand. Then I heard the blast of Mac's revolver—that big old .44 he'd probably liberated from his father. Then I heard him laugh.

"That's not very funny, Mackie," I said.

"Now, don't whine and complain, Ed," he said. "You want to be a real hunter like me, you gotta learn to stay awake."

We never did get a deer with handguns. But that's when I had my first little doubts about Mackie, and about the cowboy type in general. But I still loved him. Worshiped him, in fact. I was caught in the grip of the Western myth. Anybody said a word to me against cowboys, I'd jump down his throat with my spurs on. Especially if Mac was standing nearby.

Sometimes I'd try to ride those broncs that he brought in, trying to prove that I could be a cowboy too. Trying to prove it more to myself than to him. I'd be on this crazy, crackpot horse, going up, down, left, right, and inside out. Hanging on to the saddle horn with both hands. And Mac would sit on the corral fence, throwing beer bottles at us and laughing. Every time I got thrown off, Mac would say, "Now get right back on there, Ed. Quick, quick. Don't spoil 'im."

It took me a long time to realize I didn't have to do that kind of work. And it took me another thirty years to realize that there's something wrong at the heart of our most popular American myth—the cowboy and his cow.

You may have guessed by now that I'm thinking of criticizing the livestock industry. And you are correct. I've been thinking about cows and sheep for many years. Getting more and more disgusted with the whole business. There are some Western cattlemen who are nothing more than welfare parasites. They've been getting a free ride on the public lands for over a century, and I think it's time we phased it out. I'm in favor of putting the public lands livestock grazers out of business.

First of all, we don't need the public lands beef industry. Even beef lovers don't need it. According to most government reports (Bureau of Land Management, Forest Service), only about 2 percent of our beef, our red meat, comes from the eleven Western states. By those eleven I mean Montana, Nevada, Utah, Colorado, New Mexico, Arizona, Idaho, Wyoming, Oregon, Washington, and California. Most of our beef, aside from imports, comes from the Midwest and the East, especially the Southeast—Georgia, Alabama, Florida—and from other private lands across the nation. More than twice as many beef cattle are raised in the state of Georgia than in the sagebrush empire of Nevada. And for a very good reason: back East, you can support a cow on maybe half an acre. Out here, it takes anywhere from twenty-five to fifty acres. In the red rock country of Utah, the rule of thumb is one section—a square mile—per cow.

Since such a small percentage of the cows are produced on public lands in the West, eliminating that industry should not raise supermarket beef prices very much. Furthermore, we'd save money in the taxes we now pay for various subsidies to these public lands cattlemen. Subsidies for things like "range improvement"—tree chaining, sagebrush clearing, mesquite poisoning, disease control, predator trapping, fencing, wells, stock ponds, roads. Then there are the salaries of those who work for government agencies like the BLM and the Forest Service. You could probably also count in a big part of the salaries of the overpaid professors engaged in range-management research at the Western land-grant colleges.

Moreover, the cattle have done, and are doing, intolerable damage to our public lands—our national forests, state lands, BLM-administered lands, wildlife preserves, even some of our national parks and monuments. In Utah's Capital Reef National Park, for example, grazing is still allowed. In fact, it's recently been extended for another ten years, and Utah politicians are trying to make the arrangement permanent. They probably won't get away with it. But there we have at least one case where cattle are still tramping about in a national park, transforming soil and grass into dust and weeds.

Overgrazing is much too weak a term. Most of the public lands in the West, and especially in the Southwest, are what you might call "cowburnt." Almost anywhere and everywhere you go in the American West you find hordes of these ugly, clumsy, stupid, bawling, stinking, fly-covered, disease-spreading brutes. They are a pest and a plague. They pollute our springs and streams and rivers. They infest our canyons, valleys, meadows, and forests. They graze off the native bluestem and grama and bunch grasses, leaving behind jungles of prickly pear. They trample down the native forbs and shrubs and cactus. They spread the exotic cheat grass, the Russian thistle, and the crested wheat grass. *Weeds.*

Even when the cattle are not physically present, you'll see the dung and the flies and the mud and the dust and the general destruction. If you don't see it, you'll smell it. The whole American West stinks of cattle. Along every flowing stream, around every seep and spring and water hole and well, you'll find acres and acres of what range-management specialists call "sacrifice areas"—another understatement. These are places denuded of forage, except for some cactus or a little tumbleweed or maybe a few mutilated trees like mesquite, juniper, or hackberry.

I'm not going to bombard you with graphs and statistics, which don't make much of an impression on intelligent people anyway. Anyone who goes beyond the city limits of almost any Western town can see for himself that the land is overgrazed. There are too many cows and horses and sheep out there. Of course, cattlemen would never publicly confess to overgrazing, any more than Dracula would publicly confess to a fondness for blood. Cattlemen are interested parties. Many of them will not give reliable testimony. Some have too much at stake: their Cadillacs and their airplanes, their ranch resale profits and their capital gains. (I'm talking about the corporation ranchers, the land-and-cattle companies, the investment syndicates.) Others, those ranchers who have only a small base property, flood the public lands with their cows. About 8 percent of the federal land permittees have cattle that consume approximately 45 percent of the forage on the government rangelands.

Beef ranchers like to claim that their cows do not compete with deer. Deer are browsers, cows are grazers. That's true. But when a range is overgrazed, when the grass is gone (as it often is for seasons at a time), then cattle become browsers too, out of necessity. In the Southwest, cattle commonly feed on mesquite, cliff rose, cactus, acacia, or any other shrub or tree they find biodegradable. To that extent, they compete with deer. And they tend to drive out other and better wildlife. Like elk, or bighorn sheep, or pronghorn antelope.

How much damage have cattle done to the Western rangelands? Large-scale beef ranching has been going on since the 1870s. There's plenty of documentation of the effects of this massive cattle grazing on the erosion of the land, the character of the land, the character of the vegetation. Streams and rivers that used to flow on the surface all year round are now intermittent, or underground, because of overgrazing and rapid runoff.

Our public lands have been overgrazed for a century. The BLM knows it; the Forest Service knows it. The Government Accounting

Office knows it. And overgrazing means eventual ruin, just like strip mining or clear-cutting or the damming of rivers. Much of the Southwest already looks like Mexico or Southern Italy or North Africa: a cow-burnt wasteland. As we destroy our land, we destroy our agricultural economy and the basis of modern society. If we keep it up, we'll gradually degrade American life to the status of life in places like Mexico or southern Italy or Libya or Egypt.

In 1984 the Bureau of Land Management, which was required by Congress to report on its stewardship of our rangelands—the property of all Americans, remember—confessed that 31 percent of the land it administered was in "good condition," 42 percent in "fair condition," and 18 percent in "poor condition." And it reported that only 18 percent of the rangelands were improving, while 68 percent were "stable" and 14 percent were getting worse. If the BLM said that, we can safely assume that range conditions are actually much worse.

What can we do about this situation? This is the fun part—this is the part I like. It's not too easy to argue that we should do away with cattle ranching. The cowboy myth gets in the way. But I do have some solutions to overgrazing.

I'd begin by reducing the number of cattle on public lands. Not that range managers would go along with it, of course. In their eyes, and in the eyes of the livestock associations they work for, cutting down on the number of cattle is the worst possible solution—an impossible solution. So they propose all kinds of gimmicks. More cross-fencing. More wells and ponds so that more land can be exploited. These proposals are basically a maneuver by the Forest Service and the BLM to appease their critics without offending their real bosses in the beef industry.

I also suggest that we open a hunting season on range cattle. I realize that beef cattle will not make very sporting prey at first. Like all domesticated animals (including most humans), beef cattle are slow, stupid, and awkward. But the breed will improve if hunted regularly. And as the number of cattle is reduced, other and far more useful, beautiful, and interesting animals will return to the rangelands and will increase.

Suppose, by some miracle of Hollywood or inheritance or good luck, I should acquire a respectable-sized working cattle outfit. What would I do with it? First, I'd get rid of the stinking, filthy cattle. Every single animal. Shoot them all, and stock the place with real animals, real game, real protein: elk, buffalo, pronghorn antelope, bighorn sheep, moose. And some purely decorative animals, like eagles. We need more eagles. And wolves. We need more wolves. Mountain lions and bears. Especially, of course, grizzly bears. Down in the desert, I would stock every water tank, every water hole, every stock pond, with alligators.

You may note that I have said little about coyotes or deer. Coyotes seem to be doing all right on their own. They're smarter than their enemies. I've never heard of a coyote as dumb as a sheepman. As for deer, especially mule deer, they, too, are surviving—maybe even thriving, as some game and fish departments claim, though nobody claims there are as many deer now as there were before the cattle industry was introduced in the West. In any case, compared to elk the deer is a second-rate game animal, nothing but a giant rodent—a rat with antlers.

I've suggested that the beef industry's abuse of our Western lands is based on the old mythology of the cowboy as natural nobleman. I'd like to conclude this diatribe with a few remarks about this most cherished and fanciful of American fairy tales. In truth, the cowboy is only a hired hand. A farm boy in leather britches and a comical hat. A herdsman who gets on a horse to do part of his work. Some ranchers are also cowboys, but many are not. There is a difference. There are many ranchers out there who are bigtime farmers of the public lands—our property. As such, they do not merit any special consideration or special privileges. There are only about 31,000 ranchers in the whole American West who use the public lands. That's less than the population of Missoula, Montana.

The rancher (with a few honorable exceptions) is a man who strings barbed wire all over the range; drills wells and bulldozes stock ponds; drives off elk and antelope and bighorn sheep; poisons coyotes and prairie dogs; shoots eagles, bears, and cougars on sight; supplants the native grasses with tumbleweed, snakeweed, povertyweed, anthills, mud, dust, and flies. And then leans back and grins at the TV cameras and talks about how much he loves the American West. Cowboys are also greatly overrated. Consider the nature of their work. Suppose you had to spend most of your working hours sitting on a horse, contemplating the hind end of a cow. How would that affect your imagination? . . .

Do cowboys work hard? Sometimes. But most ranchers don't work very hard. They have a lot of leisure time for politics and belly-aching. Anytime you go into a small Western town you'll find them at the nearest drugstore, sitting around all morning drinking coffee, talking about their tax breaks.

Is a cowboy's work socially useful? No. As I've already pointed out, subsidized Western range beef is a trivial item in the national beef economy. If all of our 31,000 Western public land ranchers quit tomorrow, we'd never miss them. Any public school teacher does harder work, more difficult work, more dangerous work, and far more valuable work than any cowboy or rancher. The same thing applies to registered nurses and nurses' aides, garbage collectors, and traffic cops. Harder work, tougher work, more necessary work. We need those people in our complicated society. We do not need cowboys or ranchers. We've carried them on our backs long enough.

"This Abbey," the cowboys and their lovers will say, "this Abbey is a wimp. A chicken-hearted sentimentalist with no feel for the hard realities of practical life." Especially critical of my attitude will be the Easterners and Midwesterners newly arrived here from their Upper West Side apartments, their rustic lodges in upper Michigan. Our nouveau Westerners with their toy ranches, their pickup trucks with the gun racks, their pointy-toed boots with the undershot heels, their gigantic hats. And, of course, their pet horses. The *instant rednecks*.

To those who might accuse me of wimpery and sentimentality, I'd like to say this in reply. I respect real men. I admire true manliness. But I despise arrogance and brutality and bullies. So let me close with some nice remarks about cowboys and cattle ranchers. They are a mixed lot, like the rest of us. As individuals, they range from the bad to the ordinary to the good. A rancher, after all, is only a farmer, cropping the public rangelands with his four-legged lawnmowers, stashing our grass into his bank account. A cowboy is a hired hand trying to make an honest living. Nothing special.

I have no quarrel with these people as fellow humans. All I want to do is get their cows off our property. Let those cowboys and ranchers find some harder way to make a living, like the rest of us have to do. There's no good reason why we should subsidize them forever. They've had their free ride. It's time they learned to support themselves.

In the meantime, I'm going to say goodbye to all you cowboys and cowgirls. I love the legend, too—but keep your sacred cows and your dead horses off of my elk pastures.

■ CONSIDERATIONS OF MEANING AND METHOD

1. Understanding the original context of a piece of writing, including its audience, can help us understand a writer's purpose and consequently his or her strategies, especially in argumentation. In Abbey's case, however, an understanding of audience could raise more questions than it answers about purpose. Who is Abbey's audience at the University of Montana likely to consist of? Where in his argument does he appeal to his audience, and where does he provoke them? What could his purpose be in such provocation?

2. Abbey spends almost the first third of his essay recounting his personal experiences. What is his purpose in doing so? What would the essay lack if this portion of it were missing?

3. What is the fundamental problem that demands a solution, according to Abbey? What evidence does he cite to prove that the problem exists? Abbey offers specific reasons, or arguments, in support of his position that cattle should be removed from public lands. What are these reasons?

4. Which of Abbey's proposed solutions to the problem are serious, and which are not? Do his more ludicrous suggestions undermine his serious ones?

5. One of Abbey's objectives in "Even the Bad Guys Wear White Hats" is to debunk the myth of "the cowboy as natural nobleman." How does he establish himself as someone qualified to do this? How, specifically, does Abbey characterize cowboys and ranchers, and how does this characterization run contrary to our "most cherished and fanciful of American fairy tales"? What does the cowboy myth have to do with Abbey's arguments against private grazing on public lands?

6. Although Abbey's tone in this essay is humorous, it is impassioned and it is also confrontational. What was your personal response to his tone? Do you think Abbey's purpose is more to entertain, to incite an emotional response, or to propose real solutions?

7. Which classic strategies in effective, fair, and logical argumentation does Abbey abide by, and which does he defy? Overall, do you consider this an effective argument? Why or why not?

8. Abbey makes no bones about his bias. Does Sharman Apt Russell's essay offer enough information and a range of views to provide an adequate complement to Abbey's essay? What additional sources of information or points of view would be helpful in pro-

viding you with a more complete picture of the public lands debate?

■ POSSIBILITIES FOR WRITING

1. Voice is the quality in writing that most clearly reveals the personality of the writer. Edward Abbey's voice—his personality—comes across vividly in "Even the Bad Guys Wear White Hats," for better or worse in terms of the effectiveness of his argument. Cultivation of a distinctive writing voice is, generally speaking, something that instructors encourage in their students; yet voice can be difficult to manage. In a personal essay for your instructor and your classmates, discuss the importance of voice in your own writing. How would you characterize your voice as a writer? In what kinds of writing is your voice most pronounced and why? In what kinds of writing is it most subdued and why? Are you comfortable with your voice as a writer? Are other people, including your instructors, comfortable with it?

2. Write an argument urging a change in an existing policy (in your household, in your dorm, in your school's administration, in your local, state, or federal government—there are many possibilities). Choose a subject about which you feel strongly and about which you know a fair amount already. Research your subject carefully to fill any gaps that exist in your knowledge or understanding. In your argument, state and explain the problem and propose and defend your solution. Consider carefully to whom the argument is addressed, and when you are finished writing, deliver your argument to your reader. Remember the essential ingredients of an argument: a claim to be supported, an audience to read or hear it, exigence (the importance, timeliness, or occasion for the argument), and reasons to support the claim.

■ CYNTHIA RIGGS
Access to Public Lands: A National Necessity

Cynthia Riggs was born in Martha's Vineyard, Massachusetts, in 1931. She received her undergraduate degree in Geology from Antioch College, and her work over the years has allowed her to pursue both her scientific interests and her enjoyment of writing. Riggs lived and worked in Washington, D.C., much of her life. One of her first jobs was with the Smithsonian Institution in Washington. In 1963, she accompanied scientists on a marine expedition to the Antarctic and was asked by the Smithsonian to write up a report of the fifteen-year project of which this research expedition was a part. Subsequently, she wrote brochures and other materials for the Smithsonian, explaining the Institution's scientific research to the public. For many years, Riggs edited Petroleum Today, *a publication of the American Petroleum Institute in Washington. Riggs also holds a captain's license and during her time in Washington, D.C. operated tour boats on the Potomac River and worked as a "delivery captain," piloting boats for their owners to locations in the Caribbean and elsewhere.*

Riggs has developed a career, which she still pursues, as a freelance writer, covering subjects ranging from llamas to aquaculture for a wide variety of corporate publications and popular magazines. Her essay "Access to Public Lands: A National Necessity," which grew out of a freelance assignment, originally appeared in 1984 in Exxon USA, *a publication of the Exxon Corporation. The point of the assignment, says Riggs, was to present a point of view which favored the harvesting of natural resources on public lands, while making the distinction between heritage lands (such as the Grand Canyon) which need to be preserved and less distinguished tracts of public land which may as well be put to use through exploration and development. In conducting research for her article, Riggs says, factual accuracy was key, since Exxon's public image was at stake. Riggs says that, in understanding issues of public land use, it is important to consider all sides in the argument. It is her view that we must strive for "a balance between development and preservation." Riggs lives today in Martha's Vineyard, in the house (built in 1750) in which her mother was born, and is currently at work on two romance novels and a murder mystery.*

Quick! Name America's largest landowner. No, not the King Ranch. No, not the Bank of America. No, Exxon isn't even in the running. The answer is the federal government. Of America's 2,271 million acres, 720 million belong to Uncle Sam. Add another 966 million underwater acres of the country's continental shelf, and you've got an impressive bit of real estate there.

In terms of the nation's resources, that vast range of public property represents enormous volumes of timber, grass, and minerals. Copper, zinc, gold, vanadium, tantalum, iron, and silver are among dozens of metallic minerals mined on federal lands. In energy minerals alone, government land may contain more than half the nation's remaining resources. According to the Department of Energy, this includes 85 percent of the nation's crude oil, 40 percent of natural gas, 40 percent of uranium, 35 percent of coal, 80 percent of oil shale, 85 percent of tar sands, and 50 percent of geothermal resources.

What does this mean to those of us who don't even own a 50- by 100-foot lot? Like others who visit national parks and camp in national forests and photograph national monuments, we consider these lands our heritage. Divide it among us, and we'd each have something like three acres apiece. Like all landowners, we'd like those three acres cared for, protected, preserved. It's nice to be a landowner. But there's the rub. Each of us also needs farmland for crops, rangeland for grazing, timber for homes, metals for machines, and energy for heat and fuel. For these, we must turn increasingly to those same public lands of ours where such resources are still to be found.

"No one can feel happy about intrusions upon the wilderness," writes Dr. Charles F. Parks, professor of geology at Stanford University, in his book, *Earthbound.* "It is justified only by the urgency of the need."

The need is urgent, and getting more so. Yet tens of millions of acres of public lands have been closed to mineral development by law or administrative actions. As of early 1983, only 162 million acres of federal onshore land and 13 million acres of offshore land were under lease for oil and natural gas exploration and production.

And the trend is away from development and toward preservation. In many cases the economic use of land is prohibited in favor of a single-purpose use, such as preserving an area where a species of bird may nest, setting aside territory for grizzly bears, reestablishing a prairie ecosystem, or saving a historic site. From this clear need to protect a specific site, the drive for preservation has overwhelmed the concept of multiple use until today vast acreages of federal lands are permanently closed without reason or need, often without an evaluation of the land's aesthetic, biological, recreational, and economic resources. Would-be users—miners, skiers, cattle and sheep ranchers, farmers, campers, timber harvesters, energy firms—are affected.

Groups opposed to the multiple use of federal lands defend their stand in strong language: " . . . the industrial juggernaut must not further degrade the environment . . ." says an official of the Wilderness Society. Authors of the original law governing mineral extraction on federal lands are called a "rapacious gaggle of politicos" motivated by "cupidity and corruption." Under the appealing slogan, "Preserve the Wilderness," the Society fights to keep federal lands out of the hands of the "destroyers."

Who are the destroyers?

"Anyone who uses a sheet of paper, who drives an automobile, who has a telephone, a radio, a refrigerator," Dr. Parks says. "Anyone who owns a television set or uses artificial light. Anyone who heats a home, who applies paint, hammers a nail, or flushes a toilet. Even the staunchest of preservationists is such a destroyer."

Are environmentalists hypocritical, then?

Not really. Most hold their convictions with the best of intentions and genuine good will. They fear that without the strongest of safeguards, all public lands would be subject to indiscriminate development. They see bulldozers coming over every horizon. Yet most federal lands have no potential for mining or oil. Mineral lodes and oil-and-gas-bearing structures are not common. Their very rarity is what gives their development such high priority. The U.S. Geological Survey has identified 260 million of its on-shore acres in the lower 48 states as worth exploring for petroleum, which is a small percentage of the total acreage of federal lands. Of that, oil or gas deposits might lie beneath no more than one out of 10 of those acres. Were oil exploration encouraged to the fullest, few Americans would ever see signs of it. Nor would development, as conducted under today's environmental regulations, result in more than temporary change to the land.

Nonetheless, some environmental professionals continue to insist that more land should be set aside as wilderness. Robert Cahn, Washington editor for *Audubon Magazine,* writing of land within Alaska Wildlife Refuges, says that "the national interest might be served better by wilderness than by development." Cahn praises the Alaska National Interest Lands Conservation Act (which added 10 new national parks, 44 million acres to the National Park, and 56 million acres to the National Wilderness Preservation System) as "the greatest land-protection law in modern history."

And so it is. Yet land withdrawals of such magnitude must inevitably have serious implications for the American economy. "Civilized people want and must have raw materials, especially energy, at moderate prices," emphasizes Dr. Parks. "Nations have gone to the extreme of war to obtain them. For this reason, if for no other, those who advocate the preservation of large wilderness areas known to contain valuable and necessary raw materials are not going to prevail."

Other scientists confirm this view. Dr. William Conway, director of the New York Zoological Society and Bronx Zoo, advises, "It is absolutely impractical to imagine that the human race will not develop the undeveloped lands that remain on this earth." And he calls for a collaborative effort for development and conservation.

Similarly, public officials worried for America's welfare deplore extremes in the name of the environment. John B. Crowell, Jr., Assistant Secretary of Agriculture for Natural Resources and Environment, speaking at an Audubon Society meeting on pressures on the land, told his audience, "We are concerned that additions to the wilderness system be made with careful consideration of the costs . . . of foregoing the long-term availability of resources such as timber, minerals, oil and gas, geothermal power, developed recreation, and forest production."

The wilderness of which he speaks is one of several categories of the federal land system, which includes national parks and national monuments. The former now encompasses 68 million acres of land of exceptional natural, historic, or recreational value; the latter, a much smaller volume, covering the smallest area compatible with proper care or management. National monuments may be single buildings, such as Ford's Theatre in Washington, D.C., or an area of special geologic interest, such as the 211,000-acre Dinosaur National Monument in Utah and Colorado.

Mineral extraction is prohibited in national parks and national monuments.

Wildlife preserves account for almost 90 million acres of federal lands. Almost 54 million acres were added in 1980, all in Alaska. Petroleum exploration and production is permitted by law on wildlife refuges, provided proper environmental precautions are taken. In practice, however, few leases have been granted for such activities in these areas.

Wild and scenic rivers comprise another one million acres in the 49 states other than Alaska, and five million acres in Alaska. This relatively small percentage of federal land has a large impact on energy development because it limits access to other lands. Seismic or exploration crews cannot work across or near scenic rivers, and pipeline rights of way are restricted. Another federal land designation that limits economic use is that of National Grasslands and Wetlands. Petroleum operations are permitted legally, but administrative delays in granting leases drag on for months and even years. Military reservations make up another 30 million acres, and on these lands, public use of all kinds is tightly restricted. Indian lands generally have not presented an access problem, and tribal councils have worked with oil companies to make oil exploration and production compatible with Indian use—and economically desirable.

Two land programs particularly inhibiting to economic development are the Wilderness Preservation System, set up in 1964, and the Endangered Species Act. Together, these programs present a tangle of confusing and sometimes contradictory regulations.

The Wilderness Act defines wilderness as "an area where the earth and its community of life are untrammeled by man, where man himself is a visitor who does not remain." A wilderness area must be at least 5,000 acres in area, roadless, and unimproved. The wilderness program has grown from nine million acres to 80 million acres. If land now under study is added to the system, the wilderness area could be doubled to 167 million acres. The wilderness designation puts land off limits to all but a few users, such as backpackers. Motorized vehicles are prohibited, and road and permanent facilities are not allowed.

Some groups feel this is the way it should be. "Just because (land) is there, it's important, whether you or I or anyone else can get at it or not," says Stephen Chapman, of Minnesota's Clean Air, Clean Water Unlimited. "Perhaps (the land) is even better because we can't get to it."

Of wilderness, an article in *Harper's* magazine explains that "The wilderness concept appears valid if it is recognized for what it is—an attempt to create what are essentially 'ecological museums' in scenic and biologically significant areas of the lands. But 'wilderness' in the hands of environmentalists has become an all-purpose tool for stopping economic activity as well."

Conveniently ignored in all of this is the fact that most government land is not suitable for the "wilderness" category proposed for it. It has little aesthetic or recreational value. It has nothing in common with those spectacular parks such as Yellowstone, Yosemite, the Grand Canyon, or the Grand Teton. When land of scientific and recreational value is subtracted from the total, hundreds of millions of acres remain that can and should contribute to the national welfare through practical use. Its value as a source of raw materials far exceeds its value for recreation or science. Yet these lands, too, are often locked up with the rest.

Ignored, too, is the fact that the environmental impact of such economic activities as oil and gas extraction is slight, temporary, and carried out under strict guidelines that allow the land to revert eventually to its natural state. Yet it continues to be an article of faith among environmental activists that oil and gas activities equate with wholesale and permanent destruction which can be prevented only by prohibiting access to areas where the presence of hydrocarbons is suspected.

The Endangered Species Act is another law that has been widely used to stop economic activity. The story of the snail darter is well known. This small, minnow-sized fish, found in an area about to be inundated by construction of the Tellico Dam, a part of the TVA system, was pronounced an endangered species. As a result, construction of the multimillion-dollar dam was delayed for years at immense cost while scientists studied the possibility of relocating the fish to a new habitat. Eventually, it was discovered that snail darters are not all that uncommon, and the species was removed from the endangered list. But not until millions of dollars and valuable time had been lost.

Even private land is not exempt from the government's land policies. According to the Chase Manhattan Bank, about 30 percent of private land in the lower 48 states "has been effectively withdrawn by the need to comply with mind-boggling environmental laws and regulations. All this without any explicit analysis of the energy loss associated with alternate land uses."

Should Americans worry about the loss of energy resources? Some say no. We have enough oil and gas now, goes the argument. Let's lock up the land until we need its raw materials.

Yet the argument collapses in the face of the facts:

- America imports one-third of its oil at a cost of $50 billion a year.
- America consumes two barrels of oil from its reserves for each barrel of new oil found.
- On today's oil search, tomorrow's energy security depends.

Oil development is a long-range proposition. From the time a decision is made to prospect for oil, some 10 years may be needed to go through the lengthy process of looking for, finding, testing, developing, and producing oil into the nation's supply system. If the oil search is not pressed today, there won't be enough to go around tomorrow.

This reality lends a sense of urgency to the need to resolve a growing impasse over access to public lands. Arbitrary barriers to exploration and development of minerals on most public lands are neither wise nor necessary. A policy of careful, orderly, and steady development is preferable to one of nothing today followed by a crash program tomorrow when the awful truth sinks in.

Isn't that what you would prefer for your three acres? Should you be among the few to claim three acres in the Grand Canyon, you would certainly vote to protect it. But if you are among the many with three parched acres of sagebrush, tumbleweed, and alkali dust in Nevada's Basin and Range Province, or in the frozen bleak and barren tundra of North Alaska, your decision might well be, "Let's see if there isn't some badly needed oil under that land."

■ CONSIDERATIONS OF MEANING AND METHOD

1. What claims of fact does Riggs make in the first two paragraphs of her essay? Do you accept these claims as valid, based on her evidence? Does she state any warrants in these two paragraphs? What claims of value does she make in the third paragraph, and what warrants? In this paragraph, are claims supported by evidence? In paragraph five, Riggs's claim is that "The need is urgent, and getting more so." Where does she offer evidence to support this claim? Is the evidence adequate? Is the warrant based on this claim and evidence convincing?

2. Riggs refers to several expert sources to help support her position. Are her sources credible? Is Riggs's use of them convincing? What qualifies Riggs herself as a source? To what extent is she biased? What effect, if any, does her bias have on the credibility of her argument?

3. Where in her argument does Riggs acknowledge opposing views? Where does she accept them, and where does she refute them?

4. According to Riggs, oil companies are frustrated by the difficulties they encounter in acquiring leases on certain federal lands where such development is technically permitted. What sorts of lands are these, and to what does Riggs attribute the difficulty in acquiring leases? On which federal lands have oil companies been most successful in acquiring leases? Why?

5. In wilderness areas, mineral extraction is prohibited. What reasons does Riggs offer in her arguments that this policy is unfair and impractical? Are you convinced by her reasons? Riggs also claims that "the environmental impact of such economic activi-

ties as oil and gas extraction is slight, temporary, and carried out under strict regulations that allow the land to revert eventually to its natural state." What makes this claim convincing or unconvincing?

6. In the second-to-last paragraph, Riggs calls the "barriers to exploration and development of minerals on most public lands" "arbitrary" and maintains that they are "neither wise nor necessary." To what extent has her argument succeeded in convincing you of this?

■ POSSIBILITIES FOR WRITING

1. In conclusion, Riggs urges us to pursue "a policy of careful, orderly, and steady development" of public lands. She asks the rhetorical question in her closing paragraph, "Isn't that what you would prefer for your three acres?" In an essay, respond to Riggs by answering this question. Consider her point about the difference between lands (such as the Grand Canyon) she deems worth protecting and lands ("acres of sagebrush, tumbleweed, and alkali dust") she deems not worth protecting. This will be an argumentative essay that, in some degree, affirms or refutes Riggs's argument.

2. In her essay, Riggs refers to the Endangered Species Act and specifically to the case of the snail darter. The presence of this endangered fish in the area of Tellico Dam did indeed delay for years and at considerable economic cost construction of that dam. A similar and more recent example of the economic consequences of protection of an endangered species is the Northern spotted owl and its effects on the logging industry in the Northwest. Research the case of the snail darter, that of the Northern spotted owl, or a similar case. Pay careful attention to learning the facts of the case, including the history and premises of the Endangered Species Act. As you research the controversy involved, make sure you understand the range of views. What conclusions do you draw? To what extent should endangered species or habitats dictate economic development and progress? Write an argument, using the case you have researched as a specific example, addressing this question.

■ BY PHAM
Public Lands Should Remain Public

In the following introduction, student writer By Pham states his reasons for offering a counterargument to Cynthia Riggs's essay, "Access to Public Lands: A National Necessity." To help support his argument, Pham also refers to Edward Abbey's essay, "Even the Bad Guys Wear White Hats"; Noel Perrin's essay from Chapter 6, "Forever Virgin: The American View of America" (page 369); and an additional source, Bruce Hamilton's essay "Unfinished Business," which Pham located in his university library.

From son of a peasant farmer to pre-med student, I have traveled a bumpy road, learning every step of the way. I was born in 1973 in Hue, Vietnam, the exact date not known. My family immigrated first to Hong Kong, where we spent six grueling months in a refugee camp, and then to America in 1979, with the help of the Holy Family Catholic Church of Yakima, Washington.

From that point on, my family had to struggle to survive in the worst part of town. Working and saving religiously for thirteen years, my family and I moved out of "The Hole," but I will never forget the influences it had upon me. For me, living in low-income housing in a bad part of town deprived me of a lot of things, open space being one of them. There was never enough land for me to roam in and explore freely; the parks were too dangerous and I had no way of getting access to safer areas. The land that I was able to explore I did so meticulously.

Understanding the value of public lands compelled me to write the essay "Public Lands Should Remain Public" because I was furious after reading Cynthia Riggs's essay "Access to Public Lands: A National Necessity." Riggs insists that more public lands be made accessible to development by large corporations. I don't know what made me angrier, what she said or the reasons behind why she was saying it. She targets readers who are not sure of their position on the subject. She tries to persuade them to think the way she does. My purpose is to try to push the same audience in the opposite direction.

Cynthia Riggs says in her essay, "Access to Public Lands: A National Necessity" (published in 1984), that the U.S. government owns 720 million acres of land, roughly one-third of the total 2,271 million acres that lie within American borders. We already know from Edward Abbey's essay, "Even the Bad Guys Wear White Hats," that a great deal of public land in the Southwest has been ruined by private cattle grazing. Riggs suggests that more of the already cattle-trampled, strip-mined, eroded, and polluted public lands be made available to large corporations, like Exxon, the one that holds copyright to Riggs's essay, because there is a lot of public land and there are a lot of natural resources left to be extracted from it. Cynthia Riggs maintains that the government lands probably contain more than half of the nation's remaining natural resources, including 85 percent of its crude oil, 40 percent of its natural gas, and 40 percent of its uranium. In recent years the pressure to make these lands accessible to big business has increased due to our energy crisis.

It is this kind of "green light" attitude that Noel Perrin was writing about in his essay "Forever Virgin: The American View of America" that leads to the destruction of the most valuable natural resource of all: undisturbed nature. Noel Perrin wrote that Americans perceive nature as being infinite, never running out of resources. If Cynthia Riggs had lived in the time of the early European conquests of North America, she would undoubtedly have been an expansionist, without any inclination toward the preservation of nature. We can no longer afford this attitude of recklessness that allows Americans to be careless with their natural resources, not realizing that once they are gone, they are gone forever.

The fact that in recent years the need for new resources has increased because of an energy shortage does not make the exploitation of public lands for oil and other natural resources a necessity. Although we now know how much we can gain from solar energy, we have not yet fully utilized the power of the sun. Research is also being done in the areas of fusion and other renewable energy sources. Why don't we invest more in this research? Isn't nature worth it?

In her essay, Cynthia Riggs paints a picture of large corporations as being helpless, even selfless, in seeking to reap the benefits of resource-rich public lands in America. She says that "The need is urgent, and getting more so. Yet tens of millions of acres of public lands have been closed to mineral development by law or administrative actions. As of early 1983, only 162 million acres of federal onshore land and 13 million acres of offshore land were under lease for oil and natural gas exploration and production."

I don't know whether to view this argument as for or against easy access to public lands by private corporations. For one thing, the term "public lands" is very specific. It means that those lands designated as "public lands" are just that: they belong to the public. If access to these lands is made available to large private corporations without the consent of the public, then American democracy has broken down. If these lands belong to the public, the public should determine how these lands are to be used. Furthermore, when Cynthia Riggs acknowledges that 162 million acres of federal onshore land were under lease for extraction of natural resources, I think she means that to be a low number. In fact, that is almost 25 percent of the total acres belonging to the government. I would perceive this portion as being very substantial.

Furthermore, the large corporations that are depicted as being so helpless have connections within the government, primarily through the U.S. Forest Service and the Bureau of Land Management (BLM). The U.S. Forest Service was set up in 1905 to safeguard forest preserves, and the BLM was established in 1946 to preserve open range. These are the same rangelands that Edward Abbey describes as "cowburnt." Both of these agencies and others, such as the National Park Service (founded in 1916) and the U.S. Fish and Wildlife Service (founded in 1940), were set up to prevent abuse, but have gone astray from their missions. The U.S. Forest Service and the BLM have developed uncomfortably close relationships with commercial interests. Bruce Hamilton, in his 1989 article in *Sierra,* "Unfinished Business," tells us that "According to a recent Forest Science report, Forest Service district rangers agree with conservationists less than 5 percent of the time and with developers more than 47 percent of the time" (50). Even the National Forest Management Act of 1976, which was supposed to help plan for better conservation of national forests, has failed to relieve the pressure from big business to harvest resources from public lands.

The Bureau of Land Management has come to have a very poor reputation in the eyes of conservationists and the public, those people whose side they are supposed to be on. An investigation by the U.S. General Accounting Office concluded that "The BLM has often placed the needs of commercial interests such as livestock permittees and mine operators ahead of other users. . . . As a result, some permittees have come to view the use of these lands as a property right for private benefit" (qtd. in Hamilton 50). In this case, the agency designed to prevent land abuse is actually promoting it. This evidence has prompted some to rename the BLM, replacing the previous misnomer with the "Bureau of Livestock and Mining" (Hamilton 50).

Should public lands be open to big business like Exxon, the same company whose ship, the Exxon Valdez, wrecked in Alaska's waters, destroying that coastal ecosystem for years to come? Cynthia Riggs claims that companies who would be searching for resources would leave public lands in very good condition. I think Exxon has proved in what condition it will leave the land.

Public lands should remain public. Cynthia Riggs's depiction of big business as being helpless against the will of the public and the agencies formed to protect public lands is misleading. Big business is powerful enough to influence the most powerful government agencies. We need to preserve the limited natural resources that we still have despite the aims of money-craving millionaires who seek to take advantage of the government and the public. The survival of our environment depends upon the choices we make. If we destroy it, what of nature will our children have to enjoy?

Additional Source

Hamilton, Bruce. "Unfinished Business." *Sierra* Sept./Oct. 1989: 48–51.

■ CONSIDERATIONS OF MEANING AND METHOD

1. What reasons does Pham offer to support his claim that, despite energy shortages, "exploitation of public lands for oil and other natural resources" is not a necessity? Did his reasons convince you? Why or why not?

2. Riggs states in her essay that "tens of millions of acres of public lands have been closed to mineral development by law or administrative actions. As of early 1983, only 162 million acres of federal onshore land and 13 million acres of offshore land were under lease for oil and natural gas exploration and production." Pham responds to this statement with two points of his own. What are they? Do you find his response appropriate and his points valid? Why or why not?

3. Pham claims that Riggs "paints a picture of large corporations as being helpless, even selfless, in seeking to reap the benefits of resource-rich public lands in America." How does Pham counter this depiction? What picture does he paint of corporate developers of public lands?

4. Pham claims that large corporations "have connections within the government, primarily through the U.S. Forest Service and the Bureau of Land Management. . . ." What sources and what evidence does he cite to support this claim? What fundamental criticism does Pham level against the U.S. Forest Service and the Bureau of Land Management? Do you think this criticism is valid?

5. To counter Riggs's claim that oil companies will leave public lands in good condition, Pham points to the Exxon Valdez oil spill as evidence that they will not. Does this provide a fair and convincing counterargument?

6. Does Pham's final paragraph provide a persuasive conclusion to his argument? Why or why not?

■ **POSSIBILITIES FOR WRITING**

1. Pham claims that "the most valuable natural resource of all" is "nature undisturbed." This is a claim of value. Examine the assumptions that lie behind it, and consider the extent to which you agree or disagree with the statement. In an essay based on logic and reasoning, develop an argument supporting or refuting this statement.

2. Through library research, investigate in depth the history and consequences of one particular mining, timber, or oil drilling operation at a federally owned onshore or offshore site. Has the operation been controversial? If so, why? What issues were involved, and who has participated in the controversy? Who has profited from this development? What have the negative environmental impacts been, if any? To your mind, does this particular example further the argument for or the argument against development of public lands by private corporations? Does it suggest the need for particular changes in policy or practices? Write an argumentative essay for your class based on your investigation and the conclusions you draw from it.

Animal Rights

■ **PETER SINGER**
When Are Experiments on Animals Justifiable?

Animal rights advocate and philosopher Peter Singer was born in Melbourne, Australia, in 1946. He received both B.A. and M.A. degrees from the University of Melbourne and an advanced degree in philosophy from University College at Oxford in England. He has taught at Oxford University, New York University, and La Trobe University in Australia, and is currently a professor of philosophy at Monash University in Australia. Although his best-known writings to date promote animal rights, his current research encompasses a broad range of applied ethics, including bioethics.

When Singer taught at Oxford University in the early 1970s, he came to know a group of people who had adopted vegetarianism on ethical grounds; persuaded by their arguments that mistreatment of animals in any form, including eating them, could not be morally justified, Singer joined them. His first book, Democracy and Disobedience, *was published in 1974. Following quickly on its heels, in 1975, came two more books: a collection of writings,* Animal Rights and Human Obligations, *edited by Singer and Tom Regan, another key proponent of animal rights; and Singer's classic,* Animal Liberation: A New Ethic for Our Treatment of Animals. *The excerpt included here is from this latter work.*

Peter Singer was the first to coin the term "speciesism," by which he means "a prejudice or attitude of bias toward the interests of members of one's own species and against those of members of other species." Singer argues that speciesism provides the rationale for use of animals in scientific research and as products, and that speciesist assumptions are almost always morally unjustifiable. Many critics have applauded Singer's attempts to place the emotional issue of animal rights within the context of a reasoned, philosophical argument. Critic C. G. Luckhardt in the New York Times Book Review *says that "the great strength of this book lies in shifting the burden of argument to those who would maintain that animals ought to be excluded from our sphere of moral concern." Other critics have found Singer's arguments, though reasonable, somewhat naive. Nick Totton in the* Village Voice *observes that Singer's "arguments are lucid, but really quite beside the point: they depend firstly on the axiom that there is a network of ethical values somehow built into the universe, and secondly upon the fond hope that conformity with such values is the primary intention of human beings." As you read "When Are Experiments on Animals Justifiable?" note the construction of Singer's argument, based on reasoning and logical sequence.*

When are experiments on animals justifiable? Upon learning of the nature of many contemporary experiments, many people react by saying that all experiments on animals should be prohibited immediately. But if we make our demands as absolute as this, the experimenters have a ready reply: Would we be prepared to let thousands of humans die if they could be saved by a single experiment on a single animal?

This question is, of course, purely hypothetical. There never has been and there never could be a single experiment that saves thousands of lives. The way to reply to this hypothetical question is to pose another: Would the experimenter be prepared to carry out his experiment on a human orphan under six months old if that were the only way to save thousands of lives?

If the experimenter would not be prepared to use a human infant then his readiness to use nonhuman animals reveals an unjustifiable form of discrimination on the basis of species, since adult apes, monkeys, dogs, cats, rats, and other mammals are more aware of what is happening to them, more self-directing, and, so far as we can tell, at least as sensitive to pain as a human infant. (I specified that the human infant be an orphan to avoid the complications of the feelings of parents, although in so doing I am being overfair to the experimenter, since the nonhuman animals used in experiments are not orphans and in many species the separation of mother and young clearly causes distress for both.)

There is no characteristic that human infants possess to a higher degree than adult nonhuman animals, unless we are to count the infant's potential as a characteristic that makes it wrong to experiment on him. Whether this characteristic should count is controversial—if we count it, we shall have to condemn abortion along with experiments on infants, since the potential of the infant and the fetus is the same. To avoid the complexities of this issue, however, we can alter our original question a little and assume that the infant is one with severe and irreversible brain damage that makes it impossible for him ever to develop beyond the level of a six-month-old infant. There are, unfortunately, many such human beings, locked away in special wards throughout the country, many of them long since abandoned by their parents. Despite their mental deficiencies, their anatomy and physiology is in nearly all respects identical with that of normal humans. If, therefore, we were to force-feed them with large quantities of floor polish, or drip concentrated solutions of cosmetics into their eyes, we would have a much more reliable indication of the safety of these products for other humans than we now get by attempting to extrapolate the results of tests on a variety of other species. The radiation experiments, the heatstroke experiments, and many other experiments . . . could also have told us more about human reactions to the experimental situation if they had been carried out on retarded humans instead of dogs and rabbits.

So whenever an experimenter claims that his experiment is important enough to justify the use of an animal, we should ask him whether he would be prepared to use a retarded human at a similar mental level to the animal he is planning to use. If his reply is negative, we can assume that he is willing to use a nonhuman animal only because he gives less consideration to the interests of members of other species than he gives to members of his own—and this bias is no more defensible than racism or any other form of arbitrary discrimination.

Of course, no one would seriously propose carrying out the experiments . . . on retarded humans. Occasionally it has become known that some medical experiments have been performed on humans without their consent, and sometimes on retarded humans; but the consequences of these experiments for the human subjects are almost always trivial by comparison with what is standard practice for nonhuman animals. Still, these experiments on humans usually lead to an outcry against the experimenters, and rightly so. They are, very often, a further example of the arrogance of the research worker who justifies everything on the grounds of increasing knowledge. If experimenting on retarded, orphaned humans would be wrong, why isn't experimenting on nonhuman animals wrong? What difference is there between the two, except for the mere fact that, biologically, one is a member of our species and the other is not? But *that*, surely, is not a morally relevant difference, any more than the fact that a being is not a member of our race is a morally relevant difference.

Actually the analogy between speciesism and racism applies in practice as well as in theory in the area of experimentation. Blatant speciesism leads to painful experiments on other species, defended on the grounds of its contribution to knowledge and possible usefulness for our species. Blatant racism has led to painful experiments on other races, defended on the grounds of its contribution to knowledge and possible usefulness for the experimenting race. Under the Nazi regime in Germany, nearly 200 doctors, some of them eminent in the world of medicine, took part in experiments on Jews and Russian and Polish prisoners. Thousands of other physicians knew of these experiments, some of which were the subject of lectures at medical academies. Yet the records show that the doctors sat through medical reports of the infliction of horrible injuries on these "lesser races" and then proceeded to discuss the medical lessons to be learned from them without anyone making even a mild protest about the nature of the experiments. The parallels between this attitude and that of experimenters today toward animals are striking. Then, as now, the subjects were frozen, heated, and put in decompression chambers. Then, as now, these events were written up in a dispassionate scientific jargon. The following paragraph is taken from a report by a Nazi scientist of an experiment on a human being, placed in a decompression chamber; it could equally have been taken from accounts of recent experiments in this country on animals:

> After five minutes spasms appeared; between the sixth and tenth
> minute respiration increased in frequency, the TP [test person]
> losing consciousness. From the eleventh to the thirtieth minute res-
> piration slowed down to three inhalations per minute, only to cease
> entirely at the end of that period . . . about half an hour after
> breathing had ceased, an autopsy was begun.

Then, as now, the ethic of pursuing knowledge was considered sufficient justification for inflicting agony on those who are placed beyond the limits of genuine moral concern. Our sphere of moral concern is far wider than that of the Nazis; but so long as there are sentient beings outside it, it is not wide enough.

To return to the question of when an experiment might be justifiable. It will not do to say: "Never!" In extreme circumstances, absolutist answers always break down. Torturing a human being is almost always wrong, but it is not absolutely wrong. If torture were the only way in which we could discover the location of a nuclear time bomb hidden in a New York City basement, then torture would be justifiable. Similarly, if a single experiment could cure a major disease, that experiment would be justifiable. But in actual life the benefits are always much, much more remote, and more often than not they are nonexistent. So how do we decide when an experiment is justifiable?

We have seen that the experimenter reveals a bias in favor of his own species whenever he carries out an experiment on a nonhuman for a purpose that he would not think justified him in using a human being, even a retarded human being. This principle gives us a guide toward an answer to our question. Since a speciesist bias, like a racist bias, is unjustifiable, an experiment cannot be justifiable unless the experiment is so important that the use of a retarded human being would also be justifiable.

This is not an absolutist principle. I do not believe that it could *never* be justifiable to experiment on a retarded human. If it really were possible to save many lives by an experiment that would take just one life, and there were *no other way* those lives could be saved, it might be right to do the experiment. But this would be an extremely rare case. Not one tenth of one percent of the experiments now being performed on animals would fall into this category. . . .

It should not be thought that medical research would grind to a halt if the test I have proposed were applied, or that a flood of untested products would come onto the market. So far as new products are concerned it is true that, as I have already said, we would have to make do with fewer of them, using ingredients already known to be safe. That does not seem to be any great loss. But for testing really essential products, as well as for other areas of research, alternative methods not requiring animals can be and would be found. Some alternatives exist already and others would develop more rapidly if the energy and resources now applied to experimenting on animals were redirected into the search for alternatives.

At present scientists do not look for alternatives *simply because they do not care enough about the animals they are using.* I make this assertion on the best possible authority, since it has been more or less admitted by Britain's Research Defence Society, a group which exists to defend researchers from criticism by animal welfare organizations. A recent article in the *Bulletin* of the National Society for Medical Research (the American equivalent of the Research Defence Society) described how the British group successfully fought off a proposed amendment to the British law regulating experiments that would have prohibited any experiment using live animals if the purpose of that experiment could be achieved by alternative means not involving animals. The main objections lodged by the Research Defence Society to this very mild attempt at reform were, first, that in some cases it may be cheaper to use animals than other methods, and secondly, that: "in some cases alternatives may exist but they may be unknown to an investigator. With the vast amount of scientific literature coming out of even a very narrow field of study it is possible that an investigator may not know all that is now known about techniques or results in a particular area." (This ignorance would make the experimenter liable to prosecution under the proposed amendment.)

What do these objections amount to? The first can mean only one thing: that economic considerations are more important than the suffering of animals; as for the second, it is a strong argument for a total moratorium on animal experiments until every experimenter has had time to read up on the existing reports of alternatives available in his field and results already obtained. Is it not shocking that experimenters may be inflicting agony on animals only because they have not kept up with the literature in their field—literature that may contain reports of methods of achieving the same results without using animals? Or even reports of similar experiments that have been done already and are being endlessly repeated?

■ CONSIDERATIONS OF MEANING AND METHOD

1. When are experiments on animals justifiable, according to Singer?

2. Singer compares human infants with nonhuman animals. What is the basis of his comparison? How and why does he amend the comparison as he builds his argument in the first five paragraphs of the essay? How does the comparison function logically? What kind of emotional impact does it have?

3. At the beginning of paragraph five, Singer states that "whenever an experimenter claims that his experiment is important enough to justify the use of an animal, we should ask him whether he would be prepared to use a retarded human at a similar mental level to the animal he is planning to use." Has he convinced you that this is a fair question to ask a researcher? At the beginning of the next paragraph, Singer admits, "Of course, no one would seriously propose carrying out the experiments . . . on retarded humans." If his argument has been successful thus far, what is the next logical conclusion?

4. Singer draws an analogy, which he says "applies in practice as well as theory," between speciesism and racism. Do you consider the comparison valid? Why or why not? How does the analogy advance Singer's argument?

5. Singer asserts that speciesism is unjustifiable. Can you anticipate logical arguments that might counter his assertion?

6. What evidence does Singer cite to support his claim that "At present scientists do not look for alternatives [to animal research] *simply because they do not care enough about the animals they are using*"? What conclusions does Singer draw from the evidence? Do you, as Singer does, find it "shocking that experimenters may be inflicting agony on animals only because they have not kept up with the literature in their field . . . "?

■ POSSIBILITIES FOR WRITING

1. Singer points out that alternatives to animal experimentation do exist, and he maintains that "others would develop more rapidly if the energy and resources now applied to experimenting on animals were redirected into the search for alternatives." Investigate

alternatives to animal experimentation. What alternatives currently exist, which are most successful, and how widely have they been implemented? What stumbling blocks exist in discovery and implementation of alternative experimentation methods? Does the future look promising for alternatives to animal experimentation? Report, orally or in an essay for your class, what you discover through your research. Your research and the conclusions you draw from it may well lead you to an argument. For example, you might argue that more aggressive measures need to be taken to encourage or even to force researchers to adopt alternatives to animal experimentation. Or you might argue that alternative research methods are less productive than experiments on animals or too expensive to be widely implemented. Whatever your argument is, be sure to examine and address the assumptions of value behind it.

2. Animals are widely used in product testing as well as for medical research, and many people who would find the use of animals reprehensible in testing products such as face cream or floor polish would sanction their use in the cancer research lab. However, distinctions between "vital" and "nonvital" research are not always so easy to make. Would you condone the use of animals, for example, in the testing of cosmetic surgery techniques? How would you define "vital" research? Explore, in thinking and library research, the gray area between vital and nonvital research. Locate in your research one or two examples of research, using animals, which could be considered either vital or nonvital, and explore the implications in a report or an essay for your class.

■ **DAVID QUAMMEN**

Animal Rights and Beyond: The Search for a New Moral Framework and a Righteous Gumbo

See the headnote for David Quammen's "The Face of a Spider" in Chapter 4 (page 235) for biographical information.

David Quammen's essay "Animal Rights and Beyond: The Search for a New Moral Framework and a Righteous Gumbo" is in effect an elaborate book review, taken from his collection of essays Natural Acts: A Sidelong View of Science and Nature *(1985). In the essay, Quammen, in his typically accessible and entertaining style, responds to the fundamental arguments put forth by two key animals rights advocates: Peter Singer, in his book,* Animal Liberation *(1975), and Tom Regan, in his book* The

*Case for Animal Rights (1983). Although Quammen admires the
attempts both men make at "applying the methods of systematic
philosophy to an important and long-neglected question" and
respects them for "fighting the good fight," he questions the line
each draws in distinguishing between species that deserve our
moral consideration and those that do not. In this essay, as in "The
Face of a Spider," Quammen explores the fundamental question,
"How should a human behave toward the members of other living
species?"*

Do non-human animals have rights? Should we humans feel
morally bound to exercise consideration for the lives and well-being
of individual members of other animal species? If so, how much consideration, and by what logic? Is it permissible to torture and kill? Is
it permissible to kill cleanly, without prolonged pain? To abuse or
exploit without killing? For a moment, don't think about whales or
wolves or the California condor; don't think about the cat or the
golden retriever with whom you share your house. Think about
chickens. Think about laboratory monkeys and then think about lab
rats and then also think about lab frogs. Think about scallops. Think
about mosquitoes.

It's a Gordian question, by my lights, but one not very well suited
to Alexandrian answers. Some people would disagree, judging the
matter simply enough settled, one way or the other. *Of course they
have rights. Of course they don't.* I say beware any such snappy,
steel-trap thinking. Some folk would even—this late in the evolution
of human sensibility—call it a frivolous question, a time-filling diver-
sion for emotional hemophiliacs and cranks. *Women's rights, gay
rights, now for Christ sake they want ANIMAL rights.* Notwithstanding the ridicule, the strong biases toward each side, it is certainly
a serious philosophical issue, important and tricky, with almost endless implications for the way we humans live and should live on this
planet.

Philosophers of earlier ages, if they touched the subject at all, were
likely to be dismissive. Thomas Aquinas announced emphatically
that animals "are intended for man's use in the natural order. Hence
it is no wrong for man to make use of them, either by killing or in
any other way whatever." Descartes held that animals are merely machines. As late as 1901, a moral logician named Joseph Rickaby (who
happened to be a Jesuit, but don't necessarily hold that against him)
declared: "Brute beasts, not having understanding and therefore not

being persons, cannot have any rights. The conclusion is clear." Maybe not quite so clear. Recently, just during the past decade, professional academic philosophers have at last begun to address the matter more open-mindedly.

Two thinkers in particular have been influential: an Australian named Peter Singer, an American named Tom Regan. In 1975 Singer published a book titled *Animal Liberation,* which stirred up the debate among his colleagues and is still treated as a landmark. Eight years later Tom Regan published *The Case for Animal Rights,* a more thorough and ponderous opus that stands now as a sort of companion piece to the Singer book. In between there came a number of other discussions of animal rights—including a collection of essays edited jointly by Singer and Regan. Despite the one-time collaboration, Peter Singer and Tom Regan represent two distinct schools of thought: They reach similar conclusions about the obligations of humans to other animals, but the moral logic is very different, and possibly also the implications. Both men have produced some formidable work and both, to my simple mind, show some shocking limitations of vision.

I've spent the past week amid these books, Singer's and Regan's and the rest. It has been an edifying experience, and now I'm more puzzled than ever. I keep thinking about monkeys and frogs and mosquitoes and—sorry, but I'm quite serious—carrots.

Peter Singer's view is grounded upon the work of Jeremy Bentham, that eighteenth-century British philosopher generally known as the founder of utilitarianism. "The greatest good for the greatest number" is a familiar cartoon version of what, according to Bentham, should be achieved by the ethical ordering of society and behavior. A more precise summary is offered by Singer: "In other words, the interests of every being affected by an action are to be taken into account and given the same weight as the like interests of any other being." If this much is granted, the crucial next point is deciding what things constitute *interests* and who or what qualifies as a *being.* Evidently Bentham did not have just humans in mind. Back in 1789, optimistically and perhaps presciently, he wrote: "The day *may* come when the rest of the animal creation may acquire those rights which never could have been withholden from them but by the hand of tyranny." Most philosophers of his day were inclined (as most in our day are still inclined) to extend moral coverage only to humans, because only humans (supposedly) are rational and communicative. Jeremy Bentham took exception: "The question is not, Can they *reason?* nor, Can they *talk?* but, Can they *suffer?*" On this crucial point, Peter Singer follows Bentham.

The capacity to suffer, says Singer, is what separates a being with legitimate interests from an entity without interests. A stone has no interests that must be respected, because it cannot suffer. A mouse can suffer; therefore it has interests and those interests must be weighed in the moral balance. Fine, that much seems simple enough. Certain people of sophistic or Skinnerian bent would argue that there is no proof a mouse can in fact suffer, that it's merely an anthropomorphic assumption; but since each of us has no proof that *anyone* else actually suffers besides ourselves, we are willing, most of us, to grant the assumption. More problematic is that very large gray area between stones and mice.

Peter Singer declares: "If a being suffers, there can be no moral justification for disregarding that suffering, or for refusing to count it equally with the like suffering of any other being. But the converse of this is also true. If a being is not capable of suffering, or of enjoyment, there is nothing to take into account." Where is the boundary? Where falls the line between creatures who suffer and those that are incapable? Singer's cold philosophic eye travels across the pageant of living species—chickens suffer, mice suffer, fish suffer, um, lobsters most likely suffer, *look alive, you other creatures!*—and his damning stare lands on the oyster.

No I'm not making this up. The oyster, by Singer's best guess, doesn't suffer. Its nervous system lacks the requisite complexity. Therefore, while lobsters and crawfish and shrimp possess inviolable moral status, the oyster has none. It is a difficult judgment, Singer admits, by no means an infallible one, but "somewhere between a shrimp and an oyster seems as good a place to draw the line as any, and better than most."

Moral philosophy, no one denies, is an imperfect science.

Tom Regan takes exception with Singer on two important points. First, he disavows the utilitarian framework, with its logic that abuse or killing of animals by humans is wrong because it yields a net *overall* decrease in welfare, among all beings who qualify for moral status. No, argues Regan, that logic is false and pernicious. The abuse or killing is wrong in its *essence*—however the balance comes out on overall welfare—because it violates the rights of those individual animals. Individual rights, in other words, take precedence over the maximizing of the common good. Second, in Regan's opinion the capacity to suffer is not what marks the elect. Mere suffering is not sufficient. Instead he posits the concept of *inherent value,* a complex and magical quality possessed by some living creatures but not others.

A large portion of Regan's book is devoted to arguing toward this concept. He is more uncompromisingly protective of certain creatures—those with rights—than Singer, but he is also more selective; the hull of his ark is sturdier, but the gangplank is narrower. According to Regan, individual beings possess inherent value (and therefore inviolable rights) if they "are able to perceive and remember; if they have beliefs, desires, and preferences; if they are able to act intentionally in pursuit of their desires or goals; if they are sentient and have an emotional life; if they have a sense of the future, including a sense of their own future; if they have a psychophysical identity over time; and if they have an individual experiential welfare that is logically independent of their utility for, and the interests of, others." So Tom Regan is not handing rights around profligately, to every cute little beast that crawls over his foot. In fact we all probably know a few humans who, at least on a bad night, might have trouble meeting those standards. But how would Regan himself apply them? Where does he see the line falling? Who qualifies for inherent value, and what doesn't?

Like Singer, Regan has thought this point through. Based on his grasp of biology and ethology, he is willing to grant rights to "mentally normal mammals of a year or more."

Also like Singer, he admits that the judgment is not infallible: "Because we are uncertain where the boundaries of consciousness lie, it is not unreasonable to advocate a policy that bespeaks moral caution." So chickens and frogs should be given the benefit of the doubt, as should all other animals that bear a certain degree of anatomical and physiological resemblance to us mentally normal mammals.

But Regan does not specify just what degree.

The books by Singer and Regan leave me with two very separate reactions. The first combines admiration and gratitude. These men are applying the methods of systematic philosophy to an important and much-neglected question. Furthermore, they don't content themselves with just understanding and describing a pattern of gross injustice; they also emphatically say *Let's stop it!* They are fighting a good fight. Peter Singer's book in particular has focused attention on the outrageous practices that are routine in American factory farms, in "psychological" experimentation, in research on the toxicity of cosmetics. Do you know how chickens are dealt with on the large poultry operations? How veal is produced? How the udders of dairy cows are kept flowing? Do you know the sorts of ingenious but pointless torment that thousands of monkeys and millions of rats endure, each year, to fill the time and the dissertations of uninspired graduate students? If you don't, by all means read Singer's *Animal Liberation.*

The second reaction is negative. Peter Singer and Tom Regan, it seems to me, share a breathtaking smugness and myopia not too dissimilar to the brand they so forcefully condemn. Theirs is a righteous and vigorous smugness, not a passive and unreflective one. But still.

Singer inveighs against a sin he labels *speciesism*—discrimination against certain creatures based solely upon the species to which they belong. Regan uses a slightly less confused and less clumsy phrase, *human chauvinism,* to indicate roughly the same thing. Both of them arrive (supposedly by sheer logic) at the position that vegetarianism is morally obligatory: To kill and eat a "higher" animal represents absolute violation of one being's rights; to kill and eat a plant evidently violates nothing at all. Both Singer and Regan claim to disparage the notion—pervasive in Western philosophy since Protagoras—that "Man is the measure of all things." Both argue elaborately against anthropocentrism, while creating new moral frameworks that are also decidedly anthropocentric. Make no mistake: Man is still the measure, for Singer and Regan. The test for inherent value has changed only slightly. Instead of asking *Is the creature a human?,* they simply ask *How similar to human is similar enough?*

Peter Singer explains that shrimp deserve brotherly treatment but oysters, so different from us, are fair game for the gumbo. In Tom Regan's vocabulary, the redwood tree is an "inanimate natural object," sharing that category with clouds and rocks. But some simple minds would say: Life is life.

■ CONSIDERATIONS OF MEANING AND METHOD

1. Quammen, as Singer does, opens his essay with a fundamental question, followed by a series of consequentially related questions. Does Quammen's essay answer his fundamental question? What is his purpose, or purposes, in writing?

2. Quammen advises his readers to "beware of . . . snappy, steel-trap thinking" when considering the complex moral question of

animal rights. Singer, in "When Are Experiments on Animals Justifiable?" admits that "This is not an absolutist principle. I do not believe that it could *never* be justifiable to experiment on a retarded human." (Would it be fair to assume, by inference, that Singer does not believe that it could *never* be justifiable to experiment on nonhumans?) How flexible is Quammen in his thinking? How rigid in his thinking is Singer?

3. Voice in writing can be defined as the sense of the writer's personality that comes across in his or her use of language. Quammen's writing voice is quite distinctive. Make a list of a half dozen or so sentences from the essay which demonstrate Quammen's voice and compare them in class with other students' examples. How would you characterize Quammen's voice? How does voice contribute to the effectiveness of Quammen's writing? For what audience would it be most and least effective?

4. In the third paragraph, Quammen provides a brief history of past philosophers' views on the rights of animals, or the lack thereof. On what assumptions are these views based?

5. Explain the premises of Singer's argument for animal rights. Explain the premises of Regan's argument for animal rights. In what crucial respects do the conclusions drawn by the two men differ? Explain the meaning and appropriateness of Quammen's metaphor, "the hull of his [Regan's] ark is sturdier, but the gangplank is narrower."

6. On what grounds does Quammen praise the work of Peter Singer and of Tom Regan? On what grounds does he criticize it? To what extent do you agree or disagree with his criticism?

■ POSSIBILITIES FOR WRITING

1. Which animals, including human beings, would you consider entirely "off limits" for experimentation? Why these animals? What distinguishes them from other animals? In a reasoned argument, attempt to justify where you would draw the line. If and when reason fails you, on what do you base your determination? If your determination is not based entirely upon reason, why should your reader consider it valid?

2. In an analytical essay for readers familiar with the works, compare the two essays by Quammen included in this text, "The Face of a Spider" (in Chapter 4) and "Animal Rights and Beyond." How do the two essays reflect upon each other, extending Quammen's discussion of what should guide human behavior to-

ward members of other living species? What are your own conclusions?

3. In "Animal Rights and Beyond," Quammen praises Singer in particular for bringing to public attention, in his book *Animal Liberation*, "the outrageous practices that are routine in American factory farms, in 'psychological' experimentation, in research on the toxicity of cosmetics." Through research, investigate this subject (or one particular area of it) in depth. One of your sources could be Singer's book. What are these practices? Have practices improved over the past twenty years? If so, as a consequence of what? Report in writing on what you discover and argue, if appropriate, for the need for further improvements.

■ ANNE POLLOCK
Animal Rights: Alternative Approaches

In her statement, student writer Anne Pollock explains what motivated her to learn more about the positions that animal rights activists take in promoting their cause.

I am from Buffalo, New York. When I got to college, I was clueless about what I wanted to do for the rest of my life. I took a lot of random classes just to try to find areas that I was interested in and, as it stands now, I am thinking about majoring in English or communications, or possibly both. I may want to pursue journalism in the future. I really enjoy writing, but I have problems when it comes to personal writing, where I have to reveal myself in some way. This is a kind of writing that I think I need to work on, but I don't know if I'll ever be really good at it. I much prefer investigative writing and writing in which I have a point to prove.

The assignment that produced this piece required everyone in the class to find an article from a magazine or journal and summarize its points. I picked this particular article because we had been doing a lot of reading on animal testing in class and it resparked my interest in the topic. I am a vegetarian myself and have been since eighth grade. When I was younger, I was involved, to a small extent, in the fight for animal rights. My period of activism did not last long because I felt alienated by the extremism of other supporters of the cause; I could not see how their radical tactics were going to solve the problem. My belief in animal rights has not changed, but now I carry out my beliefs as an individual. Reading articles on the subject made me wonder again

if there were alternatives out there for people who were concerned,
as I was, with the rights of animals, but who were seeking a middle
ground, and in reading and writing about Tom Regan and Gary
Francione's article, "A Movement's Means Creates Its Ends," I
hoped to discover the answer to this question.

It is often the case in this country that extremists' views are the
only ones represented. This leaves those who are either unable or not
ready to commit to radical philosophies out in the cold. This is how I
have felt about the animal rights debate. I was, therefore, quite excited to find an article by Tom Regan and Gary Francione called "A
Movement's Means Creates Its Ends," which not only describes the
platform of animal rights activists but also the platform of a group I
had been unaware of, the animal welfarists.

This group's more tolerant attitude toward others' beliefs encouraged me. Animal welfarists seek a kinder treatment of animals but do
not espouse the goal of "*total* liberation of nonhuman animals from
human tyranny" as do the animal rights activists. Animal welfarists
are committed to the pursuit of "gentle usage" of animals (40). They
believe it morally permissible to use nonhumans for medical research
to benefit humans but think humans should try to minimize suffering. Thus, whereas animal rights activists oppose in principle all use
of animals by humans in which the animal does not benefit too and
seek to abolish all such current "exploitation" in practice, welfarists
seek to reform current practices of animal treatment, differentiating
between legitimate use and abuse. They believe this is a goal that all
animal advocates can work toward together. This goal may seem very
reasonable until it is understood through the eyes of an animal rights
activist.

Although Regan and Francione articulate clearly and fairly the animal welfarists' point of view, the article explicitly promotes the perspective of animal rights activists. Animal rights activists who dis-
avow the philosophy of animal welfare believe one cannot support
"reformist means," as the welfarists do, and expect to come up with
"abolitionist ends," which is the only outcome the animal rights activists will settle for (40). They state that the philosophies of animal
rights and animal welfare are separated by irreconcilable differences,
and that not only are the practical reforms grounded in animal welfare morally at odds with those sanctioned by the philosophy of animal rights, but that the enactment of animal welfare measures actually impedes the achievement of animal rights. Animal rights

philosophy rests on the "moral inviolability of the individual, both human or nonhuman" (40). Its goal is to abolish all exploitation of animals, and the welfarists' hope to limit as much as possible the suffering of these animals is clearly not going to accomplish this.

One cannot suppose that making animal research more humane will persuade people in the future to stop using animals in research. It seems as though just the opposite might happen, leading to an "*indefinite perpetuation* of such exploitation" (40). An example illustrating the way in which animal testing has become legitimized in the name of animal "welfare" is the federal Animal Welfare Act, which was seen by many as being a step forward in the struggle to end exploitation of animals. The Act sets standards to govern the care and use of animals in experimentation. Amendments to the Act in 1985 were supported by welfarists but despised by many animal rights activists because, they say, it gives vivisectors a legal basis for justification of use of animals in laboratories. Animal rights activists argue that the Animal Welfare Act has been used by the biomedical industry as a public relations gimmick since they can identify themselves with animal welfare rather than animal exploitation in pointing to their conforming to standards set by the Animal Welfare Act.

Animal rights activists claim that the Animal Welfare Act is dangerous in that it gives the public a false sense of security, the mistaken impression that because regulations governing the care and use of animals in medical research exist, these animals are not being abused. The Animal Welfare Act does prohibit "'unnecessary' animal suffering, but *leaves to the . . . discretion of vivisectors* what constitutes 'necessity'" (40–41). The Act requires research facilities to have Institutional Animal Care and Use Committees to regulate the treatment of animal subjects, providing them with "protection equivalent to that provided by human experimentation review committees." Human experimentation, however, "requires the *informed consent* of the human subject," a concept that cannot be carried over to animal experimentation (41). These examples show how nonabolitionist tactics, although usually well-intentioned, are simply not effective and are, in fact, contrary to animal advocacy from an animal rights point of view.

It is the belief of many nonabolitionist animal advocates that abolitionist philosophy favors inaction to gradual reform. Regan and Francione say that this is a misunderstanding. A gradual approach to end animal exploitation is perfectly consistent with the animal rights activists' beliefs, as long as the steps that are taken "are abolitionist in nature" and lead somehow to the eventual end of all experimentation on animals. Any steps taken must put an end to at least a small aspect of animal testing. It is not enough to seek less cruel treatment of animals if, in the process, one in effect condones the perpetuation of experimentation.

There is currently a fundamental division between animal rights activists and animal welfarists within the animal advocacy movement. Some believe that this internal division will harm the cause of animal advocacy, slow its progress and dilute its power. The error in this belief lies in the assumption that there was unity to begin with. Although it is possible for the two groups to coexist, it would be impracticable for them to unite because they have fundamentally different goals. The abolitionists, or animal rights activists, believe that animal rights organizations should pursue animal rights campaigns. They do not condone the spending of human and economic resources on projects that seek to promote the welfare of animals by improving conditions and treatment but do not vindicate the rights of these nonhumans. Although animal rights activists value individual acts of kindness and amelioration of animal suffering, expanding the movement's philosophies to include everyone who has a concern for animals "would be to adopt views that are so broad as to be meaningless." This would merely serve to "frustrate, rather than forward, the achievement of animal rights goals." When an animal rights organization attempts to be all things to all people, it will ensure that animal rights will remain an "unattainable ideal" (42).

Regan and Francione conclude with the idea that "the philosophy of animal rights views the systematic exploitation of animals as a symptom of a society that tolerates the systematic exploitation of 'the other,' including those human 'others' who lack the . . . means to resist oppression" (43). The animal rights activists believe that all exploitation of both humans and nonhumans must be stopped.

I find that the arguments that Regan and Francione present in favor of the more extremist position on animal rights are quite convincing. They seem to point to the conclusion that the issue of animal rights is one which requires those involved to take a strong stand if they are truly hoping to further the cause of the movement.

Source

Regan, Tom, and Gary Francione. "The Animal 'Welfare' vs. 'Rights' Debate: A Movement's Means Creates Its Ends." *The Animals' Agenda* 12:1 (Jan./Feb. 1992): 40–43.

■ CONSIDERATIONS OF MEANING AND METHOD

1. What was the question that motivated Pollock's investigation? Did she find the answers she was looking for? What is Pollock's conclusion? Did it surprise you?

2. The article Pollock located in the library is coauthored by Tom Regan and Gary Francione. Was this a promising source to investigate in the search for a "middle ground" in the animal rights debate? Why or why not?

3. Pollock's essay summarizes Regan and Francione's article. Try to locate this article in your library. If you are successful in finding it, bring it to class to share. Read the article and compare it to Pollock's essay. Is Pollock's essay a good summary? If you had written a summary of the article, how would it have differed?

4. Explain in your own words the differences between the position of animal welfarists and that of animal rightists. Does Pollock explain these differences well? Do you believe these two positions are fundamentally incompatible? Do you think dissension among animal advocates threatens to weaken the movement's progress? Why or why not?

5. In paragraph eight of her essay, Pollock writes that animal rightists view "the systematic exploitation of animals as a symptom of a society that tolerates the systematic exploitation of 'the other,' including those human 'others' who lack the . . . means to resist oppression." Is this concept clear to you? Explain and speculate about it. If it is not clear in the essay, how could it be made more so?

■ POSSIBILITIES FOR WRITING

1. Some animal rights activists have employed radical tactics to achieve their goals, including breaking into labs in order to "liberate" animals used in research or dowsing fur coats with paint. These tactics are akin to those employed by other radical environmentalists (called by some environmental warriors and by others environmental terrorists) in their attempts to stop whaling, logging, and other practices that they find morally and/or environmentally reprehensible. Are these radical tactics justifiable? Write an argument explaining and defending your position. Research one or two cases in which these tactics have been employed, and use them to illustrate and support your argument.

2. Consumers' environmental concerns, including those about the welfare and rights of animals, are reflected in the products they

buy. Today, labels on shampoo bottles boast that no animals were used in testing the product; tuna cans carry the dolphin-free symbol. How much of an impact has the animal rights movement had on the American consumer? Investigate the questions through research. Do you think environmental marketing is a marketing ploy or consumer fad, or is it sincere and here to stay?

Genetic Engineering

■ **AMY VIRSHUP**
Perfect People?

Amy Virshup says that she became interested in the subject of genetic testing through a friend who is a physician specializing in cystic fibrosis. As her friend marveled at recent breakthroughs and talked about how much they were going to change her job, Virshup became intrigued. "Once I started researching the piece (which took me over a year to report and write)," says Virshup, "I realized that the new science brought with it serious ethical dilemmas involving our attitudes toward disability, abortion, gender selection, and the 'perfectibility' of human beings."

"For me," she continues, "the way to approach these kinds of questions is never in the abstract, but in the particular. Therefore, I talked not only to medical ethicists and researchers, but also to genetic counselors, to physicians treating children with illnesses, and most important, to mothers and fathers who'd used the tests and had to deal with their implications." Since the most common test for genetic abnormalities is amniocentesis, used primarily to detect Down syndrome, Virshup talked with parents of Down children about how they had dealt with their children's disability, and she observed at a school for Down children in New York to see for herself the varying levels of achievement that these children possess. "Interestingly," reports Virshup, "Jason Kingsley, the son of the woman in the piece, has just written a book about living with Down syndrome." Virshup says that she tried "to tell the story as much as possible from the perspectives of the people I'd interviewed, even when I disagreed. My goal was to put the reader in the position of a parent, doctor, or researcher and get him or her to ask, 'What would I do in that situation?'"

Amy Virshup was born in 1960. She holds a B.A. in philosophy *from Tufts University. She has been a writer and an editor at* New York *and* Manhattan *magazines and* The Village Voice. *She was a* John S. Knight Fellow in journalism at Stanford University during the 1994–95 academic year.*

Susan and Tom Murphy* have glimpsed the future. In the spring of 1984, when Susan was four months pregnant with their second child, they learned that their firstborn, sixteen-month-old Sarah,* had cystic fibrosis, an inherited, incurable disease that can mean a short, difficult life for its victims. Sarah would likely need constant medication and daily sessions of strenuous physical therapy. To make matters worse, no one could say whether the child Susan was carrying also had the disease.

Their doctor advised the Murphys to consider having an abortion. But they decided to have the baby, and after five tense months, their son was born—without the disease. Though both Tom and Susan wanted a large family, neither was willing to risk conceiving another child who might get CF.

Within two years, the Murphys changed their minds. By then, researchers abroad had found a way to home in on the gene that causes CF, and a prenatal test had become available in the United States for families who already had a child with the disease. A door had been opened for the Murphys, and they decided they could chance another pregnancy. Tom, Susan, and Sarah had preliminary analyses of their DNA—the body's basic genetic material—and Susan became pregnant in September 1986.

Just nine weeks into her pregnancy, she had chorionic villus sampling (CVS), a recently developed twenty-minute procedure similar to amniocentesis. The CVS material was sent to the lab, and the Murphys could only wait—and worry—for ten days. They'd never decided just what they would do if the news was bad, but abortion was a real option. The day before Thanksgiving, they got the news: Their unborn child did not have CF.

Suddenly, without much time to ponder the moral and ethical implications, Americans are being thrust into the age of the tentative pregnancy. For many, the decision to have a child is made not at conception but when the lab sends back the test results. "The difference between having a baby twenty years ago and having a baby today," says ethics specialist Dr. John Fletcher of the National Institutes of

---

*Names marked with an asterisk have been changed.

Health, "is that twenty years ago, people were brought up to accept what random fate sent them. And if you were religious, you were trained to accept your child as a gift of God and make sacrifices. That's all changing."

Over the last decade, genetics has been revolutionized: Using remarkable new DNA technology, molecular biologists can now diagnose in the womb inherited diseases like CF, hemophilia, Huntington's chorea, and Duchenne muscular dystrophy. Genetics is advancing at unprecedented speed, and important breakthroughs are announced almost monthly.

Since each person's DNA is distinct, the potential uses of genetic testing seem limitless: It could settle paternity suits, take the place of dental records or fingerprints in forensic medicine, identify missing children, warn about a predisposition to diseases caused by workplace health hazards. By the mid-1990s, geneticists should be able to screen the general population for harmful genes and test—at birth—a person's likelihood of developing certain types of cancer, high blood pressure, and heart disease.

Besides the prenatal tests now commonly in use, doctors may have a blood test that screens fetal cells in a mother's bloodstream and determines the fetus's sex and whether it has any chromosomal disorders or inherited genetic diseases. Work toward the ultimate goal—gene therapy—has already begun.

But this technological wizardry has some vehement opponents. A French government committee made up of doctors and lawyers recently called for a three-year moratorium on prenatal genetic tests because of the fear that they would lead to "ethically reprehensible attempts to standardize human reproduction for reasons of health and convenience." This is similar to the objection that anti-abortionists have always raised and now extend to genetic testing. (The Vatican, in its recent "instruction" on birth technology, condemned any prenatal test that might lead to abortion.) These days, though, right-to-lifers are finding themselves with some odd allies—feminists, ethics specialists, and advocates for the handicapped who are unsettled by the implications of the new genetics. The tests, they argue, will winnow out fetuses so that only "acceptable products" will be born, thus devaluing the lives of the handicapped.

Other critics fear that services for the handicapped will be cut back and that people will be saddled with new responsibilities rather than new opportunities—after all, never before have parents had such an ability to choose whether to accept a child with an inherited condition. In addition, they claim that the sophisticated tests will give employers and insurers the ability to discriminate on genetic grounds. (A 1982 study found that eighteen major American companies—Dow Chemical and du Pont among them—had done some sort of genetic testing.)

Strong as the opposition is, it's not likely that the genetic revolution will be stopped: Few people, given the chance to avoid the emotional, physical, and economic burdens of raising a handicapped child, are likely to refuse it. The widespread use of prenatal tests parallels the advance of feminism. As more and more women made careers, the tests took on added importance—especially since many working women are putting off childbirth until their midthirties, when chromosomal abnormalities are more common.

"I didn't feel I had a choice," says advertising executive Judith Liebman, who became pregnant for the second time at 40. "It wasn't 'Is CVS sophisticated enough that I want to take the risk?' The choice was 'Look, they're doing this test, they're recommending I take it because of my age, so I have to go with the medical profession and say that it's okay to take it.'"

As sociologist Barbara Katz Rothman Writes in *The Tentative Pregnancy,* her study of genetic testing, "In gaining the choice to control the quality of our children, we may rapidly lose the choice not to control the quality, the choice of simply accepting them as they are."

"The Luddites had a point," says Rothman. "Not all technology is good technology, and not everything needs to be done faster and better."

Mount Sinai geneticist Fred Gilbert is tracking the CF gene. Like Gilbert, his lab is casual, low-key; the most spectacular thing about it is its slightly begrimed view. Notes are taped to shelves, a stack of papers and manila folders sits atop a file cabinet, and several odd-looking blue plastic boxes lined with paper towels are arrayed on the counter (they are used to separate pieces of DNA). Flipping through a loose-leaf binder of test results, Gilbert, a burly man with a dark, full beard, talks about his patients like an old-fashioned family doctor—this father drinks, that mother is overburdened, another family's religious views have made it impossible for them to abort—but he knows most of them only from the reports of their genetic counselors and from their DNA, which is shipped to him from cities all over the country.

Two years ago, Gilbert began offering a biochemical enzyme test developed in Europe for cystic fibrosis; then, when DNA probes became available, in January 1986, he started running DNA diagnoses as well (both tests are about 95 percent accurate and are used to back each other up). Now Gilbert and his team extract DNA from the cells of families at risk for CF—his patients include a tenant farmer, an executive of a large firm, and several welfare families—expose it to gene probes that have been tagged with radioactivity, and then study photographs of the DNA, looking for the pattern that means the disease is present. Since CF is inherited recessively, there is a one-in-four chance in each pregnancy that the child might have the disease.

This test can be used only by families who already have a child with the disease, but many people are betting on a CF screening test for the general population. After all, CF is the most common inherited disease in whites, striking about one child in 2,000. And now that scientists have moved in on the gene—in April, a British research team announced that it had found a marker that is even closer to it and may turn out to be the gene itself—development may be imminent. Since the test will be highly lucrative for its developer, there's a great incentive to come up with one; by one estimate, half the genetics labs in the country are looking for the CF gene. Gilbert, however, is not making money. Since the test he is using is still experimental, he is offering it at a minimal fee; for those who cannot afford it, the test is done free.

Even so, response to the test has been slow. The eight labs in the country offering DNA diagnosis have done about 400 tests, and Gilbert has completed just fifteen prenatal diagnoses using DNA. One problem is that some cystic-fibrosis specialists have been slow to tell their patients about the test. (The Murphys, for example, didn't learn about the test from their doctor; *they* had to tell *him* it was available.) The Cystic Fibrosis Foundation has also stayed away from the test, afraid of the association with abortion, and Gilbert gets no funds from it. . . .

Emily Perl Kingsley considers herself a feminist; a member of NOW, she has belonged to the Abortion Rights Action League. At 47, Kingsley has won four Emmys as a writer for *Sesame Street,* and sometime in the next year, CBS will broadcast a film she wrote. But when she thinks about prenatal testing, Kingsley finds her feminism running up against her feelings about disability rights, her belief in a woman's right to choose to have an abortion colliding with her belief in the value of the lives of handicapped children. Her son, Jason, thirteen, has Down syndrome. "When you lose me," says Kingsley, "is when you say that the world would be better off without people like my son. I can't go along with that. The only drawback to Down is the pain that he will experience. I would do anything to save him that pain—short of killing him."

Though she was offered amniocentesis during her pregnancy, Kingsley passed on it (a decision she says she has never regretted). At 34, she was a year short of the cutoff date, and at the time, amnio was a risky procedure. Kingsley and her husband, Charles, were both on their second marriage, and both were sure they wanted the child. When Jason was born, their obstetrician suggested they might put him in an institution, tell their families he'd died, and try again. Instead, they took him home to Chappaqua and enrolled him in infant-stimulation classes designed to saturate Down children with information and activity.

Infant-stimulation classes were a new concept then, and the Kingsleys had no assurance that they'd be of any real help; today, Jason functions at a high level for a Down-syndrome child. Though he will probably never drive a car, live without some supervision, or go to Yale, Jason can read and write, manage in social situations, and follow complex directions. (He has also appeared on *Sesame Street* and other television shows.) "The idea that you ought to abort a child because he might turn out like my son is *crazy* to me," says Kingsley. "It's crazy."

For Kingsley and other disability-rights activists, their movement is a rerun of the civil-rights and feminist fights of the sixties and seventies, and their goals—acceptance by and access to the mainstream of society—are similar. "No one's entitled to tell us, 'No, you can't. Your kid isn't smart enough. Not smart enough to swim on this beach. Not smart enough to play with the kids in this group.' A lot of the things that they get away with saying to us—if they said, 'You can't get into this class because your skin is black . . . '"

This time around, though, they find themselves edging toward agreement with people who probably fought on the other side in those earlier battles—right-to-life activists and those on the political right who are opposed not only to prenatal testing but to all abortion. (Many disability-rights supporters don't object to abortion in general, only to abortion to prevent the birth of a handicapped child.)

Still, even within the movement, there's no consensus on prenatal testing. The disabled and their families, after all, are of no particular political persuasion, socioeconomic class, or religion. Instead, they are united by accidents of birth and chance. Though one woman who works with the mentally retarded claims that "the lives of the disabled are debased each time a disabled child is aborted," a large number of activists are unwilling to take a stand on prenatal diagnosis. Their concern, they say, is those who have already been born.

Most, like Carol Levine, an ethics specialist at the Hastings Center in Briarcliff Manor, feel that the severity of the disease must come into play—that a short life followed by a painful death might better be avoided, but that life in a wheelchair is not grounds for abortion. "There's a difference," says Levine, "between being able to test for a lethal disease like Tay-Sachs and a disease like cystic fibrosis that people are living with—not to great old age, but it's not incompatible with life and even productive, happy life. So the choices that people will make are inevitably going to be colored by the differences in the conditions. I think it's pointed up even more in Huntington's disease, where people live to be 50. Would we have been better off without Woody Guthrie [folksinger], who died of Huntington's? Well, I don't think anybody would say that. But is there a right answer? I don't think so."

Not everyone whose child would be affected by a disease chooses abortion: Of the fifteen pregnancies Fred Gilbert has studied with DNA probes, four have come up positive for CF, and half of those families kept the children. Parents who are told their child has Down syndrome can put him up for adoption; there are waiting lists of families happy to take Down babies. Even some Roman Catholic hospitals are now offering prenatal diagnosis (without abortion), on the theory that parents who know about their child's problems will be able to cope with them better. The numbers they see are dramatically lower than those at secular hospitals: At Creighton University Medical Center in Omaha, about 5 prenatal tests are done a month; New York Hospital, which is three times as large, does approximately 39 a *week*. And for some disabilities the abortion rate is high—91 percent of the women who get a positive diagnosis for Down syndrome terminate their pregnancies (many women who don't feel they could do it simply do not take the test).

"We're all genetic messes," says the National Institutes of Health's John Fletcher. "There's no such thing as perfection, and there never will be." Yet each year, more people are searching for it. In Manhattan, about 50 percent of the women at risk for chromosomal abnormalities have prenatal diagnosis, while nationwide, the number of such women using the tests has more than doubled since 1977 (to about 20 percent). An Indiana hospital that did ten amnios in 1971 now does fifteen a *week*. In New York state, 40 percent of women 35 and over had some form of prenatal test in 1984, up from about 5 percent in 1977. As the tests become routine, the definition of abortable defects may become wider and, some people fear, parents may reject a potential child for what seem to be frivolous reasons. Ever more genetic hurdles might be set up, and in order to be born a fetus might have to clear them all.

"Anything that has an aspect of mental retardation is already quite unacceptable for most people," says Carol Levine. "I think that the limits of tolerability will be stretched very far. More and more things will be seen as disabilities, and smaller disabilities will be seen less tolerably than they are now. And a society that isn't tolerant of diversity is one that is bereft of imagination and creativity."

Prenatal diagnosis may also change our notion of parental responsibility. "To know that you're bringing forth a child who has to use a wheelchair. . . . With a few curb cuts, life in a wheelchair is not a tragedy," says Barbara Katz Rothman. "But then you're going to look at this particular kid who's going to say to you, 'I am in this wheelchair because you thought it was a good idea.' And there's going to be an element of truth in that. And that's an incredible responsibility to take on in a society that's not supportive of people in wheelchairs, people with mild retardation, people with any kind of problem. I think there's going to be a certain attitude: 'This isn't an act of God anymore that could happen to anybody; this is your selfish choice, lady.'"

But who can blame parents for wanting their children to be healthy? Though the treatments for diseases like CF and Duchenne muscular dystrophy have improved in recent years, there is still no cure for most of them, and victims may face frequent hospitalization and even early death. And though the lives of the disabled have improved immeasurably in the last decade, as federal regulations ensuring rights of the handicapped have been put into effect, discussions with the parents of handicapped children, and with those who work with them, reveal just how difficult life with a mentally or physically disabling condition can be. They speak of how hard it is to find a class for their child, of bus drivers who won't stop for people in wheelchairs, of New York's lack of simple amenities, like curb cuts, and, most important, of the cruel treatment their children receive, both from other youngsters and from adults.

"The burdens of raising a kid with Down syndrome have practically nothing to do with the child," says Emily Kingsley. "If anything, the child is easy. The burdens are the attitudes and prejudices you meet from people. Having to overcome their queasiness or whatever it is. People are afraid. 'My God, what if that happened to me?' Isn't it neater to keep these people in the closet and not have to think about them, not have to face them, not have to make ramps for them?"

For many women who work, it is almost impossible to visualize raising a severely handicapped child. "I think the real lives of women, especially women who work outside the home, mean that the juggling act implied in motherhood is already very, very tough," says Rayna Rapp, a New School anthropologist who has been studying prenatal diagnosis for the last three years. "And compared with most Western societies, we have fewer social services, fewer maternity benefits, less day care. All of those very large-scale factors go into an assessment at the time of a life crisis. You're not thinking in general about what it means to be the mother of *a* child; you're thinking rather specifically about how your life will change to become the parent of a disabled child, right now and here. And I'm not arguing that if the services were perfect everybody would go ahead and have a disabled baby. But I think some people might have a very different sense of it if the climate around disability and disability services was transformed."

Rapp, 41, is a quick, small woman with shaggy brown hair. She began her anthropological study of prenatal diagnosis after going through the experience herself. Pregnant for the first time at 36, Rapp saw amnio as part of the trade-off she had to make because she had devoted 10 years of her life to her academic and political concerns. As it turned out, she was one of the unlucky 2 percent: The fetus was diagnosed as having Down.

"When Nancy [her genetic counselor] called me twelve days after the tap," Rapp wrote in a *Ms.* article about her amnio, "I began to scream as soon as I recognized her voice. . . . The image of myself, alone, screaming into a white plastic telephone is indelible." Rapp and her husband, Mike Hooper, decided to have an abortion.

"It was a decision made so that my husband and I could have a certain kind of relationship to a child and to each other and to our adult lives," says Rapp. "It had a lot to do with a sense of responsibility, starting out life as older parents. That was the choice, to have delayed childbearing to do the other things we had done in life. And that meant we had to confront something that was very, very upsetting. But in some senses, I wouldn't have wished away the last ten years of my life in order not to have faced the decision.

"Paradoxically," says Rapp, "there's less choice for people who are better educated to understand prenatal diagnosis. The more you know about this technology, the more likely you are to feel its necessity. But unless the conditions under which Americans view, deal with, and respond to a range of disabling conditions are also put up for discussion about choice—until that larger picture changes—I think it's real hard for many, many people to imagine making a choice other than abortion for something like Down."

In fact, as screening tests for inherited diseases like CF, Huntington's, and the muscular dystrophies become available in the next decade, it's likely that many couples—especially urban, middle-class ones—will consider them a normal part of pregnancy. And as prenatal diagnosis is done earlier in pregnancy, the likelihood that prospective parents will decide to have an abortion for one of those conditions will probably also increase. That attitude is deeply disturbing to opponents of the tests, including Dr. Brian Scully, a Catholic infectious-diseases specialist who works with CF patients at Columbia-Presbyterian Medical Center. Scully, who grew up in Ireland, is opposed to genetic testing—for any condition—that leads to abortion. "The idea that I'm only going to have a child if it's going to be a perfect child, that I'll only accept a baby if it's an acceptable baby—I don't sympathize with that at all," says Scully. "I don't want children to have cystic fibrosis. But to say that if you have cystic fibrosis I'm not going to have you, I think that's wrong."

In 1985, Scully denounced the tests in a letter to *The Lancet*, a widely read British medical journal. In return, he got a note from a London biochemist who, in Scully's words, "rationalized that it was just that they were helping nature. A proportion of babies are lost because of defects naturally—I forget what that proportion is—but he felt that they were just supporting nature, and weeding out the undesirable, imperfect children. And he felt that was fine. I would say, Why not wait until they're born, and you can get everybody."

Like other decisions forced on us by advancing technology, the choice involved in genetic testing can exceed one's moral grasp. And while Scully raises an important argument, the pro-choice position is just as cogent: Can parents who have seen one child suffer with a disease be forced to risk having another? Should people be told they must have a child—even one they don't feel capable of caring for? And, in the case of a disease like Tay-Sachs, does anyone benefit from the child's being born? Parents must make all those decisions for themselves—not lightly, but with awareness of the real moral weight of the final choice. And there's no right answer, a fact that Susan Murphy acutely understands. "I don't think that you should judge people by the decisions they make, whether it's to terminate or not to terminate a pregnancy," she says. "Because you don't know what hell they went through."

■ CONSIDERATIONS OF MEANING AND METHOD

1. Why does Virshup open "Perfect People?" with the case of Susan and Tom Murphy and not, for example, with paragraph five, which offers an overview of the subject at hand?

2. What does Virshup (and author Barbara Katz Rothman) mean by "tentative pregnancy"? In what way have the meaning and implications of this term changed as a consequence of genetic testing?

3. What genetic tests are currently available? How common are they? What is the "ultimate goal" of genetic testing? What options, as a consequence of negative results of genetic tests, exist for parents today?

4. Make a chart listing the advantages of genetic testing in one column and the problems these tests pose in another column. Which advantages can be seen as problems, and vice versa? To your mind, do advantages outweigh problems, or do problems outweigh advantages?

5. Who were the Luddites?

6. In what ways do Emily Perl Kingsley's strongly held beliefs collide over the issue of prenatal testing? Compare Kingsley's decisions and the reasons behind them with Rayna Rapp's. Are you inclined to empathize more with Kingsley, or with Rapp, or do you agree with Susan Murphy when she says, "I don't think that you should judge people by the decisions they make, whether it's to terminate or not to terminate a pregnancy. . . . Because you don't know what hell they went through."

7. Virshup reports that "Of the fifteen pregnancies Fred Gilbert has studied with DNA probes, four have come up positive for CF [cystic fibrosis], and half of those families kept the children."

Virshup also reports that "91 percent of women who get a positive diagnosis for Down syndrome terminate their pregnancies." Do either of these statistics surprise you as you consider them separately, or comparatively? Why or why not?

8. In "Perfect People?" it is Virshup's goal to investigate and report a range of views and experiences related to genetic testing and, consequently, to decisions to terminate or not to terminate fetuses affected by genetic disease or disability. Did she give fair coverage? Was she able to maintain objectivity? Can you detect her own views in the essay? Point to examples from the text to support your answers to these questions.

■ POSSIBILITIES FOR WRITING

1. According to Virshup, most ethicists, like Carol Levine, "feel that the severity of the disease must come into play—that a short life followed by a painful death might better be avoided, but that life in a wheelchair is not grounds for abortion." To what extent do you agree or disagree, and why? Respond in a written argument for members of your class or one addressed to the ethicists who share this view.

2. Carol Levine observes that as time goes on and genetic tests become routine, "More and more things will be seen as disabilities, and smaller disabilities will be seen less tolerably than they are now. And a society that isn't tolerant of diversity is one that is bereft of imagination and creativity." How would you define "disability"? What, in your mind, in an "abortable defect"? In writing, speculate upon possible future consequences of genetic testing and abortion as they relate to tolerance of disability and discuss Levine's point about the deficit of imagination and creativity in an intolerant society.

3. Can you anticipate any socioeconomic consequences of genetic testing and gene therapy that Virshup does not mention in her essay? Speculate upon these effects in an essay or in a short story set, as is Aldous Huxley's novel *Brave New World*, in the future.

■ JEREMY RIFKIN

A Heretic's View on the New Bioethics

An outspoken opponent of biotechnology—and especially of genetic engineering—Jeremy Rifkin has long been a social activist and has written and lectured widely on subjects related to economics and ethics. Born in 1945 in Denver, Colorado, Rifkin earned his B.A. in economics at the University of Pennsylvania and an M.A. in international relations from the Fletcher School of Law and Diplomacy at Tufts University. In 1967, he helped organize the first national protest against the war in Vietnam, and in the late 1960s he worked for Volunteers in Service to America in Harlem in New York City. In the early 1970s, Rifkin moved to Washington, D.C., where, discouraged by the commercialization of the nation's bicentennial celebration, he founded the People's Bicentennial Commission to focus national attention on economic democracy. His first books, How to Commit Revolution American Style *(1973) and* Common Sense II: The Case Against Corporate Tyranny *(1975), both edited with John Rossen, and* Own Your Own Job: Economic Democracy for Working Americans *(1977) grew out of this period.*

In 1977, Rifkin established the Foundation on Economic Trends. The principal focus of the foundation has been to monitor developments in biotechnology and genetic engineering. In the 1980s, Rifkin was successful in blocking or delaying field tests of genetically altered microorganisms designed for use in agriculture and animal husbandry. Human genetic engineering is of particular concern to Rifkin. "A Heretic's View on the New Bioethics" is from his widely read and most controversial book Algeny *(1983), whose title is a play on the word "alchemy," relating the medieval quest to transform ordinary metals into gold to the current quest to manipulate genes. In the essay, Rifkin maintains that "once we decide to begin the process of human genetic engineering, there is really no logical place to stop," so we should not start. Who is to say that "myopia, color-blindness, left-handedness" might not be considered genetic "disorders"? "Indeed, what is to preclude a society from deciding that a certain skin color is a disorder?" he asks.*

Rifkin has been praised for his long view and his attempts to hold scientists morally responsible for the technologies they develop, but he has also been widely criticized, most fervently by scientists themselves. Both Rifkin's critics and his supporters point to his lack of scientific credentials. The first group claims that since he is not a scientist, he lacks both the facts and an understanding of basic scientific principles and subtle scientific issues; the second group maintains that science needs to be monitored by ethicists, like Rifkin, who are outside the scientific community. Rifkin is concerned, as he told one interviewer, that

. . . even though we profess to be a democratic republic, we give over much of our individual responsibility for decision making to elites, especially scientific and corporate elites. . . . I'm afraid we're going to lose the sense of a democratic republic if we don't start to assert our rightful role and participate in the political process. I don't think you have to be a physicist to speak up and speak out on the issues of nuclear power and nuclear bombs and nuclear war. I don't think you have to be a chemist to be informed and to speak out on the questions of petrochemical pollution in the environment. And I certainly don't think you have to be a molecular biologist to be informed about the issues on genetic engineering and to speak out forcefully and passionately and intelligently on those issues.

Darwin's world was populated by machine-like automata. Nature was conceived as an aggregate of standardized, interchangeable parts assembled into various functional combinations. If one were to ascribe any overall purpose to the entire operation, it would probably be that of increased production and greater efficiency with no particular end in mind.

The new temporal theory of evolution replaces the idea of life as mere machinery with the idea of life as mere information. By resolving structure into function and reducing function to information flows, the new cosmology all but eliminates any remaining sense of species identification. Living things are no longer perceived as carrots and peas, foxes and hens, but as bundles of information. All living things are drained of their aliveness and turned into abstract messages. Life becomes a code to be deciphered. There is no longer any question of sacredness or inviolability. How could there be when there are no longer any recognizable boundaries to respect? Under the new temporal theory, structure is abandoned. Nothing exists at the moment. Everything is pure activity, pure process. How can any living thing be deemed sacred when it is just a pattern of information?

By eliminating structural boundaries and reducing all living things to information exchanges and flows, the new cosmology provides the proper degree of desacralization for the bioengineering of life. After all, in order to justify the engineering of living material across biological boundaries, it is first necessary to desacralize the whole idea of an organism as an identifiable, discrete structure with a permanent set of attributes. In the age of biotechnology, separate species with separate names gradually give way to systems of information that can be reprogrammed into an infinite number of biological combinations. It is much easier for the human mind to accept the idea of engineering a system of information than it is for it to accept the idea of engineering a dog. It is easier still, once one has fully internalized the notion that there is really no such thing as a dog in the traditional sense. In the coming age it will be much more accurate to describe a dog as a very specific pattern of information unfolding over a specific period of time.

Life as information flow represents the final desacralization of nature. Conveniently, humanity has eliminated the idea of fixed biological borders and reduced matter to energy and energy to information in its cosmological thinking right at the very time that bioengineers are preparing to cut across species boundaries in the living world.

The New Ethics

Civilization is experiencing the euphoric first moments of the next age of history. The media are already treating us to glimpses of a future where the engineering of life by design will be standard operating procedure. Even as the corporate laboratories begin to dribble out the first products of bioengineering, a subtle shift in the ethical impulse of society is becoming perceptible to the naked eye. As we begin to reprogram life, our moral code is being similarly reprogrammed to reflect this profound change in the way humanity goes about organizing the world. A new ethics is being engineered, and its operating assumptions comport nicely with the activity taking place in the biology laboratories.

Eugenics is the inseparable ethical wing of the age of biotechnology. First coined by Charles Darwin's cousin Sir Francis Galton, eugenics is generally categorized in two ways, negative and positive. Negative eugenics involves the systematic elimination of so-called biologically undesirable characteristics. Positive eugenics is concerned with the use of genetic manipulation to "improve" the characteristics of an organism or species.

Eugenics is not a new phenomenon. At the turn of the century the United States sported a massive eugenics movement. Politicians, celebrities, academicians, and prominent business leaders joined together in support of a eugenics program for the country. The frenzy over eugenics reached a fever pitch, with many states passing sterilization statutes and the U.S. Congress passing a new immigration law in the 1920s based on eugenics considerations. As a consequence of the new legislation, thousands of American citizens were sterilized so they could not pass on their "inferior" traits, and the federal government locked its doors to certain immigrant groups deemed biologically unfit by then-existing eugenics standards.

While the Americans flirted with eugenics for the first thirty years of the twentieth century, their escapades were of minor historical account when compared with the eugenics program orchestrated by the Nazis in the 1930s and '40s. Millions of Jews and other religious and ethnic groups were gassed in the German crematoriums to advance the Third Reich's dream of eliminating all but the "Aryan" race from the globe. The Nazis also embarked on a "positive" eugenics program in which thousands of S.S. officers and German women were carefully selected for their "superior" genes and mated under the auspices of the state. Impregnated women were cared for in state facilities, and their offspring were donated to the Third Reich as the vanguard of the new super race that would rule the world for the next millennium.

Eugenics lay dormant for nearly a quarter of a century after World War II. Then the spectacular breakthroughs in molecular biology in the 1960s raised the specter of a eugenics revival once again. By the mid-1970s, many scientists were beginning to worry out loud that the potential for genetic engineering might lead to a return to the kind of eugenics hysteria that had swept over America and Europe earlier in the century. Speaking at a National Academy of Science forum on recombinant DNA, Ethan Signer, a biologist at M.I.T., warned his colleagues that

> this research is going to bring us one more step closer to genetic engineering of people. That's where they figure out how to have us produce children with ideal characteristics. . . . The last time around, the ideal children had blond hair, blue eyes and Aryan genes.

The concern over a re-emergence of eugenics is well founded but misplaced. While professional ethicists watch out the front door for telltale signs of a resurrection of the Nazi nightmare, eugenics doctrine has quietly slipped in the back door and is already stealthily at work reorganizing the ethical priorities of the human household. Virtually overnight, eugenics doctrine has gained an impressive if not an impregnable foothold in the popular culture.

Its successful implantation into the psychic life of civilization is attributable to its going largely unrecognized in its new guise. The new eugenics is commercial, not social. In place of the shrill eugenic cries for racial purity, the new commercial eugenics talks in pragmatic terms of increased economic efficiency, better performance standards, and improvement in the quality of life. The old eugenics was steeped in political ideology and motivated by fear and hate. The new eugenics is grounded in economic considerations and stimulated by utilitarianism and financial gain.

Like the ethics of the Darwinian era, the new commercial eugenics associates the idea of "doing good" with the idea of "increasing efficiency." The difference is that increasing efficiency in the age of biotechnology is achieved by way of engineering living organisms. Therefore, "good" is defined as the engineering of life to improve its performance. In contrast, not to improve the performance of a living organism whenever technically possible is considered tantamount to committing a sin.

For example, consider the hypothetical case of a prospective mother faced with the choice of programming the genetic characteristics of her child at conception. Let's assume the mother chooses not to have the fertilized egg programmed. The fetus develops naturally, the baby is born, the child grows up, and in her early teenage years discovers that she has a rare genetic disease that will lead to a premature and painful death. The mother could have avoided the calamity by having that defective genetic trait eliminated from the fertilized egg, but she chose not to. In the age of biotechnology, her choice not to intervene might well constitute a crime for which she might be punished. At the least, her refusal to allow the fetus to be programmed would be considered a morally reprehensible and irresponsible decision unbefitting a mother, whose duty it is always to provide as best she can for her child's future well-being.

Proponents of human genetic engineering contend that it would be irresponsible not to use this powerful new technology to eliminate serious "genetic disorders." The problem with this argument, says the *New York Times* in an editorial entitled "Whether to Make Perfect Humans," is that "there is no discernible line to be drawn between making inheritable repairs of genetic defects, and improving the species." The *Times* rightly points out that once scientists are able to repair genetic defects, "it will become much harder to argue against adding genes that confer desired qualities, like better health, looks or brains."

Once we decide to begin the process of human genetic engineering, there is really no logical place to stop. If diabetes, sickle cell anemia, and cancer are to be cured by altering the genetic makeup of an individual, why not proceed to other "disorders": myopia, color blindness, left-handedness? Indeed, what is to preclude a society from deciding that a certain skin color is a disorder?

As knowledge about genes increases, the bioengineers will inevitably gain new insights into the functioning of more complex characteristics, such as those associated with behavior and thoughts. Many scientists are already contending that schizophrenia and other "abnormal" psychological states result from genetic disorders or defects. Others now argue that "antisocial" behavior, such as criminality and social protest, are also examples of malfunctioning genetic information. One prominent neurophysiologist has gone so far as to say, "There can be no twisted thought without a twisted molecule." Many sociobiologists contend that virtually all human activity is in some way determined by our genetic makeup, and that if we wish to change this situation, we must change our genes.

Whenever we begin to discuss the idea of genetic defects, there is no way to limit the discussion to one or two or even a dozen so-called disorders, because of a hidden assumption that lies behind the very notion of "defective." Ethicist Daniel Callahan penetrates to the core of the problem when he observes that "behind the human horror at genetic defectiveness lurks . . . an image of the perfect human being. The very language of 'defect,' 'abnormality,' 'disease,' and 'risk,' presupposes such an image, a kind of proto-type of perfection."

The idea of engineering the human species is very similar to the idea of engineering a piece of machinery. An engineer is constantly in search of new ways to improve the performance of a machine. As soon as one set of imperfections is eliminated, the engineer immediately turns his attention to the next set of imperfections, always with the idea in mind of creating a perfect piece of machinery. Engineering is a process of continual improvement in the performance of a piece of machinery, and the idea of setting arbitrary limits to how much "improvement" is acceptable is alien to the entire engineering conception.

The question, then, is whether or not humanity should "begin" the process of engineering future generations of human beings by technological design in the laboratory. What is the price we pay for embarking on a course whose final goal is the "perfection" of the human species? How important is it that we eliminate all the imperfections, all the defects? What price are we willing to pay to extend our lives, to ensure our own health, to do away with all the inconveniences, the irritations, the nuisances, the infirmities, the suffering, that are so much a part of the human experience? Are we so enamored with the idea of physical perpetuation at all costs that we are even willing to subject the human species to rigid architectural design?

With human genetic engineering, we get something and we give up something. In return for securing our own physical well-being we are forced to accept the idea of reducing the human species to a technologically designed product. Genetic engineering poses the most fundamental of questions. Is guaranteeing our health worth trading away our humanity?

People are forever devising new ways of organizing the environment in order to secure their future. Ethics, in turn, serves to legitimize the drive for self-perpetuation. Any organizing activity that a society deems to be helpful in securing its future is automatically blessed, and any activity that undermines the mode of organization a society uses to secure its future is automatically damned. The age of bioengineering brooks no exception. In the years to come a multitude of new bioengineering products will be forthcoming. Every one of the breakthroughs in bioengineering will be of benefit to someone, under some circumstance, somewhere in society. Each will in some way appear to advance the future security of an individual, a group, or society as a whole. Eliminating a defective gene trait so that a child won't die prematurely; engineering a new cereal crop that can feed an expanding population; developing a new biological source of energy that can fill the vacuum as the oil spigot runs dry. Every one of these advances provides a modicum of security against the vagaries of the future. To forbid their development and reject their application will be considered ethically irresponsible and inexcusable.

Bioengineering is coming to us not as a threat but as a promise; not as a punishment but as a gift. We have already come to the conclusion that bioengineering is a boon for humanity. The thought of engineering living organisms no longer conjures up sinister images. What we see before our eyes are not monstrosities but useful products. We no longer feel dread but only elated expectation at the great possibilities that lie in store for each of us.

How could engineering life be considered bad when it produces such great benefits? Engineering living tissue is no longer a question of great ethical import. The human psyche has been won over to eugenics with little need for discussion or debate. We have already been convinced of the good that can come from engineering life by learning of the helpful products it is likely to spawn.

As in the past, humanity's incessant need to control the future in order to secure its own well-being is already dictating the ethics of the age of biotechnology. Engineering life to improve humanity's own prospects for survival will be ennobled as the highest expression of ethical behavior. Any resistance to the new technology will be castigated as inhuman, irresponsible, morally reprehensible, and criminally culpable.

■ CONSIDERATIONS OF MEANING AND METHOD

1. Many of Rifkin's critics—most of them scientists—have questioned his qualifications in writing about scientific subjects, including genetic engineering. Do you consider Rifkin well qualified to write about this subject or lacking in qualifications? Explain.

2. How, according to Rifkin, have ideas about evolution themselves evolved since Darwin, and as a consequence of what factors? What does Rifkin mean by the "desacralization of nature"?

3. How can the Nazis' campaign of genocide against the Jews and other ethnic and religious groups and their promotion of the "Aryan" race during the 1930s and 1940s be seen in terms of positive and negative eugenics? Do you think biotechnology increases the risk of "a resurrection of the Nazi nightmare"? If so, how? If not, why?

4. Rifkin says that, while we guard against eugenic practices of the past, "eugenics doctrine has quietly slipped in the back door and is already stealthily at work reorganizing the ethical priorities of the human household." How does "the new commercial eugenics" disguise itself, according to Rifkin? Why is it so hard to resist?

5. What does Rifkin say is the assumption hidden behind the term "defect" when it is applied to human beings? What do we stand to gain, and what do we stand to lose in correcting human "defects"? Do you agree with Rifkin's position?

6. Which sources cited by Virshup could be used to support Rifkin's position on genetic engineering? How? Which could be used to refute Rifkin's position? How?

7. What is Rifkin's fundamental point in the final section of the essay? How would you describe his tone? In what ways does

tone here differ from tone in the rest of the essay? As Rifkin's reader, how do you respond to his tone in the conclusion?

■ POSSIBILITIES FOR WRITING

1. Rifkin asks, "What price are we willing to pay to extend our lives, to ensure our own health, to do away with all the inconveniences, the irritations, the nuisances, the infirmities, the suffering, that are so much a part of the human experience?" From a personal perspective, respond to this question in writing.

2. Rifkin also writes, "With human genetic engineering, we get something and we give something up." In an argumentative essay, compare what Rifkin thinks we will gain and lose through human genetic engineering with what you think we will gain and lose. What conclusions do you draw as you weigh gains and losses? To support your position, you might refer to other essays in this chapter's cycle of readings about genetic engineering, to the excerpt from Aldous Huxley's *Brave New World* in Chapter 5 (page 274), or to readings in Chapter 7.

3. Rifkin suggests that at some point in the not-so-distant future, a woman who decides against a genetic screening of her unborn child might be held morally, if not legally, responsible should that child develop a genetically inherited disease later in life. Do you find this scenario feasible? Why or why not? As a consequence of genetic technologies, what hypothetical scenarios can you envision? In an essay, speculate on the feasibility of Rifkin's hypothetical case as well as on ones you might envision.

■ STEPHEN JAY GOULD
On the Origin of Specious Critics

Evolutionary biologist Stephen Jay Gould is widely respected among scientists and widely appreciated among educated lay readers for his ability, in his writings about evolution and natural history, to convey front-line scientific concepts in "superbly witty and literate fashion to anyone willing to grapple with slippery and subtle ideas," according to reviewer David Graber. Gould's essays are a regular feature in Natural History *magazine, where his column, "This View of Life," appears, and many of them have been collected and published in his books, which include* Ever Since Darwin *(1977),* The Panda's Thumb *(1980),* The Mismeasure of Man *(1981),* Hen's Teeth and Horse's Toes *(1983),* The Flamingo's

Smile *(1985), and* Wonderful Life: The Burgess Shale and the Nature of History *(1989). In his essays, Gould often illustrates scientific principles by examining a fascinating, frequently peculiar particular—the extra "thumb" of the giant panda or the flamingo's inverted jaw, for instance. This is more than literary technique. Gould, with paleontologist Niles Eldredge, has developed the now widely accepted evolutionary theory of* punctuated equilibrium, *which holds that evolution occurs not in a steady continuum, but through more radical and abrupt changes within small populations.*

Gould was born in 1941 in New York City. He has said that he decided at five years old to become a paleontologist—though he did not yet know the word—when he first saw the Tyrannosaurus rex *at the American Museum of Natural History. Gould earned his A.B. degree from Antioch College and his Ph.D. from Columbia University. He has taught geology and biology at Harvard University since 1967. For his writings he has received scores of both literary and scientific awards, including the American Book Award in science for* The Panda's Thumb *and the National Book Critics Circle Award in general nonfiction for* The Mismeasure of Man.

Gould, like Jeremy Rifkin, is concerned about the social effects and implications of science. Despite an inclination on Gould's part to sympathize with Rifkin's fears about the potential misuse of genetic engineering, in "On the Origin of Specious Critics," Gould takes fierce exception with Rifkin, criticizing what he sees as Rifkin's lack of understanding of the field of evolutionary theory, his factual inaccuracies, his unfair tactics in arguing his position, and his fundamental belief that, because there is the potential for abuse, research in genetic engineering should not be pursued. "You don't throw out the printing press because it once printed Mein Kampf," *Gould insisted to one reviewer. "There are enormously beneficial medical and agricultural uses that are potential and even actual, and there are other things like cloning that you would not want to do. All technology has power, and power can be used in good and bad ways. It has to be scrutinized, but you don't turn off the power because of its potential misuse." "On the Origin of Specious Critics" was originally published in 1985 in* Discover, *a popular science magazine. As you read Gould's critique of Rifkin's book* Algeny, *note the logical and rhetorical strategies he employs in mounting his arguments.*

Evolution has a definite geometry well portrayed by our ancient metaphor, the tree of life. Lineages split and diverge like the branches of a tree. A species, once distinct, is permanently on its own; the branches of life do not coalesce. Extinction is truly forever, persistence a personal odyssey. But art does not always imitate nature. Biotechnology, or genetic engineering, has aroused fear and opposition because it threatens to annul this fundamental property of life—to place genes of one species into the program of another, thereby combining what nature has kept separate from time immemorial. Two concerns—one immediate and practical, the other distant and deep—have motivated the opposition.

Some critics fear that certain conjunctions might have potent and unanticipated effects—creating a resistant agent of disease or simply a new creature so hardy and fecund that, like Kurt Vonnegut's *ice-nine*, it spreads to engulf the earth in a geological millisecond. I am not persuaded by these excursions into science fiction, but the distant and deeper issue does merit discussion: What are the consequences, ethical, aesthetic, and practical, of altering life's fundamental geometry and permitting one species to design new creatures at will, combining bits and pieces of lineages distinct for billions of years?

Jeremy Rifkin has been the most vocal opponent of genetic engineering in recent months. He has won court cases and aroused fury in the halls of science with his testimony about immediate dangers. However, his major statement, a book titled *Algeny* (for the modern alchemy of genes), concentrates almost entirely on the deep and distant issue. His activities based on immediate fears have been widely reported and rebutted. But *Algeny*, although it was published more than a year ago, has not been adequately analyzed or dissected. Its status as prophecy or pretension, philosophy or pamphleteering, must be assessed, for *Algeny* touts itself as the manifesto of a movement to save nature and simple decency from the hands of impatient and rapacious science.

I will state my conclusion—bald and harsh—at the outset: I regard *Algeny* as a cleverly constructed tract of anti-intellectual propaganda masquerading as scholarship. Among books promoted as serious intellectual statements by important thinkers, I don't think I have ever read a shoddier work. Damned shame, too, because the deep issue is troubling and I do not disagree with Rifkin's basic plea for respecting the integrity of evolutionary lineages. But devious means compromise good ends, and we shall have to save Rifkin's humane conclusion from his own questionable tactics.

The basic argument of *Algeny* rests upon a parody of an important theme advanced by contemporary historians of science against the myth of objectivity and inexorable scientific progress: science is socially embedded; its theories are not simple deductions from observed facts of nature, but a complex mixture of social ideology (often unconsciously expressed) and empirical constraint. This theme is liberating for science; it embodies the human side of our enterprise and depicts us as passionate creatures struggling with limited tools to understand a complex reality, not as robots programmed to convert objective information into immutable truth. But in Rifkin's hands the theme becomes a caricature. Rifkin ignores the complex interplay of social bias with *facts* of nature and promotes a crude socioeconomic determinism that views our historical succession of biological worldviews—from creationism to Darwinism to the new paradigm now supposedly under construction—as so many simple reflections of social ideology.

From this socioeconomic determinism, Rifkin constructs his specific brief: Darwinian evolutionism, he asserts, was the creation of industrial capitalism, the age of pyrotechnology. Arising in this context as a simple reflection of social ideology, it never had any sound basis in reason or evidence. It is now dying because the age of pyrotechnology is yielding to an era of biotechnology—and biotech demands a new view of life. Darwinism translated the industrial machine into nature; biotech models nature as a computer and substitutes information for material parts.

Darwinism spawned (or reflected) evil in its support for exploitation of man and nature, but at least it respected the integrity of species (while driving some to extinction) because it lacked the technology to change them by mixture and instant transmutation. But the new paradigm dissolves species into strings of information that can be reshuffled at will.

The new temporal theory of evolution replaces the idea of life as mere machinery with the idea of life as mere information. All living things are drained of their aliveness and turned into abstract messages. There is no longer any question of sacredness or inviolability. How could there be when there are no longer any recognizable boundaries to respect? In the age of biotechnology, separate species with separate names gradually give way to systems of information that can be reprogrammed into an infinite number of biological combinations.

But what can we do if we wish to save nature as we know it—a system divided into packages of porcupines and primroses, cabbages and kings? We can seek no help from science, Rifkin claims, for science is a monolith masquerading as objective knowledge, but really reflecting the dominant ideology of a new technological age. We can only make an ethical decision to "re-sacralize" nature by respecting the inviolability of its species. We must, for the first time in history, decide *not* to institute a possible technology, despite its immediately attractive benefits in such areas as medicine and agriculture.

I have devoted my own career to evolutionary biology, and I have been among the strongest critics of strict Darwinism. Yet Rifkin's assertions bear no relationship to what I have observed and practiced for 25 years. Evolutionary theory has never been healthier or more exciting. We are experiencing a ferment of new ideas and theories, but they are revising and extending Darwin, not burying him. How can Rifkin construct a world so different from the one I inhabit and know so well? Either I am blind or he is wrong—and I think I can show, by analyzing his slipshod scholarship and basic misunderstanding of science, that his word is an invention constructed to validate his own private hopes. I shall summarize my critique in five charges:

1. Rifkin does not understand Darwinism, and his arguments refute an absurd caricature, not the theory itself. He trots out all the standard mischaracterizations, usually confined nowadays to creationist tracts. Just three examples: "According to Darwin," Rifkin writes, "everything evolved by chance." Since the complexity of cellular life cannot arise by accident, Darwinism is absurd: "According to the odds, the one-cell organism is so complex that the likelihood of its coming together by sheer accident and chance is computed to be around $1/10^{78436}$." But Darwin himself, and Darwinians ever since, always stressed, as a cardinal premise, that natural selection is not a theory of randomness. Chance may describe the origin of new variation by mutation, but natural selection, the agent of change, is a conventional deterministic process that builds adaptation by preserving favorable variants.

Rifkin then dismisses Darwinism as a tautology; fitness is defined by survival, and the catch phrase "survival of the fittest" reduces to "survival of those that survive"—and therefore has no meaning. Darwin resolved this issue, as Darwinians have ever since, by defining fitness as predictable advantage before the fact, not as recorded survival afterward (as we may predict the biomechanical improvements that might help zebras outrun or outmaneuver lions; survival then becomes a testable consequence).

Rifkin regards Darwinism as absurd because "natural selection makes no room for long-range considerations. Every new trait has to be immediately useful or it is discarded." How, therefore, can natural selection explain the origin of a bird's wing, since the intermediate forms cannot fly: What good is five per cent of a wing? The British biologist St. George Jackson Mivart developed this critique in 1871 as the argument about "incipient stages of useful structures." Darwin met the challenge by adding a chapter to the sixth edition of the *Origin of Species*. One need not agree with Darwin's resolution, but one does have a responsibility to acknowledge it. Darwin argued that intermediate stages performed different functions; feathers of an incipient wing may act as excellent organs of thermoregulation—a particular problem in the smallest of dinosaurs, which evolved into birds.

Rifkin displays equally little comprehension of basic arguments about evolutionary geometry. He thinks that *Archaeopteryx* has been refuted as an intermediate link between reptiles and birds because some true birds have been found in rocks of the same age. But evolution is a branching bush, not a ladder. Ancestors survive after descendants branch off. Dogs evolved from wolves, but wolves (though threatened) are hanging tough. And a species of *Australopithecus* lived side by side with its descendant *Homo* for more than a million years in Africa.

Rifkin doesn't grasp the current critiques of strict Darwinism any better. He caricatures my own theory of punctuated equilibrium [that evolution moves in fits and starts rather than by slow, steady change] as a sudden response to ecological catastrophe: "The idea is that these catastrophic events spawned monstrous genetic mutations within existing species, most of which were lethal. A few of the mutations, however, managed to survive and become the precursors of a new species." But punctuated equilibrium, as Niles Eldredge and I have always emphasized, is about ordinary speciation (taking tens of thousands of years) and its abrupt appearance at low scales of geological resolution, not about ecological catastrophe and sudden genetic change.

Rifkin, it appears, understands neither the fundamentals of Darwinism, its current critiques, nor even the basic topology of the evolutionary tree.

2. Rifkin shows no understanding of the norms and procedures of science: he displays little comprehension of what science is and how scientists work. He consistently misses the essential distinction between fact (claims about the world's empirical content) and theory

(ideas that explain and interpret facts)—using arguments against one to refute the other. Against Darwinism (a theory of evolutionary mechanisms) he cites the British physiologist Gerald Kerkut's *Implications of Evolution,* a book written to refute the factual claim that all living creatures have a common ancestry, and to argue instead that life may have arisen several times from chemical precursors—an issue not addressed by Darwinism. (Creationist lawyers challenged me with the same misunderstanding during my cross-examination at the Arkansas "equal time" trial three years ago, in which the creationists unsuccessfully fought for compulsory presentation of their views in science classrooms.) Rifkin then suggests that the entire field of evolution may be a pseudo science because the great French zoologist Pierre-Paul Grassé is so critical of Darwinism (the theory of natural selection might be wrong, but Grassé has devoted his entire life to study the fact of evolution).

Science is a pluralistic enterprise, validly pursued in many modes. But Rifkin ignores its richness by stating that direct manipulation by repeatable experiment is the only acceptable method for reaching a scientific conclusion. Since evolution treats historically unique events that occurred millions of years ago, it cannot be a science. Rifkin doesn't seem to realize that he is throwing out half of science—nearly all of geology and most of astronomy, for instance—with his evolutionary bath water. Historical science is a valid pursuit, but it uses methods different from the controlled experiment of Rifkin's all-encompassing caricature—search for an underlying pattern among unique events, and retrodiction (predicting the yet undiscovered results of past events), for example.

3. Rifkin does not respect the procedures of fair argument. He uses every debater's trick in the book to mischaracterize and trivialize his opposition, and to place his own dubious claims in a rosy light. Just four examples:

The synecdoche (trying to dismiss a general notion by citing a single poor illustration). He suggests that science knows nothing about the evolutionary tree of horses, and has sold the public a bill of goods (the great horse caper, he calls it), because one exhibit, set up at the American Museum of Natural History in 1905, arranged fossil horses in order of size, not genealogy. Right, Jeremy, that was a lousy exhibit, but you might read George Gaylord Simpson's book *Horses* to see what we do know.

The half quote (stopping in the middle so that an opponent appears to agree with you, or seems merely ridiculous). Rifkin quotes

me on the argument about incipient stages of useful structures discussed a few paragraphs ago: "Harvard's Stephen Jay Gould posed
the dilemma when he observed, 'What good is half a jaw or half a
wing?'" Sure, I posed the dilemma, but then followed it with an entire essay supporting Darwin's resolution based on different function
in intermediate stages. Rifkin might have mentioned it and not ad-
duced me in his support. Rifkin then quotes a famous line from Darwin as if it represented the great man's admission of impotence:
"Darwin himself couldn't believe it, even though it was his own theory that advanced the proposition. He wrote: 'To suppose that the
eye, with all of its inimitable contrivances . . . could have been formed
by natural selection, seems, I freely confess, absurd in the highest
possible degree.'" But Rifkin might have mentioned that Darwin follows this statement with one of his most brilliant sections—a documentation of nature's graded intermediates between simple pinhole
eyes and the complexity of our own, and an argument that the power
of new theories resides largely in their ability to resolve previous ab-
surdities.

Refuting what your opponents never claimed. In the 1950s, Stanley
Miller performed a famous experiment that synthesized amino acids
from hypothetical components of the earth's original atmosphere.
Rifkin describes it with glaring hype: "With great fanfare, the world
was informed that scientists had finally succeeded in forming life
from nonlife, the dream of magicians, sorcerers, and alchemists from
time immemorial." He then points out, quite correctly, that the experiment did no such thing, and that the distance from amino acid to
life is immense. But Miller never claimed that he had made life. The
experiment stands in all our text books as a demonstration that some
simple components of living systems can be made from inorganic
chemicals. I was taught this 25 years ago; I have lectured about it for
15 years. I have never in all my professional life heard a scientist say
that Miller or anyone else has made life from non-life.

Refuting what your opponents refuted long ago. Rifkin devotes a
whole section to ridiculing evolution because its supporters once advanced the "biogenetic law" that embryos repeat the adult stages of
their ancestry—now conclusively refuted. But Darwinian evolutionists did the refuting more than 50 years ago (good science is self-
correcting).

4. Rifkin ignores the most elementary procedures of fair scholarship. His book, brought forth as a major conceptual statement about
the nature of science and the history of biology, displays painful ig-

norance of its subject. His quotations are primarily from old and discredited secondary sources (including some creationist propaganda tracts). I see no evidence that he has ever read much of Darwin in the original. He obviously knows nothing about (or chooses not to mention) all the major works of Darwinian scholarship written by modern historians. His continual barrage of misquotes and half quotes records this partial citation from excerpts in hostile secondary sources.

His prose is often purple in the worst journalistic tradition. When invented claims are buttressed by such breathless description, the effect can be quite amusing. He mentions the geneticist T. H. Morgan's invocation of the tautology argument discussed previously in this essay: "Not until Morgan began to suspect that natural selection was a victim of circular reasoning did anyone in the scientific community even question what was regarded by all as a profound truth. . . . Morgan's observation shocked the scientific establishment." Now, I ask, how does he know this? He cites no evidence of any shock, even of any contemporary comment. He quotes Morgan himself only from secondary sources. In fact, everything about the statement is wrong, just plain wrong. The tautology argument dates from the 1870s. Morgan didn't invent it (and Darwin, in my opinion, ably refuted it when Morgan was a baby). Morgan, moreover, was no noble knight sallying forth against a monolithic Darwinian establishment. When he wrote his critique in the 1920s, natural selection was a distinctly unpopular theory among evolutionists (the tide didn't turn in Darwin's favor until the late 1930s). Morgan, if anything, *was* the establishment, and his critique, so far as I know, didn't shock a soul or elicit any extensive commentary.

5. *Algeny* is full of ludicrous, simple errors. I particularly enjoyed Rifkin's account of Darwin in the Galapagos. After describing the "great masses" of vultures, condors, vampire bats, jaguars, and snakes that Darwin saw on these islands, Rifkin writes: "It was a savage, primeval scene, menacing in every detail. Everywhere there was bloodletting, and the ferocious, unremittent battle for survival. The air was dank and foul, and the thick stench of volcanic ash veiled the islands with a kind of ghoulish drape." Well, I guess Rifkin has never been there; and he obviously didn't bother to read anything about these fascinating islands. Except for snakes, none of those animals live on the Galapagos. In fact, the Galapagos house no terrestrial predators at all; as a result, the animals have no fear of human beings and do not flee when approached. The Galapagos are unusual, as

Darwin noted, precisely because they are not scenes of Hobbes's *bellum omnium contra omnes* (the war of all against all). And, by the way, no thick stench or ghoulish drape either; the volcanic terrains are beautiful, calm, and peaceful—not in eruption when Darwin visited, not now either.

Jeremy Rifkin, in short, has argued himself, inextricably, into a corner. He has driven off his natural allies by silly, at times dishonest, argument and nasty caricature. He has saddled his legitimate concern with an extremism that would outlaw both humane and fascinating scientific research. His legitimate brief speaks for the integrity of organisms and species. It would be a bleak world indeed that treated living things as no more than separate sequences of information, available for disarticulation and recombination in any order that pleased human whim. But I do not see why we would reject all of genetic engineering because its technology might, one day, permit such a perversion of decency in the hands of some latter-day Hitler—you may as well outlaw printing because the same machine that composes Shakespeare can also set *Mein Kampf.* The domino theory does not apply to all human achievements. If we could, by transplanting a bacterial gene, confer disease or cold resistance upon an important crop plant, should we not do so in a world where people suffer so terribly from malnutrition? Must such an event imply that, tomorrow, corn and wheat, sea horses and orchids will be thrown into a gigantic vat, torn apart into genetic units, and reassembled into rows of identical human servants? Eternal vigilance, to recombine some phrases, is the price of technological achievement.

The debate about genetic engineering has often been portrayed, falsely, as one of many battles between the political left and right—leftists in opposition, rightists plowing ahead. It is not so simple; it rarely is. Used humanely for the benefit of ordinary people, not the profits of a few entrepreneurs, this technology need not be feared by the left. I, for one, would rather campaign for proper use, not abolition. If Rifkin's argument embodies any antithesis, it is not left versus right, but romanticism, in its most dangerous anti-intellectual form, versus respect for knowledge and its humane employment. In both its content and presentation, *Algeny* belongs in the sordid company of anti-science. Few campaigns are more dangerous than emotional calls for proscription rather than thought.

I have been so harsh because I believe that Rifkin has seriously harmed a cause that is very dear to me and to nearly all my scientific colleagues. Rifkin has placed all of us beyond the pale of decency by arguing that scientific paradigms are simple expressions of socioeconomic bias, that biotech implies (and will impose) a new view of organisms as strings of separable information (not wholes of necessary integrity), and that all scientists will eventually go along with this heartless idea. Well, Mr. Rifkin, who then will be for you? Where will you find your allies in the good fight for respect of evolutionary lineages? You have rejected us, reviled us, but we are with you. We are taxonomists, ecologists, and evolutionists—most of us Darwinians. We have devoted our lives to the study of species in their natural habitats. We have struggled to understand—and we greatly admire— the remarkable construction and operation of organisms, the product of complex evolutionary histories, cascades of astounding improbability stretching back for millions of years. We know these organisms, and we love them—as they are. We would not dissolve this handiwork of four billion years to satisfy the hubris of one species. We respect the integrity of nature, Mr. Rifkin. But your arguments lack integrity. This we deplore.

■ CONSIDERATIONS OF MEANING AND METHOD

1. What qualifies Gould to write about this subject? How do his and Jeremy Rifkin's qualifications compare? Does Gould have any identifiable bias?

2. Compare the structure of Gould's critique of Jeremy Rifkin's book *Algeny* with the structure of a formal argument described in this chapter's introduction. How closely, and in what specific respects, does Gould's argument resemble this classic model? In this argument, what is Gould's most fundamental claim? Who is his audience? What is the essay's exigence? What key reasons does Gould offer in support of his claim?

3. Do you think Gould offers an accurate and fair summary of Rifkin's views? What in Rifkin's argument does Gould accept as valid? To what does he take fundamental exception? Do his criticisms of Rifkin seem legitimate to you? Why or why not?

4. Gould accuses Rifkin of indulging in logical fallacies and unfair tactics in argumentation. What are these? Do you find these criticisms convincing? Why or why not?

5. Gould refers to Rifkin in the third person throughout most of the essay, but in the final paragraph he addresses Rifkin directly. What might Gould's reasons have been for doing this? Did you find this technique effective? Why or why not?

- POSSIBILITIES FOR WRITING

1. In an analysis of structure and style, compare Rifkin's and Gould's essays. How are they similar and different in terms of audience, purpose, point of view, and strategy in argumentation? Do you think one argument is a more difficult kind to make than the other? If so, why?

2. Rifkin argues that "Once we decide to begin the process of human genetic engineering, there is really no logical place to stop," so we should not start. Gould argues, "I do not see why we should reject all of genetic engineering because its technology might, one day, permit . . . a perversion of decency in the hands of some latter-day Hitler. . . . " With which view do you tend to agree more, and why? In what respects does your own view differ from both Rifkin's and Gould's? Explain and argue for your position, and address your essay to Rifkin, Gould, or both.

- JENNIFER HARRIS
American Eugenics Society II?

In her statement, student writer Jennifer Harris introduces herself and explains her purpose in learning and writing about the history of eugenics in relation to current questions about the social implications of genetic engineering.

I am currently a sophomore majoring in geological and environmental sciences. My specific interests include geology and water resources. I am from Salem, Oregon, where I enjoy hiking in the mountains, playing sports, and spending time with my family and friends. I hope to return to the Northwest to live and to work in the future. I enjoy writing about environmental issues and about my experiences in nature; however, I often find it difficult to communicate my experiences in a clear manner without losing the emotion that I feel toward my subject.

My desire to know more about genetic engineering was sparked by an article that I read in the fall of my freshman year. I was amazed to learn from the article that it was technically possible to correct genetic defects by altering a person's genes. I was also scared by the fact that many scientists did not know where to draw the line in defining "genetic defect." For this paper, I chose to use the article "Controlling the Genetic Arsenal" by Daniel Kelves as my secondary source because it contained a thorough account of the history of eugenics and because it made me question whether genetic engineering was a legitimate practice. The article was written in a clear, simple manner that allowed the common reader like me to understand some basic facts about eugenics and genetic engineering. It was also written by a credible author.

My essay is, for the most part, a summary of the Kelves article. The audience for my essay includes people who are interested in having a basic understanding of the history of eugenics and how eugenics is related to genetic engineering. My purpose is to give my reader a sense of how eugenics influenced people's lives in the past and how genetic engineering may be encouraged or even mandated in the future because of economic pressures. This essay is not intended to fully educate the reader about eugenics or genetic engineering, but rather to encourage him or her to read more about the subject and to consider seriously the implications of supporting new advances in genetic engineering.

Ethical debates rage worldwide over such issues as abortion and animal rights. But perhaps one of the most controversial topics today in the area of science and ethics involves genetic testing and genetic engineering—the cutting and splicing of genetic material to allow scientists not only to study but also to correct several genetic defects. Many people question the morality of manipulating genes in order to create more perfect individuals. While genetic testing is used primarily to predict hereditary disabilities and illnesses such as Down syndrome and cancer, who is to say that in the future it won't be used to test for blond hair, blue eyes, or an athletic physique, or that genetic engineering won't be used to design "perfect people"? Current fears about manipulation of human genes have arisen in part because of our experience in the first half of this century with laws and organizations that actively promoted a more "suitable" (that is, white, Protestant, and middle or upper-middle class) society.

One organization that campaigned for such a society was the American Eugenics Society, formed in 1923. It consisted of white middle class professionals, scientists, and physicians. "They took crime, slums, and rampant disease to be symptoms of social pathologies that they attributed primarily to biological causes," according to Daniel J. Kelves, professor of humanities at the California Institute of Technology, in his article "Controlling the Genetic Arsenal" (68–69). It was an exclusive organization that did not tolerate "unsuitable" people.

The American Eugenics Society was formed primarily to promote the ideas of Francis Galton, a younger first cousin to Charles Darwin. Francis Galton was the first to use the word "eugenics" in the late nineteenth century as a name for one of his human improvement programs. Galton took this word from a Greek root meaning "good in birth" or "noble in heredity." Since then, eugenics has become associated with genetic engineering. Eugenics is the study of the hereditary improvement of the race by genetic control. This control is provided by discoveries and advances in the field of genetic engineering.

There are two types of eugenics: positive and negative. Positive eugenics refers to the manipulation of human breeding in order to produce a superior race. Negative eugenics aims to restrict immigration and to discourage humans perceived as being inferior from reproducing. Positive eugenics was practiced primarily at the local and state level in the United States. The Kansas State Fair held a contest in which families were judged according to breeding standards. But while positive eugenics was encouraged in a few areas of the country, "much more was done in the name of negative eugenics, notably by means of eugenic sterilization laws," according to Professor Kelves (71). By the late 1920s, twenty-four states had enacted eugenic sterilization laws primarily targeting prisoners and mentally deficient or "feebleminded" persons. These laws allowed "state prisons and other institutions to perform vasectomies or tubal ligations on inmates who were epileptic, insane, or 'feebleminded'. . . . These laws were declared constitutional in the 1927 U.S. Supreme Court decision, *Buck* v. *Bell*" (71).

The case of *Buck* v. *Bell* involved an eighteen-year-old mentally deficient woman in an institution. At the time that her sterilization case came to trial, she was the mother of an illegitimate, mentally deficient child, and her mother was living in the same institution. Justice Oliver Wendell Holmes, Jr., declared that "three generations of imbeciles are enough" (qtd. in Kelves 71). The young woman lost the case and was forced to adhere to the sterilization laws.

By 1941, nearly 36,000 Americans had been sterilized, according to Professor Kelves. California was the leading advocate for these laws, sterilizing more people than all other states combined. But the sterilization laws were not confined to this country. In fact, it is possible that in Germany, during Adolf Hitler's campaign for an Aryan race, the "sterilization measures were partly inspired by the California law," Professor Kelves claims (71).

As well as sterilization laws, immigration laws took root in the United States in the 1920s as a result of new genetic standards. In 1922, the decision in the case *Ozawa* v. *United States* allowed racial disqualifications to be included in naturalization laws. This discrimination was aimed at blacks and Asians.

Although the negative eugenics movement lost many of its supporters because of Hitler's campaign, it still has the potential to gain support in the future. According to Professor Kelves, one powerful incentive to support negative eugenics may be economic. In 1988, the European Commission—the executive arm of the twelve-nation European Community—termed genetic developments "predictive medicine." Predictive medicine aims to protect individuals from illnesses to which they are genetically vulnerable and to prevent the transmission of genetic illnesses such as diabetes and cancer to the next generation. If there were a decrease in the number of illnesses, the rate of increase in health expenditures would slow. Because a portion of health care costs are paid by taxes, and hence by citizens, many citizens are supporting the use of genetic engineering and are encouraging other people to support it as well. Many taxpayers believe that they should not have to pay health care costs for individuals with avoidable genetic diseases or disabilities.

Along with some taxpayers advocating the use of genetic engineering, the government may also encourage the use of it, according to Professor Kelves. He states that "public officials may feel pressure to encourage or even to compel people not to bring genetically marked children into the world—not for the sake of the gene pool but in the interest of keeping public-health costs down" (73).

As the government and taxpayers gain greater influence over people's decisions regarding the practice of genetic engineering, they begin to resemble the state governments and the American Eugenics Society in the earlier part of the century. Are we allowing ourselves to become members of American Eugenics Society II? Maybe we need to take a step back from the genetics movement and examine where it is leading us so we don't get ourselves involved in something we will regret—like national riots over sterilization laws.

Source

Kelves, Daniel J. "Controlling the Genetic Arsenal." *Wilson Quarterly* 16:2 (1992): 68–76.

■ CONSIDERATIONS OF MEANING AND METHOD

1. What question or questions motivated Harris's investigation? Was the Kelves article a good source to consult, given the ques-

tions Harris had? What makes Kelves, as Harris says in the introduction to her essay, "a credible author"?

2. How much did you know about the eugenics movement in the United States in the 1920s before reading Harris's essay? Did you find any of the historical facts Harris cites surprising? Why or why not?

3. Compare Harris's definitions of positive and negative eugenics with Rifkin's. Compare the examples Harris and Rifkin offer to illustrate positive and negative eugenics practices in recent history. Do these definitions and examples conflict in any way? Taken together, how do they expand your understanding of eugenics? How do they offer perspective on the current genetic technology debate?

4. Do you find the European Commission's equation of negative eugenics and "predictive medicine" disturbing? Why or why not? What role do you think economic considerations should play in the genetic engineering debate?

5. Beyond summarizing Kelves's article, does Harris state any position of her own in this essay? If so, what is it, and where does she state it?

■ Possibilities for Writing

1. Harris says that her essay "is not intended to fully educate the reader about eugenics or genetic engineering, but rather to encourage him or her to read more about the subject and to consider seriously the implications of supporting new advances in genetic engineering." For you, what are the most crucial implications of this new technology? Through an investigation of additional secondary sources, try to find answers to questions raised in your mind by Harris's essay.

MAKING CRITICAL CONNECTIONS:
QUESTIONS FOR DISCUSSION, RESEARCH, AND WRITING

1. In the cycle of readings on land use, you read two essays (Russell's investigation and Abbey's argument) about personal and public dimensions of the specific issue of private grazing on public lands in the Southwest, and two essays (Riggs's argument and Pham's counterargument) about some of the more general issues involved in the debate about private use of public lands (though these essays focus primarily on oil exploration and extraction). Aldo Leopold's essay "The Land Ethic" in Chapter 7 provides an additional point of reference on this topic. After considering this cycle of readings, what questions remain unanswered for you about the use of public lands—general questions or specific ones? What information, perspectives, or positions are missing from this cycle of readings, and how would having access to them help you achieve a more complete understanding of the issues involved? Is there a related issue that was brought to mind by the readings but was not fully addressed in them that you would like to explore? In class, compile with other students a collaborative list of these questions. Such questions provide the ideal motivation for further research. Select one of the more intriguing questions on the list, and attempt to discover the answer through an investigation into an additional primary or secondary source. Orally or in an investigative or argumentative essay, share with other students in your class what you learned through your research and explain how your additional source contributes to your understanding, relating it to readings in the land use cycle in this text. Finally, together with other students in your class who have investigated the public lands use issue further, compile a collaborative bibliography on the subject.

2. In the reading cycle about animal rights, what information or perspectives are missing? Acquire additional information or perspectives on the issue through research. Since this reading cycle emphasizes secondary sources and theoretical issues, you might concentrate your investigation of a particular aspect of the animal rights debate on primary sources, supplemented as necessary with secondary source material. For example, consider interviewing researchers who use animals in their research. What, for them, justifies animal experimentation? Do they have reservations about it? In their daily work, do they consider ethical issues much? Or you might interview animal rights activists—especially those who have been involved in illegal protests or interventions to prevent animal experimentation. How do they justify their methods? What is the insider's view of the politics of the animal

rights movement? Or, to supplement secondary research on marketing and consumer issues, you might conduct a survey to gather information about the extent to which animal rights issues influence people's habits and attitudes about products they do or do not buy. Report on the results of your investigation in a research report, or use your investigation as the basis for a documented argument.

3. Using genetic engineering as a case in point and drawing upon the readings which comprise the cycle on genetic engineering in this chapter, respond in writing or in discussion to Lewis Thomas's thesis in "Making Science Work" (Chapter 7): "Technology should be watched closely, monitored, criticized, even voted in or out by the electorate, but science itself must be given its head if we want it to work" (page 457). To what extent do you agree or disagree with Thomas? In what ways might genetic engineering technologies be "watched . . . , monitored, criticized," or "voted in or out"? If you encounter gaps in your understanding of this complex subject, fill them through additional primary or secondary research.

4. In the closing paragraph of "Perfect People?" Amy Virshup writes, "Like other decisions forced upon us by advancing technology, the choice involved in genetic testing can exceed one's moral grasp." In a class brainstorming session, consider cases other than genetic testing in which technologies force decisions upon us that may exceed our "moral grasp." Choose one of these examples as the subject of an investigation through research and a written argument.

5. Spend part of a class session listing possible topics for research essays related to the extremely broad subject of human relationships with the natural world. List topics under disciplinary and professional headings—for example, history, government, anthropology, biology, physics, earth science, political science, social science, psychology, education, economics, literature, law, medicine, business, agriculture, international relations. Try to keep the topics as specifically focused as possible; you might try phrasing them in the form of questions. As you compile this list of possible research topics, make note of which topics relate to more than one field or discipline. For example, a topic about rain forest ecology might relate to anthropology, biology, economics, agriculture, or international relations, depending upon how the topic is focused. Consider which topics you might be interested in exploring in a multiple-source research report or documented argument.

APPENDIX

WEAVING THE THREADS: AN OVERVIEW OF THE RESEARCH PROCESS

Many excellent textbooks devote themselves entirely to exploring the many facets of researching and writing documented essays. It will be impossible, in this brief Appendix, to cover all aspects of research and documented writing. But this overview will give you a sense of the scope of this kind of endeavor, along with an idea of how to begin researching a subject of interest to you, and of how your research and writing might come to fruition in a multiple source essay.

First you should understand the difference between a *single-source essay* and a *multiple-source essay.* If you are asked to write an essay in which you draw from only one primary or secondary source, you are writing a single-source essay. If you are asked to write a multiple-source essay, you will draw upon a variety of primary and/or secondary source material. There are many examples of both single-source and multiple-source essays throughout this book.

Student works in this anthology include both single-source and multiple-source essays. Jennifer Donaldson's "Silent Sufferers: A Response to Alice Walker's 'Am I Blue?'" in Chapter 5 and Anne Pollock's "Animal Rights: Alternative Approaches" and Jennifer Harris's "American Eugenics Society II?", both in Chapter 8, are single-source essays.

Multiple-source essays include Kiran Pandeya's fact sheet, "Rough-legged Hawk" in Chapter 2, Benjamin Jun's "Consciousness" in Chapter 7, and By Pham's "Public Lands Should Remain Public" in Chapter

8. Student Zach Perron's essay, "When Habitats Overlap: Increasing Contacts between Mountain Lions and Humans," included on page 624 in this Appendix, is an example of a complex multiple-source essay.

Many of the seeds of successful research and documented writing have been planted in earlier chapters of this text. By the time you read this Appendix, you will probably have already learned a great deal about using research tools and about many rhetorical strategies that would apply in writing documented essays with a variety of purposes. You have learned, for example, that evidence comes in many forms: from observation and personal experience as well as from outside sources, including primary and secondary source material. You have learned investigative techniques and reasons for searching out information in one kind of source as opposed to another as you research your subject. You have learned, too, some ways in which to evaluate your sources, whether to verify facts or to detect bias. You are now in an excellent position to undertake a more complicated research and documented writing process.

THE DOCUMENTED REPORT AND THE DOCUMENTED ARGUMENT: WHAT KIND OF RESEARCH ESSAY ARE YOU BEING ASKED TO WRITE?

You'll recall from the introduction to Chapter 8 that there are differences between investigative writing and argumentative writing: investigations report, and arguments persuade. When you are asked to write a research paper in college, you should make sure you understand the nature and purpose of the assignment. Are you expected to write a *documented report* or a *documented argument?*

If you are being asked to learn, through research, as much as you can about your subject and then to coordinate and report what you learn in a documented essay without interpreting, taking a stand, or proposing a solution, your assignment is to write a documented report. The purpose of your paper will be to inform. If you are expected to analyze the evidence you gather in research and from that analysis develop a thesis by which you promote a particular interpretation, take a stand on an issue, or propose a solution to a problem, your assignment is to write a documented argument. Although your argument will be based on investigation and one of its purposes will be to inform, its ultimate purpose is to persuade.

THE RESEARCH
AND RESEARCH WRITING PROCESS

The process of researching and writing the documented essay is complex not simply because research essays tend to be longer than other kinds of essays that you write in college, but also because in them you must balance and interweave often complicated (sometimes even contradictory) material from multiple primary and/or secondary sources. If you are writing a documented argument, you will be challenged by having to integrate this source material with your own observations, thoughts, and analysis. Throughout your analysis, you will want to retain control over the ideas you are writing about.

Any good writing, including research writing, represents an involved writing process, including stages of prewriting, drafting, and revision. In addition to the various stages of the writing process, though, a good research paper will be built on a many-layered research process. The stages of the research and research writing process that you will encounter will probably include:

    I. *Selecting a Topic*
       A. Choosing a topic
       B. Focusing the topic

    II. *Conducting Preliminary Research*
       A. Consulting reference sources
       B. Focusing the topic further

    III. *Compiling a Working Bibliography*
       A. Selecting possible sources
       B. Scanning possible sources
       C. Making bibliography cards
       D. Writing annotations

    IV. *Close Reading and Note Taking*
       A. Making note cards
       B. Recording summaries, paraphrases, and quotations
       C. Avoiding plagiarism

    V. *Outlining*
       A. Articulating a tentative thesis
       B. Organizing your thinking
       C. Organizing your evidence

    VI. *Drafting*
       A. Opening

      B. Writing from your outline
      C. Integrating and documenting source material
      D. Closing
  VII. *Revising*
      A. Re-visioning
      B. Editing

One major consideration not mentioned in the outline above is the question of which documentation style you will use in your research essay. This Appendix includes a discussion of documentation practices and styles on pages 616–24. Right now, though, let's take a closer look at what's involved at each stage of the research and research writing process outlined above.

Selecting a Topic

Most research and research writing assignments you receive in college courses will leave the choice of a specific topic relatively open within the context of subject material covered in the course. There is a wonderful freedom in selecting from among open topics, but there is a challenge as well. Which, among a nearly infinite variety of possible topics, will make for a good topic for your research essay? The answer, first and foremost, depends upon your interest. Research and research writing are generally long and involved processes, and it is essential that your research be provoked and *sustained* by a topic that truly interests you. Avoid choosing a topic about which you think you already know everything, or about which you have a lot of prejudgments. Instead choose a topic that you know *something* about—enough to realize that you want to know more. This is an opportunity for you to dig deeply within a subject, to answer questions that you may have long, or perhaps only recently, wondered about. It is your opportunity to develop expertise in a subject that matters to you.

Once you have identified a general topic—as, for example, Zach Perron did in choosing the general topic of mountain lions—you will have to focus your topic more specifically. You can do this by asking the "what about" question: *Well, what about mountain lions?* Perron decided that one of the things that interested him most about mountain lions was the fear that this animal inspires in most people—an attitude, he suspected, that arose more from misconceptions about the animal's behavior than from reality. He decided to focus his topic more narrowly on interaction between mountain lions and human beings. It is helpful to articulate your focused topic as a question, a question that will motivate your research. In Zach Perron's case, this question was *What happens when mountain lions and human beings come into direct contact?*

Perron had heard about cases in which lions had attacked livestock or human beings and had been hunted down and shot, and, because of his appreciation for this formidable animal, he knew something—but wanted to know more—about its behavior. In narrowing a research topic, you will rather quickly reach the limits of your current knowledge and understanding. In order to focus your topic any more specifically, you will have to undertake some preliminary research, probably in the reference room of your library.

Conducting Preliminary Research

You can get an overview of your topic from a variety of *reference sources.* A reference source will help you define your topic and locate primary and secondary source material relevant to it. Reference sources include three kinds of sources:

- *People.* The reference librarian in your school or local library can be a valuable source of information. It is part of his or her job to help you discover ways in which you might approach and examine your topic, locating other reference sources as well as primary or secondary source material relevant to the topic in your library. A useful reference source might also exist in the form of other people—experts in your subject area— who can recommend both other reference sources and relevant primary or secondary source material.

- *Dictionaries, encyclopedias, and other sources of general knowledge.* These reference sources will not only give you the most fundamental background on your subject, they will also suggest ways in which very broad subjects might be focused into more specific topics. We are all familiar with general dictionaries like *Webster's New Collegiate Dictionary* and general encyclopedias like *The Encyclopedia Britannica.* In your library, you will also find specialized dictionaries (many with extended entries, more like encyclopedia entries than simple definitions) and specialized encyclopedias. For example, the *McGraw-Hill Dictionary of Scientific and Technical Terms,* the *Dictionary of Symbols* by J. E. Cirlot, the *Encyclopedia of Anthropology,* or the *Encyclopedia of Religion and Ethics* might help you in your initial investigations of specialized subjects.

- *Card catalogs and indexes.* These reference sources will let you know of the existence of books, articles in magazines and newspapers, films, government documents, and other secondary sources relevant to your topic. Catalogs and indexes may exist in printed form or in electronic form.

Your school library may have a good old-fashioned card catalog system in which you can look up on cards in drawers the books your library owns by subject, author, or title. Increasingly, however, library collections are cataloged electronically. If this is the case at your library, you will look for books in your library's collection on-line, at a computer terminal, but the fundamental principle is the same: you will find books cataloged by subject, author, and title.

Most of us are familiar with general indexes to periodical literature—that is, to articles in newspapers and magazines. The *Reader's Guide to Periodical Literature* is a general index many students have used before they enter college, and it is a good source for locating articles in a broad range of general subject areas. But, as is the case for dictionaries and encyclopedias, many specialized indexes exist that will help you locate periodical literature within specific subject areas. For example, the *Humanities Index,* the *Social Sciences Index,* the *Music Index,* the *Index Medicus,* or the *National Newspaper Index* can help you focus your search for periodical source material according to specific disciplines or formats. The more specialized the index is, the more specialized the publications included within it will be, and the more specialized the publications are, the more technical the articles they include are likely to be. Some indexes exist only in printed form, but more and more exist, as do catalogs of libraries' book collections, on-line. Some indexes are stored on CD-ROM. Your reference librarian can help you learn how to access reference sources, whether they are printed or electronically stored.

Once you have gotten a sense of what information is available on your topic, as well as the ways in which other people have defined and analyzed the topic, breaking it down into more specific categories, you will have a better sense of how, in your research, you would like to approach it. At this point, you should be able, with new information, to narrow your topic even more.

You might wonder why it is preferable to work with a narrow rather than a broad topic. There are several reasons. If your assignment is to analyze a topic in a documented argument, it is difficult to accomplish this analysis when the overview, the topic itself, is very broad. You are likely to find yourself in the position of reporting general information from widely available source material—in other words, going over the same ground that countless others have already traveled—rather than analyzing a facet of the subject in depth and therefore more originally. You are also likely to find yourself, if you are working with a topic that is too broad, writing at an abstract or theoretical level, if not an obvious one, lacking specific, concrete illustrations, examples, and other kinds of evidence that will make your investigations and arguments more accessible, more worthwhile, and livelier for both you and your reader. It is difficult to engage a topic actively when you feel that there is little opportunity for you to analyze it; you may feel that you are simply taking dictation from your sources.

Until you get into the library and begin to realize how much material is available on your topic, you might fear that there will not be enough source material upon which to build your research and your paper, and so you may be resistant to limiting your topic. Most students find in preliminary research, however, that rather than there being too little material, there is too much. Limiting your topic, then, is essential if you want to say something of real significance in the relatively short time and space you have to complete the project—say, a few weeks and perhaps ten pages. Narrowing your topic is an ongoing process: the more you find out about your topic in the course of your research, the more you will continue to refine its focus.

Compiling a Working Bibliography

A working bibliography is a list of particular bibliographic possibilities. It should reflect the results of your preliminary research, an initial though careful scanning of primary and secondary material you think you might end up using in your research paper. Later, as you investigate these sources more closely, you may decide that not all of these sources will be of use to you, and so you will drop some from your final bibliography; you will also probably add new sources as you come upon them in the course of your ongoing research.

As much as possible, you should aim for variety in your choice of secondary sources, which could include books, articles, reviews, government documents, or documentary films, among other possibilities. Some research topics lend themselves well to inclusion of primary source material in the form of interviews or surveys; other topics do not lend themselves well, or even at all, to these sources of information.

Keep your motivating question, the purpose of your research, solidly in mind as you compile secondary sources for a working bibliography, and remember that various sources lend themselves to various uses. Most research papers will require some amount of background material. Often, this kind of material is best retrieved from books about the subject you are investigating; these will provide a context for your subject. Articles in periodical sources will probably focus on more specific aspects or applications of general subjects. A news article will probably give you an historical or "current events" perspective. Articles in popular magazines (for example, *Time* or *Newsweek*) will give you basic information but will also be likely to focus on popular understanding and current attitudes related to your subject, since these articles are written for general readers with an immediate interest rather than specialized readers with an ongoing, evolving interest. Articles in professional journals will be written by authors with expertise; these articles will be even more specifically focused, and they may be highly technical since their audience is other specialists. Consider what kinds of information, and combinations of information, will best serve your purposes in answering the question motivating your research.

In compiling a working bibliography, you will need to develop techniques for quickly scanning secondary sources to gauge their applicability to your research; you will probably not want to engage in close reading at this early stage. Much can be ascertained about a book or an article from its title, including its subtitle. But this might not give you enough information. In your printed or electronic card catalog, there will be a brief description of the contents of books which you should take note of. In scanning a book itself, look over the table of contents: chapter titles or the titles of essays in a collection will tell you more specifically whether or not, or to what degree, the material in the book will be of use in your investigation of your topic. You might also quickly scan the introduction to a book to get a better sense of its contents. Some indexes to periodical literature will supply *abstracts*. These are brief but concrete summaries of the article itself and are highly useful in determining applicability.

Many instructors will ask you to submit a working bibliography so that they can gather from it the direction your preliminary research is taking you. Frequently, instructors will ask for an *annotated bibliography*. Annotations are very brief summaries of the source you plan to use. Generally, a couple of sentences will do. You might compose a one-sentence description of the contents of the source itself, and another sentence to indicate how you think this particular source will serve you as you explore your topic.

Whether or not you are required to submit a working bibliography before you submit your research paper, and whether or not this working bibliography includes annotations, you will want to record all of your bibliographic possibilities carefully, whether they are primary or secondary sources; bibliography cards are an excellent place to do this. It is important to record all relevant information on these cards, even if you are not certain that you will end up using the source. For books, you will want to record the library call number. You will also want to record the full name(s) of author(s) or editor(s), complete title (including subtitle), city of publication, publisher, and date. If you are using part of a book—for example, an essay within an edited collection, you will also need to include the author, title, and inclusive page numbers of the part of the book you are using. An example of a bibliography card for a book source is shown below.

Kevin Hansen   *[call number]*

Cougar: The American Lion

Flagstaff, Arizona: Northland Publishing

1992

116 pages

historical overview: recent
depredation studies

For articles in periodical publications (including magazines, journals, or newspapers), you will record full name(s) of author(s), complete title of article, title of the periodical, date and/or volume and issue numbers, and inclusive page numbers (for newspaper articles, this includes the section of the paper). Here is an example of a bibliography card for a periodical source:

> Nancy Worth
>
> "When Good Lions Go Bad"
>
> *Outdoor Life*
>
> Jan. 1991
>
> pp. 56 and 78–80
>
>   hotspots of human/cougar contact

Complete bibliographic information will be essential when you compose your list of works cited, and you do not want to be in the position later of having to return to the library to find essential information that you forgot to record in your preliminary research. You might also find it useful to record a brief annotation—a description of the contents of the source—on each bibliography card (as shown in the examples on page 606 and above).

Close Reading and Note Taking

Although researchers develop and individually tailor techniques and strategies that work best for them, some techniques and strategies seem to work generally better than others. Many researcher-writers find that using note cards to record information and ideas gathered in close reading of source material helps them to develop their thinking and organize their material most efficiently. If you have been using bibliography cards to record bibliographic information, you might consider adding note cards to your research card collection. Information recorded on note cards is much easier to pull together when the time comes to create a formal outline than information scattered helter-skelter in a notebook.

A note card might look like this:

> Hansen, *American Lion*   depredation
>
> One lion killed 59 sheep in one night, Nevada
>
> p. 60

At the upper left-hand corner of your card, you will write the author's last name and an abbreviated title. This reference will tie in to the full reference of this source recorded on a separate bibliography card. At the upper right-hand corner of the card, you will indicate a heading that will help you place this card within your outline. (Some researcher-writers develop rough, working outlines before or in the process of examining their sources closely.) Below this you will record specific information from this source, whether in the form of facts or statistics, summary, paraphrase, or quotation. Finally, at the bottom of the card, you will record the page number on which you found this information in your source. Use a new note card to record each new idea, piece of information, or quotation.

A *summary* is a statement in your own language of a broad idea expressed by your source. In recording information on a note card in the form of a summary, you might be reducing an idea contained within several paragraphs or several pages of your source into a few sentences of your own. A *paraphrase* differs from a summary in scope; in a paraphrase, you will state in your own language a specific idea or specific information from your source. Sometimes you will want to record direct *quotations* from sources on your note cards. When you are recording quotations on note cards, accuracy is essential: you must be careful to include quotation marks and to copy the quotation exactly as it appears in your source. If you leave out any words of a sentence as you copy it from your source, indicate this with an ellipsis (. . .), and if what you delete includes the end of a sentence in your source, indicate this with an ellipsis plus a period (. . . .). If you add any of your own words in linking chunks of quoted material, put your own words (no more than a word or short phrase to provide clarification) in brackets ([ ]). Accuracy at the stage of note taking is extremely important, because if you don't record quotations accurately in your notes, you won't transcribe them accurately in your paper. Inaccuracy, even if it is inadvertent, is one of the leading causes of plagiarism.

Whether you are recording information or ideas from sources on note cards in the form of summaries, paraphrases, or quotations, make sure you cite specific page references to indicate exactly where in your source you found them. When you make specific reference to your sources in your paper, you will need these page references.

It is a good idea, as you take notes, to paraphrase more frequently than you quote. You will want to record quotations when it is not only the idea that is important to you, but the language itself—when the author has expressed an idea unusually well, or there is something about the language itself that you might wish to comment on. Unless there is something particularly appealing or compelling about the author's exact wording, paraphrase the information or idea, or use a combination of paraphrase and quotation (but take care to record quoted key words and phrases accurately). If your note taking consists mostly of transcribing quotations, you are really just taking dictation from your sources; when you paraphrase and summarize, restating ideas from sources in your own language, you will understand them more fully, and you will analyze and relate them more actively. Both summarizing and paraphrasing help you to internalize the information and ideas you encounter in your sources.

It is crucial, as you examine your sources carefully and record what you find in them on note cards, and as you get closer to drafting your documented essay, that you have a good understanding of what plagiarism is and how to avoid it. *Plagiarism* is more than the theft of language from another source; it is also the theft of information and ideas from another source. As you take notes, remember that in your paper you must credit your sources for the information, ideas, *and* language you draw from them. Your analysis of your sources, the ways in which you compare them, and the conclusions you draw from them are your own, original work.

As you learn more and more about your subject through your scrutiny of source material, original ideas will come to you—ideas about how to relate information and sources and how to organize and express your thoughts. You should also record these ideas on note cards as you go. Since these ideas express your original thinking they will, especially in a documented argument, provide the backbone of your paper, its direction and its reason for being.

Outlining

As you read and evaluate your sources, developing a deeper, more specific and sophisticated understanding of your subject, the thesis of your research essay will begin to come into focus. Possible answers to the question that has been motivating and focusing your research have probably already occurred to you as you have examined your sources closely; now it is time to articulate the question's most fundamental answer in the form of a tentative thesis. This thesis will help you direct and shape your formal outline.

Many researcher-writers undertake their close examination of primary and secondary source material with a rough outline, based on preliminary research, before them, to help chart their course; other researcher-writers allow a rough outline to develop in the course of close examination of source material. Whichever approach you choose, you should, after completing the bulk of your indepth research, have a sense not only of what the most fundamental answer to your motivating question is (your tentative thesis), but of what main points your essay should cover and what background or contextual information you will need to provide in order to establish exigence and to lay a foundation of understanding for your reader. You should also have a sense of how you will use your primary and secondary sources to provide information and to support your assertions.

A formal outline is essential in drafting a multiple-source research essay because these essays are complex, and in them you will need to develop your thinking over a sustained time and to coordinate evidence from many different sources. This formal outline, therefore, should indicate not only your organizational strategy, but how and where you intend to use your source material. See Zach Perron's outline (pp. 625–628), upon which he based the drafting of his research essay, as an example of a detailed outline that maps both organizational strategy and use of source material. You might find it useful to state your motivating question in the introductory portion of the outline and your thesis in its conclusion. Be aware, however, that as you compose your outline, and even as you draft your paper, your thesis may continue to evolve, since writing, after all, is a way of thinking. It is also quite possible that in your formal outline, as in Perron's, you will map out more than you can realistically cover in the space available to you in your research paper.

In composing and in reviewing your outline before settling down to the job of drafting your documented essay, refer to the following checklist to see if your outline is working to help you develop your thinking and map your use of source material:

- Does your thesis answer your motivating question? Can you articulate your thesis statement in a sentence or two? Take multiple (evolving) stabs at it.

- In the number of pages you have, can you cover as much ground as you've mapped out? If you have taken on too much, is there anything tangential in your outline? Consider relative importance and emphasis: which points are of central importance, and which are of marginal importance? Can you delete or reduce the emphasis of some points without losing completeness or coherence?

- Consider exigence. Will your reader have a sense early on in your essay of why and how your subject is important? Consider the question, *So what?* or *What's at stake?* Anticipate how you will draw the reader in in the introduction.

- How much background is necessary for the reader to have a context of understanding in reading your paper (history, definition of terms, theory, technical information)? How much background or contextual information is too little, enough, too much? Will the paper be top-heavy with background information? Consider how such information will balance with the real business of the paper.

- Consider relative emphasis within the headings of your outline. Are the points you present as being of equal importance really of equal importance? Are points *I, II, III, IV* (and so on) balanced, of equivalent weight and emphasis? Compare points *A, B, C, D; 1, 2, 3, 4;* and *a, b, c, d* similarly.

- Are you listing or relating ideas? A good outline, at all its levels (*I, A, 1, a,* and so on), should reflect not only the points and the evidence you intend to include, but also how these points and items relate to one another. When you analyze, you consider how points and evidence might fall within specific categories. In this light, consider the following questions:

    - How will you work major transitions between key points—between *I* and *II,* for example, or between *A* and *B?*

    - How will you organize within more detailed categories—between *1, 2,* and *3* or between *a, b,* and *c,* for example? Are these random lists or do they represent a logical sequence? How do items relate? Anticipate how you might cover these details in drafting your essay—in a single paragraph? In more than one paragraph?

- Scan your outline for distribution of evidence. Are your points well-supported by evidence from your various sources? Are you relying too much on one particular source? Are there gaps of evidence, points for which you will need to establish more support with further research?

As you consider this final point of the checklist, remember that, especially in a documented argument, part of your job will be to analyze and to draw your own conclusions. Thus, particularly toward the end of your essay, you will probably be relying less on your sources and more on your own analysis. This is appropriate. After all, you have, through your research and your thinking, earned your own expertise and a right to speak from this expertise.

Drafting

A comprehensive and detailed outline, based on thorough research and careful thinking, is a giant step toward your finished research essay. You may find that the drafting of your paper is, if not exactly "easy," at least more relaxed if you are working from a solid outline. As you draft your research essay, you don't want to be preoccupied with figuring out which points deserve coverage and which do not, the fundamental organization of your material, and what it is you intend to explain or prove in your paper. This is the work involved in outlining. Rather, at the drafting stage, you will want to pay most attention to the writing—to the question of how most effectively to express your ideas and explain and illustrate your points in service of your thesis.

As you write, you will continue to develop your thoughts. If a new idea occurs to you in the process of drafting, you can afford, with a good outline as your point of reference, to explore it—to incorporate or to abandon it—without losing yourself and your fundamental ideas in the process. In your draft, you are fleshing out your ideas, thinking through your arguments, arranging your evidence, and modifying your organization. As with any kind of writing at the draft stage, you should try not to get bogged down with details. You will have the opportunity to revise and edit once your draft is complete.

You will be considering a great many questions about how best to articulate your thinking and incorporate your evidence as you draft your documented essay. Perhaps most pressing, however, will be questions about how best to open your essay, how to integrate material from sources smoothly, and how most effectively to close your essay.

Within the first couple of paragraphs, your reader should know precisely what the subject of your research essay is and why he or she should feel compelled to read about it. Therefore, you will need to be clear early on in indicating the topic of your paper while at the same time capturing your reader's interest. Consider, as you open your paper, who your reader is and why you have researched and are writing about the topic you've chosen. What kind of relevance is your topic likely to have in your reader's life? In providing contextual or background information early in your essay, consider your reader's level of expertise and the extent to which he or she is likely to be familiar with your topic and its implications. Having an accurate picture of your reader and your reasons for writing will direct the early content and style of your essay.

The successful integration of source material will be determined to a large extent by the degree to which you have engaged and analyzed this material. Simple lists of evidence from sources will do you no good unless they serve to illustrate or prove a point that you wish to make, and they will not lead you naturally to your next point unless you have analyzed the evidence and have drawn conclusions from it. Keep in mind the fundamental structure of claim, evidence, and warrant discussed in the introduction to Chapter 7 (page 408):

A claim (an assertion) $\longrightarrow$
is supported or illustrated by evidence $\longrightarrow$
which gives rise to a warrant (a statement which clarifies the relationship between claim and evidence).

When you introduce an idea or make a claim, back it up with evidence from personal experience, observation, reasoning, or from source material. But don't stop there. Analyze and draw conclusions from it: How do your claim and your evidence relate? Where do they lead you? Your warrants will lead you to your next point, and will help you relate ideas. Your warrants are where your most original thinking resides, and they form the heart of your essay. In writing from sources, you will want to use your source material to explain, illustrate, and prove your ideas; you don't want to feel used by your sources. Warrants will help you retain intellectual control of your work, even when you are drawing from sources.

In closing your documented essay, examine the honesty of the conclusions you draw. Is your most fundamental warrant justified by the evidence? Are you acknowledging the true complexity of your subject? Your closing paragraphs are your last opportunity to speak to your reader. Avoid reiterating the introduction or summarizing the body of the essay here. What is the most essential point, the kernel of thought or implication you would like to leave your reader pondering?

Revising

As you revise your documented essay, you should bear in mind something you already know: there is a difference between revising (or re-visioning) and editing. Approach the revision process from the most fundamental to the most particular points of your essay.

In early revision, you will want to pay attention to the large questions that apply to your essay as a whole:

- Is your thesis clear?
- Are the main points you make clearly stated and clearly related?
- Have you supplied adequate contextual and background information?

In the middle stages of revision, consider development of ideas and evidence at the paragraph level:

- Are your key points thoroughly developed and adequately supported with evidence?
- Have you related your points clearly, establishing in transitions between paragraphs the relationships between ideas?
- Are there any major tangents or over- or under-emphases in coverage?

In the late stages of revision, consider clarity and style at the sentence level:

- Are you explaining specific ideas clearly enough?
- Are you including evidence in support of specific points and citing evidence from sources accurately?
- Are you analyzing and drawing conclusions from your evidence as you go?
- Are you being wordy?
- Are your tone and writing style appropriate to your audience and purpose?

In the final stages of revision, the editing stage, format your essay properly and check for grammatical and spelling errors as well as for accuracy in documentation.

The following questions are designed for conducting a peer review, which can be extremely helpful in testing the effectiveness of drafts of the research essay on an outside reader. These questions will also help you focus your own revision, with or without a peer review exchange.

1. Who is the author's audience? What is his or her purpose in writing? Is this a documented report or a documented argument?

2. Does the author establish the subject, stating the key question or problem, early on? When you have finished the paper, look back at the introduction. Did it give you a good idea of what the author actually did address in the rest of the paper? What is the author's thesis, the main point or argument? Does it appear in an appropriate place?

3. Does the paper reach a conclusion or does it merely stop? Does the conclusion repeat the introduction? Do introduction and conclusion fit together naturally as a kind of question and answer? Are conclusions well-earned?

4. Does the author provide necessary background information? Is there enough? Is any superfluous? (Consider the author's audience.)

5. Is the information organized in the most effective way? Do the ideas follow each other in a logical sequence? Do key points relate to the central idea? Does the author provide clear transitions, relating ideas? Are there any places that are confusing?

6. Are the points that the author is trying to make developed to their fullest extent? Does the paper bring up any interesting points that you would like to see developed further? Is there needless material that should be omitted?

7. Are the author's statements supported adequately with evidence and/or examples? Is evidence relevant? Is it convincing? Does the author provide a clear context for the evidence, introducing it clearly and following it with comment or analysis?

8. Does the author integrate source material—facts and figures, summaries, paraphrases, and quotations—fluidly in his or her text? Does he or she rely too heavily upon quotations or on any one source? Are there any quotations that might just as well be paraphrased?

9. Are there any grammatical or mechanical errors (including problems with punctuation) that the author will need to focus attention on in rewriting? Are there any consistent problems with diction, usage, or misused words that you can point out to the author?

10. Beyond mechanical and grammatical errors, comment on the author's writing style. Does the author vary sentence structure? Are there too many short, choppy sentences or ones that are overly complex and need to be broken up? Does the author choose precise words? Is there any wordiness?

11. Does the writer use correct form in internal citations of source material? Is the bibliography in correct form?

12. How, specifically, can the author improve this paper?

13. What are the draft's particular strengths?

DOCUMENTATION STYLES

Documentation styles vary among disciplines of study and sometimes even within a single discipline. The documentation style you choose to use in any given research essay is not a random choice; it should be based on the discipline in which you are writing and the audience for, and purpose of, your work. The most common and widely accepted documentation styles are the MLA (Modern Language Association) author/page style for documented writing in the humanities; the APA (American Psychological Association) author/date style for documented writing in the social sciences; and the CBE (Council of Biology Editors) number system for writing in the sciences.

Variations in form between each of these three documentation styles may seem somewhat arbitrary, but the most fundamental differences, at least, are not. In each style, primary and secondary sources are documented in ways that emphasize the particular aspects of information that are most important within each discipline. For example, in the MLA documentation style for writing in the humanities, internal citations require author and specific page references, emphasizing the text of the source itself. In the APA documentation style for writing in fast-changing fields in the social sciences, where current information is so important, internal citations require author and date as well as, in most cases, specific page references. Because the CBE documentation style for writing in the sciences is often used in reporting and documenting original reports of scientific research, a number system is used, keying internal citations—(1), (2), (3), and so on—with entries in the bibliography which are arranged sequentially rather than alphabetically; this system emphasizes the original research, while allowing the research-writer to acknowledge outside sources responsibly.

Your choice of which documentation style to use in any given research essay will depend not only on the discipline in which your topic falls; it will depend as well on the context in which your paper is written. For example, although Zach Perron's documented essay (pp. 628–40) cites scientific studies of the behavior of mountain lions, its purpose is broader than this. He is also interested in history, myths and misconceptions, and popular attitudes relating to his subject. The paper is intended to be read by a general audience, not an audience of science specialists. Since the paper was written within the context of a humanities course, Perron chose the MLA style as his form of documentation.

It is not possible to explain and to illustrate all three of the most widely used documentation styles here. If the APA or the CBE style is appropriate to the documentation of your research essay, you will find these documentation styles explained and illustrated in other sources. This Appendix will provide explanations and examples of the MLA documentation style. Whichever documentation style you choose in writing your research essay, be consistent in your use of it. Don't change documentation styles in midstream.

Whichever documentation style you choose, you are obliged to cite sources in two ways: with internal citations in the text of your essay and in your bibliography. In the MLA style, your internal citations will be parenthetical. Currently, in most disciplines and documentation styles, parenthetical citations are preferred over footnotes. The fundamental information in parenthetical citations in the MLA format will be the author's last name and a specific page reference. In your bibliography, which in the MLA style is titled "Works Cited," you will list all the outside sources that you have referred to specifically within your paper.

MLA DOCUMENTATION STYLE

Parenthetical Citations

In parenthetical citations, you must give enough information so that your reader will be able to identify your source in your list of works cited. In most cases, the author's last name and page reference are all you need in a parenthetical citation. Place citations as close as possible to the information to which they apply, but preferably at the end of a sentence. The following examples will illustrate the most common types of parenthetical references.

AN ENTIRE WORK

If you refer to a whole work in your text—a book or an article, for example—you will not need specific page references. If you include the author's name in the text of your essay, you will not even need a parenthetical citation.

> In *Brave New World,* Aldous Huxley describes a society in which individuality is sacrificed for social stability.

A WORK BY A SINGLE AUTHOR

If you do not refer to the author by name in your text, you will need to include both the author's name and the page reference in your parenthetical citation with no comma between them.

> One study in the Hirakud area of Orissa, India, found that people living in the neighborhood of an aluminum factory suffered from fluorosis (Samal 375).

If you give the author's name in the text of your essay, you need only include the page reference in your parenthetical citation.

> Steven Rice, in an article about environmental considerations in research and development, claims that "All environmental attentions and efforts are . . . directed at the need to protect employee and public health and welfare" (59) rather than to protect the environment for its intrinsic value.

MORE THAN ONE WORK BY THE SAME AUTHOR

If there is more than one work by the same author in your list of works cited, you will need to include in your parenthetical citation a brief title so that your reader will be able to distinguish between these works. If you include the author's name in your text, you need only refer to the title and page number in your parenthetical citation.

> W. G. Nawlakke stresses that although the alum actually removes the fluoride from the water, the addition of lime and bleaching powder are necessary steps in the de-fluoridation process because they help separate the

pollutants from and disinfect the water, respectively ("Water Treatment" 818).

If you refer to the author and to the title of the work in text, you need only include the page reference in your internal citation.

In one article, "Water Treatment Technology for Removal of Excess Fluoride," W. G. Nawlakke stresses that although the alum actually removes the fluoride from the water, the addition of lime and bleaching powder are necessary steps in the de-fluoridation process because they help separate the pollutants from and disinfect the water, respectively (818).

If you refer neither to the author nor to the title in text, you will include both in your parenthetical citation, with a comma separating name from title.

Although the alum actually removes the fluoride from the water, the addition of lime and bleaching powder are necessary steps in the de-fluoridation process because they help separate the pollutants from and disinfect the water, respectively (Nawlakke, "Water Treatment" 818).

A WORK BY TWO OR THREE AUTHORS

If the work you are citing was written by two or three authors, cite in text and in parenthetical citation as you would a work by a single author.

According to Alastair Gunn and P. Aarne Vesilind, environmental ethics is a "young and highly volatile field" (31).

Environmental ethics is a "young and highly volatile field" (Gunn and Vesilind 31).

A WORK BY MORE THAN THREE AUTHORS

If the work you are citing in a parenthetical reference was written by three authors or more, give the name of the first author, followed by *et al.*, which means "and others," with no comma between them.

Using American technology to feed a world of five billion human beings an American diet would require 7.1×10^{12} liters of oil per year, a rate which would dry up world oil reserves in fewer than twelve years (Pimentel et al. 32).

A WORK BY A CORPORATE AUTHOR

Give the name of a corporate author (which could be an organization, association, or government agency) in text or in parenthetical citation, as you would a personal author.

> The Colorado River Commission of the State of Arizona pointed out in a 1928 report that California's river systems held four times more water than the entire Colorado River Basin (3).

> As early as 1928, it was widely recognized that California's river systems held four times more water than the entire Colorado River Basin (State of Arizona, Colorado River Commission 3).

A WORK WITHOUT A STATED AUTHOR

Some works, including some news articles as well as pamphlets and flyers, have no stated authors. These you will refer to by title, shortened if the title is long, in your parenthetical reference. The following citation refers to a pamphlet, the full title of which is *Sunshine: Free Cooking Power* (and which would be listed alphabetically in the Works Cited list under this title). The pamphlet has no numbered pages.

> Solar cookers can be used to cook virtually all foods and are of relatively simple construction *(Sunshine)*.

This next example cites a magazine article with no stated author.

> Forty years ago, Phoenix was a community with a population of 100,000. Now it is a metropolis numbering more than two million. In the same period of time, the Los Angeles metropolitan area has grown from 4.4 million to 13.5 million people ("Till the River Runs Dry" 32).

INDIRECT SOURCES

If you run across a reference in one source to another source, and the source referred to seems especially promising, you should make every effort to track down that original source. If that source is unavailable to you, you may cite it indirectly. If the original source is quoted in the second-hand source, and you wish also to use the original author's language, cite the original author's name in your text, and in your internal citation use the abbreviation *qtd. in* (for "quoted in"), followed by reference to the second-hand source. If the second-hand source paraphrases or summarizes the original source and you wish to cite it similarly, or if you wish to paraphrase a quotation from the original source cited in the second-hand one, use *cited in*, instead of *qtd. in*, as above.

> Carol M. Browner, U.S. Environmental Protection Agency (EPA) administrator, recently stated in a congressional hearing that critics of Superfund are "skewing a program that has done a lot of good for the public" (qtd. in de Saillan 43).

> Terry Mansfield, a mountain lion expert with the California Department of Fish and Game, notes that there is a much higher probability of being hit by lightning than there is of being attacked by a cougar (cited in Sunderland 9E).

TWO OR MORE WORKS BY DIFFERENT AUTHORS IN THE SAME CITATION

Sometimes you will use information or ideas in your writing which you found reference to in more than one source. Separate these citations with semicolons.

> Superfund critics point out repeatedly that only a small number—currently about 200 sites—have been declared officially clean, and there are more than 1,200 toxic sites on Superfund's "National Priority List" ("Cleaning Up Superfund" 7; de Saillan 44).

ORIGINAL INTERVIEWS, SURVEYS, AND POLLS

In making reference to original research that you yourself have conducted in the form of interviews, surveys, or polls, describe the source of your information in your parenthetical citation.

> According to Dave Muffly, who directs the Oaks Regeneration Project in Palo Alto, California, destruction of young trees by rodents, resulting in a 40 percent attrition rate, is the most serious problem the Project faces (interview).

It is a good idea to introduce, and provide the qualifications of your source in the text of your essay when feasible. For example, if you were to write, "According to Dr. Sylvia Rosen, Director of Health and Human Services for the city of . . . ," you would accomplish two things. First, you would clearly distinguish information, ideas, or quotation from this source from what came before it. Second, in supplying important information about the source's qualifications, you enhance credibility. Your parenthetical citation, which in this case will probably consist of a page reference, will signal the end of reference to this particular source, setting it apart from what will follow.

Works Cited

In your "Works Cited," you will provide a list of all the primary and secondary sources to which you refer specifically in your internal citations. The idea is to supply your reader with the bibliographic information he or she will need to locate these sources.

In the MLA documentation style, entries in the list of works cited will be arranged alphabetically by the author's last name or by the title of the work if there is no author. Most book entries will consist of three units of information, including

- the full name of the *author,* last name first, with a comma separating last and first name, followed by a period;
- the full *title* of the book, italicized or underlined and with first letters of major words capitalized, followed by a period; and
- *publication data,* including city of publication (followed by a colon), brief name of the publisher (followed by a comma), and latest copyright date (followed by a period).

For most articles in periodical publications, there are also three units of information, including

- the full name of the author, as above;
- the full title of the article, placed in quotation marks and with first letters of major words capitalized, with a period inside the final quotation mark; and
- publication data, which for periodicals will vary according to the type of periodical, but will include the full title of the periodical (underlined, with first letters of major words capitalized), the date of publication, and the page numbers on which the article appears.

In periodical entries, no punctuation appears following the title of the periodical title, a colon introduces the page numbers, and, if the periodical gives both a volume number and a date, the date appears in parentheses.

Note that when you cite parts of books (including essays within edited collections and entries in encyclopedias, for example) or articles in newspapers or periodical publications, your entry will provide inclusive page numbers. Indent the second line of any entry that exceeds one line five spaces, so that the alphabetical arrangement can be easily scanned.

What follows are some of the most common forms for compiling your list of Works Cited in the MLA documentation style.

A BOOK BY ONE AUTHOR

Fradkin, Philip L. *A River No More.* New York: Knopf, 1981.

MORE THAN ONE WORK BY THE SAME AUTHOR

Shaw, Harley. *Mountain Lion Field Guide.* Phoenix: Arizona Game and Fish Department, 1983.

___. *Soul Among Lions: The Cougar as Peaceful Adversary.* Boulder, CO: Johnson Books, 1989.

A BOOK BY TWO AUTHORS

Silver, Cheryl Simon, and Ruth S. Defries. *One Earth, One Future.* Washington, D.C.: National Academy Press, 1990.

AN ESSAY BY ONE AUTHOR IN AN EDITED COLLECTION

Hay, John. "The Nature Writer's Dilemma." In *On Nature: Nature, Landscape, and Natural History.* Ed. Daniel Halpern. San Francisco: North Point Press, 1987. 7–10.

AN ARTICLE IN AN ENCYCLOPEDIA

"Oaks." *Scientific Encyclopedia.* 1976 ed.

A PUBLICATION BY A CORPORATE AUTHOR
OR GOVERNMENT AGENCY

Environmental Protection Agency. *The Superfund Program: Ten Years of Success.* Washington, D.C.: Government Printing Office, 1991.

AN ARTICLE IN A PERIODICAL NUMBERED BY VOLUME AND ISSUE

Fineman, Mark. "A Scheme to Harness India's Sacred Waters Brings Tempers to a Boil." *Smithsonian* 21.8 (1990): 118–130.

AN ARTICLE IN A MONTHLY PERIODICAL

Carrier, Jim. "The Colorado: A River Drained Dry." *National Geographic* June 1991: 4–35.

AN ARTICLE IN A WEEKLY PERIODICAL

Smith, Emily T., and Mimi Bluestone. "The Global Greenhouse Finally Has Leaders Sweating." *Business Week* 1 Aug. 1988: 74–76.

AN ARTICLE IN A NEWSPAPER

Sunderland, Bill. "Are Mountain Lions a Threat to Humans?" *San Jose Mercury News* 22 Oct. 1992: 9E.

AN ARTICLE OR PUBLICATION WITH NO STATED AUTHOR

"This Little Water Went to Market." *The Economist* 4 Aug. 1990: 19–20.

Sunshine: Free Cooking Power. Pamphlet. Sacramento, CA: Solar Box Cookers International, 1992.

A FILM

Dr. Strangelove. Dir. Stanley Kubrick. Columbia Pictures, 1963.

AN INTERVIEW

Muffly, Dave. Dir. Oaks Regeneration Project, Palo Alto, CA. Personal interview. 20 Feb. 1993.

■ ZACH PERRON

When Habitats Overlap: Increasing Contacts between Mountain Lions and Humans

Student Zach Perron has this to say about himself and about his choice of subject, his research, and his writing of his research essay about interaction between mountain lions and human beings:

I was born and raised in Palo Alto, California. I have not officially declared a major and am currently considering such varied options as earth systems, English, psychology, and communications. My career plans are undecided as well; ideally, I would like to be in a field that combines education, the natural environment, and science writing.

Writing had always come easily to me before I entered college. Once there, I found that college writing was markedly different from that in high school. Bringing my writing up to a college level has been difficult, but I find that when I am dealing with a subject that holds my interest (such as mountain lions), the words just kind of flow out onto the page.

This particular assignment was of special importance to me. For as long as I can remember, I have had a fascination with large cats. For this assignment, then, I was well motivated to do the research, and writing about a subject that means so much to me was not at all difficult. My audience for this paper was the general reader; I purposely left out much of the highly technical information I found in my research so the paper would be easily understood by a general audience. My purpose was to educate people as to the true relationship between these magnificent cats and humans, to dispel rumors and ensure that the truth be known.

Formal Outline
for Research Paper

When Habitats Overlap: Increasing Contacts between Mountain Lions and Humans

Note: In the source references, there are two numbers for each source. The first is the page number the information is found on in the source, and the second is a reference to the notecard it is recorded on.

Motivating Question: What happens when mountain lions and human beings come into direct contact?

   I. Introductory paragraph. General information. Stuff that will get readers interested while giving them a brief background on lions, their interaction with humans since settlers arrived in North America, persecution, and need to know more.
      A. Lions' shrinking range (Milstein 19, #19; Hansen 106, #18)
      B. Myths and misconceptions (Milstein 20, #20; Hansen 20, #4; McCall vi, #11)
      C. Panic about increase in sightings
      D. *Thesis statement: Despite increased contacts between cougars and humans in recent years, it is possible to achieve a peaceful coexistence of these two species with sound management techniques and broader public education.*

II.   Early history of the mountain lion in the United States
   A.   Native American views of cougar
      1.   Names they gave it (McCall 9, #99)
      2.   Why they revered it (Acuff in Hansen 55, #97)
   B.   First European interaction
      1.   First non-native sightings (Hansen 2, #84 & #85)
      2.   Attitude of colonialists (Hansen 56, #96)
   C.   Widespread extermination of lion from 17th to 20th century = threatened extinction
      1.   Spanish missionaries and bounty systems (Milstein 20, #98)
      2.   Dates cougar was eliminated from certain states (Hansen 57, #95)
      3.   Animal Damage Control
         a.   History (Hansen 57, #70)
         b.   Statistics (Hansen 57, #70)
      4.   Trapping/hunting (Shaw 131, #16)
         a.   Yellowstone: elimination of predators that kill "tourist-pleasing" wildlife (Milstein 20, #73)
         b.   Methods of killing (Laycock 14, #75)
            i.   "Will-Call" hunts (Hansen 63, #75)
            ii.   "Shootout" hunts (Hansen 63, #71)
   D.   Current range
      1.   Western states/Canada
      2.   Lions' resistance to extermination (Shaw 131, #78)

III.   Studies of mountain lions
   A.   Difficulty in studying due to remote range and secretive nature
   B.   Hornocker's preliminary studies
      1.   Lion habitat (Hansen 23, #49; McCall 16, #111)
   C.   More recent studies
      1.   Population density & social interaction (Weaver 2, #66)
      2.   Home ranges/establishment of home territory (Weaver 2, #66; Hansen 11, #34; Pennisi 410, #35; Hansen 25, #39 & #40)
         a.   Immature, transient, resident (Shaw 2–3, #65)
      3.   Predator/prey relations (Hansen 21, #48; Hansen 50–51, #50; Hansen 48, #51; McCall 5, #54; McCall 11, #55)
         a.   Stalkers (Seidensticker in Hansen 27, #52)
         b.   Diet mostly deer (Ackerman in Hansen 44, #49; Beier & Barrett 81, #57)
         c.   Opportunistic hunters

IV.   Depredation
   A.   A real problem, but sometimes exaggerated (Hansen 15, #116; Hansen 60, #117; Guggisberg in Hansen 61, #118)

B. Incidents of/reasons for depredation
  1. Carlsbad Caverns and Guadalupe Mountains National Parks (Milstein 19, #120; Milstein 23, #131 & #132)
  2. Shaw's studies, Arizona (Shaw 96, #123; Shaw 95, #129 & #130)
     a. Greatest losses of livestock in Southwest
     b. When deer aren't available, calves the next best thing (opportunistic)
  3. California (Laycock 13, #121 & #122; Weaver 5, #124; Hansen 15, #125; Hansen 60, #126 & #127; Weaver 10, #128)
C. Lethal vs. nonlethal control methods
  1. Killing individual lions doesn't work; transients will repopulate area (Milstein 19, #120)
  2. Hansen's suggestions for nonlethal control (Hansen 61, #119)
     a. steer rather than cow/calf operations
     b. open terrain
     c. electric fences
     d. large dogs
V. Direct interaction
  A. Attacks on humans rare (Beier & Barrett 90, #94; Laycock 12, #6; Laycock 15, #7; Laycock 17, #8)
  B. Attacks increasing as human and lion populations grow (Hansen 72, #89)
    1. More lions
       a. Restrictions on hunting (Hansen 72, #88; Weaver 13, #80, #81, #82; Mansfield in Beier & Barrett 5, #68)
       b. Explosions in deer populations
    2. More people
       a. Urban/wilderness interfaces
       b. Increased park visitation
  C. Attack hotspots
    1. Vancouver Island
       a. Nearly 40% of recorded attacks in 100 years occurred here (Beier & Barrett Appendix)
       b. Reason: high use, limited space (Hamilton in Worth 56, #105 & #9; Laycock 15, #104)
    2. Big Bend National Park (Milstein 23, #100; Beier & Barrett Appendix)
       a. Cats adapting to humans (Milstein 23, #101)
       b. Juveniles most dangerous (Milstein 23, #103)
    3. Caspers Wilderness Park
       a. Lawsuits from two attacks on children (Hansen 72, #106; Laycock 16, #107)

     b. County temporarily closes park; bans kids under 18 from park (Hansen 72, #106; Laycock 16, #109)

     c. Objections to lawsuits and ban

       i. Cougars' right to open space (Laycock 16, #108)

       ii. Inherent risks in visiting wilderness

   D. Keeping attacks in perspective

     1. Many more deaths caused by deer, dogs, bees, lightning (Hansen 71, #87; Sunderland 9E #112; Benshimon & Brophy 79, #115)

VI. Steps to protect lions and the public

   A. Management

     1. Nonlethal controls to reduce depredation

   B. Funding

     1. Further research

     2. Conservation of habitat (Torres interview)

       a. Wildlife corridors (Beier & Barrett 25–26, #43; Harris & Gallagher in Hansen 74, #44; Harris in Hansen 75, #3)

       b. California funds for habitat improvement (Laycock 17, #76)

   C. Public education

     1. Informational pamphlets/warnings

       a. Drawbacks: alarmist (Carson interview)

     2. Campfire programs

       a. Portola State Park (Carson interview)

VII. Concluding paragraph

   A. Contacts will increase as human and lion populations rise

   B. Knowledge = sound management

   C. Both species' right to thrive

   D. Protecting diversity

When Habitats Overlap: Increasing Contacts between Mountain Lions and Humans

When settlers arrived in the New World, the mountain lion's range was more widespread than that of any other large predator in the Western Hemisphere. Over the past 250 years, the range of this magnificent animal has been reduced to twelve western states, with a remnant population in Florida and a population of unknown size in Central and South America. The mountain lion, or cougar, as it is often called, is one of the most misunderstood animals on the continent. The elusive nature of *Felis concolor* has perpetuated fantastic myths and legends, most of which originated in the creative imaginations of people who caught only glimpses of the large feline. Early on, the cats acquired a bad reputation that, for the most part, persists today. President Theodore Roosevelt, an avid hunter, described the lion as the "big horse-killing cat, destroyer of the deer and lord of stealthy murder with a heart craven and cruel" (qtd. in Milstein 20). Misconceptions, coupled with recent increases in cougar sightings in areas of human habitation, have generated unreasonable public fears of a ruthless, bloodthirsty species intent on killing both humans and livestock. Wildlife managers and biologists are currently studying cougars in an effort to determine their true role in nature and relationship to human beings. Despite increased contacts between cougars and humans in recent years, it is possible to achieve a peaceful coexistence of these two species with sound management techniques and broader public education.

Before Europeans arrived in the New World, the mountain lion had been revered for centuries by Native Americans for its cunning and stealth. The Zuni followed cougars and scavenged their kills, a source of food that constituted a substantial part of their diet. When they weren't following the cats, Zuni hunters carried lion fetishes, which they believed gave them good luck when hunting deer. To the Cherokee, the cougar was "Klandaghi," the lord of the forest. To the Creeks, it was "Katalgar," the greatest of wild hunters (McCall and Dutcher 9). D. S. Acuff, in his 1988 Master's thesis, "Perceptions of the Mountain Lion 1825–1986," at the University of California at Davis, maintains that the cougar was most respected because of the ease with which it captured its prey, a trait admired by tribes that themselves relied on hunting for their sustenance (cited in Hansen 55). The Native Americans had a sense of the fundamental role the mountain lion played in the balance of nature.

European colonization of the New World marked the beginning of the end of the mountain lion's reign in North America. The first sighting of a mountain lion by a white man in the Western Hemisphere was recorded by Amerigo Vespucci, who in 1500 saw one of the great cats on the shore of South America. Thirteen years later, the first sighting by a white man in North America was reported near the Florida Everglades (Hansen 2). The first Europeans to arrive in what is today the United States tended to divide animals into one of two categories: beneficial (edible wild game and livestock) and injurious (virtually all other birds and animals) (Hansen 56). Unfortunately, the cougar fell into the latter group, and so was widely exterminated as settlers moved from east to west. The unabashed slaughter of the mountain lion is perhaps understandable, though not justifiable. For all of history, human beings have feared the unknown. The mountain lion, a creature more often heard (its cry sounds much like a woman's scream) than seen, struck fear in the hearts of settlers who did the one thing in their power to make the frontier "safe": they killed the lion.

The last cougar in Vermont was shot in 1881, the last in Pennsylvania in 1891. By the turn of the century, the lion was, for all intents and purposes, extinct east of the Mississippi River (Hansen 57). In the West, as early as the seventeenth century, Spanish missionaries gave a live bull for each dead mountain lion surrendered to them by native Californians (Milstein 20), and bounty systems lasted well into the nineteenth century. Such persecution is not a relic of the distant past, nor was it restricted to the mountain lion. In 1931, the Animal Damage Control Act sanctioned the killing of all creatures "injurious to agriculture, horticulture, forestry, husbandry, game, or domesticated animals." From 1937 to 1970, the Animal Damage Control unit of the Department of Agriculture was responsible for the deaths of over 7,000 cougars, 23,000 bears, 450,000 bobcats, and almost three million coyotes (Hansen 57; 59).

Mountain lions might well have been wiped out entirely had it not been for the remoteness of some of the lion's haunts. Harley Shaw, a wildlife biologist with the Arizona Game and Fish Department who has studied lions in the Southwest for over twenty years, says, "The vastness of lion habitat, the secretiveness of the species, its resistance to poisoning, and the ability of the lion to recolonize empty habitat thwarted every effort aimed toward its complete elimination. The lion exists today due to its own invulnerability; not to any altruism on the part of the human species" (*Soul among Lions* 131). Although efforts to drive the mountain lion to total extinction failed, the lion population has nonetheless been decimated. The current range of the cougar, though still impressive, is but a fraction of what it once was.

Even in the western United States and Canada, the last stronghold of the mountain lion in North America, the cat has not been extensively studied. Its secretive nature and large home territory make population studies difficult. Today, it is generally accepted that the best way to study the cat is by radio telemetry, a system too expensive and complex for the average biologist. As a result, studies of lions have been limited, and much remains to be learned about most aspects of their lives. Nonetheless, studies that have been completed have provided much new information, ranging from population estimates to detailed experiments on predator/prey relations, home ranges, and interaction with humans.

The first modern research on mountain lions began in 1969, when biologist Maurice Hornocker and his colleagues began a study in central Idaho. Hornocker pioneered radio telemetry technology with the cats, tracking several felines in a 200-square-mile section of the Idaho Primitive Area (now called the Frank Church River of No Return Wilderness), the largest single wilderness area in the contiguous United States. Although much of Hornocker's work has been revised by research involving better technology in recent years, his study revealed preliminary data on social organization, territorial behavior, and family structure of the mountain lion (cited in McCall and Dutcher 16). Perhaps the most important information to come out of his study was the identification of what made for suitable lion habitat. Hornocker and other biologists, including John Seidensticker, have concluded that lions only inhabit areas that have a proper combination of vegetation, topography, prey density, and prey vulnerability (Hansen 23). More recent studies have determined that even in areas in which lion populations are relatively high, as few as six to seven adult cats may inhabit every 100-square-miles of habitat (Weaver 2). Interestingly, the distribution of cougars appears to be limited not so much by the abundance of prey as by social interactions between cats.

This social interaction has been studied by several researchers in recent years. Cats can be divided into one of three categories, depending on their age: immature (offspring of adults that are traveling with their mother), transient (independent young lions searching for a home range of their own), or resident (adults that use established home ranges and are reproductively active) (Shaw, *Field Guide* 2–3). The home territory for a male ranges from 25 to 500 square miles, while that of females falls between eight and 400 square miles. The home range of a male will overlap the territories of several females, allowing one tom to breed with many females each year (Hansen 24–25). The only time two adults will be found together is during the breeding season, a period of time as limited as a single week. After the cubs are born, the mother will raise her young until they are eighteen months old, at which time she will abandon them, forcing them to locate their own home territory. At this point, the young lions become transients. The dispersal of these cats away from their area of birth reduces inbreeding, thus diversifying gene pools (Hansen 11).

Transients often cause the most problems with humans and livestock because they are forced to the edge of wilderness in search of their own territories (Pennisi 410).

The relationship between mountain lions and their prey is another subject that has been more widely researched in recent years. Very few people have witnessed a lion making a kill in the wild. For years, fantastic myths surrounded how it was done. In frontier times, a popular story circulated about a cougar who had killed an 800-pound cow, then scaled a ten-foot fence with it in its jaws (Hansen 48). Mountain lions are known as "stalking" predators (Seidensticker cited in Hansen 27), referring to their method of capture, which very much resembles that of a house cat: using vegetation as a shield, the cat will slink slowly toward its prey, then at close range launch itself at the animal and attempt to break its neck. In the wild, the preferred prey of lions is deer. In Utah, for example, deer constitute 80 percent of the cougar's diet (Ackerman cited in Hansen 44). During their five-year study in southern California, Paul Beier and Reginald Barrett determined that cats in Orange County ate deer almost 60 percent of the time, with opossum and coyote rounding out their diet (81). While cougars will feed on a wide variety of prey, taking down a single deer is much more efficient for them than killing many smaller mammals. It is a popular misconception that lions always feed on sick or old individuals; rather, as opportunistic hunters, they will kill whatever they can, be it sick or healthy.

Unfortunately, this opportunism occasionally results in depredation, the loss of livestock to wildlife, one of two main sources of major conflict between humans and mountain lions. No one knows the extent to which cougars are responsible for lost cattle and sheep. It has been documented, however, that coyotes and domestic animals are responsible for more deaths than cougars (Hansen 60). Yet ranchers continually complain that lion depredation is driving them out of business. Fred Lindzey, a wildlife biologist with the United States Fish and Wildlife Service, partly concurs with this point of view: "Although depredation is a small problem industry-wide, local ranchers can be significantly affected" (qtd. in Hansen 60). Isolated instances of lion depredation have attracted a great deal of attention, such as that of a lion that killed fifty-nine sheep in one night in Nevada (Hansen 60). More usual depredation patterns have been extensively studied, especially in New Mexico, Arizona, and Texas.

Wildlife biologist Shaw reports that the greatest losses of livestock to lions occur in the Southwest, especially in Arizona and New Mexico. In his five-year study of cougar behavior at the Spider and Cross U Ranches, he determined that 30 percent of the lion diet was livestock, especially calves. However, Shaw himself admits that this statistic isn't representative of lions everywhere; indeed, it actually isn't representative of the lions even in his study area. During his study, the deer population around the ranches was abnormally low, perhaps because of low rainfall during that period of time or increased deer hunting. In any event, it was clear to Shaw that the cats didn't have their normal food source in its normal abundance, and as a result they fed on the next available large prey, livestock. Shaw also noted that the deer population is lowest in the late winter and early spring, the time when the calf population is highest (*Soul among Lions* 95–96). This further demonstrates that lions are opportunistic hunters, for when the native prey population is low, they turn to the calves, which are abundant at that time, in their attempts to survive.

In areas in which relatively high rates of depredation have occurred, many ranchers' first impulse has been, perhaps understandably, to track and kill the offending lions. Research has revealed, however, that this method of depredation control is not all that effective. Trapping and killing cougars that reside in one particular area is at best a temporary solution since transient lions will simply repopulate available territories (Milstein 19). Short of total eradication of lion populations in vast areas of the United States where livestock happens also to be raised (a "solution" so radical that, fortunately, few advocate it), killing lions in an attempt to solve depredation problems seems to be impractical.

A more effective way to reduce depredation is the use of "nonlethal control methods." Kevin Hansen, drawing upon his longtime experience as a National Park Service ranger in lion and livestock country, compiles suggestions of these methods from several sources in his book *Cougar: The American Lion.* In areas of heavy lion depredation, Hansen suggests that cattle ranchers switch to steer operations instead of cow/calf operations, since the large steers would present too formidable a kill for a lion. Another idea is grazing livestock in open areas, reducing the chances of a cougar attack since the cats need cover to stalk their prey. For smaller pastures, electric fences may be installed, which would not only reduce lion depredation but coyote depredation as well. As a last suggestion, Hansen encourages the use of guard dogs, especially those of large breeds

(61). All of these ideas are sound management strategies, providing good protection against cougars without harming the cats or the livestock.

Besides depredation, the other main source of conflict between cougars and humans is direct interaction: specifically, attacks on people. Researcher Beier compiled a history of attacks from 1890 to 1990, defining an attack as an incident when the lion bit, scratched, or knocked down a person. Beier found that there were only nine attacks resulting in ten human deaths and forty-four non-fatal attacks in this 101-year period (Beier and Barrett 90). When the chances of an attack are so slight, widespread fears seem unwarranted. Stanley Young, a federal biologist for forty years, says, "The almost universal fear of the puma [mountain lion] is based mainly on its mysterious ways, size, and power to do harm, not on its aggressiveness, for as a rule it is notoriously timid in relation to man" (qtd. in Laycock 15). Maurice Hornocker, the wildlife biologist who pioneered cougar research in the early 1970s, says of interaction between man and cat that as "a large predatory animal that can be dangerous . . . has to be viewed that way. But this doesn't mean that we should do away with all mountain lions any more than we would try to kill all the mice in a valley because one got into the camp oatmeal" (qtd. in Laycock 17).

It is true, however, that in the last twenty years mountain lion attacks on humans have increased. One reason many naive people cite for this increase is that the lions are getting more aggressive. This is entirely false. The simple explanation is that the populations of both people and cats are growing, and with the rise in numbers of both species, encounters in the wild are bound to go up (Hansen 72). In many areas of the western United States and Canada, suburban developments and heavily visited public park lands have overlapped traditional lion habitats as well as lands that are being repopulated by lions. The number of lions is increasing mainly due to changes in the legal status of the cat. For example, following California's declaration of the mountain lion as a nongame species in the early 1970s, the state's lion population rose from a 1972 estimate of approximately 2,100 (Weaver 13) to current estimates of between 4,100 and 5,700 animals (Mansfield cited in Beier & Barrett 5). The cougar is still considered a game species in many states and Canadian provinces, but there are now limits on the number of cats that can be taken each season (Hansen 89). Lion populations have also grown in many areas due to increases in deer populations, since with higher concentrations of lions' primary food source, more kittens grow to adulthood.

There have been three main hotspots of cougar/human interaction in North America: Vancouver Island, British Columbia; Big Bend National Park, Texas; and in southern California, specifically in Caspers Wilderness Park. Due to the limited area of Vancouver Island, the highest concentration of incidents has occurred there. Paul Beier, in his analysis of the history of lion attacks in North America, cites twenty attacks on the island since 1890, resulting in three deaths (Beier and Barrett Appendix), roughly 40 percent of all attacks since that time. Don Hamilton, a conservation officer employed by the Ministry of Environment on Vancouver Island, investigates about 130 cougar cases annually. Of these, thirty-five to forty cats are killed or moved to another location. Hamilton has a grim outlook on the future of contacts between cougars and humans on the island: "Like it or not, cougars eat meat," he says. "People are meat" (qtd. in Worth 56).

In 1984, federal biologists began a study of cougar/human interaction in Big Bend National Park in Texas, another hotspot of direct contact. This study, prompted by two attacks within four months on visitors in a heavily used section of the park (Beier and Barrett Appendix; Milstein 23), yielded some interesting results. Raymond Skiles, a resource management ranger at the park, summarized them this way: "The lions had become so accustomed to people they seemed to have lost their usual fear of humans. We found cats in their day rest areas right near busy trails where people were carrying on all the time, and they [the cats] didn't seem to be disturbed at all" (qtd. in Milstein 23). The study showed that mountain lions can learn to take people in stride, just as they've adjusted to other pressures placed on them by man, such as habitat loss and hunting. That the two species interact in such close proximity might seem dangerous, yet the fact that there hasn't been another attack in the area in nearly ten years dispels the need to be overly concerned. Another result of the Big Bend study is that biologists there think that juvenile cats present the most risk to humans since they may not be used to foraging for themselves and may have been pushed to the edges of older lions' territories in search of their own (Milstein 23).

A third hotspot of cougar/human encounters lies in Caspers Wilderness Park in Orange County, California, where in 1986 a five-year-old girl was mauled by a lion. She suffered a fractured skull, partial paralysis, and a serious eye injury. The parents were furious that they had not been warned about lions prior to entering the park and filed a multi-million dollar lawsuit against assorted defendants.

They claimed that "those named in the suit knowingly harbored a dangerous animal" (Laycock 16). The parents won the lawsuit and were awarded two million dollars in compensation (Hansen 72). Only a few months later, a six-year-old boy was also attacked in the park when he stopped to tie his shoe. Before his father was able to drive the cat off with a knife, the child suffered multiple lacerations of the head, chest, and back. The parents of the second child filed a similar lawsuit. As a result of these two attacks, the Orange County Board of Supervisors voted to close the park for two months. One local politician called for the slaughter or relocation of every lion in the area, but the proposal was vehemently opposed by hundreds of environmentalists defending the cougars' right to open space (Laycock 16). Six years later, though, in 1992, Orange County officials, yielding to a vocal minority opinion, banned all children under the age of 18 years from the park (Hansen 72). The fact that children can no longer enjoy the beauty of this wilderness area is very unfortunate indeed.

No one denies that the trauma suffered by these attack victims and their families is tremendous, but many believe that the lawsuits were unfounded. When people enter a wilderness area, they are accepting the innate risks associated with that wilderness, be it falling off a cliff, being bitten by a rattlesnake, or being pounced by a cougar. If park personnel issued warnings about every conceivable danger contained in their nature area, visitors might be unduly alarmed. They might spend more time at the entrance station reading warning brochures than on the trails, or they might be frightened away entirely from the experience of the outdoors that parks seek to provide.

Short of complete eradication of lions, there is not a single management strategy that would completely alleviate the chances of a lion attacking a human. Following incidents such as the attacks at Caspers Wilderness Park, many people do inevitably call for the removal of all lions from the wild. The question "Shouldn't lions be killed to make the wild safer for humans?" is continually tossed around and debated after every cougar attack. However, we should keep this question in the correct perspective.

The chances of being attacked by a cougar in the wild are remote. Between 1890 and 1990, Beier counted only ten deaths, an average of only one death every decade (Beier and Barrett, Appendix). Ironically, deer, the cat's main prey, bring about many more deaths than those caused by the predator: in 1989 alone, 130 people died as a result of deer-related injuries, mostly in vehicular accidents (Benshimon and Brophy 79). Domestic dogs kill eighteen to twenty people annually. Bees kill over forty people annually, and rattlesnakes are responsible for twelve deaths each year (Hansen 71). Terry Mansfield, a mountain lion expert with the California Department of Fish and Game, notes that there is a much higher probability of being hit by lightning than there is of being attacked by a cougar (cited in Sunderland 9E).

Yet humans tend to fear what they cannot control and do not understand, and the cougar remains wild and relatively mysterious. As a result, mountain lions have faced unwarranted persecution over the years. Fortunately, however, despite increased contact between humans and lions and persistent lion hysteria, the current trend is toward conservation rather than eradication. Most wildlife managers and more and more ranchers and ordinary citizens seem to understand that, as human and mountain lion habitats increasingly overlap, our goal should be both to maintain viable lion populations and public safety. The question, of course, is how best to accomplish these goals.

In order to protect the interests of both mountain lions and human beings, we need to continue to re-evaluate management strategies, provide for adequate funding for further study and habitat conservation, and increase public understanding. Ranchers should be actively encouraged to use nonlethal control methods to reduce lion depredation. Ranchers who run steer operations, graze livestock in open areas, install electric fences, and use guard dogs have less of a chance of being severely affected by lion depredation.

Funds must be made available for both further study of the mountain lion and for habitat protection. Although much has been learned about these elusive animals, we need to know more about mountain lions in order to know how best to protect them and ourselves. An intensive field study of mountain lions can cost many thousands of dollars. Habitat protection is even more expensive, but well worth the investment. California Department of Fish and Game program coordinator Steve Torres recommends the implementation of a statewide conservation program for the cougar (interview). In preserving additional lion habitat, we would not only protect the cougar but many species falling below it in the food chain. We should remember that in reducing the range of the mountain lion, we are disrupting whole ecosystems that become unbalanced without a top predator to control animal populations.

Some conservationists have suggested the implementation of "wildlife corridors." In many areas, open space preserves are separated by roads, small towns, and in some cases even cities. This fragmented habitat not only provides isolated home ranges, but also increases the likelihood of interaction since the cats need to pass through areas of human habitation in order to reach the next block of open space. Beier and Barrett recommend preserving small corridors of wilderness between larger areas, such as state or regional parks. But there are several factors that would influence the success of these movement corridors, such as width, available cover, lighting, roads, and other disturbances (25–26). Corridors cannot be in entirely open areas, and they must be devoid of street lighting and free of unrestrained pets (especially domestic dogs). Such specific areas are difficult to locate and often fall on private property, making acquisition difficult. However, in 1990, the people of California approved a new law which, in addition to forbidding mountain lion hunting in the state until the year 2020, earmarks $30 million of the state's budget each year to improve habitat for both lions and deer (Laycock 17), hopefully making the acquisition of wildlife corridors easier.

A general increase in public knowledge of mountain lions is essential to ensure a peaceful coexistence between human beings and the cats. With greater understanding, people's fears of the cougar, which may be disproportionate to real risk, might be relieved. One option that is becoming more and more common is the distribution of informational pamphlets about cougars at the headquarters of open space areas, similar to those about bears that have been distributed in some national parks for some time. This option, however, has been criticized by some as being alarmist or as simply being a legal disclaimer. Some fear that handouts detailing the statistics of mountain lion attacks may be counterproductive to parks' missions; some visitors might perceive only the risk, not the rarity, of lion attacks and refrain from spending time in the outdoors (Carson interview).

A better option, perhaps, are educational programs presented by park personnel in a friendly, informal fashion. For example, Portola State Park in California has recently implemented a campfire program series, offered by park rangers and naturalists every weekend night for people camping in the park. One of the programs is entitled "Wildcats of the Santa Cruz Mountains: The Truth about Mountain Lions and Bobcats" (Carson interview). This program is effective because it gives a complete picture and targets those who are most likely to profit from the information it provides: people who spend a lot of time in the outdoors and who have an ongoing interest in the subject.

As more Americans visit the wilderness and as suburban areas continue to expand into lion habitat, contacts between the two species will keep increasing. Separating fact from longstanding fiction about the mountain lion is the first step in educating the public about this magnificent animal, and an understanding of mountain lion behavior is the foundation of sound management policies. Americans seem to be more willing now than in the past to accept the premise that, although the interests of our own species are crucial, the interests of other species are important as well. Although we cannot fully control the mountain lion any more than we can control mountains or weather, we can achieve a more peaceful coexistence with this wild predator. In fact, we must, if we wish to maintain into the next century anything resembling the rich diversity of life the first Americans experienced on the continent hundreds of years ago.

Works Cited

Beier, Paul, and Reginald H. Barrett. *The Cougar in the Santa Ana Mountain Range, California.* Berkeley: Department of Forestry and Resource Management, University of California at Berkeley, 1993.

Benshimon, D., and M. Brophy. "Man Killers." *Men's Health* Apr. 1992: 79.

Carson, Chris. Portola State Park Ranger. Personal interview. 3 Aug. 1994.

Hansen, Kevin. *Cougar: The American Lion.* Flagstaff: Northland Publishing, 1992.

Laycock, George. "Cougars in Conflict." *Audubon Nature Yearbook.* Ed. Les Line. Des Moines, IA: Meredith Corporation, 1991. 11–17.

McCall, Karen, and Jim Dutcher. *Cougar: Ghost of the Rockies.* San Francisco: Sierra Club Books, 1992.

Milstein, Michael. "The Hidden Lion." *National Parks* Jan./Feb. 1990: 19–23, 44.

Pennisi, Elizabeth. "Heavy Cougar Traffic at City Edges." *Science News* 26 June 1993: 410.

Shaw, Harley. *Mountain Lion Field Guide.* Phoenix: Arizona Game and Fish Department, 1983.

___. *Soul among Lions: The Cougar as Peaceful Adversary.* Boulder, CO: Johnson Books, 1989.

Sunderland, Bill. "Are Mountain Lions a Threat to Humans?" *San Jose Mercury News* 22 Oct. 1992: 9E.

Torres, Steve. California Department of Fish and Game. Telephone interview. 20 Jan. 1994.

Weaver, Richard A. *Status of the Mountain Lion in California with Recommendations for Management.* Sacramento: State of California Department of Fish and Game, 1982.

Worth, Nancy. "When Cats Go Bad." *Outdoor Life* Jan. 1991: 56, 78–80.

Acknowledgments

Journal excerpt, April 3, 1871, by John Muir, from *John of the Mountains*, edited by Linnie Marsh Wolfe. Copyright © 1938 by Wanda Muir Hanna. Copyright © renewed 1966 by John Muir Hanna and Ralph Eugene Wolf. Reprinted by permission of Houghton Mifflin Co. All rights reserved.

"Estes Park, Colorado, October" by Isabella Bird from *A Lady's Life in the Rocky Mountains* by Isabella L. Bird. Copyright © 1960 by the University of Oklahoma Press. Used by permission.

"November 3, 9, and 14" from *The Snow Leopard*. Copyright © 1978 by Peter Matthiessen, used by permission of Viking Penguin, a division of Penguin Books USA, Inc.

"Day Seventeen" and "Day Eighteen" from *Winter Brothers*, copyright © 1980 by Ivan Doig, reprinted by permission of Harcourt Brace and Company.

"White-headed Eagle" by John James Audubon from *Ornithological Biography* (Dover Publications, Inc.). Reprinted by permission of Dover Publications.

Chapter 1 from *Black Boy* by Richard Wright. Copyright © 1937, 1942, 1944, 1945, by Richard Wright. Copyright © renewed 1973 by Ellen Wright. Reprinted by permission of HarperCollins Publishers, Inc.

Preface to *The Way to Rainy Mountain* by N. Scott Momaday first published in *The Reporter*, January 26, 1967. Reprinted from *The Way to Rainy Mountain*, N. Scott Momaday, © 1969, the University of New Mexico Press. Used by permission.

"Ponds" copyright © 1978 by Lewis Thomas. Originally appeared in the *New England Journal of Medicine*. From *The Medusa and the Snail* by Lewis Thomas. Used by permission of Viking Penguin, a division of Penguin Books USA, Inc.

Excerpt from *Basin and Range* by John McPhee. Copyright © 1980, 1981 by John McPhee. Reprinted by permission of Farrar, Straus and Giroux, Inc.

"A Very Warm Mountain" by Ursula K. Le Guin. Copyright © 1980 by Ursula K. Le Guin; first appeared in *Parabola*; reprinted by permission of the author and the author's agent, Virginia Kidd.

"The Changing Year" by Rachel L. Carson from *The Sea around Us*, revised edition by Rachel L. Carson. Copyright © 1950, 1951, 1961, by Rachel Carson; renewed 1979, 1989 by Roger Christie. Reprinted by permission of Oxford University Press.

"Falling for Apples" from *Second Person Rural* by Noel Perrin. Copyright © 1980 by Noel Perrin. Reprinted by permission of David R. Godine, Publisher, Inc.

"Sojourner" from *Teaching a Stone to Talk* by Annie Dillard. Copyright © 1982 by Annie Dillard. Reprinted by permission of HarperCollins Publishers, Inc.

"Rules of the Game: Rodeo" from *The Solace of Open Spaces* by Gretel Ehrlich. Copyright © 1985 by Gretel Ehrlich. Used by permission of Viking Penguin, a division of Penguin Books USA, Inc.

"Building Fence" by Maxine Kumin. Copyright © 1981 by Maxine Kumin, from *In Deep—Country Essays*. Used by permission of Viking Penguin, a division of Penguin Books USA Inc.

"Becoming Feral" from *A Country Year: Living the Questions* by Sue Hubbell, copyright © 1983, 1984, 1985, 1986 by Sue Hubbell. Reprinted by permission of Random House, Inc.

"On Being a Scientific Booby" from *Plaintext*, by Nancy Mairs, reprinted by permission of the University of Arizona Press, copyright © 1986.

Rights and Beyond" copyright © June 1984 by David Quammen. This article originally appeared in *Outside* Magazine.

"Perfect People?" by Amy Virshup from *New York* magazine, July 27, 1987. Reprinted by permission of Amy Virshup.

"A Heretic's View on the New Bioethics" by Jeremy Rifkin from *Algeny.* Copyright © 1983 by Foundation on Economic Trends. Reprinted by permission of Writers and Artists Agency.

"On the Origin of Specious Critics" by Stephen Jay Gould. Reprinted by permission of Stephen Jay Gould. This article originally appeared in *Discover* magazine, January, 1985.

Index